DEFINING INTERNATIONAL AGGRESSION: the search for world peace; a documentary history and analysis, by Benjamin B. Ferencz. Oceana, 1975. 2v bibl 75-16473. 75.00 set. v.1, ISBN 0-379-00271-X; v.2, ISBN 0-379-00272-8. C.I.P.
In 1974 the U.N. General Assembly adopted a definition of "aggression." It was the culmination of 30 years' work by various committees of the U.N. and really the culmination of several hundred years' work by legal and political philosophers and writers. In these two volumes, Benjamin B. Ferencz, a lawyer, has brought together most of the more recent important documents in this quest — those originating under the auspices of the League of Nations, the post-W.W. II trials, and the U.N. And his hundred-or-so pages of historical survey and textual analysis of some of these documents should be most useful. The volumes ought to be in even the smallest undergraduate library collections in the fields of international law or U.N. affairs.

DEFINING INTERNATIONAL AGGRESSION

Volume 1

DEFINING INTERNATIONAL AGGRESSION

THE SEARCH FOR WORLD PEACE
A Documentary History and Analysis

by
BENJAMIN B. FERENCZ

With An Introduction By
LOUIS B. SOHN

Volume 1

1975
OCEANA PUBLICATIONS, INC.
DOBBS FERRY, NEW YORK

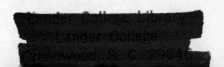

Library of Congress Cataloging in Publication Data
    Main entry under title:

    Defining international aggression, the search for world
        peace.

    1. Aggression (International law) I. Ferencz,
Benjamin B., 1920-
JX4471.D43   341.5'8   75-16473
ISBN 0-379-00271-X (v.1)
ISBN 0-379-00272-8 (v.2)

Manufactured in the United States of America

To

Gertrude

for her patience

If we our strength should all together join,
Viewing each other's welfare as our own,
If we should each exact full punishment
From evil doers for the wrongs they do,
The shameless violence of wicked men
Against the innocent would not prevail;
Guarded on every hand and forced to pay
The penalties which their misdeeds deserve,
They soon would cease to be, or few become.

Menander (3rd Cent. B.C.)

Cited by Grotius in The Law of
War and Peace (1648) Book I,
Chap. V. Sec. II, Kelsey Transl.
(1925).

Author's Preface

It seems only fair to explain to the reader how I came to write this book. When I was still a student at the Harvard Law School, a third of a century ago, one of the more interesting ways of earning my keep involved some research on the efforts under the Treaty of Versailles to bring the German Kaiser and others to trial for crimes committed during World War I. The knowledge thus acquired eventually led to an assignment in World War II which brought me into several of the Nazi concentration camps as they were liberated. This in turn led to a post with the prosecution staff at the subsequent Nuernberg trials, where there was further opportunity to consider the human as well as the legal consequences of aggressive war.

Being deeply moved by those experiences I spent a good many years thereafter in trying to obtain restitution for the victims of Nazi persecution. What seemed to me even more important than the punishment of the criminals or the rescue and rehabilitation of the survivors was the need to prevent the recurrence of the events which had given rise to the unprecedented tragedies.

There was never any doubt in my mind that aggression was the greatest of all human crimes and that the cause of world peace would be served if those responsible, no matter how high their rank or station, might be held to culpable account. It had been the hope of many of us at Nuernberg that some day there would be created a permanent judicial-type machinery with international authority to cope with the disputes which give rise to offenses against the peace and other crimes against humanity. The failure of States to be able to agree on a definition of aggression was the excuse given to defer any further efforts in that direction. In fact the governments were too engrossed in advancing their own immediate cause by every means within their power to be hampered by the visions of idealistic dreamers.

It seemed worthwhile therefore to try to encourage a definition by writing on the subject and the problems. It is with considerable trepidation that I have dared to re-tread the early historical paths which have been so well hewn by such respected scholars as Professors Julius Stone, Myres McDougal and others. It was an unavoidable frame of reference for the developments after the Second World War.

During the past few years I was the only unpaid, nongovernmental observer regularly to attend the meetings of the

Special Committee on the Question of Defining Aggression. If the collection of background materials and my observations will make it easier for the reader to understand how a consensus definition was reached and what it really means I will not consider my effort to have been completely in vain.

Benjamin B. Ferencz

New Rochelle, New York
December 1974

CONTENTS

VOLUME 1

DOCUMENTS

PART ONE: THE TRADITION OF WAR AND THE
           ASPIRATION FOR PEACE

PART TWO: THE AFTERMATH OF WORLD WAR II

18. Report of Robert H. Jackson, U.S. Rep. to the International Conference on Military Trials (ICMT),
London, 1945

Dept. of State Publ. 3080, International Org. and
Conf. Series II, European and British Commonwealth 1, June 26, August 8, 1945 (Extracts)

19. Nazi Conspiracy and Aggression, Vol. 1

VOLUME 2

DOCUMENTS

PART THREE: THE UNITED NATIONS MOVES TO DEFINE
AGGRESSION

General Assembly, Official Records (GAOR)

PART FOUR   AGGRESSION DEFINED BY CONSENSUS

INTRODUCTION

by

Louis B. Sohn

Bemis Professor of International Law,

Harvard Law School

After more than fifty years of international discussions, the General Assembly of the United Nations has finally approved a definition of aggression. The issue was first raised in the League of Nations in 1923 and was revived by the Soviet Union in 1950. Neither the International Law Commission nor the first three special committees appointed for the purpose by the General Assembly could agree on a definition. Finally, the fourth committee, established in 1967, after seven sessions reached a consensus on a definition of aggression in the strict sense of the term, abandoning the more complicated attempt to define also ideological and economic aggression.

The definition is not an ideal one and in the final debate many speakers expressed reservations about some of its provisions. Nevertheless, it was generally accepted that the consensus reached in the special committee was so fragile and so carefully balanced that it would have been dangerous to reopen in the Assembly the issues which were carefully papered over by the committee.

The definition has a quadruple purpose: to serve as a guideline to the Security Council, to deter the taking by the aggressor of any of the proscribed acts, to help mobilize public opinion in case of aggression and to facilitate immediate assistance to the victim of aggression by other States.

The definition forms part of a consistent effort of the United Nations to develop a code of basic rules of international law, implementing the cryptic provisions of the Charter of the United Nations. Adopted unanimously or by consensus, these rules are binding on the world community as authoritative interpretations of the Charter. They don't have an independent force, but draw their binding power from the Charter itself, which is the cornerstone of the world constitutional law.

As the definition has been accepted explicitly or implicitly by all the Members of the United Nations including the permanent members of the Security Council, it should be considered as binding on the Council as well. Of course, the definition is not an exhaustive one and permits the Security Council to determine that acts not enumerated in the definition constitute aggression. It also allows the Council to determine that in view of the relevant circumstances of a particular case certain acts, though falling under the definition, do not constitute aggression. Nevertheless, in view of the overwhelming support behind the definition, it should be difficult for the Council to disregard it in a concrete situation clearly falling under the definition.

To understand the new definition, it is not enough to look at its text. The preparatory materials of the special committee and earlier struggles to arrive at a definition need to be considered by any careful interpreter and decision-maker. To make this possible, Mr. Benjamin B. Ferencz has prepared a collection of relevant materials. It provides a thorough documentary history of this intricate subject and should be of great assistance to all concerned. Mr. Ferencz has followed this topic for some thirty years and is well qualified to provide such a comprehensive guide to this complicated chapter of the international legislative process. This collection constitutes an important contribution to the history of international law. For once, those who contended that this job will never be finished have been found to be too pessimistic, and the story told in this book has reached a satisfactory ending. The end of one story is, of course, only the beginning of another, and we have to wait many years before we will know what impact this document has had on the development of international relations. Perhaps some day the author will prepare another book about the practical applications of the new definition.

PART ONE

THE TRADITION OF WAR AND THE ASPIRATION FOR PEACE

PART ONE:

THE TRADITION OF WAR
AND
THE ASPIRATION FOR PEACE

Six tapestries adorn the halls of the Palace of Nations at Geneva. They tell the story of man's progress and aspirations. The artists depict the evolution of social life from the family, to the clan, the village, the feudal estates, the national State, and finally a universal Federation in which all people of all races are joined in a circle of peace. It has taken some 6000 years of man's recorded history to approach the frontiers of a world order in which equality and tranquility are combined. All this time man has lived and died with violence. What has endured is the unquenchable hope that, some day, the current of history will sweep away the prevailing anarchy whereby peoples and states decide for themselves when they may assault their neighbors. The determination to curb aggression is evidenced by the striving to define it.[1]

The awareness of the interdependence of all life on earth is a new reality. Transnational interaction for a better world now blossoms in areas which were unimagined only a few decades ago. Problems of population control and socio-economic transformation engage the combined attention of all nations. Food, energy, the seas, the sky and the air we breathe are increasingly the objects of both international competition and cooperation, as man comes to recognize that his survival depends upon a rational and equitable distribution of all vital resources. As long as violence, and the fear of violence, continue to drain the substance of life and destroy its quality, the legitimate aspirations for a more just society must remain dangerously frustrated. The proliferating capacity for thermonuclear annihilation intensifies the urgency for an effective system of peaceful change. If nations do not decide soon to replace the present pattern of systematic slaughter by a rule of reason, there may be no one left to make the choice.

Scholars and statesmen have labored for over half a century to fashion the framework of an agreed understanding delimiting the tolerable uses of armed force. Their efforts reflect the doubts, the retreats, the vacillation, and the dissents which characterize a peaceful alteration of any existing social order. The process whereby

3

the concept of "aggression" was defined must be viewed not merely in the perspective of the past, or the hesitant reality of the present, but also as part of the dream of the future.

(1) A Glance at History to the First World War.   (to 1918)

We are told that it was at least 400 years before Christ that the Chinese philosopher, Mo Ti, urged that international aggression be abandoned and that wars be outlawed as the greatest of all crimes. [2] Yet, man's history is a chronicle of bloodshed and war. The Ancient Greek city States, despite their high level of civilization, clashed and destroyed themselves in the Pelopennesian Wars. The Empire of Alexander the Great, enlightened and humanistic for its time, was torn asunder by the conflicting Hellenistic Kingdoms. In the 2nd and 3rd centuries B.C. Rome spread its power over vast empires which it governed by Roman law in relative tranquility for almost two centuries, before it too succumbed to internal upheaval. The growth of Byzantium, the expansion of Islam, and the emergence of the Papacy were accompanied by constant conflict against infidels, dissidents or invaders.

In Feudal Europe of the Middle Ages it was the absolute pre-rogative of the sovereign to employ force of arms as an instrument of national policy. War was the approved and lawful method of resolving disputes. As long as there existed some central authority, such as the Catholic church, which, by virtue of Divine Right, could determine that only one cause was "just", and the other "unjust", and which could then apply the sanctions of excommunication and interdiction, it was not necessary that States which were not directly involved in the conflict should take action in support of either side. On the contrary, it was their duty to limit the scope of the conflict by remaining neutral. [3]

Those not directly involved were abjured by Grotius to "do nothing whereby he who supports a wicked cause may be rendered more powerful, or whereby the movements of him who wages a just war may be hampered." [4] The duty to refrain from aiding one who "supports a wicked cause" is essentially the idea of not helping an aggressor. It is the root of what is found today in the U.N. Charter provisions which call upon Members to "refrain from giving assistance to any State against which the United Nations is taking preventive or enforcement action". [5] The policy, which has variously been labelled neutrality, non-discrimination, non-interference, restraint, or even indifference, was later to be coupled with a more positive duty to come to the aid of the victim of aggression. The transition from the requirement of simple restraint to the obligation of positive action was, however, a development which took at least two centuries.

Grotius had also urged that disputes be settled by independent judges or arbiters in order to limit the ceaseless wars which were plaguing Europe.[6] The merit of the idea was recognized, but it took almost three centuries for it to be accepted, and then only in part, so that it remained ineffective. The essential ingredient of compulsory jurisdiction was repeatedly rejected.

Leagues of Protestant Princes fought Leagues of Catholic Princes and when the 30 Years' War was ended by the Peace of Westphalia in 1648, the Holy Roman Empire was replaced by a new system of independent and equal national States. The fine art of diplomacy and the creation of religious, territorial or political alliances were the principle means to be employed in order to obtain or retain positions of power.

With the increase of commerce, the rise of colonialism, and growing nationalist feeling, the inadequacy of the existing methods of preventing violence soon became increasingly apparent. A number of distinguished thinkers in various parts of the world began to see the outlines of a better system. William Penn, the British Quaker, urged that a "Sovereign Court" be established to deal with disputes between States. If any State refused to submit its dispute or accept the decision of the court all of the other States would unite against the recalcitrant one, which would also have to pay reparations and all the expenses incurred in mounting the allied armies.[7] Rousseau proposed international Federations in 1761.[8] Kant's "Essay on Eternal Peace" favored a "Völkerbund" or Federal Union of Nations.[9]

In 1838 Jeremy Bentham proposed that there be a "common court of judicature for the decision of differences between the several nations."[10] At about the same time, the American peace advocate, William Ladd, proposed a "Congress of Nations" to deal with "the intercourse of nations in peace and war."[11] None of these proposals had any visible impact, until the beginnings of a breakthrough occurred at the start of the 20th century.

It was in 1899 that the Czar of Russia, unable to bear the burdens of rearmament, and faced with the fact that France and Germany had recently equipped their armies with new artillery pieces, convened the First Hague Peace Conference of 26 States for the Friendly Settlement of International Disputes.[12] Although the disarmament efforts failed, the Conferences of 1899, and its successor in 1907, did produce new and widely accepted rules for the conduct of war, and a convention was drafted for the Pacific Settlement of International Disputes.[13] It contained a formal plan of mediation, but only "as far as circumstances allow". It was considered

5

"desirable" that strangers to a dispute should offer their good offices, but it was specifically provided that such mediation or good offices "have exclusively the character of advice and never have binding force". A Permanent Court of Arbitration was established, but attempts to make recourse to arbitration compulsory were unsuccessful.[14]

The value of third-party intervention was perceived but compulsory jurisdiction of an objective international body was not something which the States were prepared to accept in 1899 or 1907, any more than they would accept it in the future years when the Covenant of the League of Nations was considered, or the International Court of Justice was founded.

In the early nineteen hundreds, with conflict seething in the Balkans, a number of private groups, societies, and individuals, took up or actively espoused the idea of a League of Nations to help prevent war.[15] The idea received too little support to prevent the outbreak of World War I. It was to be taken up again, this time more seriously, as the casualties of the war began to be counted.

Millions of soldiers and millions of civilians had perished in the battles. Many millions more had been wounded or had succumbed to epidemics or famine. In the face of such disaster there arose a universal call for some new system which might put an end to armed conflict. President Woodrow Wilson became the most articulate spokesman for a new organization "to guarantee peace and justice throughout the world." Addressing a Joint Session of Congress on January 8, 1918, President Wilson outlined the basis for peace. His "14 Points" culminated with a call for "A general association of nations . . . under specific covenants for the purpose of affording mutual guarantees of political independence and territorial integrity to great and small states alike."[16] The world had grown weary of aggression and its consequences.

(2) The League of Nations

(a) The Peace Conference and the Covenant (1918–1920).

The war over and the dead buried, all men's hearts cried out for a better order of society. The world's leaders were to assemble in Paris for a Peace Conference which was intended to prove that the enormous losses were not in vain. The concept of a League of Nations envisioned an association of governments freely chosen by their peoples and meeting together in a democratic process to maintain harmony and peace in the world. The League would enact, develop and enforce international laws for the benefit of society as

6

a whole, and would create new institutions to resolve whatever controversies might arise, and to impose whatever sanctions might be required to enforce its judgments. Such at least was the dream. [17]

Toward the end of 1917 a Supreme Inter-Allied War Council had been established at Versailles to render the war efforts more effective. Following the same pattern, the four major Powers – France, England, Italy and the United States, joined by Japan, designated their Premiers and Foreign Ministers to form a Council of Ten to prepare the terms of the treaty of peace. It convened what came to be known as "The Paris Peace Conference". Numerous special commissions were designated to deal with the many problems which were anticipated once an armistice was signed.

The Commission to Study the Responsibility of the Authors of the War concluded that Germany and Austria, as well as Turkey and Bulgaria, had declared war "in pursuance of a policy of aggression, the concealment of which gives to the origin of this war the character of a dark conspiracy against the peace of Europe". [18] Article 231 of the Versailles treaty called for the surrender of the Kaiser for trial by an allied court. Here can be seen the forerunner of the concept that aggressive war was a crime against peace for which there could be international criminal responsibility of the head of state. [19]

The Commission considered the problem of establishing a "high tribunal" which could try offenders not merely for the traditional war crimes, but also for the acts which brought about the war. The United States disapproved of the idea of an international tribunal and the possibility of legal charges against Heads of State for such vague concepts as "Crimes against Humanity". [20] It would take the suffering of one more world war to bring about a reversal of the U.S. position.

Undoubtedly the most important Commission established at the Paris Peace Conference was the one assigned the problem of creating the League of Nations and drafting the Covenant which would guide the actions of the League. The Committee, under the chairmanship of President Woodrow Wilson, who had become the foremost champion of the League idea, included some of the most respected intellectual and moral leaders of the time. [21] They were, however, not unmindful of the political realities of the society in which they lived. After 4 months of intensive effort, and some watering down, a Covenant of the League was adopted on April 28, 1919. (DOCUMENT 1).

The Covenant of the League set forth its purpose "to achieve international peace and security" through "international law" and "the maintenance of justice". Effective control was vested in the founding Members. Germany was excluded, and newcomers would only be admitted upon approval of two-thirds of the Assembly and

acceptance of the rules regarding military forces and armaments. [22]
The League proposed to act through an Assembly, representing each
Member, and a Council consisting of the major allied powers together
with a limited number of other representatives whom they would select from time to time. [23] The President of the United States was, by
the specific terms of the Covenant, to summon the first meeting. [24]

Recognizing that the maintenance of peace required a reduction
of national armaments, the Covenant called for a permanent Commission to study and advise on the subject. [25] This was a very weak
substitute for an international military force which had initially
been proposed by the French but which had been rejected. [26]

The first formal consideration of the question of aggression
appeared in Art. 10 of the Covenant. The Members undertook

> to respect and preserve as against external aggression
> the territorial integrity and existing political independ-
> ence of all Members of the League. In case of any such
> aggression or in case of any threat or danger of such ag-
> gression the Council shall advise upon the means by which
> this obligation shall be fulfilled.

It may be noted that by the reference to "such aggression"
the Covenant restricted the types of aggression with which it was
concerned. Its attention was focused on external aggression against
the territorial integrity and existing political independence of all
Members. It has been argued that Art. 10 was, for President Wilson,
the key article and one which would protect small states from the
ambitions of the great. [27] The reading of the text tends to support
a conclusion that it was, as finally accepted, designed to preserve
the existing boundaries and political structure of the Members from
being overturned by any external forces. The existing democracies
would band together to "make the world safe for Democracy".

Art. 11 was a catch-all, authorizing the League to "take any
action which might be deemed wise and effectual to safeguard the
peace of nations". Members agreed that any dispute likely to lead
to rupture would be submitted to arbitration or consideration by
the Council. [28] A clause added that in no case would Members resort
to war "until three months after the award" or report of the
Council.

War continued to be a recognized and permissible alternative,
despite the general preambular provision of "the obligation not to
resort to war". Traditional diplomacy remained the primary technique for reconciliation of differences. It was left to the Members
themselves to decide whether a dispute was suitable for submission
to arbitration. If arbitration was agreed upon, then other Members
were bound not to go to war against the party which accepted the
arbitral award. [29] It was also left to the parties themselves to

decide whether an issue should be submitted to the Permanent Court of International Justice which was subsequently established. [30]

If the parties did not decide to submit to arbitration or judicial settlement, they were obliged to submit the dispute to the Council. The Council, however, could only issue a report and make recommendations. If the Council, after excluding the parties to the dispute, reached a unanimous agreement, the other Members were only obliged to remain neutral, or "not go to war with any party to the dispute which complies with the recommendation of the report". In the absence of unanimity by the Council the Members were free to do as they saw fit. [31] How to close this "gap in the Covenant", was to become a source of later deliberation.

If any Member did in fact go to war without waiting for the three months prescribed in Art. 12, or against a Member who had complied with an arbitral award, or decision, or who had accepted the unanimous recommendations of the Council, then ipso facto that violator would "be deemed to have committed an act of war against all other Members". Under such circumstance the Members undertook to subject the Covenant-breaking State to sanctions including the severance of all trade or financial relations. There were general promises of mutual assistance and agreement of free passage to the forces of any Member cooperating to defend the Covenant. Violators could be expelled from the League. [32]

Although all obligations inconsistent with the terms of the Covenant were to be abrogated, [33] it was specifically stated that the Covenant would not affect the validity of regional understandings for securing the maintenance of peace, such as the Monroe Doctrine. [34] This discordant provision, inserted at the last moment, was intended to placate the United States Senate. It marred the Covenant, antagonized many, and failed to achieve its purpose.

The basic security plan of the Covenant was:

1. All arms were to be brought under the control of the Council,
2. Private manufacture of arms would be prohibited,
3. Members would exchange full information about armaments,
4. Aggression against any Member would be recognized, and,
5. Effective sanctions would immediately be employed against the aggressor.

The plan failed in every single point.

Despite all the safeguards and the retention of almost complete freedom of action, the isolationist United States Senate refused to give its consent to the Treaty. The failure of the world's richest and most powerful nation to accept the Covenant or to become a Member of the League was bound to destroy the possibility of the League ever becoming an effective instrumentality for world peace.

While the United States vacillated, or went its own way, the other major powers were determined to organize the League and to try to establish security systems as envisioned by the Covenant and the Versailles Treaty. The League Council proceeded to establish its rules, set up the Secretariat, and convene the Assembly.[35] At its first meeting the Assembly accepted the text of the Statute of the Permanent Court of International Justice, although the proposal of the Distinguished Jurists Committee, that the Court have compulsory jurisdiction, was rejected by the great powers.[36] The Committee of Jurists had also recommended the establishment of an International Criminal Court to try crimes against the universal law of nations. The Assembly, on advice of the Third Committee, rejected the idea, noting that there was as yet no international penal law recognized by all nations.[37] A resolution of the International Law Association that there was an urgent need for an International Criminal Court was largely ignored.[38]

The Assembly appointed a Temporary Mixed Commission for the Reduction of Armaments (T.M.C.) which consisted of a committee of experts from various fields. It supplemented the work of the purely military Permanent Advisory Commission on Military, Naval and Air Questions (P.A.C.), which was charged with responsibility for submitting plans for disarmament and security. The T.M.C. was to produce the first scheme for mutual security and disarmament.

(b) The Draft Treaty of Mutual Assistance (1923)

During the Third Assembly in 1922, the Council was requested to have the T.M.C. prepare for submission to governments, a Treaty of Mutual Guarantee embodying certain principles which the Assembly laid down.[39] (DOCUMENT 2 (a)) The treaty would have to recognize 1) that no disarmament scheme could be fully successful unless it was universal; 2) that armament reduction would only be acceptable to many governments if they received in exchange a guarantee of the safety of their country; 3) that such a guarantee should provide immediate and effective assistance in the event any signatory was attacked; and lastly that the guarantees would only be called into play if the government attacked had previously agreed to reduce its arms. The guarantee and disarmament were interdependent. One was the reward for the other.

The plan could be carried out in whole or in part by either general or partial treaties. The T.M.C. was also asked to consider the possibility of concluding similar agreements on a regional basis.[40]

By the following year the Fourth Assembly had before it the proposed text of the document which had gone through several drafts and was now called a Treaty of Mutual Assistance. (DOCUMENT NO. 2 (b)) It was seen as the suggested method for implementing Art. 8 of the Covenant. The first of its 18 Articles, declared: "aggressive war is an international crime", which the High Contracting Parties agreed not to commit. The parties jointly and severally undertook to furnish assistance to any signatory which was the object of a war of aggression, provided it had conformed to the disarmament requirements.[41] A party threatened by aggression could also summon the Council of the League.[42] The Council was expected to decide, within 4 days, which party was the object of aggression and whether they were entitled to claim assistance.[43] The other parties were then to furnish whatever assistance the Council considered likely to be the most effective.[44] The aggressor could also be charged with reparations.[45] The parties were obliged to recognize the compulsory jurisdiction of the Permanent Court with regard to interpretations of the Treaty.[46]

The key to triggering the whole defensive system was action by the Council determining which party was the aggressor. The Council, as in the Covenant, would have to act unanimously, excluding only those parties which were engaged in hostilities. It was anticipated that such a determination could be made within four days. Yet nowhere in the Treaty was there any definition of what would constitute an act of aggression.

An exculpatory sentence was contained in Art. 1 in which it was stated that it would not be a war of aggression if a State was acting pursuant to a unanimous recommendation of the Council, a verdict of the Permanent Court or an arbitral award, providing there was no intent (by the party resorting to war), to violate the political independence or territorial integrity of the party which refused to accept the award. This was the only reference to the intent of the parties, an element which was to become the subject of great debate over the many years during which the subject of aggressive war was to be considered.

It was not long before objections were raised against the obvious deficiencies in the proposed Treaty.[47] Several Delegations expressed the opinion that "under the conditions of modern warfare it would seem impossible to decide, even in theory, what constitutes a case of agression".[48] The previous definition of aggression had been "mobilization or the violation of a frontier", and this double test, they said, had now lost its value, since now whole countries were mobilized, frontiers were hard to ascertain, and actions by air or naval forces could disregard frontiers. Even "armed forces" could not be identified since irregular troops or police forces could be used. They perceived that the problem of support for armed bands, or indirect aggression would also have to be resolved, but it is doubtful whether they realized that it would still be debated half a century later.

Having noted the difficulty of defining aggression the Delegates tried to set forth precise criteria of what seemed to them to be essential military steps before aggression could be committed. The sequence of preparing for aggression, from a military point of view, would have to be: The organization of industrial mobilization, the collection of stocks of raw materials, the setting up of war industries, the preparation for and the actual military mobilization, and finally hostilities. By the time the character of such steps was recognized it would be too late to act to avert war.

The Delegates also looked to other, non-military, criteria which might give the examiner some impression of whether aggression was about to take place. This included the political attitude and propaganda of the possible aggressor, the attitude of the press and population, and policies on the international market, but these were considered too vague to allow preventive action. They concluded therefore that every aggression "gives rise to a 'particular case' which does not come within the scope of a general treaty". [49]

A Special Committee of the Temporary Mixed Commission commented on the definition of aggression. (DOCUMENT 2 (c)) The Members noted that it would be theoretically desirable, if it could be done, to set down an exact definition of aggression which the Council could then simply apply to determine which party was the aggressor. They agreed, however, that, in the light of the views expressed by the P.A.C., and some of the Delegates, such a precise definition was not possible. They did not, however, seem quite as pessimistic as their professional military colleagues. In their view "If the troops of one power invade the territory of another, this fact in itself constitutes a presumption that the first power has committed a wrongful act of aggression". [50] Here we see the beginnings of the doctrine, which was later to be universally accepted, that the onus rests with the State which is the first to invade, but it only gives rise to a presumption of aggression.

The Special T.M.C. Committee Members recognized that the presumption was not conclusive and that where troops were close to each other it might be difficult to ascertain which party had acted first. They suggested therefore that, as a matter of tactic, the Council try first to arrange a separation of forces wherever there seemed to be a conflict brewing. Some of the Members felt that refusal to agree to a separation would be either proof that the refusing party was the aggressor or could lead to such an inference. [51] The Committee agreed that a large scale attack by one party upon the territory of another would be decisive evidence of aggression. (The reference to a "large scale" attack seemed to anticipate the preclusion of "minor incidents", a point which was to appear again in the 1970's.) Similarly, a surprise attack by poison gas from the air would be decisive.

The Members were inclined to agree that it would not be possible to draw up a precise definition and that whatever definition was accepted would still face the difficulty of being interpreted when applied to specific circumstances in the light of the other elements mentioned by the P.A.C. They felt therefore that the best policy might be for the Council to call upon the parties to abstain, or to cease hostilities and agree to be bound by either the recommendation of the Council or a decision of the Permanent Court. The invitation might "be accompanied by an intimation that the party which refused would be considered the aggressor".[52]

The Committee concluded:

"It is clear, therefore, that no simple definition of aggression can be drawn up, and that no simple test of when an act of aggression has actually taken place can be devised. It is, therefore, clearly necessary to leave the Council complete discretion in the matter, merely indicating that the various factors mentioned above may provide the elements of a just decision."[53]

The factors indicating aggression were summarized as:

(a) Actual industrial and economic mobilization, which could be carried out by a State or "by persons or societies on foreign territory". The Committee thereby anticipated that the organization of subversive activities abroad might constitute an element in determining aggression.

(b) "Secret military mobilization by the formation and employment of irregular troops, or by a declaration of a state of danger of war which would serve as a pretext for commencing hostilities". The use of armed bands and mobilization under a pretext of defense would also indicate an aggressive design.

(c) "Air, chemical or naval attack".

(d) "The presence of armed forces of one party on the territory of another".

(e) Refusal to withdraw forces behind the line indicated by the Council.

(f) "A definitively aggressive policy" and the refusal to submit the dispute to the Council or the Permanent Court, and to refuse to accept the recommendation or decision rendered. The Committee recognized the difficulties but felt that the Council would "probably be in a position to form an opinion as to which of the parties is really actuated by aggressive intentions".[54]

The Council referred the Draft Treaty of Mutual Assistance to a Committee of Jurists which found even more difficulties. The Jurists did not like the reference to "aggressive war" and preferred to characterize as an international crime a war which was "contrary to the provisions of the Covenant".[55]

The Draft Treaty of Mutual Assistance was sent to all governments, including those not Members of the League, for comments to be submitted to the Council. It did not take long for the United States, England, Russia and Germany to make clear their absolute opposition. (DOCUMENT 3 (a)) Almost every government recognized that the Council could not possibly act quickly or reliably unless and until there were some clear criteria to make it possible to decide which of two warring states was the aggressor. The Draft Treaty of Mutual Assistance was dead.[56]

(c) The Protocol for the Pacific Settlement of International Disputes (1924)

An American group drew up an amended treaty of mutual guarantee which was submitted to the League Assembly in 1924. (DOCUMENT 3 (b)) The plan, which also contained various resolutions on disarmament and sanctions, was deceptively simple. It was a contract with a sanction attached. Aggressive war was denounced as "an international crime".[57] The Contracting Parties undertook not to commit it.[58] The Permanent Court would decide whether aggression had been committed.[59] It was recognized that certain preparatory acts not amounting to a state of war could be aggressive and were prohibited.[60] Even in the absence of a state of war, the use of military force would be an act of aggression, unless it was taken "for the purpose of defense against aggression or the protection of human life". Mobilization was deemed preparation for aggression. Any signatory claiming violation could submit the case to the Permanent Court, and any signatory failing to accept the jurisdiction of the Court within 4 days would be deemed an aggressor.[61] Economic sanctions or force could be applied against an aggressor within the discretion of each signatory.[62]

Under the American plan there was no need to involve the Council of the League, to which the United States did not belong. The problem of deciding whether aggression had been committed was relegated to the Court, which presumably would be able to make a just determination. The key point was that the parties could not resort to force but would have to submit their dispute to an impartial judicial body for binding determinaton. The willingness to submit to arbitration or adjudication was seen as the test of whether a party was guilty of aggression. What was meant by "defense against aggression", or military force used for "the protection of human life", was not explained in the American Plan. It was rather obvious from past U.S. attitudes that such questions would be decided by each sovereign State.

The American Plan, although considered and compared with other plans, was never accepted or even seriously debated. (DOCUMENT 3 (c)) It was merged into a new plan put forward by the

British and the French which sought to combine various elements from the aborted Treaty of Mutual Assistance and the American proposal.

The official title of the new proposal was "The Protocol for the Pacific Settlement of International Disputes". (DOCUMENT 3 (d)) It sought to combine into one agreement the key elements of Arbitration, Security and Disarmament. It was designated a "Protocol" to make it clear that it was considered a document to implement, and not replace, the provisions of the Covenant of the League. A report of the First Committee, prepared by Mr. Politis of Greece, and a report by Mr. Benes, Rapporteur of the Third Committee, dealt more comprehensively than ever before with the question of determining the aggressor. (DOCUMENT 3 (e))

Mr. Politis noted that the object of the Protocol was to guarantee security of states by developing methods for the pacific settlement of disputes "and the effective condemnation of aggressive war".[63] Compulsory arbitration was the fundamental basis of the proposed system. The "gap in the Covenant", which allowed war under certain circumstances, was to be closed by prohibiting all wars of aggression. "No purely private war between nations will be tolerated".[64] Under Art. 2 of the protocol the signatories agreed not to go to war against any other signatory "except in case of resistance to acts of aggression" or pursuant to the agreement of the Council or the Assembly. "The right of legitimate self-defense continues" said Mr. Politis. "The State attacked retains complete liberty to resist by all means in its power any acts of aggression of which it may be the victim".[65] A state could participate in collective measures of force, it authorized by the League, and it would then be acting, not on its own, but as an agent of the world community.

The signatories would be bound to accept compulsory jurisdiction of the Permanent Court, although they could do so with a wide range of possible reservations.[66] The procedures for settling disputes as laid down in the Covenant were to be strengthened.[67] National sovereignty was protected in that matters held by the Court to be within the domestic jurisdiction of a state were not subject to compulsory arbitration.[68] Amicable methods of settlement prescribed by the Covenant were not to be excluded.[69] The signatories would undertake "to abstain from any act which might constitute a threat of aggression".[70]

Art. 10 of the draft Protocol was a key article. Under its terms any state resorting to war in violation of the Covenant or the Protocol was to be condemned as an aggressor. Violation of the rules for demilitarized zones was equivalent to a resort to war. Refusal to submit a dispute to the prescribed pacific settlement procedures was itself an act of aggression, unless the Council unanimously decided otherwise. Thus, under the new plan, positive action by the Council was required to negate the presumption of aggression which arose from failing to submit the dispute to peaceful settlement. Refusal to accept an armistice, or the violation of its terms, was also an act of aggression, immediately calling forth the prescribed sanctions by the other signatory states.

The sanctions were economic, financial and military, and reparations were to be paid by the aggressor.[71] Signatory states specifically undertook to participate in an International Conference for the Reduction of Armaments which was set for Geneva on June 15, 1925, thereby showing the close connection between the entire Protocol and the ultimate disarmament objectives.[72]

The effectiveness of the Protocol depended upon the speedy identification of the aggressor. "There are two aspects to the problem", said Mr. Politis. "First, aggression has to be defined, and secondly, its existence has to be ascertained".[73] The Committee considered the definition of aggression to be a relatively easy matter. That state would be the aggressor which:

"resorts in any shape or form to force in violation of the engagements contracted by it under the Covenant (if, for instance, being a Member of the League of Nations, it has not respected the territorial integrity or political independence of another Member of the League) or under the present Protocol (if, for instance, being a Signatory of the Protocol, it has refused to conform to an arbitral award or to a unanimous decision of the Council)".[74]

The use of force in violation of the Covenant or refusal to accept the award of the Court or the unanimous decision of the Council was aggression.

Ascertaining whether aggression had occurred was considered to be much more difficult. "When one country attacks another, the latter necessarily defends itself, and when hostilities are in progress on both sides, the question arises which party began them".[75] Unanimous decision by the Council, even excluding the parties in dispute, was not considered a satisfactory approach since it subjected the defending State to the hazard that some Council Member might not be prepared to recognize a certain use of force as aggressive. Majority vote of the Council would also not be satisfactory since those who didn't concur could hardly be expected to apply sanctions as required by the agreement. The Protocol framers thought they found the solution by having created a presumption that aggression had occurred unless certain procedures were followed, and thereby having shifted the burden of proof of aggression until the unanimous decision of the Council might rule otherwise. The presumption of aggression would arise when a resort to war was accompanied by: 1) A refusal to accept the procedure of pacific settlement or to submit to the decision resulting therefrom; 2) Violation of the provisions of the Protocol prohibiting rearmament while a dispute was under advisement; or 3) Disregarding a decision that the dispute concerned was a purely domestic matter, and refusing to submit that question to the Council or the Assembly for possible conciliation. [76]

In the absence of the conditions giving rise to the presumption it was still up to the Council to decide whether or not aggression existed. If it acted unanimously there would be no problem, but if the Council could not agree, then it could call for an armistice by two-thirds vote. The party refusing to honor such an armistice would thereby be rendered an aggressor. A determination of aggression would automatically bring into play all of the sanctions and obligations of the guarantor states.

An important point was made that even a state acting against an aggressor does not possess entire freedom of action. "The force employed by it must be proportionate to the object in view and must be exercised within the limits and under the conditions recommended by the Council". [77]

The Third Committee under the chairmanship of Mr. Benes, assigned the task of drafting the articles dealing with the question of sanctions and disarmament, believed they were on the threshold of a new form of political life. Mr. Benes recognized that each state would still remain the judge of what sanctions it would apply, but it would no longer be the judge of what it should do. The sanctions would vary with the nature of the aggression. Under the system of the Covenant each party could decide for itself whether the unanimous decision of the Council regarding which state was the aggressor was justified and whether the obligation to apply economic sanctions was operative at all. Under the propsed new system of the Protocol it was the Council which would decide which state was the aggressor and sanctions would be required "loyally and effectively". Mr. Benes considered that both previous loopholes had been closed - the one allowing the Council's recommendations not to be followed, and the further possibility that the Council itself might fail to reach unanimity so that no determination of aggression would exist and no sanctions would be required. [78] If both States were held to be aggressors then economic and financial sanctions, but not military sanctions, would be applied against both. [79]

In calling for acceptance of the new system, Mr. Benes reminded the Assembly: "The peace of the world is at stake". [80] The Protocol was adopted unanimously, but by its terms it was to come into effect only upon ratification by the requisite number of states, and only upon the condition that the plan for the reduction of armaments went into effect. [81] There was the catch!

Although France immediately announced full support for the Protocol, the enthusiasm at Geneva did not carry over to other distant capitals. In England a Conservative Government had just ousted the Labour Party. Commonwealth members found no joy in the prospect of having to apply sanctions to maintain European boundaries. The idea of compulsory arbitration was as unpopular in the Foreign Office as it was in the U.S. Senate. By the time the Council met in March 1925 the fate of the Protocol was sealed. Like the Draft Treaty of Mutual Assistance before it, the Protocol for the Pacific Settlement of International Disputes was to be discarded into the trashcan of man's unrealized dreams.

(3) Early Security Plans Outside the League

(a) The Treaty of Mutual Guarantee and the Treaties of Locarno (1925)

As the funeral for the Geneva Protocol was being prepared the German government proposed a "Rhineland Pact" between Germany, France, Britain and Italy to guarantee the Franco-German frontier and the territorial status of the Rhine. This provided the British with the incentive to put aside the discussion of the Protocol in favor of disarmament arrangements between governments directly concerned with specific problems. The delegations turned their eyes toward a new series of conferences which were to take place in 1925 in Locarno.

The series of agreements which emerged were designed to deal with some of the specific disputes then threatening the peace of the nations concerned.

The basic document, which was the model for similar agreements between France and Poland, and France and Czechoslovakia, was the Treaty of Mutual Guarantee between Germany, Belgium, France, Great Britain and Italy. (DOCUMENT 4) It was intended to supply certain supplementary guarantees within the framework of the Covenant. The parties agreed to maintain the inviolability of the frontiers fixed in the Treaty of Versailles.[82] Germany and Belgium and also Germany and France, as the principal parties in dispute, agreed not to resort to war against each other, except, in "the exercise of the right of legitimate defense". Self defense was contemplated if one party violated the undertaking not to attack, invade, or resort to war, or if there was a "flagrant breach" of the Versailles provisions relating to a demilitarized zone, providing "such breach constitutes an unprovoked act of aggression and by reason of the assembly of armed forces in the demilitarized zone immediate action is necessary". . . [83] (Underlining added.) No explanation of what facts would signify that the action was either "flagrant", "unprovoked" or "aggression" was offered.

18

Resort to war would also be permissible if it was done pursuant to Art. 16 of the Covenant, or a decision taken by the Assembly or the Council under Art. 15, but in the latter case only if it was directed against "a state which was the first to attack". [84]

Differences were to be settled by peaceful means and conflicts were to be submitted to judicial decision which the parties agreed to accept. Other problems would go to a newly created Conciliation Commission, and if the Commission's proposals or other arbitral or judicial decisions, were not accepted the question would go to the Council of the League to be dealt within the limits prescribed by the Covenant. [85]

During the Locarno meetings no one paid much attention to the question of trying to define aggression, or of trying to pin down precisely what was meant by "flagrant", "unprovoked", or some of the other vague terms in the Treaty. The defects were concealed by an event which occurred within 10 days after the Locarno meetings were concluded and which was to raise public hopes that a procedure for peaceful settlement of disputes had finally been devised.

A border incident occurred between Greece and Bulgaria, both Members of the League, which caused the Secretary General of the League to convene the Council to deal with a threat of war. The British, French and Italians joined to put an end to the hostilities. There was an immediate cease-fire, withdrawal from occupied territories, appointment of a commission to investigate and report to the Council, and agreement by both parties to be bound by the Council's decision. The Council found that the pleas of both sides that they had acted in self defense were unjustified, that responsibility was divided and that some reparations should be paid by Greece. This success, coupled with the new treaties signed at Locarno, seemed to confirm the impression that the Covenant could work effectively without any more detailed agreements than those already concluded.

The Locarno Treaty went into force in September 1926. Under the illusion that nothing more was required, attention was directed during the next few years to additional bilateral or multi-lateral security arrangements.

With the states on her western flank forming alliances the Soviet Union began to look to her own defenses. In 1925 she signed a Treaty of Friendship and Neutrality with Turkey, in which the parties agreed to refrain from aggression, to form no alliances with others, and to refrain from any hostile act in the event of hostilities with third parties. [86] The following year Russia went a step further, and in her Treaty of Non-Aggression with Lithuania the parties also agreed to a conciliation commission to resolve differences which might arise between them. [87] A year after that in its Treaty of Guarantee and Neutrality with Persia the Soviets were to go even further, and prohibit acts of subversion or the organization of any groups directed against the government of the other party. [88]

19

The major powers, the United States, Germany and Russia, were outside the League and yet no effective decisions regarding world peace could be concluded without them. 1926 was a year which concentrated on the problems connected with the admission of Germany into the League and the enforcement of the Versailles Treaty. The Senate of the United States had made it clear that although it would authorize U.S. signature to the statute for the World Court, it would be subject to the reservation that "such adherance shall not be taken to involve any legal relation on the part of the United States to the League of Nations". . . . The Court could only act on matters affecting the United States if the United States agreed, and even this restricted adherence to the Court could not be construed to "require the United States to depart from its traditional policy of not intruding upon, interfering with, or entangling itself in the political questions of policy or internal administration of any foreign state" or "to imply a relinquishment by the United States of its traditional attitude toward purely American questions".[89] It was within the framework of the planned Disarmament Conference that more effective cooperation was to be sought.

(b) The Preparatory Commission for the Disarmament
Conference and Model Treaties of Non-Aggression
(1926-1928)

The United States, Germany and the Soviet Union, although not Members of the League, played an active role in the preparations for the Disarmament Conference foreseen by the Versailles Treaty and the Covenant. The Commission to prepare the conference appointed a Committee on Arbitration and Security which was to consider the entire question of reducing the need for armaments by providing alternate forms of security to the participants. It was clear that there could be no feeling of safety until there was some guarantee that collective and effective sanctions would be applied promptly in the event of aggression. A prerequisite for such action was a method for determining without delay which State was in fact the aggressor. The provisions of the Covenant were vague and other early efforts at definition had been inconclusive.

While the Disarmament Conference was being prepared the International Law Association, the Inter-Parliamentary Union, and the First International Congress of Penal Law, under the leadership of Prof. V.V. Pella of Bucharest, urged that an international court be established to deal with international crimes, and particularly with aggression.[90] On September 24, 1927 the Assembly resolved "That all wars of aggression are, and always shall be, prohibited" and denounced wars of aggression as "an international crime". (DOCUMENT 5) No definition of aggression was attempted, but the subject attracted growing attention by the Committee on Arbitration and Security.

Mr. Politis, the Rapporteur dealing with the security question, presented a comprehensive overview of the prevailing situation. (DOCUMENT 6) He recognized that security depended upon guarantees: 1) That a State would not be attacked; and 2) That if attacked it would receive prompt and effective aid from other countries. This was the scheme behind Art. 10 and 16 of the Covenant. The requirement of unanimity by the Council was only one of the elements making the outcome uncertain. Disarmament depended upon security, and security, according to the Committee, was dependent upon arbitration. All were interdependent. Not only did states have to be free from the danger of aggression but they would also have to be free from the fear of aggression, if they were expected to disarm.

Mr. Politis recognized that a world security pact would be desirable but, in the light of past experience, he did not consider that feasible. Instead he urged that there be created a series of regional pacts to supplement the existing treaties then being concluded among many states in search of mutual security. The Draft Treaty of Mutual Assistance of 1923, the Protocol of 1924, and the Rhine Pact of 1925 could serve as useful models for new regional treaties which would exclude recourse to war, establish procedures to settle disputes without violence, and prescribe a system of mutual assistance in the event of breach. He noted that:

> "It will be essential to make it quite plain that the condemnation related only to aggressive war ... Force may still be resorted to for purposes of legitimate defense, in the application of Art. 16 of the Covenant, in execution of a decision of the Assembly or Council of the League, or when action is undertaken, in virtue of Art. 15, Par. 7, of the Covenant, against a State guilty of aggression". [91]

For the purposes of a regional security pact Mr. Politis felt that it would be sufficient, despite the difficulty of determining unprovoked aggression, to say that the term "aggressor":

> "shall be applicable to any contracting state that resorts to force in violation of the undertakings entered into by it in the regional pact; for example, if it offers armed resistance to a final decision".

Mr. Rutgers submitted a Memorandum on Articles 10, 11 and 16 of the Covenant. [92] In dealing with the question of defining aggression he concluded that he did not feel called upon to offer a precise definition but considered it more practical to "enumerate some of the facts which, according to circumstances, may serve as evidence that aggression has taken place". He felt that any attempt to lay down rigid or absolute rules would, in the existing circumstances, not lead to any practical result. "It must be recognized" said Mr. Rutgers, "that the results which it (the Council) will obtain cannot be regarded as complete or as applicable to every case. A particular act may be deemed to raise, or not to raise, a presumption of aggression having regard to the circumstances under which it was committed." [93]

In searching for criteria which would be useful in determining acts of aggression, Mr. Rutgers looked to past treaties, the proceedings of the Assembly and Council, and the records of the Draft Treaty of Mutual Assistance. These were extracted to include: "Invasion", "attack on a considerable scale launched by one State on the frontiers of another State", "a surprise attack by aircraft ... with the aid of poisonous gases", "actual industrial and economic mobilization, carried out locally or by persons or societies on foreign territory", "secret military mobilization by the formation of irregular troops, or by pretending that there was the danger of war and using that as a pretext for commencing hostilities", "air, chemical or naval attack", "the presence of armed forces ... on the territory of another", or the refusal to withdraw behind a line indicated by the Council. A "definitely aggressive policy" and a refusal to let the Council or the Permanent Court decide the issue were additional factors to be considered.

To these elements, which the Special Committee of the Temporary Mixed Commission had already listed, the Rutgers Committee added that the violation of certain undertakings would also signify aggression, such as the refusal to abide by agreed methods for the pacific settlement of disputes or to observe military restrictions which had been accepted. [94] The Committee listed many of the treaties which contained military restrictions such as the partial demilitarization of certain areas, and noted that a violation "would in many circumstances - in the absence of any express stipulation - raise a presumption of aggression". [95]

Mr. Rutgers agreed with Mr. Politis that the violation of a demilitarized zone, such as set forth in the Rhine Pact, would justify the legitimate right of defense, but it was coupled with the condition that it be "an unprovoked act of aggression" requiring immediate defensive action to meet the assembly of forces by the other side. The Committee endorsed the rules laid down in the Rhineland Pact, according to which the guarantor states could intervene immediately in case of a "flagrant violation" of the demilitarized zone, providing it was considered an "unprovoked act of aggression" calling for immediate response. The Council would then be seized of the question and could by unanimous decision, excluding the belligerent parties, determine the issue. The provisions of the Protocol of Geneva were also referred to approvingly, according to which the burden of proof was to be shifted, and a state was to be presumed the aggressor, unless the Council unanimously decided otherwise, if the State refused to accept the procedure for pacific settlement, violated an injunction of the Council, or disregarded a decision that the dispute was a purely domestic matter.

"It is clear", said Mr. Rutgers, "that the nature and extent of the cooperation which the parties to the dispute are willing to afford to the Council cannot fail to exercise considerable influence upon the decision of that body". The degree of cooperation therefore was to be another indicator of aggression.

In considering how to implement the Council's broad authority under Art. 11, to "take any action" to safeguard the peace, Mr. Rutgers felt that no code of procedure could be established as a guide. "The infinite variety of events that may occur in political life cannot be confined in advance in watertight compartments". [96] The role recommended to the Council was to keep in close touch with the situation through its Members and their diplomatic agents, and to try to reconcile differences by reminding the parties of their treaty obligations, by sending commissions of inquiry, by trying directly to settle the issues, and by trying to mitigate the effects of any rupture which might have taken place. Having thus become deeply involved in trying to prevent, limit, or put an end to the hostilities, it was felt by the Committee that the Council's interaction with the problem would make it possible for the Council Members to determine which State was really the aggressor. Said the committee:

"It is not necessarily the State to whose conduct the crisis was originally due which is to be regarded as the aggressor; in certain eventualities it might possibly be the other party which ought to be regarded as the aggressor, if it has deliberately refused to conform to the Council's recommendations". [97]

It was noted that the recommendation of the Council would not only influence the parties and face them with the possibility that failure to comply would trigger coercive measures against them, but it would also serve as a source for influencing public opinion.

"It must be recognized", said Mr. Rutgers, "that it would be extremely desirable to arrive at a generally accepted interpretation which would put an end to many controversies". [98] The trouble was that there were no rules, and Mr. Rutgers feared that the existence of hard and fast criteria would force a nation to decide whether there had been "resort to war" at a time when there was still room for doubt, and thereby destroy the possibility for mediation by the Council before hostilities began. In short, clear cut criteria might hamper the chances for a peaceful settlement.

The Rutgers Committee concluded:

"A hard-and-fast definition of the expression 'aggression' (Art. 10), and 'resort to war' (Art. 16) would not be free from danger, since it might oblige the Council and the Members of the League to pronounce on a breach of the Covenant and apply sanctions at a time when it would still be preferable to refrain for the moment from measures of coercion. There would also be the risk that criteria might be taken which, in unforeseen circumstances, might lead to a State which was not in reality responsible for hostilities being described as an aggressor".[99]

After noting that committee members had differed, the Assembly adopted the resolution put forth by the Committee, which simply stated that the criteria of aggression contained in the Committee's documents usefully summarized the studies previously made. [100]

The Arbitration and Security Committee, finding itself bogged down in general discussions about ambiguous phraseology, and recognizing the impossibility of making any substantial progress in having the major powers accept binding interpretations, turned its attention to the drafting of a wide assortment of Model Treaties which States might choose if they were inclined to seek their security safeguards by such means.

A "General Act" called for the pacific settlement of all disputes by arbitration, conciliation or judicial determination, or a combination of all three. A choice of treaties or conventions gave the signatories the option of coupling the renunciation of force, with guarantees of mutual assistance against a violator. The Model Treaties of non-aggression, either on a collective or a bilateral basis, provided that the parties would not "attack or invade each other or resort to war". A specific exception was made, however, if the action was taken as part of a right of legitimate defense in opposing an attack, invasion or act of war. Force was also permissible if taken pursuant to Article 15 Paragraph 7 and Article 16 of the Covenant, or pursuant to a decision of the Assembly or the Council. The Assembly of 1928 approved and recommended the nine models presented for selection.[101] The General Act was the only one which actually came into force, only to be repudiated a few years after its birth.

(c) The General Treaty for the Renunciation of War, - (The Kellogg-Briand Pact) (1928)

The work of the League was overshadowed by the leading international event of 1928. On the 10th anniversary of the U.S. entry into the war the French Foreign Minister, Aristide Briand, had sent a message to the American people calling for an agreement with the United States mutually outlawing war as an instrument of national policy.[102] The United States had thereupon prepared its own draft of such a treaty and circulated it to a number of governments on June 23, 1928. It was accompanied by an explanatory note, which stated:

"There is nothing in the American draft of an anti-war treaty which restricts or impairs in any way the right of

24

self-defense. That right is inherent in every sovereign state and is inherent in every treaty. Every nation is free at all times and regardless of treaty provisions to defend its territory from attack or invasion and it alone is competent to decide whether circumstances require recourse to war in self-defense...Express recognition by treaty of this inalienable right, however, gives rise to the same difficulty encountered in any effort to define aggression. It is the identical question approached from the other side. Inasmuch as no treaty provision can add to the natural right of self-defense, it is not in the interest of peace that a treaty should stipulate a juristic conception of self-defense since it is far too easy for the unscrupulous to mold events to accord with an agreed definition".[103]

The General Treaty for the Renunciation of War as an instrument of National Policy, popularly known as the Kellogg-Briand Pact, or the Pact of Paris, was signed in Paris on August 27, 1928. (DOCUMENT 7) It was eventually ratified by almost all of the countries of the world. It consisted of only two brief articles. Recourse to war was renounced as an instrument of national policy, and the parties pledged that the solution of all disputes would never be sought except by pacific means.

The interpretation which the U.S., and Great Britain, put on the treaty destroyed the hope that it could really be effective in achieving its noble goals. The U.S. right to self-defense encompassed not merely the territory of the U.S. but also any other area in which the U.S. decided that it had a vital interest. The British considered their domain to include all territories under British sovereignty.[104] Under such circumstances it was obvious why there was no desire to define aggression. Almost every act of war could be justified under the guise of self-defense. A war of aggression would never again be waged - except in self-defense. The Pact was, in fact, a plan for maintaining the peace by guaranteeing the status quo. It was doomed to failure - but that became apparent only later.

(4) The Road to World War Two

(a) The Beginning of the End   (1929-1932)

The world economic crisis of 1929 diverted public attention from the problems of disarmament. The United States and Great Britain were working on arrangements to diminish the size of their Navies and the League's Preparatory Commission for the Disarmament Conference remained nearly paralyzed. German proposals to improve the means of preventing war by having states agree in advance to accept the recommendations of the Council were debated, together with Finland's plan to arrange for funds in advance which might be available to any state threatened with aggression. [105] Problems of minorities and reparations were in the fore. Nationalism and militarism were on the rise. At the end of 1930 the Preparatory Commission closed five years of its work. Its disarmament proposals inspired no enthusiasm.

When the Assembly met in 1931 it was in an atmosphere of gloom. A sub-committee had been set up to consider amendments to the Covenant, in order to bring the Covenant into harmony with the Pact of Paris. The Rapporteur was M. Henri Rolin of Belgium, and his report considered the question of self-defense and aggression.

M. Rolin concluded:

". . .in the present state of the law, the satisfactory enumeration of the distinctive characteristics either of aggression or of legitimate self-defense appears difficult and even impossible". [106]

He referred to the report which M. de Brouckere had made in 1926 which had noted some of the difficulties in drawing the line between aggression and self-defense. A victim of aggression could, for example, become the aggressor unless the defense was "proportionate to the seriousness of the attack and justified by the imminence of the danger".

The Committee felt that "assistance given spontaneously by a Member of the League to another Member which has been the victim of flagrant aggression would not constitute a violation of the prohibition of recourse to war". The intervening state, once having decided who was the aggressor, did not have to wait for a decision of the Council on that subject, but could apply the sanctions foreseen in the Covenant. What those sanctions might be was best left to the individual Member's discretion. The Committee saw no acceptable way to improve the situation. States were not ready, even theoretically, to increase their obligations, and the Committee felt there was no viable alternative but to rely on the good faith of the Members. [107]

A General Convention to Improve the Means of Preventing War was signed in Geneva on Sept. 26, 1931, by representative of 22 States, but it contained nothing more than precautionary steps designed to prevent incidents from growing into wars. [108]

The Assembly, not knowing what else it could do, looked for action to the Disarmament Conference which was scheduled to take place in February 1932. Before the Disarmament Conference could meet, Japan, in clear violation of the restrictions against the use of armed force in both the Covenant and the Kellogg Pact, invaded Manchuria. Japan argued that she was acting against lawless elements in self-defense, to protect her vital interests in line with the doctrine expressed by the U.S. and British governments when they ratified the Pact of Paris! [109]

Under the League's interpretation of Article 11 of the Covenant, unanimous action by the Council was required before it could take any action to safeguard the peace. With Japan in opposition, the Council was legally stymied. The United States was not ready to risk coercive action against Japan. Britain, also in the midst of a depression, would not act alone, and France, fearing a rearmed Germany, had no desire to engage Japan as an additional enemy. Russia feared to offend Japan. Without any one of the major powers being willing to take coercive action, or to apply the sanctions envisaged by the Covenant, it became all too obvious that the League was only a paper tiger.

As the Disarmament Conference was assembling, Japan extended its attack to Shanghai. China, as authorized by Art. 15 of the Covenant, called for action by the Assembly. A time-consuming investigation was made in an attempt to settle the dispute. The League, after an objective report was received, rejected the arguments of self-defense. [110] On March 27, 1933 Japan withdrew from the League. The demonstration of power by Japan exposed the weakness of the League. What most states considered to be a clear act of aggression had taken place, vast territories had been seized from a member of the League, and the League proved itself impotent to do anything about it. The rift in the wall of the League would soon bring the entire structure tumbling down.

(b) The Futile Disarmament Conference   (1932-1934)

The Worldwide Disarmament Conference, which had been planned and hoped for since the end of the war, was attended by all of the 64 nations of the world, with the exception of 4 small Latin American countries. France began by putting on the table an elaborate plan according to which the most dangerous weapons would be set aside to be used only in self-defense or on orders of the League's Council. A standing international police force would be created for use by the Council. Compulsory arbitration would be required. Aggression would be defined, and an effective system of sanctions would apply in case of breaches of either the anticipated new Disarmament Convention or the Covenant. (DOCUMENT 8) The plan was far ahead of its time. In 1932 the great powers caught up in internal political turmoils, suffering from economic uncertainties and beset by fears, were not prepared to accept any such commitments.

During the first year of its existence the Disarmament Conference was bogged down in debates about which weapons could be classified as defensive or offensive, and whether adequate security against aggression could be provided if such weapons were eliminated or reduced. Germany withdrew from the Conference until a formula was presented which seemed to assure her that she would receive equality of rights. While they were talking disarmament, most of the major powers were, despite major depressions, rearming. A war was in progress and a greater war was already brewing.

On November 14, 1932 France put forth a new proposal for collective security, prohibiting economic relations with the aggressor and refusing to recognize any situation brought about in violation of an international undertaking. There would be a right to assistance in case of aggression and a special fact-finding commission to report to the Council.[111] This too came under consideration in 1933.

Despairing of any effective action by the Disarmament Conference, the Soviet Union continued to enter into treaties of non-aggression with its neighboring States. The Treaty with Finland declared:

"Any act of violence attacking the integrity and inviolability of the territory or the political independence of the other High Contracting Party shall be regarded as an act of aggression, even if it is committed without declaration of war and avoids warlike manifestations." [112]

It was thereby recognized that a declaration of war might be irrelevant and that aggression could take many forms. The Soviet Treaty with Latvia spoke of "any act of aggression directed against the other" and "acts of violence directed against the territorial integrity and inviolability or the political independence of the other."[113] The use of different terms implied that there was a distinction between acts of "aggression" and acts of "violence." The Treaty with Estonia prohibited "political agreements manifestly directed in an aggressive sense against the other party."[114] The Treaty with Poland prohibited "aggressive action."[115] Nowhere were these distinctions explained, and it must have occurred to some of the parties that until there was a more precise formulation the effectiveness of such treaties was questionable. It would not be long before the Soviet Union would seek to correct the shortcoming.

The existence of a disarmament conference did not deter the major powers from channelling arms to two South American states actively engaged in hostilities. Between Paraguay and Bolivia lay a large undeveloped region known as The Chaco. Each country claimed it, and eventually the border skirmishes exploded into war. Both belligerents were members of the League bound to uphold the Covenant and both had ignored the obligation to submit the dispute to peaceful settlement. The League was brushed aside as the parties tried to settle the dispute by force of arms or via various commissions of South American States acting under U.S. domination. [116]

In May 1933 Paraguay, in an attempt to stop the flow of munitions to Bolivia, formally declared the existence of a state of war. When the League intervened by sending a Commission to the scene, the proposals of the Commission were rejected by Paraguay. Her neighbors were not ready to impose sanctions by breaking off economic and financial relations. The Assembly urged an arms embargo only against Paraguay. In response Paraguay notified its decision to withdraw from the League. When peace came a few years later it was not as a result of the effective functioning of the League but rather a consequence of the exhaustion of both parties. [117]

In a territorial dispute between Colombia and Peru, League action was equally ineffective, although the conflict was settled before large-scale fighting erupted.[118] The lesson had been learned from Japan that the League could be flouted with near impunity.

(c) The Proposed Soviet Definition of Aggression and the Politis Report (1933)

When the World Disarmament Conference reconvened in 1933 its prospects for success were anything but inspiring. As the debate resumed on the French Plan for General Disarmament and the Organization of Peace, the Soviet Delegate, M. Litvinoff, stated the position of his government on the whole subject. (DOCUMENT 9) He noted that the U.S.S.R. was the only country in the world which had destroyed the capitalist system, and which was being boycotted by the majority of States. In such circumstances he felt that no State could be expected to submit itself to the judgment of any international body composed of those who were clearly hostile to it. The French proposal for international sanctions inevitably gave rise to the questions, "How is the aggressor to be determined, and who is to determine the aggressor". [119]

While rejecting the impartiality of any of the existing agencies which might determine the aggressor, the Soviet representative felt that should the establishment of such organs come up for discussion it would have to be recognized that his government would be entitled to the same measure of impartiality and fairness expected by other States. He did not anticipate that the fulfillment of that legitimate demand would encounter much difficulty. The implication was that an objective international forum would be acceptable to the U.S.S.R.

The key problem for M. Litvinoff was that there was no universally acknowledged definition of aggression, and as long as there were different interpretations, and States continued to insist, as had been done by the U.S. and the U.K., when signing the Kellogg-Briand Pact, that they alone could decide when they were acting in self-defense, no international tribunal would ever be able to identify the aggressor in any armed conflict. Said M. Litvinoff:

"if we wish to see in action the Briand-Kellogg Pact, together with the extension proposed by the French delegation, and to secure the minimum of authority, impartiality
and confidence to the international organ to be called into
life by these extensions, we shall have to give it instructions for its guidance, and that means, first of all, defining war and aggression and the distiction between aggression and defense, and once for all condemning those fallacious justifications of aggression with which the past has
familiarized us". [120]

Mr. Litvinoff then presented a comprehensive definition of
aggression for consideration. The Soviet draft definition consisted
of a preamble and three paragraphs. The Preamble recognized the
right of all states to independence, security, territorial inviolability
and self-defense within its own frontiers, and that the definition was
a guide to an international organ which might be called upon to
determine the aggressor. The opening substantive article declared
that the aggressor would be that State which was the first to take
any one of five different actions: (a) A declaration of war; (b) Invasion of another state; (c) Bombardment of territory or attacking
another State's armed forces; (d) Landing armed forces on another
State's territory, or remaining there longer than permitted; and
(e) Naval blockade. The Second paragraph, which was considered the
most important, listed various situations which were frequently used
to justify aggression, and specifically excluded them as a valid
excuse for an attack. "No considerations whatsoever of a political,
strategical or economic nature", in particular the internal situation
of a State or any of its acts or laws, would justify any State being the
first to take any one of the five prohibited acts of aggression. It
would be permissible under the Third paragraph, however, for an
endangered State to match the threat of mobilized armed forces on
its frontier. [121]

It may be recalled that in 1924 the Soviet Union had opposed
the Draft Treaty of Mutual Assistance, partly because they thought
it impossible to define the aggressor. They recognized then that a
"first strike" might, under certain circumstances be defensive. [122]
Now the picture had changed.

"We make no pretensions to absolute definitions", said M.
Litvinoff, "since such are hardly possible or conceivable . . . We
are ready to admit the imperfections of the document we are placing
before you; we are ready to listen to your objections, to advance and
accept amendments, additions and the like". [123] The principles
which were important to the Soviet delegate were the inviolability of
recognized frontiers, and non-interference in the affairs, development, legislation, or administration of another State. It would take
over 40 years for the Soviet proposals, with modifications, to be
accepted.

The Belgian Delegation submitted a proposal on the fact-finding procedure to be followed in case of aggression or threat of aggression. Both the Soviet and the Belgian proposals were referred to the Political Commission of the Disarmament Conference. The reactions of some of the Members can best be seen from some of the Minutes. (DOCUMENT 10)

The Chinese Delegate, representing a country which was widely regarded as being a victim of aggression at that time, bemoaned the discrepancy between theory and practice. He was, however, prepared to support the Soviet definition. Norway and France appreciated the Soviet reference to international organs, and Poland approved the Soviet ideas. The German delegate noted the deterent character of a definition but felt it should be more elastic. [124] Mr. Anthony Eden, speaking for the United Kingdom, made it clear that he considered the attempt to draw up a precise definition of aggression to be a waste of time. [125] Sweden favored increasing the Council's powers,[126] and Japan wanted to be sure that all of the facts were considered. [127] The United States representative also challenged the utility of a rigid definition. He thought it wiser to establish criteria which each government might find helpful in reaching a decision on aggression. [128] His interest in retaining independence of action was unmistakable. Italy shared the doubts of England and the United States.

The question of defining aggression was accordingly referred to still another committee, the Committee on Security Questions, consisting of 17 nations, under the Chairmanship of M. Politis, which was also charged with considering the Belgian Proposal and a United Kingdom proposal for consultation and good offices to prevent hostilities. [129]

The Politis Report of May 24, 1933 (DOCUMENT 11) proposed that the definition of aggression be contained in a specific act which would become part of the proposed General Convention for the Reduction and Limitation of Armaments. The draft Act was annexed, and the report contained a brief commentary on each of the articles, which were based on the Soviet definition submitted by M. Litvinoff.

The preamble had been reworded without much substantive change. Which party was the first to use force remained the decisive determinant of aggression, but a reservation was added making the determination subject to the agreements in force between the parties to the dispute. This was aimed at safeguarding the possibility of taking steps prescribed by such other agreements as the Covenant, without thereby committing an aggressive act. [130] The reservation brought a new element of uncertainty, into the definition.

The acts which would constitute aggression remained essentially unchanged, although there were slight improvements in wording and sequence. A declaration of war, invasion, attack on territory, vessels or aircraft, with or without a declaration of war, naval blockade, and finally

"provision of support to armed bands formed in its territory which have invaded the territory of another State, or refusal, notwithstanding the request of the invaded State, to take in its own territory all measures in its power to deprive those bands of all assistance or protection".[131]

The Soviet draft had spoken of "landing" or "introducing" armed forces into another State without permission, or "infringement of the conditions of such permission".[132] The Politis Committee varied not merely the terms, since "provision of support" was much broader, but it also added a new concept, which had not previously been recognized, - that the failure to take whatever steps were within ones power to restrain armed bands was in itself an act of aggression. The Committee recognized that the measures which were within a State's power to take would have to be determined in each case, and this too was a new element of flexibility.[133]

Some members felt that the Soviet draft went too far in its article describing that no considerations of any kind could be used to justify aggression. The Committee was prepared to agree that:

"No political, military, economic or other considerations may serve as an excuse or justification for the aggression referred to in Article 1".

but they preferred, with some reservations, to add a Protocol instead of the long Soviet list illustrating the scope of the non-exculpating acts. They agreed that a listed act of aggression would constitute sufficient "provocation" to justify retaliation by acts of a similar nature.[134]

Even within the Committee itself, Germany, Hungary, Italy, Spain, Switzerland and the U.K. showed a preference for an elastic definition which would permit all the circumstances to be taken into account for consideration by an international body which could either resort to arbitration, if it could not agree unanimously, or could regard as the aggressor that state which refused to cease hostilities.[135]

M. Politis also submitted a draft of a European Security Pact. (DOCUMENT 12) It did not seek to impose new obligations of mutual assistance since such obligations would not have been accepted.[136] It did, however reproduce certain clauses from the proposed Act Defining Aggression, and hoped thereby to give it broader acceptance. What was omitted from the definition was the listing of naval blockade as an act of aggression, since it was thought that blockade should not always involve an obligation to provide assistance.[137]

The Politis Report came before the General Commission for discussion. (DOCUMENT 13) In explaining his report M. Politis noted that the definition had the advantage that it warned States of the acts they must not commit. Public opinion would now be able to form a judgment. The definition would facilitate the work of an international organ charged with responsibility for determining the aggressor, which by virtue of the definition would be less tempted to seek political grounds to excuse aggression. [138] The definition was designed so that it could be accepted by all States. In the absence of universality, however, it would only bind those agreeing to accept its terms. Using force to assist a victim of aggression would not be aggression.

In declaring that more progress had been made in his committee than had been possible for the past 10 years, M. Politis expressed appreciation for the Soviet initiative, even though the Soviet Union was not a member of the League. He felt the progress was possible because they had separated the definition of aggression from the question of sanctions which was a separate issue, and they had separated the term "aggressor" from the term "war", which was itself ambiguous. The definition dealt only with "resort to force" and not the existence of a state of "war" in the strict sense. [139] This, said M. Politis, was the greatest success of the Conference to date.

M. Politis found no opposition to the Belgian proposal for the creation of fact-finding bodies to investigate alleged acts of aggression. [140] As for the Act Defining Aggression, however, the reception was, as expected, quite different.

Spain was clearly opposed. [141] Germany wanted more elasticity and picked up the discrepancies between the Act and the draft of a European Pact for security in that the latter did not include blockade as an act of aggression. A few days before President Franklin D. Roosevelt had sent a message proposing:

"That all the nations of the world should enter into a solemn and definite pact of non-aggression. That they should solemnly reaffirm the obligations they had assumed to limit and reduce their armaments and, provided these obligations were faithfully executed by all signatory Powers, individually agree that they would send no armed force of whatsoever nature across their frontiers". [142]

This new development provided the German representative with the excuse to call for further study and coordination. [143] Mr. Eden had already voiced the objections of Great Britain, which were strongly shared by Italy, Hungary and Bulgaria. [144]

Wellington Koo of China supported the Act and felt that objections could be met by agreeing that the enumerated acts of aggression were not exhaustive. [145] The main support for M. Politis came from M. Paul-Boncour of France. He called the definition "one of the keystones, if not the chief keystone, of the edifice of mutual international security . . . ". [146]

In replying to the objections raised in two days of debate, M. Politis invited those who had amendments to make them. With this opening the President called for some of the most articulate advocates, - Mr. Dougalevski of the USSR and Mr. Politis, on the one hand, and in opposition, Mr. Eden of the U.K. and Mr. de Madariaga of Spain, to meet again and try to reconcile their views. [147] Whether they ever met again does not appear from the available records. One conclusion is clear - they were never to reach agreement.

(d) The League Crumbles (1933-1940)

The atmosphere at the Disarmament Conference was one of confusion, mistrust and apathy. The discussions in the Committees failed to influence what was happening in the world outside of the meeting halls in Geneva. As Germany under Hitler began to mobilize and demand disarmament by the other European countries or equality for Germany, those who considered themselves threatened began to scramble for new alliances. [148]

The USSR sought to reinforce its regional security system with a ring of buffer states. On July 3, 1933 a Convention for the Definition of Aggression was signed by the USSR and Romania, Poland, Afghanistan, Persia, Latvia, Estonia and Turkey, and later acceded to by Finland. It accepted the precise wording of the definition of aggression as recommended by the Politis Committee on May 24, 1933, "until such time as those rules shall become universal". Within the next two days similar agreements were signed with Czechoslovakia, Turkey and Yugoslavia, and then Lithuania. (DOCUMENT 14)

In September 1934 Russia joined the League in the hope that some League members might come to her defense if Germany attacked. [149] On October 14, 1933 Germany, refusing to bow to the "Diktat von Versailles" withdrew from the Disarmament Conference and from the League. [150] Rearmament and not disarmament became the order of the day.

In the following year nations were too busy planning to commit or defend against aggression to be concerned with defining it. Italy's aggression against Ethiopia found the great powers in the League too frightened, and too divided, to take effective action as envisioned by the Covenant and the many subsequent treaties. They talked and argued while the Italian armies marched. The limited economic sanctions which were applied were too little and too late. [151]

Man's attempt to set up a new world order of peace was now sliding down a very slippery slope. It was Hitler's turn to defy the League. His remilitarization of the Rhineland violated the Versailles Treaty and successfully challenged the Treaty of Locarno. The States affected, despite the legal authority and the moral basis for action, pursued instead their own national interests and did nothing to stop the German defiance. No State could rely on the Covenant or the League for protection against aggression. King Alexander of Yugoslavia was murdered while on a state visit to Marseilles in Oct. 1934. France urged the League to take effective action against political crimes. The answer was to appoint a committee to prepare a convention against terrorism and for the establishment of an international criminal court. [152]

Beginning in 1936, until the spring of 1939, German and Italian ''volunteers'' fought side by side with rebels seeking to overthrow the Spanish government. The government's call for an urgent meeting of the Council to deal with the clear case of aggression produced nothing but diplomatic maneuvering. [153]

On July 5, 1937, Afghanistan, Iraq, Iran and Turkey signed a treaty in which they all agreed to refrain from any act of aggression against any of them. (DOCUMENT 15) The signatories recognized the need to define aggression and self-defense. The treaty set forth specifically when force was permissible and not permissible. Any one of 4 listed acts was deemed to be an act of aggression: Declaration of war, invasion, attack against the territory, vessels or aircraft of another State, or directly or indirectly aiding an aggressor. Legitimate self-defense was permissible, and it was specifically defined as resistance to one of the listed acts of aggression. Action pursuant to Art. 16 of the Covenant was not to be considered as aggression, nor action taken pursuant to a decision of the Assembly or Council, or under Art. 15 of the Covenant, if it was directed against a State which attacked first. Action taken to assist a State which was subject to attack in violation of the Pact of Paris would also be permissible. Although blockade was not listed as an act of aggression and assistance to armed bands was also omitted, each of the parties undertook to prevent the formation or activities of armed bands within its borders, if such bands might subvert the established institutions of the other.[154] The treaty was a very substantial improvement on similar non-aggression pacts of the past, but adhesion to traditional views was still very strong.

By 1937 the committee of distinguished jurists which had been appointed in 1934, completed its draft Convention for the Prevention and Punishment of Terrorism and the establishment of an International Criminal Court. No State, other than India, was prepared to ratify it. [155]

The few remaining years of the League are a story of vacillation, apprehension and retreat. The obligations of the Covenant became scraps of paper as States began to return to the international anarchy which had marked the condition of the world before the outbreak of World War I. With the world racing to rearm the question of disarmament disappeared from the agenda, and with it all further discussion of the definition of aggression.

At the Harvard Law School a group of distinguished scholars

35

were completing their work on a Draft Convention on the Rights and Duties of States in Case of Aggression. Their study could only define aggression in very general terms as

> resort to armed force by a State when such resort has been duly determined, by a means which the State is bound to accept, to constitute a violation of an obligation. [155a]

As each State declared that it alone would be the judge of its own action, all hope of collective security was abandoned. In the face of threats of aggression nations praying for peace stood paralyzed, and hoped that the threat would somehow disappear if sufficient concessions were made. Czechoslovakia was annexed and the issue was not even brought to the League. On September 1, 1939 Germany invaded Poland. The League was silent. World War II was on the way.

On November 30, 1939, Soviet troops invaded Finland, seizing territory which the Finn's had refused to lease, although deemed vital for Soviet defense. Finland and the Soviet Union were bound by the Covenant, they were both parties to the Pact of Paris, both had signed a non-aggression pact in 1932, and Finland had acceded to the 1933 Soviet Convention for the Definition of Aggression. It was a perfect test case, and Finland called for a meeting of the Council in accordance with Art. 15 of the Covenant. The Council and the Assembly acted. (DOCUMENT 16)

An objective report set forth the violations by the Soviet Union of its treaty obligations and the Covenant. The facts were compared with the definition of aggression. [156] "The Soviet Government", said the Report, "is also directly contravening the very definite obligations laid down in the Convention for the Definition of the Aggressor which it signed and in the preparation of which it took a decisive part".[157]

In the 20th year of its life, for the first time in its history, in addition to appealing to its members to provide material and humanitarian assistance to Finland, the Assembly and the Council declared the Soviet Union to be no longer a Member of the League. [158] Some measure of financial assistance was provided to Finland, but having already lost all respect and influence the League could no longer be effective. Following upon the acts of aggression by Japan, Italy and Germany, in which the League had hesitated to exercise its power, it was, in the words of M. Paul-Boncour of France, "a tardy awakening of the universal conscience". [159]

The Assembly adjourned within the next two weeks and the League's agencies began to flee for refuge to other parts of the world. The system of security which had been envisioned by the Covenant had failed. Not having learned the lessons of history, and not being ready to take the steps required to identify aggression and to repel it, the world was doomed to redouble and relive the horrors of the past.

PART TWO

THE AFTERMATH OF WORLD WAR II

PART TWO:

THE AFTERMATH OF WORLD WAR II

(1) The San Francisco Conference and the Birth of the U.N.
    Charter   (Apr. 25-June 26, 1945)

With war raging in Europe, President Roosevelt and Prime
Minister Churchill met on board ship and issued "The Atlantic
Charter". The declaration of "Four Freedoms" which it contained
was reminiscent of Wilson's "14 Points". Once more the hope was
expressed that a just social order would be created in which man
could live in freedom from fear. In 1942 the Allies met in Washington, endorsed the principles of the Atlantic Charter, and adopted the
name "United Nations". Plans were being made to bring before the
bar of justice those who had been responsible for the crimes committed. [160]

Proposals for the structure of the new international parliament were considered by the United States, Great Britain, Russia
and China when they met at Dumbarton Oaks, in Washington, D.C. in
1944. At Yalta, in 1945, the "Big Three", with victory in sight,
summoned the United Nations to send delegates to San Francisco to
prepare the final instrument for a new world order to which the
United States pledged its full support. [161] The "Dumbarton Oaks
Proposals" were taken as the basis for the discussions which were
to lead to the United Nations Charter. (DOCUMENT 17 (a))

It was the plan of the Conference to enforce peace and security
by assuring the speedy assembly of forces of such magnitude as to
deter or suppress any aggression which might arise. The Security
Council was to be given a wide grant of authority. The great Powers,
which would have to bear the brunt of any military or economic
obligations, were to act in the Council by unanimous decision. [162]
The shortcomings of the League were to be corrected by giving the
Council authority to enforce its decisions - an element of compulsion
which was absent from the Covenant.

The primary purpose of the new organization was "to maintain
international peace and security; and to that end to take effective
collective measures for the prevention and removal of threats to
the peace and the suppression of acts of aggression or other

37

breaches of the peace...".[163] In using the words "other breaches of the peace" in addition to the term "aggression", it was intended to allow the Council to act, even if the unlawful duress was something less than aggression, providing the improper means of coercion posed a threat to the security of a State.[164]

Chapter VIII, Sec. B of the Dumbarton Oaks proposal charged the Security Council with responsibility for determining the existence of aggression, and the means necessary to restore peace. The Committee assigned to make recommendations on that particular article soon came face to face with the problem of defining aggression.[165]

The Czech delegate expressed concern about the danger inherent in allowing the Council to have complete discretion. (DOCUMENT 17 (b)) He drew attention to the Convention on the Definition of Aggression which his government, and others, had signed in July 1933.

The Bolivian representative, in a very perceptive and far sighted declaration, considered that a definition of aggression was absolutely essential to a system of world security. (DOCUMENT 17 (c)) He also saw the need for a mechanism of international justice which would take into account the economic and social well-being of the great masses of the peoples. The definition, which Bolivia proposed be written into the Charter, listed as aggression: "invasion, by armed force, of a foreign territory, declaration of war, attack by land, sea or air forces, aid lent to armed bands for the purposes of invasion, the intervention of a state in the internal or external policy of another, refusal to submit the cause of belligerence to the procedures of peaceful solution, or refusal to comply with a decision pronounced by a court of international justice."[166] The actual wording proposed by Bolivia as amendments to the Charter contained slight variations, but the importance of a definition and its general content was clearly recognized.[167]

The Philippine Delegation proposed that the definition of aggression be written into the Charter, and that it also prohibit attack on public vessels, or supplying any form of aid to any armed band, faction or group, or the establishment of agencies abroad to conduct subversive propaganda. (DOCUMENT 17 (d)) Iran and Egypt agreed that the Charter should include a "clear and exact definition of the term 'aggressor'," but no specific definition was offered.[168]

Greece noted that the existence of the veto power might prevent any determination of who was the aggressor, and therefore recommended that the determination be made by the vote of 7 members of the Security Council and not merely the big Powers. (DOCUMENT 17 (e)) Along similar lines, Mexico submitted that the General Assembly should have a hand in determining which state was the aggressor.[169] New Zealand wanted concurrence by majority vote of the assembly before sanctions could be applied.[170] Peru was concerned about possible "economic aggression", which it felt should be studied by the Assembly.[171]

The four-Powers themselves had proposed an amendment which would have required the Security Council, in determining which state was the aggressor, to take into account any failure to comply with provisional measures recommended by the Council for the restoration of peace. (DOCUMENT 17 (f)) This was interpreted as a partial definition of aggression, for it implied that failure to accept the Council's recommendation might lead to the conclusion that the recalcitrant state was the aggressor.[172] Other participating governments had other suggestions. (DOCUMENT 17 (g))

The definition of aggression, and whether it should be included in the Charter, was given protracted consideration by the responsible committee. (DOCUMENT 17 (h)) The United States and the United Kingdom led the majority in opposition. The conclusion finally reached, as reported by M. Paul-Boncour, was to omit any definition of aggression from the Charter and "to leave to the Council the entire decision as to what constitutes a threat to the peace, a breach of the peace, or an act of aggression." (DOCUMENT 17 (i)) With the closing of the San Francisco Conference, the United Nations Charter was born.

President Harry Truman, addressing the 50 nations assembled, declared: "By this Charter, you have given reality to the ideal of that great statesman of a generation ago - Woodrow Wilson."[173] Jan Christian Smuts, who had been one of the fathers of the League idea, was among those invited to speak. He saw the Charter as a working plan "for a unified front of peace-loving people against future aggressors." The old veteran of both war and peace conferences warned: "Unless the spirit to operate it is there, the best plan or machine may fail."[174] When M. Paul-Boncour, who had pleaded in vain for effective action by the League, rose to speak he echoed the sentiments of the American President, and expressed the conviction than an international force would be formed to enforce the decisions of the Security Council in suppressing aggression. He recalled the words of Pascal: . . . "Justice without strength is a mockery." "The United Nations," he said, "and more especially the great nations with a permanent seat on the Council, must remain truly united. The whole efficacy of the Charter depends on this unity."[175] All of the distinguished statesmen assembled at San Francisco knew, or should have known, that the problem of world peace was not one of conceiving plans or Charters, but of implementing them.

(2) The London Conference and The Charter of the International Military Tribunal (June–Aug.1945)

While the victorious states were busy at San Francisco, preparations were being made for the trial of the major war criminals. The United States had prepared a plan which was accepted in principle by the Foreign Ministers of Britain, the Soviet Union and France. "Launching a war of aggression" would be charged as a criminal act, along with "invasion by force or threat of force . . . or initiation of war in violation of international law or treaties." (DOCUMENT 18 (a))

President Truman appointed Robert H. Jackson to undertake the preparations for the United States. Mr. Jackson, having taken leave as an Associate Justice of the U.S. Supreme Court, submitted a comprehensive plan to the new American President. (DOCUMENT 18 (b)) "We propose to charge". said Justice Jackson, "that a war of aggression is a crime." He referred to the Geneva Protocol of 1924, the 1927 League Resolution on Aggression, the Kellogg-Briand Pact, and other international instruments, as ample authority for a strengthened international law whose goal would be "to make war less attractive to those who have governments and the destinies of people in their power." [176]

The four Allied Powers met in London for the purpose of drawing up a Charter setting forth the law and the procedures to be applied by the planned International Military Tribunal. In delineating the range of crimes over which the court would have jurisdiction, the initial draft followed the line of the original United States proposal. (DOCUMENT 18 (c)) Within a few days, however, the United States felt that there should be some clarification of what would constitute "launching a war of aggression", and suggested: "an invasion of another country in the absence of an attack upon, invasion of, or declaration of war against such country." (DOCUMENT 18 (d)) This inartistic formulation implied that aggression was equivalent to invasion and that there could be a legitimate military defense in response to invasion, attack or declaration of war by another country.

Justice Jackson felt that the tribunal should not be drawn into a propaganda discussion by allowing the Germans to argue that they were provoked into war as a defensive action, and that the best way to avoid that hazard was to have an agreed definition of aggression included in the Charter of the Tribunal. He expressed the view that the definition used in the Soviet Treaty of July 3, 1933 would be suitable, but that other treaties might usefully be consulted. (DOCUMENT 18 (e)) The French were prepared to condemn the "policy of aggression" in breach of treaties and in violation of international law, but without any definition. (DOCUMENT 18 (f)) The discussion which followed showed the basic differences in approach among the distinguished international lawyers.

Professor André Gros of France did not believe that aggressive war could be considered a crime since there had never before been any sanctions connected with such an offense.[177] General Nikitchenko, of the Soviet Supreme Court, wanted to avoid any argument which might arise from varying interpretations of what was or was not a crime under international law. His primary concern was not to make international law for the future but to punish the Nazi criminals. He felt that if the San Francisco delegates had been unable to define aggression and had left it to the United Nations, those drawing the IMT Charter should do the same.[178]

Mr. Jackson, having been a former U.S. Attorney General, wanted a precise specification of the elements of the crime being charged.[179] The British tried to find compromise formulas to satisfy the French, and finally submitted a draft which they said was insisted upon by the USSR. (DOCUMENT 18 (g)) In the face of the strong opposition, the United States dropped its proposal for including in the IMT Charter what was essentially the Soviet definition of aggression. (DOCUMENT 18 (h)) After a few minutes of discussion the additional British suggestion was accepted to drop the caption "Crime of War", and substitute "Crimes against Peace," which encompassed the planning, preparation, initiation or waging of a war of aggression. (DOCUMENT 18 (i)) The Charter was agreed and adopted. (DOCUMENT 18 (j)) Aggression was nowhere defined.

The Charter was soon adhered to by 19 nations and was to receive the approval of the General Assembly of the United Nations.[180] It formed the basis for the first criminal indictment in history of leaders of a nation charged with personal responsibility for aggressive war.

(3) The Nuernberg War Crimes Trials   (Aug. 1945-June 1949)

The indictment presented to the International Military Tribunal accused the major Nazi war criminals of a common plan or conspiracy to commit crimes against peace, war crimes, and crimes against humanity, as defined in the Charter. (DOCUMENT 19 (a)) "Mobilization for aggressive war", and the initiation of "aggressive war" were among the offenses charged. Specific reference was made to violations of the Hague Agreements of 1899 and 1907, the Versailles Treaty, the Locarno Pacts of 1925, the Pact of Paris of 1928, and various Non-Aggression Agreements.[181]

When Justice Jackson rose to make his opening statement, he denounced aggressive war as "the greatest menace of our times." (DOCUMENT 19 (b)) In outlining the law of the case, Justice Jackson criticized the Charter for having omitted a definition of aggression. He felt constrained to close the gap in the criminal indictment by a recital from the Soviet Conventions of 1933.[182]

In it's judgment, the International Military Tribunal said: "To initiate a war of aggression . . . is not only an international crime; it is the supreme international crime differing only from other war crimes in that it contains within itself the accumulated evil of the whole." (DOCUMENT 20) The court was unmoved by the defense arguments that at the time the alleged criminal acts were committed aggressive war was not generally considered a crime, that no statute had defined aggressive war, that no penalty had ever been fixed for its commission, and that no prior court had ever been established to try the offense. The judgment observed that the maxim nullum crimen sine lege was a general principle of justice designed to protect those who did not know they were doing wrong. In the face of the historical record and the wealth of international agreements requiring resort to peaceful means before resort to armed violence, and declaring aggressive war to be a crime, it was the judgment of the court that some of the defendants must have known that they were acting in defiance of law "when in complete deliberation they carried out their designs of invasion and aggression."[183]

Said the Tribunal: "The invasion of Austria was a premeditated aggressive step in furthering the plan to wage aggressive wars against other countries."[184] The action against Austria, not having resulted in the outbreak of war and not having been so charged in the indictment, was not held to be "aggressive war." So too the attack on Czechoslovakia was condemned as an aggressive act, although it was not charged as a crime against peace in the indictment. "The invasion of Poland was most plainly an aggressive war."[185] "The invasion of Belgium, Holland and Luxemborg was entirely without justification. It was carried out in pursuance of policies long considered and prepared, and was plainly an act of aggressive war."[186] Germany's action against Greece and Yugoslavia was described as "aggressive war,"[187] and the attack launched against the Soviet Union was called "plain aggression."[188]

On the basis of the facts before the court, the Tribunal concluded that the convicted German leaders had been responsible for premeditated and unprovoked attacks and invasions of peaceful neighboring States, and that by the use of armed force in violation of accepted international obligations, they were, by any permissible standard, guilty of a Crime against Peace. Nowhere did the International Military Tribunal define "aggressive war".

Hitler had committed suicide. Hermann Göring, who was about

to do the same, was held to be "the moving force for aggressive war." Rudolph Hess, who was Deputy to the Fuehrer, and General Keitel, Chief of the High Command, together with his deputy Jodl, von Neurath and von Ribbentrop, top foreign policy advisors, were found guilty of the charge of having committed crimes against peace because of their leading role in support of Germany's aggressive actions. Alfred Rosenberg and Admiral Raeder, who helped plan the attack on Norway, were also found guilty. Death by hanging was the sentence imposed on Göring, Ribbentrop, Keitel, Rosenberg, and Jodl.

Was this only "victor's justice", or was it the beginning of a new rule of law? Surely it was the hope of the American prosecutors, at least, that what was done at Nuernberg would help establish a new era of peace. "The ultimate step in avoiding periodic wars," said Justice Jackson,

". . .is to make statesmen responsible to law. . .While this law is first applied against German aggressors. . .it must condemn aggression by any other nations, including those who sit here now in judgement. . .This trial represents mankind's desperate effort to apply the discipline of the law to statesmen who have used their powers of state to attack the foundations of the world's peace and to commit aggressions against the rights of their neighbors. . . This trial is part of the great effort to make the peace more secure. One step in this direction is the United Nations organization, which may take joint political action to prevent war if possible, and joint military action to insure that any nation which starts a war will lose it". [189]

In his final report to the President, Justice Jackson expressed the view that "all who have shared in this work have been united and inspired in the belief that at long last the law is now unequivocal in classifying armed aggression as an international crime instead of a national right." [190]

The principles laid down by the International Military Tribunal were carried forward in a dozen subsequent trials prosecuted by Justice Jackson's successor, General Telford Taylor. [191] A new law, enacted by the four occupying powers, Control Council Law No. 10, set out the procedure for continued trials in the different zones of occupation. (DOCUMENT 21) It restated and somewhat expanded the principles of the London Charter of the IMT. "Initiation of invasions of other countries" was specifically listed as a crime against peace, in addition to "planning, preparation, initiation or waging a war of aggression." It was made clear that the offense of Crimes against Humanity could be committed by a government against its own nationals even if there did not exist a state of war. [192]

In four of the subsequent trials held at Nuernberg, 52 defendants were charged with crimes against peace. Only 5 were convicted.

One of the tribunals, consisting of American judges charged with carrying out international law, considered the subject at length in a decision against leading officials of the German Foreign Office and other Ministries. (DOCUMENT 22) The court went a step further than the IMT. After reviewing Nazi threats and pressures against Austria, the majority concluded that even though "Austria fell without a struggle . . . the invasion was aggressive . . . "[193] The campaign of duplicity and the massing of overwhelming force was recognized as a violation of both the letter and spirit of the Kellogg Pact. "It is not reasonable to assume that an act of war, in the nature of an invasion, whereby conquest and plunder are achieved without resistance, is to be given more favorable consideration than a similar invasion which may have met some military resistance." [194]

In considering the invasion of Denmark the court said: "Military necessity is never available to an aggressor as a defense for invading the rights of a neutral."[195] It was the League which had applied that very principle in ousting the Soviet Union for its invasion of Finland. The arguments of German self-defense and justification were considered and repudiated because of Germany's prior violation of international law. Germany was condemned as an aggressor, and other states were justified in helping those attacked and joining with others who had previously come to the aid of the victim.[196]

One of the judges was unable to agree that invasion without war could constitute a crime against peace. In his dissenting opinion, Judge Leon W. Powers, who had come to Nuernberg from the Supreme Court of Iowa, said: "Many acts may be aggressive that are short of war. They may merit the condemnation of all right-thinking people, but unless they involve a breach of the peace, it would be an abuse of language to call them 'crimes against peace'."[197] Furthermore, the crime, according to him, was the initiation of the war and not the participation in it, and a person could only be held criminally responsible if he knowingly engaged in activity to induce or support his government in initiating a war which he knew to be a war of aggression and if he had some influence in bringing about the action of his government.[198]

In reporting on the subsequent Nuernberg trials, General Taylor, who was to become a Professor of Law at Columbia University, concluded that the major contribution which the Nuernberg trials made to the preservation of peace and the establishment of world order was the framing of certain principles of law, which when applied in the judicial process, added enormously to the body and the living reality of international penal law. "No principle", said Telford Taylor, "deserves to be called such unless men are willing to stake their consciences on its enforcement."[199] Some years later, in denouncing the United States action in Vietnam, he was to criticize his own government for having failed to learn the lessons it sought to teach the rest of the world at the time of Nuernberg.[200]

(4) The Tokyo War Crimes Trial   (1946-1948)

While the trial of major Nazi offenders was in progress at Nuernberg, preparations were under way for the trial of Japanese War Criminals in the Far East. A charter of the International Military Tribunal for the Far East, based very largely on the London Charter for the Nuernberg court, was approved on January 19, 1946. (DOCUMENT 23 (a)) In describing "Crimes against Peace" the Tokyo Charter added that a war of aggression could be either "declared or undeclared". This clarification was also to find a place when aggression was to be defined by consensus many years later.

In addition to charges of war crimes and crimes against humanity, the indictment accused 28 defendants of 36 counts of Crimes Against Peace, including conspiracy, and having "planned and prepared a war of aggression and a war in violation of international law, treaties and agreements and assurances", or having "initiated a war of aggression". All the defendants were also accused of having "waged a war of aggression." (DOCUMENT 23 (b)) The particulars were spelled out in two appendixes, including a list of the treaties and international agreements which had been violated.

The Tokyo Tribunal, composed of members from 11 nations, met for almost two years before rendering its very extensive judgment covering some 1500 pages. (DOCUMENT 24) In holding the Charter to be a valid expression of existing international law, the Tokyo court followed the Nuernberg Tribunal. It relied on the Pact of Paris as evidence that aggressive war was a crime. [201] The majority did not feel that the absence of an agreed definition of aggression was a bar to conviction for the offense. Japan's actions were seen as unprovoked attacks prompted by the desire to seize the possessions of the victim states, and by any definition that would have to be characterized as a war of aggression. [202] Eight of the judges fully supported the judgment and verdicts, but Justice Roling of the Netherlands dissented in part, and Justice Pal, of India, was in fundamental disagreement. [203]

Almost all of the defendants were formulators of government policy and were convicted of conspiracy to wage aggressive war, of having waged aggressive war, as well as violations of the laws of war. Seven of the accused were sentenced to death and, after review and appeal, were executed. The others received long prison sentences.

One of the keenest analysts of the Tokyo trials concluded that the greatest contribution of the tribunal was not to succumb to the feeling amidst the tensions of the new post-war conflict, that their task was a futile one. "They elected to reaffirm as an act of faith,

45

their conviction that war was not a necessary concomitant of international life and that acknowledged principles of law and justice were fully applicable to nations and their leaders." [204]

We have seen that throughout history man's hope was sustained by his faith. The aspiration for peace could not alone destroy the tradition of war. The suffering of World War I gave rise to the hope that a League of Nations would provide a new order of tranquility and justice, but the refusal to relinquish the practices of the past led to an even greater holocaust. From the ashes of World War II new hope was born, and there arose again in the United Nations Charter and the war crimes trials the yearning that the force of law might finally replace the law of force.

Notes

Abbreviations Used

AJIL - American Journal of International Law

GAOR - General Assembly, Official Records

ICMT - International Conference on Military Trials

IMT - International Military Tribunal

L.o.N. - League of Nations

LNOJ - League of Nations, Official Journal

LNTS - League of Nations, Treaty Series

UNCIO - The United Nations Conference on International
        Organization

Notes

PART ONE:

THE TRADITION OF WAR
AND
THE ASPIRATION FOR PEACE

1. In a learned text reviewing the quest for a definition of aggression Prof. Julius Stone concluded that the hopes of securing peace by inventing a precise mechanically operating definition was "a snare and a delusion". Aggression and World Order, ix (1958). Professors Myres McDougal and Florentino P. Feliciano, in a brilliant analysis of the factors which decision makers would have to consider in determining the limits of permissible and impermissible coercion, rejected a defeatist view, and concluded that it was intellectually possible and practically indispensible to clarify the policy of international coercion in order to enhance minimum order and optimum human dignity. Law and Minimum World Public Order, Chap. 3 (1961). Other outstanding studies include: Komarnicki, W., La Définition de l'Aggresseur dans le Droit International Moderne (1949); Aroneanu, E., La Définition de l'Aggression; Exposé Objectif (1958). More recent studies to which the present author is also deeply indebted include: Broms, B., The Definition of Aggression in the United Nations (1968), Thomas, A. and Thomas A.J. Jr., The Concept of Aggression in International Law, (1972), Schwebel, S. M., Aggression, Intervention and Self-Defense in Modern International Law, II Recueil des Cours (1972).

2. Harley, J., _Documentary Textbook of the U.N._, 2 (1950).

3. See Nussbaum A., _A Concise History of the Law of Nations_ (1947); See Wright, Q., _A Study of War_ (1965), for an intensive historical study of war and related problems.

4. _The Law of War and Peace_, Vol. III, cap. 17, Sec. 3 (1625), cited in Scott, J.B. Ed. Classics of International Law (1925) at 786.

5. Art. 2 Sec. 5.

6. See Note 4 _supra_ at 560-561.

7. See _Selections from the Work of William Penn_, ed. I. Sharpless (1915), "Essay Toward the Present and Future Peace of Europe" (1693). Reprinted in Int'l Conciliation, No. 394 (1943).

8. _Jugement sur la Paix Perpetuelle_, English Ed. Vaughan C.E.

9. World Peace Foundation (1914). Also Kant, _Perpetual Peace_, Smith, C. Trans. (1903).

10. _The Work of J. Bentham_, part viii, Bouring's Ed. "_Plan for a Universal and Perpetual Peace_". Also Grotius Soc. Publ. Texts for Students of Int'l Relations, No. 6. (1927).

11. _An Essay on a Congress of Nations_, Carnegie End. (1916), See Beales, _The History of Peace_ (1931).

12. See Scott J.B., _The Hague Conventions and Declarations of 1899 and 1907_.

13. _Malloy's Treaties_ II, 2020-2022, 2228-2229.

14. See Scott, J.B. _The Hague Peace Conferences_, I, 321-385 (1909).

15. See Marburg, T., _Development of the League of Nations Idea_, Ed. by J.H. Latane, 2 Vols. (1932). In 1917, it was stated that aggressive war was a crime against mankind. See _Text on International Law_, Academy of Sciences of USSR, Moscow at 403.

16. _U.S. Documents_, Serial No. 7443, Doc. No. 765. See also Cong. Rec. May 29, 1916, at 8854, for a typical Wilson speech saying: " . . . the world is even now on the eve of a great consumation . . . when coercion shall be summoned not to the service of a political ambition or selfish hostility, but to the service of a common order, a common justice and a common peace."

17. See Smuts, J.C., The League of Nations, A Practical Suggestion (1918). For much of the background material concerning the origins and growth of the League and its history see also Walters, F.P., A History of the League of Nations (1960).

18. German White Book Concerning the Responsibility of the Authors of the War, 15-24, Carnegie Endow. (1924).

19. See Glueck, S., War Criminals-Their Prosecution and Punishment, 19-36, (1944) for a summary of action taken against war criminals pursuant to the Versailles Treaty.

20. See Memorandum of Reservations by the United States, 14 A.J.I.L. 95-154 (1920).

21. See Day, C. "The Atmosphere and Organization of the Peace Conference, in House and Seymour, Eds. What Really Happened at Paris 16-18 (1921); For a comprehensive text see Temperly, H.W.V., A History of the Peace Conference of Paris (1920) See also Miller, D.H., The Drafting of the Covenant (1928).

22. Art. 1.

23. Art. 4 Subsequent amendments increased the non-permanent members from four to six, and later to nine.

24. Art. 5.

25. Art. 8, and 9.

26. See Walters, Note 17 supra at 61-63.

27. Id. at 48.

28. Art. 12. Later amendments made it clear that the court to which such disputes would be referred would be the Permanent Court of International Justice described in Art. 14. For amended Covenant see Secretariat of the League of Nations, Ten Years of World Co-operation (1930).

29. Art. 13.

30. Art. 14.

31. Art. 15.

32. Art. 16.

33. Art. 20.

34. Art. 21.

35. See LNOJ (1920).

36. See LNOJ 33-38 (1920).

37. See L.O.N. Records of the First Assembly, Third Committee, 10th Meeting, p. 764.

38. See Report of the Thirty-First Conf. of the Int'l Law Assoc. held in Buenos Aires in 1922, Vol. I, p. 74.

39. Resolution XIV. Text contained in DOCUMENT 2 (a) at 114.

40. Resolution XV.

41. See Art. 2.

42. See Art. 3.

43. See Art. 4.

44. See Art. 5.

45. See Art. 10.

46. See Art. 15.

47. See DOCUMENT 2 (a) 114-120.

48. Id. at 116.

49. Id. at 118; See also Zimmern, A., The League of Nations and the Rule of Law, 1918-1935 (1939) for an analysis of the vacillation by Members of the League.

50. DOCUMENT No. 2 (c) at 183.

51. Id. at 183-184 Para. 4.

52. Id. 184 Para. 7.

53. Id. 184 Para. 8.

54. Id. 185.

55. LNOJ Spec. Supp.No. 16, 209-210 (1923).

56. See Cooke, W.H. and Stickney, E. Eds. Readings in European International Relations Since 1879, 946 (1931).

57. DOCUMENT 3 (b), Art. 1.

58. Id. Art. 2.

59. Id. Art. 3.

60. Id. Art. 4.

61. Id. Art. 5.

62. Id. Art. 8.

63. DOCUMENT 3 (e) at 197.

64. Id.

65. Id. at 198.

66. Id. Art. 3.

67. Id. Art. 4.

68. Id. Art. 5.

69. Id. Art. 6.

70. Id. Art. 8.

71. Id. Art. 11-15

72. Id. Art. 17

73. Id. at 204.

74. Id.

75. Id.

76. See Id. 204-205.

77. Id. 206.

78. Id. 209.

79. Id. 210.

80. Id. 212.

81. Art. 21.

82. DOCUMENT 4, Art. 1.

83. Id. Art. 2.

84. Id.

85. See Id. Art. 3,5.

86. See LNTS (1935) 335-357, Dec. 17, 1925.

87. See LNTS (1927) 152-154, Sept. 28, 1926.

88. LNTS (1931) 292-293, Oct. 1. 1927.

89. Cong. Record, Vol. 67, 2824-2825 (Jan. 27, 1926).

90. See Report of the 34th Conference of the International Law
Association, 110 (1926); Union Interparlementaire, XXIII Conference, 205-242; Premier Congrès International de Droit Pénal, Actes
du Congrès. Prof. Pella was to be the outstanding champion of the
idea of an International Penal Court until his death in New York in
1952. See 46 AJIL 709-710.

91. DOCUMENT 6, at 17.

92. Id. 24-40.

93. Id. at 25.

94. Id.

95. Id. at 26.

96. Id. at 28.

97. Id. at 31.

98. Id. at 32-33.

99. Id. at 40.

100. LNOJ, Spec. Supp. No. 64, 113-115 (1928).

101. See LNOJ, Spec. Supp. No. 63 (1928); Resolutions and Recommendations Adopted by the Assembly During its Ninth Ordinary Session, Sept. 3 to 26th, 1928 contains the Assembly Resolution at p. 16, and the General Act at Annex 1, p. 20-26, as well as texts of the Model Treaties. At about the same time a Pan-American Conference meeting in Havana resolved to prohibit all aggression and declared that a "war of aggression constitutes an international crime against the human species". See Proceedings of the Amer. Society of Int'l Law, 22nd Annual Meeting, 14-15 (1928).

102. See N.Y. Times, April 6, 1928, p. 5.

103. See Proc. of Amer. Soc. of Int'l Law, (1928) at 143; Notes exchanged between the U.S. and other Powers, in Shotwell, J.T. War as an Instrument of National Policy and its Renunciation in the Pact of Paris (1929); Miller, H., The Peace Pact of Paris (1928). See also Sohn, L.B. Cases on U.N. Law 935 (1956).

104. See note 103 supra, and Meyers, Origins and Conclusion of the Paris Pact (1929). For different views see Wright, Q. "The Meaning of the Pact of Paris", 27 AJIL 39 (1933), and Borchard, E.M. Ed. Comment, "War and Peace", 27 AJIL 114 (1933).

105. See Walters, note 17 supra. at 382.

106. LNOJ, Spec. Supp. No. 94, 145-149, at 146 (1931).

107. See Id. at 149.

108. L.o.N. Conf. for Red. of Armaments, Vol. II, 313-321, Series of L.o.N. Public. IX Disarmament 1935, IX:4. A violation of the restrictions was prima facie evidence of having resorted to war. See Art. 5.

109. See the LNOJ and Records of the Assembly and the Council (1932); Lauterpacht, "Resort to War and the Interpretation of the Covenant during the Manchurian Dispute" 28 AJIL 43-60 (1934); See also Willoughby, W.W., The Sino-Japanese Controversy and the League of Nations (1935). Japan's "Doctrine", the Monroe Doctrine and England's "Monroe Doctrine" are compared at 627-654.

110. See Hudson, M., The Verdict of the League: China and Japan in Manchuria (1933); The Final Report appears in 27 AJIL 119-152 (1933).

111. See Conf. Doc. D-146, LN Conf. for Red. of Armaments, Conference Documents, Vol. II, 435, Series of L.o.N. Public. IX Disarmament 1935, IX:4.

112. LNTS (1935) 395-399, Jan. 21, 1932.

113. LNTS (1934) 123-125, Feb. 5, 1932.

114. LNTS (1932) 305-307, May 4, 1932.

115. LNTS (1933) 49-51, July 25, 1932.

116. See Jessup, P.C., and Wood, B. The Chaco Award, The Independent Jour. of Columbia Univ. Dec. 9, 1938. See also editorial 33 AJIL 126 (1939).

117. See LNOJ, Spec. Supp. No. 132, 47-51 (1934); Spec. Supp. No. 133, 49; 28 AJIL 138-217, Supp. (1934). See also Proceedings of the Commission of Inquiry and Conciliation, Mar. 13-Sept. 13, 1929, Washington, D.C.

118. See Woolsey, L.H., "Leticia Dispute Between Columbia and Peru", 27 AJIL 317-324 (1933), and 29 AJIL 94-99 (1935).

119. DOCUMENT 9 at 236.

120. Id. at 237.

121. Id. at 237-238

122. See supra. DOCUMENT 3, at 138.

123. DOCUMENT 9 at 239.

124. DOCUMENT 10 at 52.

125. Id. at 53.

126. Id. at 54.

127. Id. at 55.

128. Id.

129. Id. at 56; See Conf. Doc. D. 157. Mar. 16, 1933, Conf. Docs. Vol. II, p. 476.

130. DOCUMENT 11 at 4-5.

131. Id. at 16.

132. See DOCUMENT 9 at 238, Art. 1 (d).

133. See DOCUMENT 11 at 9.

134. Id. at 10.

135. See Id. at 4.

136. See DOCUMENT 12 at 4. The draft submitted by the U.K. provided that in case of a breach of the Pact of Paris the parties would meet, but any action would require the concurrence of the major Powers. See Conf. D. 157 (1), Mar. 16, 1933.

137. DOCUMENT 12 at 7.

138. DOCUMENT 13 at 500.

139. See Id. at 502.

140. See DOCUMENT 12 supra. at 18.

141. See DOCUMENT 13 at 547-548.

142. See Minutes of the General Commission, Series B, Vol. II, p. 462, May 19, 1933. Text in Official Documents, AJIL (1933) at 155; See Finch, G.A., Ed. Comment, "A Pact of Non-Aggression" 27 AJIL 725 (1933).

143. DOCUMENT 13 at 549.

144. See Id. at 550-552. The subject was also discussed at 510-517, which have not been reproduced as part of the document.

145. Id. at 551.

146. Id. at 552.

147. Id. at 557. On June 18, 1934 it was reported that the recommended conversations to define aggression had not yet been held. See Conf. D/C.G./C.S.S./2 at 14. In July M. Dougalevsky died.

148. See Anti-War Treaty of Non-Aggression and Conciliation signed at Rio de Janeiro, Oct. 10, 1933 by six South American States, LNTS (1935) 405-413. In view of the U.K.'s refusal to assume any new obligations on the continent, and hesitation by other States, only new regional arrangements seemed feasible. See Conf. D./C.G. 169 (1) July 5, 1934. Conf. Docs. Vol. III, April 1936. IX Disarm. 1936 IX.4.

149. See Walters, note 17 supra. at 579-585.

150. See Id. at 550, 565, 768. The withdrawal was made final and irrevocable on Dec. 12, 1937, a day after Italy gave notice of withdrawal from the League.

151. See Serup, A. L'Article 16 du Pacte et son Interpretation dans le Conflit Italo-Ethiopien 58-100 (1938).

152. See LNOJ, 15th Year, No. II, 1760, 1839-1840 (1934).

153. See Padelford, N.J. International Law and Diplomacy in the Spanish Civil Strife, 121-143 (1939).

154. DOCUMENT 15 at 27.

155. See Historical Survey of the Question of Int'l Criminal Jurisdiction, U.N. Memo. Doc. A/CN.4/7 Rev. 1 (1949). See also Proceedings of the Int'l Conf. on the Repression of Terrorism, Geneva, Nov. 1-16, 1937, Official No. C.94.M.47. 1938 (V). Series of L.o.N. Publ. V Legal V.3.

155 (a). See 33 AJIL Supp. 821-909 at 811 (1939). The study also contains a comprehensive bibliography. The Harvard definition was similar to one suggested by Quincy Wright in 1935. See "The Concept of Aggression in International Law", 9 AJIL 373 (1935) at 395.

156. DOCUMENT 16 at 539.

157. Id. at 540.

158. See Id. at 508,540.

159. Id. at 507.

PART TWO:

THE AFTERMATH OF WORLD WAR II

160. See <u>Punishment for War Crimes</u>; The <u>Inter-Allied Declaration signed at St. James's Palace</u>, London, on 13 Jan. 1942, and relative documents (Issued by the Inter-Allied Information Committee, London, 1942), 3-4. See also <u>The Moscow Declaration on German Atrocities</u>, 1 Nov. 1943, U.N. Information Org., London, Information Paper No. 1.; Dept. of State Bull. Nov. 6, 1943, at 308-309.

161. See <u>U.S. Dept. of State Bulletin</u>, Feb. 18, 1945, London, H.M. Stationary Office, (Misc. No. 5 (1945), Cmd. 6598.

162. See 11 <u>UNCIO</u> 232-235, Report of Commission III, Doc. 1170, III/13, June 23, 1945.

163. DOCUMENT 17 (a) at 2.

164. See 6 <u>UNCIO</u> 703, Doc. 723, I/1/A/19, June 1, 1945.

165. Committee 3 of Commission III. See Russell, R.B., <u>A History of the U.N. Charter - The Role of the U.S. 1940-1945</u> (1958) For U.S. refusal to define aggression see p. 564.

166. DOCUMENT 17 (c) at 579.

167. See <u>Id.</u> at 585.

168. See 3 <u>UNCIO</u> 459, Doc. 2 G/7 (q) (1), and G/14 (m), May 5, 1945.

169. See 3 <u>UNCIO</u> 376, Doc. 2, G/7 (c) (1) at 13, May 5, 1945.

170. See 3 <u>UNCIO</u> 486, Doc. 2, G/14 (f) at 3, May 1, 1945.

171. See 3 <u>UNCIO</u> 596, Doc. 2, G/14 (u), May 6, 1945.

172. For discussion see 12 <u>UNCIO</u> 341-342, 348-349, May 19, 1945.

173. 1 <u>UNCIO</u> 718, June 26, 1945.

174. <u>Id.</u> at 710-711.

175. Id. at 700.

176. DOCUMENT 18 (b) at 53.

177. See DOCUMENT 18 (f) at 295.

178. Id. at 298.

179. See Id. at 300.

180. For a comprehensive discussion of the legal character of the IMT see Woetzel, R.K., The Nuremberg Trials in International Law, 40-96 (1962).

181. DOCUMENT 19 (a) at 73-81.

182. DOCUMENT 19 (b) at 166.

183. DOCUMENT 20 at 49.

184. Id. at 21.

185. Id. at 34.

186. Id. at 40.

187. Id. at 42.

188. Id. at 45.

189. DOCUMENT 19 (b) at 172.

190. ICMT XII, Dec. 29, 1947. See Sohn, L.B., Cases on World Law (1950), Sec. 5 on War Crimes and the Crime of War. A bibliography is at 967-974.

191. See Taylor, T., Final Report to the Secretary of the Army on the Nuernberg War Crimes Trials Under Control Council Law No. 10, Washington D.C., 15 Aug. 1949.

192. Compare Charter Art. 6 (c) with Control Council Law No. 10, Art. II (1) (c).

193. DOCUMENT 22 at 330.

194. Id. at 331.

195. Id. at 334.

196. See Id. at 336.

197. Trials of War Criminal Before the Nuernberg Military Tribunals, Vol. XIV at 882.

198. Id. at 889.

199. See Final Report, note 191 supra. at 112.

200. See Taylor, T., Nuremberg and Vietnam: An American Tragedy (1970).

201. See DOCUMENT 24 at 25-26.

202. See Id. at 994.

203. For an excellent analysis of the Tokyo trial see Horwitz, S., The Tokyo Trial, International Conciliation No. 465, Nov. 1950. See also International Military Tribunal for the Far East - The Dissenting Judgment of Justice R.B. Pal, published in 1953.

204. Id. at 575. For comparisons between the Nuernberg and Tokyo trials see Woetzel, op.cit.supra. note 180, at 226-232; Keenan and Brown, Crimes against International Law, 1-56 (1950); Appleman, J.A., Military Tribunals and International Crimes (1954).

DOCUMENTS

PART ONE

THE TRADITION OF WAR AND THE ASPIRATION FOR PEACE

The Covenant of the League of Nations.

THE HIGH CONTRACTING PARTIES,

In order to promote international co-operation and to achieve international peace and security

by the acceptance of obligations not to resort to war.

by the prescription of open, just and honourable relations between nations,

by the firm establishment of the understandings of international law as the actual rule of conduct among Governments, and

by the maintenance of justice and a scrupulous respect for all treaty obligations in the dealings of organised peoples with one another,

Agree to this Covenant of the League of Nations.

ARTICLE I.

The original Members of the League of Nations shall be those of the Signatories which are named in the Annex to this Covenant and also such of those other States named in the Annex as shall accede without reservation to this Covenant. Such accession shall be effected by a declaration deposited with the Secretariat within two months of the coming into force of the Covenant. Notice thereof shall be sent to all other Members of the League.

Any fully self-governing State, Dominion or Colony not named in the Annex may become a Member of the League if its admission is agreed to by two-thirds of the Assembly, provided that it shall give effective guarantees of its sincere intention to observe its international obligations, and shall accept such regulations as may be prescribed by the League in regard to its military, naval and air forces and armaments.

Any Member of the League may, after two years' notice of its intention so to do, withdraw from the League, provided that all its international obligations and all its obligations under this Covenant shall have been fulfilled at the time of its withdrawal.

ARTICLE 2.

The action of the League under this Covenant shall be effected through the instrumentality of an Assembly and of a Council, with a permanent Secretariat.

ARTICLE 3.

The Assembly shall consist of Representatives of the Members of the League.

The Assembly shall meet at stated intervals, and from time to time as occasion may require at the Seat of the League or at such other place as may be decided upon.

The Assembly may deal at its meetings with any matter within the sphere of action of the League or affecting the peace of the world.

At meetings of the Assembly each Member of the League shall have one vote, and may have not more than three Representatives.

ARTICLE 4.

The Council shall consist of Representatives of the Principal Allied and Associated Powers, together with Representatives of four other Members of the League. These four Members of the League shall be selected by the Assembly from time to time in its discretion. Until the appointment of the Representatives of the four Members of the League first selected by the Assembly, Representatives of Belgium, Brazil and Spain and Greece shall be members of the Council.

With the approval of the majority of the Assembly, the Council may name additional Members of the League whose Representatives shall always be members of the Council; the Council with like approval may increase the number of Members of the League to be selected by the Assembly for representation on the Council.

The Council shall meet from time to time as occasion may require, and at least once a year, at the Seat of the League, or at such other place as may be decided upon.

The Council may deal at its meetings with any matter within the sphere of action of the League or affecting the peace of the world.

Any Member of the League not represented on the Council shall be invited to send a Representative to sit as a member at any meeting of the Council during the consideration of matters specially affecting the interest of that Member of the League.

At meetings of the Council, each Member of the League represented on the Council shall have one vote, and may have not more than one Representative.

ARTICLE 5.

Except where otherwise expressly provided in this Covenant or by the terms of the present Treaty, decisions at any meeting of the Assembly or of the Council shall require the agreement of all the Members of the League represented at the meeting.

All matter of procedure at meetings of the Assembly or of the Council, including the appointment of Committees to investigate particular matters, shall be regulated by the Assembly or by the Council, and may be decided by a majority of the Members of the League represented at the meeting.

The first meeting of the Assembly and the first meeting of the Council shall be summoned by the President of the United States of America.

ARTICLE 6.

The permanent Secretariat shall be established at the Seat of the League. The Secretariat shall comprise a Secretary General and such secretaries and staff as may be required.

The first Secretary General shall be the person named in the Annex ; thereafter the Secretary General shall be appointed by the Council with the approval of the majority of the Assembly.

The secretaries and staff of the Secretariat shall be appointed by the Secretary General with the approval of the Council.

The Secretary General shall act in that capacity at all meetings of the Assembly and of the Council.

The expenses of the Secretariat shall be borne by the Members of the League in accordance with the apportionment of the expenses of the International Bureau of the Universal Postal Union.

ARTICLE 7.

The Seat of the League is established at Geneva.

The Council may at any time decide that the Seat of the League shall be established elsewhere.

All positions under or in connection with the League, including the Secretariat, shall be open equally to men and women.

Representatives of the Members of the League and officials of the League when engaged on the business of the League shall enjoy diplomatic privileges and immunities.

The buildings and other property occupied by the League or its officials or by Representatives attending its meetings shall be inviolable.

ARTICLE 8.

The Members of the League recognise that the maintenance of peace requires the reduction of national armaments to the lowest point consistent with national safety and the enforcement by common action of international obligations.

The Council, taking account of the geographical situation and circumstances of each State, shall formulate plans for such reduction for the consideration and action of the several Governments.

Such plans shall be subject to reconsideration and revision at least every ten years.

After these plans shall have been adopted by the several Governments, the limits of armaments therein fixed shall not be exceeded without the concurrence of the Council.

The Members of the League agree that the manufacture by private enterprise of munitions and implements of war is open to grave objections. The Council shall advise how the evil effects attendant upon such manufacture can be prevented, due regard being had to the necessities of those Members of the League which are not able to manufacture the munitions and implements of war necessary for their safety.

The Members of the League undertake to interchange full and frank information as to the scale of their armaments, their military, naval and air programmes and the condition of such of their industries as are adaptable to war-like purposes.

ARTICLE 9.

A permanent Commission shall be constituted to advise the Council on the execution of the provisions of Articles 1 and 8 and on military, naval and air questions generally.

ARTICLE 10.

The Members of the League undertake to respect and preserve as against external aggression the territorial integrity and existing political independence of all Members of the League. In case of any such aggression or in case of any threat or danger of such aggression the Council shall advise upon the means by which this obligation shall be fulfilled.

ARTICLE 11.

Any war or threat of war, whether immediately affecting any of the Members of the League or not, is hereby declared a matter of concern to the whole League, and the League shall take any action that may be deemed wise and effectual to safeguard the peace of nations. In case any such emergency should arise the Secretary General shall on the request of any Member of the League forthwith summon a meeting of the Council.

It is also declared to be the friendly right of each Member of the League to bring to the attention of the Assembly or of the Council any circumstance whatever affecting international relations which threatens to disturb international peace or the good understanding between nations upon which peace depends.

ARTICLE 12.

The Members of the League agree that if there should arise between them any dispute likely to lead to a rupture, they will submit the matter either to arbitration or to inquiry by the Council, and they agree in no case to resort to war until three months after the award by the arbitrators or the report by the Council.

In any case under this Article the award of the arbitrators shall be made within a reasonable time, and the report of the Council shall be made within six months after the submission of the dispute.

ARTICLE 13.

The Members of the League agree that whenever any dispute shall arise between them which they recognise to be suitable for submission to arbitration and which cannot be satisfactorily settled by diplomacy, they will submit the whole subject-matter to arbitration.

Disputes as to the interpretation of a treaty, as to any question of international law, as to the existence of any fact which if established would constitute a breach of any international obligation, or as to the extent and nature of the reparation to be made for any such breach, are declared to be among those which are generally suitable for submission to arbitration.

For the consideration of any such dispute the court of arbitration to which the case is referred shall be the court agreed on by the parties to the dispute or stipulated in any convention existing between them.

The Members of the League agree that they will carry out in full good faith any award that may be rendered, and that they will not resort to war against a Member of the League which complies therewith. In the event of any failure to carry out such an award, the Council shall propose what steps should be taken to give effect thereto.

ARTICLE 14.

The Council shall formulate and submit to the Members of the League for adoption plans for the establishment of a Permanent Court of International Justice. The Court shall be competent to hear and determine any dispute of an international character which the parties thereto submit to it. The Court may also give an advisory opinion upon any dispute or question referred to it by the Council or by the Assembly.

ARTICLE 15.

If there should arise between Members of the League any dispute likely to lead to a rupture, which is not submitted to arbitration in accordance with Article 13, the Members of the League agree that they will submit the matter to the Council. Any party to the dispute may effect such submission by giving notice of the existence of the dispute to the Secretary General, who will make all necessary arrangements for a full investigation and consideration thereof.

For this purpose the parties to the dispute will communicate to the Secretary General, as promptly as possible, statements of their case, with all the relevant facts and papers, and the Council may forthwith direct the publication thereof.

The Council shall endeavour to effect a settlement of the dispute, and if such efforts are successful, a statement shall be made public giving such facts and explanations regarding the dispute and the terms of settlement thereof as the Council may deem appropriate.

If the dispute is not thus settled, the Council either unanimously or by a majority vote shall make and publish a report containing a statement of the facts of the dispute and the recommendations which are deemed just and proper in regard thereto.

Any Member of the League represented on the Council may make public a statement of the facts of the dispute and of its conclusions regarding the same.

If a report by the Council is unanimously agreed to by the members thereof other than the Representatives of one or more of the parties to the dispute, the Members of the League agree that they will not go to war with any party to the dispute which complies with the recommendations of the report.

If the Council fails to reach a report which is unanimously agreed to by the members thereof, other than the Representatives of one or more of the parties to the dispute, the Members of the League reserve to themselves the right to take such action as they shall consider necessary for the maintenance of right and justice.

If the dispute between the parties is claimed by one of them, and is found by the Council, to arise out of a matter which by international law is solely within the domestic jurisdiction of that party, the Council shall so report, and shall make no recommendation as to its settlement.

The Council may in any case under this Article refer the dispute to the Assembly. The dispute shall be so referred at the request of either party to the dispute, provided that such request be made within fourteen days after the submission of the dispute to the Council.

In any case referred to the Assembly, all the provisions of this Article and of Article 12 relating to the action and powers of the Council shall apply to the action and powers of the Assembly, provided that a report made by the Assembly, if concurred in by the Representatives of those Members of the League represented on the Council and of a majority of the other Members of the League, exclusive in each case of the Representatives of the parties to the dispute, shall have the same force as a report by the Council concurred in by all the members thereof other than the Representatives of one or more of the parties to the dispute.

ARTICLE 16.

Should any Member of the League resort to war in disregard of its covenants under Articles 12, 13 or 15, it shall *ipso facto* be deemed to have committed an act of war against all other Members of the League, which hereby undertake immediately to subject it to the severance of all trade or financial relations, the prohibition of all intercourse between their nationals and the nationals of the covenant-breaking State, and the prevention of all financial, commercial or personal intercourse between the nationals of the covenant-breaking State and the nationals of any other State whether a Member of the League or not.

It shall be the duty of the Council in such case to recommend to the several Governments concerned what effective military, naval or air force the Members of the League shall severally contribute to the armed forces to be used to protect the covenants of the League.

The Members of the League agree, further, that they will mutually support one another in the financial and economic measures which are taken under this Article, in order to minimise the loss and inconvenience resulting from the above measures, and that they will mutually support one another in resisting any special measures aimed at one of their number by the covenant-breaking State, and that they will take the necessary steps to afford passage through their territory to the forces of any of the Members of the League which are co-operating to protect the covenants of the League.

Any Member of the League which has violated any covenant of the League may be declared to be no longer a Member of the League by a vote of the Council concurred in by the Representatives of all the other Members of the League represented thereon.

ARTICLE 17.

In the event of a dispute between a Member of the League and a State which is not a Member of the League, or between States not Members of the League, the State or States not Members of the League shall be invited to accept the obligations of Membership in the League for the purposes of such dispute, upon such conditions as the Council may deem just. If such invitation is accepted, the provisions of Articles 12 to 16 inclusive shall be applied with such modifications as may be deemed necessary by the Council.

Upon such invitation being given the Council shall immediately institute an inquiry into the circumstances of the dispute and recommend such action as may seem best and most effectual in the circumstances.

If a State so invited shall refuse to accept the obligations of Membership in the League for the purposes of such dispute, and shall resort to war against a Member of the League, the provisions of Article 16 shall be applicable as against the State taking such action.

If both parties to the dispute when so invited refuse to accept the obligations of Membership in the League for the purposes of such dispute, the Council may take such measures and make such recommendations as will prevent hostilities and will result in the settlement of the dispute.

ARTICLE 18.

Every treaty or international engagement entered into hereafter by any Member of the League shall be forthwith registered with the Secretariat and shall as soon as possible be published by it. No such treaty or international engagement shall be binding until so registered.

ARTICLE 19.

The Assembly may from time to time advise the reconsideration by Members of the League of Treaties which have become inapplicable and the consideration of international conditions whose continuance might endanger the peace of the world.

ARTICLE 20.

The Members of the League severally agree that this Covenant is accepted as abrogating all obligations or understandings *inter se* which are inconsistent with the terms thereof and solemnly undertake that they will not hereafter enter into any engagements inconsistent with the terms thereof.

In case any Member of the League shall, before becoming a Member of the League have undertaken any obligations inconsistent with the terms of this Covenant, it shall be the duty of such Member to take immediate steps to procure its release from such obligations.

ARTICLE 21.

Nothing in this Covenant shall be deemed to affect the validity of international engagements, such as treaties of arbitration or regional understandings like the Monroe doctrine, for securing the maintenance of peace.

ARTICLE 22.

To those colonies and territories which as a consequence of the late war have ceased to be under the sovereignty of the States which formerly governed them and which are inhabited by peoples not yet able to stand by themselves under the strenuous conditions of the modern world, there should be applied the principle that the well-being and development of such peoples form a sacred trust of civilisation and that securities for the performance of this trust should be embodied in this Covenant.

The best method of giving practical effect to this principle is that the tutelage of such peoples should be entrusted to advanced nations who by reason of their resources, their experience or their geographical position can best undertake this responsibility, and who are willing to accept it, and that this tutelage should be exercised by them as Mandatories on behalf of the League.

The character of the mandate must differ according to the stage of the development of the people, the geographical situation of the territory, its economic conditions and other similar circumstances.

Certain communities formerly belonging to the Turkish Empire have reached a stage of development where their existence as independent nations can be provisionally recognised subject to the rendering of administrative advice and assistance by a Mandatory until such time as they are able to stand alone. The wishes of these communities must be a principal consideration in the selection of the Mandatory.

Other peoples, especially those of Central Africa, are at such a stage that the Mandatory must be responsible for the administration of the territory under conditions which will guarantee freedom of conscience and religion, subject only to the maintenance of public order and morals, the prohibition of abuses such as the slave trade, the arms traffic and the liquor traffic, and the prevention of the establishment of fortifications or military and naval bases and of military training of the natives for other than police purposes and the defence of territory, and will also secure equal opportunities for the trade and commerce of other Members of the League.

There are territories, such as South-West Africa and certain of the South Pacific Islands, which, owing to the sparseness of their population, or their small size, or their remoteness from the centres of civilisation, or their geographical contiguity to the territory of the Mandatory, and other circumstances, can be best administered under the laws of the Mandatory as integral portions of its territory, subject to the safeguards above mentioned in the interests of the indigenous population.

In every case of mandate, the Mandatory shall render to the Council an annual report in reference to the territory committed to its charge.

The degree of authority, control, or administration to be exercised by the Mandatory shall, if not previously agreed upon by the Members of the League, be explicitly defined in each case by the Council.

A permanent Commission shall be constituted to receive and examine the annual reports of the Mandatories and to advise the Council on all matters relating to the observance of the mandates.

ARTICLE 23.

Subject to and in accordance with the provisions of international conventions existing or hereafter to be agreed upon, the Members of the League :

(*a*) will endeavour to secure and maintain fair and humane conditions of labour for men, women, and children, both in their own countries and in all countries to which their commercial and industrial relations extend, and for that purpose will establish and maintain the necessary international organisations ;

(*b*) undertake to secure just treatment of the native inhabitants of territories under their control ;

(*c*) will entrust the League with the general supervision over the execution of agreements with regard to the traffic in women and children, and the traffic in opium and other dangerous drugs ;

(*d*) will entrust the League with the general supervision of the trade in arms and ammunition with the countries in which the control of this traffic is necessary in the common interest ;

(*e*) will make provision to secure and maintain freedom of communications and of transit and equitable treatment for the commerce of all Members of the League. In this connection, the special necessities of the regions devastated during the war of 1914–1918 shall be borne in mind ;

(*f*) will endeavour to take steps in matters of international concern for the prevention and control of disease.

ARTICLE 24.

There shall be placed under the direction of the League all international bureaux already established by general treaties if the parties to such treaties consent. All such international bureaux and all commissions for the regulation of matters of international interest hereafter constituted shall be placed under the direction of the League.

In all matters of international interest which are regulated by general conventions but which are not placed under the control of international bureaux or commissions, the Secretariat of the League shall, subject to the consent of the Council and if desired by the parties, collect and distribute all relevant information and shall render any other assistance which may be necessary or desirable.

The Council may include as part of the expenses of the Secretariat the expenses of any bureau or commission which is placed under the direction of the League.

ARTICLE 25.

The Members of the League agree to encourage and promote the establishment and co-operation of duly authorised voluntary national Red Cross organisations having as purposes the improvement of health, the prevention of disease and the mitigation of suffering throughout the world.

ARTICLE 26.

Amendments to this Covenant will take effect when ratified by the Members of the League whose Representatives compose the Council and by a majority of the Members of the League whose Representatives compose the Assembly.

No such amendment shall bind any Member of the League which signifies its dissent therefrom, but in that case it shall cease to be a Member of the League.

Annex.

I. ORIGINAL MEMBERS OF THE LEAGUE OF NATIONS SIGNATORIES OF THE TREATY OF PEACE.

UNITED STATES OF AMERICA.
BELGIUM.
BOLIVIA.
BRAZIL.
BRITISH EMPIRE.
   CANADA.
   AUSTRALIA.
   SOUTH AFRICA.
   NEW ZEALAND.
   INDIA.
CHINA.
CUBA.
ECUADOR.
FRANCE.
GREECE.
GUATEMALA.

HAITI.
HEDJAZ.
HONDURAS.
ITALY.
JAPAN.
LIBERIA.
NICARAGUA.
PANAMA.
PERU.
POLAND.
PORTUGAL.
ROUMANIA.
SERB-CROAT-SLOVENE STATE.
SIAM.
CZECHO-SLOVAKIA.
URUGUAY.

STATES INVITED TO ACCEDE TO THE COVENANT.

ARGENTINE REPUBLIC.
CHILI.
COLOMBIA.
DENMARK.
NETHERLANDS.
NORWAY.
PARAGUAY.

PERSIA.
SALVADOR.
SPAIN.
SWEDEN.
SWITZERLAND.
VENEZUELA.

II. FIRST SECRETARY GENERAL OF THE LEAGUE OF NATIONS.

The Honourable Sir James Eric DRUMMOND, K.C.M.G., C.B.

III. Opinion of the Permanent Advisory Commission Regarding Assembly Resolutions XIV and XV[1].

The Permanent Advisory Commission, which met at Geneva from April 16th to 23rd, 1923, to consider Assembly Resolutions XIV and XV with regard to Treaties of Mutual Guarantee was unable, in consequence of divergencies in the instructions given to members by their respective Governments to express a unanimous opinion on this matter.

The British Delegation, not having received instructions from its Government, was, unable to take part in the discussion.

The Italian Delegation stated that it was unable to discuss the question of partial treaties.

SUMMARY.

A. Opinion of the Belgian, Brazilian, French and Swedish Delegations in regard to :

I. General conditions to be fulfilled by any Treaty of Guarantee

II. Difficulties inherent in any Treaty of Guarantee

III. The value of a General Treaty

---

[1] *Resolution XIV (a).* The Assembly, having considered the report of the Temporary Mixed Commission on the question of a general Treaty of Mutual Guarantee, being of opinion that this report can in no way affect the complete validity of all the Treaties of Peace or other agreements which are known to exist between States; and considering that this report contains valuable suggestions as to the methods by which a Treaty of Mutual Guarantee could be made effective, is of the opinion that :

(1) No scheme for the reduction of armaments, within the meaning of Article 8 of the Covenant, can be fully successful unless it is general.

(2) In the present state of the world, many Governments would be unable to accept the responsibility for a serious reduction of armaments unless they received in exchange a satisfactory guarantee of the safety of their country.

(3) Such a guarantee can be found in a defensive agreement which should be open to all countries, binding them to provide immediate and effective assistance in accordance with a pre-arranged plan in the event of one of them being attacked, provided that the obligation to render assistance to a country attacked shall be limited in principle to those countries situated in the same part of the globe. In cases, however, where, for historical, geographical, or other reasons, a country is in special danger of attack, detailed arrangements should be made for its defence in accordance with the above-mentioned plan.

(4) As a general reduction of armaments is the object of the three preceding statements, and the Treaty of Mutual Guarantee the means of achieving that object, previous consent to this reduction is therefore the first condition for the Treaty.

This reduction could be carried out either by means of a general Treaty, which is the most desirable plan, or by means of partial treaties designed to be extended and open to all countries.

In the former case, the Treaty will carry with it a general reduction of armaments. In the latter case, the reduction should be proportionate to the guarantees afforded by the Treaty.

The Council of the League, after having taken the advice of the Temporary Mixed Commission, which will examine how each of these two systems could be carried out, should further formulate and submit to the Governments for their consideration and sovereign decision the plan of the machinery, both political and military, necessary to bring them clearly into effect.

(b) The Assembly requests the Council to submit to the various Governments the above proposals for their observations, and requests the Temporary Mixed Commission to continue its investigations, and, in order to give precision to the above statements, to prepare a draft Treaty embodying the principles contained therein.

Resolution XV. The Assembly,

Whilst declaring that the reduction of armaments contemplated by Article 8 of the Covenant cannot achieve its full effect for world-peace unless it be general :

Desires to emphasise the importance of regional agreements for the purpose of reducing armaments — agreements which, if necessary, might even go beyond the measures decided upon in respect of general reduction ;

And requests the Council to ask the Temporary Mixed Commission to take into consideration, during its subsequent work, the possibility of recommending the conclusion of similar agreements to States which might be concerned.

B. Opinion of the Belgian, Brazilian and French Delegations in regard to :
 . IV. Partial treaties and regional agreements.

C. Opinion of the Swedish Delegation in regard to :
 IV. Partial Treaties.

D. V. Conclusions and Résumé of the Belgian, Brazilian and French Delegations.

E. Observations by the Spanish and Italian Delegations (otherwise in agreement
 with almost all the considerations of a military nature set forth in the preceding Opinions), to which the Japanese Delegation adheres in principle :

 I. General conditions to be fulfilled by any Treaty of Guarantee.
 II. General Treaty.
 III. Conclusion.

———

A.

The BELGIAN, BRAZILIAN, FRENCH and SWEDISH DELEGATIONS express the following
opinions in regard to :

 I. The general conditions to be fulfilled by any Treaty of Guarantee.
 II. The difficulties inherent in any Treaty of Guarantee.
 III. The value of a General Treaty.

I. GENERAL CONDITIONS TO BE FULFILLED BY ANY TREATY OF GUARANTEE, WHETHER GENERAL OR PARTIAL.

Our object is to prevent war and not to bring progressively into action the forces which
will carry a war to a successful conclusion. Any system which did not *immediately* confront
the aggressor with forces considerably superior to his own would be fundamentally unsound :
instead of stopping the conflict at the beginning, it would allow it time to develop, and would
thus lead to a *long war*, with all the irreparable damage and loss of life which such a war
involves.

This postulate implies the following conditions :

(a) The system to be established should be such that the aggressor :

Could not even imagine the possibility of coming into conflict with it (ideal solution) ;

Would be very quickly crushed in a *short* war (acceptable solution) ;

Would have no hope of success in a long war (dangerous solution).

(b) In no case must a State which is attacked suffer invasion.

This condition assumes the existence of a mutual guarantee which can be *brought into
action immediately*. The necessity of such a guarantee is proportionate to the directness
of the threat which overshadows a country owing to " historical, geographical or other "
circumstances, which entail, for some countries, the " special dangers " recognised by the
Assembly.

(c) As war is carried on in every sphere, mutual assistance must also be given in every sphere.
It is not, however, equally effective in all the forms and in all the combinations of circumstances
considered.

*The only form of assistance which is really effective at the beginning of a war is military,
naval or air assistance.*

Other forms of assistance — economic, financial, etc. — can only play a subsidiary
part, which, however great its importance, is only felt, as a rule, in course of time, during a
long war. Moreover, the very nature of these forms of assistance renders it impossible
to estimate the guarantees that they afford, and consequently to apply one of the principles
laid down in Resolution XIV — namely, that the reduction of armaments should be
" proportionate to the guarantees " offered by the Treaty.

*(d) If the assistance is to be " immediate and effective " it must be given " in accordance
with a pre-arranged plan "*, as stated in Resolution XIV ; and if this pre-arranged plan, which
will necessarily involve detailed provision, is to be carried out without delay — that is, without
discussion — it is important that it should be made an *integral part* of the treaty of guarantee.

(e) As the methods of attack and defence are constantly changing, it is essential :

That any treaty of guarantee involving reductions in armaments should be *periodically
revised* with a view to maintaining its efficacy ;

That some form of control should be exercised with the double object of revealing secret
armaments or preparations before it is too late, and of ensuring that the guarantee nations
maintain a minimum quantity of sufficiently modern armaments to enable them to fulfil,
if necessary, their obligation to provide assistance. Even if it is practicable to ensure by some
form of control that each State maintains the minimum quantity of armaments which it
has undertaken to maintain, it will be very difficult, if not impossible, to exercise control in
respect of excess of armaments in an effective manner and without infringing the sovereignty
of the States required to submit to such control.

To sum up, it will be seen that a treaty of mutual guarantee should *in theory :*

Take instant effect with a force which would discourage any idea of aggression, would protect the State attacked from invasion and would shorten the war ;

Include in its text a detailed and pre-arranged plan of common action in every sphere, but particularly in the sphere of military, naval and air operations ;

Organise some form of preventive control ;

Provide for periodical revisions.

II. DIFFICULTIES INHERENT IN ANY TREATY OF GUARANTEE.

The conditions considered above have already brought to light the difficulties involved in the conclusion of treaties of guarantee. It will now be observed that, *by their very nature, though in varying degrees according to the system of which they are a part,* treaties of this kind contain inevitable weaknesses.

(a) In the first place, the guarantees to be given from outside will in all cases be of less intrinsic value than similar guarantees secured to a State by its own resources. A few obvious reasons may readily be given in connection with armed forces providing assistance.

The preparations for their action cannot be carried so far ;

Their arrival at the seat of operations will be subject to many risks (delay or interruption to land transport in foreign territory, or of sea transport if the command of the sea is not assured) ;

The plan of concentration (and to some extent the plan of operations) will be known to so many persons that it will be impossible to preserve that *secrecy* which is an essential factor of success in war ;

The value of the auxiliary forces will vary and will depend upon their organisation, arms, officers, training and individual qualities.

(b) The relative value of foreign intervention will depend upon the peace-time military organisation of the co-operating State. If a long war is to be avoided, the *initial operations* must be regarded as *decisive.* To ensure their success, it is better that units of comparatively small value should be *immediately available* at the outset than that better-trained troops should arrive *too late.* Now, those countries which only maintain small professional armies, and for which mobilisation involves the training of their national man-power, will not be able to put any considerable effectives into the field until after several months, if not longer.

(c) Foreign troops, the despatch of which depends on the goodwill of their Governments and on a vote of their Parliaments, will never be available with *certainty and in every event.* This point brings us to the following question, which is of capital importance and governs the whole problem :

(d) How can the mutual assistance provided for by a treaty of guarantee be automatically brought into play ?

It is not enough merely to repeat the familiar formula, " unprovoked aggression ": for under the conditions of modern warfare it *would seem impossible to decide, even in theory, what constitutes a case of aggression. Thus :*

Aggression should be *defined in the treaty ;*

The signs should be visible, so that the treaty may be *applicable ;*

Lastly, the signs should be *universally recognised,* in order to make the operation of the treaty *certain.*

1. DEFINITION OF AGGRESSION.

Hitherto, aggression could be defined as mobilisation or the violation of a frontier. This double test has lost its value.

Mobilisation, which consisted, until quite recently, of a few comparatively simple operations (calling up of reserves, purchases or requisitions and establishment of war industries, *after the calling up of the men*), has become infinitely more complicated and more difficult both to discover at its origin and to follow in its development. In future, mobilisation will apply not merely to the army but *to the whole country before the outbreak of hostilities* (collection of stocks of raw materials and munitions of war, industrial mobilisation, establishment or increased output of industries). All these measures which give evidence of an *intention* to go to war may lead to discussions and conflicting interpretations, thus securing *decisive* advantages to the aggressor unless action be taken.

The violation of a frontier by " armed forces " will not necessarily be, in future, such an obvious act of violence as it has hitherto been. The expression "armed forces" has now become somewhat indefinite, as certain States possess police forces and irregular troops which may or may not be legally constituted, but which have a definite military value. Frontiers themselves are not easy to define, since the treaties of 1919-1920 have created neutral zones, since political and military frontiers no longer necessarily coincide, and since air forces take no account of either.

Moreover, the passage of the frontier by the troops of another country does not always mean that the latter country is the aggressor. Particularly in the case of small States, the object of such action may be to establish an initial position which shall be as advantageous as possible for the defending country, and to do so before the adversary has had time to mass his superior forces. A military offensive of as rapid a character as possible may therefore be a means, and perhaps the only means, whereby the weaker party can defend himself against the stronger. It is also conceivable that a small nation might be compelled to make use of its air forces in order to forestall the superior forces of the enemy and take what advantage was possible from such action.

Finally, the hostilities between two naval Powers generally begin on sea by the capture of merchant vessels, or other acts of violence — very possibly on the high seas outside territorial waters. The same applies to air operations, which may take place without any violation of the air frontiers of States.

These few considerations illustrate some of the difficulties inherent in any attempt to define the expression "cases of aggression" and raise doubt as to the possibility of accurately defining this expression *a priori* in a treaty, *from the military point of view*, especially as the question is often invested with a political character.

2. Signs which betoken an Impending Aggression.

But, even supposing that we have defined the circumstances which constitute aggression, the existence of a case of aggression must be *definitely established*. It may be taken that the signs would appear in the following order :

1. Organisation on paper of industrial mobilisation.
2. Actual organisation of industrial mobilisation.
3. Collection of stocks of raw materials.
4. Setting-on-foot of war industries.
5. Preparation for military mobilisation.
6. Actual military mobilisation.
7. Hostilities.

Numbers 1 and 5 (and to some extent Number 2), which are in all cases difficult to recognise, may, in those countries which are not subject under the Peace Treaties to any obligation to disarm, represent precautions which every Government is entitled to take.

Number 3 may be justified by economic reasons, such as profiting by an advantageous market or collecting stocks in order to guard against the possible closing of certain channels of supply owing to strikes, etc.

Number 4 (setting-on-foot of war industries) is the first which may be definitely taken as showing an intention to commit aggression; it will, however, be easy to conceal this measure for a long period in countries which are under no military supervision.

When Numbers 6 and 7 are known to have taken place, it is too late.

3. Universal Recognition of Impending Aggression.

In the absence of any indisputable test, Governments can only judge by an *impression* based upon the most various factors, such as :

The political attitude of the possible aggressor ;

His propaganda ;

The attitude of his Press and population ;

His policy on the international market, etc.

Now, the impression thus produced *will not be the same* on the nations which are directly threatened as upon the guarantor nations ; thus, as every Government has its own individual standpoint, no simultaneous and universal agreement as to the imminence of an attack is possible.

It will be seen, in short, that the first act of war will precede the outbreak of military hostilities by several months or even more, and that there is no reason to expect any unanimous agreement as to the signs which betoken the imminence of danger. There is therefore a risk that the mutual assistance would only come into action in reply to military mobilisation or hostilities on the part of the aggressor. Such assistance, not being *preventive*, will always come *too late*, and will therefore only allow of a slight reduction in the individual provision which must be made by each nation for the organisation of its own defence.

Despite these points, in which " collective guarantees " are inferior to " national guarantees ", we must not abandon the former class, nor must we give up our attempts to strengthen them. They involve, however, important results as regards the latter class, and those results we must now enumerate.

(a) Whatever external guarantees may be in contemplation, no country can be expected, if attacked, to refrain from mobilising as quickly as possible all its forces of every kind. Such a country must therefore maintain, in peace-time, armaments proportionate to possible attacks and so organised that complete mobilisation will be easy at any time.

(b) The final decision as to the value of external support and the efficiency of the machinery by which this supports is to be brougt into action must necessarily be left to each of the Goverments concerned. Vhe same stipulation should therefore apply to the reductions in armaments which may be rendered possible by these new guarantees. *Any ideal of a scale of armaments calculated* a priori *on a more or less arbitrary basis is thus excluded.* As each Government remaids the sole judge of the minimum quantity of armaments which is necessary for its security, it is *only* to the extent to wihch external support takes the place of a portion of the national armamants that the latter can and should be reduced.

Further, it will be advisable, in calculating the " substitutiod value " of external support, to find a suitable and variable co-efficient of reduction which will express the relation of each of the elements making up this support to the corresponding elements in the national forces.

(c) As the word " guarantee " implies the idea of real security, it would be preferable, in order to avoid misleading public opinion, to refer to the treaty as one of " mutual assistance " rather than of " mutual guarantee ".

III. GENERAL TREATY.

It would doubtless be highly desirable that as many countries as possible should automatical come, in one form or another, to the assistance of any one or more of their number which may be attached.

The principle of a guarantee of this kind is laid down, in theory, in Article 10 of the Covenant of the League. Il would be well, however, to strengthen this principle by means of a *General Treaty for the practical application of those articles of the Covenant which relate to it, although the* amendment adopted by the Second Assembly must seriously reduce the efficacy of the economic weapon placed in the hands of the League by Article 16.

The ideal and the practical do not, however, always coincide ; and it must be asked in this case whether the vagueness which so often characterises general contracts can be reconciled with the *degree of confidence* which would be implied by any considerable reduction in the armaments of each State. This question can only be answered by taking the following points in order :

(a) Is a general treaty of mutual assistance, defining the obligations under Articles 10 and 16 of the Covenant, calculated, in case of war, to provide effective support for the State attacked ; and, if so, in what form ?

A distinction must be drawn between wars in which an attacked State is *directly* involved and those in which such a State would be obliged to intervene *as a co-operating State.* In the former case the important points for the country concerned are the nature and value of the support *immediately* available from abroad ; in the latter case, the chief importance attaches to the obligations which the country must undertake and the burdens it will thus incur. A further distinction must be drawn regarding the *actual nature of the war*, according as its form is predominantly military (land warfare) or predominantly naval (sea warfare). In other words, *the necessity of adapting armaments to the nature and magnitude of the dangers* against which they are intended to guard involves the basing of all calculations upon *potential offensive power of the possible aggressor.* Even this first condition appears to be incompatible with the very nature of a general treaty, which should be *valid in all cases of aggression*; for every aggressor gives rise to a " particular case " which does not come within the scope of a general treaty.

Similarly, a country which has decided to attack at a convenient moment will take measures to destroy, at least for a considerable time, the efficacy of the only weapon which could come immediately into action under a general treaty — *the blockade.* It would, of course, be difficult for small or average countries, whose resources and industrial capacity are limited, to carry out in all its various forms such a preparation for attack. But a treaty of guarantee which only gave security against the weak would be immoral and valueless. Now a guarantee against the strong could only be provided by a *continental* study of the potential offensive power of all possible aggressors. To attain this object, therefore, a general treaty would have to be *split up into a series of separate treaties*, each of which would provide in the greatest detail against a certain hypothetical case of aggression The treaty would thus retain no characteristics which could be called general, except the name.

It may readily be imagined that the different risks involved may incline some Governments towards the idea of a general treaty and others towards that of partial treaties. For the former class, the risks consist in naval dangers, which may interfere with or close their channels of supply without striking directly at their national existence. For the latter class, the danger represents the direct threat of an invasion of their territory. Though the former class of Government may consider general guarantees of a more or less vague and uncertain character to be sufficient, the other Governments cannot be so easily satisfied. In any case, *this distinction may in course of time lose its validity* as a result of the increasingly far-reaching changes which will probably be introduced by air warfare. The value of natural barriers will decrease in proportion, as they can be more easily crossed by large air forces, and as, without regard to distance, a nation becomes immediately vulnerable in its population and resources of every kind, wherever they may be situated.

If we start from the assumption that, at least *in a land war, the first few months of operations* will be decisive, the question which arises is what military, naval or air assistance can be given *immediately,* or with very little delay, by any country to any other country which is attacked.

From the military standpoint, this assistance will depend upon the time taken by the co-operating State to mobilise, on transport facilities and on the organisation of channels of supply and special bases for each nationality. It is well known that the action of land forces cannot be efficient unless detailed preparations have been made for it. Thus the scheme of transport should comprise the selection of the lines of transport and, in some cases, of alternative lines, their equipment for military transport, and the formation of a technical staff to ensure the immediate working of the lines in case of need, should the ordinary staff not be available (owing to strikes or any other reason). The plan of supply would require the compulsory collection of stocks of material for the various expeditionary forces. It is clear that, while such preparations could be carried out for a limited number of countries under certain definite conditions, they become *technically impossible* if an attempt is made to apply them to a very large number of States simultaneously, *owing to the great variety of the hypothetical cases for which provision must be made.*

From the naval standpoint, the technical problem is, comparatively, simpler. Naval forces are not subject to the same conditions of mobilisation as land forces. The number of possible cases to be considered appears to be smaller, and the potential naval power of possible enemies can be more easily determined. Nevertheless, the naval forces of the co-operating States will not necessarily be concentrated at the moment of the outbreak of war. Their use also involves the necessity of drawing up a plan of action, of ensuring its execution, of establishing bases of supply, etc. ; and, while recognising that naval forces are more quickly available than land forces, we must be under no illusion regarding the very relative rapidity with which they can be brought into action.

The naval forces of a number of Powers are often composed of units whose qualities (seagoing capability, radius of action, etc.) seriously diminish the possibility of their employ. This circumstance adds still further to the difficulties of a practical application of a general treaty from the fact that the employment of such naval forces must necessarily be limited to special theatres of operations.

Furthermore, *their action may be technically ineffective,* particularly at the outset, in many land wars. They cannot guard against the invasion of a country, and their effect as instruments of a blockade is only felt during the course of a *long* war.

From the air standpoint, it is generally admitted that the immediately available air forces are those which can start from aerodromes situated not more than 250 kilometres from their objectives. Beyond that radius they cannot act, unless previous preparations have been made for their transport and supply. Now, immediate action will be of great importance as regards defence, to prevent the passage of enemy bombing machines, and, as regards the offensive, to impede the enemy's concentration. Under these conditions, the available air forces will generally be confined to those which can be provided by the adjacent countries. As these countries will undoubtedly retain their fighting machines for their own defence, we can only reckon upon a contingent of bombing machines.

The impossibility of satisfying, by means of a general treaty, the principles laid down by the Assembly of " immediate and effective assistance in accordance with a pre-arranged plan " is rendered still more obvious by another consideration. The number and variety of the possible cases to be considered in a single continent is further complicated by the fact that *any country may be, at different times, assisted or assisting,* and *that its position may change in the course of a single war.* Reserving for later consideration the problem of deciding whether aggression has been committed (which, as will be seen below, is insoluble in the case of a general treaty), we may therefore lay it down that the military, naval or air assistance afforded by such a treaty would be uncertain, and would in any case come too late to *protect a State from invasion* if attacked and to ensure, in every event, the decisive success of the initial operations.

(b) Can the military, naval or air support given by a general treaty be calculated with sufficient exactitude to allow Governments to reduce their armaments below the minimum now considered necessary by them, such reduction being proportionate to the guarantees afforded by the treaty ?

It has been seen to be impossible, owing to the number and variety of the possible cases, to determine the nature and value of the assistance to be given in each of these cases by each of the States signatory to a general treaty. It follows that no relation can be established between two factors, one of which (guarantees) remains *indefinite,* while the other (reduction of armaments) should be *definite.* Some States may display sufficient confidence in the co-operating countries to consider that their risks are not so great as to debar them from consenting to a certain reduction of armaments. But it is also possible that other States may be requested, in the name of international co-operation, to increase the military burden which they formerly regarded as sufficient for their own defence. For, though certain countries run special risks, " owing to their historical and geographical situation ", others may consider that, from both these points of view, their own situation renders them comparatively immune from the threat of immediate danger.

It is therefore possible that a general treaty may lead to certain reductions of armaments, *but it is impossible to state this definitely, and still more so to indicate without further evidence how far these reductions would go.* They would, in any case, be based, not upon organised and actual assistance, as was recommended by the Assembly, but on a feeling of confidence which has no connection with the principles embodied in Resolution XIV.

(c) As the military, naval or air support afforded by a general treaty could not be immediately or sufficiently effective, what would be the nature and the value of the other forms of assistance (economic, financial, etc.), and could they lead to reductions of armaments ?

One of the advantages of a general treaty would, of course, consist in the fact that it would assure the State attacked of a measure of economic, industrial and financial assistance which would enable it to fill any gaps of this nature in its national organisation. It must be clearly realised, however, that, in the case of a general treaty, every State which entered the war *without knowing the limits of its liabilities would, to a large extent, retain its own resources for its own use.* The assistance given in the forms which we have mentioned would, moreover, only be felt after a certain lapse of time, and its full value would only be seen in a *long* war. Having no influence on the initial operations, it would not allow of any reduction in peace-time armaments. And even if such a reduction were contemplated, it could not be made proportionate to the assistance expected, as no definite relation can be established between, for example, an amount of *financial support* and a *reduction of effectives.*

(d) In what contingencies would mutual assistance be required, and by what procedure could it be brought into action so that the participating States could place full reliance upon it and thus gain the necessary confidence to reduce their national armaments ?

This question touches the most delicate point in the problem. We need only refer to what has been said above regarding the weaknesses inherent in any treaty of guarantee (pages 120 to 122) in order to realise the impossibility, in the case of a general treaty, of bringing mutual assistance into action *in time.*

According to the suggestions put forward in the report of the Temporary Mixed Commission, the machinery would work somewhat on the following lines :

The threatened country would approach the Council of the League, giving information regarding the plans of its general staff, the forces which it could put in the field, the total forces which it considered necessary to achieve success, the countries which, in its opinion, should supply these forces, and its plans for their employment. The Council, with the assistance of the Permanent Advisory Commission, would consider how far these applications were reasonable and practical, and would invite the Governments concerned to take all necessary steps to furnish the forces required.

It is needless to attempt to prove that, even if this machinery could work, it would work with a *slowness* which would be inadmissible. It is impossible to solve in a few days, or even in a few weeks, a problem of preparation which, *merely in its technical aspect, supposing all the political difficulties to have been overcome, would require months.*

Such an argument would, moreover, assume that the vital question as to whether there was aggression had been decided. Independently of the fact that the " territorial " definition of aggression as a violation of the frontier is altogether too general and, as has been explained on pages 120 to 122, in no way corresponds to the realities of modern warfare, it would appear that the actual procedure suggested by the Temporary Mixed Commission could not be carried into effect either within the limits indicated by the Commission or even within substantially wider limits. In other words, *a State threatened by direct attack would find no guarantee in a Treaty the text of which did not contain a precise statement of the actual hostilities which that State might have to fear.*

The foregoing considerations afford evidence of the danger involved in a Treaty of Guarantee which merely lays down principles and, as appears to be suggested in the last paragraph of Resolution XIV, admits that " the plan of the machinery, both political and military, necessary to bring them clearly into effect " might only be established " subsequently ". The difficulties which would be experienced in drawing up such a plan would doubtless lead to its postponement, and possibly even to its abandonment. Nothing would remain but a treaty which, from the point of view of *guarantees,* would be a mere sham, while, from the point of view of the *reduction of armaments,* it would appear to hold out a prospect of relief on a large scale to a public which had been deluded and lulled into a sense of false security.

DOCUMENT 2 (b)

III. Text of the Treaty of Mutual Assistance.

Preamble.

The High Contracting Parties, being desirous of establishing the general lines of a scheme of mutual assistance with a view to facilitate the application of Articles 10 and 16 of the Covenant of the League of Nations, and of a reduction or limitation of national armaments in accordance with Article 8 of the Covenant " to the lowest point consistent with national safety and the enforcement by common action of international obligations ", agree to the following provisions :

Article 1.

The High Contracting Parties solemnly declare that aggressive war is an international crime and severally undertake that no one of them will be guilty of its commission.

I. Pact of non-aggression.

A war shall not be considered as a war of aggression if waged by a State which is party to a dispute and has accepted the unanimous recommendation of the Council, the verdict of the Permanent Court of International Justice, or an arbitral award against a High Contracting Party which has not accepted it, provided, however, that the first State does not intend to violate the political independence or the territorial integrity of the High Contracting Party.

Article 2.

The High Contracting Parties, jointly and severally, undertake to furnish assistance, in accordance with the provisions of the Present Treaty, to any one of their number should the latter be the object of a war of aggression, provided that it has conformed to the provisions of the present Treaty regarding the reduction or limitation of armaments.

II. General assistance.

Article 3.

In the event of one of the High Contracting Parties being of opinion that the armaments of any other High Contracting Party are in excess of the limits fixed for the latter High Contracting Party under the provisions of the present Treaty, or in the event of it having cause to apprehend an outbreak of hostilities, either on account of the aggressive policy or preparations of any State party or not to the present Treaty, it may inform the Secretary-General of the League of Nations that it is threatened with aggression, and the Secretary-General shall forthwith summon the Council.

Menace of aggression

The Council, if it is of opinion that there is reasonable ground for thinking that a menace of aggression has arisen, may take all necessary measures to remove such menace, and in particular, if the Council thinks right, those indicated in sub-paragraphs (a), (b), (c), (d) and (e) of the second paragraph of Article 5 of the present Treaty.

The High Contracting Parties which have been denounced and those which have stated themselves to be the object of a threat of aggression shall be considered as especially interested and shall therefore be invited to send representatives to the Council in conformity with Articles 4, 15 and 17 of the Covenant. The vote of their representatives shall, however, not be reckoned when calculating unanimity.

Article 4.

In the event of one or more of the High Contracting Parties becoming engaged in hostilities, the Council of the League of Nations shall decide, within four days of notification being addressed to the Secretary-General, which of the High Contracting Parties are the objects of aggression and whether they are entitled to claim the assistance provided under the Treaty.

Hostilities

The High Contracting Parties undertake that they will accept such a decision by the Council of the League of Nations.

The High Contracting Parties engaged in hostilities shall be regarded as especially interested, and shall therefore be invited to send representatives to the Council (within the terms of Articles 4, 15 and 17 of the Covenant), the vote of their representative not being reckoned when calculating unanimity; the same shall apply to States signatory to any partial agreements involved on behalf of either of the two belligerents, unless the remaining Members of the Council shall decide otherwise.

Article 5.

The High Contracting Parties undertake to furnish one another mutually with assistance in the case referred to in Article 2 of the Treaty in the form determined by the Council of the League of Nations as the most effective, and to take all appropriate measures without delay in the order of urgency demanded by the circumstances.

Measures of assistance.

In particular, the Council may:

(a) Decide to apply immediately to the aggressor State the economic sanctions contemplated by Article 16 of the Covenant, the Members of the League not signatory to the present Treaty not being, however, bound by this decision, except in the case where the State attacked is entitled to avail itself of the Articles of the Covenant;

(b) Invoke by name the High Contracting Parties whose assistance it requires. No High Contracting Party situated in a continent other than that in which operations will take place shall, in principle, be required to co-operate in military, naval or air operations;

(c) Determine the forces which each State furnishing assistance shall place at its disposal;

(d) Prescribe all necessary measures for securing priority for the communications and transport connected with the operations;

(e) Prepare a plan for financial co-operation among the High Contracting Parties with a view to providing for the State attacked and for the States furnishing assistance the funds which they require for the operations;

(f) Appoint the Higher Command and establish the object and the nature of his duty.

The representatives of States recognised as aggressors under the provisions of Article 4 of the Treaty shall not take part in the deliberations of the Council specified in this Article. The High Contracting Parties who are required by the Council to furnish assistance, in accordance with sub-paragraph (b), shall, on the other hand, be considered as especially interested, and, as such, shall be invited to send representatives, unless they are already represented, to the deliberations specified in sub-paragraphs (c), (d), (e) and (f).

ARTICLE 6.

III. Complementary defensive agreements.

For the purpose of rendering the general assistance mentioned in Articles 2, 3 and 5 immediately effective, the High Contracting Parties may conclude, either as between two of them or as between a larger number, agreements complementary to the present Treaty exclusively for the purpose of their mutual defence and intended solely to facilitate the carrying out of the measures prescribed in this Treaty, determining in advance the assistance which they would give to each other in the event of any act of aggression.

Such agreements may, if the High Contracting Parties interested so desire, be negotiated and concluded under the auspices of the League of Nations.

ARTICLE 7.

Complementary agreements, as defined in Article 6, shall, before being registered, be examined by the Council with a view to deciding whether they are in accordance with the principles of the Treaty and of the Covenant.

In particular, the Council shall consider if the cases of aggression contemplated in these agreements come within the scope of Article 2 and are of a nature to give rise to an obligation to give assistance on the part of the other High Contracting Parties. The Council may, if necessary, suggest changes in the texts of agreements submitted to it.

When recognised, the agreements shall be registered in conformity with Article 18 of the Covenant. They shall be regarded as complementary to the present Treaty, and shall in no way limit the general obligations of the High Contracting Parties nor the sanctions contemplated against the aggressor State under the terms of this Treaty.

They will be open to any other High Contracting Party with the consent of the signatory States.

ARTICLE 8.

The States parties to complementary agreements may undertake in any such agreements to put into immediate execution, in the cases of aggression contemplated in them, the plan of assistance agreed upon. In this case they shall inform the Council of the League of Nations, without delay, concerning the measures which they have taken to ensure the execution of such agreements.

Subject to the terms of the previous paragraph, the provisions of Articles 4 and 5 above shall also come into force both in the cases contemplated in the complementary agreements and in such other cases as are provided for in Article 2 but are not covered by the agreements.

ARTICLE 9.

IV. Demilitarised zones.

In order to facilitate the application of the present Treaty, any High Contracting Party may negotiate, through the agency of the Council, with one or more neighbouring countries for the establishment of demilitarised zones.

The Council, with the co-operation of the representatives of the parties interested, acting as Members within the terms of Article 4 of the Covenant, shall previously ensure that the establishment of the demilitarised zone asked for does not call for unilateral sacrifices from the military point of view on the part of the High Contracting Parties interested.

ARTICLE 10.

The High Contracting Parties agree that the whole cost of any military, naval or air operations which are undertaken under the terms of the present Treaty and of the supplementary partial agreements, including the reparation of all material damage caused by operations of war, shall be borne by the aggressor State up to the extreme limits of its financial capacity.

The amount payable under this article by the aggressor shall, to such an extent as may be determined by the Council of the League, be a first charge on the whole of the assets and revenues of the State. Any repayment by that State in respect of the principal money and interest of any loan, internal of external, issued by it directly or indirectly during the war shall be suspended until the amount due for cost and reparations is discharged in full.

V. Cost of intervention.

ARTICLE 11.

The High Contracting Parties, in view of the security furnished them by this Treaty and the limitations to which they have consented in other international treaties, undertake to inform the Council of the League of the reduction or limitation of armaments which they consider proportionate to the security furnished by the general Treaty or by the defensive agreements complementary to the general Treaty.

The High Contracting Parties undertake to co-operate in the preparation of any general plan of reduction of armaments which the Council of the League of Nations, taking into account the information provided by the High Contracting Parties, may propose under the terms of Article 8 of the Covenant.

This plan should be submitted for consideration and approved by the Governments, and, when approved by them, will be the basis of the reduction contemplated in Article 2 of this Treaty.

The High Contracting Parties undertake to carry out this reduction within a period of two years from the date of the adoption of this plan.

The High Contracting Parties undertake, in accordance with the provisions of Article 8, paragraph 4, of the Covenant, to make no further increase in their armaments, when thus reduced, without the consent of the Council.

VI. Disarmament.

ARTICLE 12.

The High Contracting Parties undertake to furnish to the military or other delegates of the League such information with regard to their armaments as the Council may request.

ARTICLE 13.

The High Contracting Parties agree that the armaments determined for each of them, in accordance with the present Treaty, shall be subject to revision every five years, beginning from the date of the entry into force of this Treaty.

ARTICLE 14.

Nothing in the present Treaty shall affect the rights and obligations resulting from the provisions of the Covenant of the League of Nations or of the Treaties of Peace signed in 1919 and 1920 at Versailles, Neuilly, St. Germain and Trianon, or from the provisions of treaties or agreements registered with the League of Nations and published by it at the date of the first coming into force of the present Treaty as regards the signatory or beneficiary Powers of the said Treaties or agreements.

VII. Protocol. Maintenance of existing treaties.

ARTICLE 15.

The High Contracting Parties recognise from to-day as *ipso facto* obligatory, the jurisdiction of the Permanent Court of International Justice with regard to the interpretation of the present Treaty.

Compulsory jurisdiction of the Court.

ARTICLE 16.

The present Treaty shall remain open for the signature of all States Members of the League of Nations or mentioned in the Annex to the Covenant.

States not Members shall be entitled to adhere with the consent of two-thirds of the High Contracting Parties with regard to whom the Treaty has come into force.

Signature.

ARTICLE 17.

Partial adhesion. Any State may, with the consent of the Council of the League, notify its conditional or partial adherence to the provisions of this Treaty, provided always that such State has reduced or is prepared to reduce its armaments in conformity with the provisions of this Treaty.

ARTICLE 18 [1].

Ratification. [The present Treaty shall be ratified and the instruments of ratification shall be deposited as soon as possible at the Secretariat of the League of Nations.

It shall come into force:

In Europe when it shall have been ratified by five States, of which three shall be permanently represented on the Council ;

In Asia when it shall have been ratified by two States, one of which shall be permanently represented on the Council;

In North America when ratified by the United States of America;

In Central America and the West Indies when ratified by one State in the West Indies and two in Central America;

In South America when ratified by four States;

In Africa and Oceania when ratified by two States.

With regard to the High Contracting Parties which may subsequently ratify the Treaty, it will come into force at the date of the deposit of the instrument.

The Secretariat will immediately communicate a certified copy of the instruments of ratification received to all the signatory Powers.

It remains understood that the rights stipulated under Articles 2, 3, 5, 6 and 8 of this Treaty will not come into force for each High Contracting Party until the Council has certified that the said High Contracting Party has reduced its armaments in conformity with the present Treaty or has adopted the necessary measures to ensure the execution of this reduction, within two years of the acceptance by the said High Contracting Party of the plan of reduction or limitation of armaments.]

ARTICLE 19 [1].

Denunciation. [The present Treaty shall remain in force for a period of fifteen years from the date of its first entry into force.

After this period, it will be prolonged automatically for the States which have not denounced it.

If, however, one of the States referred to in Article 18 denounces the present Treaty, the Treaty shall cease to exist as from the date on which this denunciation takes effect.

This denunciation shall be made to the Secretariat of the League of Nations, which shall, without delay, notify all the Powers bound by the present Treaty.

The denunciation shall take effect twelve months after the date on which notification has been communicated to the Secretariat of the League of Nations.

When the period of fifteen years referred to in the first paragraph of the present Article has elapsed, or when one of the denunciations made in the conditions determined above takes place, if operations undertaken in application of Article 5 of the present Treaty are in progress, the Treaty shall remain in force until peace has been completely re-established.]

---

[1] See page 206 §d.

ANNEX 4.

————

COMMENTARY ON THE DEFINITION OF A CASE OF AGGRESSION.

Drawn up by a Special Committee of the Temporary Mixed Commission[1].

1. It would be theoretically desirable to set down in writing, if it could be done, an exact definition of what constitutes an act of aggression. If such a definition could be drawn up, it would then merely remain for the Council to decide in each given case whether an act of aggression within the meaning of this definition had been committed.

It appears, however, to be exceedingly difficult to draw up any such definition. In the words of the Permanent Advisory Commission, "under the conditions of modern warfare, it would seem impossible to decide even in theory what constitutes an act of aggression".

2. Hitherto, according to the opinion expressed by certain members of the Permanent Advisory Commission, in the report drawn up by that Commission, "aggression could be defined as mobilisation or the violation of a frontier. This double test has lost its value".

It is further stated that:

"Mobilisation, which consisted, until quite recently, of a few comparatively simple operations (calling up of reserves, purchases or requisitions and establishment of war industries, after the calling-up of the men), has become infinitely more complicated and more difficult both to discover at its origin and to follow in its development. In future, mobilisation will apply not merely to the army but *to the whole country before the outbreak of hostilities* (collection of stocks of raw materials and munitions of war, industrial mobilisation, establishment or increased output of industries). All these measures, which give evidence of an *intention* to go to war, may lead to discussions and to conflicting interpretations, thus securing *decisive* advantages to the aggressor unless action be taken."

3. Similarly, in the view of the Permanent Advisory Commission, the test of the violation of a frontier has also lost its value.

The report states:

"The violation of a frontier by 'armed forces' will not necessarily be, in future such an obvious act of violence as it has hitherto been... The passage of the frontier by the troops of another country does not always mean that the latter country is the aggressor. Particularly in the case of small States, the object of such action may be to establish an initial position which shall be as advantageous as possible for the defending country, and to do so before the adversary has had time to mass his superior forces. A military offensive of as rapid a character as possible may therefore be a means, and perhaps the only means, whereby the weaker party can defend itself against the stronger. It is also conceivable that a small nation might be compelled to make use of its air forces in order to forestall the superior forces of the enemy and take what advantage was possible from such action.

"Finally, the hostilities between two naval Powers generally begin on sea by the capture of merchant vessels or other acts of violence — very possibly on the high seas outside territorial waters. The same applies to air operations which may take place without any violation of the air frontiers of States."

Nevertheless it is still conceivable that in many cases the invasion of a territory constitutes an act of aggression and, in any case, it is important to determine which State had violated the frontier.

If the troops of one Power invade the territory of another, this fact in itself constitutes a presumption that the first Power has committed a wrongful act of aggression.

But, apart from the considerations already given, this is not entirely conclusive. When armies have been practically in contact on the frontier which divides their respective countries, it may be exceedingly difficult to obtain conclusive evidence as to which of them first crossed the frontier; and, once the frontier is crossed and hostilities have begun, it may not be possible to know from the geographical position of the troops alone which State was guilty.

4. In order to avoid such a case arising, the Council might desire, in certain cases where such a course could be followed without disadvantage to either party, either before hostilities began or even after they had begun, to invite both parties to withdraw their troops a certain

————

[1] This Committee was composed as follows:
Lord Robert Cecil (Chairman), Count Bonin-Longare, M. Janssen, M. Jouhaux, Rear-Admiral Kiyokawa, Colonel Lohner, Admiral Marquis de Magaz, General de Marinis Stendardo di Ricigliano, Lieut.-Colonel Réquin, Rear-Admiral Segrave.

distance behind a given line. It might be that such a request could be made by the Council with the intimation that, if either party refused to accede to it, such refusal would be considered as an element in deciding which was the aggressor[1].

5. There may, of course, be other cases in which some action of one of the parties will simplify the matter by proving it clearly to be the aggressor. If, for example, one Power carried out a large-scale attack upon the territory of the other, that would be conclusive. Similarly, a surprise attack by poison gas, executed from the air on the territory of the other party, would be decisive evidence.

6. It may, however, be accepted that no satisfactory definition of what constitutes an act of aggression could be drawn up. But even supposing that such a definition were possible, there would still be difficulty in determining when an act of aggression within the meaning of this definition has actually taken place. In the view of the Permanent Advisory Commission, the signs of an intention of aggression would appear in the following order:

(1) Organisation on paper of industrial mobilisation.
(2) Actual organisation of industrial mobilisation.
(3) Collection of stocks of raw materials.
(4) Setting on foot of war industries.
(5) Preparation for military mobilisation.
(6) Actual military mobilisation.
(7) Hostilities.

Numbers (1) and (5) (and to some extent Number (2)), which are in all cases difficult to recognise, may, in those countries which are not subject under the Peace Treaties to any obligation to disarm, represent precaution which every Government is entitled to take.

Number (3) may be justified by economic reasons, such as profiting by advantageous markets or collecting stocks in order to guard against the possible closing of certain channels of supply owing to strikes, etc.

Number (4) (Setting on foot of war industries) is the first which may be definitely taken as showing an intention to commit aggression: it will, however, be easy to conceal this measure for a long period in countries which are under no military supervision.

When Numbers (6) and (7) are known to have taken place, it is too late.

In the absence of any indisputable test, Governments can only judge by an *impression* based upon the most various factors, such as:

The political attitude of the possible aggressor:
His propaganda;
The attitude of his press and population;
His policy on the international market, etc.

7. One of the conclusions which follows from the above contentions set forth in the report of the Permanent Advisory Commission is that, quite apart from the material sides of the aggressive intention, the real act of aggression may lie not so much in orders given to its troops by one of the parties as in the attitude which it adopts in the negotiations concerning the subjects of dispute. Indeed, it might be that the real aggression lies in the political policy pursued by one of the parties towards the other. For this reason it might perhaps appear to the Council that the most appropriate measure that could be taken would be to invite the two parties either to abstain from hostilities or to cease the hostilities they have begun, and to submit their whole dispute to the recommendation of the Council or the decision of the Permanent Court of International Justice, and to undertake to accept and execute whatever recommendation or decision either of these bodies might give. Such an invitation might again be accompanied by an intimation that the party which refused would be considered to be the aggressor.

8. It is clear, therefore, that no simple definition of aggression can be drawn up, and that no simple test of when an act of aggression has actually taken place can be devised. It is therefore clearly necessary to leave the Council complete discretion in the matter, merely indicating that the various factors mentioned above may provide the elements of a just decision.

---

[1] Count Bonin-Longare and General de Marinis state that they would prefer that this article should be suppressed.

M. Jouhaux prefers the original text, which runs as follows: " In order to avoid such a case arising, it might well be that the Council of the League might desire, either before hostilities began or even after they had begun, to invite both parties to withdraw their troops to a certain distance behind a given line. It might be that such a request could be made by the Council with the intimation that whichever party refused to accede to it would be considered the aggressor".

These factors may be summarised as follows:

(a) Actual industrial and economic mobilisation carried out by a State either in its own territory or by persons or societies on foreign territory.

(b) Secret military mobilisation by the formation and employment of irregular troops or by a declaration of a state of danger of war which would serve as a pretext for commencing hostilities.

(c) Air, chemical or naval attack carried out by one party against another.

(d) The presence of the armed forces of one party in the territory of another.

(e) Refusal of either of the parties to withdraw their armed forces behind a line or lines indicated by the Council [1].

(f) A definitely aggressive policy by one of the parties towards the other, and the consequent refusal of that party to submit the subject in dispute to the recommendation of the Council or to the decision of the Permanent Court of International Justice and to accept the recommendation or decision when given.

9. In conclusion, it may be pointed out that in the case of a surprise attack it would be relatively easy to decide on the aggressor, but that in the general case, where aggression is preceded by a period of political tension and general mobilisation, the determination of the aggressor and the moment at which aggression occurred would prove very difficult.

But it must be remembered that in such a case the Council, under the provisions of the Covenant, will have been engaged in efforts to avoid war and may therefore probably be in a position to form an opinion as to which of the parties is really actuated by aggressive intentions.

Annex 3.

———

TREATY OF MUTUAL ASSISTANCE

REPLIES FROM GOVERNMENTS

———

Contents

TREATY OF MUTUAL ASSISTANCE

ACTION TAKEN BY THE COUNCIL AND THE COMMISSIONS
OF THE LEAGUE ON THE RESOLUTIONS ADOPTED BY THE ASSEMBLY
AT ITS FOURTH SESSION

Resolution I. — Draft Treaty of Mutual Assistance.

"The Assembly:

"Having taken cognisance of the Draft Treaty of Mutual Assistance Drawn up by the Temporary Mixed Commission and amended by the Third Committee as a result of an exchange of views between its members, some of whom spoke in their personal capacity;

"Considering that this discussion has revealed some divergences of view and, further, that a large number of Governments have not yet expressed their opinions on Resolution XIV of the third Assembly:

"Decides to request the Council to submit the Draft Treaty of Mutual Assistance to the Governments for their consideration, asking them to communicate their views in regard to the aforesaid draft Treaty."

In conformity with this resolution, the Council, in September 1923, decided to empower the Secretary-General to circulate to all the Governments of Members of the League the report of the Third Committee of the Assembly on the Draft Treaty of Mutual Assistance, together with the report of the Temporary Mixed Commission to the Assembly on the same subject, and the Minutes of the Third Committee.

In accordance with the decision of the Assembly, the letter from the Secretary-General drew the attention of the Governments of the Members of the League to the fact that, in order that the work of co-ordinating the opinions of the Governments with regard to the Draft Treaty might be taken in hand in sufficient time for the consideration of the next Assembly, it would be of the greatest utility that these opinions should reach the Secretariat of the League as early as possible in the year. The Council, in December, decided to extend this communication to States non-Members of the League, and a letter to that effect was sent by the Secretary-General on January 9th, 1924.

During its March session, the Council noted that only three Governments had by then replied to the first letter of the Secretary-General, dated October 25th, 1923. It adopted the following resolution:

"The Council:

"In view of Resolution I of the Assembly, in accordance with which the Draft Treaty of Mutual Assistance was submitted to the Governments for their consideration, with the request that they should communicate their views in regard to the said draft;

"Considering that it is important that the next Assembly should be in a position to examine the draft again in the light of the views of the Governments:

"Instructs its President to approach all States Members of the League of Nations which have not yet communicated their views on this subject, requesting them to be good enough to do so, in order that their views on the Treaty of Mutual Assistance may reach the Secretariat in time to be submitted to the next Assembly."

All the replies so far received by the Secretariat are included in the present document.

REPLY FROM THE FINNISH GOVERNMENT.

[*Translation.*]   January 18th, 1924

The Finnish Government considers that it is one of the primary duties of the League of Nations to secure the definite establishment and effective application of the guarantee provided for in Article 10 of the Covenant, and to develop the principles laid down therein. The Finnish Government, therefore, wishes to express its appreciation of the efforts made to create a system of mutual guarantee on the lines laid down in Resolution XIV of the third Assembly, and especially of the endeavour, first, to place on a solid and practical basis the logical relation which ought to exist between the right to security and the duty of reducing or limiting armaments — a relation the establishment of which is undoubtedly required by the spirit of the Covenant — and, secondly, to enlarge the community of nations for the purpose of the application — in the interests of the world's peace — of Articles 8, 10 and 16 of the Covenant. If, notwithstanding, my Government ventures to submit certain remarks on the scheme of mutual assistance drawn up by the Third Committee of the fourth Assembly, it is due to the fact that the problem is of wide general interest, and that its discussion from every point of view is indispensable.

I. — In accordance with the principle laid down in Article 14 of the draft, and with the definition of the aims of the Treaty given in the preamble, the Finnish Government considers that the Treaty of Mutual Assistance should be directed, above all, to the progressive consolidation of the League of Nations.

The draft Treaty of Assistance establishes the principle that a State which is not a Member of the League of Nations may participate in the organisation of mutual assistance. The Powers signatory to the Treaty of Assistance, which seeks to facilitate and direct the application of the two fundamental principles contained in Articles 10 and 16 of the Covenant, would therefore include States outside the League of Nations and not bound by the League's judicial system. Difficult as it may be to incorporate a Power which remains outside the League of Nations in an organisation depending for its motive power on the Council of the League, the Finnish Government cannot but express its satisfaction at the enlargement, whether immediate or not, of the League's sphere of action.

A serious difficulty results from another unavoidable anomaly in the system provided for in the draft Treaty, *i.e.*, the fact that a Member of the League of Nations might not be a party to the Treaty of Assistance. As the compulsory character of the Covenant and of the obligations based upon it will not and cannot suffer any limitation in consequence of the new Treaty, it will be necessary to fix a definite line of demarcation between the obligations resulting from the Covenant and those based upon the Treaty of Assistance. This appears essential, in view of the fact that States Members of the Council may have to deal with matters concerning the application of the Treaty of Assistance without themselves being parties to the Treaty, and, further, that the Council may have the same dispute submitted to it in its two distinct capacities; in the absence of unanimity, it could take no action as the organ of the organisation of assistance, but it could perhaps, composed in a slightly different manner, take action as an organ acting in virtue of the Covenant. It should be emphasised that the application of Articles 10 and 16 of the Covenant ought, in all fairness, to affect in equal measure all the Members of the League. In the opinion of the Finnish Government, only vital political and practical considerations could justify an arrangement whereby Members of the League of Nations would remain outside the new organisation of assistance.

Anxious to assist the common cause by exploring every avenue which may lead to the general acceptance of the Treaty, the Finnish Government feels bound to observe that, in view of the provisions of paragraph 4, Article 16 of the Covenant, the relation between the right to security and the duty of reducing or limiting armaments could, in its opinion, be established in another form than that adopted in the draft Treaty.

II. — The Government is fully aware of the difficulties raised by the requirement that all decisions of the Council should be unanimous — a principle which can only be justified on the ground that it is an unavoidable consequence of the virtual identity of the Council sitting as an executive organ of the League of Nations and, as such, ruled by this principle, with the Council acting as the motive power of the organisation of assistance. As long as the principle of unanimity remains a fundamental rule of the Covenant, it seems difficult to propose the acceptance of a contrary principle for the Treaty of Assistance. Nevertheless, the Finnish Government feels justified in suggesting two necessary modifications on this point:

(1) The declaration provided for in Article 4, paragraph 1, for the purpose of deciding which States are the objects of aggression, is only a statement of fact. On purely logical grounds it would, therefore, seem natural that such a declaration should be made by a majority vote. Even if a decision as to the measures to be taken requires unanimity, the Council could hardly declare itself incompetent to settle this question of fact; the consequences of applying the unanimity rule to this case might be equivalent to a denial of justice.

(2) Could not this hard-and-fast rule be modified, as regards the measures provided for in Article 5, by applying the principle established in the Convention on the neutralisation of the Aaland Islands, to the effect that, if unanimity cannot be obtained, each of the High

Contracting Parties will be authorised to take the measures which the Council may recommend by a two-thirds majority ? The Finnish Government ventures to recommend that, with a view to rendering easier the working of the Treaty, an application of this principle should be considered.

Mention should also be made of the grave drawback resulting from the connection between the general guarantee and the complementary agreements provided for in Article 6, tautologically defined in Article 7 as agreements "complementary to the present Treaty". It is clear from the provisions of the Treaty that a State which is party to a complementary agreement may refuse to carry out the obligation incumbent on it in virtue of this agreement as long as the Council has not succeeded in obtaining the unanimity required to decide, first, that there is a threat of aggression; secondly, which is the aggressor; and lastly, what measures should be taken in virtue of Article 5.

III. — Article 3 lays down with justice that any State "party or not to the present Treaty" and therefore conceivably not a Member of the League of Nations, may be denounced on account of its aggressive policy or hostile intentions. If there is reasonable ground for thinking that a menace of aggression has arisen, the Council may take, among other measures, those indicated in sub-paragraphs (a),(b), (c), (d) and (e) of the second paragraph of Article 5. The application of these measures necessarily presupposes a decision as to which Power is threatening aggression (or which is the presumed aggressor), and which is the victim of the aggression. The Council may therefore be called upon to deal with a question concerning a State which is not a Member of the League of Nations. The Finnish Government views this contingency with satisfaction, especially because this point of view entirely corresponds with the opinion it maintained before the Permanent Court of International Justice and the Assembly and Council of the League of Nations.

Article 3, paragraph 1, lays down that any State, party or not to the Treaty, may be denounced on account of its aggressive policy. But, in paragraph 3, the only States considered as liable to denunciation are the High Contracting Parties; it is these States which must be invited to send representatives to the Council. Why is the invitation of a State which, though not party to the Treaty of Assistance, may be denounced by a Contracting Party not expressly authorised on the analogy of Article 17 of the Covenant ? The draft requires to be completed on this point.

For the same reasons, Article 4, paragraph 3, should be modified in order to make it quite clear that it is not with the High Contracting Parties *alone*, when engaged in hostilities, that the assistance organisation is concerned, and consequently that the measures laid down in the second paragraph of Article 5 may be applied in respect of a State which is not party to the Treaty, both in the circumstances indicated in Article 4 and in those described in Article 3.

IV. — The draft Treaty is also insufficiently clear owing to the fact that it does not indicate how the Council is to accomplish the important duties imposed upon it by Article 5 of the Treaty. How will it employ the forces which each State furnishing assistance will have to place at its disposal ? How will it prepare a plan for co-operation when it has no permanent military organisation ready for action at the required moment ? Does Article 5 take for granted that an organisation of this kind would be established in advance? The silence of the draft Treaty on this point is the more incomprehensible as Resolution XIV assumes that an organisation of this kind will be created. This resolution says: "The Council of the League ...... should further formulate and submit to the Governments for their consideration and sovereign decision the plan of the machinery, both political and military, necessary to bring them (*i.e.*, the systems of achieving a general reduction of armaments) clearly into effect." In these circumstances, it might be expected that the draft Treaty would expressly stipulate that such machinery should be set up.

It is equally necessary, in the opinion of the Finnish Government, that the plans for financial co-operation provided for in sub-paragraph (e) of the second paragraph of Article 5 should be prepared in advance, in order to allow States victims of an aggression, the resources of which are insufficient for their national defence, to obtain the contemplated assistance at the outset of hostilities.

V. — According to Article 17, any State may notify its conditional or partial adherence to the proposed Treaty. It goes without saying that a State will not by such conditions or reservations be able to evade its obligations under the Covenant. Hence, the nature and extent of these conditions should be clearly defined, and also — what is even more important — the rights which may be claimed by these States, the position of which should be determined on a basis of perfect reciprocity.

The somewhat vague terms of Article 17 lend themselves to the interpretation that a State could adhere to the Treaty of Assistance even with the reservation that it should not be required to take any part in carrying out the economic measures provided for in the Treaty. But such a reservation would be quite inadmissible, as it is in contradiction with the fundamental rules of the Covenant. If conditional or partial adherence were to be equivalent to an attempt to evade certain obligations imposed by the Covenant, the Finnish Government would regard it as a "shirking of responsibilities" entirely contradictory to the principles of solidarity and co-operation laid down in the Covenant.

The article in question should also be considered from another point of view. Resolution XV of the third Assembly lays down the principle that certain countries which are in a special geographical position may conclude regional agreements of such a character as to make it possible to take measures for the reduction of armaments even exceeding those decided upon in respect of general reduction. Further, the Assembly recognised that special measures would have to be taken for the defence of countries which, for historical, geographical or other reasons, were in special danger of attack. But it is clear that the Council's task will be made even more difficult if, on account of the accentuated reduction of armaments in neighbouring countries, it is obliged to look to more distant countries for the special guarantees indicated above. The Finnish

Government therefore considers that the provisions of Article 17 should be modified so as to render partial or conditional adherence to the Treaty impossible in cases when the States in question intend to conclude regional agreements for the purpose of reducing their armaments to a greater extent than is provided for in the general scheme.

VI. — The procedure regarding the preparation of the general plan for the reduction of armaments as laid down in Article 11 of the Treaty seems destined in practice to give rise to serious difficulties. The first paragraph of this article obliges the High Contracting Parties to inform the Council of the reduction or limitation of armaments which they consider proportionate to the security furnished by the general Treaty or by the complementary defensive agreements, in order to enable the Council to prepare a general plan for the reduction of armaments on the basis of this information. But at the moment when the High Contracting Parties have to fulfil this obligation, they will probably not be possessed of any exact information in regard to the actual assistance on which they can count, in the event of danger, by virtue of the decisions taken by the Council under the terms of Article 5. There is reason to fear, therefore, that they will be unable to take such assistance into account when supplying information to the Council of the League, and that they will be unable to furnish the latter with a sound basis for its calculations or to fulfil the obligation expressly imposed by the first paragraph of Article 11 of the Treaty and accepted by them.

VII. — While it will be difficult to bring the Treaty of Assistance into effect, it will be easy to denounce it. The terms of Article 19 do not make it clear that the Treaty cannot be denounced in the course of the first fifteen years. If it can be denounced during the first period of fifteen years, and especially if denunciation on the part of a permanent Member of the Council, i.e., of a Great Power, is sufficient not only to break up the contractual community formed by the States situated in the same continent, but to invalidate the whole Treaty, it must be admitted that the security furnished by the Treaty will be very slender.

VIII. — In comparison with the foregoing considerations, the note of the Committee of Jurists with regard to the term "aggressive war" is only of secondary importance; this term, although not strictly in accordance with the Covenant, is preferable to the amendments proposed by the Committee. The Committee also states that the Covenant "authorises, by implication, war in the case of States which comply with a unanimous recommendation by the Council and, in general, in the case of all parties to a dispute in which the Council fails to reach a unanimous recommendation." It should, however, be pointed out that whether a war is legitimate and whether it is in conformity with the Covenant are matters which do not depend solely on the formal and incidental question as to whether the Council has come to a unanimous decision or not, but rather on the actual facts of the case in point. For instance, a war may be contrary to Article 10 of the Covenant without being unanimously disapproved of by the Council. When the Committee describes as an international crime a war which violates the provisions of the Covenant. this is tautology as far as the Members of the League are concerned, while the States non-Members of the League would probably not recognise an act forbidden by the Covenant as an international crime unless it appeared as such in the light of the general principles of international law.

IX. — In the opinion of the Finnish Government, it would be preferable to make the co-operation of the Council in the conclusion of agreements concerning demilitarised zones optional and not obligatory as proposed in Article 9. But such agreements should, for the same reasons as in the case of the agreements referred to in Article 6, be regarded as complementary to the Treaty, and as such be subject to examination by the Council and to registration in conformity with Article 18 of the Covenant.

X. — Article 3 only deals with cases in which the State which fears the aggressive policy or preparations of another State appeals to the Council. But under Article 11 of the Covenant, any war or threat of war, whether immediately affecting any of the Members of the League or not, involves the immediate summoning of the Council and justifies any Member of the League in requesting the Council to meet.

Again, Article 15 (paragraphs 9 and 10) of the Covenant lays down that a question with which the Council has already dealt, in virtue of these provisions, may be laid before the Assembly. According to the Treaty of Assistance, the Assembly would play no part in the disputes with which the Treaty deals. It goes without saying, however, that the Treaty of Assistance does not take precedence over the Covenant, and that the option of laying a question before the Assembly still exists if the question at issue also calls for investigation under the terms of the Covenant. In consequence, this option should be expressly specified in the Treaty.

In its keen desire to further the efforts of the League of Nations in favour of an effective reduction of armaments based upon increased national security, the Finnish Government has considered it necessary to formulate certain objections to which the draft Treaty submitted to it gives rise. It expresses the sincere hope that the organs of the League of Nations will be able to solve satisfactorily this fundamental problem and to carry out successfully this task of completing the League's organisation and of safeguarding the interests of peace throughout the world.

(Signed) WENNOLA.

REPLY FROM THE ESTHONIAN GOVERNMENT.

[*Translation.*]   January 22nd, 1924.

In reply to your Note C.L.105, dated October 25th, 1923, concerning the draft Treaty of Mutual Assistance, I have the honour, on behalf of the Government of the Esthonian Republic, to inform you as follows.

The Esthonian Government has watched with interest and keen sympathy the work in which the League of Nations has been engaged for over a year in order to find a practical scheme which will enable the different Governments to reduce their armaments. The Esthonian Government congratulates the League of Nations on the first important fruits of this work — the draft Treaty of Mutual Assistance adopted by the fourth Assembly — and expresses its lively satisfaction at the attainment of so notable a result.

The Esthonian Government recognises the exceptional competence of the Temporary Mixed Commission and of the Third Committee of the Assembly, and is well aware that these Committees have spared no efforts to ensure that this scheme, while remaining true to the high general ideals upon which it is based, should at the same time be realisable in practice in the existing situation of world politics; the Esthonian Government does not, therefore, deem it necessary to offer any detailed comments on the draft adopted by the fourth Assembly, although it has given the proposals its most careful consideration. Its object, in the present communication, is rather to declare that it approves of the draft Treaty and is prepared to adhere to it, whenever it shall have been given its final form.

The Esthonian Government would, however, have preferred that the first article of the Treaty should have retained the concise and exact form in which it was originally drafted. Similarly, it believes that the Treaty would prove more effective if all the Contracting States undertook the same obligations and received in return the same guarantees; and, finally, it considers that a simple general Treaty would have been preferable to a Treaty supplemented by special agreements. However, it is well aware that concessions had to be made on these points in order that the draft should prove acceptable to as many States as possible, and also because these concessions rendered its pratical application easier.

In regard to Article 18 of the draft, the Government of the Republic desires, in particular, to state that it approves the conditions for the coming into force of the Treaty in Europe as laid down in that article — which requires ratification by five States, three of which must be States permanently represented on the Council. It is, however, essential, in the view of the Esthonian Government, that the expiration of the Treaty should be made subject to the same conditions: in other words, that the Treaty must not cease to be in force in Europe until, out of the five ratifying States, less than three of the States which are permanent Members of the Council continue to be parties to the Treaty.

Finally, Esthonia, as a State which has accepted the optional clause for the compulsory jurisdiction of the Permanent Court of International Justice, and which is vitally interested in the complete elimination of war as an expedient for the settlement of international disputes, expresses its confident hope that the League of Nations will succeed, in a not distant future, in making the Treaty of Mutual Assistance an accomplished fact, and that the largest possible number of States will adhere to it.

(Signed) F. AKEL,
Minister.

REPLY FROM THE BELGIAN GOVERNMENT.

[*Translation.*]   February 8th, 1924.

I have the honour to communicate to you the views of the Belgian Government on the draft Treaty of Mutual Assistance, prepared by the Temporary Mixed Commission and amended by the Third Committee of the Assembly, which you were good enough to forward to me with your letter dated October 25th last.

The draft is based on two leading principles, to which the Government has already signified its assent, namely, the necessity of making the disarmament of each State proportionate to the guarantees of security furnished to it, and the combination of partial defensive agreements with the Treaty of General Guarantee.

The Belgian Government readily gives its adherence to the general lines of the draft, but it feels bound to submit the following observations, which have been suggested to it by a detailed examination of the articles.

The draft Treaty is closely connected with the Covenant of the League of Nations, of which it forms, to a certain extent, a supplement. Consequently, the existence, in the draft Treaty and the Covenant, of two different terminologies in regard to the definition of the kind of war which the Contracting Parties undertake not to wage against each other presents serious practical disadvantages which have been pointed out in the Note from the Committee of Jurists appointed to consider the text of the draft Treaty.

The Government therefore adopts the view of this Committee and proposes to draft Articles 1 and 2 as follows, specifying in article 2 the articles of the Covenant to which it refers:

Article 1. "The High Contracting Parties solemnly declare that a war waged in violation of the provisions of the Covenant is an international crime and severally undertake that no one of them will be guilty of this crime.

Article 2. "The High Contracting Parties jointly and severally undertake to furnish assistance, in accordance with the provisions of the present Treaty, to any of their number which, after having reduced its armaments in conformity with the provisions of the present Treaty, is the object of a war prohibited by the Covenant of the League of Nations either on account of its origin (Article 10 of the Covenant) or of its aims (Articles 12–15 of the Covenant)."

The textual amendments to these two articles do not in any way impair the value of the draft Treaty from the point of view of the military guarantees which it will add to the Covenant. The amendments do not affect the main advantage which the draft has to offer, namely, that the Contracting Parties substitute for limited engagements to furnish military assistance on certain occasions (Articles 10 to 15 of the Covenant) engagements which are both more precise and more extensive.

Article 5 of the draft lays down that in the cases referred to in Article 2 of the Treaty the High Contracting Parties shall furnish one another mutually with assistance in the form determined by the Council of the League of Nations, which has the right to "require", if necessary, the High Contracting Parties to furnish military assistance to one of their number.

Article 9 provides for the establishment of demilitarised zones. It would be desirable to define what is meant by this term, in order that the Council of the League of Nations may be enabled to take steps to establish zones of this kind.

Article 10 places upon the aggressor State the cost of the operations and of the damage caused, up to the extreme limits of its financial capacity.

Provision should be made for the case in which this financial capacity may prove inadequate. It might be stipulated that, in the event of the total or partial insolvency of the aggressor State, the cost of that part of the damage for which no reparation has been made would be borne by the High Contracting Parties in the proportion fixed by the Council of the League of Nations, which could take into account for this purpose the amount of their respective contributions to the expenses of the League of Nations.

Under the terms of *Article 11*, it will not be possible to alter the plan for the reduction of armaments, when once approved by the various Governments, until a period of five years has elapsed. But the situation might be considerably changed if a new State were admitted or if a State were excluded, and certain countries might thereby lose part of the security upon which they had relied.

Should such a situation arise, it should be laid down that the reduction of armaments by the signatory States might be modified accordingly, after the Council has considered the request put forward by the countries concerned or by any one of their number.

In *Article 12* no method of investigation is laid down to determine whether each State has actually reduced its armaments in accordance with the Treaty, or, on the other hand, whether it is still in a position to furnish the forces which are required of it.

Anxiety to avoid infringing State sovereignty was apparently the consideration which militated against the introduction of supervision of this kind. In order to provide a safeguard on this point, a system of supervision might be instituted, acceptable to the parties concerned, which could be carried out on identical lines in every country by a Commission composed of representatives of all the Powers signatory to the Treaty.

Article 12 of the draft Treaty contains no mention of sanctions. This omission might be repaired by stipulating that a refusal to communicate the necessary information could be pleaded by one of the High Contracting Parties as *prima-facie* evidence that the armaments of the High Contracting Party which fails to supply the information exceed the limits allowed it under the present Treaty. In such a case, Article 3 of the Treaty might be applied.

The Belgian Government is in favour of the following text proposed by the Committee of Jurists for Article 14:

Article 14. "Nothing in the present Treaty shall affect the rights and obligations resulting from the provisions of the Covenant of the League of Nations or of the Treaties of Peace signed in 1919 and 1922 at Versailles, Neuilly, St. Germain and Trianon and in 1923 at Lausanne, or from the provisions of treaties or agreements registered with the League of Nations at the date of the conclusion of the present Treaty."

The Belgian Government considers that more complete guarantees should be required in the event of the adherence to the Treaty of States non-Members of the League of Nations, as provided in the second paragraph of Article 16.

It proposes that such adherences should be subject to the consent of two-thirds of the High Contracting Parties in respect of which the Treaty has come into force, and subject also to the unanimous consent of those of the High Contracting Parties which are permanently represented on the Council of the League of Nations and in respect of which the Treaty has come into force.

Article 17 would gain in precision if it were drafted as follows:

"Any State may, with the consent of the Council of the League of Nations and subject to the provisions of the second paragraph of Article 16, notify its conditional or partial adherence to the provisions of this Treaty, provided always that such State has reduced or is prepared to reduce its armaments in conformity with the provisions of this Treaty."

Article 18 of the draft does not appear sufficiently explicit. It refers to the date at which the Treaty of Guarantee will enter into force in respect of the various countries. The following wording is proposed:

"The present Treaty shall be ratified and the instruments of ratification shall be deposited as soon as possible at the Secretariat of the League of Nations. It shall come into force:

"In Europe when it shall have been ratified by *five European States*, of which three shall be permanently represented on the Council of the League of Nations;

"In Asia when it shall have been ratified by *two Asiatic States*, one of which shall be permanently represented on the Council of the League of Nations;

"In North America when it shall have been ratified by the United States of America;

"In Central America and the West Indies when it shall have been ratified by two States in Central America and one of the West Indies;

"In Africa and Oceania when ratified by *two States in those continents*."

The rest of the article would remain as in Article 18 of the draft Treaty.

As a matter of less moment I may add that, although the Government gives its general approval to the commentary on the definition of a case of aggression prepared by the special committee of the Temporary Mixed Commission, it must nevertheless make the following reservations:

Paragraph 6 includes, among the signs of an intention of aggression, the organisation on paper of industrial mobilisation. It would, however, appear hardly possible to prohibit a country from examining the theoretical question of industrial mobilisation and still less possible to consider such an investigation as an act of aggression.

Moreover, according to Paragraph 8 (*e*), the refusal of either of the parties to withdraw its armed forces behind a line or lines indicated by the Council may also be considered as an act of aggression.

The Government's view is that when military operations have once been begun they cannot be subjected to any restrictions of this kind. If imposed upon countries with territory of small depth, such as Belgium, the withdrawal of the troops might have serious consequences which would menace the strategical position of the army.

(Signed) JASPAR.

REPLY FROM THE UNION OF SOCIALIST SOVIET REPUBLICS.

[*Translation*]   March 12th, 1924.

The Federal Government of the Union of Socialist Soviet Republics has examined with the utmost care the draft Treaty of Mutual Assistance which was drawn up by the Temporary Mixed Commission of the League of Nations, amended by the Third Committee of the fourth Assembly of the League and forwarded to the Commissariat for Foreign Affairs by the Secretariat in its letter of January 9th.

The Federal Government of the Union maintains the negative attitude which it has frequently expressed with regard to the " League of Nations " in its present form and as at present constituted. It nevertheless feels under an obligation to do everything in its power to assist in lightening the military armaments which oppress all nations in averting the risk of war.

In contradistinction to the provisions of the draft Treaty, the Federal Government of the Union considers it desirable to separate the question of the limitation of armaments from that of establishing an international organisation for the prevention of war. It regards the adoption of measures by all Governments for the limitation of armaments as so grave and urgent a task that it is imperative that the question should be raised immediately, independently of other problems which are more difficult to solve. On more than one occasion, *e.g.* at the Genoa Conference and at the Disarmament Conference held at Moscow, the Soviet Government has endeavoured to draw the attention of other Governments to this question and to obtain an agreement for a general and proportionate limitation of armaments. Although these efforts have not been crowned with success, it would still insist on the urgent need for an international examination of this problem. In the opinion of the Soviet Government, it is perfectly possible at the present moment to fix the maximum strengths of the standing armies and of the naval and aerial forces of each State, taking as a basis the area of its territory, the figures of its population and the amount of its public revenue and also taking count of the special local considerations of certain States. The Soviet Government considers that this limitation of armaments should be accompanied by the fixing of war budgets. It regards as indispensable the simultaneous disbandment by all the Contracting Parties of their irregular military forces. Subject to slight modifications, it approves of the proposal contained in Article 9 of the draft Treaty that each Contracting Party should be authorised to negotiate with the neighbouring States the establishment of controlled frontier zones. It recommends the institution of frontier zones of equal width on both sides, within which only a strictly limited number of regular troops could be stationed under the control of mixed commissions. This system has already been put into force as between the Union and Finland. The Soviet Government has proposed to its other neighbours in the West the adoption of the same system, but so far without success. The Soviet Government would recommend the general adoption of this measure.

The general limitation of armaments could, in the opinion of the Soviet Government, be carried out, without the participation of the League of Nations, by a general congress convened for the purpose, which would appoint its own executive organ for the purpose of putting into effect such decisions as might be taken.

The Committees and the Assembly of the League of Nations have approached the problem from the opposite angle. They have made the limitation of armaments depend upon the solution of the extremely complicated question of an international organisation for the prevention of wars, and in this way they have delayed it for an indefinite period. The third Assembly of the League of Nations decided that the limitation of armaments should be preceded by a general treaty of guarantee against aggression, which should itself be preceded by the obtaining of general consent to the limitation of armaments. In the report of the Third Committee of the fourth Assembly, this point is expressed as follows : the treaty of guarantee and disarmament are interdependent ; there arises, in addition to the dependence of disarmament upon the guarantee, a further dependence of the guarantee on the necessary disarmament. Consequently, the Third Committee of the fourth Assembly proposed the following procedure : first, a general contractual guarantee is established in principle ; next, each State determines the limitation which it considers it can effect in its armaments ; subsequently, the Council of the League of Nations draws up the general plan for the limitation of armaments ; then the adhering States agree to put this plan into operation within a fixed period ; and it is only then that the treaty of guarantee comes into force. The Soviet Government is of opinion that the whole system of interdependence between disarmament and the treaty of guarantee merely delays the realisation of the immediate practical object — namely, the general limitation of armaments. This object, which is perfectly feasible and practicable in itself, is made conditional upon the execution of a plan the putting into force of which is hardly possible at the present time.

The Soviet Government feels that in an epoch such as ours, when the policy of all States is wholly dominated by their separate interests, any attempt to establish a system of international equity and of protection for the weak nations against the strong by means of an international organisation is sure to fail. In the whole of its policy, the Soviet Government is endeavouring to help in dissipating world antagonism, in preventing war and in defending the weak nations against the strong. It is fully prepared to discuss any plan, whatever it may be, which is designed to achieve the same objects. But it categorically refuses to co-operate in carrying out plans the execution of which might furnish a weapon to certain States or groups of States for the satisfaction of their separate interests or aggressive dessings and thus merely envenom the present international situation.

The Soviet Government therefore rejects any plan for an international organisation which implies the possibility of measures of constraint being exercised by any international authority whatsoever against a particular State. In the present state of international relations, a system of that kind would inevitably become, in the hands of a dominant group of Powers, an instrument of aggressive policy against other Powers. The Soviet Government considers that the establishment of an international organisation is at present both right and desirable, but only for the purpose of effecting the amicable settlement of all disputes, without application of penalties or measures of constraint. This world organisation might, in its opinion, take the form of general congresses of all Governments, which would arrive at agreements voluntarily with regard to the questions in which they were interested without any measure of constraint being employed against certain of them.

The draft Treaty of Mutual Assistance is based upon two original plans — that of Viscount Cecil and that of Colonel Réquin. These two plans are themselves based upon opposite principles. In accordance with the views expressed above, the Soviet Government rejects them both. The former places extremely wide powers in the hands of the Council of the League of Nations in all domains of international life. Most of these powers have been retained in the final draft : for instance, the Council of the League of Nations is to decide within a period of four days, in the event of hostilities, which of the belligerents is the aggressor, and all the Contracting Powers are then obliged to submit to its decision and take part in the struggle against the State in question. The Soviet Government objects, in the most emphatic and definite manner, to the attribution to a group of States of such wide powers, which are equivalent to an international dictatorship.

Moreover, the Soviet Government denies the possibility of determining in the case of every international conflict which State is the aggressor and which is the victim. There are, of course, cases in which a State attacks another without provocation, and the Soviet Government is prepared, in its conventions with other Governments, to undertake, in particular cases, to oppose attacks of this kind undertaken without due cause. But in the present international situation, it is impossible in most cases to say which party is the aggressor. Neither the entry into foreign territory nor the scale of war preparations can be regarded as satisfactory criteria. Hostilities generally break out after a series of mutual aggressive acts of the most varied character. For example, when the Japanese torpedo-boats attacked the Russian fleet at Port Arthur in 1904, it was clearly an act of aggression from a technical point of view, but, politically speaking, it was an act caused by the aggressive policy of the Czarist Government towards Japan, who, in order to forestall the danger, struck the first blow at her adversary. Nevertheless, Japan cannot be regarded as the victim, as the collision between the two States was not merely the result of the aggressive acts of the Czarist Government but also of the imperialist policy of the Japanese Government towards the peoples of China and Korea. The Soviet Government considers, therefore, that it is absolutely impossible to adopt the system of deciding which State is the aggressor in the case of each conflict and making definite consequences depend upon such decision.

Colonel Réquin's plan is based not on the attribution of extraordinary powers to the Council of the League of Nations but on the recognition of individual agreements between groups of States for the prevention of aggression, together with the communication of these agreements to the Council of the League of Nations. In the final draft, this plan is incorporated in the form of supplementary regional agreements between States for the prevention of aggression, subject to the preliminary examination of such agreements by the Council of the League of Nations.

The Soviet Government fully realises that the conclusion of local agreements between certain States is inevitable in the present state of international relations. It considers, however, that it is quite inadmissible that they should receive recognition from an international organisation or that they should be regarded as beneficial in the prevention of wars. It regards as even more inadmissible the obligation imposed on the other Contracting States to give assistance, in the event of hostilities, to these coalitions of Powers.

The Soviet Government absolutely refuses to accept the reservation contained in the draft Treaty confirming the Treaties of Versailles, Neuilly, Saint Germain and Trianon. The Soviet Government took no part in the conclusion of these treaties and maintains an entirely negative attitude with regard to the provisions contained in them.

While willingly responding to the invitation addressed to it to communicate its opinion regarding the draft Treaty of Mutual Assistance, the Soviet Government emphatically protests against that article of the draft whereby the adhesion of States not Members of the League of Nations is only possible with the consent of two-thirds of the signatories. The Soviet Government has no intention of addressing such a request to the Powers signatory to the Treaty or of appearing to ask for their indulgence. The Soviet Government always negotiates with other Governments on a footing of equality.

In any case, the essential object of the drafts communicated to the Soviet Government — *viz.* disarmament and the averting of the risk of war — cannot be achieved, even partially or, indeed, to any degree whatsoever, without the participation of the Soviet Republics.

(Signed) George Tchitcherin,
People's Commissary for Foreign Affairs
of the Union of Socialist Soviet Republics.

REPLY FROM THE LATVIAN GOVERNMENT.

[*Translation*]

Riga, March 22nd, 1924.

With reference to your letter No. C. L. 105, dated October 25th, 1923, I have the honour to inform you that, in accordance with the resolution adopted by the fourth Assembly of the League of Nations, the Latvian Government has considered the draft Treaty of Mutual Assistance and has instructed me to communicate to you its opinion thereon.

The Latvian people are eminently peace-loving, and the Government has invariably been anxious to contribute to the development of good relations between all countries. The Government accordingly desires, in the first instance, to pay a tribute to the work of the League of Nations for the consolidation of the peace of the world.

The Government cannot do other than approve the draft taken as a whole. If, however, it makes a few observations on certain clauses in the draft, its only object is to increase the efficacy of the measures provided for in the draft.

In accordance with its frequently reiterated conviction that the best method of preventing disturbances of the peace consists in unanimous co-operation between all nations on the basis of mutual equality, and taking into consideration the present political situation, the Government approves the principle of partial agreements as a practical measure for guaranteeing the safety of States. The Government will, however, give its support to any endeavour in the field of mutual assistance the object of which is to render the general treaty more effective.

Among other obligations imposed on the Council by the draft Treaty and also by the Covenant is a military obligation :

(a) The Council shall decide, within four days of notification being addressed to the Secretary-General, which of the High Contracting Parties are the objects of aggression and whether they are entitled to claim the assistance provided under the Treaty (Article 4).

(b) The Council determines the form of assistance (Article 5).

(c) The Council may act as intermediary between two or more neighbouring countries for the establishment of demilitarised zones (Article 9).

(d) Under the Covenant and draft Treaty (Article 11) it is the duty of the Council to prepare a general plan for the reduction of armaments and to supervise the execution of such plan by the High Contracting Parties, and also to undertake the revision of armaments provided for in Article 13 of the Treaty.

(e) The Council receives and considers information on the armaments of the High Contracting Parties furnished by the latter to the military or other delegates of the League (Article 12).

(f) Finally, in accordance with the intentions of the Treaty and in order to enhance its efficacy, the Council obviously must prepare in advance some plan of military action, based on the terms of the Treaty, to meet cases in which political circumstances make a resort to arms a possible eventuality; the Council would also be called upon to direct the execution of such a plan.

Under present conditions the Council cannot carry out these obligations without consulting military experts — a somewhat protracted process, which, moreover, would not provide all the desired guarantees. The Government accordingly thinks that these disadvantages might be obviated with the help of a permanent military organisation which would possess qualifications greatly exceeding those possessed by experts selected *ad hoc*. The Government merely puts forward this idea, which it is ready to support when this subject comes up for discussion ; it will not at the present moment go into details of the organisation, which would be within the competence of the Temporary Mixed Commission.

Article 17 admits of conditional or partial adherence to the provisions of the Treaty, the object obviously being to give States which, but for this clause, would abstain, an opportunity of adhering to the Treaty. States which, however, adhered to the Treaty in a conditional or partial form would only assume certain vaguely defined obligations and would, in certain cases and to the same extent as those States which adhered unconditionally, derive all the advantages resulting from the fact that the latter States had assumed in *toto* the obligations under the Treaty. The Latvian Government fears that a situation of this kind would seriously impair the efficacy of the general treaty and would tend to increase the number of States adhering under special privileged conditions.

Article 19 should be amended in such a way that the Treaty could only be denounced at the end of the fourteenth year. As the Treaty involves a genuine reduction of armaments, it should only be possible to denounce it upon the expiration of the period in question.

(*Signed*) L. SEJA,
Minister for Foreign Affairs.

REPLY FROM THE BULGARIAN GOVERNMENT.

[*Translation.*]

Sofia, June 10th, 1924.

The Bulgarian Government congratulates the League of Nations on its untiring efforts to evolve a general plan for the reduction of armaments, and on having produced, as a first result of these efforts, the draft of a Treaty of Mutual Assistance. Desirous of doing all that lies in its power to assist the League of Nations in its work in the cause of peace, the Bulgarian Government has subjected the draft to the most careful examination and declares that it approves it. If feels, however, that it should make certain observations which it considers important.

The Treaty of Mutual Assistance should be regarded as the continuation and development of the system of the Covenant of the League of Nations, for the preamble and Articles 8 and 9 of the Covenant provide for the general reduction of armaments.

The Bulgarian Government is firmly convinced that a general reduction of armaments is one of the most effective means of diminishing the danger of war, and earnestly hopes that the efforts of the League of Nations to this end will result in guaranteeing peace to a world, which has been so sorely tried.

But, although nearly six years have elapsed since the signing of the Covenant, the promises contained in Articles 8 and 9 have not been fulfilled. Side by side with countries which have voluntarily reduced their armaments, or which have been obliged to disarm under treaties, are to-day other countries which have maintained formidable armaments.

The inequality thus established is not favourable to the cause of general peace, since experience has, unfortunately, proved that armed countries cannot always resist the temptation of employing their forces, particularly when they are not in the right. The need for a general reduction of armaments was therefore never more urgent. Finally, it seems highly desirable that the undertaking to reduce armaments should be given a more positive form and that the general plan for this reduction should be laid down in the Treaty itself. The period of two years provided for in Article 11 of the draft might well be reduced to one year.

The Treaty of Mutual Assistance must be universal and general and must include all civilised countries : this principle was laid down in paragraph 1 of the Resolution XIV of the third Assembly. It is widely recognised that the partial grouping of countries possesses the great defect of giving rise to the formation of rival groups, which paves the way for a return to the former military alliances, and these constitute a danger to peace. For these reasons, partial agreements should only be permitted if they are concluded under the auspices of the League of Nations, and if their purely defensive character is established beyond all doubt.

It would also be desirable, in order that war should be eliminated as a means for settling international disputes, to enlarge the field of the application of compulsory arbitration, and to recommend that all the Contracting Parties should adhere to the optional clause concerning the obligatory jurisdiction of the Permanent Court of International Justice.

(Signed) Ch. KALFOFF,
Bulgarian Minister for Foreign Affairs.

REPLY FROM THE GOVERNMENT OF THE UNITED STATES OF AMERICA.

Washington, June 16th, 1924.

The Secretary of State of the United States of America has the honour to acknowledge the receipt of a communication of the Secretary-General of the League of Nations submitting, by direction of the Council of the League of Nations, the draft Treaty of Mutual Assistance, proposed by the Third Committee to the fourth Assembly, and requesting the expression of the views of the Government of the United States.

In reply it may be said that the Government of the United States is most desirous that appropriate agreements should be reached to limit armament and thus to reduce the heavy burdens of expenditure caused by unnecessary and competitive outlays in providing facilities and munitions of war. The desire and purpose of this Government were fully manifested when the great military and naval Powers were invited by the President of the United States to send representatives to meet in conference at Washington in 1921 for the purpose of considering the limitation of armaments. While that Conference resulted in the conclusion of an important Naval Treaty between the United States of America, the British Empire, France, Italy and Japan for the limitation of capital fighting ships, it was found to be impossible to obtain an agreement for the limitation of the tonnage of auxiliary naval craft or to make any progress in the direction of limitation of land forces. The Government of the United States, having reduced its own armaments, continues to cherish the hope that the desired result in the case of other Powers may be achieved, and it notes with keen and sympathetic interest every endeavour to that end. In this spirit the draft Treaty submitted has been carefully considered.

It appears from the preamble of the Treaty that it has been formulated with the desire " of establishing the general lines of a scheme of mutual assistance with a view to facilitate the application of Articles 10 and 16 of the Covenant of the League of Nations, and of a reduction or limitation of national armaments in accordance with Article 8 of the Covenant ' to the lowest point consistent with national safety and the enforcement by common action of international obligations ' ".

The following provisions of the draft Treaty may be especially noted :

" *Article 2.* — The High Contracting Parties, jointly and severally, undertake to furnish assistance, in accordance with the provisions of the present Treaty, to any one of their number should the latter be the object of a war of aggression, provided that it has conformed to the provisions of the present Treaty regarding the reduction or limitation of armaments.

" *Article 3.* — In the event of one of the High Contracting Parties being of opinion that the armaments of any other High Contracting Party are in excess of the limits fixed for the latter High Contracting Party under the provisions of the present Treaty, or in the event of it having cause to apprehend an outbreak of hostilities, either on account of the aggressive policy or preparations of any State party or not to the present Treaty, it may inform the Secretary-General of the League of Nations that it is threatened with aggression, and the Secretary-General shall forthwith summon the Council.

" The Council, if it is of opinion that there is a reasonable ground for thinking that a menace of aggression has arisen, may take all necessary measures to remove such menace and, in particular, if the Council thinks right, those indicated in sub-paragraphs *(a)*, *(b)*, *(c)*, *(d)* and *(e)* of the second paragraph of Article 5 of the present Treaty.

" The High Contracting Parties which have been denounced and those which have stated themselves to be the object of a threat of aggression shall be considered as especially interested and shall therefore be invited to send representatives to the Council in conformity with Articles 4, 15 and 17 of the Covenant. The vote of their representatives shall, however, not be reckoned when calculating unanimity.

" *Article 4.* — In the event of one or more of the High Contracting Parties becoming engaged in hostilities, the Council of the League of Nations shall decide, within four days of notification being addressed to the Secretary-General, which of the High Contracting Parties are the objects of aggression and whether they are entitled to claim the assistance provided under the Treaty.

" The High Contracting Parties undertake that they will accept such a decision by the Council of the League of Nations.

" The High Contracting Parties engaged in hostilities shall be regarded as especially interested, and shall therefore be invited to send representatives to the Council (within the terms of Articles 4, 15 and 17 of the Covenant), the vote of their representative not being reckoned when calculating unanimity ; the same shall apply to States signatory to any partial agreements involved on behalf of either of the two belligerents, unless the remaining Members of the Council shall decide otherwise.

" *Article 5.* — The High Contracting Parties undertake to furnish one another mutually with assistance in the case referred to in Article 2 of the Treaty in the form determined by the Council of the League of Nations as the most effective, and to take all appropriate measures without delay in the order of urgency demanded by the circumstances.

" In particular, the Council may :

" *(a)* Decide to apply immediately to the aggressor State the economic sanctions contemplated by Article 16 of the Covenant, the Members of the League not signatory to the present Treaty not being, however, bound by this decision, except in the case where the State attacked is entitled to avail itself of the Articles of the Covenant ;

" *(b)* Invoke by name the High Contracting Parties whose assistance it requires. No High Contracting Party situated in a continent other than that in which operations will take place shall, in principle, be required to co-operate in military, naval or air operations ;

" *(c)* Determine the forces which each State furnishing assistance shall place at its disposal ;

" *(d)* Prescribe all necessary measures for securing priority for the communications and transport connected with the operations ;

" *(e)* Prepare a plan for financial co-operation among the High Contracting Parties with a view to providing for the State attacked and for the States furnishing assistance the funds which they require for the operations ;

" *(f)* Appoint the Higher Command and establish the object and nature of his duty.

" The representatives of States recognised as aggressors under the provisions of Article 4 of the Treaty shall not take part in the deliberations of the Council specified in this article. The High Contracting Parties which are required by the Council to furnish assistance in accordance with sub-paragraph *(b)* shall, on the other hand, be considered as especially interested and, as such, shall be invited to send representatives, unless they are already represented, to the deliberations specified in sub-paragraphs *(c)*, *(d)*, *(e)* and *(f)*. "

Without attempting an analysis of these provisions, or of other provisions of the draft Treaty, it is quite apparent that its fundamental principle is to provide guarantees of mutual assistance and to establish the competency of the Council of the League of Nations with respect to the decisions contemplated, and, in view of the constitutional organisation of this Government and of the fact that the United States is not a Member of the League of Nations, this Government would find it impossible to give its adherence.

The Government of the United States has not failed to note that, under Article 17 of the draft Treaty, " any State may, with the consent of the Council of the League, notify its conditional or partial adherence to the provisions of this Treaty, provided always that such State has reduced or is prepared to reduce its armaments in conformity with the provisions of this Treaty ", but it would not serve a useful purpose to consider the question of a conditional or partial adherence on the part of the Government of the United States when the conditions imposed would of necessity be of such a character as to deprive adherence of any substantial effect.

REPLY FROM THE AUSTRALIAN GOVERNMENT.

Melbourne, July 4th, 1924.

The Commonwealth Government has given most careful consideration to the draft Treaty of Mutual Assistance and other relevant documents forwarded with your letter C.L. 105. 1923. IX of October 25th, 1923.

The Commonwealth Government earnestly desires to assist in every way to secure the maintenance of world peace, and realises that a general reduction of armaments is essential as a preliminary step in the pursuit of this objective.

As regards the application of this principle to Australia, it may be stated definitely that, being a young country, Australia, in the adoption of measures for her own defence, has not yet attained the lowest point consistent with national safety ; and therefore the obligation relating to reduction or limitation of armaments is without that special significance for us which it has for other and older States.

The particular national and geographical situation of Australia needs emphasis. We are a small population, forming part of the British Empire and occupying a continent ; and in this respect our position is entirely different from that of any European State. It follows that any treaty of mutual assistance specially designed to meet European conditions could be made applicable to Australia only after considerable reservation. This latter observation is specially warranted, in view of the provisions of Article 5 *(b)* of the draft Treaty, from which it must be inferred that the Continent of Europe was chiefly in mind when the Treaty was being drafted.

Resolution XIV of the third Assembly affirms the undeniable proposition that, in the present state of the world, serious reduction of armaments can only be accepted in exchange for a satisfactory guarantee of safety ; and it is in the light of this proposition that the Government of the Commonwealth of Australia has approached this important question.

The obligations of the draft Treaty, concisely stated, are :

(a) To reduce armaments in return for a guarantee of security ;
(b) To keep a striking force available for duty at the call of the League,

and the provisions of Article 5 *(b)* of the Treaty have a special significance for Australia in this connection, in as much as they take no account of the fact that she is the sole occupant of a continent.

Article 5 *(b)* provides :

" In particular the Council may invoke by name the High Contracting Parties whose assistance it requires. No High Contracting Party situated in a continent other than that in which operations will take place shall, in principle, be required to co-operate in military, naval or air operations."

The result of this article, in its application to Australia, is that no nation signatory to this Treaty would be under any obligation to come to the assistance of Australia if she were attacked, and Australia herself would not be obliged to render assistance to anybody. In other words, there is neither obligation to assist nor guarantee of receiving assistance so far as Australia is concerned.

Additionally, the following views are expressed in connection with certain other provisions of the Treaty.

Article 5 of the draft Treaty, which authorises the Council to take measures and give directions, goes far beyond the provisions of Article 16 of the Covenant, under which the Council may only recommend action.

The proposal in Article 6 for complementary defensive agreements between individual Members of the League is an indication that the general treaty by itself would not be fully effective. Apart from other objections to this system of partial treaties, it is very difficult to see what part Australia could have in the linking-up of these treaties.

The question whether it would be possible for the Council to determine, within four days of the notification of hostilities, which nation is the aggressor is a most important one. The uncertainty of agreement on this matter within the prescribed time, or at all, seriously jeopardises the effective use of forces at the disposal of the League.

The foregoing are the main reasons why this draft Treaty is not acceptable to the Commonwealth Government. The Government thinks, however, that useful avenues of enquiry have been opened up by the report. That this particular scheme of international guarantees does not prove acceptable need not discourage the friends of the League. The League has done, and can still do, much to concentrate the moral force of the world on the urgent necessity for the solution of this great problem, and to devise means to that end.

(Signed) S. M. BRUCE,
Prime Minister.

REPLY FROM THE BRITISH GOVERNMENT.

London, July 5th, 1924.

His Majesty's Government have examined with the utmost care the report of the Third Committee of the fourth Assembly, the resolution of the fourth Assembly of the League of Nations and the report for 1923 of the Temporary Mixed Commission on the reduction of armaments, together with the other documents enclosed in your letter of October 25th, 1923. They desire to place on record their appreciation of the prolonged and exhaustive investigations which have been made into the important subject of treaties of mutual assistance as a step towards the reduction or limitation of armaments.

2. There is no question to which His Majesty's Government attach greater importance than the reduction or limitation of armaments, for they recognise that, as stated in Article 8 of the Covenant, the maintenance of peace, which is the principal object of the League of Nations, requires the reduction of national armaments to the lowest point consistent with national safety and the enforcement by common action of international obligations. For this very reason, they hold that any measures designed to bring about the reduction or limitation of armaments must be subjected to the most careful scrutiny before adoption. No greater calamity to the cause which they have at heart can be imagined than that any scheme adopted by the League should, when submitted to the test of reality, fail owing to defects which ought to have been foreseen in advance. It is vital, therefore, that, before the League of Nations takes the responsibility of making any recommendations to its Members, it should satisfy itself that the scheme recommended is in all respects reliable and effective.

3. Out of the twenty-six nations whose replies are published with the report of the Temporary Mixed Commission, only a very small number are able to express unqualified acceptance of Resolution XIV adopted at the third session of the Assembly, which forms the basis of the reports now under consideration. The objections to the various proposals for treaties of mutual guarantee or assistance which have been considered by the League are to be found in the report of the Third Committee itself, as well as in the reports of experts and the opinions of Governments included in the documents circulated to Members of the League. From these detailed criticisms there emerge certain objections of principle which up to the present time do not appear to have been adequately met.

4. The main criticisms of the proposed treaty fall under two heads, which may be expressed in an interrogative form: Are the guarantees contained therein sufficient to justify a State in reducing its armaments? Are the obligations to be undertaken towards other States of such a nature that the nations of the world can conscientiously engage to carry them out?

5. In regard to the first group of criticisms, it is generally conceded that if a treaty of mutual assistance is to prove effective in bringing about a reduction of armaments, its stipulations must be such that the parties thereto can assume with absolute confidence not only that in the contingencies for which it provides it will be brought into operation with certainty, but also that it will effectually accomplish its purpose.

6. The effectiveness of the scheme will be seen to depend to a considerable extent on the ability of the Council of the League to determine, by unanimous vote of all Members not concerned in the dispute, which nation is the aggressor. This difficult question has to be settled within a period of four days from the notification of hostilities to the Secretary-General. It is unnecessary here to deal at length with the difficulties which might confront the Council in reaching agreement on such a point within the stipulated time, or the likelihood that unanimity might never be reached at all on a really controversial issue, since these considerations are fully discussed in the documents circulated to the various Governments. In this connection, the " commentary on the definition of a ' case of aggression ' ", drawn up by a Special Committee of the Temporary Mixed Commission, in collaboration with certain technical members of the Permanent Advisory Commission, is of great interest. The commentary does not provide a solution of the difficulty. It is stated therein more than once that no satisfactory definition of what constitutes an " act of aggression " could be drawn up

Consequently, the report does not provide that element of certainty and reliability which is essential if the League of Nations is to recommend the adoption of the treaty by its Members as a basis for reduction in armaments.

7. Another important objection of principle is the long delay which is liable to occur before the forces at the disposal of the League of Nations can be brought into effective operation against an aggressor State. It is not until after the determination by the Council of the question which State is the aggressor, which is likely to occupy the whole of the four days permitted by the draft Treaty, that the Council can begin to take the necessary steps for bringing pressure, whether military or economic, to bear on the aggressor. Economic pressure is admittedly slow in operation. As regards military pressure, all the technical experts who have advised the organs of the League on the subject are agreed that no military assistance can be considered immediate and effective unless it be given in accordance with a pre-arranged plan. It is obvious, however, and was recognised by the Third Committee of the fourth Assembly, that in the case of a general treaty of assistance plans can rarely be pre-arranged. They would therefore have to be drawn up, after the question which was the aggressor State had been determined, by the naval, military or air officers designated by the Council of the League to command the international forces. The experience of the recent world-war does not justify the assumption that where the forces of several nations are involved the immediate acceptance, much less the rapid execution, of plans of operations can with certainty be counted on. The possibility will always exist that the States most favourably situated for providing the necessary force may at a given moment not be in a position to do so, owing to commitments elsewhere, the state of public opinion, or the political condition of the country at the time. The appointment of the higher command will itself involve delay. The Council will have great difficulty in reaching a unanimous decision, for no nation places its troops under a foreign command without very careful considerations. A system which involves prolonged delays before the first step in bringing military pressure to bear on an aggressor nation can be taken does not reach that standard of effectiveness which is essential.

8. The necessary measures to carry the general guarantees into effect are, moreover, made dependent upon the explicit consent of each individual State which may be called upon to render assistance as a permanent or *ad hoc* Member of the Council. This consideration can but strengthen His Majesty's Government in the view that the guarantee afforded by the draft Treaty is so precarious that no responsible Government will feel justified in consenting to any material reduction of its armaments in return. If, as His Majesty's Government feel convinced, this is the case, the whole object of the Treaty is lost and its conclusion is objectless. His Majesty's Government, indeed, go further. They are persuaded, after careful examination of the draft scheme, that, if the obligations created by the Treaty be scrupulously carried out, they will involve an increase rather than a decrease in British armaments. The report of the Temporary Mixed Commission for 1922 stated that, " in the case of armed assistance, certain forces, such as aircraft and warships, are the most readily available and therefore the most likely to be asked for and to be effective in the initial stages of the war ". It is the considered opinion of the British Naval Staff that a treaty such as is proposed will, if properly carried out, necessitate an increase in the British naval forces. His Majesty's Government cannot avoid the belief that the position will be the same in other countries.

9. It was owing to the recognition of the defects inherent in any general treaty of mutual assistance that the proposal was made to super-impose on a general treaty a system of partial treaties between groups of countries. It has been urged against such partial treaties that their conclusion by one group of States is likely to bring about the formation of competing groups, and that the result will be a reappearance of the former system of alliances and counter-alliances, which in the past has proved such a serious menace to the peace of the world. The proposal to meet this objection by bringing the partial treaties under the control of the League does not overcome the difficulty, particularly so long as important nations remain outside the League, and His Majesty's Government cannot but recognise the force of the above criticism.

10. A further objection to the scheme for partial treaties to be embodied in the Treaty of Mutual Assistance is the opening that would be afforded for conflict between the Council of the League and individual Governments. Under Article 4 of the draft Treaty it will be the duty of the Council to decide which of two belligerents is the aggressor. Under Article 8, States parties to a partial treaty will be at liberty to decide the point for themselves, before it is decided by the Council. The possibility of disagreement between the Council and States between which a partial treaty is operative is one which cannot be contemplated with equanimity.

11. The obligations involved in the proposed treaty are of such a nature that several of the nations whose opinions are forwarded with the report of the Temporary Mixed Commission have been unable to accept them. In this connection, His Majesty's Government desire to draw particular attention to the following extract from a letter to the Secretary-General of the League from the Government of Canada, dated June 19th, 1923 :

" It is intended that the obligation to render assistance shall be limited in principle to those countries situated in the same part of the globe. While Canada is situated in the North-American Continent, she is a nation forming part of the British Empire, and it seems difficult to devise a scheme which would give due effect to these conflicting considerations. In any case, it seems very unlikely that the Canadian people in the present circumstances would be prepared to consent to any agreement binding Canada to give assistance as proposed to other nations, and the Government therefore does not see its way to a participation in the Treaty of Mutual Guarantee. "

12. The draft Treaty further appears to involve an undesirable extension of the functions of the Council of the League. Under Article 16 of the Covenant, the Council can only recommend action, while even under Article 10 it can only *advise*. By Article 5 of the draft Treaty, the Council is authorised to decide to adopt various measures. Thus the Council would become an executive body with very large powers, instead of an advisory body. In any event, the Council of the League is a most inappropriate body to be entrusted with the control of military forces in operation against any particular State or States.

13. For the reasons which have been enumerated, the draft Treaty, in the eyes of His Majesty's Government, holds out no serious prospect of advantage sufficient to compensate the world for the immense complication of international relations which it would create, the uncertainty of the practical effect of its clauses, and the consequent difficulty of conducting national policy.

14. His Majesty's Government, therefore, have come to the conclusion that the adoption of the text included in the report of the Third Committee of the fourth Assembly cannot be recommended. They are, however, far from admitting that the careful study of these questions has been fruitless. The years of patient investigation which have been devoted to this subject by the various organs of the League are themselves a proof of the desire of nations Members of the League to find a solution to the difficult question of reduction and limitation of armaments. This sentiment finds strong expression in practically all the replies of the various nations published with the report of the Temporary Mixed Commission. If this study has not so far resulted in the submission of a draft treaty of mutual assistance in an acceptable form, the reports which have been under consideration nevertheless contain some encouraging and suggestive passages as to other lines of enquiry which might be followed with useful results.

15. It is the policy of His Majesty's Government that, whenever a favourable opportunity presents itself, the Governments of the world should meet in conference with the object of devising a scheme or schemes for the reduction of armaments. Such a conference should include the Governments of countries which are not yet Members of the League, and which are therefore not represented at the Assembly. At this conference every suggestion for the reduction of armaments, including the suggestion contained in the proposed Treaty of Mutual Assistance, would be open on its merits for full exploration and examination, and His Majesty's Government, in finding themselves unable to support the proposal submitted by the Third Committee of the fourth Assembly, desire to make it clear that there is no intention to prejudge in any way the further consideration of the proposed Treaty by the conference, which it is their policy to bring together, or help to bring together, whenever a favourable opportunity is presented. It is not within the province of His Majesty's Government, nor would it be wise on the present occasion, to attempt to formulate anything in the nature of an exhaustive category of the proposals which may be brought before such a conference. Among constructive proposals which have been already discussed are those defining zones of demilitarisation between States, safeguarding special frontiers under some form of international control, granting further powers to the International Court, and so on. His Majesty's Government believe that they ought to keep themselves free to consider any and every practicable proposal, and commit themselves at present only to a pledge to do everything in their power to bring about agreements that will have as an immediate effect a substantial reduction in armaments. On the practical side, it is noticeable that an advance in the reduction of armaments has already been made in Central and South America, and in the carrying-out of the recommendations of the Washington Conference.

(Signed) J. Ramsay MacDonald,
Prime Minister.

REPLY FROM THE CANADIAN GOVERNMENT.

Ottawa, July 9th, 1924.

The Canadian Government has very earnestly considered the proposed Treaty of Mutual Assistance submitted to it by you in your communications of October 25th, 1923, and April 11th, 1924, and has also examined the documents accompanying the draft. Realising the vital importance of the subject and the devoted labour the formulation of the draft Treaty has entailed, and notwithstanding its profound sympathy with the objects sought to be attained, the Canadian Government finds itself unable to conclude that these objects would be promoted by the arrangement suggested. It concurs generally with the conclusions on the subject expressed by the Government of Great Britain and submits only the following brief observations.

The position of Canada in the British Empire is such that, in spite of the fact that the application of the Treaty to the continent of North America is by its terms conditioned upon its ratification by the United States of America, the question of Canada's adherence to it has a more practical aspect than it would otherwise have. Apart from indications that the Government of the United States of America was likely to find the plan acceptable in principle, Canada has already indicated disapproval of the interpretation of the terms of Article 10 of the Covenant as implying an obligation upon her to intervene actively under that article. The proposed Treaty creates an obligation wider in its extent and more precise in its implications than any which Article 10 could be interpreted as imposing, and it proposes, moreover, to transfer the right to decide upon the scope of the action Canada should take from the Canadian Parliament to the Council of the League of Nations. It is true that, for the purpose of deciding upon the assistance to be given by Canada, the Council would include a Canadian representative and that the draft limits the liability of a signatory in another continent to measures not involving naval, military or air operations. But the presence of a Canadian representative on the Council would hardly compensate for the, at least nominal, transfer of authority, and, again, Canada's position in the British Empire affects the protection afforded her by the continental limitation of which in any event the utility is uncertain since it appears doubtful if hostile action can widely or indeed safely be undertaken by any State upon the principle of limited liability.

For these reasons and those expressed in the communication of the Government of Great Britain above referred to, the Canadian Government is of the opinion that the nature of the proposed Treaty is such that so far as it purports to impose a future obligation to take specific action in circumstances incapable of present definition, it would be hopeless to expect the people of Canada to accept it, and it is also of opinion that, even if those provisions of the draft were generally approved and brought into operation, their effect would neither be to minimise the danger of war nor to bring about any useful limitation of armaments. On the other hand, the Canadian Government considers that every extension by general agreement of the facilities for formal, regular, early and informed public discussion of possible causes of war is to be welcomed. It omits to deal more at large with such of the provisions of the draft Treaty as appear to be designed to bring about such an extension only because it conceives that those would not appear in their present form if the draft were confined to provisions of that character.

(Signed) Mackenzie KING,
Prime Minister.

REPLY FROM THE GERMAN GOVERNMENT.

[Translation from the German.]   Berlin, July 24th, 1924.

The German Government has examined with interest the draft of a treaty of mutual assistance which you forwarded to it in your letter of January 9th, 1924. In view of the great importance of the problem dealt with in the draft, the Government considered it advisable to obtain the views on the matter of certain German experts of repute. These experts, viz. :

Professor HOETZSH, Member of the Reichstag ;
Professor KAAS, Prelate and Member of the Reichstag ;
Professor KAHL (Geheimer Justizrat), Member of the Reichstag ;
Dr. KRIEGE (Wirklicher Geheimer Rat), Ministerial Director ;
Professor MEINECKE (Geheimer Regierungsrat) ;
Count MONTGELAS, Infantry General, retired ;
Dr. SCHIFFER, former Minister of the Reich and Member of the Reichstag ; and
Professor SCHÜCKING, Member of the Reichstag ;

have embodied the results of their investigation in a memorandum. In forwarding this memorandum to you, I have the honour to observe that the views to which expression is given therein are also the views of the German Government.

(Signed) STRESEMANN.

The draft of a Treaty of Mutual Assistance submitted to us is dominated by the idea of disarmament which the League of Nations has hitherto been unable to realise. In its opening sentence, the Covenant of the League of Nations incorporated in the Treaty of Versailles sets forth as its object the promotion of " international co-operation " and the achievement of " international peace and security by the acceptance of obligations not to resort to war ". According to Article 8 and the Preamble to Part V of the Treaty of Versailles, the demand for " a general limitation of the armaments of all nations " shall serve to effect the realisation of this main motive. In order to render the nations capable and willing to fulfil this demand, a scheme is placed at their disposal for the peaceful settlement of their disputes, and arrangements are, at the same time, made for opposing with united forces any party who shall evade or ignore their obligations and resort instead to arms. This scheme however, has not proved effective. The contractual disarmament provided for has not materialised. There are serious gaps in the legal protection afforded by the Covenant. In many cases it tolerates war or the use of force ; and it fails to provide adequate guarantee that, in the event of illicit war, the culpable party shall be disabled with sufficient rapidity.

This shortcoming the draft under consideration seeks to make good by proceeding from the new starting-point that aggressive warfare must be prohibited. A war of aggression is declared in principle to be an international crime and is categorically interdicted. The object of such a war is assured of the speediest assistance against the aggressor. The assurance of this assistance is to involve the obligation to proceed to the reduction or limitation of one's own armaments and to co-operate in the construction of a general scheme of disarmament. Moreover, protection against an aggressor is immediately coupled with the disarmament which it is intended to render possible, so that it is only to be accorded if the party menaced has fulfilled the stipulations concerning the reduction or limitation of armaments.

The object of this draft treaty is thus clearly defined. Its significance and value are beyond all manner of doubt. But whether the method adopted for the achievement of that object is practicable and appropriate is open to serious question.

For intervention on the part of the contracting parties, the war must be shown to be a war of aggression. But, save for the purely negative definition contained in Article 1, paragraph 2, the draft gives no interpretation of the term. Nor is it, indeed, able to give such an interpretation. The question who is the aggressor in a war — just like the question who is responsible for a war — cannot, as a rule, be answered according to the immediate and superficial features of the case ; it is a problem which can be solved only after careful recognition and appreciation of all the many intrinsic and extrinsic factors which have contributed to originate it. Its solution involves a task of historic research and the application of international law, and this, in its turn, implies the reference to all sources, the disclosure of all records, the examination of witnesses and experts, as well as the taking of all sorts of other evidence. This demands time — an amount of time, indeed, which only scientific enquiry can assume. But, in the case before us, the verdict would have to be pronounced forthwith ; for hereupon would depend the intervention, and upon the speediness of the intervention its very success. Looked at, therefore, from this point of view, it appears absolutely logical that the draft treaty appoints a period of only four days for the decision. But the logic of this stipulation does not, in any way, alter the fact that, in the great majority of cases, it would be impossible to issue a decision of an objectively exhaustive and conclusive character within such a limited period.

This impossibility is not lessened but only enhanced by the character of the organ to be entrusted with making the decision. This organ is to be the Council of the League of Nations. Its members are chosen with a political perspective ; they act, not according to their own convictions and free judgment, but on the instructions of their respective Governments. Their votes are accordingly influenced by the special political interests of their various countries, and any resolution adopted bears the nature not of an impartial verdict but of a political decree. True, the immediately interested parties will have no vote (it is to be assumed that this applies also to the States regularly represented on the Council, though the draft treaty only expressly excludes from voting States not represented on the Council and merely admitted to the proceedings in special cases). But with the interlocking of political relations the interests of a Power immediately concerned will very frequently be safeguarded by other Powers not directly involved. This heightens the danger of no decision whatever being reached, inasmuch as it must be unanimously adopted. A single partisan of the aggressor will suffice to prevent the latter from being subjected to an adverse decision and effectively to nullify the entire claim to assistance on the part of the party attacked. On the other hand, the Council of the League of Nations is given the control of economic, military, communicational and financial measures of an incisive character, and is thereby placed in a position to dictate to the individual States participation in a coalition war with the ultimate result that the effects of the war may be more serious for these participators than for the original parties to the dispute.

To entrust a body of purely political orientation with such enormous powers is a very hazardous proceeding. But the situation becomes still more serious when, instead of action being taken by the Council of the League of Nations itself, the parties to the complementary defensive agreements permitted by the draft treaty adopt the initiative. Where such a complementary agreement has been concluded, the separate allies who, by virtue of their agreement, hold a partisan position from the very outset, are *ipso facto* legitimised to declare the case for assistance as established and to act accordingly. True, they must in this case inform the Council of the League of Nations without delay of the steps they have taken, and the Council has then to consider the situation just as it would have done if it had dealt with it from the first. But even if it should unanimously adopt a resolution contrary to the decision of the separate allies — which as regards a coalition of any significance and the actual situation created by it would certainly be a very rare occurrence — practically it would scarcely be possible to direct those who had hitherto marched as the confederates of one party into the camp of the other.

Considering the unequal status of armaments now prevailing, especially on the European continent, the military action provided for in the draft will be absolutely unfeasible in the event of an illegal attack being made by a strong military Power, not to speak of a group of strong military Powers allied by special agreement. The assistance provided for in the draft treaty will not be feasible until the inequalities of the status of armament have been removed by raising the standard of permissible armament in one direction and lowering it in another according to objectively ascertained requirements. But, as a matter of fact, in this direction the draft treaty contents itself with taking no steps ; it leaves it entirely to the personal judgment of the various contracting parties to decide the extent to which they will reduce or limit their armaments and give their assent to the general scheme of disarmament.

It is also left to free agreement between contiguous States to establish demilitarised zones. While the draft treaty rightly demands that no " unilateral sacrifice from the military point of view " shall be required on the part of one of the interested Powers, a mechanical special equality will nevertheless not suffice, since consideration must be given to the difference of the circumstances decisive for military operations. Apart from local, natural and artificial conditions, this difference will also noticeably exist in the disproportion of armaments.

Keeping all this in view, it is difficult to recognise in the draft treaty any progress as compared with the Covenant. Frequently, indeed, the contrary appears to be the case in regard to inherent ideas. This is particularly so with the complementary defensive agreements, which, though they have perhaps their formal authorisation in Article 21 of the Covenant, are something materially different from the special agreements permitted by that article and contravene, indeed, the very spirit of the Covenant. Their admission means practically the sanctioning of the existing system of group alliances and military conventions, the system of secret diplomacy and the balance-of-power policy ; consequently it would form a serious menace to the peace of the world ; for a State against which such a special agreement is directed would feel itself to be continually threatened and in its turn would endeavour to protect itself by military agreements with other States ; in other words, military conventions challenge the conclusion of fresh military conventions and render illusory the leading notion of the League of Nations, which is to replace the grouping of Powers by international organisation.

It must further be remembered that the contracting parties of the proposed Treaty of Mutual Assistance and the Members of the League of Nations will not, by any means, necessarily be identical. Consequently, the simultaneous existence of the new treaty and of the Covenant would create a most awkward uncertainty as to the competency of the two. In stressing the fact that its articles do not in any way affect the rights and duties emanating from the Covenant of the League of Nations, the draft treaty reveals the difficult complications which must arise from a State being a Member of the League of Nations, a signatory of the Treaty of Mutual Assistance, a party to a complementary defensive agreement — or to several such agreements — or being able to make use of the right to declare its merely conditional or partial adherence to the draft treaty. Under these circumstances, it is clearly a tempting and easy matter for a State to evade its obligations by playing off the articles of the one treaty against those of the other.

But, further, the Treaty is to leave unaffected not only the Covenant of the League of Nations but also the Treaties of Versailles, Neuilly, St. Germain and Trianon. If, therefore, Germany were to adhere to the new treaty, her situation would be intolerably ambiguous and would involve her in well-nigh incalculable danger. Disarmed almost to the point of impotency, she would have to reckon with being drawn resistless and defenceless into all sorts of conflicts, and to look on while her unprotected territory became the battlefield of foreign Powers. The mere fulfilment of the obligation to permit transit and traffic through the country to one party would render her a prey to the other, inasmuch as the latter would be given a convenient pretext for treating her as an enemy State. The fact, moreover, that her adherence would require a two-thirds majority of the votes of the principal contracting parties reveals even more drastically the disproportion between the adverse character of the conditions under which Germany could join and the advantages which might accrue to her from doing so.

If we really wish to promote that realisation of disarmament, of such essential import to the League of Nations, we must not follow the lines laid down in the new draft treaty. They are lines which neither touch nor run parallel with the principles of the Covenant but which diverge further and further from them. Only an organic development of the Covenant can bring success — not a heterogeneous adjunct thereto. What we need is not an accumulation of treaties and agreements side by side with the Covenant but an intensification and refinement of the Covenant itself. This development cannot be achieved by opposing force to force. Illegal force will only be driven from the world by opposing it with justice whereby the force employed to meet injustice will be justified and hallowed. Forbid the forcible settlement of disputes ; forbid the forcible attempt to obtain one's supposed rights altogether. Interdict all special agreements which shelve or contravene the general treaty. Remove all hindrances left by former treaties. Side by side with the Court of International Justice for purely legal disputes, create a court of arbitration for political conflicts and endow it with every guarantee for the juridicial independence of its members. Decree compulsory adherence thereto as well as to the Permanent Court of International Justice. Endow both courts with the right and the duty to issue provisional injunctions *uti possidetis*, especially in reference to the ostensibly peaceful occupation of foreign territory. Appoint an organ which shall oppose the peace-breaker with the weight of the League of Nations in order to carry into effect the decrees and all other decisions of the Court of Arbitration and of the Court of International

Justice. Above all, make disarmament obligatory upon all nations. Finally, see to it that the justified wishes of the population for an adjustment of frontiers be met by means of properly regulated legal procedure. Remember that development never ends, and that, unless you wish it to find vent on some violent eruption, you must not make the bootless attempt to curb and enclose it. No, we must give it free progress along the lines of right and justice. So, and only so, will it be possible to provide the premises for the vigorous efficacy of the League of Nations ; so, and only so, to create the possibility of an energetic growth of its authority ; so, and only so, to prepare the way for that universality of its membership without which it will never be able to fulfil its great task. Then Germany, too, would no longer need to hesitate whether she should, on condition of equality of rights, enter the community of nations united in the League and to co-operate in the maintenance of peace on the footing of justice and righteousness.

Berlin, July 5th, 1924.

| *(Signed)* | HOETZSCH | KAAS | KAHL | KRIEGE |
| | MEINECKE | MONTGELAS | SCHIFFER | SCHUCKING. |

REPLY FROM THE NETHERLANDS GOVERNMENT.

[Translation.]   The Hague, July 30th, 1924.

In your letter C.L. 105 of October 25th, 1923, you submitted for consideration by the Netherlands Government, in accordance with the Council's decision of September 29th, and a resolution of the fourth Assembly, the draft Treaty of Mutual Assistance drawn up by the Third Committee of that Assembly. In the same letter you requested me to communicate Her Majesty's Government's opinion on the draft.

In reply, I beg to refer to the letter which I sent you on June 23rd, 1923, and in which the Netherlands Government, in compliance with a request made by you, stated its opinion on the resolution adopted by the third Assembly concerning the question of treaties of mutua. guarantee. The Royal Government mentioned the doubts which it had entertained from the outset as to whether the putting into effect of the treaties of guarantee would really achieve the proposed object — namely, the reduction of armaments. The Government questioned whether it was justifiable to assume that the universality which is essential for this purpose would be achieved more easily or more rapidly by means of the Treaty of Guarantee than by the Covenant of the League of Nations, or to suppose that a system of military co-operation which did not provide the necessary legal guarantees that the assistance to be given should only be granted to States in a position to claim it rightfully would be likely to create between countries that atmosphere of peace and confidence by which alone the reduction of armaments could be realised.

Further, the Government raised the question whether the system contemplated in the above-mentioned resolution was in accordance with the principles and spirit of the Covenant, and whether its adoption would promote the development of the League of Nations.

After taking cognisance of the discussions at the fourth Assembly, the Netherlands Government continued its enquiry into these questions and made a most careful examination of the draft Treaty. As a result of that examination, it has not been led to modify its original point of view ; rather, it is confirmed in its opinion.

I presume that it was not the object of your circular letter to invite the Governments to give in their replies a detailed criticism of the various articles in the draft Treaty. I shall accordingly confine myself to referring to the speech of the first delegate of the Netherlands at the plenary meeting of the Assembly on September 29th, 1923. In his speech, Jonkheer Loudon drew attention to the inadequate interdependence established in the draft Treaty between the guarantee and the reduction of armaments ; he emphasised the preponderating weight given to partial treaties under the proposed system. The standpoint of Her Majesty's Government on this question is in complete agreement with the views expressed by the first delegate on that occasion.

The report submitted by the Permanent Advisory Commission in April 1923 showed that, in application, the principle of the mutual guarantee would necessarily result in the conclusion of separate treaties specifying in detail the terms upon which the Contracting States would assist one another in case of aggression. Accordingly separate treaties form an essential constituent of the system proposed in the draft. Without contesting the right of States to conclude separate and original treaties of this nature, the Netherlands Government is of opinion that it would be contrary to the principles and spirit of the Covenant to expand the conclusion of such agreements into a system and to make them in a way the basis of the international commonwealth. Indeed, this system would rather appear likely to give rise to serious alarm with regard to the maintenance of peace.

Further, the Netherlands Government entertains some doubt whether the draft Treaty would accelerate the reduction of armaments stipulated in Article 8 of the Covenant. In view of the preponderating position given to separate agreements, the proposed system involves a risk that, in practice, the limitations specified in that article would cease to be regarded as a maximum which should not be exceeded, and would come to be regarded rather as a minimum which the Contracting Parties would be entitled to demand from one another. The result might be that the weaker Powers would lose their freedom to decide on their own authority alone the various questions relating to the organisation of their armaments.

In the Government's opinion, the foregoing objections would become decisive if the legal guarantees which are intended to control the operation of the proposed system were to fail. It must be admitted that in this respect the draft is far from satisfactory. Its failure on this point may be best inferred from Article 8, which provides for the automatic operation of the machinery of assistance.

While maintaining, therefore, its objections to the draft Treaty, the Netherlands Government remains fully aware of the great importance for the entire world of the question of the reduction of armaments, and, again, the necessity of finding some method of arriving at a solution of this vital problem. Instead of employing for this purpose a system of an essentially military character based on the use of force, Her Majesty's Government thinks that it is chiefly essential to encourage the development of all the various institutions of the League of Nations and to give practical proof in international life and in relations between States of the League's spirit of conciliation, co-operation and mutual discussion. Once the League becomes universal, and once the States are genuinely and fully prepared to comply with the provisions and spirit of the Covenant, more particularly in regard to the peaceful consideration and settlement of disputes likely to lead to a rupture, that atmosphere of international security and confidence will be created which is both the most powerful argument for the general reduction of armaments and, at the same time, the essential condition thereof. Her Majesty's Government, which was among the first to adopt as obligatory the jurisdiction of the Permanent Court of International Justice, will constantly endeavour to strengthen the legal guarantees desired by the League of Nations and to give that body the universal character which is indispensable to its efficacy. The Government cannot, however, support proposals which would establish an organisation resting on might rather than on right, thus resulting in the creation of political groups on a military basis and, in consequence, in the disruption of the international commonwealth, instead of promoting the ideal of unity and general collaboration, which is one of the fundamental principles of the League of Nations.

(Signed) V. KARNEBEEK.

REPLY FROM THE PORTUGUESE GOVERNMENT.

[*Translation.*]   Lisbon, August 1st, 1924.

The Portuguese Government, having examined the draft Treaty of Mutual Assistance and the documents accompanying your letter of October 25th, 1923, has the honour to inform you:

1. That the Government of the Republic accepts in principle the provisions of the Treaty of Mutual Assistance ;
2. That, nevertheless, it considers the guarantees afforded in case of aggression to be inadequate and the indispensable definition of what constitutes aggression to be insufficiently clear and definite ;
3. That the Portuguese delegation to the fifth Assembly has been instructed by the Government to give its opinion on the details of the Treaty if the latter is again brought up for discussion.

(Signed) V. GARDINE.

REPLY FROM THE CHINESE GOVERNMENT.

[*Translation.*]   Rome, August 2nd, 1924.

I have the honour to inform you that my Government has given careful consideration to the draft Treaty of Mutual Assistance which you submitted to it in your communication of October 25th, 1923 (C.L. 105. 1923. IX), and to the documents accompanying the draft Treaty.

The Chinese Government considers that, taken as a whole, the text of this Treaty may be regarded as acceptable, as the draft is well calculated to promote the aims of those who are working to ensure universal peace and a reduction of armaments.

The Chinese Government wishes to point out, however, that it will continue to adhere to the plan drawn up by its Ministry of War in 1922 for the reduction of the strength of its army from 1,500,000 to 800,000 men. The latter figure may be still further reduced to the absolute minimum compatible with the armaments of the other Powers and the requirements of internal security.

As regards its naval forces, the Chinese Government wishes to repeat once more the reservation it has already put forward on several occasions to the effect that it must take into account the special position of the country. Its existing naval forces are far from sufficient for the defence of its coast line, which exceeds 3,000 nautical miles, and of its rivers ; in the opinion of experts a fleet of at least 500,000 tons would be required, to say nothing of the construction of naval bases and arsenals.

The Chinese Government intends to send you a communication later in regard to its air armaments, in respect of which it also begs to refer you to the letter which I had the honour to send you on July 30th, 1923.

(Signed) Ts. F. TANG.

REPLY FROM THE SPANISH GOVERNMENT.

[Translation.]   Madrid, August 4th, 1924.

The Spanish Government has examined the terms of the draft Treaty with all the attention and care which a document of such world-wide importance merits, and in the drawing-up of which the Government of His Majesty had zealously co-operated. It was, at the same time, important not to lose sight of the special position of Spain, or of the fact that, like all countries, she is obliged to see that her present means of defence are not replaced by means which may be less effective.

. The Spanish Government was accordingly led to consider the close connection between the main points of the scheme, *i.e.* the decision as to when " aggression " has taken place and the application thereafter of effective pressure on the aggressor State. It quickly realised that it was difficult, if not impossible, to define an " act of aggression ", although it is upon this definition that all subsequent action depends. For the purposes of this action, the scheme confers upon the Council powers which are perhaps even more extensive than those it possesses in virtue of the Covenant itself. We may therefore anticipate that, in practice, misgivings may be felt by countries which are not represented on the Council, since they will be compelled to act in accordance with the latter's decisions.

Further, even assuming that aggression is defined by the Council, one is inclined to think, on examination of the terms of the scheme, that the economic or military action which followed would only be carried out slowly by reason of its collective character. In these circumstances, the Government of His Majesty feels that the guarantees afforded by this scheme, however great its merits, may not inspire sufficient confidence to enable a Government conscious of its responsibilities to make a serious reduction in the national armaments.

These considerations should not be taken to indicate that the Government of His Majesty fails to appreciate the eminent desirability of continuing investigations for the purpose of attaining the result desired, by means of an agreement even more universal than the preliminary one which will only bind the present Members of the League of Nations. The Spanish Government realises, however, that it will require long and persevering effort to attain, by means of a general limitation of armaments, a state of mutual confidence which will dispel even the suspicion of action contrary to the free development of the creative energy of mankind. The Spanish Government is likewise persuaded that it is possible to work to this end, to prepsare the way for this universal brotherhood, and to strengthen the Covenant which expressetis ideals, by means of other agreements which would give a contractual form to the idea of compulsory arbitration.

In the opinion of the Government of His Majesty this era of fraternity and concord may be attained by means of a general treaty, and not by partial agreements. Partial agreements, even if they were under the supervision of the League of Nations (assuming that the League could overcome the difficulties involved in such supervision), would — though based on high ideals in so far as they originated from motives of self-defence — soon be vitiated by realities and by the human tendency to partiality for one's own cause, and would consequently deteriorate into an unfortunate survival of a past which we trust will never return.

For these reasons, the Government of His Majesty regrets that it cannot adhere to the draft Treaty of Mutual Assistance communicated in your Note, C.L. 105 of October 25th, 1923. It is of opinion, nevertheless, that the work which has been taken in hand should be zealously pursued and it is prepared to co-operate wholeheartedly in finding a method of quelling at the outset, by means of united action, any threat of armed conflict. Such action would constitute the most effective and valid guarantee for peace.

(Signed) Marquis DE MAGAZ,
Head of the Government ad interim.

REPLY FROM THE GOVERNMENT OF THE KINGDOM OF THE SERBS, CROATS AND SLOVENES.

[Translation.] August 7th, 1924.

The Government of the Kingdom of the Serbs, Croats and Slovenes has given repeated proofs of its earnest desire to ensure the maintenance of peace. It cannot therefore fail to express its wholehearted admiration for the efforts which have been made with a view to diminishing the danger of war, in the future, by a Treaty of Mutual Assistance and by the reduction of armaments. It has consequently examined, with the greatest care, the draft of this Treaty transmitted to it with your letter C.L. 105 of October 25th, 1923.

In the opinion of this Government, a Treaty of Assistance should be general, at least as regards Europe ; further, the measures which it provides should be effective and should guarantee *absolute security* to each signatory State.

The Government is, moreover, of opinion that the general reduction of armaments is *impossible until some practical solution has been found for the problem of assistance.*

Mutual assistance should be absolute and unconditional ; it should be immediately effective both as regards time and the forces employed, and it should be founded on the maintenance of the *status quo*. It should come into action automatically and rapidly as soon as the need for it is felt. Unfortunately, these requirements are not sufficiently met by the draft submitted to the Royal Government.

In cases of aggression, the draft provides for a procedure which, in the opinion of the Royal Government, could, in most cases, only be set in motion and could only produce its final result — *i.e.* the action taken against the aggressor (if any such action follows, for even that is not certain) — slowly and with considerable delay. As any delay would place the aggressor State in a favourable situation as compared with its victim, especially if the latter were a small Power, the effect of intervention would thus be weakened. The State assisted, whose territory would be invaded and laid waste, would have difficulty in repairing the devastation, even if it obtained reparation for the damage caused by the enemy. This has been clearly proved by the example of the *last war*.

In view of the above considerations and without going further into the details of the scheme, the Serb-Croat-Slovene Government feels that it could not entrust its safety to the guarantees provided by the draft.

The Royal Government, looking confidently to the future and earnestly desiring to assist in finding a solution for the difficult question of the reduction and limitation of armaments, which is indissolubly bound up with that of guarantees, will readily continue to co-operate in the work which has thus been begun and the final success of which has undoubtedly been advanced by the results already obtained.

(Signed) Dr. V. MARINKOVITCH,
Minister for Foreign Affairs.

REPLY FROM THE NORWEGIAN GOVERNMENT.

Christiania, August 14th, 1924.
[Translation.]

The Royal Government does not think it necessary for the moment to submit the observations which might be suggested by a detailed consideration of the various provisions of the draft Treaty of Mutual Assistance.

When Norway adhered to the Covenant of the League of Nations, the greatest importance was attached, as appears from my predecessor's letter of July 17th, 1923, to maintaining absolutely intact the right of the country's constitutional authorities to decide for themselves in regard to this country's participation in military operations. This right would become illusory if the draft Treaty were adopted, since, according to Articles 3 and 5 of the draft, it is for the Council of the League to take a formal *decision* regarding the employment of military force. The Norwegian Government is unable to concur in such a proposal. In general, it is opposed to the adoption of treaties of guarantee which so largely increase the obligations imposed upon the Members of the League by the Covenant.

Moreover, as already stated in my predecessor's letter of July 17th, 1923, the Royal Government considers that, in virtue of Article 8 of the Covenant, the Members of the League have already undertaken to reduce their armaments without other guarantees than those provided in the Covenant. The Royal Government is most anxious to promote general disarmament and will do all that lies in its power to bring it about ; but it is of opinion that this result cannot be attained by the conclusion of a general treaty of mutual guarantee supplemented by special defensive agreements. Nor does it think that the guarantee of security which a number of States have found it necessary to demand before materially reducing their armaments can be provided by means of a treaty of military assistance. In its opinion, this security can rather be attained by the consistent pursuance of a peaceful policy on the part of the States themselves and by working for the reduction of armaments in every country, without having recourse to a system of military guarantee. The all-essential consideration is to develop progressively co-operation between nations in support of peace and justice, and to fortify international organisation without assigning to military strength so predominant a place as is given to it in the draft Treaty of guarantee under consideration.

As Resolution XIV of the third Assembly points out, no plan for the reduction of armaments can fully succeed unless it is general : the draft Treaty now submitted to the various Governments stipulates therefore that, subject to certain conditions, every country may adhere thereto. In the opinion of the Royal Government it is probable that a plan of military assistance would result in the formation of groups of Powers and would consequently create a situation which experience has shown to contain the seeds of war. For this reason also, the Royal Government feels unable to give its support to the scheme.

(Signed) J. L. MOWINCKEL.

REPLY FROM THE POLISH GOVERNMENT.

[*Translation.*]   Warsaw, August 16th, 1924.

. . . .

The Polish Government has no desire to criticise this complex document, which is the result of three years' continuous, devoted work in the cause of peace by certain eminent and exceptionally qualified men. On the contrary, the Polish Government is happy to pay tribute to the endeavours made to secure general disarmament by means of the establishment of a system of guarantees for the security of the different countries.

The Government of the Republic considers that a general Treaty of Mutual Assistance should be the most forcible manifestation of that international solidarity which is the very basis of the League of Nations.

Its chief anxiety being to safeguard the territorial integrity and independence of the country, as is the duty of every responsible Government, the Polish Government hastens to give its adhesion to the principle of establishing preliminary guarantees, already recognised as essential in Resolution XIV of the third Assembly.

In the opinion of the Polish Government, the realisation of this principle, which is closely associated with the undertakings entered into in Articles 10 and 16 of the Covenant, which is incorporated in the Treaties of Peace, would constitute a valuable means of defending the political integrity and independence of the various countries.

Thereby it is laid down that any attack upon a country's heritage, which is the most heinous of all international crimes, will involve the operation of a complicated system of mutual assistance, military, economic, financial and political.

The reduction or limitation of national armaments, in conformity with the provisions of Article 8 of the Covenant, can only be made possible by putting into practice a scheme of guarantees facilitating the application of Articles 10 and 16 of the Covenant. By the universal authority which it enjoys, the League of Nations is able to achieve this task, on which the peace of the world depends. The Polish Government, therefore, will always assist in the work of international pacification undertaken by the League.

The Polish Government has given very careful consideration to the draft Treaty forwarded to it. Subject to the observations on points of detail which it will put forward during the discussions of the Assembly, it desires to submit below certain remarks which it considers of particular importance.

I. It is evident that the first decision to be taken by the Council will be whether or not an act of aggression has been committed. The work of the Temporary Mixed Commission and the Commentary drawn up by the Special Committee in co-operation with certain members of the Perma ent Advisory Commission show that, failing an exact definition of the word " aggression ", the chief difficulty which the Council would encounter in the matter would be the impossibility of establishing the fact that an act of aggression had really been committed, of deciding which was the aggressor State and, consequently, of putting the different clauses of the Treaty into effect.

The Polish Government considers, however, that this circumstance cannot be held to be an insurmountable obstacle to the putting into force of a scheme designed to be a decisive contribution to the establishment of a new era in international relations.

In the opinion of the Polish Government, the fact should be recognised beyond all doubt that, quite apart from and independently of the " material signs of the aggressive intention ", which preoccupied the authors of the Commentary, the mere invasion of the territory or viola- tion of the frontier of a neighbouring State constitutes not merely a presumption that an international crime has been committed but a wrongful act, which is a decisive factor in aggression, determining the immediate operation of the provisions for mutual assistance. Further, the task of the Council would be assisted if a detailed list of the measures to be regarded by it as expressive of an aggressive intention were appended to the Treaty. The list, which would be drawn up by a special committee of experts, should take into account improvements in military science and the conditions of modern warfare.

II.   In the view of the Government of the Republic, the ideal of international solidarity, which is the foundation of the Covenant, the new international charter, should inspire every endeavour to create equal conditions of security for all States and so enable the work of disarmament to be undertaken in a practical manner.

It should, however, be stated that the favourable situation in which certain countries are placed as regards their security handicaps the full and complete realisation of the principle of international solidarity in the field of general assistance. It is accordingly the duty of responsible Governments, while duly making allowance for the present state of affairs, to seek for the means of arriving at immediate and effective assistance as provided for in Resolution XIV of the third Assembly.

For the moment these guarantees can only be realised by means of the complementary agreements specified in Article 6 to 8 of the draft, since these agreements are designed to regulate beforehand the assistance which the signatory States would give one another in the event of a specific act of aggression being committed. As they would be disassociated from the schemes for general assistance laid down in the Treaty, the operation of which is subordinate to a system of decisions by the League, and as they would be both carefully drawn up according to pre-arranged plans, which could be immediately put into operation, the complementary agreements constitute the only genuine guarantees capable of realising the reduction of armaments.

III.   .Again, we must take into consideration the fact that the geographical, economic or political situation of certain countries or groups of countries would seem to indicate the necessity of bearing in mind that all the High Contracting Parties might not be required to support to the same extent the burdens of the engagements contained in the provisions of the draft.   In certain cases, for example, effective financial aid might beneficially supple- ment the military assistance suitable to the particular conditions of the countries concerned.

Further, with a view to increasing the practical value of the draft so far as possible in time of war, it would be well to establish and specify beforehand the various means of coercion to be placed at the disposal of the Council.   The list of these means should be kept up to date and regularly communicated to the Members of the League of Nations.

For this purpose every State adhering to the Treaty of Mutual Assistance should be required to declare :

(1)   The extent and kind of assistance which it expects from the Council under the terms of the Treaty, and the assistance which it is able to give to the other High Contracting Parties ;

(2)   The limit to the reduction of its armed forces.

Being thus in possession of the requisite information for regulating without restriction the operation of the various kinds of pressure to be brought to bear on the aggressor State, the Council would also be free to determine the individual rights and obligations of the High Contracting Parties in such conditions as were acceptable to each.

IV.   The application of the principle of international solidarity might, in the view of the Polish Government, be immediately displayed in a general way by the universal reprobation of the act of aggression.   The most suitable means might be the suspension of diplomatic relations with the aggressor by all countries signatories to the Treaty.   If a stipulation of this kind were introduced into the Treaty, it would also be an effective means of completing Article 16 of the Covenant.

V.   The Polish Government considers that the practical value of the Treaty might be enhanced by a stipulation establishing the system of guarantee at the time of the settlement of a dispute.

The only provision in the draft which refers, and that in an indirect manner, to the con- ditions governing the termination of a dispute is Article 1.   Under the terms of this article, even in case of a war which shall not be considered as a war of aggression, no State shall violate the political independence and territorial integrity of any of the High Contracting Parties.   There is, therefore, all the more ground for laying down that, in an aggressive war which, under the authority of the Council, has mobilised the united forces of the High Contracting Powers against the attacking country, the settlement of the dispute and the peace negotiations must be designed to include international guarantees safeguarding the territorial integrity and political independence of the countries attacked.

Accordingly, it is essential that at this all-important moment for the attacked country, the powers and duties of the Council should be at least as decisive and extensive as at the beginning of the dispute or during the procedure regulating the assistance provided for in the Treaty.

VI. Although the Polish Government is far from ignoring the importance of the principle of unanimity which is the basis of the League's procedure, it thinks that the moral authority of the Council, in whose hands the peace of the world would be placed in the event of a threat of war, might be weakened by the strict application of this principle to the procedure contemplated in Articles 3 and 4 of the draft Treaty. The decisions of the Council, when the latter is summoned to organise combined action on the part of the High Contracting Parties against the aggressor, might run the risk of remaining inoperative, if any single High Contracting Party voted in opposition to the others. The Polish Government is of opinion that, in cases where unanimity is impossible to obtain, the Council might take a majority decision.

VII. Under the terms of Article 16 of the draft, States which are not Members of the League shall be entitled to adhere to the Treaty with the consent of two-thirds of the High Contracting Parties with regard to whom the Treaty has come into force. The Polish Government considers it extremely desirable, in view of the character of the Treaty, which is a natural corollary to the Covenant, that States desiring to adhere should first give *effective guarantees* as specified in Article 1, paragraph 2, of the Covenant.

(Signed) SKRZYNSKI,
Minister for Foreign Affairs.

REPLY FROM THE CZECHOSLOVAK GOVERNMENT.

[*Translation.*] ·
Prague, August 17th, 1924.

The Government of the Czechoslovak Republic desires to tender its thanks to the Secretariat of the League of Nations for forwarding to it the various documents regarding the discussion at the fourth Assembly in September 1923 on the question of the Treaty of Mutual Assistance and the limitation and reduction of armaments. The Czechoslovak Government has examined these documents with the closest attention and it desires to pay tribute to the devoted work of all those who have contributed to the collection of the valuable information, the highly important material and the ideas, which must be recognised by all, as springing from the highest and most generous motives.

The Czechoslovak Government, since the establishment of the Republic, has followed with special attention and zeal all matters tending to settle the great question of general disarmament and the question closely connected with it — namely, that of security and the prevention of future wars. Czechoslovakia herself, after having, at the beginning of her independent existence, taken certain military measures and having obtained such armaments as were indispensable for her immediate security, has latterly become somewhat reassured as to the stability of the general situation and has consequently begun to effect progressive reductions in her expenditure on armaments and proposes to continue to do so.

Having thus given practical proof of her conception of the principles and aims of the League of Nations, she attaches the greatest importance to all efforts to assure a more permanent and definite peace. The future of the smaller nations is, in her opinion, guaranteed only by an international system, in which, as a result of obligations freely entered into, all the nations, without thought of national egoism, undertake to offer determined resistance to evil with all the material means at their disposal, even in cases in which their own interests are only affected indirectly or from the moral point of view.

It is the aim of the League of Nations to arrive by progressive stages at such a state of affairs. This goal can probably be reached in various ways; and for the last five years the League of Nations has made every effort to find such ways and to decide which is the most likely to succeed. The Government of the Republic considers it immaterial which method is adopted; it considers it essential, however, that every effort should be made to find a method; that such efforts should be unceasing; that the real object of them should never be lost sight of and that a positive result should be finally attained.

This positive result it desires for two reasons :

(1) It is essential, after the Great War, that the nations should at last enjoy the assurance of a quieter life and the certainty of a lasting peace ;

(2) It is essential that the League of Nations should not meet with any check in this matter. For this question is the very essence of the League, its main object and, in the opinion of the Czechoslovak Government, its justification.

For some years past, the League of Nations has been endeavouring, by means of the efforts of its important organisations, to find a way by which these objects may be attained. One such way was thought at last to have been found in the proposal for a Treaty of Mutual Assistance drawn up by the Third Committee of the fourth Assembly.

The Czechoslovak Republic, to which this question has been submitted for opinion, adheres to its general policy and to its principle of examining, without prejudice or reservation, all proposals embodying the objects of the League and ventures to lay before you its candid and definite views on this matter.

I. The Czechoslovak Government considers the idea of the Treaty of Mutual Assistance capable of achieving what the League of Nations desires to achieve. The Czechoslovak Government is not aware, at the moment, of any other means by which this object can be attained and is doubtful if, indeed, other means exist. After full consideration, therefore, it accepts the idea of the Treaty of Mutual Assistance submitted to it for consideration as a basis for further efforts to bring about general disarmament and the security of nations. It accepts it as a basis, but is at the same time prepared to abandon it directly any plan is presented that is easier of realisation, more effective in result, and less open to objections than this draft Treaty. The Czechoslovak Government itself recognises these objections.

Until it sees a better method, the Czechoslovak Government considers it to be its duty, in view of the obligations entered into in regard to the League of Nations, to make every effort to improve the present proposal, to remove these drawbacks and to endeavour to bring it to a successful issue.

It is in this spirit that the Czechoslovak Government now declares itself a firm supporter of the Treaty of Mutual Assistance, but it would, at the same time, submit certain reservations in regard to various articles of the Treaty.

There is, in the first place, in the opinion of the Czechoslovak Government, a question of principle which should be further considered : in the case of aggression, the Council of the League would have to decide by unanimous vote which party is responsible for the aggression and what measures are to be taken against such party. Without considering the principle underlying this question, including the necessity of respecting the sovereignty of States in matters of such importance, the Czechoslovak Government is in favour, in such cases, of applying the principle of a majority vote pure and simple. It ventures, therefore, to submit reservations in regard to the article in question.

There are other reservations of less importance which it would desire to submit. The question of demilitarised zones appears to a small country in quite a different light from that in which it appears to large States whose territory cannot, therefore, fall easily and at a single blow into the hands of the enemy.

Finally, we have reservations to make in regard to Articles 13 and 18; the point in question is that of the revision of armaments which is permitted to individual States if the conditions of their security should change or deteriorate. Furthermore, it is necessary, from our point of view, to reconsider the question of the assistance which is to be given by other States to a State which is the object of aggression solely in cases where the Council has certified that the State in question has reduced its armaments in accordance with its undertakings. Again, disputes might arise as to whether the State in question had fulfilled its engagements or not ; the Czechoslovak Government reserves the right on this point, as in the case of the other articles referred to, to submit during the coming discussion amendments to the text which, in its opinion, might tend to its general improvement. It intends, moreover, to propose certain amendments to the articles regarding partial defensive treaties.

II. There are certain general observations which inevitably occur to all those who, responsible to their country and to international public opinion, do not wish to treat lightly questions of such importance and are endeavouring to approach the very heart of the proposal submitted to us. From this point of view, the Czechoslovak Government has followed with the closest attention all official and unofficial expressions of opinion in the various countries regarding the question of the Treaty of Mutual Assistance and disarmament.

There is, in the first place, one important and serious objection to the very principle upon which the whole text of the Treaty is based : that is, the interdependence between security and the progressive reduction of armaments. This principle signifies, indeed, that there shall be no reduction of armaments except in proportion to the security furnished to any State attacked by the guarantee of the other States.

The following objection immediately arises : Does not the Covenant in Article 8 simply and unconditionally impose upon all the Members of the League the obligation to proceed to the reduction of armaments ?

The Czechoslovak Government considers that such an interpretation of the Covenant is entirely wrong. It is of opinion that Article 8 must necessarily be supplemented by Articles 10 and 16, that one cannot be applied without the other, and that Articles 10 and 16 express simply and solely the idea of security which, in the draft Treaty in question, is still further accentuated and transferred, so to speak, from the theoretical plane of the Covenant into the practical sphere of the Treaty of Mutual Assistance.

It has been said, and rightly said, that the Treaty of Mutual Assistance is "an extension of the Covenant". I would say, further, it is *the putting into concrete, practical form of the Covenant,* and more especially of Articles 10 and 16. Finally, it appears to me that the idea of interdependence between security and the reduction of armaments is essentially inherent in the Covenant and entirely in keeping with its spirit. The Czechoslovak Government has never interpreted those articles of the Covenant in any other manner.

If, therefore, the Council of the League and the Assembly are endeavouring to put into practice the principles of the Covenant, they can only follow the method indicated by the principles expressed in the Treaty of Mutual Assistance, that is to say, they can only put into force the idea of disarmament, by developing at the same time the principles contained in Articles 10 and 16.

111

The Czechoslovak Government cannot conceal the fact that a certain amount of anxiety has for some time past been apparent in public opinion in its country. Public opinion in Czechoslovakia has not failed to note that for the last two years repeated attempts have been made in the League of Nations to reduce the importance of Article 10, to lessen its significance to the point of rendering it ineffective in the event of any real threat of aggression against a smaller country. I rather fear that these tendencies led to more or less positive results during the Fourth Assembly.

I venture to add that such tendencies appear to me contrary to the spirit of the Covenant and, in such a case, to the Covenant itself ; the League of Nations would thereby lose much of its value and its real moral importance, and the very basis of the League would be jeopardised.

The Czechoslovak Government was therefore delighted to see the opposite tendency developing, the tendency to enhance the importance of the great principle of the Covenant contained in Article 10.

In conclusion, the Government of the Czechoslovak Republic is of opinion that to emphasise the interdependence of two essential principles — security and the reduction of armaments — is not to add a fresh condition to the execution of the Covenant but, on the contrary, to act in the spirit of the Covenant and to give it the true significance which it should always possess.

III. There is a whole series of other objections of principle which appear perhaps still more important. They may be summed up as follows :

The Treaty of Mutual Assistance cannot have the desired result and will be ineffective for the following reasons :

(a) A unanimous decision of the Members of the Council is required to decide which party is the aggressor. In practice, however, it is impossible to believe that in a really serious case unanimity could be obtained.

(b) In case of aggression it is necessary to act promptly ; but the procedure laid down for the Council not only rules out, a priori, any such prompt action, but even precludes the possibility of a prompt agreement as to the military or other measures to be taken, the strategic plan of campaign, etc.

(c) The authors of the Treaty were indeed alive to this difficulty, and they finally adopted, as a complement to the general guarantees of the Treaty, the further special guarantee of the partial defensive Treaties, thus reverting to the old system of alliances, which encourage the formation of rival groups and are contrary to the spirit of the Covenant.

(d) In addition to this ineffectiveness as a practical instrument, and to its reversion to the pre-war system of alliances, the scheme contains a final and serious disadvantage. It weaves a whole web of grave international obligations, without in any way advancing the general cause ; and these obligations are so complex that they seem likely to be a source of fresh difficulties rather than a means of avoiding disputes.

If these criticisms were justified, they would amount to a final condemnation of all schemes for a treaty of mutual assistance. Their arguments may be summed up as follows: You are seeking to create a system of obligations which will not procure the advantages desired and promised, but which will justify the formation of mischievous alliances — admittedly indefensible, from a moral point of view — and will provoke fresh international difficulties.

IV. The acceptance of such criticisms would, however, amount to a blank negation of the whole conception of the League of Nations; and, if they are justified, it would follow that the idea of the League of Nations, as now constituted and as conceived by its authors, is impracticable.

What is the essential basis of any conception of a League of Nations ? Is it not the desire for universal and lasting peace ; is it not the demand that the community of nations should guarantee the independence and freedom of each of its members ; is it not the endeavour to make the brotherhood of nations a reality, and at the same time to offer an effective bar to any violation of public right or justice by using measures of constraint against those who commit such a crime against the law of nations ?

In spite of these criticisms — which in our view are only justified up to a certain point in regard to the present Treaty — the Czechoslovak Government remains firm in its loyalty to the League of Nations ideal. It believes that it would be only a half-way measure to seek the final abolition of war through efforts for the reduction and limitation of armaments — since, in practice, we can never contemplate complete disarmament. For the question at once arises : would it not be possible to begin a war with reduced armaments and reduced supplies of munitions ? Would it not be possible to violate the conventions establishing the demilitarised zones, or the other less important conventions ? Is it not a fact that in the last war some States entered into the struggle almost without armaments, and only took steps to supply their requirements during the course of hostilities ? And how are we going to act, and how is the League of Nations going to act, if such cases arise in future ? Should we not be failing in our duty as Members of the League if we did not foresee such eventualities and prepare to guard against them ?

The fact is that to endeavour to prevent wars by the reduction or limitation of armaments is to mistake the means for the end, thus committing a fundamental error. The employment of the means — even with a large measure of success — in no way implies that the goal has been attained.

The question which I have just raised is one which will always have to be faced by the League of Nations, particularly by the smaller nations which are so much exposed to aggression.

If, in spite of the reduction of armaments and of all these conventions, a State attacks one of its neighbours, notwithstanding its reduced armaments and in violation of its pledged word, what policy are we going to adopt ?

There are certain States whose social and economic structure enables them to increase so rapidly their supplies of the arms and munitions required for the scientific and technical warfare of to-day that their neighbours might be easily and rapidly overwhelmed if they possessed no other form of guarantee.

V.   These are very disturbing questions ; they all lead back to the fundamental question : Do we desire, and is it in our power to prevent, wars ? Is it in our power to guarantee the safety of nations which may be the victims of aggression, and are we prepared to adopt measures of constraint in case of a violation of public right ?

If the answer is *No*, let us say so frankly and not blind ourselves with illusions. Let us expose the naked truth, before the eyes of the whole world, and particularly of certain small nations which are especially concerned about their future. For these nations have both the right and the duty of acquainting themselves with the facts and of shaping their policy accordingly. The world would draw the inevitable though somewhat melancholy conclusion — which, nevertheless, would be much better than uncertainty or the kind of vague hopefulness which at present prevails — that the League of Nations in its full idealistic sense is an impracticable idea, and that it must continue to play — no doubt an important — but still a secondary role as an organisation which may often be usefully employed for subsidiary tasks, but which is incapable of solving the real problems of international relationship, and in particular the most burning problem which now confronts humanity — the problem of permanent and durable peace.

If the answer is *Yes*, let us set to work without hesitation, let us redouble our efforts and strive to eradicate the defects in the schemes to secure the safety, liberty and independence of the peoples.

In the present case we might get rid of some of the difficulties in the way of the draft Treaty of Mutual Assistance by adopting the principle of a majority in place of a unanimous vote for decisions in cases of aggression. This suggestion does not entail any amendment to the Covenant. The Covenant is not involved ; we are simply concerned here with the stipulations of a new treaty to be freely accepted by the High Contracting Parties. The principle of decisions by a majority vote would thus only apply within the ambit of the treaty, and would not necessarily entail any amendments to the Covenant. The results would quickly be evident.

We might also make a bold effort to hasten the procedure by which the Council is to afford assistance. We could arrange for the partial treaties to be operated under the supervision of the League. I am fully alive to the defects of the partial treaties. But these treaties exist, they will continue to exist, and no one has hitherto ventured to maintain that they would be contrary to the spirit of the Covenant, seeing that they must contain a clause to the effect that they can only become operative if compatible with the Covenant.

We are told, as a serious objection, that partial treaties are imperfect and even dangerous instruments. To that I would reply that every human institution has two aspects — its good side and its bad side, and that it may always be diverted to wrong uses. We do not stop using knives because it is easy to cut our fingers with them !

In this case we are concerned with a great idea, the development of which is being watched with anxiety and hope by a large section of mankind. Let us have the courage to recognise that, in order to realise so great an ideal and to attain so great a goal, it is necessary to take risks : we must choose the lesser evil. I prefer to accept the principle of the partial treaties, which certainly involve some difficulties — though it should be easy to surmount them if we grapple with them vigorously — rather than to abandon the idea of a Treaty of Mutual Assistance and so virtually condemn the very ideal of the League of Nations. Even the strictest moralists do not scruple, in their daily lives, to practise the rule of choosing the lesser evil. If all nations had practised this rule in political affairs, we should long ago have entered the era of eternal peace between nations.

VI.   The last argument which the Czechoslovak Government would advance in favour of giving effect to the Treaty of Mutual Assistance is as follows : Why should we not adopt both courses simultaneously ? Why not seek to improve, and carry out, by successive stages, the scheme for security through a treaty of mutual assistance, and at the same time proceed with the necessary steps and measures for the conclusion of special conventions concerning the demilitarised zones, the specially exposed frontiers, the extension of arbitration, etc. ? Neither of these courses excludes the other. On the contrary, they mutually assist and supplement one another, and by thus supplementing one another they will mutually eliminate the objections which are peculiar to each.

To conclude, the Czechoslovak Government believes that the idea of the Treaty of Mutual Assistance is one which cannot be abandoned without the danger of provoking — particularly among the smaller nations — the impression that they can never obtain even comparative safety, and that in the last resort it will always be the force in the hands of the most powerful nations which will decide their rights and destinies. My Government, however, holds that there are other paths by which we may approach the same objective and that the use of these paths does not exclude that of this particular scheme, so that our efforts to attain the desired end by these paths should be continued. The Government of the Republic draws particular attention to the principle of compulsory arbitration, which it endeavours to apply in its own policy, whenever there is an opportunity for doing so.

Confident in its belief in a genuine human idealism — a belief which has inspired the views expressed in this letter — the Government of the Republic is convinced that the combination of methods which it has indicated offers the right, and indeed, the only path, to the solution of the great problem of disarmament and of a universal and durable peace.

(Signed) Dr. EDUARD BENES.

REPLY FROM THE FRENCH GOVERNMENT.

[*Translation.*]

Paris, August 19th, 1924.

The French Government has examined with the closest attention and the fullest sympathy the report of the Third Committee of the fourth Assembly and the draft Treaty of Mutual Assistance, both of which you communicated to it in your letter of October 25th, 1923.

Before expressing any opinion on the text of the Treaty, the French Government desires to confirm the favourable opinion which it expressed on June 15th, 1923, as to the proposals put forward in Resolution XIV of the third Assembly, and at the same time to state more definitely its views on certain points. These are the necessity of establishing, as the third Assembly proposed, an indissoluble connection between the terms *security* and *armaments*, and of making any scheme for the reduction of armaments contingent upon the prior provision of mutual assistance in an immediate and effective form. Accordingly, as, in the opinion of the French Government, no reduction of armaments can be effected unless external support of equivalent value and equal rapidity in operation is forthcoming, any *a priori* scale of reduced armaments calculated on a more or less arbitrary basis must be rejected absolutely.

So far from awaiting the organisation, in the form of a treaty, of mutual assistance on the principles laid down by the third Assembly, the French Government has already — since it regards the Covenant of the League of Nations as constituting in itself a general treaty of mutual assistance affording the most valuable *moral* guarantees — effected the full reduction of armaments, which such guarantees rendered possible for France. This operation has taken the form of a reduction of the period of military service with the colours by 50 per cent, of the number of divisions of the line by 25 per cent, and of naval tonnage by over 50 per cent as compared with 1914. The French Government would emphasise that the reduction of national armaments can only be considered *as a whole* and with close reference to the guarantees of security; the various kinds of armament (land, sea and air) must not be taken separately, since, at least in the case of France, they constitute an *indissoluble* unit.

Further, since the primary condition of any organisation for mutual assistance is mutual confidence in the international obligations assumed by States, it is clear that no State could be admitted to such an organisation unless it had given, in the words of Article 1 of the Covenant of the League of Nations, " effective guarantees of its sincere intention to observe its international obligations ".

In its letter of June 15th, 1923, to which reference has already been made, the French Government suggested a solution, the principle of which was embodied in the draft treaty by the Temporary Mixed Commission and by the Third Committee of the Assembly. This suggestion was that, according to the varying requirements of different countries in the matter of security, two forms of assistance should be combined.

The first would be military, immediate and practically automatic. It would be furnished by defensive agreements designed to meet certain specific possibilities of war, the intention being that the scope of these agreements should subsequently be enlarged by the adhesion of a greater number of countries.

The second form of assistance would be general, progressive in development, and conditional. It would be furnished by a general treaty for the application of Articles 10 and 16 of the Covenant, and under certain conditions the defensive agreements mentioned above would be incorporated in this treaty.

The foregoing is a statement of the position taken up by the French Government with regard to the draft Treaty of Mutual Assistance after the third Assembly had adopted Resolution XIV and before the Treaty had even been drafted.

The French Government, after an exhaustive study of the draft, unreservedly approves the manner in which it combines the two forms of assistance — individual and general — in accordance with its own suggestion made in 1923. It also endorses the fundamental principles embodied in the preamble and in Article 1, namely :

(1) The *object* of the Treaty — a combination of *mutual assistance* (Articles 10 and 16 of the Covenant) with the *reduction or limitation of armaments* (Article 8 of the Covenant).

(2) The *solemn reprobation of aggressive warfare*, which will, it hopes, have the desired result of protecting political independence and territorial integrity — the foundations of peace in the modern world.

The principle of *general* mutual assistance, to be afforded by all countries, is the outcome of the conception of international solidarity. While fully realising the heavy mutual obligations which this principle may require the States to assume, the French Government feels that it is not possible in honour to repudiate obligations once assumed by the act of adhesion to the Covenant. Its own intention, therefore, is to contract, so far as is compatible with the requirements of its own security, such obligations as are alone capable of giving vitality to the principle of international solidarity and of putting it gradually into effect through the practical organisation of mutual assistance between States. It was with this conception before her that France signed the Covenant of the League of Nations, and that in 1923 the French Government endorsed Resolution XIV of the third Assembly.

It must be admitted that, in the event of aggression, the *practical value* of *general* assistance alone would seem likely to be very slight from the military standpoint, for its operation would be problematic, conditional, and gradual ; regarded in this aspect, therefore, this form of assistance would not seem adequate to justify any considerable reduction in armaments.

Nevertheless, by improving general conditions of security, it might in course of time encourage such reductions. It would in any event have an incontestable *moral* value, combined with practical *economic and financial* efficacy. Indeed, any attempt to provide for the progressive organisation of general mutual assistance ought probably to begin with economic and financial assistance, which must not be confused with the economic measures to be taken against aggressors under Article 16 of the Covenant. This economic and financial assistance would be claimed and received from all States as a kind of insurance premium against the spread of the plague of war.

It is not, however, conceivable that any treaty of mutual assistance should afford less effective guarantees than those offered by the Covenant itself. Assistance should therefore be required, from one continent to another, not only in an economic and financial form but also, whenever possible, in the form of naval, air and even military co-operation.

While it concurs in the necessity of organising and developing the system of general assistance provided for in Articles 2 to 5 of the draft Treaty, the French Government is of opinion that immediate steps should be taken to ensure the security of countries which, " for historical, geographical or other reasons ", are "in special danger of attack", as specified in Resolution XIV of the third Assembly. That is indeed the object of the supplementary defensive agreements whose conditions of validity and operative machinery are laid down in Articles 6 to 8. The French Government is of opinion that such agreements will continue to be necessary until the military form of general assistance can be made "immediate and effective ".

In the opinion of the French Government, the criticisms to which these agreements have been subjected were fully answered in the debates at the Third Committee of the fourth Assembly, inasmuch as they clearly showed that it was no longer possible honestly to regard these agreements as similar to the old type of alliance and as being vitiated by the defects ascribed to those alliances. Whereas these alliances were secret and limited, the proposed agreements are to be public, and to be open to subsequent adhesion by other States. The Council is to consider and decide whether they can be incorporated in the general treaty as constituting the most effective instruments for the application of the principle of international solidarity. There is good ground for hoping, therefore, that the Governments would consider it to their advantage to submit such agreements to the Council in order to qualify for the benefits of general assistance, and would accordingly waive their incontestable right to conclude such agreements without reference to the general Treaty of Mutual Assistance or to the Covenant of the League.

While, however, it is essential that these agreements should be subject to certain conditions as a guarantee of their purely defensive character, they must not be deprived of their *raison d'être*, namely, their *efficacy*, which depends entirely upon their coming automatically into effect in certain previously specified cases. The French Government is anxious to make it clear that mutual assistance should not be brought automatically into play in every case of aggression but only in certain flagrant cases *recognised as casus fœderis in advance by the Council* when the defensive agreements were submitted to it. In these specified cases, *and in no others*, the defensive agreement would carry with it the right to general assistance on the one condition that the Council should have acknowledged *the existence of the facts*. In other words, there could be no uncertainty as to the Council's decision if there arose one of the cases of aggression clearly defined in the agreements.

Nevertheless, while approving the draft as a whole as being in principle in conformity with its own policy, the French Government desires to offer comments on certain points of the text submitted to it. The following are the principal points which have engaged its attention :

(1) Though it is difficult to define specifically *all* cases of aggression, it is undoubtedly possible to specify the most flagrant cases, which would in themselves furnish a solid foundation for the provisions of the draft Treaty.

(2) The difficulty which the Council would experience in deciding within four days which party was the aggressor suggests that it might suffice to require such decision to be reached as speedily as possible, *e.g.* within not more than a fortnight.

(3) Failing a unanimous decision on the part of the Council as to which States was the aggressor, provision should be made for a majority vote ; in this event, the High Contracting Parties would retain full freedom to take such action as they thought necessary for the upholding of right and justice. The vote should be open to all representatives, except those of the parties *actually engaged* in hostilities.

(4) There is some danger that the operation of mutual assistance might be paralysed by the rule requiring a unanimous vote of the Council, and it would therefore be better to require only a two-thirds majority.

(5) It would also be desirable to define more clearly the provisions of Article 18, and especially to provide for the case of a State being attacked during the period between the ratification of the Treaty and the approval by the Governments of the scheme for the reduction of armaments. Such a State ought undoubtedly to be entitled to the benefits of mutual assistance during the period in question.

In offering these observations, and in suggesting some of the amendments which it thinks necessary, the French Government has been anxious to show that, while the existing draft cannot be regarded as final, there is no reason for giving up hope of rendering it generally acceptable. The French Government will always be ready to consider any proposal likely to contribute to the satisfactory solution of the problem of security, provided always that the reduction of armaments is to be proportionate to the value of the commensurable guarantees afforded by the scheme adopted, and it maintains its belief that, following the policy of international solidarity set forth in Resolution XIV of the third Assembly, a solution, which will meet that Assembly's unanimous desire, can eventually be reached.

(Signed) HERRIOT.

REPLY FROM THE LITHUANIAN GOVERNMENT

Kovno, August 22nd, 1924.

[*Translation.*]

The Lithuanian Government views with great satisfaction the results so far obtained by the League of Nations in the important question of the reduction and limitation of armaments, and fully accepts the principles on which the draft Treaty of Mutual Assistance is based, since they will, in its view, strengthen international confidence and will afford States a guarantee of security in return for the reduction of their armaments.

The Lithuanian Government feels bound to point out, however, that the guarantees of security offered by the draft Treaty are open to serious criticism, and that the assistance provided for in the draft might not prove sufficient to enable States to reduce their armaments without jeopardising their national security. At the same time, it is the Lithuanian Government's opinion that the draft Treaty of Mutual Assistance marks an important step towards the realisation of the aim set before the Members of the League of Nations by Article 8 of the Covenant.

The Lithuanian Government considers, however, that the draft Treaty, in the form voted by the Third Committee of the fourth Assembly, contains certain serious gaps to which it would venture to call the attention of the League of Nations.

In the Preamble of the draft it is stated that the aim of the Treaty is to establish the general lines of a scheme of Mutual Assistance with a view to facilitate the application of Articles 10 and 16 of the Covenant ; in other words, the Powers adhering to the Treaty would, among other things, undertake to respect one another's territorial integrity. This provision obviously presupposes that frontiers have been regularly established and are recognised by the States concerned. Unfortunately, cases exist where there is no frontier regularly established by treaty or recognised by the States concerned, and where serious controversies on territorial questions have arisen. A striking example of this is the Lithuanian-Polish dispute regarding Vilna, with which the League is only too familiar. The Lithuanian Government could not undertake to come to the assistance of Poland, should the latter be the victim of an act of aggression, unless and until she restores Vilna, the age-long capital of Lithuania, together with the adjacent territory, which Poland now occupies in violation of treaties and of her own international engagements.

Moreover, the Lithuanian Government takes the view that States participating in the Treaty of Mutual Assistance should undertake not to resort to force for the purpose of settling international disputes, and also to accept the compulsory arbitration and obligatory jurisdiction of the Permanent Court of International Justice.

The Lithuanian Government accordingly ventures to propose that the following two provisions should be inserted in the draft Treaty of Mutual Assistance :

(1) The reference, in the Preamble, to Article 10 of the Covenant of the League of Nations shall in no wise prejudge already-existing disputes between States adhering to this Treaty ;

(2) The Contracting Parties undertake to adhere to the optional clause regarding the jurisdiction of the Permanent Court of International Justice.

In view of the special circumstances in which Lithuania is placed, the Lithuanian Government can only adhere to the draft Treaty of Mutual Assistance on condition that the two provisions which it has suggested are adopted.

(Signed) V. CARNECKIS,
Minister for Foreign Affairs.

REPLY FROM THE ITALIAN GOVERNMENT.

[*Translation from the Italian.*]   Rome, August 25th, 1924.

The Royal Government has examined with the closest attention the draft Treaty of Mutual Assistance, drawn up by the Temporary Mixed Commission and amended by the Third Committee of the last Assembly of the League.

In confirmation of the statements in my note dated June 10th, 1923, the Royal Government cannot but regard with satisfaction any proposal which aims, directly or indirectly, at the reduction of armaments ; and accordingly it would welcome the conclusion of a general treaty of mutual guarantee, freely accepted by all nations, if the intention and the practical effect of such treaty contributed to that end.

Resolution XIV of the third Assembly and the draft Treaty now submitted to the Governments for consideration, contemplate that the guarantees of security offered to the different countries to enable them to reduce their armaments might take the form of a general treaty and of partial and regional agreements.

With reference to the conclusion of partial and regional agreements, the Royal Government shares the misgivings which were authoritatively expressed in the course of the preparatory work on the draft. It fears that, so far from furthering, they may jeopardise the operation of the general treaty as a means of securing peace.

As regards the provisions of Article 4 of the draft Treaty, to the effect that, in the event of hostilities, the Council of the League of Nations will determine within four days which of the High Contracting Parties is the victim of aggression and will accordingly set the machinery of the guarantee in motion against the aggressor, the Royal Government feels bound to express the opinion that in most cases it will be extremely difficult, if not impossible, for the Council to decide, within the brief period allowed, which party is the aggressor and which the victim ; for it is not easy to define what either in law or in fact constitutes aggression.

Lastly, the Royal Government considers that, if the great humanitarian object of the Treaty is to be attained, a larger number of adhesions will be necessary than is contemplated in Article 18 of the draft ; this, indeed, should be an essential condition for the operation of the Treaty.

_____

(*Signed*) MUSSOLINI.

REPLY FROM THE ROUMANIAN GOVERNMENT.

[*Translation.*]   Bucarest, August 25th, 1924.

The Roumanian Government has given its careful consideration to the report on the draft Treaty of Mutual Assistance which you transmitted to us in your letter of October 25th, 1923.

Pursuing as she does an eminently peaceful policy, no country would welcome with greater satisfaction than Roumania the attainment of general disarmament, but, in view of her geographical position and of the special dangers to which it exposes her, the Roumanian Government is clearly unable to assume the grave responsibility of reducing the national armaments unless it is offered real and effective guarantees of security.

It is therefore in the light of this vital consideration that we have examined the draft prepared by the Temporary Mixed Commission and amended by the Third Committee.

After most careful consideration we have been obliged to come to the conclusion that the draft is not of a nature to provide us with real and effective guarantees.

If a treaty of mutual guarantee is to be really effective and if it is not to expose the States which disarm to serious danger, it appears to us that it is an essential condition that the treaty should be a general treaty.

As long as there exist, side by side with the countries which disarm, countries which continue to arm, it is impossible for true disarmament to be attained or for serious guarantees to be offered for countries which consent to follow such a policy.

Resolution XIV of the third Assembly bears witness to the truth of this when it says in point I that " No scheme for the reduction of armaments within the meaning of Article 8 of the Covenant can be really successful unless it is general ".

Not only, however, does the present situation preclude the plan from having a really general character, but the procedure which has been adopted renders it possible for certain Members of the League of Nations to evade their most important obligations.

For this reason Article 17, which provides for the possibility of conditional or partial adhesion, appears to us particularly liable to deprive the pact of mutual guarantee of its real efficacy.

Again, we consider that it would, if necessary, be possible to accept even a scheme which was not definitely general in character if mutual assistance in case of aggression were so organised as to ensure the maximum aid and security to countries against which an act of aggression was committed.

Unfortunately, the draft does not seem to us to provide the requisite guarantees even from this point of view.

1. It does not define the facts which constitute aggression. It leaves the decision of this vital point to the Council.

2. It fails to provide for sufficiently rapid action in case of aggression, as it does not state the time limits within which the necessary decisions must be taken. The seriousness of this omission, from the point of view of the State threatened, is obvious.

3. It does not provide for adequate assistance in case of aggression, as the determination of the military contingents is left to the discretion of the Council, which may even confine itself to taking merely economic measures.

4. It attempts to combine and to dovetail into each other a number of over-complicated and over-intricate systems of mutual guarantees, whereas the first requisites of the situation are simplicity and speed.

5. As regards the period during which disarmament is to be carried out, there is no clause definitely stating whether a country which is actually reducing its army can rely on the assistance of the other signatory States in the event of aggression.

6. Lastly, Article 19 lays down that denunciation by one of the great Powers permanently represented on the Council renders the Treaty invalid, thus simultaneously depriving the signatory States which have reduced their armies of every guarantee. This is, in our opinion, quite inadmissible.

In these circumstances, the Roumanian Government considers that the present draft does not offer adequate guarantees to ensure the success of a policy of general disarmament.

If the League of Nations, whose praiseworthy efforts to ensure the establishment of world peace we warmly appreciate, succeeds in discovering a system which obviates the drawbacks mentioned above and provides more effective guarantees for the security of countries which agree to disarm, the Roumanian Government will be glad to give its support.

Having achieved her national unity, Roumania needs to devote all her resources to the work of consolidation and progress incumbent upon her, and is therefore most anxious to relieve her budget of the military burdens imposed by the present general situation.

(Signed) J. G. Duca,
Minister of Foreign Affairs.

REPLY FROM THE SWEDISH GOVERNMENT.

[*Translation.*]   Stockholm, August 25th, 1924.

. . . .

The object of the present draft Treaty is to facilitate the carrying-out of an international reduction of armaments which, according to Article 8 of the Covenant, is one of the duties of the League of Nations.

The Royal Government considers it of capital importance that the League of Nations should take, as soon as possible, effective steps to carry out this important duty. If all the States, whose attitude in this matter might in any way concern Sweden agreed to reduce their armaments simultaneously, the Swedish Government would also be prepared to adhere to an agreement upon equitable terms.

The authors, in working out this draft Treaty, hoped no doubt that by so doing, they would be taking the first step towards the reduction of armaments. It is, however, extremely doubtful whether the desired result can be attained by a Treaty of this kind. This Treaty does not provide for any binding undertaking by the signatory Powers to reduce their armaments, but only a promise on the part of each Power to bring about, as far as that Power considers possible, a reduction or limitation of its armaments and to co-operate with the other signatory Powers in a general plan for the reduction of armaments. Even these restricted engagements would be dependent on the carrying-out of the system of guarantees provided for in the Treaty. It is, therefore, probable that the whole question of disarmament would be postponed until the Treaty had been accepted. The Royal Government has serious doubts as to the advisability of thus combining the two questions, especially since past experience had clearly revealed the difficulties that would have to be overcome in order to make the Treaty acceptable to the majority of States.

The principal idea underlying the Treaty is that the contracting parties should undertake to give assistance to any party who is a victim of a war of aggression on condition that the State attacked has conformed to the terms of the Treaty in the clauses relating to the reduction of armaments.

The Royal Government wishes, in the first place, to stress the fact that the nature of the engagement in question has given rise to certain differences of interpretation on an essential point. By the terms of Article 2 of the Treaty, such an engagement should only be carried out " in accordance with the provisions of the present Treaty " ; one of these provisions, however, is contained in the last paragraph of Article 5, which lays down that a decision regarding the military assistance to be furnished to the State attacked can only be valid if such decision has been taken unanimously by the Members of the Council of the League of Nations, including the State whose assistance has been called for.

A recognised authority on the subject has pointed out, in reference to the provisions of Articles 2 and 5 mentioned above, that any State has the right to decide for itself whether or not, in any case that arises, it will furnish military assistance to the State which is the victim of an aggression, and that the Treaty in this respect only involves a moral obligation. If this interpretation is correct and it is therefore possible for a State to refuse to adhere to a decision of the Council concerning the measures for assistance without such a refusal neing considered a breach of the Treaty, there is no doubt that the value of the Treaty is begligible as a guarantee. We cannot therefore see that the acceptance of the Treaty would remove the hesitation shown by certain States in the matter of the reduction of their armaments.

The Royal Government, however, has grounds for putting another interpretation on the Treaty. The Government is of the opinion that the draft Treaty really implies, for the contracting parties, a strictly obligatory engagement to furnish military assistance to one another, leaving the State whose assistance is asked for free, of course, to form an opinion at the meeting of the Council, whether aggression has been committed or not. If this interpretation is admitted, the Treaty must call forth serious objections on the part of the Swedish Government.

According to the Government's statement in the letter which it had the honour to address to you on June 1st, 1923, on the subject of the draft Treaty then submitted, the Government and the Rikstag had, in the course of the discussions preceding the entry of Sweden into the League of Nations, carefully examined the extent of the obligations which this country's entry into the League would involve. They had considered the fact to be of special importance that their adhesion to the League did not involve the obligation for Sweden to renounce the right of herself considering the question of her possible participation in any military sanctions taken by virtue of Article 16 of the Covenant. There is no reason to believe that public opinion in Sweden has changed on this subject. There are still less grounds for believing that the Rikstag would be disposed to assume the obligation of furnishing military assistance to an extent beyond that provided for in the above-mentioned article.

Such, however, would be the consequence of the draft. Whereas the sanctions, whether economic or military, stipulated in the Covenant would only be applicable in the case of sudden aggression — a method of action which, under Article 13 of the Covenant, all Members of the League of Nations have declared themselves prepared to abandon unconditionally — the Powers signatory to the Treaty would, under the terms of the draft, be obliged in addition to take part in military operations in the event of a State resorting to war merely on the failure of the conciliation procedure provided for under Article 15 of the Covenant to result in a unanimous recommendation by the Council. Even should a State resort to war in pursuance of a decision by the Permanent Court of International Justice or an arbitral tribunal or, finally, on a unanimous recommendation by the Council under Article 15 of the Covenant, a war of this nature might, in certain circumstances, call for military measures on the part of the signatory Powers. The latter would, under Article 1 of the draft, be obliged to intervene if there were ground for supposing that the aggressor intended to violate the political independence or the territorial integrity of another State.

Further, the Royal Government considers that the extension of the system of sanctions contained in the Covenant is inacceptable, since it is not accompanied by a corresponding extension of the rules contained in the Covenant for the solution of international disputes. If it is desired to apply military sanctions in a general manner to a State which embarks upon a war of aggression, specific stipulations must be made that all disputes which cannot be settled in a friendly manner should be submitted to the decision of a tribunal or other international authority, which would of course be a great step forward, but one for which the majority of States is not yet ripe.

If, again, the draft is examined from the point of view of the security against attacks, which acceptance of the draft is to secure for the signatory Powers, it is impossible not to express certain doubts concerning the efficacy of the guarantees contained in it. Even if the only guarantee under consideration in the present case were the less extensive guarantee mentioned in Article 16 of the Covenant — which obliged the Members of the League automatically to apply the economic blockade to the aggressor State — we cannot be sure that we could invariably rely on the assistance of all States without exception, which is a necessary condition for the effective working of the system. We could even less certainly rely on the execution by all countries, at the proper moment, of the military undertakings stipulated in the Treaty. The Treaty can only become operative if the Council unanimously decides which of the opposing States is the aggressor and unanimously take certain decisions regarding the assistance to be furnished. The organisation of the Council, however, does not fit it for this kind of work. The Council is a political organisation consisting of persons who act under the instructions of their Governments. We cannot help feeling that the decisions taken by a body of this character might sometimes be influenced by political considerations.

If a single Member of the Council voted upon considerations other than those of justice and truth, the whole system of guarantees would break down. Again, the task incumbent upon the Council under the draft of deciding within four days by whom the act of aggression had been committed appears extremely difficult and even impracticable, particularly since the Treaty, as worded, contains no directions for the Council in cases in which it may be calley upon to define the term, " war of aggression ". The extremely interesting commentard on the definition of the case of aggression drawn up by the Temporary Mixed Commission and annexed to the draft gives an idea of the difficulties with which the Council will be confronted in this matter.

It is very natural, in view of the purely relative efficacy of the proposed system, that the general Treaty should contain a stipulation suggesting that the signatory States should separately conclude, either as between two of them or as between a larger number, complementary defensive agreements and should determine in them the nature and extent of the assistance which they would undertake to furnish one another. Agreements of this nature are already in existence and are not incompatible with the Covenant. If, however, the view of the Royal Government is accepted that separate agreements of this kind tend to the formation of mutually hostile groups of Powers and consequently to involve certain dangers to Peace, the agreements proposed under the Treaty cannot be contemplated without certain misgivings. The stipulations under which a certain measure of control is conferred upon the Council as regards these agreements are not, in the opinion of the Royal Government, sufficient to remove the disadvantages inherent in the system.

The Royal Government has not yet dealt with Article 17 of the Treaty, which provides for the possibility, subject to the Council's consent, of conditional or partial adhesion to the stipulations of the Treaty. There is no exact definition of the scope of this stipulation, a fact which may also be inferred from the proceedings of the Third Committee of the 1923 Assembly. Obviously, from the Swedish point of view, partial adhesion, under which the country would be free from certain obligations stipulated in the Treaty, would meet with fewer objections than unconditional adhesion. As the Treaty does not mention the advantages to be gained by partial adhesion, it would appear that it is for the Council to take a decision in the matter should occasion arise. We could only, however, expect advantages which would counterbalance the obligations assumed. If these obligations did not include military participation, there would accordingly be no compensation at all.

In view of the considerations set forth above, the Royal Government is of opinion :

That acceptance of the draft does not offer States which sign the Treaty any advantages which would counterbalance the risks inherent in adhesion ;

That, under these circumstances, there is no prospect of the Treaty obtaining general acceptance ; and

That in consequence it is not desirable to make the realisation of disarmament as specified in Article 8 of the Covenant depend upon the acceptance of the Treaty.

The Royal Government, therefore, much regrets to inform you that it does not consider that Sweden should adhere to a treaty of this nature.

(Signed) E. Marks de Wurtemberg.

REPLY FROM THE GOVERNMENT OF URUGUAY.

Montevideo, August 7th, 1924.

The Uruguayan Government has given careful consideration to the draft Treaty of Mutual Assistance adopted by the Third Committee of the fourth Assembly, concerning which this Government has been asked by the President of the Council, in his note C. L. 48. 1924. IX, of April 11th last, to give an opinion.

In general, the Uruguayan Government considers that the Committee's conclusions are in accordance with the spirit of the Covenant and with the high ideals of the League of Nations. It ventures, however, to make a few observations, which it hopes will be taken into consideration when the treaty comes up for discussion.

Uruguay, like almost all South American countries, is in a very peculiar position as regards the putting into operation of the machinery of mutual guarantee set up under the draft Treaty.

It is only natural that, in the draft Treaty, account should have been taken mainly of the geographical, economic and military situation in Europe, because, in the first place, the dangers and possibilities of conflict on that continent are more immediate, and also because (as the question has been dealt with in a European atmosphere) the special circumstances to which the situation in Europe daily, and almost hourly, gives rise have necessarily been taken into account.

The assistance which Members of the League would, in accordance with the instructions of the Council, be called upon to furnish to a State when it is attacked may be very easy and expeditious in Europe, where means of communication have the advantage of being very rapid, where it can be known almost immediately what country will go to the assistance of another, and where such co-operation can be given without any appreciable delay.

The position of the Members of the League in this part of the world is very different. Communications with countries in other continents, are slow and at times difficult ; it may therefore happen that measures for cooperation and effective assistance can only be carried out when the situation has become virtually irretrievable.

Within the continent itself, or even in each district of the continent, the position is no better. Uruguay, for instance, owing to the difficulty of communications, is further from the northern countries of South America than from all, or nearly all, the countries of Europe.

If, in accordance with the terms of paragraph *b* of Article 5, mutual guarantee is limited, as regards participation in military, naval and air operations, to the countries belonging to the continent where the conflict, or danger of conflict, arises, a threatened country situated at one end of the American continent may be said, at least in certain circumstances, to be left completely unprotected. Such a country therefore would have to assume all the obligations imposed upon it by the draft Treaty and would be obliged to furnish such military assistance as the Council required in accordance with the terms of the Treaty, without being in a position itself to receive the co-operation and military assistance for which provision is made.

The situation would be even less satisfactory if the continental divisions fixed by Article 18 for the whole of America are taken to mean that American countries are to be grouped into three divisions for the purposes of the Treaty, for in that case no State of Northern or Central America would be obliged to come to the assistance of any South American State requiring military assistance. Article 18, to which we refer, differs fundamentally from Article 25 of the draft formerly submitted by Lord Robert Cecil, because the latter treated the whole of the American continent as a single unit for the purposes of the treaty whereas the text now submitted for consideration to the various Governments provides for three continental divisions, as mentioned above.

The Uruguayan Government recognises that the sole object of this continental grouping is to facilitate the observance of such text as may finally be adopted, with a view to ensuring earlier ratification by the countries concerned. This Government, however, feels or at least fears, that in practice the arrangements suggested in the present draft may be taken to mean — by an extension of the principle that co-operation is limited to continental divisions — that the grouping adopted for ratification will, in short, be the grouping which shall govern the execution of the military obligations imposed by the treaty.

The Uruguayan Government expects that in the course of the discussions to which the draft text will give rise, amendments will be proposed which will meet these objections. In addition the Uruguayan delegates will undoubtedly avail themselves of such opportunity to present a full and thorough explanation of them, and any other proposals which may be made, when the Assembly comes to consider the problem.

(Signed) Alvaro SARALEGUI.

REPLY FROM THE GREEK GOVERNMENT.

[*Translation.*]   Athens, August 12th, 1924.

I. The object of the draft under consideration is to enforce the observance of signed treaties and, by the promise of mutual assistance between nations, to render possible a reduction of armaments.

II. This latter point, which is the crux of the whole question, has been taken into serious consideration by the Greek Government which, on its own initiative, has found it possible to take certain measures which testify to its desire to reduce its military forces to a minimum.

Greece has accordingly :

(a) Reduced the period of military service from 24 months to 18 months,

(b) Reduced her ordinary military expenditure by diminishing the sums appropriated for this purpose in her Budget.

(c) Although the population of Greece has increased by a quarter since 1913, while 200 square kilometres have been added to her territory, Greece has reduced the number of her Army Corps from 5 to 4 and that of her Divisions from 15 to 12.

These measures sufficiently demonstrate Greece's willingness to restrict her armaments and her sincere desire to contribute, to the peaceful solution of disputes.

III. The Greek Government is therefore in favour of the conclusion of a Treaty of Mutual Assistance which would provide the basis of a general agreement leading to the limitation of armaments while guaranteeing the security of the signatory States.

The Greek Government does not consider, however, that the draft in itself provides sufficient guarantees of peace or that it is likely to bring about the reduction of armaments.

Indeed, a Treaty of Mutual Assistance, owing to its general character and the large number of eventualities for which the Contracting States would have to be prepared, would oblige them to keep considerable military resources at their immediate disposal, and the final result would be an increase rather than a reduction in military expenditure.

IV. The Greek Government also fears that a general treaty would be ineffective.
The Treaty could only be put into operation with the consent of all the signatory States; this would necessarily be a somewhat slow process; and even after this consent had been obtained it would be necessary to discuss the military measures to be taken, the composition of the contingents, the organisation of the higher command and the plan of campaign. Discussion of all these points would take too much time for the security of the countries attacked not to be jeopardised, and we fear that in many cases the Council would find itself faced with accomplished facts before a decision had been reached.

V. In these circumstances the Greek Government considers that the measure which has most to recommend it from the practical point of view is the conclusion of complementary agreements (Article 6 of the draft).

Such agreements would obviate the delays and imperfections of a general pact, and as every country would know exactly what eventualities it might be called upon to face and would share the risks and responsiblities with certain other States, it would know exactly how far it could reduce its armaments.

VI. However, we consider two conditions to be absolutely essential if these separate treaties are to retain their defensive character and are not to become pacts of aggression:

(1) The text of the complementary treaties must immediately be registered with the League of Nations.

(2) The exclusive purpose of the contracting parties must be to ensure the observance of signed treaties.

The Greek Government is prepared to give its consideration to agreements of this nature which in its opinion would be particularly effective.

(Signed) Roussos,
Minister of Foreign Affairs.

Letter from the Greek Government.

[*Translation.*]   Athens, August 12th, 1924.

In communicating to the Secretariat of the League of Nations its reply regarding the draft Treaty of Mutual of Assistance, the Greek Government desires to point out that, quite apart from the general considerations set forth in this reply, Greece finds herself in a very special position.

Her territorial status and nearly all the vital questions affecting her national life are governed by the Treaties of Neuilly and Lausanne.

(a) As regards the Treaty of Neuilly, however, Bulgaria has consistently violated its military clauses for the last three years and;

(b) The Treaty of Lausanne imposes on Turkey no restrictions in regard to her military and naval forces.

In order to provide for her security, Greece is therefore obliged to take military measures which she would have been glad to be able to reduce if she had been placed in more favourable circumstances.

(Signed) Roussos,
Minister of Foreign Affairs.

REPLY FROM THE BULGARIAN DELEGATION.

[*Translation.*[Geneva, September 5th, 1924.

It is with considerable surprise that I have noted the letter of the Greek Government dated August 12th, 1924, and published by the Secretariat of the League of Nations in document A. 35. 1924. IX. of September 1st, 1924.

Contrary to the statement contained in that letter, I have the honour to declare that Bulgaria has loyally and fully carried out all the military clauses of the Treaty of Neuilly, which has indeed been duly recorded on several occasions by the Inter-Allied Commissions established for this purpose.

I should be very glad if you would kindly give this letter the same publicity that the Secretariat has given to the letter of the Greek Government.

(Signed) Ch. Kalfoff,
Minister for Foreign Affairs,
First Delegate of Bulgaria.

REPLY FROM THE SIAMESE GOVERNMENT

Geneva, September 22nd, 1924.

On the instructions of His Excellency the Minister for Foreign Affairs, I have the honour to acknowledge the receipt of your communications to him of October 23rd, 1922; March 9th, May 9th, October 25th, 1923, and April 11th, 1924, with reference to the proposed Treaty of Mutual Assistance and to express the views of His Majesty's Government on this subject as follows:

His Majesty's Government would heartily welcome any practical scheme making possible a general and universal limitation of armaments. It is also of opinion that, before armaments can practically be limited, some effective guarantee of protection is necessary. But the question is : How can this guarantee of protection be made effectual ? His Majesty's Government is not yet satisfied with the present draft of the Treaty of Mutual Assistance, which is largely framed for conditions in Europe and fails to satisfy the situation in Asia, the difficulty of which lies in the fact that Asia is largely composed of : (1) a group of unhomogeneous States, where unsettled conditions make the problem difficult ; and (2) of territories held by European Powers.

Supposing that a European colony were the aggressor, it would not be improbable that the attack would be made with European land and naval forces drawn from the mother-country. To guarantee sufficient protection, therefore, to make possible a reduction of armaments, the proposed Treaty must provide for rendering by one mother-country of European assistance in the case of aggression with European forces by the colony of another mother-country. This the Treaty as drafted apparently fails to do, as Article 18 provides for its coming into force separately in different continents.

Apart from the shortcomings of the proposed draft Treaty, the present draft, from the Asiatic view-point, is open to other serious objections. It leaves open too large room for argument in the determination of whether or not a given war is aggressive ; protection to be adequate must be based upon promises which are precise and leave no loopholes for argument and evasions. His Majesty's Government is impressed with the observations and remarks concerning Articles 1 and 2 by the Committee of Jurists, yet their solution does not altogether give satisfaction. Under their proposal, protection would be afforded in disputes referred to the Council of the League only in the case when the Council makes a unanimous report. If unanimity is not reached, apparently even an aggresive war, so long as Article 10 is not violated, is not forbidden by the Covenant.

If a treaty or regional agreement can be drafted which will give Siam practical and effective protection, His Majesty's Government would be glad to sign it. But the peculiarity of Siam's geographical situation and the absence of no through international railway communications between non-contiguous Asiatic countries make the question of limitation of armaments problematical. Until adequate security is given, Siam cannot sign away her right to maintain an army sufficient for her protection. His Majesty's Government strongly favours compulsory arbitration, whether this is accompanied by disarmament or not. It also strongly favours disarmament provided that this is accompanied by adequate security.

His Majesty's Government is eager to find a solution of the difficulty involved and to find some form of treaty of mutual assistance or of compulsory arbitration which will adequately give security and will do all in its power to co-operate in finding some solution. His Majesty's Government would heartily welcome an arbitration treaty signed by all nations. If this proves impossible His Majesty's Government would suggest, as a possible solution of the Asiatic situation, a joint treaty of compulsory arbitration signed by Asiatic States together with those European States having colonies in Asia.

I will be grateful if you will be good enough as to bring the above views of His Majesty's Government to the notice of the Third Committee of the Fifth Assembly.

(Signed) CHAROON,
Siamese Representative to the League of Nations.

REPLY FROM THE JAPANESE GOVERNMENT.

[*Translation.*[Geneva, September, 3rd, 1924.

The Japanese Government fully appreciates the spirit which animates the draft Treaty of Mutual Assistance. It accepts the fundamental principle that security and disarmament are interdependent. Accordingly, it has examined in the most sympathetic spirit the draft Treaty in the light of the present situation in Japan and in the world as a whole. It ventures, however, to submit a few remarks on the measures proposed.

It considers that the provisions of Article 4 form the basis for putting in motion the machinery of mutual assistance and that they are the fundamental conditions on which the possibility of attaining our common end, the reduction of armaments, depends. It is of opinion, however, that it will be difficult in practice for the Council to give a precise definition of aggression and to decide within so short a period which is the aggressor State.

It also considers that the arguments against supplementary agreements are not entirely devoid of foundation since such agreements might easily lead to the formation of opposing groups even among the Members of the League of Nations and might thus produce a result entirely different from that which we are endeavouring to secure.

(Signed) Y. SUGIMURA,
Assistant Director of the Japanese
League of Nations Bureau.

Annex 4.

DRAFT TREATY OF DISARMAMENT AND SECURITY PREPARED BY AN AMERICAN GROUP

DECLARATION OUTLAWING AGGRESSIVE WAR.

Chapter I. — Outlawry of Aggressive War.

Article 1. — The High Contracting Parties solemnly declare that aggressive war is an international crime. They severally undertake not to be guilty of its commission.

Article 2. — A State engaging in war for other than purposes of defence commits the international crime described in Article 1.

Article 3. — The Permanent Court of International Justice shall have jurisdiction, on the complaint of any Signatory, to make a judgment to the effect that the international crime described in Article 1 has or has not in any given case been committed.

Chapter II. — Acts of Aggression.

Article 4. The High Contracting Parties solemnly declare that acts of aggression, even when not amounting to a state of war, and preparations for such acts of aggression, are hereafter to be deemed forbidden by international law.

Article 5. In the absence of a state of war, measures of force by land, by sea or in the air taken by one State against another and not taken for the purpose of defence against aggression or for the protection of human life shall be deemed to be acts of aggression.

General or partial mobilisation may be deemed to be preparation for an act of aggression.

Any Signatory which claims that another Signatory has violated any of the terms of this Declaration shall submit its case to the Permanent Court of International Justice.

A Signatory refusing to accept the jurisdiction of the Court in any such case shall be deemed an aggressor within the terms of this Declaration.

Failure to accept the jurisdiction of the Court within four days after notification of submission of a claim of violation of this Declaration shall be deemed a refusal to accept the jurisdiction.

Article 6. The Court shall also have jurisdiction on the complaint of any Signatory to make a judgment to the effect that there has or has not in any given case been committed a violation of international law within the terms of Article 4.

Article 7. The Court shall, in any case, have the power to indicate, if it considers that circumstances so require, any provisional measures which ought to be taken to reserve the respective rights of either party.

Pending the final decision, notice of the measures suggested shall forthwith be given to the parties.

Chapter III. — Sanctions.

Article 8. In the event of any High Contracting Party having been adjudged an aggressor pursuant to this Declaration, all commercial, trade, financial and property interests of the aggressor shall cease to be entitled, either in the territory of the other signatories or on the high seas, to any privileges, protection, rights or immunities accorded by either international law, national law or treaty.

Any High Contracting Party may in such case take such steps toward the severance of trade, financial, commercial and personal intercourse with the aggressor and its nationals as it may deem proper, and the High Contracting Parties may also consult together in this regard.

The period during which any such economic sanction may be continued shall be fixed at any time by the Court at the request of any Signatory.

In the matter of measures of force to be taken, each Signatory shall consult its own interests and obligations.

Article 9. If any High Contracting Parties shall be adjudged an aggressor by the Permanent Court of International Justice, such Power shall be liable for all damage to all other High Contracting Parties resulting from its aggression.

Chapter IV. — Decrees of the Permanent Court.

Article 10. The High Contracting Parties agree to accept the judgment of the Permanent Court of International Justice as to the fulfilment or violation of the contracts of this Declaration.

Any question arising under this Declaration is *ipso facto* within the jurisdiction of the Court.

Article 11. If a dispute arising under this Declaration shall be submitted to the Permanent Court of International Justice, it is for the Court to decide as to its jurisdiction and also whether or not its degree has been complied with.

Article 12. The High Contracting Parties, recognising that excessive armaments constitute a menace of war, agree to participate in the Permanent Advisory Conference on Disarmament decided upon by the Fifth Assembly of the League of Nations.

Article 13. The present Declaration shall be ratified. The ratifications shall be deposited as soon as possible with the Secretary-General of the League of Nations.

Any Signatory to this Declaration desiring to withdraw therefrom may give notice thereof to the Secretary-General of the League of Nations. Such notice shall take effect one year from the date of deposit thereof and only as to the Signatory so withdrawing.

Notice of each ratification and of each withdrawal shall be communicated by the Secretary-General of the League of Nations to each Signatory hereto.

RESOLUTION CONCERNING THE DECLARATION OUTLAWING AGGRESSIVE WAR.

1. The Assembly unanimously declares its approval of the Declaration Outlawing Aggressive War which was prepared by the Third Committee of the Assembly and submitted to the Assembly for its approval.

2. The said Declaration shall be submitted within the shortest possible time to the Members of the League of Nations for adoption in the form of a protocol duly ratified and declaring their recognition of this Declaration. It shall be the duty of the Council to submit the Declaration to the Members

The said protocol shall likewise remain open for signature by States not Members of the League of Nations.

3. As soon as this protocol has been ratified by the majority of the Members of the League the said Declaration shall go into force.

DISARMAMENT RESOLUTION "A"

1. The Assembly, having considered the Report of the Temporary Mixed Commission and having also considered the replies of the various Governments commenting on the proposed Treaty of Mutual Assistance, reaffirms the principles set forth in Resolution XIV of the Third Assembly.

2. Furthermore, the Assembly is of the opinion that all the Nations of the world, whether or not Members of the League of Nations, should agree:

(a) to limit or reduce their armaments to the basis necessary for the maintenance of peace and national security;

(b) to study the ways and means for future reduction of armaments either as between all Nations or as between any two of them.

3. The Assembly is further of the opinion that reciprocal agreements between two or more neighbouring countries for the establishment of demilitarised zones would facilitate the security necessary to progressive disarmament.

4. In order to facilitate the reduction and limitation of armaments, the Assembly requests the Council to call a Permanent Advisory Conference upon disarmament which shall meet periodically at intervals of not less than once every three years.

Invitations to participate in this Permanent Conference shall be sent to all Nations whether Members of the League or not.

The said Conference should from time to time consider the further codifying of the principles of international law, particularly in relation to acts of aggression and preparations for such acts.

In this regard the Conference should take into account matters upon the security of the Powers represented and the steps taken toward disarmament.

The recommendations of the Conference shall be submitted to the Powers for their adoption, and shall also be transmitted to the Permanent Court of International Justice.

The said Conference should publish periodical reports concerning the actual conditions of the armaments of the Powers.

The said Conference should advise the Powers concerning measures to be taken to ensure the carrying-out of the principles of the present Resolution, and it may prepare draft treaties for the establishment of demilitarised zones and for the further promotion of disarmament and peace.

5. The said Conference should appoint a Permanent Technical Committee.

6. The said Conference or its Permanent Technical Committee should give advice on technical questions to the Permanent Court of International Justice at the request of said Court.

7. The expenses of the said Conference and of its agencies should be borne by the Powers in the proportions of their respective budgets for defence.

DISARMAMENT RESOLUTION "B"

1. Considering that, by the terms of Article 8 of the Covenant of the League of Nations:

"The Members of the League undertake to interchange full and frank information as to the scale of their armaments, their military, naval and air programmes and the condition of such of their industries as are adaptable to warlike purposes",

the Assembly, in order to facilitate the carrying out of the said engagement, requests the Council to set up a Commission charged with the duty of making the necessary official examinations and reports.

2. The said Commission shall proceed under such regulations as the Council and the Assembly shall from time to time approve.

3. Subject to such regulations, the members of the Commission shall be entitled, when they deem it desirable, to proceed to any point within the territory of any Member of the League or to send sub-commissions or to authorise one or more of their members so to proceed on behalf of the Commission.

4. The Members of the League will give all necessary facilities to the said Commission in the performance of its duties.

5. All reports made by the said Commission shall be communicated to the Members of the League.

DISARMAMENT RESOLUTION "C".

The Assembly, taking account of the provisions of the Declaration Outlawing Aggressive War, is of opinion that:

1. Powers which have ratified the said Declaration may, subject to the following provisions, conclude, either as between two of them or as between a larger number, agreements complementary to the said Declaration, exclusively for the purpose of their mutual defence and intended solely to facilitate the carrying-out of the measures prescribed in said Declaration, determining in advance the assistance which they would give to each other in the event of any act of aggression.

Such agreements may, if the High Contracting Parties interested so desire, be negotiated and concluded under the auspices of the Council.

2. Complementary agreements as defined in the preceding paragraph shall, before being registered, be examined by the Council with a view to deciding whether they are in accordance with the principles of said Declaration and of the Covenant.

In particular, the Council shall consider if the cases of aggression contemplated in those agreements are of a nature to give rise to an obligation to give assistance on the part of the other High Contracting Parties.

The Council may, if necessary, suggest changes in the texts of the agreements submitted to it.

When recognised, the agreements shall be registered in conformity with Article 18 of the Covenant. They shall be regarded as complementary to the said Declaration and shall in no way limit the general obligations of the High Contracting Parties nor the sanctions contemplated against an aggressor under the terms of the said Declaration.

They will be open to any other High Contracting Party to said Declaration with the consent of the Signatory States.

3. In all cases of aggression, for which provision is made in the agreement constituting a defensive group, the High Contracting Parties which are members of such group may undertake to put into operation automatically the plan of assistance agreed upon between them; and in all other cases of aggression or menace or danger of aggression directly aimed at them, they will consult each other before taking action, and will inform the Council of the measures which they are contemplating.

4. The Council, taking into account the reports and opinions of the Commission set up under Resolution B of this Assembly, shall, at any time when requested, consider summarily whether: (a) the armaments of any State are in excess of those fixed under the provisions of any agreement relating to reduction or limitation of armaments; or (b) the military or other preparations of any State are if such a nature as to cause apprehension of aggression or an eventual outbreak of hostilities.

5. If the Council shall, upon such request, be of the opinion that there is reasonable ground for thinking that a menace of aggression has arisen, the parties to the defensive agreements hereinbefore mentioned may put into immediate execution the plan of assistance which they have agreed upon

6. If the Council shall, upon such request, not be of the opinion that a menace of aggression has arisen, a public report to the effect shall be made, and in such case no State shall be under

any obligation to put into execution any plan of assistance to which it is a party; but any Member of the League, believing itself to be threatened with a menace of aggression, notwithstanding the fact that the Council has not been of such opinion, may forthwith notify the Council to that effect, and such Member shall thereupon have full liberty of action in military or other preparations for defence, subject, however, to the limitations as to armament which are imposed by any treaty now in force.

DOCUMENT 3 (c)

Annex 5.

GENERAL SCHEME
.OF THE PROVISIONS OF THE DRAFT TREATY OF MUTUAL ASSISTANCE
AS COMPARED WITH THE REPLIES OF THE GOVERNMENTS (ANNEX 3)
AND THE DRAFT BY AN AMERICAN GROUP (ANNEX 4).

I. The Draft and the Covenant.

1. *Connection between the Draft Treaty and the Covenant (Analysis).*

Attention must be drawn at the outset to the close connection between the Draft Treaty and the Covenant.

In a certain sense it may be said that the entire scheme is implicitly contained in paragraphs 2 to 4 of Article 8 of the Covenant.

From this point of view the Draft Treaty might be considered as the practical method which the Temporary Mixed Commission would recommend to the Council for the purpose of carrying out the task entrusted to it in the paragraphs of Article 8 of the Covenant cited above.

The logical connection between this Article of the Covenant and the Treaty is clearly seen in Resolution XIV.

The Commission called upon to draw up a plan for the reduction of armaments begins by stating the fact that a certain number of States cannot contemplate such a reduction unless they receive in exchange a guarantee of security.

Hence the necessity of strengthening the feeling of international confidence by developing those stipulations in the Covenant which may be considered as an effort towards a mutual guarantee of security.

Hence also the general rule upon which the draft Treaty is based: that the guarantee and disarmanent are interdependent.

It should, however, be emphasised that this rule is only the outcome of practical experience and is in no way the expression of a principle in law.

Accordingly, the Treaty of Guarantee would appear as the measure recommended by the Commission for the purpose of adapting to the present situation the obligations contained in Article 7 of the Covenant.

Finally, with regard to adherence, the Draft Treaty might not include certain States signatories to the Covenant, while on the other hand it allows of the adherence, under certain conditions, of States which are not at present Members of the League of Nations. The draft scheme includes. moreover, an article contemplating partial adherence or adherence conditional upon reciprocity,

2. *Objections made by Governments.*

One of the criticisms most frequently levelled against the Draft Treaty is that the guarantees provided do not imply with sufficient clearness a reduction of armaments.

The Draft Treaty has been drawn up in order to give effect to Article 8 of the Covenant, which requires the Council to draw up plans for the reduction of armaments.

In the view of certain countries, the additional idea of guarantee upon which this reduction is made to depend is not contained in Article 8 of the Covenant.

Other Governments have maintained that the undertaking in Article 8, entered upon when signing the Covenant of the League of Nations, implied an unconditional reduction of armaments as being in itself an adequate means of ensuring the peace of the world. The idea of mutual assistance in exchange for the reduction of armaments is not, in their opinion, contained in the Covenant.

In addition, a certain number of special criticisms have been formulated. One country, for instance, maintained that it did not come within the scope of Article 8 of the Covenant, being a new country in process of devleopment, and not having as yet acquired the minimum of armaments compatible with its national security.

It has also been observed that the proposed system could not be brought into full operation until the League of Nations had become a universal organisation, and that the Covenant itself could secure this condition more easily than could the Treaty of Mutual Assistance.

Finally, attention should be drawn to the attitude adopted by certain members of the Commission, who held that if the Draft provided exclusively for the extension of the Covenant in the matter of material guarantees, this would represent a one-sided development of the League of Nations. In the opinion of these delegations, concurrently with this development of material guarantees, there should be a development of the legal and moral elements in the Covenant. They specially insisted on the importance of asking those States which would in practice enjoy the guarantee offered them by the draft treaty for guarantees of a "wise" policy (respect for the stipulations of the Covenant providing for the registration and publication of international treaties and adherence to the optional clause in the Statute of the Court of International Justice).

3. *Suggestions and Proposals.*

The treaties of assistance should provide for assistance from one continent to another, not only in the economic and financial sphere but also, wherever possible, in the naval, air and even military sphere.

The undertakings to be entered upon by the different States might be adapted to their particular circumstances. The Council should acquaint itself with the nature of the coercive forces which these States could place at its disposal, the limit of possible reductions in their armaments, and the extent and nature of the assistance which they expect. The Council would then be in a position to determine the rights and obligations of each State.

A scheme for the reduction of armaments should be incorporated in the Treaty of Mutual Assistance.

Any Treaty of Mutual Assistance should provide for the settlement of disputes and should confer upon the Council powers to negotiate peace as decisive and extensive as its powers for regulating assistance.

II. AGGRESSIVE WAR.

1. *Analysis of the Draft.*

The Third Committee of the Fourth Assembly adopted the view of the Temporary Mixed Commission as to the advantage to be gained by causing the draft Treaty of Mutual Assistance, with a view to the reduction of armaments, to open with a solemn declaration condemning all aggressive war. This is the idea of Article 1 of the Draft Treaty.

It would no doubt have been preferable for this article to retain the clear and concise form given it by the Temporary Mixed Commission. The Third Committee felt itself obliged, however, to add to the text a precise definition of a case of legitimate war, that is to say, that of a State a party to a dispute having accepted the unanimous recommendation of the Council, the verdict of the Permanent Court of International Justice, or an arbitral award declaring war against another Contracting Party which had not accepted the decision of one of the international institutions.

Thus, even with this exception clearly and honestly recognised and admitted, Article 1 still remains a solemn pact of non-aggression, the spirit of which should rule the application of the draft Treaty of Mutual Assistance.

2. *Objections made by Governments.*

The criticism most frequently formulated on this point has emphasised the difficulty of defining an act of aggression. This difficulty has re-appeared in the replies of several Governments.

It has further been pointed out that, even if the States Members of the League of Nations recognised an act prohibited by the Covenant as an act of aggression, States non-members of the League were under no obligation to take the same view.

3. *Suggestions and Proposals.*

A large number of countries propose that arbitration should be made compulsory and that its field of application should be enlarged.

One country proposes the creation, side by side with the International Court, of a special organisation for the settlement of political disputes.

It is also proposed that a regular procedure should be established for frontier rectifications.

4. *Analysis of the American Group Draft* (Articles 1, 2, 3, 10 and 11).

Article 1 has been taken over from the draft Treaty of the Temporary Mixed Commission. It acquires, however, a new character; it is no longer a mere declaration and statement of intention, but a contract with a sanction attached.

Article 2 is a further step of definition. It is kept in very general terms. The systematic and detailed definition of aggression will be established later by the organisation created by the Powers (Permanent Court of International Justice and Permanent Advisory Conference).

Articles 10 and 11 form the conclusion to the part of the treaty concerning the outlawry of aggressive war, and contain the stipulations which establish the distinction being made between police measures and measures of aggression. These two articles constitute a further safeguard against the possible bad faith of an aggressor.

III. The Guarantee — Disarmament.

1. *Analysis of the Draft.*

The close practical connection which exists between guarantees and disarmament for States adhering to the Treaty finds expression in Articles 2, 3, 4 and 5 of the Draft. This question has already received due consideration in our study of the connection between the Draft and the Covenant. It will here be sufficient to note that the pledge of guarantees in exchange for the reduction of armaments is clearly expressed in Article 2, Articles 3, 4 and 5 being no more than provisions for the application of Article 2.

The operation of the guarantee and of the reduction of armaments, according to these articles of the draft, would be as follows:

1. The general guarantee is established in principle and defined by the Treaty — first stage.
2. In the case of certain States the guarantee is supplemented by special treaties.
3. Each State estimates what reduction in armaments it can effect in consequence of this single or double operation of guarantees — second stage.
4. The Council, upon examination of these estimates, works out the scheme of reduction in accordance with Article 8 of the Covenant — third stage.
5. The States, having given their adherence to the plan, undertake to apply it as regards themselves within a period of time fixed by the Treaty — fourth stage.
6. Once this undertaking has been given, the guarantee is put into effect — the provisions of Article 8 of the Covenant regarding disarmament are on the way to practical realisation.

2. *Objections made by Governments.*

The chief criticism has been that by the terms of the Treaty each State estimates for itself what reduction in armaments it can effect in consequence of the operation of the guarantees, and that there is therefore no certainty that the Treaty will lead to any appreciable reduction of armaments.

Some States indeed have maintained that the Treaty might compel them to increase their military preparations.

It has also been observed that the synchronism in the entering into force of the guarantees provided and the execution of the scheme for reducing armaments is not sufficiently emphasised, and would meet with many difficulties in application.

3. *Suggestions and Proposals.*

It is proposed that the measures which the Council may recommend in application of Article 16 of the Covenant should be taken by a two-thirds majority. It is also proposed that the decision to put into execution the measures of mutual assistance might be likewise given by a two-thirds majority of the Council.

———————

One country proposes that the organisation of mutual assistance should start with economic and financial help to the country attacked, this being the counterpart of the economic and financial sanctions against the aggressor provided for in Article 16.

———————

One country observes that it would be expedient to prepare in advance the plans for financial co-operation.

———————

Another proposal is that, should the aggressor be financially incapable of paying reparations, the outstanding sums might be shared between the High Contracting Parties in a certain proportion.

———————

As regards military sanctions, one proposal aims at providing the Council with a permanent military organisation.

With regard to the reduction of armaments, it is proposed that this reduction should be investigated in all countries by a commission of members belonging to all the Signatory States. Refusal to submit to investigation would be *primâ facie* evidence of guilt.

———————

One reply is to the effect that the reduction of armaments should be examined as a single question, no distinction being drawn between the different forms of armament.

4. *Analysis of the American Group Draft.*

(Articles 8 and 9).

Article 8 is the heart of the whole Treaty. For the first time a method has been found which leaves the High Contracting Parties free to apply the enforcement of the Treaty or not, as they see fit, and which yet secures an enforcement that is real and adequate. This article does not imply any surrender of national sovereignty.

The sanctions are divided into economic and military. In the latter case, the Article expressly stipulates that each Signatory shall be entirely free. Naturally, the other articles of the Treaty prevent it transforming this military action into aggression.

In the economic sanction, the High Contracting Parties do not bind themselves to take any acts contrary to their own interests. But they are free to do all manner of things as against an aggressor with reference to his property rights on the high seas or within their own frontiers. In a word, the aggressor is outlawed and deprived of any security for his property in other lands. Automatically he loses his own security throughout the whole world.

Article 9 applies the principle of reparation. This is a normal consequence of the recognition of aggressive war as a crime.

(Articles 12 and 13).

Article 12 has been drafted in very general terms. The Treaty calls for a continuous study of the problem and provides the means for it.

In principle, however, the Treaty relies more upon the measures described in Part I for securing a lessening of armaments than upon the mutual agreements for disarming.

Article 13 is an incomplete statement of an important measure. More should be done both to develop this article and to secure its application in special instances.

(Articles 12, 14, 15, 16 and 17).

The necessity of having a Conference on Disarmament is recognised on all hands. But this Conference must be periodic. If a Conference recurs automatically, the questions in dispute can be brought up without involving the national honour of any of the Parties to it.

The organisation must be permanent in order to deal with the technical questions which are involved in measures of disarmament in their relation to new discoveries in chemistry and mechanics.

(Articles 18, 19, 20, 21 and 22).

This part embodies not only a provision of the Covenant of the League of Nations but a device which has been frequently recommended in the interests of the pacification of Europe. The institution of a Commission entrusted with the duty of investigating how the various High Contracting Parties were carrying out the terms of the present Treaty could hardly be objected to by a Power which entered into its obligations in good faith.

(Articles 23, 24 and 25).

This part of the Treaty overcomes one of the principal criticisms directed against the Covenant and the Draft Treaty of Mutual Assistance. It limits the prerogatives of the Council so that the latter would be hardly more than an advisory body.

Under the terms of the present Treaty, the Council would tend more and more to become an instrument of conciliation, and its administrative functions would become inoperative.

But the Council's sphere of action would remain a large and important one. Its competence in the political sphere would remain unaffected.

This limitation of the Council's competence, in comparison with the Treaty of Mutual Assistance, must not be regarded as lessening its validity; on the contrary, it would in reality strengthen the Council's position in the sphere in which its influence is necessary and legitimate.

IV. Definition of Aggression.

1 *Analysis of the Draft.*

Article 4 defines the conditions of intervention by the Council of the League of Nations, and, if necessary, that of all the States Signatories, in case of aggression.

All the Commissions which have collaborated directly or indirectly in the Draft have realised the extreme difficulty of defining a case of aggression.

The Draft Treaty is accompanied by a "Commentary on the Definition of a Case of Aggression" drawn up by a special Committee of the Temporary Mixed Commission, with the co-operation of certain technical experts of the Permanent Advisory Commission, and following upon the study of the question by the latter Commission. The Third Committee recommended that this commentary should be forwarded to the respective Governments for information.

2. *Objections by the Governments.*

The Draft Treaty is — it has been said — an infringement of the sovereign rights of the States, in that it requires the Signatories to abdicate part of their sovereignty in favour of the Council and to bind themselves to accept its decision, both in regard to the determination of cases of aggression and in regard to the despatch of military forces.

The rule concerning unanimity would, moreover, paralyse the Council in its decisions.

In the opinion of many States, moreover, it appeared difficult for the Council to come to an agreement in regard to the determination of a case of aggression within a period of four days, or indeed, within any time-limit. Certain of those States, therefore, pointed out that the guarantee of assistance given by the Treaty could not, in these circumstances, enable them to reduce their armaments.

Finally, in the opinion of certain States, the procedure provided for, even if applied in despite of the rule of unanimity, would entail delays which the aggressor might utilise for destroying the State which had been attacked. This danger would be especially great in the case of certain States in unfavourable geographical circumstances (remoteness from States which could give assistance, or specially vulnerable frontiers)

3. *Suggestions and Proposals.*

Many countries propose that the Council should take the decision regarding the determination of the aggressor by a majority vote.

It is proposed that the decision of the Council should be taken within a time limit of a fortnight.

One country suggests that, with a view to facilitating the task of the Council, a specific list should be drawn up of measures which might be considered to constitute an intention of aggression.

4. *Analysis of the American Group Draft* (Articles 4, 5, 6 and 7).

This chapter deals with acts leading to competition in armaments and even to war itself. It constitutes an effort to avert the menace of aggression. It is not, however, applicable to provocative acts of a political nature which lie outside the technical sphere of aggression. The intervention of the Court is strictly limited to the interpretation of the terms of the Treaty itself.

Article 5 is one of the principal articles of the Treaty. It contains a definition of aggression: the aggressor is the one who refuses to accept the jurisdiction of the Court.

V. COMPLEMENTARY AGREEMENTS.

1. *Analysis of the Draft.*

The discussions in the Third Committee of the last Assembly which resulted in Resolution XIV brought to light the difficulties of a technical character connected with the establishment of a guarantee.

Certain States which, for various reasons, believed themselves to be especially threatened insisted, without denying the great moral and political value of the general guarantee, on the impossibility of risking a reduction of their armaments in exchange for a general guarantee of assistance, of which the technical preparation, the rapidity and the efficacy would be problematical.

The technical experts not only in these countries but also in the countries represented on the Permanent Advisory Commission, decided unanimously, as may be seen from the reports of the Permanent Advisory Commission, that assistance could not be regarded as immediate and effective unless it were carried out according to a previously arranged plan.

This condition, which practical circumstances made it necessary to accept, at least in certain specific cases, made it, in the opinion of some technical experts, indispensable that there should be added to the General Treaty of Guarantee defensive agreements of a more restricted character, allowing military conventions to be concluded in view of possible threats of aggression.

The introduction of this idea into the general system of the Treaty of Guarantee provoked grave objections. The Temporary Mixed Commission and the Third Committee endeavoured to reconcile the two points of view, the one in favour of the General Treaty and the other in favour of the General Treaty supplemented by special treaties.

The majority of the Commission considered, for the political reasons referred to above and for many other reasons based on the necessities of practical every-day politics, that they should maintain in their draft the system of supplementary defensive agreements. The Third Committee thought that these agreements should be submitted to the Council for consideration. It was on this condition that certain delegations declared themselves prepared to withdraw their opposition to the principle of special treaties.

Consequently, the special treaties do not share the benefits of the general guarantee until they have been recognised by the Council as not being contrary to the spirit of the Covenant and as coming within the general framework of the General Treaty of Mutual Assistance.

They must, in consequence, be registered with and published by the League of Nations (Article 7).

2. *Objections put forward by Governments.*

The objections raised against the supplementary treaties all originate in the fear that the old systems of alliances which proved so dangerous to the peace of Europe may be re-established under that name.

The adversaries of the supplementary treaties have observed that the very existence of these treaties implies suspicion and mistrust of a State or group of States. The body of States signatory to the General Treaty would consequently be divided, and this division would merely be aggravated

PROTOCOL FOR THE PACIFIC SETTLEMENT
OF INTERNATIONAL DISPUTES.

Adopted by the Fifth Assembly on October 2nd, 1924.

————

Animated by the firm desire to ensure the maintenance of general peace and the security of nations whose existence, independence or territories may be threatened;

Recognising the solidarity of the members of the international community;

Asserting that a war of aggression constitutes a violation of this solidarity and an international crime;

Desirous of facilitating the complete application of the system provided in the Covenant of the League of Nations for the pacific settlement of disputes between States and of ensuring the repression of international crimes; and

For the purpose of realising, as contemplated by Article 8 of the Covenant, the reduction of national armaments to the lowest point consistent with national safety and the enforcement by common action of international obligations;

The undersigned, duly authorised to that effect, agree as follows:

Article 1.

The signatory States undertake to make every effort in their power to secure the introduction into the Covenant of amendments on the lines of the provisions contained in the following articles.

They agree that, as between themselves, these provisions shall be binding as from the coming into force of the present Protocol and that, so far as they are concerned, the Assembly and the Council of the League of Nations shall thenceforth have power to exercise all the rights and perform all the duties conferred upon them by the Protocol.

Article 2.

The signatory States agree in no case to resort to war either with one another or against a State which, if the occasion arises, accepts all the obligations hereinafter set out, except in case of resistance to acts of aggression or when acting in agreement with the Council or the Assembly of the League of Nations in accordance with the provisions of the Covenant and of the present Protocol.

Article 3.

The signatory States undertake to recognise as compulsory, *ipso facto* and without special agreement, the jurisdiction of the Permanent Court of International Justice in the cases covered by paragraph 2 of Article 36 of the Statute of the Court, but without prejudice to the right of any State, when acceding to the special protocol provided for in the said Article and opened for signature on December 16th, 1920, to make reservations compatible with the said clause.

Accession to this special protocol, opened for signature on December 16th, 1920, must be given within the month following the coming into force of the present Protocol.

States which accede to the present Protocol after its coming into force must carry out the above obligation within the month following their accession.

Article 4.

With a view to render more complete the provisions of paragraphs 4, 5, 6, and 7 of Article 15 of the Covenant, the signatory States agree to comply with the following procedure:

1. If the dispute submitted to the Council is not settled by it as provided in paragraph 3 of the said Article 15, the Council shall endeavour to persuade the parties to submit the dispute to judicial settlement or arbitration.
2. (*a*) If the parties cannot agree to do so, there shall, at the request of at least one of the parties, be constituted a Committee of Arbitrators. The Committee shall so far as possible be constituted by agreement between the parties.

    (*b*) If within the period fixed by the Council the parties have failed to agree, in whole or in part, upon the number, the names and the powers of the arbitrators and upon the procedure, the Council shall settle the points remaining in suspense. It shall with the utmost possible despatch select in consultation with the parties the arbitrators and their President from among persons who by their nationality, their personal character and their experience, appear to it to furnish the highest guarantees of competence and impartiality.

    (*c*) After the claims of the parties have been formulated, the Committee of Arbitrators, on the request of any party, shall through the medium of the Council request an advisory opinion upon any points of law in dispute from the Permanent Court of International Justice, which in such case shall meet with the utmost possible despatch.
3. If none of the parties asks for arbitration, the Council shall again take the dispute under consideration. If the Council reaches a report which is unanimously agreed to by the members thereof other than the representatives of any of the parties to the dispute, the signatory States agree to comply with the recommendations therein.
4. If the Council fails to reach a report which is concurred in by all its members, other than the representatives of any of the parties to the dispute, it shall submit the dispute to arbitration. It shall itself determine the composition, the powers and the procedure of the Committee of Arbitrators and, in the choice of the arbitrators, shall bear in mind the guarantees of competence and impartiality referred to in paragraph 2 (*b*) above.
5. In no case may a solution, upon which there has already been a unanimous recommendation of the Council accepted by one of the parties concerned, be again called in question.
6. The signatory States undertake that they will carry out in full good faith any judicial sentence or arbitral award that may be rendered and that they will comply, as provided in paragraph 3 above, with the solutions recommended by the Council. In the event of a State failing to carry out the above undertakings, the Council shall exert all its influence to secure compliance therewith. If it fails therein, it shall propose what steps should be taken to give effect thereto, in accordance with the provision contained at the end of Article 13 of the Covenant. Should a State in disregard of the above undertakings resort to war, the sanctions provided for by Article 16 of the Covenant, interpreted in the manner indicated in the present Protocol, shall immediately become applicable to it.
7. The provisions of the present article do not apply to the settlement of disputes which arise as the result of measures of war taken by one or more signatory States in agreement with the Council or the Assembly.

Article 5.

The provisions of paragraph 8 of Article 15 of the Covenant shall continue to apply in proceedings before the Council.

If in the course of an arbitration, such as is contemplated in Article 4 above, one of the parties claims that the dispute, or part thereof, arises out of a matter which by international law is solely within the domestic jurisdiction of that party, the arbitrators shall on this point take the advice of the Permanent Court of International Justice through the medium of the Council. The opinion of the Court shall be binding upon the arbitrators, who, if the opinion is affirmative, shall confine themselves to so declaring in their award.

If the question is held by the Court or by the Council to be a matter solely within the domestic jurisdiction of the State, this decision shall not prevent consideration of the situation by the Council or by the Assembly under Article 11 of the Covenant.

Article 6.

If in accordance with paragraph 9 of Article 15 of the Covenant a dispute is referred to the Assembly, that body shall have for the settlement of the dispute all the powers conferred upon the Council as to endeavouring to reconcile the parties in the manner laid down in paragraphs 1, 2 and 3 of Article 15 of the Covenant and in paragraph 1 of Article 4 above.

Should the Assembly fail to achieve an amicable settlement:

If one of the parties asks for arbitration, the Council shall proceed to constitute the Committee of Arbitrators in the manner provided in sub-paragraphs (*a*), (*b*) and (*c*) of paragraph 2 of Article 4 above.

If no party asks for arbitration, the Assembly shall again take the dispute under consideration and shall have in this connection the same powers as the Council. Recommendations embodied in a report of the Assembly, provided that it secures the measure of support stipulated at the end of paragraph 10 of Article 15 of the Covenant, shall have the same value and effect, as regards all matters dealt with in the present Protocol, as recommendations embodied in a report of the Council adopted as provided in paragraph 3 of Article 4 above.

If the necessary majority cannot be obtained, the dispute shall be submitted to arbitration and the Council shall determine the composition, the powers and the procedure of the Committee of Arbitrators as laid down in paragraph 4 of Article 4 above.

Article 7.

In the event of a dispute arising between two or more signatory States, these States agree that they will not, either before the dispute is submitted to proceedings for pacific settlement or during such proceedings, make any increase of their armaments or effectives which might modify the position established by the Conference for the Reduction of Armaments provided for by Article 17 of the present Protocol, nor will they take any measure of military, naval, air, industrial or economic mobilisation, nor, in general, any action of a nature likely to extend the dispute or render it more acute.

It shall be the duty of the Council, in accordance with the provisions of Article 11 of the Covenant, to take under consideration any complaint as to infraction of the above undertakings which is made to it by one or more of the States parties to the dispute. Should the Council be of opinion that the complaint requires investigation, it shall, if it deems it expedient, arrange for enquiries and investigations in one or more of the countries concerned. Such enquiries and investigations shall be carried out with the utmost possible despatch and the signatory States undertake to afford every facility for carrying them out.

The sole object of measures taken by the Council as above provided is to facilitate the pacific settlement of disputes and they shall in no way prejudge the actual settlement.

If the result of such enquiries and investigations is to establish an infraction of the provisions of the first paragraph of the present Article, it shall be the duty of the Council to summon the State or States guilty of the infraction to put an end thereto. Should the State or States in question fail to comply with such summons, the Council shall declare them to be guilty of a violation of the Covenant or of the present Protocol, and shall decide upon the measures to be taken with a view to end as soon as possible a situation of a nature to threaten the peace of the world.

For the purposes of the present Article decisions of the Council may be taken by a two-thirds majority.

Article 8.

The signatory States undertake to abstain from any act which might constitute a threat of aggression against another State.

If one of the signatory States is of opinion that another State is making preparations for war, it shall have the right to bring the matter to the notice of the Council.

The Council, if it ascertains that the facts are as alleged, shall proceed as provided in paragraphs 2, 4, and 5 of Article 7.

Article 9.

The existence of demilitarised zones being calculated to prevent aggression and to facilitate a definite finding of the nature provided for in Article 10 below, the establishment of such zones between States mutually consenting thereto is recommended as a means of avoiding violations of the present Protocol.

The demilitarised zones already existing under the terms of certain treaties or conventions, or which may be established in future between States mutually consenting thereto, may at the request and at the expense of one or more of the conterminous States, be placed under a temporary or permanent system of supervision to be organised by the Council.

Article 10.

Every State which resorts to war in violation of the undertakings contained in the Covenant or in the present Protocol is an aggressor. Violation of the rules laid down for a demilitarised zone shall be held equivalent to resort to war.

In the event of hostilities having broken out, any State shall be presumed to be an aggressor, unless a decision of the Council, which must be taken unanimously, shall otherwise declare:

1. If it has refused to submit the dispute to the procedure of pacific settlement provided by Articles 13 and 15 of the Covenant as amplified by the present Protocol, or to comply with a judicial sentence or arbitral award or with a unanimous recommendation of the Council, or has disregarded a unanimous report of the Council, a judicial sentence or an arbitral award recognising that the dispute between it and the other belligerent State arises out of a matter which by international law is solely within the domestic jurisdiction of the latter State; nevertheless, in the last case the State shall only be presumed to be an aggressor if it has not previously submitted the question to the Council or the Assembly, in accordance with Article 11 of the Covenant.

2. If it has violated provisional measures enjoined by the Council for the period while the proceedings are in progress as contemplated by Article 7 of the present Protocol.

Apart from the cases dealt with in paragraphs 1 and 2 of the present Article, if the Council does not at once succeed in determining the aggressor, it shall be bound to enjoin upon the belligerents an armistice, and shall fix the terms, acting, if need be, by a two-thirds majority and shall supervise its execution.

Any belligerent which has refused to accept the armistice or has violated its terms shall be deemed an aggressor.

The Council shall call upon the signatory States to apply forthwith against the aggressor the sanctions provided by Article 11 of the present Protocol, and any signatory State thus called upon shall thereupon be entitled to exercise the rights of a belligerent.

Article 11.

As soon as the Council has called upon the signatory States to apply sanctions, as provided in the last paragraph of Article 10 of the present Protocol, the obligations of the said States, in regard to the sanctions of all kinds mentioned in paragraphs 1 and 2 of Article 16 of the Covenant, will immediately become operative in order that such sanctions may forthwith be employed against the aggressor.

Those obligations shall be interpreted as obliging each of the signatory States to co-operate loyally and effectively in support of the Covenant of the League of Nations, and in resistance to any act of aggression, in the degree which its geographical position and its particular situation as regards armaments allow.

In accordance with paragraph 3 of Article 16 of the Covenant the signatory States give a joint and several undertaking to come to the assistance of the State attacked or threatened, and to give each other mutual support by means of facilities and reciprocal exchanges as regards the provision of raw materials and supplies of every kind, openings of credits, transport and transit, and for this purpose to take all measures in their power to preserve the safety of communications by land and by sea of the attacked or threatened State.

If both parties to the dispute are aggressors within the meaning of Article 10, the economic and financial sanctions shall be applied to both of them.

Article 12.

In view of the complexity of the conditions in which the Council may be called upon to exercise the functions mentioned in Article 11 of the present Protocol concerning economic and financial sanctions, and in order to determine more exactly the guarantees afforded by the present Protocol to the signatory States, the Council shall forthwith invite the economic and financial organisations of the League of Nations to consider and report as to the nature of the steps to be taken to give effect to the financial and economic sanctions and measures of co-operation contemplated in Article 16 of the Covenant and in Article 11 of this Protocol.

When in possession of this information, the Council shall draw up through its competent organs:

1. Plans of action for the application of the economic and financial sanctions against an aggressor State;
2. Plans of economic and financial co-operation between a State attacked and the different States assisting it;

and shall communicate these plans to the Members of the League and to the other signatory States.

Article 13.

In view of the contingent military, naval and air sanctions provided for by Article 16 of the Covenant and by Article 11 of the present Protocol, the Council shall be entitled to receive undertakings from States determining in advance the military, naval and air forces which they would be able to bring into action immediately to ensure the fulfilment of the obligations in regard to sanctions which result from the Covenant and the present Protocol.

Furthermore, as soon as the Council has called upon the signatory States to apply sanctions, as provided in the last paragraph of Article 10 above, the said States may, in accordance with any agreements which they may previously have concluded, bring to the assistance of a particular State, which is the victim of aggression, their military, naval and air forces.

The agreements mentioned in the preceding paragraph shall be registered and published by the Secretariat of the League of Nations. They shall remain open to all States Members of the League which may desire to accede thereto.

Article 14.

The Council shall alone be competent to declare that the application of sanctions shall cease and normal conditions be re-established.

Article 15.

In conformity with the spirit of the present Protocol, the signatory States agree that the whole cost of any military, naval or air operations undertaken for the repression of an aggression under the terms of the Protocol, and reparation for all losses suffered by individuals, whether civilians or combatants, and for all material damage caused by the operations of both sides, shall be borne by the aggressor State up to the extreme limit of its capacity.

Nevertheless, in view of Article 10 of the Covenant, neither the territorial integrity nor the political independence of the aggressor State shall in any case be affected as the result of the application of the sanctions mentioned in the present Protocol.

Article 16.

The signatory States agree that in the event of a dispute between one or more of them and one or more States which have not signed the present Protocol and are not Members of the League of Nations, such non-Member States shall be invited, on the conditions contemplated in Article 17 of the Covenant, to submit, for the purpose of a pacific settlement, to the obligations accepted by the States signatories of the present Protocol.

If the State so invited, having refused to accept the said conditions and obligations, resorts to war against a signatory State, the provisions of Article 16 of the Covenant, as defined by the present Protocol, shall be applicable against it.

Article 17.

The signatory States undertake to participate in an International Conference for the Reduction of Armaments which shall be convened by the Council and shall meet at Geneva on Monday, June 15th, 1925. All other States, whether Members of the League or not, shall be invited to this Conference.

In preparation for the convening of the Conference, the Council shall draw up with due regard to the undertakings contained in Articles 11 and 13 of the present Protocol, a general programme for the reduction and limitation of armaments, which shall be laid before the Conference and which shall be communicated to the Governments at the earliest possible date, and at the latest three months before the Conference meets.

If by May 1st, 1925, ratifications have not been deposited by at least a majority of the permanent Members of the Council and ten other Members of the League, the Secretary-General of the League shall immediately consult the Council as to whether he shall cancel the invitations or merely adjourn the Conference to a subsequent date to be fixed by the Council so as to permit the necessary number of ratifications to be obtained.

Article 18.

Wherever mention is made in Article 10, or in any other provision of the present Protocol, of a decision of the Council, this shall be understood in the sense of Article 15 of the Covenant, namely, that the votes of the representatives of the parties to the dispute shall not be counted when reckoning unanimity or the necessary majority.

Article 19.

Except as expressly provided by its terms, the present Protocol shall not affect in any way the rights and obligations of Members of the League as determined by the Covenant.

Article 20.

Any dispute as to the interpretation of the present Protocol shall be submitted to the Permanent Court of International Justice.

Article 21.

The present Protocol, of which the French and English texts are both authentic, shall be ratified.

The deposit of ratifications shall be made at the Secretariat of the League of Nations as soon as possible.

States of which the seat of government is outside Europe will be entitled merely to inform the Secretariat of the League of Nations that their ratification has been given; in that case, they must transmit the instrument of ratification as soon as possible.

So soon as the majority of the permanent Members of the Council and ten other Members of the League have deposited or have effected their ratifications, a *procès-verbal* to that effect shall be drawn up by the Secretariat.

After the said *procès-verbal* has been drawn up, the Protocol shall come into force as soon as the plan for the reduction of armaments has been adopted by the Conference provided for in Article 17.

If within such period after the adoption of the plan for the reduction of armaments as shall be fixed by the said Conference, the plan has not been carried out, the Council shall make a declaration to that effect; this declaration shall render the present Protocol null and void.

The grounds on which the Council may declare that the plan drawn up by the International Conference for the Reduction of Armaments has not been carried out, and that in consequence the present Protocol has been rendered null and void, shall be laid down by the Conference itself.

A signatory State which, after the expiration of the period fixed by the Conference, fails to comply with the plan adopted by the Conference, shall not be admitted to benefit by the provisions of the present Protocol.

In faith whereof the undersigned, duly authorised for this purpose, have signed the present Protocol.

DONE at Geneva, on the second day of October, nineteen hundred and twenty-four, in a single copy, which will be kept in the archives of the Secretariat of the League and registered by it on the date of its coming into force.

DOCUMENT 3 (e)

Annex 13.

ARBITRATION, SECURITY
AND REDUCTION OF ARMAMENTS.

General Report submitted to the Fifth Assembly on behalf of the First and Third Committees by M. Politis (Greece), Rapporteur for the First Committee, and M. Benes (Czechoslovakia), Rapporteur for the Third Committee.

I. — Introduction.

After being examined for several years by the Third Committee, the problem of the reduction of armaments has this year suddenly assumed a different, a wider and even an unexpected form.

Last year a draft Treaty of Mutual Assistance was prepared, which the Assembly sent to the Members of the League for their consideration. The replies from the Governments were to be examined by the Fifth Assembly.

At the very beginning of its work, however, after a memorable debate, the Assembly indicated to the Third Committee a new path. On September 6th, 1924, on the proposal of the Prime Ministers of France and Great Britain, M. Edouard Herriot and Mr. Ramsay MacDonald, the Assembly adopted the following resolution:

"The Assembly,
"Noting the declarations of the Governments represented, observes with satisfaction that they contain the basis of an understanding tending to establish a secure peace:
"Decides as follows:
"With a view to reconciling in the new proposals the divergences between certain points of view which have been expressed and, when agreement has been reached, to enable an international conference upon armaments to be summoned by the League of Nations at the earliest possible moment:
"(1) The Third Committee is requested to consider the material dealing with security and the reduction of armaments, particularly the observations of the Governments on the draft Treaty of Mutual Assistance, prepared in pursuance of Resolution XIV of the Third Assembly and other plans prepared and presented to the Secretary-General since the publication of the draft Treaty, and to examine the obligations contained in the Covenant of the League in relation to the guarantees of security which a resort to arbitration and a reduction of armaments may require;
"(2) The First Committee is requested:
"(a) To consider, in view of possible amendments, the articles in the Covenant relating to the settlement of disputes;
"(b) To examine within what limits the terms of Article 36, paragraph 2, of the Statute establishing the Permanent Court of International Justice might be rendered more precise and thereby facilitate the more general acceptance of the clause;
and thus strengthen the solidarity and the security of the nations of the world by settling by pacific means all disputes which may arise between States."

This resolution had two merits; first, that of briefly summarising all the investigations made in the last four years by the different organisations of the League in their efforts to establish peace and bring about the reduction of armaments, and, secondly, that of indicating the programme of work of the Committees in the hope that, with the aid of past experience, they would at last attain the end in view.

The Assembly had assigned to each Committee a distinct and separate task; to the First Committee, the examination of the pacific settlement of disputes by methods capable of being applied in every case; to the Third Committee, the question of the security of nations considered as a necessary preliminary condition for the reduction of their armaments.

Each Committee, after a general discussion which served to detach the essential elements from the rest of the problem, referred the examination of its programme to a Sub-Committee, which devoted a large number of meetings to this purpose.

The proposals of the Sub-Committees then led to very full debates by the Committees, which terminated in the texts analysed below

As, however, the questions submitted respectively to the two Committees form part of an indivisible whole, contact and collaboration had to be established between the Committees by means of a Mixed Committee of nine members and finally by a joint Drafting Committee of four members.

For the same reason, the work of the Committees has resulted in a single draft protocol accompanied by two draft resolutions for which the Committees are jointly responsible.

Upon these various texts, separate reports were submitted, which, being approved by the Committees respectively responsible for them, may be considered as an official commentary by the Committees.

These separate reports have here been combined in order to present as a whole the work accomplished by the two Committees and to facilitate explanation.

Before entering upon an analysis of the proposed texts, it is expedient to recall, in a brief historical summary, the efforts of the last four years, of which the texts are the logical conclusion

HISTORICAL STATEMENT.

The problem of the reduction of armaments is presented in Article 8 of the Covenant in terms which reveal at the outset the complexity of the question and which explain the tentative manner in which the subject has been treated by the League of Nations in the last few years.

> "The Members of the League recognise that the maintenance of peace requires the reduction of national armaments to the lowest point consistent with national safety and the enforcement by common action of international obligations."

Here we see clearly expressed the need of reducing the burden which armaments imposed upon the nations immediately after the war and of putting a stop to the competition in armaments, which was, in itself, a threat to the peace of the world. But, at the same time, there is recognised the duty of safeguarding the national security of the Members of the League and of safeguarding it, not only by the maintenance of a necessary minimum of troops, but also by the co-operation of all the nations, by a vast organisation for peace.

Such is the meaning of the Covenant, which, while providing for reduction of armaments properly so called, recognises at the same time the need of *common action*, by all the Members of the League, with a view to compelling a possible disturber of the peace to respect his *international obligations*.

Thus, in this first paragraph of Article 8, which is so short but so pregnant, mention is made of all the problems which have engaged the attention of our predecessors and ourselves and which the present Assembly has specially instructed us to solve, the problems of *collective security* and the *reduction of armaments*.

Taking up Article 8 of the Covenant, the First Assembly had already outlined a programme. At its head it placed a pronouncement of the Supreme Council:

> "In order to diminish the economic difficulties of Europe, armies should everywhere be reduced to a peace footing. Armaments should be limited to the lowest possible figure compatible with national security."

The Assembly also called attention to a resolution of the International Financial Conference of Brussels held a short time before:

> "Recommending to the Council of the League of Nations the desirability of conferring at once with the several Governments concerned with a view to securing a general reduction of the crushing burdens which, on their existing scale, armaments still impose on the impoverished peoples of the world, sapping their resources and imperilling their recovery from the ravages of war."

It also requested its two Advisory Commissions to set to work at once to collect the necessary information regarding the problem referred to in Article 8 of the Covenant.

From the beginning the work of the Temporary Mixed Commission and of the Permanent Advisory Commission revealed the infinite complexity of the question.

The Second Assembly limited its resolutions to the important, but none the less (if one may say so) secondary, questions of traffic in arms and their manufacture by private enterprise. It only touched upon the questions of military expenditure and budgets in the form of recommendations and, as regards the main question of reduction of armaments, it confined itself to asking the Temporary Mixed Commission to formulate a definite scheme.

It was between the Second and Third Assemblies that the latter Commission, which was beginning to get to grips with the various problems, revealed their constituent elements. In its report it placed on record that:

> "The memory of the world war was still maintaining in many countries a feeling of insecurity, which was represented in the candid statements in which, at the request of the Assembly, several of them had put forward the requirements of their national security, and the geographical and political considerations which contributed to shape their policy in the matter of armaments."

At the same time, however, the Commission stated that:

> "Consideration of these statements as a whole has clearly revealed not only the sincere desire of the Governments to reduce national armaments and the corresponding expenditure to a minimum, but also the importance of the results achieved. These facts" — according to the Commission — "are indisputable, and are confirmed, moreover, by the replies received from Governments to the Recommendation of the Assembly regarding the limitation of military expenditure."

That is the point we had reached *two years ago;* there was a *unanimous desire to reduce armaments.* Reductions, though as yet inadequate, had been begun, and there was a *still stronger desire to ensure the security of the world* by a stable and permanent organisation for peace.

That was the position which, after long discussions, gave rise *at the Third Assembly to the famous Resolution XIV* and at the Fourth Assembly *to the draft Treaty of Mutual Assistance,* for which we are now substituting the Protocol submitted to the Fifth Assembly.

What progress has been made during these four years ?

Although the Treaty of Mutual Assistance was approved in principle by eighteen Governments, it gave rise to certain misgivings. We need only recall the most important of these, hoping that a comparison between them and an analysis of the new scheme will demonstrate that the First and Third Committees have endeavoured, with a large measure of success, to dispose of the objections raised and that the present scheme consequently represents an immense advance on anything that has hitherto been done.

In the first place, a number of Governments or delegates to the Assembly argued that the guarantees provided by the draft Treaty of Mutual Assistance did not imply with sufficient definiteness the reduction of armaments which is the ultimate object of our work.

The idea of the Treaty was to give effect to Article 8 of the Covenant, but many persons considered that it did not, in fact, secure the automatic execution of that article. Even if a reduction of armaments was achieved by its means, the amount of the reduction was left, so the opponents of the Treaty urged, to the estimation of each Government, and there was nothing to show that it would be considerable.

With equal force many States complained that no provision had been made for the development of the *juridical and moral elements of the Covenant* by the side of material guarantees. The novel character of the charter given to the nations in 1919 lay essentially in the advent of a moral solidarity which foreshadowed the coming of a new era. That principle ought to have, as its natural consequence, *the extension of arbitration and international jurisdiction,* without which no human society can be solidly grounded. A considerable portion of the Assembly asked that efforts should also be made in this direction. The draft Treaty seemed from this point of view to be insufficient and ill-balanced.

Finally, the articles relating to partial treaties gave rise, as you are aware, to certain objections. Several Governments considered that they would lead to the establishment of groups of Powers animated by hostility towards other Powers or groups of Powers and that they would cause political tension. The absence of the barriers of compulsory arbitration and judicial intervention was evident here as everywhere else.

Thus, by a logical and gradual process, there was elaborated the system at which we have now arrived.

The reduction of armaments required by the Covenant and demanded by the general situation of the world to-day led us to consider the question of security as a necessary complement to disarmament.

The support demanded from different States by other States less favourably situated had placed the former under the obligation of asking for a sort of moral and legal guarantee that the States which have to be supported would act in perfect good faith and would always endeavour to settle their disputes by pacific means.

It became evident, however, with greater clearness and force than ever before, that if the security and effective assistance demanded in the event of aggression was the *condition sine quâ non* of the reduction of armaments, it was at the same time the necessary complement of the pacific settlement of international disputes, since the non-execution of a sentence obtained by pacific methods of settlement would necessarily drive the world back to the system of armed force. Sentences imperatively required sanctions or the whole system would fall to the ground.

Arbitration was therefore considered by the Fifth Assembly to be the necessary third factor, the complement of the two others with which it must be combined in order to build up the new system set forth in the Protocol.

Thus, after five years' hard work, we have decided to propose to the Members of the League *the present system of arbitration, security and reduction of armaments* — a system which we regard as being complete and sound.

That is the position with which the Fifth Assembly has to deal to-day. The desire to arrive at a successful issue is unanimous. A great number of the decisions adopted in the past years have met with general approval. There has arisen a thoroughly clear appreciation of the undoubted gaps which have to be filled and of the reasonable apprehensions which have to be dissipated. Conditions have therefore become favourable for arriving at an agreement.

An agreement has been arrived at on the basis of the draft Protocol which is now submitted to you for consideration.

II. — Analysis of the Scheme.

1. WORK OF THE FIRST COMMITTEE.

(*Rapporteur:* M. POLITIS.)

Draft Protocol for the Pacific Settlement of International Disputes.

Preamble.

The object of the Protocol, which is based upon the resolution of September 6th, 1924, is to facilitate the reduction and limitation of armaments provided for in Article 8 of the Covenant of the League of Nations by guaranteeing the security of States through the development of methods for the pacific settlement of all international disputes and the effective condemnation of aggressive war.

These general ideas are summarised in the preamble of the Protocol.

COMPULSORY ARBITRATION.

(*Articles 1 to 6, 10, 16, 18 and 19 of the Protocol.*)

I. INTRODUCTION.

Compulsory arbitration is the fundamental basis of the proposed system. It has seemed to be the only means of attaining the ultimate aim pursued by the League of Nations, viz. the establishment of a pacific and legal order in the relations between peoples.

The realisation of this great ideal, to which humanity aspires with a will which has never been more strongly affirmed, pre-supposes, as an indispensable condition, the elimination of war, the extension of the rule of law and the strengthening of the sentiment of justice.

The Covenant of the League of Nations erected a wall of protection around the peace of the world, but it was a first attempt at international organisation and it did not succeed in closing the circle sufficiently thoroughly to leave no opening for war. It reduced the number of possible wars. It did not condemn them all. There were some which it was forced to tolerate. Consequently, there remained, in the system which it established, numerous fissures, which constituted a grave danger to peace.

The new system of the Protocol goes further. It closes the circle drawn by the Covenant; it prohibits all wars of aggression. Henceforth no purely private war between nations will be tolerated.

This result is obtained by strengthening the pacific methods of procedure laid down in the Covenant. The Protocol completes them and extends them to all international disputes without exception, by making arbitration compulsory.

In reality, the word "arbitration is used here in a somewhat different sense from that which it has generally had up to now. It does not exactly correspond with the definition given by the Hague Conferences which, codifying a century-old custom, saw in it "the settlement of disputes between States by judges of their own choice and on the basis of respect for law" (Article 37 of the Convention of October 18th, 1907, for the Pacific Settlement of International Disputes).

The arbitration which is now contemplated differs from this classic arbitration in various respects:

(*a*) It is only part of a great machinery of pacific settlement. It is set up under the auspices and direction of the Council of the League of Nations.

(*b*) It is not only an instrument for the administration of justice. It is, in addition and above all, an instrument of peace. The arbitrators must no doubt seek in the first place to apply the rules and principles of international law. This is the reason why, as will be seen below, they are bound to consult the Permanent Court of International Justice if one of the parties so requests. But if international law furnishes no rule or principle applicable to the particular case, they cannot, like ordinary arbitrators, refuse to give a decision. They are bound to proceed on grounds of equity, for in our system arbitration is always of necessity to lead to a definitive solution of the dispute. This is not to be regretted, for to ensure the respect of law by nations it is necessary first that they should be assured of peace.

(*c*) It does not rest solely upon the loyalty and good faith of the parties. To the moral and legal force of an ordinary arbitration is added the actual force derived from the international organisation of which the kind of arbitration in question forms one of the principal elements; the absence of a sanction which has impeded the development of compulsory arbitration is done away with under our system.

In the system of the Protocol, the obligation to submit disputes to arbitration is sound and practical because it has always a sanction. Its application is automatically ensured, by means of the intervention of the Council; in no case can it be thrown on one side through the ill-will of one of the disputant States. The awards to which it leads are always accompanied by a sanction, adapted to the circumstances of the case and more or less severe according to the degree of resistance offered to the execution of the sentence.

2. NATURE OF THE RULES OF THE PROTOCOL.

Article 1.

The rules laid down in the Protocol do not all have the same scope or value for the future.

As soon as the Protocol comes into force, its provisions will become compulsory as between the signatory States, and in its dealings with them the Council of the League of Nations will at once be able to exercise all the rights and fulfil all the duties conferred upon it.

As between the States Members of the League of Nations, the Protocol may in the first instance create a dual regime, for, if it is not immediately accepted by them all, the relations between signatories and non-signatories will still be governed by the Covenant alone while the relations between signatories will be governed by the Protocol as well.

But this situation cannot last. Apart from the fact that it may be hoped that all Members of the League will adhere to it, the Protocol is in no sense designed to create among the States which accept it a restricted League capable of competing with or opposing in any way the existing League. On the contrary, such of its provisions as relate to articles of the Covenant will, as soon as possible, be made part of the general law by amendment of the Covenant effected in accordance with the procedure for revision laid down in Article 26 thereof. The signatory States which are Members of the League of Nations undertake to make every effort to this end.

When the Covenant has been amended in this way, some parts of the Protocol will lose their value as between the said States: some of them will have enriched the Covenant, while others, being temporary in character, will have lost their object.

The whole Protocol will remain applicable to relations between signatory States which are Members of the League of Nations and signatory States outside the League, or between States coming within the latter category.

It should be added that, as the League realises its aim of universality, the amended Covenant will take the place, as regards all States, of the separate regime of the Protocol.

3. CONDEMNATION OF AGGRESSIVE WAR.

Article 2.

The general principle of the Protocol is the prohibition of aggressive war.

Under the Covenant, while the old unlimited right of States to make war is restricted, it is not abolished. There are cases in which the exercise of this right is tolerated; some wars are prohibited and others are legitimate.

In future the position will be different. In no case is any State signatory of the Protocol entitled to undertake on its own sole initiative an offensive war against another signatory State or against any non-signatory State which accepts all the obligations assumed by the signatories under the Protocol.

The prohibition affects only aggressive war. It does not, of course, extend to defensive war. The right of legitimate self-defence continues, as it must, to be respected. The State attacked retains complete liberty to resist by all means in its power any acts of aggression of which it may be the victim. Without waiting for the assistance which it is entitled to receive from the international community, it may and should at once defend itself with its own force. Its interests are identified with the general interest. This is a point on which there can be no doubt.

The same applies when a country employs force with the consent of the Council or the Assembly of the League of Nations under the provisions of the Covenant and the Protocol. This eventuality may arise in two classes of cases: either a State may take part in the collective measures of force decided upon by the League of Nations in aid of one of its Members which is the victim of aggression; or a State may employ force with the authorisation of the Council or the Assembly in order to enforce a decision given in its favour. In the former case, the assistance given to the victim of aggression is indirectly an act of legitimate self-defence. In the latter, force is used in the service of the general interest, which would be threatened if decisions reached by a pacific procedure could be violated with impunity. In all these cases the country resorting to war is not acting on its private initiative but is in a sense the agent and the organ of the community.

It is for this reason that we have not hesitated to speak of the exceptional authorisation of war. It has been proposed that the word "force" should be used in order to avoid any mention of "war"—in order to spare the public that disappointment which it might feel when it found that, notwithstanding the solemn condemnation of war, war was still authorised in exceptional cases. We preferred, however, to recognise the position frankly by retaining the expression "resort to war" which is used in the Covenant. If we said "force" instead of "war", we should not be altering the facts in any way. Moreover, the confession that war is still possible in specific cases has a certain value, because the term describes a definite and well-understood situation, whereas the expression "resort to force" would be liable to be misunderstood, and also because it emphasises the value of the sanctions at the disposal of the community of States bound by the Protocol.

4. COMPULSORY JURISDICTION OF THE PERMANENT COURT OF INTERNATIONAL JUSTICE.

Article 3.

The general principle of the Protocol could not be accepted unless the pacific settlement of all international disputes without distinction were made possible.

This solution has been found, in the first place, in the extension of the compulsory jurisdiction of the Permanent Court of International Justice.

According to its Statute, the jurisdiction of the Court is, in principle, optional. On the other hand, Article 36, paragraph 2. of the Statute, offers States the opportunity of making the jurisdiction compulsory in respect of all or any of the classes of legal disputes affecting: (*a*) the interpretation of a Treaty; (*b*) any question of international law; (*c*) the existence of any fact which, if established, would constitute a breach of an international obligation; (*d*) the nature or extent of the reparation to be made for the breach of an international obligation. States have only to declare their intention through the special Protocol annexed to the Statute. The undertaking then holds good in respect of any other State which assumes the same obligation. It may be given either unconditionally or on condition of reciprocity on the part of several or certain other States; either permanently or for a fixed period.

So far such compulsory jurisdiction has only been accepted by a small number of countries. The majority of States have abstained because they did not see their way to accept compulsory jurisdiction by the Court in certain cases falling within one or another of the classes of dispute enumerated above, and because they were not sure whether, in accepting, they could make reservations to that effect.

It was for this reason that the Assembly in its resolution of September 6th, requested the First Committee to render more precise the terms of Article 36, paragraph 2, in order to facilitate its acceptance.

Careful consideration of the article has shown that it is sufficiently elastic to allow of all kinds of reservations. Since it is open to the States to accept compulsory jurisdiction by the Court in respect of certain of the classes of dispute mentioned and not to accept it in respect of the rest, it is also open to them only to accept it in respect of a portion of one of those classes; rights need not be exercised in their full extent. In giving the undertaking in question, therefore, States are free to declare that it will not be regarded as operative in those cases in which they consider it to be inadmissible.

We can imagine possible and therefore legitimate, reservations either in connection with a certain class of dispute or, generally speaking, in regard to the precise stage at which the dispute may be laid before the Court. While we cannot here enumerate all the conceivable reservations, it may be worth while to mention merely as examples those to which we referred in the course of our discussions.

From the class of disputes relating to "the interpretation of a treaty" there may be excluded, for example, disputes as to the interpretation of certain specified classes of treaty such as political treaties, peace treaties, etc.

From the class of disputes relating to "any point of international law" there may be excluded, for example, disputes as to the application of a political treaty, a peace treaty, etc., or as to any specified question or disputes which might arise as the outcome of hostilities initiated by one of the signatory States in agreement with the Council or the Assembly of the League of Nations.

Again, there are many possible reservations as to the precise stage at which a dispute may be laid before the Court. The most far-reaching of these would be to make the resort to the Court in connection with every dispute in respect of which its compulsory jurisdiction is recognised contingent upon the establishment of an agreement for submission of the case which, failing agreement between the parties, would be drawn up by the Court itself, the analogy of the provisions of the Hague Convention of 1907 dealing with the Permanent Court of Arbitration being thus followed.

It might also be stated that the recognition of the compulsory jurisdiction of the Court does not prevent the parties to the dispute from agreeing to resort to a preliminary conciliation procedure before the Council of the League of Nations or any other body selected by them, or to submit their disputes to arbitration in preference to going before the Court.

A State might also, while accepting compulsory jurisdiction by the Court, reserve the right of laying disputes before the Council of the League with a view to conciliation in accordance with paragraphs 1-3 of Article 15 of the Covenant, with the proviso that neither party might, during the proceedings before the Council, take proceedings against the other in the Court.

It will be seen, therefore, that there is a very wide range of reservations which may be made in connection with the undertaking referred to in Article 36, paragraph 2. It is possible that apprehensions may arise lest the right to make reservations should destroy the practical value of the undertaking. There seems, however, to be no justification for such misgivings. In the first place, it is to be hoped that every Government will confine its reservations to what is absolutely essential. Secondly, it must be recognised that, however restrictive the scope of the undertaking may be, it will always be better than no undertaking at all.

The fact that the signatory States undertake to accede, even though it be with reservations, to paragraph 2 of Article 36 may therefore be held to constitute a great advance.

Such accession must take place at latest within the month following upon the coming into force or subsequent acceptance of the Protocol.

It goes without saying that such accession in no way restricts the liberty which States possess, under the ordinary law, of concluding special agreements for arbitration. It is entirely open to any two countries signatory of the Protocol which have acceded to paragraph 2 of Article 36 to extend still further, as between themselves, the compulsory jurisdiction of the Court, or to stipulate that before having recourse to its jurisdiction they will submit their disputes to a special procedure of conciliation or even to stipulate, either before or after a dispute has arisen, that it shall be brought before a special tribunal of arbitrators or before the Council of the League of Nations rather than to the Court.

It is also certain that up to the time of the coming into force or acceptance of the Protocol accession to paragraph 2 of Article 36, which will thenceforth become compulsory, will remain optional, and that if such accession has already taken place it will continue to be valid in accordance with the terms under which it was made.

The only point which may cause difficulty is the question what is the effect of accessions given to the Protocol if the latter becomes null and void. It may be asked whether such accessions are to be regarded as so intimately bound up with the Protocol that they must disappear with it. The reply must be in the negative. The sound rule of interpretation of international treaties is that, unless there is express provision to the contrary, effects already produced survive the act from which they sprang.

The natural corollary is that any State which wishes to make the duration of its accession to Article 36 dependent on the duration of the Protocol must make an express stipulation to this effect. As Article 36 permits acceptance of the engagement in question for a specified term only, a State may, when acceding, stipulate that it only undertakes to be bound during such time as the Protocol shall remain in force.

5. STRENGTHENING OF PACIFIC METHODS OF PROCEDURE.

Article 4.

We have, in the second place, succeeded in making possible the pacific settlement of all disputes by strengthening the procedure laid down in the Covenant.

Article 4, paragraph 1.

Action by the Council with a view to reconciliation. If a dispute does not come within the compulsory jurisdiction of the Permanent Court of International Justice and if the Parties have been unable to come to an agreement to refer it to the Court or to submit it to arbitration, it should, under the terms of Article 15 of the Covenant, be submitted to the Council, which will endeavour to secure a settlement by reconciling the parties. If the Council's efforts are successful, it must, so far as it considers it advisable, make public a statement giving such facts and explanations regarding the dispute and the terms of settlement thereof as it may deem appropriate.

In this connection no change has been made in the procedure laid down by the Covenant. It appeared unnecessary to specify what particular procedure should be followed. The Council is given the utmost latitude in choosing the means most appropriate for the reconciliation of the parties. It may take advice in various quarters; it may hear expert opinions; it may proceed to investigations or expert enquiries, whether by itself or through the intermediary of experts chosen by it; it may even, upon application by one of the parties, constitute a special conciliation committee. The essential point is to secure, if possible, a friendly settlement of the dispute; the actual methods to be employed are of small importance. It is imperative that nothing should in any way hamper the Council's work in the interests of peace. It is for the Council to examine the question whether it would be expedient to draw up for its own use and bring to the notice of the Governments of the signatory States general regulations of procedure applicable to cases brought before it and designed to test the goodwill of the parties with a view to persuading them more easily to reach a settlement under its auspices.

Experience alone can show whether it will be necessary to develop the rules laid down in the first three paragraphs of Article 15 of the Covenant.

For the moment it would appear to be expedient to make no addition and to have full confidence in the wisdom of the Council, it being understood that, whether at the moment in question or at any other stage of the procedure, it will be open to the parties to come to an agreement for some different method of settlement: by way of direct understanding, constitution of a special committee of mediators or conciliators, appeal to arbitration or to the Permanent Court of International Justice.

The new procedure set up by the Protocol will be applicable only in the event of the Council's failing in its efforts at reconciliation and of the parties failing to come to an understanding in regard to the method of settlement to be adopted.

In such case, before going further, the Council must call upon the parties to submit their dispute to judicial settlement or to arbitration.

It is only in the case where this appeal — which the Council will make in the manner which appears to it most likely to secure a favourable hearing—is not listened to that the procedure will acquire the compulsory character which is necessary to make certain the final settlement of all disputes.

There are three alternatives:

(*a*) Compulsory arbitration at the request of one of the parties;
(*b*) A unanimous decision by the Council;
(*c*) Compulsory arbitration enjoined by the Council.

Appropriate methods are laid down for all three cases.

Article 4, paragraph 2.

First case of Compulsory Arbitration. — If the parties, being called upon by the Council to submit their dispute to a judicial or arbitral settlement, do not succeed in coming to an agreement on the subject, there is no question of optional arbitration, but if a single party desires arbitration, arbitration immediately becomes compulsory.

The dispute is then *ipso facto* referred to a Committee of Arbitrators, which must be constituted within such time limit as the Council shall fix.

Full liberty is left to the parties themselves to constitute this Committee of Arbitrators They may agree between themselves in regard to the number, names and powers of the arbitrators and the procedure. It is to be understood that the word "powers" is to be taken in the widest sense, including, *inter alia*, the questions to be put.

It was not considered desirable to develop this idea further. It appeared to be sufficient to state that any result which could be obtained by means of an agreement between the parties was preferable to any other solution.

It also appeared inexpedient to define precisely the powers which should be conferred upon the arbitrators. This is a matter which depends upon the circumstances of each particular case. According to the case, the arbitrators, as is said above, may fill the rôle of judges giving decisions of pure law or may have the function of arranging an amicable settlement with power to take account of considerations of equity.

It has not been thought necessary to lay this down in the form of a rule. It has appeared preferable to leave it in each case to the parties to agree between themselves to decide the matter according to the circumstances of the case

Nevertheless, consideration has been given to the possibility that the arbitrators need not necessarily be jurists. It has therefore been decided that, when called upon to deal with points of law, they shall, if one of the parties so desires, request, through the medium of the Council, the advisory opinion of the Permanent Court of International Justice, which must, in such a case, meet with the utmost possible despatch. The opinion of the Court is obtained for the assistance of the arbitrators; it is not legally binding upon them, although its scientific authority must, in all cases, exercise a strong influence upon their judgment. With a view to preventing abusively frequent consultations of this kind, it is understood that the opinion of the Court in regard to disputed points of law can only be asked on a single occasion in the course of each case.

The extension which, in the new system of pacific settlement of disputes, has been given to the advisory procedure of the Court has suggested the idea that it might be desirable to examine whether, even in such cases, it might not be well to adopt the system of adding national judges which at present only obtains in litigious proceedings, and also that of applying to the advisory procedure the provisions of Article 24 of the Statute of the Court relating to withdrawal of judges.

If the parties have not been able to come to an understanding on all or on some of the points necessary to enable the arbitration to be carried out, it lies with the Council to settle the unsettled points, with the exception of the formulation of the questions to be answered, which the arbitrators must seek in the claims set out by the parties or by one of them if the others make default.

In cases where the selection of arbitrators thus falls upon the Council, it has appeared necessary — however much confidence may be felt in the Council's wisdom — to lay down for the selection of the arbitrators certain rules calculated to give the arbitration the necessary moral authority to ensure that it will in practice be respected.

The first rule is that the Council shall, before proceeding to the selection of arbitrators, have regard to the wishes of the parties. It was suggested that this idea should be developed by conferring on the parties the right to indicate their preferences and to challenge a certain number of the arbitrators proposed by the Council.

This proposal was set aside on account of the difficulty of laying down detailed regulations for the exercise of this double right. But it is understood that the Council will have no motive for failing to accept the candidates proposed to it by the different parties nor for imposing upon them arbitrators whom they might wish to reject, nor, finally, for failing to take into account any other suggestion which the parties might wish to make. It is indeed evident that the Council will always be desirous of acting in the manner best calculated to increase to the utmost degree the confidence which the Committee of Arbitrators should inspire in the parties.

The second rule is based on the same point of view. It lays down the right of the Council to select the arbitrators and their president from among persons who, by their nationality, their personal character and their experience, appear to furnish the highest guarantees of competence and impartiality.

Here, too, experience will show whether it would be well for the Council to draw up general regulations for the composition and functioning of the compulsory arbitration now in question and of that above referred to, and for the conciliation procedure in the Council itself. Such regulations would be made for the Council's own use but would be communicated to the Governments of the signatory States.

Article 4, paragraph 3.

Unanimous decision by the Council. If arbitration is refused by both parties, the case will be referred back to the Council, but this time it will acquire a special character. Refusal of arbitration implies the consent of both parties to a final settlement of the dispute by the Council. It implies recognition of an exceptional jurisdiction of the Council. It denotes that the parties prefer the Council's decision to an arbitral award.

Resuming the examination of the question, the Council has not only the latitude which it customarily possesses. It is armed with full powers to settle the question finally and irrevocably if it is unanimous. Its decision, given unanimously by all the members other than those representing parties to the dispute, is imposed upon the parties with the same weight and the same force as the arbitration award which it replaces.

Article 4, paragraph 4.

Second case of Compulsory Arbitration. If the Council does not arrive at a unanimous decision, it has to submit the dispute to the judgment of a Committee of Arbitrators, but this time, owing to the parties being deemed to have handed their case over to the Council, the organisation of the arbitration procedure is taken entirely out of their hands. It will be for the Council to settle all the details, the composition, the powers and the procedure of the Committee of Arbitrators. The Council is of course at liberty to hear the parties and even to invite suggestions from them, but it is under no obligation to do so. The only regulation with which it must comply is that, in the choice of arbitrators, it must bear in mind the guarantees of competence and impartiality which, by their nationality, their personal character and their experience, these arbitrators must always furnish.

Article 4, paragraph 6.

Effect of, and Sanction enforcing, Decisions. Failing a friendly arrangement, we are, thanks to the system adopted, in all cases certain of arriving at a final solution of a dispute, whether in the form of a decree of the Permanent Court of International Justice or in the form of an arbitral award or, lastly, in the form of a unanimous decision of the Council.

To this solution the parties are compelled to submit. They must put it into execution or comply with it in good faith.

If they do not do so, they are breaking an engagement entered into towards the other signatories of the Protocol, and this breach involves consequences and sanctions according to the degree of gravity of the case.

If the recalcitrant party confines itself to offering passive resistance to the solution arrived at, it will first be the object of pacific pressure from the Council, which must exercise all its influence to persuade it to respect its engagements. If the Council is unsuccessful, it must propose measures calculated to ensure effect being given to the decision.

On this point the Protocol has been guided solely by the regulation contained at the end of Article 13 of the Covenant. The Council may thus institute against the recalcitrant party collective sanctions of an economic and financial order. It is to be supposed that such sanctions will prove sufficient. It has not appeared possible to go further and to employ force against a State which is not itself resorting to force. The party in favour of which the decision has been given might, however, employ force against the recalcitrant party if authorised to do so by the Council.

But if the State against which the decision has been given takes up arms in resistance thereto, thereby becoming an aggressor against the combined signatories, it deserves even the severe sanctions provided in Article 16 of the Covenant, interpreted in the manner indicated in the present Protocol.

Sphere of Application of Methods of Pacific Procedure. Necessary as the system which we have laid down is for the purpose of ensuring settlement of all disputes, in applying it, the pacific aim which underlies it must be the only guide. It must not be diverted to other purposes and used as an occasion for chicanery and tendencious proceedings by which the cause of peace would lose rather than gain.

A few exceptions to the rule have also had to be made in order to preserve the elasticity of the system. These are cases in which the claimant must be non-suited, the claim being one which has to be rejected *in limine* by the Council, the Permanent Court of International Justice or the arbitrators, as the case may be.

The disputes to which the system will not apply are of three kinds:

Article 4, paragraph 5.

1. The first concerns disputes relating to questions which, at some time prior to the entry into force of the Protocol, have been the subject of a unanimous recommendation by the Council accepted by one of the parties concerned. It is essential to international order and to the prestige of the Council that its unanimous recommendations, which confer a right upon the State accepting them, shall not be called into question again by means of a procedure based upon compulsory arbitration. Failing a friendly arrangement, the only way which lies open for the settlement of disputes to which these recommendations may give rise is recourse to the Council in accordance with the procedure at present laid down in the Covenant.

Article 4, paragraph 7.

2. The same applies to disputes which arise as the result of measures of war taken by one or more signatory States in agreement with the Council or the Assembly of the League of Nations. It would certainly not be admissible that compulsory arbitration should become a weapon in the hands of an enemy to the community to be used against the freedom of action of those who, in the general interest, seek to impose upon that enemy respect for his engagements.

In order to avoid all difficulty of interpretation, these first two classes of exceptions have been formally stated in the Protocol.

3. There is a third class of disputes to which the new system of pacific settlement can also not be applied. These are disputes which aim at revising treaties and international acts in force, or which seek to jeopardise the existing territorial integrity of signatory States. The proposal was made to include these exceptions in the Protocol, but the two Committees were unanimous in considering that, both from the legal and from the political point of view, the impossibility of applying compulsory arbitration to such cases was so obvious that it was quite superfluous to make them the subject of a special provision. It was thought sufficient to mention them in this report.

6. ROLE OF THE ASSEMBLY UNDER THE SYSTEM SET UP BY THE PROTOCOL.

Article 6.

The new procedure should be adapted to the old one, which gave the Assembly the same powers as the Council when a dispute is brought before it, either by the Council itself or at the request of one of the parties.

The question has arisen whether the system of maintaining in the new procedure this equality of powers between the two organs of the League of Nations is a practical one. Some were of opinion that it would be better to exclude intervention by the Assembly. Finally, however, the opposite opinion prevailed; an appeal to the Assembly may, indeed, have an important influence from the point of view of public opinion. Without going so far as to assign to the Assembly the same rôle as to the Council, it has been decided to adopt a mixed system by which the Assembly is, in principle, substituted for the Council in order that, when a dispute is referred to it in conformity with paragraph 9 of Article 15 of the Covenant, it may undertake, in the place of the Council, the various duties provided for in Article 4 of the present Protocol with the exception of purely executive acts which will always devolve upon the Council. For example, the organisation and management of compulsory arbitration, or the transmission of a question to the Permanent Court of International Justice, must always be entrusted to the Council, because, in practice, the latter is the only body qualified for such purposes.

The possible intervention of the Assembly does not affect in any way the final result of the new procedure. If the Assembly does not succeed in conciliating the parties and if one of them so requests, compulsory arbitration will be arranged by the Council in accordance with the rules laid down beforehand.

If none of the parties asks for arbitration, the matter is referred back to the Assembly, and if the solution recommended by the Assembly obtains the majority required under paragraph 10 of Article 15 of the Covenant, it has the same value as a unanimous decision of the Council.

Lastly, if the necessary majority is not obtained, the dispute is submitted to a compulsory arbitration organised by the Council.

In any event, as in the case where the Council alone intervenes, a definitive and binding solution of the dispute is reached.

7. DOMESTIC JURISDICTION OF STATES.

Article 5.

The present Protocol in no way derogates from the rule of Article 15, paragraph 8, of the Covenant, which protects national sovereignty.

In order that there might be no doubt on this point, it appeared advisable to say so expressly.

Before the Council, whatever be the stage in the procedure set up by the Protocol at which the Council intervenes, the provision referred to applies without any modification.

The rule is applied also to both cases of compulsory arbitration. If one of the States parties to the dispute claims that the dispute or part thereof arises out of a matter which by international law is solely within its jurisdiction, the arbitrators must on this point take the advice of the Permanent Court of International Justice through the medium of the Council, for the question thus put in issue is a legal question upon which a judicial opinion should be obtained.

The Court will thus have to give a decision as to whether the question in dispute is governed by international law or whether it falls within the domestic jurisdiction of the State concerned. Its functions will be limited to this point and the question will in any event be referred back to the arbitrators. But, unlike other opinions requested of the Court in the course of a compulsory arbitration—opinions which for the arbitrators are purely advisory—in the present case the opinion of the Court is compulsory in the sense that, if the Court has recognised that the question in dispute falls entirely within the domestic jurisdiction of the State concerned, the arbitrators will simply have to register this conclusion in their award. It is only if the Court holds that the question in dispute is governed by international law that the arbitrators will again take the case under consideration in order to give a decision upon its substance.

The compulsory character of the Court's opinion, in this case, increases the importance of the double question referred to above, in connection with Article 4, relating to the calling-in of national judges, and the application of Article 24 of the Statute of the Court in matters of advisory procedure.

While the principle of Article 15, paragraph 8, of the Covenant is maintained, it has been necessary, in order to make its application more flexible, to call in aid the rule contained in Article 11 of the Covenant, which makes it the duty of the League of Nations, in the event of war or a threat of war, to "take any action that may be deemed wise and effective to safeguard the peace of nations", and obliges the Secretary-General to summon forthwith a meeting of the Council on the request of any Member of the League. It is in this way understood that when it has been recognised that a dispute arises out of a matter which is solely within the domestic jurisdiction of one of the parties, that party or its opponent will be fully entitled to call upon the Council or the Assembly to act.

There is nothing new in this simple reference to Article 11. It leaves unimpaired the right of the Council to take such action as it may deem wise and effectual to safeguard the peace of nations. It does not confer new powers or functions on either the Council or the Assembly. Both these organs of the League simply retain the powers now conferred upon them by the Covenant.

In order to dispel any doubt which may arise from the parallel which has been drawn between Article 15, paragraph 8, and Article 11 of the Covenant, a very clear explanation was given in the course of the discussion in the First Committee.

Where a dispute is submitted to the Council under Article 15 and it is claimed by one party that the dispute arises out of a matter left exclusively within its domestic jurisdiction by international law, paragraph 8 prevents the Council from making any recommendations upon the subject if it holds that the contention raised by the party is correct and that the dispute does in fact arise out of a matter exclusively within that State's jurisdiction.

The effect of this paragraph is that the Council cannot make any recommendation in the technical sense in which that term is used in Article 15, that is to say, it cannot make, even by unanimous report, recommendations which become binding on the parties in virtue of paragraph 6.

Unanimity for the purpose of Article 15 implies a report concurred in by all the members of the Council other than the parties to the dispute. Only a report so concurred in is one which the parties to the dispute are bound to observe, in the sense that, if they resort to war with any party which complies with the recommendations, it will constitute a breach of Article 16 of the Covenant and will set in play the sanctions which are there referred to.

On the other hand, Article 11 is of different scope : first, it operates only in time of war or threat of war ; secondly, it confers no right on the Council or on the Assembly to impose any solution of a dispute without the consent of the parties. Action taken by the Council or the Assembly under this article cannot become binding on the parties to the dispute in the sense in which recommendations under Article 15 become binding, unless they have themselves concurred in it.

One last point should be made clear. The reference which is made to Article 11 of the Covenant holds good only in the eventuality contemplated in Article 15, paragraph 8, of the Covenant. It is obvious that when a unanimous decision of the Council or an arbitral award has been given upon the substance of a dispute, that dispute is finally settled and cannot again be brought either directly or indirectly under discussion. Article 11 of the Covenant does not deal with situations which are covered by rules of law capable of application by a judge. It applies only to cases which are not yet regulated by international law. In fact, it demonstrates the existence of loop-holes in the law.

The reference to Article 11 in two of the articles of the Protocol (Articles 5 and 10) has advantages beyond those to which attention is drawn in the commentary on the text of those articles. It will be an incitement to science to clear the ground for the work which the League of Nations will one day have to undertake with a view to bringing about, through the development of the rules of international law, a closer reconciliation between the individual interests of its Members and the universal interests which it is designed to serve.

8. DETERMINATION OF THE AGGRESSOR.

Article 10.

In order that the procedure of pacific settlement may be accompanied by the necessary sanctions, it has been necessary to provide for determining exactly the State guilty of aggression to which sanctions are to be applied.

This question is a very complex one, and in the earlier work of the League the military experts and jurists who had had to deal with it found it extremely difficult.

There are two aspects to the problem: first, aggression has to be defined, and, secondly, its existence has to be ascertained.

The definition of aggression is a relatively easy matter, for it is sufficient to say that any State is the aggressor which resorts in any shape or form to force in violation of the engagements contracted by it either under the Covenant (if, for instance, being a Member of the League of Nations, it has not respected the territorial integrity or political independence of another Member of the League) or under the present Protocol (if, for instance, being a signatory of the Protocol, it has refused to conform to an arbitral award or to a unanimous decision of the Council). This is the effect of Article 10, which also adds that the violation of the rules laid down for a demilitarised zone is to be regarded as equivalent to resort to war. The text refers to resort to war, but it was understood during the discussion that, while mention was made of the most serious and striking instance, it was in accordance with the spirit of the Protocol that acts of violence and force, which possibly may not constitute an actual state of war, should nevertheless be taken into consideration by the Council.

On the contrary, to ascertain the existence of aggression is a very difficult matter, for although the first of the two elements which together constitute aggression, namely, the violation of an engagement, is easy to verify, the second, namely, resort to force, is not an easy matter to ascertain. When one country attacks another, the latter necessarily defends itself, and when hostilities are in progress on both sides, the question arises which party began them.

This is a question of fact concerning which opinions may differ.

The first idea which occurs to the mind is to make it the duty of the Council to determine who is the aggressor. But, immediately, the question arises whether the Council must decide this question unanimously, or whether a majority vote would suffice. There are serious disadvantages in both solutions and they are therefore unacceptable.

To insist upon a unanimous decision of the Council exposes the State attacked to the loss of those definite guarantees to which it is entitled, if one single Member of the Council— be it in good faith or otherwise — insists on adhering to an interpretation of the facts different from that of all his colleagues. It is impossible to admit that the very existence of a nation should be subject to such a hazard. It is not sufficient to point out that the Council would be bound to declare the existence of aggression in an obvious case and that it could not fail to carry out its duty. The duty would be a duty without a sanction and if by any chance the Council were not to do its duty, the State attacked would be deprived of all guarantees.

But it would also be dangerous to rely on a majority vote of the Council. In that case, the danger would be incurred by the State called upon to furnish assistance and to support the heavy burden of common action, if it still entertained some doubt as to the guilt of the country against which it had to take action. Such a country would run the risk of having to conform to a decision with which it did not agree.

The only escape from this dilemma appeared to lie in some automatic procedure which would not necessarily be based on a decision of the Council. After examining the difficulty and discussing it in all its aspects, the First Committee believes that it has found the solution in the idea of a presumption which shall hold good until the contrary has been established by a unanimous decision of the Council.

The Committee is of opinion that this presumption arises in three cases, namely, when a resort to war is accompanied:

By a refusal to accept the procedure of pacific settlement or to submit to the decision resulting therefrom;

By violation of provisional measures enjoined by the Council as contemplated by Article 7 of the Protocol;

Or by disregard of a decision recognising that the dispute arises out of a matter which lies exclusively within the domestic jurisdiction of the other party and by failure or by refusal to submit the question first to the Council or the Assembly.

In these cases, even if there is not absolute certainty, there exists at any rate a very strong presumption which should suffice for the application of sanctions unless proof to the contrary has been furnished by a unanimous decision of the Council.

It will be noticed that there is a characteristic difference between the first two cases and the third.

In the first two cases the presumption exists when, in addition to a state of war, the special condition referred to is also fulfilled.

In the third case, however, the presumption is dependent upon three conditions: disobedience to a decision, wilful failure to take advantage of the remedy provided in Article 11 of the Covenant, and the existence of a state of war.

This difference is due to the necessity of taking into account the provisions of Article 5 analysed above, which, by its reference to Article 11 of the Covenant, renders the application of paragraph 8 of Article 15 of the Covenant more flexible. After very careful consideration it appeared that it would be unreasonable and unjust to regard as *ipso facto* an aggressor a State which, being prevented through the operation of paragraph 8 of Article 15 from urging its claims by pacific methods and being thus left to its own resources, is in despair driven to war.

It was considered to be more in harmony with the requirements of justice and peace to give such a State which has been non-suited on the preliminary question of the domestic jurisdiction of its adversary, a last chance of arriving at an amicable agreement by offering it the final method of conciliation prescribed in Article 11 of the Covenant. It is only if, after rejecting this method, it has recourse to war that it will be presumed to be an aggressor.

This mitigation of the rigid character of paragraph 8 of Article 15 has been accepted, not only because it is just, but also because it opens no breach in the barrier set up by the Protocol against aggressive war: it in no way infringes the principle — which remains unshaken — that a war undertaken against a State whose exclusive jurisdiction has been formally recognised is an international crime to be avenged collectively by the signatories of the Protocol.

When a State whose demands have been met with the plea of the domestic jurisdiction of its adversary has employed the resource provided for in Article 11 of the Covenant, the presumption of aggression falls to the ground. The aggression itself remains. It will be for the Council to decide who is responsible for the aggression in accordance with the procedure which will be described below.

Apart from the above cases, there exists no presumption which can make it possible automatically to determine who is the aggressor. But this fact must be determined, and, if no other solution can be found, the decision must be left to the Council. The same principle applies where one of the parties is a State which is not a signatory of the Protocol and not a Member of the League.

If the Council is unanimous, no difficulty arises. If, however, the Council is not unanimous, the difficulty is be overcome by directing that the Council must enjoin upon the belligerents an armistice the terms of which it will fix if need be by a two-thirds majority and the party which rejects the armistice or violates it is to be held to be an aggressor.

The system is therefore complete and is as automatic as it can be made.

Where a presumption has arisen and is not rejected by a unanimous decision of the Council, the facts themselves decide who is an aggressor; no further decision by the Council is needed and the question of unanimity or majority does not present itself; the facts once established, the Council is bound to act accordingly.

Where there is no presumption, the Council has to declare the fact of aggression; a decision is necessary and must be taken unanimously. If unanimity is not obtained, the Council is bound to enjoin an armistice, and for this purpose no decision properly speaking has to be taken: there exists an obligation which the Council must fulfil; it is only the fixing of the terms of the armistice which necessitates a decision, and for this purpose a two-thirds majority suffices.

It was proposed to declare that, in cases of extreme urgency, the Council might determine the aggressor, or fix the conditions of an armistice, without waiting for the arrival of the representative which a party not represented among its members has been invited to send under the terms of paragraph 5 of Article 4 of the Covenant.

It seemed preferable, however, not to lay down any rule on this matter at present but to ask the special Committee which the Council is to appoint for the drafting of amendments to the Covenant on the lines of the Protocol, to consider whether such a rule is really necessary.

It may in fact be thought that the Council already possesses all the necessary powers in this matter and that, in cases of extreme urgency, if the State invited to send a representative is too far distant from the seat of the Council, that body may decide that the representative shall be chosen from persons near at hand and shall attend the meeting within a prescribed period, on the expiry of which the matter may be considered in his absence.

The fact of aggression having been established by presumption or by unanimous decision of the Council or by refusal to accept or violation of the armistice, it will only remain to apply the sanctions and bring into play the obligations of the guarantor States. The Council will merely call upon them to fulfil their duty; here, again, there is no decision to be taken but an obligation to be fulfilled, and the question of majority or unanimous vote does not arise.

It is not, indeed, a matter of voting at all.

In order to leave no room for doubt, it has been formally laid down that a State which, at the invitation of the Council, engages in acts of violence against an aggressor is in the legal position of a belligerent and may consequently exercise the rights inherent in that character.

It was pointed out in the course of the discussion that such a State does not possess entire freedom of action. The force employed by it must be proportionate to the object in view and must be exercised within the limits and under the conditions recommended by the Council.

Article 18.

Likewise, in order to avoid any misunderstanding, it has been stipulated, in a special Article, that unanimity or the necessary majority in the Council is always calculated according to the rule referred to on several occasions in Article 15 of the Covenant and repeated in Article 16 of the Covenant for the case of expulsion of a Member from the League, viz., without counting the votes of the representatives of the parties to the dispute.

9. DISPUTES BETWEEN STATES SIGNATORY AND STATES NON-SIGNATORY OF THE PROTOCOL.

Article 16.

As regards the settlement of disputes arising between a State signatory and one or more States non-signatory and non-Members of the League of Nations, the new system has had to be adapted to the former system.

In order that States signatory might enjoy the essential advantages offered by the Protocol, which forbids all wars of aggression, it has been necessary to bring the rule laid down in Article 17 of the Covenant into harmony with the provisions of the Protocol. It has therefore been decided that States non-signatory and non-Members of the League of Nations in conflict with a State signatory shall be invited to conform to the new procedure of pacific settlement and that, if they refuse to do so and resort to war against a State signatory, they shall be amenable to the sanctions provided by Article 16 of the Covenant as defined by the Protocol.

There is no change in the arrangements laid down in the Covenant for the settlement of disputes arising between States Members of the League of Nations of which one is a signatory of the Protocol and the other is not. The legal nexus established by the Covenant between two such parties does not allow the signatory States to apply as of right the new procedure of pacific settlement to non-signatory but Member States. All that signatory States are entitled to expect as regards such other States is that the Council should provide the latter with an opportunity to follow this procedure and it is to be hoped that they will do so. But such States can only be offered an opportunity to follow the new procedure; they cannot be obliged to follow it. If they refuse, preferring to adhere to the procedure laid down in the Covenant, no sanctions could possibly be applied to them.

The above indicated solution of the case of States non-signatory but Members of the League of Nations appears to be so obvious as to require no special mention in the Protocol. A proposal to make a special mention of the matter was made, but after explanations had been given, the authors withdrew their suggestion, declaring that they would be satisfied with the above reference to the subject.

At first sight the difference in the way it is proposed to treat non-signatories non-Members of the League of Nations and non-signatories Members of the League may cause some surprise, for it would seem that the signatory States impose greater obligations on the first category than on the second. This, however, is only an appearance. In reality, the signatory States impose no obligations on either category. They cannot do so because the present Protocol is *res inter alios acta* for all non-signatory States, whether they are Members of the League of Nations or not. The signatories merely undertake obligations as between themselves as to the manner in which they will behave if one of them becomes involved in a conflict with a third State. But whereas, in possible conflicts with a State non-signatory and non-Member of the League, they are entirely free to take such action as they choose, in conflicts which may arise between them and States non-signatory but Members, like themselves, of the League of Nations, their freedom of action is to some extent circumscribed because both parties are bound by legal obligations arising under the Covenant.

2. WORK OF THE THIRD COMMITTEE.

(*Rapporteur:* M. BENES).

SECURITY AND REDUCTION OF ARMAMENTS.

(Articles 7 to 9, 11 to 15, 17 and 21 of the Protocol).

1. INTRODUCTION.

The special work of the Third Committee was to deal with the problem of security (sanctions) and the reduction of armaments.

The work required, above all, important political negotiations. While the question of arbitration only required one political decision of principle, namely, the acceptance of compulsory arbitration, and the remainder was principally a matter of drafting—without question an extremely difficult task—of a scheme for the application of such arbitration, the questions of security and disarmament necessitated long and laborious political negotiations; for they involved fundamental interests, questions of vital importance to the States, engagements so far-reaching as radically to change the general situation of the various countries.

Although in the work of the First Committee the Assembly had distinctly indicated in its resolution of September 6th that there was a likelihood — indeed, a necessity — of amending the Covenant, the work of the Third Committee as regards questions of security and reduction of armaments had, in conformity with the debates of the Assembly, to remain within the framework of the Covenant. Above all, it was a question of developing and rendering more precise what is already laid down in the Covenant. All our discussions, all our labours, were guided by these principles, and a delicate task was thus imposed upon us. But the spirit of conciliation which pervaded all the discussions has permitted us to resolve the two problems which were placed before us. This is, indeed, an important result, and if the solution of the problem of arbitration which has been so happily arrived at by the First Committee be also taken into consideration, we are in the presence of a system the adoption of which may entirely modify our present political life.

This is the real import of the articles of the Protocol concerning the questions of security and reduction of armaments.

2. THREAT OF AGGRESSION: PREVENTIVE MEASURES.

Article 7.

The pacific settlement of disputes being provided for in the present Protocol, the signatory States undertake, should any conflict arise between them, not to resort to preparations for the settlement of such dispute by war and, in general, to abstain from any act calculated to aggravate or extend the said dispute. This provision applies both to the period preceding the submission of the dispute to arbitration or conciliation and to the period in which the case is pending.

This provision is not unaccompanied by sanctions. Any appeal against the violation of the aforesaid undertakings may, in conformity with Article 11 of the Covenant, be brought before the Council. One might say that, in addition to such primary dispute as is or might be submitted to the Council or to some other competent organ, a second dispute arises, caused by the violation of the undertakings provided for in the first paragraph.

The Council, unless it be of opinion that the appeal is not worthy of consideration, will proceed with the necessary enquiries and investigations. Should it be established that an offence has been committed against the provisions of the first paragraph, it will be the duty of the Council, in the light of the results of such enquiries and investigations, to call upon any State guilty of the offence to put an end thereto. Any such State failing to comply will be declared by the Council to be guilty of violation of the Covenant (Article 11) or the Protocol.

The Council must, further, take the necessary measures to put an end, as soon as possible, to a situation calculated to threaten the peace of the world. The text does not define the nature of these preventive measures. Its elasticity permits the Council to take such measures as may be appropriate in each concrete case, as, for example, the evacuation of territories.

Any decisions which may be taken by the Council in virtue of this Article may be taken by a two-thirds majority, except in the case of decisions dealing with questions of procedure which still come under the general rule of Article 5, paragraph 2, of the Covenant. The following decisions, therefore, can be taken by a two-thirds majority:

> The decision as to whether there has or has not been an offence against the first paragraph;
> The decision calling upon the guilty State to remedy the offence;
> The decision as to whether there has or has not been refusal to remedy the offence;
> Lastly, the decision as to the measures calculated to put an end, as soon as possible, to a situation calculated to threaten the peace of the world.

The original text of Article 7 provided that, in the case of enquiries and investigations, the Council should avail itself of the organisation to be set up by the Conterence for the Reduction of Armaments in order to ensure respect for the decisions of that Conference. There is no longer any mention of this organisation, but this omission does not prejudice any decisions which the Conference may be called upon to take regarding the matter. It will be entirely free to set up an organisation, if it judges this necessary, and the Council's right to make use of this body for the enquiries and investigations contemplated will, *a fortiore*, remain intact.

Article 8.

Article 8 must be considered in relation to Article 2. Article 2 establishes the obligation not to resort to war, while Article 8, giving effect to Article 10 of the Covenant, goes further. The signatories undertake to abstain from any act which might constitute a threat of aggression against any other State. Thus, every act which comes within the scope of this idea of a threat of war — and its scope is sufficiently elastic — constitutes a breach of the Protocol, and therefore a dispute with which the Council is competent to deal.

If, for example, one State alleges that another State is engaged in preparations which are nothing less than a particular form of threat of war (such as any kind of secret mobilisation, concentration of troops, formation of armed bodies with the connivance of the Government, etc.), the Council, having established that there is a case for consideration, will apply the procedure which may be defined as the procedure of preventive measures; it will arrange for suitable enquiries and investigations, and, in the event of any breach of the provisions of paragraph 1 being established, will take the steps described in Article 7, paragraph 4.

3. SECURITY : SANCTIONS.

Article 11, paragraphs 1 and 2, of the Protocol in its relation to Articles 10 and 16 of the Covenant.

According to Article 10 of the Covenant, Members of the League undertake to preserve as against external aggression the territorial integrity and existing political independence of all Members of the League. In case of aggression, the Council shall advise upon the means by which this obligation shall be fulfilled.

According to Article 16, should any Member of the League resort to war in disregard of its engagements under Articles 12, 13 or 15, all other Members of the League undertake immediately to apply economic sanctions; furthermore, it shall be the duty of the Council to recommend to the several Governments concerned what effective military, naval or air forces the Members of the League shall severally contribute to the armed forces to be used to protect the engagements of the League.

At the time when they were drafted at the Peace Conference in Paris in 1919, these articles gave rise to keen controversy as to the exact scope of the engagements entered into in these provisions, that is to say, as to the nature and extent of the obligations referred to in Article 10, the exact moment at which such obligations arose, and the legal consequences of the Council recommendations referred to in Article 16, paragraph 2. This controversy continued, as is well known, in the debates here in Geneva, where the question has been discussed in previous years.

Article 11 is intended to settle this controversy. The signatories of the present Protocol accept the obligation to apply against the aggressor the various sanctions laid down in the Covenant, as interpreted in Article 11 of the Protocol, when an act of aggression has been established and the Council has called upon the signatory States immediately to apply such sanctions (Article 10, last paragraph). Should they fail so to do, they will not be fulfilling their obligations.

The nature and extent of this obligation is clearly defined in paragraph 2 of Article 11. According to this paragraph, the reply to the question whether a signatory to the Protocol has or has not fulfilled its obligation depends on whether it has loyally and effectively co-operated in resisting the act of aggression to an extent consistent with its geographical position and its particular situation as regards armaments.

The State remains in control of its forces, and itself, and not the Council, directs them, but paragraph 2 of Article 11 gives us positive material upon which to form a judgment as to whether or not the obligation has been carried out in any concrete case. This criterion is supplied by the term: *loyally and effectively*.

In answering the question whether a State has or has not fulfilled its obligations in regard to sanctions, a certain elasticity in the obligations laid down in Article 11 allows of the possibility of *taking into account, from every point of view, the position of each State which is a signatory to the present Protocol*. The signatory States are not all in possession of equal facilities for acting when the time comes to apply the sanctions. This depends upon the geographical position and economic and social condition of the State, the nature of its population, internal institutions, etc.

Indeed, during the discussion as to the system of sanctions, certain delegations declared that their countries were in a special situation by reason of their geographical position or the state of their armaments. These countries desired to co-operate to the fullest extent of their resources in resistance to every act of aggression, but they drew attention to their special conditions. In order to take account of this situation, an addition has been made to paragraph 2 of Article 11 pointing out this state of affairs and laying stress on the particular situation of the countries in question. Moreover, Article 13 of the Protocol allows such countries to inform the Council of these matters beforehand.

I would further add that the obligations I refer to are imperfect obligations in the sense that no sanctions are provided for against any party which shall have failed loyally and effectively to co-operate in protecting the Covenant and resisting every act of aggression. It should, however, be emphasised that such a State would have failed in the fulfilment of its duties and would be guilty of a violation of engagements entered into.

In view of the foregoing, the gist of Article 11, paragraphs 1 and 2, might be expressed as follows: Each State is the judge of the manner in which it shall carry out its obligations but not of the existence of those obligations, that is to say, each State remains the judge of what it will do but no longer remains the judge of what it should do.

Now that the present Protocol has defined more precisely the origin, nature and extent of the obligations arising out of the Covenant, the *functions of the Council, as provided in Articles 10 and 16, have become clearer and more definite.*

Directly the Council has called upon the signatories to the Protocol to apply without delay the sanctions provided in Article 11, it becomes a regulating, or rather an advisory, body, but not an executive body. The nature of the acts of aggression may vary considerably; the means for their suppression will also vary. It would frequently be unnecessary to make use of all the means which, according to paragraphs 1 and 2 of Article 11, are, so to speak, available for resisting an act of aggression. It might even be dangerous if, from fear of failing in their duties, States made superfluous efforts. It will devolve upon the Council, which, under Article 13 can be put in possession of the necessary data, to give *its opinion*, should need occur, as to the best means of executing the obligations which arise directly it enjoins the application of sanctions, especially as to the sequence in which the sanctions must be applied.

The practical application of the sanctions would, however, always devolve upon the Governments; the real co-operation would ensue upon their getting into touch, through diplomatic channels — perhaps by conferences — and by direct relations between different General Staffs, as in the last war. The Council would, of course, be aware of all these negotiations, would be consulted and make recommendations.

The difference between the former state of affairs and the new will therefore be as follows:

According to the system laid down by the Covenant:

1. The dispute arises.
2. In cases where neither the arbitral procedure nor the judicial settlement provided for in Article 13 of the Covenant is applied, the Council meets and discusses the dispute, attempts to effect conciliation, mediation, etc.
3. If it be unsuccessful and war breaks out, the Council, if unanimous, has to express an opinion as to which party is guilty. The Members of the League then decide for themselves whether this opinion is justified and whether their obligations to apply economic sanctions become operative.
4. The Council then has, *by a unanimous decision, to recommend* military sanctions.
5. If unanimity cannot be obtained, the Council ceasing to take action, each party is practically free to act as it chooses.

According to the new system defined in the Protocol, the situation is as follows:

1. The dispute arises.
2. The system of peaceful settlement provided for by the Protocol comes into play.
3. The Council intervenes, and if, after arbitration has been refused, war is resorted to, if the provisional preventive measures are not observed, etc., the Council decides which party is the aggressor and calls upon the signatory States to apply the sanctions.
4. This decision implies that such sanctions as the case requires — economic, financial, military, naval and air — shall be applied forthwith, and without further recommendations or decisions.

We have therefore the following new elements:

(*a*) The obligation to apply the necessary sanctions of every kind as a direct result of the decision of the Council.

(*b*) The elimination of the case in which all parties would be practically free to abstain from any action. The introduction of a system of arbitration and of provisional measures which permits of the determination in every case of the aggressor.

(*c*) No decision is taken as to the strength of the military, naval and air forces, and no details are given as to the measures which are to be adopted in a particular case. None the less, objective criteria are supplied which define the obligation of each signatory; it is bound, in resistance to an act of aggression, to collaborate *loyally and effectively* in applying the sanctions in accordance with its geographical situation and its particular situation as regards armaments.

That is why I said that *the great omission in the Covenant has been made good.*

It is true that no burden has been imposed on States beyond the sanctions already provided for in the Covenant. But, at present, a State seeking to elude the obligations of the Covenant can reckon on two means of escape:

(1) The Council's recommendations need not be followed.

(2) The Council may fail to obtain unanimity, making impossible any declaration of aggression, so that no obligation to apply military sanctions will be imposed and everyone will remain free to act as he chooses

We have abandoned the above system and both these loopholes are now closed.

Articie 11, *paragraphs* 3 *and* 4.

Paragraph 3 of Article 11 has been drafted with a view to giving greater precision to certain' provisions of Article 11, paragraph 3, of the Covenant. Article 16, paragraph 3, refers to mutual support in the application of financial and economic measures. Article 11, paragraph 3, of the present Protocol establishes real economic and financial co-operation between a State which has been attacked and the various States which come to its assistance.

As, under Article 10 of the Protocol, it may happen that both States involved in a dispute are declared to be aggressors, the question arose as to what would be the best method of settling this problem. There were three alternatives: to apply the principle contained in paragraph 1, which is practically equivalent to making a sort of police war on both parties — or to leave the matter to pursue its course, or, finally, to compel States which disturb the peace of the world to desist from acts of war by the employment of means less severe than those indicated in paragraph 1. It is the last method which has been chosen. Only economic measures will be taken against such States, and naturally they will not be entitled to receive the assistance referred to in Article 11, paragraph 3.

Article 12.

Article 16, paragraph 1, of the Covenant provides for the immediate severance of all trade or financial relations with the aggressor State, and paragraph 3 of the same Article provides, *inter alia*, for economic and financial co-operation between the State attacked and the various States coming to its assistance.

As has already been pointed out, these engagements have been confirmed and made more definite in Article 11 of the Protocol.

But the severance of relations and the co-operation referred to necessarily involve measures so complex that, when the moment arises, doubts may well occur as to what measures are necessary and appropriate to give effect to the obligations assumed under the above provisions. These problems require full consideration in order that States may know beforehand what their attitude should be.

Article 12 defines the conditions of such investigation.

It is not expressly stated that the problem will be examined by the Council in collaboration with the various Governments, but the Council will naturally, if it deems it necessary, invite the Governments to furnish such information as it may require for the purpose of carrying out the task entrusted to it under Article 12.

Article 13, *paragraph* 1.

The above explanation of Article 11, paragraphs 1 and 2, contains many references to Article 13.

As I have already pointed out, in case sanctions have to be applied, it is highly important that there should exist some organ competent to express an opinion as to the best way in which their obligations could be carried out by the signatories. As you are aware, this organ, according to the Covenant, is the Council. In order that the Council may effectively fulfil this duty, Article 13 empowers it to receive undertakings from States, determining *in advance* the military, naval and air forces which they would be able to bring into action immediately in order to ensure the fulfilment of the obligations in regard to sanctions arising, out of the Covenant and the present Protocol.

It is also necessary to emphasise the fact that the means which the States signatories to the present Protocol have at their disposal for the fulfilment of the obligations arising out of Article 11 vary considerably owing to the differences in the geographical, economic, financial, political and social condition of different States. Information as to the means at the disposal of each State is therefore indispensable in order that the Council may in full understanding give its opinion as to the best method by which such obligations may best be carried out.

Finally, as regards the question of the reduction of armaments, which is the final goal to which our efforts are tending, the information thus furnished to the Council may be of very great importance, as every State, knowing what forces will be available for its assistance in case it is attacked, will be able to judge to what extent it may reduce its armaments without compromising its existence as a State, and every State will thus be able to provide the International Conference for the Reduction of Armaments with very valuable data. I should add, moreover, that Article 13, paragraph 1, does not render it compulsory for States to furnish this information. It is desirable that States should furnish the Council with this information, but they are at liberty not to do so.

Article 13, *paragraphs* 2 *and* 3.

The provisions of Article 13, paragraphs 2 and 3, refer to the special agreements which were discussed at such length last year. In view of the fact that, according to paragraph 2, such agreements can only come into force when the Council has invited the signatory States to apply the sanctions, the nature of these agreements may be defined as follows:

Special agreements must be regarded as the means for the rapid application of sanctions of every kind in a particular case of aggression. They are additional guarantees which give weaker States an absolute assurance that the system of sanctions will never fail. They guarantee that there will always be States prepared immediately to carry out the obligations provided for in Article 11 of the Protocol.

In accordance with Article 18 of the Covenant, it is expressly stated that these agreements will be registered and published by the Secretariat, and it has also been decided that they will remain open for signature to any State Member of the League of Nations which may desire to accede to them.

4. ENDING OF SANCTIONS: PUNISHMENT OF THE AGGRESSOR.

Article 14.

Article 14 is in perfect keeping with the last paragraphs of Articles 10 and 11. In the paragraphs in question, the coming into operation of the sanctions depends upon an injunction by the Council; it therefore also devolves upon the Council to declare that the object for which the sanctions were applied has been attained. Just as the application of the sanctions is a matter for the States, so it rests with them to liquidate the operations undertaken with a view to resisting the act of aggression.

Article 15.

Paragraph 1 is similar to Article 10 of the Draft Treaty of Mutual Assistance drawn up last year.

Paragraph 2 is designed to prevent the sanctions provided for in Article 11 from undergoing any change in character during the process of execution and developing into a war of annexation.

In view of the observations of various delegations regarding the punishment of the aggressor, it should be added that it would be incorrect to interpret this article as meaning that the only penalties to be apprehended by the aggressor as the result of his act shall be the burdens referred to in paragraph 1. If necessary, securities against fresh aggression, or pledges guaranteeing the fulfilment of the obligations imposed in accordance with paragraph 1, might be required. Only annexation of territory and measures involving the loss of political independence are declared inadmissible.

"Territory" is to be taken to mean the whole territory of a State, no distinction being made between the mother-country and the colonies.

5. REDUCTION OF ARMAMENTS.

Articles 17 and 21.

Although it has not been possible to solve the problem of the reduction of armaments in the clauses of the document submitted to the Assembly for approval, our work paves the way to it and makes it possible.

The reduction of armaments will result, in the first place, from the general security created by a diminution of the dangers of war arising from the compulsory pacific settlement of all disputes.

It will also ensue from the certainty which any State attacked will have of obtaining the economic and financial support of all the signatory States, and such support would be especially important should the aggressor be a great Power, capable of carrying on a long war.

Nevertheless, for States which, owing to their geographical position, are especially liable to attack, and for States whose most important centres are adjacent to their frontiers, the dangers of a sudden attack are so great that it will not be possible for them to base any plan for the reduction of their armaments simply upon the political and economic factors referred to above, no matter what the importance of such factors may be.

It has also been repeatedly declared that many States would require to know what military support they could count on, before the convening of the Conference, if they are to submit to the Conference proposals for large reductions of armaments; this might necessitate negotiations between the Governments and with the Council before the meeting of the Conference for the reduction of armaments provided for in Article 17. The undertakings referred to in Article 13 of the Protocol should be interpreted in the light of the above.

In drawing up the general programme of the Conference, it will also be necessary, as stated in paragraph 2 of Article 17, for the Council, apart from other criteria, "to take into account the undertakings mentioned".

In view of the close interdependence of the three great problems involved, namely, the pacific settlement of disputes, sanctions against those who disturb the peace of the world, and reduction of armaments, the Protocol provides for the convening by the Council of a general Conference for the Reduction of Armaments and for the preparation of the work of such a Conference. Furthermore, the application of the clauses concerning arbitration and sanctions will be conditional on the adoption by the said Conference of a plan for the reduction and limitation of armaments.

Moreover, in order to preserve the connection between the three big problems referred to above, it is provided that the whole Protocol will lapse in the event of the non-execution of the scheme adopted by the Conference. It devolves upon the Council to declare this under conditions to be determined by the Conference itself.

The last paragraph of Article 21 provides for the case of the partial lapsing of the Protocol after it has been put into force. Should the plan adopted by the Conference be regarded as having been put into effect, any State which fails to execute it, so far as it is concerned, will not benefit by the provisions of the Protocol.

6. THE COVENANT AND THE PROTOCOL.

Article 19.

The present Protocol emphasises and defines certain obligations arising out of the Covenant. Those of which the present Protocol makes no mention are not affected in any manner. They still exist. Examples which might be quoted are those laid down in Article 16, paragraph 3, of the Covenant, namely, the obligation of the States to give one another mutual support in order to minimise the loss and inconvenience resulting from the application of the economic and financial sanctions or the obligation of the States to take the necessary steps to afford passage through their territory to forces which are co-operating to protect the covenants of the League.

Moreover, as the Swiss Delegation suggests, attention should be directed to the fact that the present Protocol does not in any way affect the special position of Switzerland arising out of the Declaration of the Council at London on February 13th, 1920. As the special position of Switzerland is in accordance with the Covenant, it will also be in accordance with the Protocol.

III. — **Conclusion.**

No further explanations need be added to these comments on the articles. The main principles of the Protocol are clear, as are the detailed provisions.

Our purpose was to make war impossible, to kill it, to annihilate it. To do this, we had to create a system for the pacific settlement of *all disputes* which might arise. In other words, it meant the creation of a system of arbitration from which no international dispute, whether legal or political, could escape. The plan drawn up leaves no loophole; it prohibits wars of every description and lays down that all disputes shall be settled by pacific means.

But this absolute character which has been given to the system of arbitration should also belong to the whole of the scheme, to the treatment of every question of principle. If there were one single gap in the system, if the smallest opening were left for any measure of force, the whole system would collapse.

Arbitration, therefore, is provided for every kind of dispute, and aggression is defined in such a way as to give no cause for hesitation when the Council has to take a decision.

These reasons led us to fill in the gaps in the Covenant and to define the sanctions in such a way that no possible means could be found of evading them, and that there should be a sound and definite basis for the feeling of security.

Finally, the Conference for the Reduction of Armaments is indissolubly bound up with this whole system: *there can be no arbitration or security without disarmament, nor can there be disarmament without arbitration and security.*

The peace of the world is at stake.

The Fifth Assembly has undertaken a work of worldwide political importance which, if it succeeds, is destined profoundly to modify present political conditions. This year great progress in this direction has been made in our work. If we succeed, the League of Nations will have rendered an inestimable service to the whole modern world. Such success depends partly upon the Assembly itself and partly upon individual Governments. We submit to the Assembly the fruit of our labours: a work charged with the highest hopes. We beg the Assembly to examine our proposals with care, and to recommend them to the various Governments for acceptance.

In this spirit and with such hopes do we request the Assembly to vote the draft resolutions 1 and 2 that are presented with this Report.

Annex 14.

ARBITRATION, SECURITY AND REDUCTION OF ARMAMENTS.

Resolution adopted by the Fifth Assembly at its meeting held on October 2nd, 1924, on the Reports of the First and Third Committees.

I. The Assembly,

Having taken note of the reports of the First and Third Committees on the questions referred to them by the Assembly resolution of September 6th, 1924:

Welcomes warmly the draft Protocol on the Pacific Settlement of International Disputes proposed by the two Committees of which the text is annexed to this resolution, and

Decides:

(1) To recommend to the earnest attention of all the Members of the League the acceptance of the said draft Protocol;

(2) To open immediately the said Protocol in the terms proposed for signature by those representatives of Members of the League who are already in a position to sign it and to hold it open for signature by all other States;

(3) To request the Council forthwith to appoint a Committee to draft the amendments to the Covenant contemplated by the terms of the said Protocol;

(4) To request the Council to convene an International Conference for the Reduction of Armaments, which shall meet at Geneva as provided by the following stipulations of Article 17 of the draft Protocol:

> "In preparation for the convening of the Conference, the Council shall draw up, with due regard to the undertakings contained in Articles 11 and 13 of the present Protocol, a general programme for the reduction and limitation of armaments which shall be laid before the Conference and be communicated to the Governments at the earliest possible date, and at the latest three months before the Conference meets.
>
> "If by May 1st, 1925, ratifications have not been deposited by at least a majority of the permanent Members of the Council and ten other Members of the League, the Secretary-General of the League shall immediately consult the Council as to whether he shall cancel the invitations or merely adjourn the Conference to a subsequent date to be fixed by the Council so as to permit the necessary number of ratifications to be obtained."

(5) To request the Council to put into immediate execution the provisions of Article 12 of the draft Protocol.

[1] TRADUCTION. — TRANSLATION.

No. 1292. — TREATY OF MUTUAL GUARANTEE[2] BETWEEN GERMANY, BELGIUM, FRANCE, GREAT BRITAIN AND ITALY, DONE AT LOCARNO, OCTOBER 16, 1925.

Official text in French. This Treaty was registered with the Secretariat, in accordance with its Article 10, on September 14, 1926, the date of its entry into force.

THE PRESIDENT OF THE GERMAN REICH, HIS MAJESTY THE KING OF THE BELGIANS, THE PRESIDENT OF THE FRENCH REPUBLIC, HIS MAJESTY THE KING OF THE UNITED KINGDOM OF GREAT BRITAIN AND IRELAND AND OF THE BRITISH DOMINIONS BEYOND THE SEAS, EMPEROR OF INDIA, HIS MAJESTY THE KING OF ITALY ;

Anxious to satisfy the desire for security and protection which animates the peoples upon whom fell the scourge of the war of 1914-18 ;

Taking note of the abrogation of the treaties for the neutralisation of Belgium, and conscious of the necessity of ensuring peace in the area which has so frequently been the scene of European conflicts ;

Animated also with the sincere desire of giving to all the signatory Powers concerned supplementary guarantees within the framework of the Covenant of the League of Nations and the treaties in force between them ;

Have determined to conclude a treaty with these objects, and have appointed as their Plenipotentiaries :

THE PRESIDENT OF THE GERMAN EMPIRE :

> Dr. Hans LUTHER, Chancellor of the Empire ;
> Dr. Gustav STRESEMANN, Minister for Foreign Affairs ;

HIS MAJESTY THE KING OF THE BELGIANS :

> M. Emile VANDERVELDE, Minister for Foreign Affairs ;

THE PRESIDENT OF THE FRENCH REPUBLIC :

> M. Aristide BRIAND, Prime Minister and Minister for Foreign Affairs ;

HIS MAJESTY THE KING OF THE UNITED KINGDOM OF GREAT BRITAIN AND IRELAND AND OF THE BRITISH DOMINIONS BEYOND THE SEAS, EMPEROR OF INDIA :

> The Right Honourable Stanley BALDWIN, M.P., First Lord of the Treasury and Prime Minister ;
> The Right Honourable Joseph Austen CHAMBERLAIN, M.P., Principal Secretary of State for Foreign Affairs ;

HIS MAJESTY THE KING OF ITALY :

> The Honourable Vittorio SCIALOJA, Senator of the Kingdom ;

---

[1] Communiquée par le Ministère des Affaires étrangères de Sa Majesté britannique.   [1] Communicated by His Britannic Majesty's Foreign Office.

[2] The ratifications were deposited at Geneva, September 14, 1926.

Who, having communicated their full powers, found in good and due form have agreed as follows :

Article 1.

The High Contracting Parties collectively and severally guarantee, in the manner provided in the following Articles, the maintenance of the territorial *status quo* resulting from the frontiers between Germany and Belgium and between Germany and France, and the inviolability of the said frontiers as fixed by or in pursuance of the Treaty of Peace signed at Versailles on June 28, 1919, and also the observance of the stipulations of Articles 42 and 43 of the said Treaty concerning the demilitarised zone.

Article 2.

Germany and Belgium, and also Germany and France, mutually undertake that they will in no case attack or invade each other or resort to war against each other.

This stipulation shall not, however, apply in the case of :

(1) The exercise of the right of legitimate defence, that is to say, resistance to a violation of the undertaking contained in the previous paragraph or to a flagrant breach of Articles 42 or 43 of the said Treaty of Versailles, if such breach constitutes an unprovoked act of aggression and by reason of the assembly of armed forces in the demilitarised zone, immediate action is necessary ;

(2) Action in pursuance of Article 16 of the Covenant of the League of Nations ;

(3) Action as the result of a decision taken by the Assembly or by the Council of the League of Nations or in pursuance of Article 15, paragraph 7, of the Covenant of the League of Nations, provided that in this last event the action is directed against a State which was the first to attack.

Article 3.

In view of the undertakings entered into in Article 2 of the present Treaty, Germany and Belgium, and Germany and France, undertake to settle by peaceful means and in the manner laid down herein all questions of every kind which may arise between them and which it may not be possible to settle by the normal methods of diplomacy :

Any question with regard to which the Parties are in conflict as to their respective rights shall be submitted to judicial decision, and the Parties undertake to comply with such decision.

All other questions shall be submitted to a conciliation commission. If the proposals of this commission are not accepted by the two Parties, the question shall be brought before the Council of the League of Nations, which will deal with it in accordance with Article 15 of the Covenant of the League.

The detailed arrangements for effecting such peaceful settlement are the subject of special Agreements signed this day.

Article 4.

(1) If one of the High Contracting Parties alleges that a violation of Article 2 of the present Treaty or a breach of Articles 42 or 43 of the Treaty of Versailles has been or is being committed, it shall bring the question at once before the Council of the League of Nations.

(2) As soon as the Council of the League of Nations is satisfied that such violation or breach has been committed, it will notify its finding without delay to the Powers signatory of the present

Treaty, who severally agree that in such case they will each of them come immediately to the assistance of the Power against whom the act complained of is directed.

(3) In case of a flagrant violation of Article 2 of the present Treaty or of a flagrant breach of Articles 42 or 43 of the Treaty of Versailles by one of the High Contracting Parties, each of the other Contracting Parties hereby undertakes immediately to come to the help of the Party against whom such a violation or breach has been directed as soon as the said Power has been able to satisfy itself that this violation constitutes an unprovoked act of aggression and that by reason either of the crossing of the frontier or of the outbreak of hostilities or of the assembly of armed forces in the demilitarised zone immediate action is necessary. Nevertheless, the Council of the League of Nations, which will be seized of the question in accordance with the first paragraph of this Article, will issue its findings, and the High Contracting Parties undertake to act in accordance with the recommendations of the Council, provided that they are concurred in by all the Members other than the representatives of the Parties which have engaged in hostilities.

Article 5.

The provisions of Article 3 of the present Treaty are placed under the guarantee of the High Contracting Parties as provided by the following stipulations :

If one of the Powers referred to in Article 3 refuses to submit a dispute to peaceful settlement or to comply with an arbitral or judicial decision and commits a violation of Article 2 of the present Treaty or a breach of Articles 42 or 43 of the Treaty of Versailles, the provisions of Article 4 of the present Treaty shall apply.

Where one of the Powers referred to in Article 3, without committing a violation of Article 2 of the present Treaty or a breach of Articles 42 or 43 of the Treaty of Versailles, refuses to submit a dispute to peaceful settlement or to comply with an arbitral or judicial decision, the other Party shall bring the matter before the Council of the League of Nations, and the Council shall propose what steps shall be taken ; the High Contracting Parties shall comply with these proposals.

Article 6.

The provisions of the present Treaty do not affect the rights and obligations of the High Contracting Parties under the Treaty of Versailles or under arrangements supplementary thereto, including the Agreements signed in London on August 30, 1924 [1].

Article 7.

The present Treaty, which is designed to ensure the maintenance of peace, and is in conformity with the Covenant of the League of Nations, shall not be interpreted as restricting the duty of the League to take whatever action may be deemed wise and effectual to safeguard the peace of the world.

Article 8.

The present Treaty shall be registered at the League of Nations in accordance with the Covenant of the League. It shall remain in force until the Council, acting on a request of one or other of the High Contracting Parties notified to the other signatory Powers three months in advance, and voting at least by a two-thirds' majority, decides that the League of Nations ensures sufficient protection to the High Contracting Parties; the Treaty shall cease to have effect on the expiration of a period of one year from such decision.

---

[1] Vol. XXX. pages 63, 75, 89 and 97, of this Series.

Article 9.

The present Treaty shall impose no obligation upon any of the British dominions, or upon India, unless the Government of such dominion, or of India, signifies its acceptance thereof.

Article 10.

The present Treaty shall be ratified and the ratifications shall be deposited at Geneva in the archives of the League of Nations as soon as possible.

It shall enter into force as soon as all the ratifications have been deposited and Germany has become a Member of the League of Nations.

The present Treaty, done in a single copy, will be deposited in the archives of the League of Nations, and the Secretary-General will be requested to transmit certified copies to each of the High Contracting Parties.

In faith whereof the above-mentioned Plenipotentiaries have signed the present Treaty.

Done at Locarno, October 16, 1925.

(L. S.)   *(Signed)*   Hans LUTHER.

(L. S.)   *(Signed)*   Gustav STRESEMANN.

(L. S.)   *(Signed)*   Emile VANDERVELDE.

(L. S.)   *(Signed)*   Aristide BRIAND.

(L. S.)   *(Signed)*   Stanley BALDWIN.

(L. S.)   *(Signed)*   Austen CHAMBERLAIN.

(L. S.)   *(Signed)*   Vittorio SCIALOJA.

FINAL PROTOCOL OF THE LOCARNO CONFERENCE.

The representatives of the German, Belgian, British, French, Italian, Polish and Czechoslovak Governments, who have met at Locarno from October 5 to 16, 1925, in order to seek by common agreement means for preserving their respective nations from the scourge of war and for providing for the peaceful settlement of disputes of every nature which might eventually arise between them,

Have given their approval to the draft Treaties and Conventions which respectively affect them and which, framed in the course of the present Conference, are mutually interdependent :

Treaty[1] between Germany, Belgium, France, Great Britain and Italy (Annex A).

Arbitration[1] Convention between Germany and Belgium (Annex B).
Arbitration[1] Convention between Germany and France (Annex C).
Arbitration[1] Treaty between Germany and Poland (Annex D).
Arbitration[1] Treaty between Germany and Czechoslovakia (Annex E).

These instruments, hereby initialled *ne varietur*, will bear to-day's date, the representatives of the interested Parties agreeing to meet in London on December 1 next, to proceed during the course of a single meeting to the formality of the signature of the instruments which affect them.

---

[1] See International Engagements Nos. 1292 to 1298, of this Volume.

DOCUMENT 5

V. RESOLUTIONS AND RECOMMENDATIONS ADOPTED ON THE REPORTS OF THE THIRD COMMITTEE.

1. DECLARATION CONCERNING WARS OF AGGRESSION.

The Assembly,

Recognising the solidarity which unites the community of nations ;
Being inspired by a firm desire for the maintenance of general peace ;
Being convinced that a war of aggression can never serve as a means of settling international disputes and is, in consequence, an international crime ;
Considering that a solemn renunciation of all wars of aggression would tend to create an atmosphere of general confidence calculated to facilitate the progress of the work undertaken with a view to disarmament ;

Declares :

(1)   That all wars of aggression are, and shall always be, prohibited ;
(2)   That every pacific means must be employed to settle disputes, of every description, which may arise between States.

The Assembly declares that the States Members of the League are under an obligation to conform to these principles.

[Resolution adopted by roll call on September 24th, 1927 (morning).]

DOCUMENT 6

C. A. S. 10

GENEVA, February 6th, 1928.

LEAGUE OF NATIONS

PREPARATORY COMMISSION
FOR THE DISARMAMENT CONFERENCE

COMMITTEE ON ARBITRATION AND SECURITY

1. Introduction to the Three Memoranda on Arbitration, Security and the Articles of the Covenant, submitted by the Chairman of the Committee in agreement with the Rapporteurs.

2. Memorandum on Arbitration and Conciliation, submitted by M. Holsti, Rapporteur.

3. Memorandum on Security Questions, submitted by M. Politis, Rapporteur.

4. Memorandum on Articles 10, 11 and 16 of the Covenant, submitted by M. Rutgers, Rapporteur.

5. Annexes.

Publications of the League of Nations

IX. DISARMAMENT
1928. IX. 3.

3.

Memorandum on Security Questions

Submitted by M. POLITIS, *Rapporteur.*

52. In this initial stage of the Committee's work the task of its rapporteur must necessarily be strictly limited.

First, we have to take a general view of the question, to examine the various treaties and agreements concluded by the States Members of the League, both between themselves and with non-member States, on the subject of security, for the purpose of diagnosing the situation as accurately as possible and obtaining some idea of the present position as regards security. Secondly, having gained our idea of the present position, we have to devise " practical measures " by which constructive work can be done at the present juncture on the lines indicated in the last Assembly's resolution.

I. PRESENT POSITION IN REGARD TO SECURITY.

53. According to the view now taken by most countries, security consists in two main guarantees : (1) that they will not be attacked by any other State ; (2) that if, nevertheless, they were so attacked, they would receive prompt and effective aid and assistance from other countries.

This is the conception embodied in the Covenant of the League. The two guarantees mentioned are to be found, more particularly, the one in Article 10 and the other in Article 16 of the Covenant.

54. The degree of security thus provided, however, is not generally regarded as adequate, because the guarantees on which it rests are left indefinite in their principle and uncertain in their application. Moreover, to diminish still further the degree of security provided under the Covenant, there is the unanimity rule, which controls the Council in setting the guarantees in motion ; for if unanimity is not secured, force may still lawfully be resorted to.

Thus security under the Covenant is subject to too many elements of uncertainty for States which feel themselves threatened to be able to decide, in the present situation, to diminish to any considerable extent the guarantees which they find in their armaments.

55. As a remedy for this, a supplementary general agreement has been suggested to fill up the gaps in the Covenant and enhance the efficacy of its provisions. Two attempts have been made to establish such an agreement. They were, however, unsuccessful, because it was felt that the scope and the uniformity of the guarantees were not suited to the present variety of conditions and the fluctuating nature of international relations.

56. At the same time, the investigations and discussions that took place on these occasions throw a fuller light on the complexity of the problem, and enable everybody to realise the nature of the bonds by which security is linked to disarmament on the one hand, and on the other to arbitration in its widest sense of procedures for pacific settlement. It is now regarded as a twofold axiom that : (1) there can be no disarmament without security, and (2) there can be no security without arbitration.

It is more and more clearly recognised that the relation between disarmament and security is not one of subordination, but of co-ordination ; neither is less important than the other, and their progress must be equal and simultaneous.

The same applies to security and arbitration. Arbitration is an essential factor in security, and is parallel to it in the same way as security is parallel to disarmament. Thus every advance in arbitration is an increase in security, and in the possibility of limiting and reducing armaments.

57. Failing a general agreement, which was for the time being impossible, an endeavour was made to find additional guarantees of security in separate agreements, so linked together as to form a coherent whole consonant with the spirit of the Covenant of the League and operating in harmony with the organisation which the Covenant sets in motion.

58. In this direction rapid progress has been made.

There are now in force 85[1] treaties of conciliation or arbitration, or conciliation and arbitration combined, which are registered with the League, and most of which embody the ideas advocated by the League. Among these there is one collective treaty binding four States. These treaties engage 38 countries, 24 of which are in Europe. Moreover, 14 States (12 in Europe) are bound by the optional clause concerning the compulsory jurisdiction of the Permanent Court of International Justice.

There are 12 separate treaties of non-aggression, three agreements embodying unilateral guarantees, and three agreements regarding unilateral respect for the political independence and territorial integrity of certain countries ; most of these treaties are collective.

There are 15 treaties of political co-operation not amounting to alliances or guarantees; there are three agreements establishing neutral zones; and there are 15 separate treaties of guarantee

---

[1] This figure indicates the number of treaties registered on February 1st, 1928. For details, see the 2nd edition of " Systematic Survey of Arbitration and Security Treaties " (document C. 663. M. 216. 1927. V).

in the form of alliances, military agreements, or pacts of friendship and co-operation, and one collective treaty of non-aggression and guarantee among five States.

The great store of information collected by the Secretariat, with a diligence and zeal for which we are greatly indebted, gives some idea of the nature, the scope, and the practical value of the engagements entered into by the various countries concerned in this immense network of treaties.

It would be interesting to see these engagements represented, particularly on a map of Europe, by lines of various shapes and thicknesses joining the capitals of the contracting States. Such a map would present, in regard to arbitration and security treaties, a picture similar to that which Europe offered at the beginning of the development of railway and telegraph systems. It should here be observed that the increase of security in Europe carries with it a like increase in other parts of the world.

59. Most of these agreements, being due to the impulse given by the League in the matter of arbitration and security, follow certain common lines. Some of them, however, make no suggestion as to the co-ordination of their systems of mutual assistance with the procedure under the Covenant, and more particularly with the action of the Council in an emergency. This is not true of the Locarno Agreements and those which follow the same lines.

60. The treaties now in force form a system which is too involved, too complex, and in some respects too uneven, for the supplementary guarantees of security which they add to those provided by the Covenant to be measured with tolerable accuracy.

In order of importance, they fall into eight main classes :

    (1) Regional collective agreements for non-aggression, pacific settlement and mutual assistance ;

    (2) Separate agreements of the same nature ;

    (3) Agreements for non-aggression ;

    (4) Collective agreements for conciliation, arbitration and judicial settlement ;

    (5) Separate agreements of the same nature ;

    (6) Arbitration agreements ;

    (7) Conciliation agreements ;

    (8) Agreements for simple political co-operation.

61. In each of these classes the practical value of the agreement varies with the nature of the contracting parties. Its value is greater if the relations between the parties are such that disputes capable of causing a rupture might be anticipated, than if their relations have long been friendly and are unlikely to be seriously disturbed.

62. The value of any agreement, however comprehensive and however important as regards the nature of the parties, is essentially relative, for the efficacy of the security which it appears to give to the parties will, in actual fact, depend largely on the position, as regards security, of other countries linked with them by ties of " solidarity of a geographical or other nature ". The security of the former varies as the security of the latter. Consequently, the security of both can only be guaranteed in practice — failing a general agreement — by a series of regional pacts completing each other and forming a harmonious whole within the framework of the League of Nations, whose system of protection would thus be amplified and reinforced.

Until such a position has been secured, the security of certain States will remain too precarious for them to be able to consent to any appreciable reduction of their armaments.

63. Though the regional and separate agreements at present in force may not give the States which have concluded them all the security they desire, it cannot be denied that they do add certain guarantees to those provided by the Covenant of the League. To realise this it will suffice to compare the situation they have brought about with the situation scarcely six years ago, at the time when by its famous Resolution XIV the Third Assembly made absolutely clear the interdependence of disarmament and security. Each one of the numerous arbitration and security agreements which have been concluded since that time has placed in the path of war an obstacle which, slight, even imperceptible as it may be, is nevertheless of some value for the consolidation of world peace.

64. But to provide a picture of the present situation in regard to security the facts already stated are not sufficient. A psychological factor must also to some extent be taken into account. Security consists in the absence of any danger of aggression ; but there are two ways of judging of this absence of danger. It may be regarded from the objective point of view of the reality or unreality of the danger, or from the subjective point of view of the feeling of the country concerned that it is or is not secure. Now it is not sufficient for third parties to realise that the circumstances of a certain country are such that no real danger threatens it. That country itself must feel the same ; from its point of view, security is life ; it cannot be expected to disarm if it feels exposed to a threat of aggression.

In the last resort, therefore, what is necessary is to implant and develop in every country that confidence without which nothing can be done. Arbitration and security agreements are a step in this direction, and their conclusion should therefore be encouraged and their scope enlarged.

II. Practical Measures for increasing the Guarantees of Security.

65. There is only one possible way of endeavouring to increase the guarantees of security, and that way consists in the conclusion of separate agreements or regional pacts of non-aggression, of pacific settlement of disputes and mutual assistance, or of non-aggression only. The more logical and the speedier method — the conclusion of a general treaty binding on all States Members of the League — must, for the time being, be excluded. After the two unsuccessful attempts made in 1923 and 1924, it would be not merely useless from the practical point of view, but dangerous to the prestige of the League, to make a third attempt ; for the objections raised to the earlier attempts still exist.

As between separate agreements and regional pacts, the latter appear in every respect preferable. They can be better and more easily brought into line with the Covenant system, and, consequently, they help more to increase the guarantees of security.

It is essential to add that this increase in the guarantees would benefit not merely the contracting parties, but indirectly, in varying degrees, every country in the world.

66. The task of the rapporteur was primarily to consider the problem of security from the point of view of the application of regional pacts. He must, however, stress the point that these pacts are necessarily based on mutual confidence and the sincere desire of all contracting parties to develop mutual co-operation. It is not for the rapporteur to make suggestions regarding the preparatory work in the political field, and for the promotion of a better understanding between the peoples which would have to be undertaken to this end, nevertheless this appears to him to be an essential part of the work of pacification.

67. The best method of encouraging the conclusion of as many regional security pacts as possible would seem to be to bring light into the minds of peoples and Governments by demonstrating the benefits which would accrue to their national interests, and to give them every inducement, by offering them models which they could adopt wholly or in part, and which they could combine and adapt as required to the peculiar circumstances affecting the countries in any given area.

No obligation would thereby necessarily be assumed by the States Members of the League. The sole aim of their co-operation would be to establish model treaties which each of them would then be free to take as a basis in any negotiations with its neighbours.

68. It would seem desirable that these models should be made as flexible as possible, alternative formulæ with one or more variants being proposed for most of their clauses. The question of security is, after all, essentially plastic ; its aspects vary in different places, and its guarantees in different circumstances.

It will be natural, however, to give primary consideration to Europe; for it is in Europe that the benefit will first be felt from the suggested system. It is there that the need of greater security is now most keenly felt ; and it is European countries that offer the most recent experience in treaty-making, which will have to be taken as a guide.

69. In this respect, the Committee will base its work on that already done by the League. Its results will have to be adjusted to the new needs which came to light during the sittings of the Preparatory Commission. The draft Treaty of Mutual Assistance of 1923, the Protocol of 1924, the Rhine Pact of 1925, and the later agreements based upon them, will furnish the general framework for the model treaties of security.

70. In these model treaties, provision has to be made for the best possible settlement of the various questions whose solution may help to assure the countries in any particular area of the highest degree of security at present conceivable.

Among these questions there are three which are so essential that they should always be dealt with in a regional security pact, if it is to achieve its object. These questions are : (1) the exclusion of recourse to war ; (2) the organisation of pacific procedures for the settlement of all disputes ; and (3) the establishment of a system of mutual assistance, linked with the functions of the Council of the League.

To each of these questions there are attached certain complementary questions, in particular : to the first, the question of demilitarised zones ; to the second, that of the refusal to accept a pacific settlement or to carry out the decision arrived at ; to the third, that of the organisation of economic, financial and military assistance.

Four other subsidiary questions deserve study with a view to enhancing the practical value of the models contemplated. They are: (1) the connection between regional pacts and the reduction of the armaments of the contracting countries ; (2) the accession of third States and their possible guarantees ; (3) the co-ordination of each regional pact with the others and with the Covenant of the League ; and (4) the guaranteeing of the territorial integrity of the contracting parties.

On each of these ten questions — which do not, of course, exhaust the subject — the following suggestions are submitted for the Committee's consideration :

71. *Exclusion of resort to war.* — The condemnation of aggressive war, already implied in the Covenant (Article 10), and considered by the Assembly on various occasions in 1923 and 1924, was publicly proclaimed in the Assembly resolution of September 24th, 1927, as tending " to create an atmosphere of general confidence calculated to facilitate the progress of the work undertaken with a view to disarmament ".

It will therefore be essential to set down this condemnation at the head of every regional security pact, and to deduce the corollary that the contracting parties " mutually undertake that they will in no case attack or invade each other or resort to war against each other ".

This is the formula employed in the Rhine Pact and in various separate agreements based upon it. It might well be suggested as a model to be followed in future regional pacts, for it is very comprehensive and perfectly clear. If it were desired to express the same idea more briefly, use might be made of the formula of the Geneva Protocol (Article 2) : " the signatory States agree in no case to resort to war ".

In any event, however, it will be essential to make it quite plain that the condemnation relates only to aggressive war, by specifying that force may still be resorted to for purposes of legitimate defence, in the application of Article 16 of the Covenant, in execution of a decision of the Assembly or Council of the League, or when action is undertaken, in virtue of Article 15, paragraph 7, of the Covenant, against a State guilty of aggression. The formula employed in this connection by the Rhine Pact (Article 2) and the separate agreements modelled upon it is to be recommended, for it could hardly be further condensed. The formula of the Geneva Protocol would be unsuitable to a regional pact, because it does not mention the hypothesis of Article 15, paragraph 7, which was necessarily excluded from the system of the Protocol. In a regional pact, the clause embodied in Article 15, paragraph 7, might, it is true, as we shall see later, be waived in disputes between the contracting parties. It would, however, necessarily have to be applied in disputes between one of them and a third party, in which it would continue to operate. In such a dispute, if the Council is not unanimous, the contracting party involved in the dispute has the right to take such action against its adversary " as it shall consider necessary for the maintenance of right and justice ". It is important that each of the other contracting parties should be able to reserve the right to make use of the same latitude in accordance with its interests.

72. *Demilitarised zones.* — The establishment of demilitarised zones between the territories of the States parties to a regional security pact, or some of them, might in principle be recommended as a measure calculated to prevent aggression and to facilitate the determination of the aggressor, should this become necessary.

In view, however, of the variety of conditions, no rigid rules should be proposed ; the greatest elasticity is necessary in this matter. Account should be taken of the configuration of the various frontiers, the relative size of the countries concerned, and the lessons to be drawn from the customs of the neighbouring countries. There may be cases in which the establishment of a demilitarised zone is impossible in practice.

There should be the same elasticity in the regulation of any demilitarised zones that the States concerned might desire to establish, particularly in regard to the temporary or permanent supervision which the contracting parties might ask the Council of the League to organise.

Violation of a demilitarised zone should not in all cases be treated as equivalent to a resort to war. Its degree of gravity depends on circumstances. It would be for the Council to judge, and to prescribe the measures to be taken in order to ensure the observance of the engagements given.

III. Organisation of Pacific Procedures.

73. The exclusion of the resort to war as a means of settling disputes necessarily implies an undertaking to settle them by pacific means. That is the rule established by the Rhine Pact and the separate agreements based upon it. It is also the corollary drawn by the Assembly resolution of September 24th, 1927, from the condemnation of wars of aggression. In every regional security pact, therefore, pacific procedures, to be followed in the event of a dispute, must be arranged for.

In this matter various systems are established in practice. There is the system which, by making arbitration compulsory without any restriction, enables a final settlement of the dispute to be reached in every case ; and there is the system which, combining arbitration (limited to certain classes of dispute) with conciliation and mediation by the Council, leaves the dispute unsettled if the Council cannot attain unanimity.

74. In order that the model regional security pacts may be as flexible as possible, it would be better not to lay down that the acceptance of a more or less comprehensive obligation to arbitrate is indispensable. Such a provision might be difficult to carry out if the number of States contemplating the conclusion of a regional pact were fairly large ; the relations of each of them with the others might not in all cases be the same, and consequently a uniform rule would be ill adapted to their diversity. This should not form an obstacle to the conclusion of the pact. It would be sufficient to stipulate that all disputes between the contracting parties should necessarily be settled by some form of pacific procedure — conciliation, arbitration, judicial proceedings, or, if necessary, mediation by the Council — without specifying the respective spheres in which each of these procedures should be applied. The necessary details might be given in special conventions already concluded, or others which each of the contracting States would be free to conclude collectively or separately with all the others or with only some of them. The essential point is that the security pact should be capable of operating, even in the absence of any such convention. All that would be specifically provided would be that any dispute, of whatever nature, which might arise between two or more contracting parties would be dealt with by conciliation or arbitration, in accordance with the previous engagements of the parties or the rules which they might agree upon in each case, and that, in the absence of any previous engagements or special agreement, or failing any award or arrangement as the result of conciliation proceedings, the question would necessarily be laid by one of the parties before the Council of the League.

It would then be understood that, if all other pacific procedures failed, the parties should submit their dispute to the Council. It would remain for them to indicate in the regional pact the details of these procedures and, in particular, the time-limit after which, failing any resort to arbitration or conciliation, the question would have to be laid before the Council.

On the other hand, it may be worth considering whether it would not be expedient to ensure that this undertaking to settle all disputes by pacific means should be made as effective as possible in practice.

75. The question which arises is this : If there were no provision for resort to the Council except under Article 15 of the Covenant, there would be a risk of the dispute being left unsettled if the Council were not unanimous. This is the position under the Locarno system. In practice, however, the risk is not serious, owing to the guarantee by third Powers. In future regional pacts, in which there would not necessarily be any such guarantee, the case would be different ; the undertaking not to resort to war might become precarious if a serious dispute were left long unsettled. It might, therefore, be wise to take steps to obviate this contingency.

At first sight, it might be thought reasonable to recommend that the contracting States should stipulate that, in the event of a resort to the Council, they undertake to hold the latter's decision as final and binding in their mutual relations, even if the decision were only reached by a simple majority or a specified majority.

A precedent for this system is to be found in the Convention of October 20th, 1921, regarding the neutralisation of the Aaland Islands, which, after maintaining the principle of unanimity in the case of the Council's being called upon to pronounce as to the violation of its provisions, adds (Article 7) : " if unanimity cannot be obtained, each of the High Contracting Parties shall be entitled to take any measures which the Council, by a two-thirds majority, recommends ".

This solution seems, however, open to a serious objection. Majority decisions of the Council, even if accepted by the parties as binding, would still, under the Covenant, have no legal effect on the other States Members of the League. Consequently, a war undertaken in contempt of such a decision would be lawful in their eyes under Article 15, paragraph 7, and would not be covered by the provisions of Article 16.

Another solution should therefore be found which, while ensuring that a final decision should be reached in every dispute, would not form an obstacle to the application of Article 16.

Without expressly recommending their adoption, one of the following suggestions might serve as a basis :

(1) It might be agreed that the Council should take a decision by a bare majority or a specified majority, but in the capacity or arbitrator. This decision, being equivalent to an arbitral award, would be covered by Article 13, and hence by Article 16, of the Covenant.

A precedent for this would be provided to some extent by the Treaty of Lausanne in the Mosul affair.

(2) It might be provided that when, in the absence of any organised system of arbitration between the parties, their dispute came before the Council, the latter should first proceed to act, in virtue of Article 15, the parties undertaking to accept its unanimous decision as final and binding upon them. Should the Council fail to reach unanimity, it would refer the dispute to a body of arbitrators, having first determined by a bare majority or a specified majority the constitution, procedure and powers of such body. In every case, therefore, in virtue either of Article 15 or of Article 13 of the Covenant, there would be a final decision, any violation of which accompanied by resort to war would undoubtedly come under the provisions of Article 16.

76. *Refusal to follow pacific procedures or to execute a decision reached.* — This contingency must be provided for, in order to ensure that the undertaking referred to in the preceding paragraph shall be effective. It must be assumed, in this case, that the recalcitrant State continues nevertheless to maintain a pacific attitude, since if it resorts to force it will at the same time be violating its obligation in regard to non-aggression, thus creating the hypothesis which will be examined in due course.

Passive resistance should involve a sanction proportionate to its degree of gravity. As in the Geneva Protocol (Article 4, paragraph 6), followed by the Rhineland Pact (Article 5), so here it would be expedient, in conformity with the spirit of the Covenant, to adhere to the rule laid down at the end of Article 13 : the question will be brought before the Council by the other party to the dispute. The Council will begin by exercising all its moral influence to persuade the recalcitrant State to respect its undertaking. Should it prove unsuccessful, it will propose what steps should be taken. The high contracting parties would be bound to conform to such proposals.

77. *Domestic jurisdiction.* — It is important to consider what provision should be made in the model security treaties for the rule laid down in Article 15, paragraph 8. In the absence of any stipulation, it is certain that if the assertion of domestic jurisdiction were submitted either to the Council or to international judges, and were recognised to be well founded, the dispute would remain unsolved. This would mean a gap — at first sight serious. It would not really constitute a direct menace to peace, since resort to force would still be prohibited : a State which was unsuccessful in obtaining a material settlement of its claim through its adversary's domestic jurisdiction having been recognised would nevertheless be obliged to maintain a pacific attitude. It would have to content itself with the general resources provided by the other articles of the Covenant of the League, in the hope of arriving in time at a settlement. If its growing

impatience drove it to acts of violence, it would have to expect legitimate defence on the part of its adversary and armed intervention on that of the other contracting States.

It is certainly not in the interests of peace to strain the patience of States who consider themselves victimised by the pressing of their rivals' rights; it is therefore desirable that, in the relations between countries bound by a regional security pact, it should always be possible in case of dispute to obtain a decision on the substance of the question. But it has to be admitted that in the present state of international law and international morality the complete renunciation of the rule laid down in Article 15, paragraph 8, would be attended by more drawbacks than advantages. Prudence, therefore, recommends that it be maintained. In order to give it greater elasticity in application, however, reference might be made, as in the Geneva Protocol (Article 5), to the rule prescribed in Article 11 of the Covenant. It would thus be understood that when, on examination, a dispute is recognised as coming within the domestic jurisdiction of one of the parties, those concerned should be fully entitled if necessary to demand that action be taken by the Council or the Assembly.

If, however, some of the States contemplating the conclusion of a regional security pact should desire in their relations with one or other of their co-contractors to renounce wholly or in part, with or without conditions, the protection afforded them by the rule of domestic jurisdiction, it should be legitimate for them to do so in special arbitration or conciliation conventions, if they undertake not to plead the said rule in specific contingencies either before the judge or before the Council.

78. *Establishment of a system of mutual assistance.* — The undertaking to refrain from aggression and to adopt pacific procedures in every case requires, in the interests of security, that the contracting parties shall be bound to offer one another guarantees against the violation of the undertakings entered into. The possible extent of this obligation in the event of refusal to follow pacific procedures or to execute a decision has already been explained in paragraph 75.

The question now calling for consideration is that of assistance in the case of a resort to force. By assistance should be understood immediate and unstinted help offered by the contracting parties to any one of their number who may be the victim of unprovoked aggression, so as to enable that State to vanquish the aggressor and to safeguard its political independence and territorial integrity.

Two main questions call for examination : *(a)* the determination of unprovoked aggression ; *(b)* the nature and extent of the assistance due to the victim of such aggression.

79. *Determination of unprovoked aggression.* — The studies pursued for the past six years by the League of Nations have demonstrated the extreme complexity of the question, which must be viewed in two aspects : unprovoked aggression must first be defined ; it must then be established.

Considered from a general standpoint, the definition of unprovoked aggression presents real difficulties, as indicated in the memorandum on Article 10 of the Covenant submitted to the Committee on Arbitration and Security.

For the purposes of a regional security pact, however, it would appear to be relatively simple. It is sufficient to say that the term " aggressor" shall be applicable to any contracting State that resorts to force in violation of the undertakings entered into by it in the regional pact ; for example, if it offers armed resistance to a final decision.

To establish unprovoked aggression is, however, very difficult, since once hostilities have begun it is not always easy to say with certainty which of the belligerents first resorted to force.

Two systems have been recommended : the first — unanimous decision by the Council, exclusive of the representatives of the belligerent parties — was proposed in 1925 and adopted at Locarno ; the second — the automatic designation of the aggressor on the basis of presumptive evidence remaining valid until discounted by unanimous decision of the Council — formed the basis of the Geneva Protocol (Article 10).

Both are open to grave objections, which are so familiar that there is no need to recall them here.

As a way out of the difficulty, serious consideration should be given to an idea which was mentioned subsidiarily in the Geneva Protocol (Article 10) and was brought up again by the French delegation in the memorandum submitted by it in 1926 to the Preparatory Disarmament Commission.

The solution suggested was to empower the Council, should it not reach unanimity as regards the determination of the aggressor, to order the belligerents to observe an armistice, the conditions of which it was to fix by a two-thirds majority, and to agree that any belligerent refusing to consent to such armistice or violating it should definitively be regarded as the aggressor.

This system might in principle be incorporated in a regional security pact, but the question as to whether the Council could decide in all cases by a majority vote calls for the closest consideration, as it is essential that that decision should be in perfect agreement with the spirit and mechanism of the Covenant.

80. *Flagrant aggression.* — It has to be considered whether this rule should not, like the Rhineland Pact, admit of exception in the case of a flagrant violation of the mutual undertaking in no circumstances to resort to war. Under the Locarno system, the guarantee becomes binding and operative directly aggression has been established by the Council, when the latter is applied to by one of the contracting parties. It is, on the other hand, optional in the case of flagrant violation of undertakings entered into before intervention by the Council, in the sense that the guarantors reserve the right themselves to judge of the genuineness of the provocation and the urgency of intervention on their part.

This system, which is quite appropriate to a situation such as the Rhineland Pact had in view, might be adopted in pacts relating to areas where the situation is analogous.

81. *Organisation of economic, financial and military assistance.* — In addition to the adaptation to regional pacts of the rules at present contemplated for financial assistance and the measures that might be taken in virtue of Article 16, the regional agreements might, so far as concerns military assistance, enable the final paragraph of the resolution adopted by the 1927 Assembly to be put into effect.

This paragraph refers to " an invitation from the Council to the several States to inform it of the measures which they would be prepared to take, irrespective of their obligations under the Covenant, to support the Council's decisions or recommendations in the event of a conflict breaking out in a given region, each State indicating that, in a particular case, either all its forces, or a certain part of its military naval or air forces could forthwith intervene in the conflict to support the Council's decisions or recommendations ".

As the British Government has observed, " it seems probable that States may well hesitate to indicate precisely what measures they would be prepared to take in hypothetical contingencies ; nor, for fear of increasing tension, or of creating it where none exists, are they likely to be willing, except in mutual agreement, to describe the contingencies in which they would be ready immediately to bring part or whole of their forces to the support of the Council's decision or recommendations. The most effective way of establishing such mutual agreement, and of placing it on record, is by the negotiation of a formal treaty ". In this connection the British Government recalled that " His Majesty's Government in Great Britain have adopted this method in the Treaty of Locarno, by which they have engaged to bring the whole of the forces of the country to the support of the League's judgment in certain definite contingencies "

82. *Aggression by third States.* — The question of aggression has hitherto been considered simply when one of the contracting parties is the victim of another contracting party. It would perhaps be expedient, in order to increase the value of regional pacts from the point of view of security, to provide for the case of aggression against a contracting party by a third State, whether a Member of the League or not. This extension of the mutual guarantee might perhaps give rise to such objections as may be deduced from the observations made in the German and British Governments memoranda. But it might be proposed as a useful variant to States which are prepared to accept it and could make provision for it, with a view to such a contingency, on the basis of Articles 15 and 16 of the Covenant, in the case of a third party, Member of the League, and Article 17 in that of a non-Member third party.

In any case, failing an extension of the mutual guarantee, in the event of aggression by a third State, it should be clearly specified in the regional pact that the contracting parties are bound towards any one of their number who may be attacked by a third State in no circumstances to assist the aggressor.

83. *Re-establishment of peace after aggression.* — It would be expedient, in regional pacts, to include a reservation as to the Council's right of examination in regard to the cessation of active mutual assistance and the re-establishment of normal relations, and also to the reparation due by the aggressor.

84. *Connection between regional pacts and disarmament.* — The idea of such a connection has formed the basis of the League's work on security. It is to be found in the Draft Treaty of Mutual Assistance of 1923 (Article 2) and in the Geneva Protocol (Articles 7, 8 and 21, paras. 5-8). It might be well to consider whether it should not be taken up again in the model security treaties, which are designed for the very purpose of facilitating and preparing for a general agreement on the reduction and limitation of armaments.

Provision might be made in them for three series of stipulations :

(a) A contracting party which was the victim of unprovoked aggression would be entitled to the promised assistance only on condition that it had conformed to the general plan framed by the League of Nations for the reduction of armaments.

(b) On the lines of Article 7 of the Geneva Protocol, in the event of conflict between two or more contracting parties, any increase in armaments or effectives that might modify the position laid down in the plan of reduction and also measures of mobilisation and, generally speaking, any act calculated to aggravate or extend the dispute, might be prohibited.

(c) It might be added that any violation of the above-mentioned undertakings could be brought by any one of the contracting parties before the Council, which would have to examine it and, if necessary, to order the enquiries and investigations to be held, and, should an offence be established, to take appropriate measures for the removal of the cause and the safeguarding of peace.

85. *Accession of third States.* — It is in keeping with the spirit of the League of Nations that regional treaties, considered in relation to the Covenant as supplementary agreements, should be open to accession by third parties. The Draft Treaty of 1923 (Article 7, paragraph 4) and the Geneva Protocol (Article 13, paragraph 3) both contained this principle. But whereas the second admitted free accession by any State Member of the League, the first restricted it to the contracting parties to the Treaty of Assistance and made it conditional on the consent of the States signatories to the special agreement.

As regards possible regional security pacts, the question arises whether : (1) they should in principle be left open, (2) accession should be open to all third States without distinction, to third States Members of the League of Nations, or only to adjacent third States Members or non-Members of the League, and (3) accession should be free or subject to certain conditions.

As regards the first point there would appear to be no possible doubt : the object in view will be more successfully achieved by open than by limited pacts.

With reference to the second point, the same reason seems to militate in favour of the admission of all third States Members or non-Members of the League.

As regards the third point, accessions without the consent of the contracting parties could hardly be admitted since reciprocity in the matter of undertakings necessarily presupposes in the States affected a certain degree of confidence which may possibly not exist as between a third Party desirous of acceding and all the contracting parties.

At most it might be admitted that, in order to preclude arbitrary refusal of the necessary consent, the Council should exercise a certain moral control in the matter. It might be possible to provide that the application for accession should only reach the contracting parties through the Council, which, taking all the circumstances into account, could, if it thought fit, attach its recommendation when forwarding the application to the States.

86. *Guarantee by third States.* — It is conceivable that third States, while unwilling to accept reciprocity in the matter of undertakings, might wish for various reasons to strengthen the efficacy of a regional pact by offering the contracting parties their guarantee, in accordance with the Locarno predecent. Their offer might be made before or after the conclusion of the regional pact. In either case its acceptance must depend upon the consent of all the parties concerned. In view, however, of the undoubted utility of third party guarantees in consolidating peace, it would be well to facilitate their acceptance by providing some procedure which would ensure that such guarantees did in fact consolidate peace.

It would accordingly seem expedient to provide that the third guarantor would have to accept in its entirety the system of assistance agreed upon between the contracting parties.

87. *Guaranteeing of the territorial integrity of the contracting parties.* — It may perhaps be questioned whether in regional security pacts the reciprocal undertaking in regard to non-aggression should be accompanied, as in the Rhineland Pact, by an individual and collective guarantee to maintain the territorial *status quo* represented by the existing frontiers between the contracting States.

This is desirable but not essential. There might be cases when to require a guarantee in regard to territorial integrity would constitute an obstacle to the conclusion of the regional pact, for any State belonging to the area in question might mistakenly see in this guarantee a crystallisation of the existing frontiers which it was not prepared to accept.

It would appear expedient, therefore, not to make this guarantee an essential condition of the regional pact.

In order to create between the contracting parties the confidence which should colour their relations, it would be sufficient to incorporate in the regional pact the ideas to be found in the Preamble to the Arbitration Treaty between Germany and Poland signed in 1925 at Locarno, namely that sincere observance of pacific procedures permits of resolving any conflicts that might arise, that respect for the rights established by treaty or resulting from the law of nations is obligatory for international tribunals, and that the rights of a State cannot be modified save with its consent. This would emphasise the spirit of legality which the parties would promise to observe in their reciprocal relations, avoiding all moral or political subterfuge or pressure.

88. *Co-ordination or regional pacts* inter se *and with the Covenant of the League of Nations.* — The need for this double co-ordination is manifest. If regional pacts, following on one another in the various parts of the world and more particularly of Europe, are to constitute the elements of a general system of security and hence promote the consolidation of peace, it is essential that they should be linked up with one another and bear a coherent and unbroken relationship to a comprehensive scheme in effective harmony with the Covenant, which represents the common law of Members of the League.

(a) In order to ensure this double co-ordination, it is expedient that regional pacts should provide for intervention by a regulating body whose jurisdiction would be recognised and accepted by all the States concerting in this conventional movement. Only the Council could perfom such a function.

As regards the manner in which it might exercise its powers of co-ordination, Article 7 of the Treaty of Mutual Assistance of 1923 supplies a model which might be followed with advantage.

Before registration, regional pacts would be examined by the Council from the point of view of their conformity with the Covenant and their connection with other regional pacts already concluded. The Council could, if necessary, suggest changes in the text of pacts submitted to it.

The Council's powers should also apply to the duration of regional pacts ; Article 8 of the Rhineland Pact furnishes a useful precedent. It might be provided that such pacts should remain in force until, on the application of one of the high contracting parties, duly notified to the other signatory Powers three months in advance, the Council by a majority of at least two thirds should declare that the League of Nations offers the high contracting parties adequate guarantees, the pacts in question then ceasing to have effect on the expiry of one year from that date.

(b) It is natural, in the second place, that the parties should themselves co-ordinate the regional agreements with any special agreements they may have concluded previously. They could, if necessary, avail themselves of the good offices of the Council to facilitate such coordination.

(c) Lastly, another point calls for attention. The development of regional security pacts, in addition to its many advantages, is attended by one serious drawback which requires to be remedied. This is the regrettable possibility that the contracting States, now enjoying greater security *vis-à-vis* third States, may be less inclined to conclude arbitration treaties with those States.

There is one way of remedying this situation and at the same time of strengthening the force of regional pacts in relation to general peace.

This is, first, that the contracting parties should undertake to conclude pacts of non-aggression with third parties upon their borders. The Protocol annexed to the Franco-Roumanian Treaty of Friendship of June 10th, 1926, furnishes a precedent.

Such an undertaking would lighten the obligation in regard to mutual assistance assumed under the regional pact.

Secondly, the contracting parties should undertake to offer to conclude treaties of conciliation and arbitration with such third parties, their neighbours, and to give their favourable consideration to any proposals of this nature coming from those third parties.

This would involve a duty similar to, but more emphatic than, that laid down in Article 48 of the Hague Convention of October 18th, 1907, for the pacific settlement of international disputes.

This undertaking would signify that each of the contracting parties agreed to accept the good offices of the others with a view to concluding treaties of conciliation and arbitration with its neighbours.

It would further have the immense advantage that public opinion would be made the judge of the peaceful intentions of the contracting parties towards third parties on their borders.

89. *Conclusion of regional pacts.* — In determining the practical means whereby the League of Nations might promote regional pacts of security, attention might be paid to the provisions of Article 6, paragraph 2, of the Draft Treaty of Mutual Assistance of 1923, which lays down that " such agreements may, if the High Contracting Parties interested so desire, be negotiated and concluded under the auspices of the League of Nations ".

But it would be possible to go even further, and the next Assembly might proclaim that if, in any specific area, two or more States desired to conclude a security pact with the other States belonging to that same area, they might apply to the Council requesting its good offices for this purpose.

If such a resolution were passed and the Council informed all the States Members of the League that it would be prepared to accept this duty, there is good reason to hope that the appeal would be answered in more than one part of Europe.

90. As regards agreements between States Members and non-Members of the League, whether security pacts or simply pacts of non-aggression, the Council might, if circumstances permitted, accept the duties already referred to, or even advise or suggest to the applicant party that it should employ the good offices of a third Power. The conclusion of agreements of this nature is desirable as a means of creating confidence alike between Members and non-Members of the League and between non-Members and the League itself.

IV. CONCLUSIONS.

91. It is impossible at present to contemplate the conclusion of a general agreement — adding to the obligations assumed under the Covenant — with a view to giving the nations greater security.

92. States which require wider guarantees of security should seek them in the form of separate or collective agreements for non-aggression, arbitration and mutual assistance, or simply for non-aggression.

93. Regional pacts comprising non-aggression, arbitration and mutual assistance represent the completest type of security agreement, and the one which can most easily be brought into harmony with the system of the Covenant. Such pacts should always include the following provisions :

    (a) A prohibition to resort to force ;
    (b) The organisation of pacific procedures for the settlement of all disputes ;
    (c) The establishment of a system of mutual assistance, to operate in conjunction with the duties of the League Council.

94. The establishment of demilitarised zones, wherever practicable, may play an important part, from a general standpoint, in consolidating and enforcing the provisions of a regional pact.

95. With a view to the pacific settlement of all disputes that may arise between them, the States contracting a regional pact might consider provisions which would bind them more closely than those of the Covenant, in the matter of arbitral procedure, so as to make good the legal deficiencies in paragraphs 7 and 8 of Article 15 of the Covenant.

96. Similarly, the parties might facilitate the designation of the aggressor by the Council, should one or more of them resort to war in violation of the undertakings entered into under the regional pact, by empowering the Council, for example, to order the belligerents to observe an armistice, the conditions of which it would determine as might be necessary.

97. The provisions of the Locarno Rhineland Pact concerning flagrant aggression might be adopted in regional pacts wherever the situation was analogous.

98. In the absence of a mutual guarantee covering the case of aggression by a third party, the regional pacts should at all events contain a clause requiring the parties in no circumstances to lend assistance to the third party guilty of aggression.

99. Apart from the adaptation to regional pacts of the rules now proposed for financial assistance and any measures which might be taken under Article 16 of the Covenant, it would be possible to insert special clauses in these pacts, embodying the suggestion made in regard to offers of military assistance in the final paragraph of the last Assembly's resolution.

100. The progress of disarmament must keep pace with that of security so that the conclusion of security pacts should facilitate and prepare for a general agreement for the reduction and limitation of armaments. The regional pacts might contain suitable clauses postulating the connection between security and disarmament.

101. The adhesion of third-party States to regional pacts is desirable. It must depend upon the consent of the contracting parties. Application for accession by a third State might be submitted through the Council, which would decide whether or not to support it.

102. It is desirable but not essential to have the guarantee of a third State; this would be possible, if it were accepted by all the parties and if the third guaranteeing State itself agreed to accept in its entirety the system of assistance agreed upon between the parties.

103. In order that greater confidence may be created between the States contracting a regional pact it is desirable that they should append to their reciprocal undertaking to refrain from aggression an individual and collective guarantee to maintain their territorial integrity. Such a guarantee, however, is not essential. It would be sufficient if the parties agreed to submit all their disputes to pacific procedure, and to recognise that respect for the rights established by treaty or resulting from the law of nations is obligatory for international tribunals, and that the rights of a State cannot be modified save with its consent.

104. It is essential that security pacts should form part of a coherent and comprehensive scheme, and should be brought into harmony with the Covenant. The Council of the League might act in this matter as a regulating organ.

105. The feeling of security enjoyed by the parties as the result of the conclusion of a regional pact should not make them less disposed to conclude treaties of non-aggression or arbitration with third parties upon their borders. Such treaties are eminently desirable, in that they would enhance the value of regional pacts as instruments of peace and would at the same time lighten the undertaking assumed in regard to mutual assistance.

106. With a view to promoting the conclusion of regional pacts it might be expedient to consider a resolution by the next Assembly inviting the Council to study the possibility of lending its good offices to States which may desire to conclude security pacts with other States.

107. Should States desire to conclude agreements with non-member States, the Council might deem it preferable to suggest that they should request the good offices of a third Power.

4.

Memorandum on Articles 10, 11, and 16 of the Covenant

Submitted by M. RUTGERS, *Rapporteur.*

I. PREFACE.

108. The programme adopted by the Committee on Arbitration and Security at its first session comprised, as a second group of questions to be studied, the " systematic preparation of the machinery to be employed by the organs of the League of Nations with a view to enabling the Members of the League to perform their obligations under the various Articles of the Covenant ".

This group of questions relates to the fifth sub-paragraph of paragraph 3 of Resolution V, adopted by the Assembly at its last ordinary session on the proposal of the Third Committee.

109. It is contemplated in this programme that — without limiting the Committee's future field of action — a study should immediately be begun of Articles 10, 11 and 16 of the Covenant and of the scheme of financial assistance to be given to States threatened with aggression :

Article 10. Study of the criteria by which aggression may be presumed.

Article 11. Study of this article, taking into account the work already done or at present in hand.

Article 16. Study of Article 16 under conditions similar to those applied to the study of Article 11 ;
Study of the scheme of financial assistance to be given to States threatened with aggression ;
Study of the above-mentioned scheme and particularly of the preliminary points raised by the Financial Committee.

(a) Study of the criteria by which aggression may be presumed and the procedure of the Council in this matter ;
(b) Right of participation by States (the question of States not Members of the League).

110. It was agreed during the debates at the last ordinary session of the Assembly that the object of this study of the articles of the Covenant was to explore the possibilities which that instrument offers, without in any way enlarging or abridging the obligations incumbent upon Members of the League, and without making any attempt to interpret the Covenant.

II. ARTICLE 10 OF THE COVENANT : STUDY OF THE CRITERIA BY WHICH AGGRESSION MAY BE PRESUMED.

Preliminary Observations.

111. Article 10 of the Covenant is worded as follows :

" The Members of the League undertake to respect and preserve as against external aggression the territorial integrity and existing political independence of all Members of the League. In case of any such aggression or in case of any threat or danger of such aggression, the Council shall advise upon the means by which this obligation shall be fulfilled. "

The Committee on Arbitration and Security is called upon to study Article 10, as also Articles 11 and 16, from the point of view of " systematic preparation of the machinery to be employed by the organs of the League of Nations with a view to enabling the Members of the League to perform their obligations under the various articles of the Covenant ". The rapporteur has been asked to examine Article 10 from the point of view of the criteria by the aid of which aggression may be presumed.

112. The rapporteur has made a careful examination of the discussions on the scope of Article 10 which followed the Canadian Government's proposal to suppress the article, as well as of the opinion bearing on the interpretation of the article which was expressed by the Committee of Jurists appointed under the Council's resolution of September 28th, 1923, and of the observations on that opinion made by a number of Members of the League.

For the rapporteur's present task, however, it does not seem necessary to consider the various points so raised. The discussions showed the extreme difficulty of obtaining unanimous agreement in advance as to what might be the full scope of the obligations under Article 10.

113. The rapporteur does not, moreover, feel called upon to offer a precise definition of the criteria by which aggression may be presumed, but considers that it would be more practical to enumerate some of the facts which, according to circumstances, may serve as evidence that aggression has taken place. Moreover, the question of acts which are evidence of aggression has already been the subject of the most exhaustive and careful study by the League of Nations and by many of its Members. These studies have led to different conclusions, and we are

constrained to believe that any attempt to lay down rigid or absolute criteria in advance for determining an aggressor would be unlikely in existing circumstances to lead to any practical result.

114. In the present connection, however, we have a valuable precedent in the report of the Committee of the Council on Article 11. That report is based on the idea that it is neither possible nor desirable to draw up a complete or exclusive statement of the measures to be taken under Article 11, or to lay down in advance any hard-and-fast rules as to their application ; but that it is of practical use, in the light of past experience and the studies and discussions on the subject, to keep in view a certain number of measures which might be employed in the future.

The rapporteur proposes to follow the same method. He is not blind to the difficulties which must be encountered. So far, it has fortunately never been necessary for the Council to determine which of two enemy States was the aggressor, and there is nothing to be drawn from actual experience in the matter. This omission, however, is to some extent balanced by the fact that certain treaties contain stipulations which constitute a practical contribution to the study of the problem.

115. In approaching this enquiry, it must be recognised that the results which it will obtain cannot be regarded as complete or as applicable to every case. A particular act may be deemed to raise, or not to raise, a presumption of aggression having regard to the circumstances under which it was committed.

Criteria for determining Aggression.

116. Some useful material in regard to criteria for determining aggression is to be found in certain treaties and in the proceedings of the Assembly and the Council of the League of Nations.

117. First among these sources of information are the results of the investigations carried out by the Permanent Advisory Commission and the Special Committee of the Temporary Mixed Commission when drawing up the Treaty of Mutual Assistance. The reports of these bodies show that certain acts would in many cases constitute acts of aggression ; for instance :

(1) The invasion of the territory of one State by the troops of another State ;

(2) An attack on a considerable scale launched by one State on the frontiers of another State ;

(3) A surprise attack by aircraft carried out by one State over the territory of another State, with the aid of poisonous gases.

The reports in question add that other cases may arise in which the problem would be simplified owing to some act committed by one of the parties to the dispute affording unmistakable proof that the party in question was the real aggressor.

There are also certain factors which may serve as a basis in determining the aggressor :

(a) Actual industrial and economic mobilisation carried out by a State either in its own territory or by persons or societies on foreign territory.

(b) Secret military mobilisation by the formation and employment of irregular troops or by a declaration of a state of danger of war which would serve as a pretext for commencing hostilities.

(c) Air, chemical or naval attack carried out by one party against another.

(d) The presence of the armed forces of one party in the territory of another.

(e) Refusal of either of the parties to withdraw its armed forces behind a line or lines indicated by the Council.

(f) A definitely aggressive policy by one of the parties towards the other, and the consequent refusal of that party to submit the subject in dispute to the recommendation of the Council or to the decision of the Permanent Court of International Justice and to accept the recommendation or decision when given.

118. The list of factors furnished by the Special Committee of the Temporary Mixed Commission might be supplemented by including the violation of certain undertakings ; for instance, refusal to submit a dispute for pacific settlement by the methods agreed upon, or failure to observe restrictions of a military nature which have been accepted.

119. As regards military restrictions, mention must be made, *inter alia*, of the following treaties, the relevant passages of which are given in the Appendix.

(a) The " Rush-Bagot Agreement " between Great Britain and the United States, concerning naval force on the Great Lakes, signed April 28th-29th, 1817.

(b) The Convention between Great Britain and China, giving effect to Article III of the Convention of July 24th, 1886, relative to Burma and Tibet, signed March 1st, 1894.

(c) The Convention between Norway and Sweden, concerning the establishment of a neutral zone, the dismantling of fortifications, etc., signed October 26th, 1905.

(d) The Treaty of Versailles.

(e) The Convention relating to the non-fortification and neutralisation of the Aaland Islands, signed on October 20th, 1920.

(f) The Treaty of Lausanne between the British Empire, France, Italy, Japan, Greece, Roumania, the Kingdom of the Serbs, Croats and Slovenes and Turkey, signed July 24th, 1923.

(g) The Treaty between Germany and Belgium, France, Great Britain and Italy, signed at Locarno on October 16th, 1925.

120. The treaties provide for the total or partial demilitarisation of certain zones. It is clear that a violation of these zones would in many circumstances — in the absence of any express stipulation — raise a presumption of aggression.

The value of these demilitarised zones as aids in determining the aggressor has already been recognised in the draft Treaty of Mutual Assistance, which states in Article 9 :

" In order to facilitate the application of the present Treaty, any High Contracting Party may negotiate, through the agency of the Council, with one or more neighbouring countries for the establishment of demilitarised zones. "

Paragraph 1 of Article 9 of the Protocol of Geneva contains the following provision :

" The existence of demilitarised zones being calculated to prevent aggression and to facilitate a definite finding of the nature provided for in Article 10 below, the establishment of such zones between States mutually consenting thereto is recommended as a means of avoiding violations of the present Protocol. "

121. Special importance was given to the demilitarised zone in the Rhine Pact. This Treaty declares that resistance offered to a violation of the Rhineland Demilitarised Zone shall be deemed to be the exercise of a legitimate right of defence, in derogation from the mutual undertaking to refrain from aggression, when such violation constitutes an unprovoked act of aggression and when, by reason of the assembly of armed forces in the demilitarised zone, immediate action is necessary. This Treaty further provides that, in case of a flagrant violation of the Demilitarised Rhineland Zone, the guarantor powers shall immediately come to the help of the party against whom such a violation or breach has been directed as soon as they have been able to satisfy themselves that this violation constitutes an unprovoked act of aggression, and that, by reason either of the crossing of the frontier or of the outbreak of hostilities or of the assembly of armed forces in the demilitarised zone, immediate action is necessary. Nevertheless, the Council of the League of Nations, which will be seized of the question if one of the contracting parties considers that the zone has been violated, will issue its findings. The contracting parties undertake in such a case to act in accordance with the recommendations of the Council, provided that they are concurred in by all the members other than the representatives of the parties which have engaged in hostilities.

122. In the event of hostilities having broken out, the Protocol of Geneva laid down explicitly that a State might be presumed to be an aggressor in the following circumstances, unless a decision of the Council, which must be taken unanimously, should declare otherwise :

(1) If it has refused to accept the procedure for a pacific settlement or to comply with the decision rendered in pursuance of that procedure.

(2) If it has violated the provisional measures enjoined by the Council to prevent preparations for war being carried on during the proceedings for pacific settlement ;

(3) Disregard of a decision recognising that the dispute lies solely within the domestic jurisdiction of the other party, if the State in question has failed or refused previously to submit the question to the Council or to the Assembly.

The Protocol further declared that a belligerent which refused to accept, or violated, an armistice enjoined by the Council was to be deemed an aggressor.

When the Council had called upon the signatory States to apply against the aggressor the sanctions provided by the Protocol, any signatory State thus called upon was thereupon entitled to exercise the rights of a belligerent.

123. The Report of the Committee of the Council on Article 11 of the Covenant points out that the action which the Council has to take in case of a conflict, in virtue of Article 11 and other articles of the Covenant, will provide it with valuable material which will assist it in determining the aggressor, in case war should break out in spite of all the efforts made to prevent hostilities, or to suspend them after they have begun. It is clear that the nature and extent of the co-operation which the parties to the dispute are willing to afford to the Council cannot fail to exercise considerable influence upon the decision of that body.

124. *Appendix to Chapter II.*

Treaties involving certain undertakings in regard to military restrictions :

(a) In 1817, Great Britain and the United States came to an agreement for the demilitarisation of the big lakes forming the frontier between the United States and Canada. This agreement was known as the " Rush-Bagot Agreement ".

(b) Great Britain concluded with China a Convention designed to ensure the maintenance of peace on the Chinese frontiers of her Asiatic possessions. This Convention was ratified in London on August 23rd, 1894. The high contracting parties undertake not to construct or maintain fortifications within a ten-mile zone along the frontier.

(c) On the dissolution of the Union of Norway and Sweden, a Convention was signed at Stockholm in October 1905, establishing a neutral zone between the two countries. This Convention can only be denounced by joint agreement.

(d) Under Article 42 of the Treaty of Versailles, Germany is forbidden to maintain or construct any fortifications either on the left bank of the Rhine or on the right bank to the west of a line drawn 50 kilometers to the east of the Rhine. Article 43 provides that " in the area defined above [*i.e.*, in Article 42] the maintenance and the assembly of armed forces, either permanently or temporarily, and military manœuvres of any kind, as well as the upkeep of all permanent works for mobilisation, are in the same way forbidden ".

(e) On October 20th, 1921, a Convention relating to the non-fortification and neutralisation of the Aaland Islands was signed. Under this Convention, Finland undertakes not to fortify that part of the Finnish Archipelago which is called " the Aaland Islands ". Article 7 of the Convention provides as follows :

" I. In order to render effective the guarantee provided in the Preamble of the present Convention, the High Contracting Parties shall apply, individually or jointly, to the Council of the League of Nations, asking that body to decide upon the measures to be taken either to assure the observance of the provisions of this Convention or to put a stop to any violation thereof.

" The High Contracting Parties undertake to assist in the measures which the Council of the League of Nations may decide upon for this purpose.

" When, for the purposes of this undertaking, the Council is called upon to make a decision under the above conditions, it will invite the Powers which are parties to the present Convention, whether Members of the League or not, to sit on the Council. The vote of the representative of the Power accused of having violated the provisions of this Convention shall not be necessary to constitute the unanimity required for the Council's decision.

" If unanimity cannot be obtained, each of the High Contracting Parties shall be entitled to take any measures which the Council by a two-thirds majority recommends, the vote of the representative of the Power accused of having violated the provisions of this Convention not being counted.

" II. If the neutrality of the zone should be imperilled by a sudden attack either against the Aaland Islands or across them against the Finnish mainland, Finland shall take the necessary measures in the zone to check and repulse the aggressor until such time as the High Contracting Parties shall, in conformity with the provisions of this Convention, be in a position to intervene to enforce respect for the neutrality of the islands.

" Finland shall refer the matter immediately to the Council. "

(f) The Treaty signed at Lausanne on July 24th, 1923, between the British Empire, France, Italy, Japan, Greece, Roumania, the Kingdom of the Serbs, Croats and Slovenes and Turkey includes a Convention relating to the regime of the Straits.

The preamble declares that the signatory Powers are desirous of ensuring in the Straits freedom of transit and navigation between the Mediterranean Sea and the Black Sea for all nations, and that they consider that the maintenance of that freedom is necessary to the general peace and the commerce of the world.

Further, Article 18 contains the following provisions :

" The High Contracting Parties, desiring to secure that the demilitarisation of the Straits and of the contiguous zones shall not constitute an unjustifiable danger to the military security of Turkey, and that no act of war should imperil the freedom of the Straits or the safety of the demilitarised zones, agree as follows :

" Should the freedom of navigation of the Straits or the security of the demilitarised zones be imperilled by a violation of the provisions relating to freedom of passage, or by a surprise attack or some act of war or threat of war, the High Contracting Parties, and in any case France, Great Britain, Italy and Japan, acting in conjunction, will meet such violation, attack, or other act of war or threat of war, by all the means that the Council of the League of Nations may decide for this purpose.

" So soon as the circumstance which may have necessitated the action provided for in the preceding paragraph shall have ended, the regime of the Straits as laid down by the terms of the present Convention shall again be strictly applied.

" The present provision, which forms an integral part of those relating to the demilitarisation and to the freedom of the Straits, does not prejudice the rights and obligations of the High Contracting Parties under the Covenant of the League of Nations. "

The Treaty of Lausanne also includes another Convention respecting the Thracian frontier. This Convention declares that the said Powers, being desirous of ensuring the maintenance of peace on the frontiers of Thrace, and considering it necessary for this purpose that certain special reciprocal measures should be taken on both sides of this frontier, have agreed (in Article 1) that from the Ægean Sea to the Black Sea the territories extending on both sides of the frontiers separating Turkey from Bulgaria and from Greece shall be demilitarised to a depth of about 30 kilometers.

According to Article 4, in the event of one of the bordering Powers whose territory forms the subject of the present Convention having any complaint to make respecting the observance of the preceding provisions, this complaint shall be brought by that Power before the Council of the League of Nations.

(g) The Treaty signed at Locarno on October 16th, 1925, between Germany, Belgium, France, Great Britain and Italy, provides in Article 2 that :

" Germany and Belgium, and also Germany and France, mutually undertake that they will in no case attack or invade each other or resort to war against each other.

" This stipulation shall not, however, apply in the case of the exercise of the right of legitimate defence, that is to say, resistance to a violation of the undertaking contained in the previous paragraph, or to a flagrant breach of Articles 42 or 43 of the said Treaty of Versailles, if such breach constitutes an unprovoked act of aggression, and, by reason of the assembly of armed forces in the demilitarised zone, immediate action is necessary. "

III. ARTICLE 11 OF THE COVENANT : STUDY OF THIS ARTICLE WITH REFERENCE TO WORK ALREADY DONE AND IN PROGRESS.

Introduction.

125. Article 11 covers all cases of armed conflict. In this respect, its scope is wider than that of Articles 10, 16 and 17 of the Covenant. It may be said that these latter articles deal with only certain of the armed conflicts covered by Article 11.

126. Under Article 11, the League of Nations has the most extensive competence. The Council can intervene in any conflict, whether the parties are Members of the League or not. It is equally competent whether there is resort to war or a threat of war, and it can take action in time to prevent hostilities or to terminate them if they have already been begun. Its authority is exercised in any war — not only in a war contrary to Articles 12, 13 and 15, but also in a war which is not contrary to those articles. If the procedure contemplated in Article 15 has failed, Article 11 remains applicable, and offers a possibility of renewing efforts to prevent war. Even if there is no threat of war, but merely circumstances affecting international relations which threaten to disturb international peace or the good understanding between nations, the case may be brought to the Council's attention.

127. The resources at the League's command are also very extensive. The extremely general terms of Article 11 — " any action that may be deemed wise and effectual to safeguard the peace of nations " — allow of all suitable measures being taken. Within the limits of its powers, and without prejudice to the rights of the Members of the League, on whom Article 11 imposes no special obligation, the Council, in consciousness of its responsibilities under the Covenant, may choose at its discretion whatever measures it thinks expedient. Moreover, proceedings under Article 11 do not in any way exclude proceedings under other provisions of the Covenant.

128. The difference between Articles 10 and 12-16 on the one hand and Article 11 on the other hand may be expressed as follows :
Article 10 protects the territorial integrity and political independence of every Member of the League against all external aggression.
Articles 12-16 prescribe the procedure to be followed in the event of disputes, and the rights and obligations thence derived by Members.
Article 11 is the essential expression of the principles of the League, and is designed to protect the interests of all. It does not impose upon Members of the League any obligations which can be rigidly specified ; the Council's action under this article is political rather than judicial.
It is in Article 11 that the moral factors and the solidarity of the Members of the League are most clearly brought out.

129. The systematic preparation of the Council's action under Article 11 has two aspects — a technical and a political aspect.
The technical aspect relates to communications of importance to the League at times of emergency. It is studied in a special chapter of this memorandum.
The political aspect has already been dealt with in the Report submitted by the Committee of the Council on point 1 (*b*) of the French proposal to the Preparatory Commission for the Disarmament Conference (document A. 14. 1927. V, pages 76 *et seq.*) (Report approved by the Assembly and the Council). The report may be said to have laid the foundations for the systematic preparation of the Council's action under Article 11. In this study, an attempt will be made to ascertain whether it can be completed.

130. It is important to make it clear at the outset that the systematic preparation of the Council's action under Article 11 can never be a code of procedure.
As was very well pointed out in the report of the Committee of the Council, it is not possible to enumerate all the measures that might be taken ; a few of them must be indicated by way of example, without underestimating or questioning the value of those which are not expressly mentioned. The infinite variety of events that may occur in international political life cannot be confined in advance in watertight compartments.
The Council will to a great extent be guided by precedent, and its experience will grow with the progress of its political work.

How Article 11 comes into Operation.

131. Any action by the Council in virtue of Article 11 presupposes that the question at issue has been officially laid before the Council.

Legally speaking, the Council cannot receive notice of a question except from a Member of the League.

It is not necessary, however, that this Member should be one of the parties to the dispute. Any Member of the League, even if not immediately affected, has the right to bring a dispute before the Council in virtue of Article 11.

132. No special form is prescribed for this purpose. Reference may be made to the dispute between Panama and Costa Rica, when the Council, meeting at Paris, had before it certain reports showing that there was tension between the two countries, and proceeded to discuss the matter.

133. Nevertheless, if, in accordance with paragraph 1 of Article 11, the Secretary-General is to be able to summon a meeting of the Council forthwith, one of the Members of the League must have requested him to do so.

134. In certain cases, Governments may think it more expedient to refer to paragraph 2 of Article 11 than to paragraph 1 of that article. If the question is thought to be sufficiently urgent, the Council can be convened without delay in accordance with the rules of procedure it has itself established. In this eventuality, a request for a meeting of the Council must be addressed to the Secretary-General.

135. It is certainly desirable that a State asking for the application of Article 11 should make reference to that article. The Council, however, in consciousness of its responsibility, will, if necessary, act in virtue of that article, even if no specific reference is made to it.

136. The Council must not interfere in disputes without a serious reason, or as long as there is still some hope of an amicable settlement.

137. In the event of war or a threat of war, the Council can always act under Article 11, paragraph 1, even if another article is invoked or if proceedings have already been entered upon in virtue of another article. This question is considered in the memorandum on arbitration and conciliation.

138. Even if a dispute is submitted to a special tribunal, it is possible in certain cases that such tension may develop between the two States as to amount to a threat of war. The Council can then intervene under Article 11. This is explicitly recognised in the Locarno agreements, where it is stated that nothing in the agreements is to be interpreted as restricting the duty of the League to take whatever action may be deemed wise and effectual to safeguard the peace of the world.

An observation to the same effect has been made in the memorandum on arbitration and conciliation.

139. Experience shows that in certain cases it may be expedient to resort to all possible means of direct conciliation, and to the good offices of third Powers, before bringing a dispute before the Council. Article 11 is sufficiently elastic to allow of this.

M. de Brouckère, delegate of Belgium, in calling the attention of the Third Committee of the last Assembly to this point, raised the question whether the Council ought not at all events to keep in touch with developments in the dispute. This suggestion is worthy of special attention. Nevertheless, if efforts of conciliation are to be successful, it may be essential that the question should be discussed by a very small number of Powers. It would seem that the parties concerned must be left full latitude to decide whether the Council should be kept informed of the developments of the case so long as the question has not actually been submitted to the Council. There have been cases in which Members of the League have thought it desirable to make such communications to the Council. Great Britain did so in the Chinese question (Declaration by the British Government concerning British policy in China, February 8th, 1927); the Albanian and Serb-Croat-Slovene Governments did so in the dispute which arose out of the arrest of the dragoman of the Serb-Croat-Slovene Legation at Tirana. It must also be remembered that the Governments Members of the Council are kept abreast of political developments by their diplomatic agents.

Application of Article 11.

(a) *Cases covered by Article 11, Paragraph 2, of the Covenant, and Similar Cases.*

140. Even if the threat of war is not an imminent threat, it may be useful, when the situation is liable to grow worse, to call the attention of the parties to the undertakings into which they have entered in virtue of the Covenant, and to urge them to refrain from any act which might increase the tension. The Council has acted in this way on several occasions — in connection with the Aaland Islands question between Sweden and Finland, the dispute between Costa Rica and Panama, the frontier disputes between Albania and her neighbours, the Mosul question between Turkey and Iraq, the incursion of armed bands from Bulgaria into neighbouring States, and the Italo-Greek incident at Corfu.

141. The Council may also send a commission to the spot, with the consent of the party to whose territories it is to proceed, to enquire into the situation on the frontier areas of the parties to the dispute ; this was done in the dispute between Turkey and Iraq.

142. The Council may also endeavour to hasten the settlement of the question actually at issue ; an example of this is the frontier dispute between Albania and her neighbours.

143. If a rupture has taken place, the Council may take steps to mitigate its effects. In the first Polish-Lithuanian dispute, it recommended the parties to re-establish consular relations and free communication, and when these efforts proved unsuccessful it requested them to entrust their interests to friendly Powers.

144. In other cases it may be useful to recommend to the parties measures which, from the military point of view, will furnish pledges of their peaceful intentions towards each other; such measures are the withdrawal of troops from the frontier, reduction of effectives, demobilisation, etc.

(b) *Cases covered by Article* 11, *Paragraph* 1.

145. The Committee of the Council points out in its report that the Council may indicate to the parties from what movements of troops, mobilisation operations and other measures of the same kind it recommends them to refrain.

146. *A fortiori,* in the hypothesis put forward in paragraph 1 of Article 11, the Council may recommend to the parties the demobilisation and other measures indicated in the preceding paragraph.

147. Experience shows that it is very often the impression of being exposed to a military threat that nullifies efforts to prevent war. We must here refer to the observations made by Sir Austen Chamberlain at the thirty-third session of the Council to the effect that all the military preparations of a State to deal its adversary a crushing blow immediately on the outbreak of war may already have been made in normal times, and may constitute a very serious threat to the opponent at a time of crisis.

148. Another important point which should be mentioned is that of the localisation of the conflict. All the Council's efforts to prevent hostilities may prove to be vain if other countries besides the parties to the dispute take military action against either of those parties. Even what are called precautionary measures or demonstrations are liable to do irreparable harm. The Council can take the same measures against third States as against the parties.

This point seems to call for the Council's special attention in cases were military alliances or conventions might operate, particularly if these agreements allow of military action being taken automatically or spontaneously. This point is examined in detail in the memorandum on security.

149. In order to terminate hostilities that have already been engaged, the Council may recommend the parties to conclude an armistice. This was done in the first Polish-Lithuanian dispute.

150. In order to keep abreast of developments during the intervals between sessions, the Council may confer powers according to the case, either on the acting President or on the rapporteur on the question at issue, or on both jointly. It may also appoint a committee of certain of its members. An instance of this is to be found in the first Polish-Lithuanian dispute. Mention may also be made of M. Briand's intervention in the Greco-Bulgarian dispute.

(c) *Special Cases.*

151. Article 11 is still applicable when the procedure under Article 15 has been exhausted. The following situations can be imagined as arising in regard to Article 15 :

(a) The Council is not able to recommend a solution unanimously.
(b) The Council is unanimous in recommending a solution, but this solution is rejected by one or both of the parties.
(c) The Council recognises that the dispute concerns a question which, under international law, is within the domestic jurisdiction of one of the parties.

152. In these hypotheses the Council may always obtain information as to what the parties propose to do after the expiry of the time-limits provided for in Article 12. It may recommend the parties to extend these time-limits. It may propose measures to prevent the situation from becoming more acute.

153. If there is a unanimous recommendation, the Council may endeavour to induce the party or parties who have rejected its solution to accept any suggestions it may make.

It may be recalled that in the hypothesis covered by Article 15, paragraph 8, the Geneva Protocol provided that, even if the question were held by the Permanent Court or by the Council to be a matter solely within the domestic jurisdiction of one State, this decision should not prevent consideration of the situation by the Council or by the Assembly under Article 11 of the Covenant.

(d) *Measures of Conservancy.*

154. It is difficult to enumerate all the steps that the Council might take as measures of conservancy under Article 11, but valuable suggestions on this point are to be found in the Locarno agreements.

These agreements provide that, if a question covered by the agreements is laid before the Council, the latter shall ensure that suitable provisional measures are taken ; and that the parties undertake to accept such measures, to abstain from all measures likely to have a repercussion prejudicial to the execution of the decision or to the arrangements proposed by the Council, and, in general, to abstain from any sort of action whatsoever which may aggravate or extend the dispute.

155. It might be suggested that, in the case of a dispute between Powers which are not signatories of the Locarno arbitration treaties, the Council should recommend the parties to enter into similar undertakings.

Final Observations.

156. The Committee of the Council points out in its report that if, notwithstanding all the measures recommended by the Council in virtue of Article 11, war is resorted to, it is probable that the Council's action will have made it possible to determine which State is the aggressor

157. It is not necessarily the State to whose conduct the crisis was originally due which is to be regarded as the aggressor ; in certain eventualities it might possibly be the other party which ought to be regarded as the aggressor, if it has deliberately refused to conform to the Council's recommendations. The prospect of this possibility will strongly influence the parties to the dispute to accept the measures proposed by the Council.

158. There is another factor of very great importance which will set up a further obstacle to prevent nations from being swept into war. As was stated in the Introduction, " it may truly be said that before the existence of the League of Nations the national points of view were the only ones of which public opinion had any cognisance in times of international crisis. The effect of the Council's debates being held in public will be not only that the opponent's point of view is likely to become better known in the other country, but also — more important still — that the official recommendations given by the Council to the parties will furnish the public in all countries with the means of forming a judgment ; this factor cannot fail to turn governing circles in the different countries concerned towards a pacific settlement.

" It is difficult to believe that the Government of any of these countries would refuse to give full publicity to the official recommendations of the Council. Indeed, such a refusal would be taken, not only by foreigners but by the people of the country itself, as very significant evidence of the real intentions of the Government. It would be a matter of vital importance to any Government to avoid incurring such discredit. "

IV. Article 16 of the Covenant : Study of this Article on the same Lines as Article 11.

Introduction.

159. The programme of work approved by the Committee on Arbitration and Security at its first session includes the study of Article 16 on lines similar to those adopted in studying Article 11.

The study of Article 11 followed M. de Brouckère's report to the Committee of the Council on Question 1 (b) of the French delegation's proposal to the Preparatory Commission for the Disarmament Conference. M. de Brouckère's report dealt with the two articles (11 and 16).

The French proposal referred to some of the questions contained in the questionnaire which had been submitted by the Council to the Preparatory Commission for the Disarmament Conference, namely :

" Question V (a). On what principles will it be possible to draw up a scale of armaments permissible to the various countries, taking into account particularly :

" 1. . . . .

" 8. The degree of security which in the event of aggression a State could receive under the provisions of the Covenant, or of separate engagements contracted towards that State ?

" (b) Can the reduction of armaments be promoted by examining possible means for insuring that the mutual assistance, economic and military, contemplated in Article 16 of the Covenant shall be brought quickly into operation as soon as the act of aggression has been committed ? "

The French proposal relating to these questions included the following passage :

" With reference to Question V (a), 8, and V (b), the Commission considers that, in order that a State should be able to calculate to what extent it can consent to the reduction or limitation of its armaments, it is essential to determine what method and what machinery are best calculated to give help to that State when attacked.

" The Commission therefore proposes to suggest to the Council :

" 1. That methods or regulations should be investigated which would :

" (a) . . . .

" (b) Enable the Council to take such decisions as may be necessary to enforce the obligations of the Covenant as expeditiously as possible. "

160. M. de Brouckère's able report on Question 1 *(b)* was discussed at the fifth session of the Committee of the Council. The latter decided, on Lord Cecil's proposal, to undertake immediately the study of five concrete proposals made in the report, and of the part of the report dealing with the measures to be taken in virtue of Article 11. The discussion of the part of the report dealing with the general principles of Article 16, and the legal force of the 1921 resolutions was postponed.

The Council, in its resolutions of December 8th, 1926, noted that the Committee of the Council proposed to submit a report on Article 16 at a later date, and, in accordance with the Committee's suggestions, it requested the Secretary-General to collect all the documents which related to the preliminary work carried out by the League in regard to this article. In pursuance of this decision, the Secretary-General obtained all the resolutions adopted by the different organs of the League with regard to Article 16, and added a memorandum summarising the measures taken by the League in this connection (document A.14.1927.V).

The study of Article 11 led to the preparation of the report approved by the Committee of the Council on March 15th, 1927, with regard to the methods and regulations which would enable the Council to take such decisions as might be necessary to enforce the obligations of the Covenant as expeditiously as possible. This report (to which Chapter III of the present memorandum referred) was approved by the Assembly at its last ordinary session.

In the present chapter we propose to continue the study of the application of Article 16.

The Resolutions of 1921.

161. The Assembly of 1921 adopted a series of amendments to Article 16. It held over the further study of the application of Article 16 for a subsequent Assembly. The latter was to take as a basis the text of Article 16 as it would stand after the ratification and entry into force of the amendments of 1921. The Assembly of 1921, being anxious to provide as far as possible a method by which Article 16 could be applied until the amendments should come into force, adopted a series of nineteen resolutions, the aim of which is indicated in the first resolution :

" 1. The resolutions and the proposals for amendments to Article 16 which have been adopted by the Assembly shall, so long as the amendments have not been put into force in the form recommended by the Covenant, constitute rules for guidance which the Assembly recommends, as a provisional measure, to the Council and to the Members of the League in connection with the application of Article 16. "

The Assembly thus desired to lay down provisional rules to be acted upon until the amendments adopted were put into force. Provisionally, and pending their ratification, these amendments and the resolutions relating thereto were to serve as guiding principles. It should be noted that more than one of the nineteen resolutions was based, not on the text of Article 16, which was in force in 1921, but on the text resulting from the 1921 amendments. M. de Brouckère's report gives a series of examples which we need not enumerate here.

The 1921 amendments have not come into force. They lack the ratification required of several Members of the Council.

Thus the state of affairs to which the first resolution quoted above refers has lasted much longer than was anticipated by the Assembly in 1921.

162. This situation is far from satisfactory. The old text is still in force, notwithstanding the numerous ratifications obtained by the 1921 amendments. The fate of these amendments depends upon the decision of a few Members only. It is desirable that this uncertainty should be put an end to by the ratification of these amendments in the near future or their final abandonment. It is worth recalling here the amendment adopted by the Assembly on October 3rd, 1921, adding to Article 26 of the Covenant a paragraph to be worded as follows : " If the required number of ratifications shall not have been obtained within twenty-two months after the vote of the Assembly, the proposed amendment shall remain without effect ". This amendment, however, has not yet obtained the necessary number of ratifications.

163. In so far as the 1921 resolutions are not compatible with Article 16 as it stands, they cannot be given force of law. Those which are in conformity with the Covenant retain their value. On the one hand, it must be recognised, as is done in M. de Brouckère's report, that neither the amendements which have not come into force nor the resolutions can impose on a Member any new obligation or release him from obligations which he has already contracted. But it cannot be denied that both the amendments and the resolutions constitute suggestions of the greatest interest. In so far as the resolutions are in agreement with the Covenant, they can be regarded as indicating the view taken by the Council and the Assembly of the scope of Article 16, and as announcing the way in which they intend to apply this article if the need should arise.

Interpretation of Article 16.

164. The study of Article 16 has given rise to more than one controversy on the exact scope of the terms of the article. In order to remedy this, is it necessary to endeavour once again to give a more or less official interpretation ? Is it necessary, for example, to define what is meant by the expression " resort to war " in the first line of the article ? It must be recognised that it would be extremely desirable to arrive at a generally accepted interpretation

which would put an end to many controversies. It is worth recalling here the words of the fourth resolution of 1921 :

> " 4. It is the duty of each Member of the League to decide for itself whether a breach of the Covenant has been committed. The fulfilment of their duties under Article 16 is required from Members of the League by the express terms of the Covenant, and they cannot neglect them without breach of their treaty obligations. "

This doctrine is generally accepted to-day, and even if it were not the Council could not invoke a text or apply a sanction to oblige a Member to obey a decision of the Council in virtue of Article 16 which that Member did not consider to be well founded. It is the Members themselves who must decide on the performance of their obligations under Article 16. It must therefore be realised that when they are called upon to take this extremely grave decision they will be guided by their own conception of their obligations under Article 16.

165. We may go even further than this. If ever the question of the application of Article 16 arose, the decision of the different countries would not depend on interpretations, however authoritative, or on the deductions of lawyers ; the great question would be whether the principle of Article 16 was or was not a living reality. To carry out the grave obligations contained in Article 16, States would have to be inspired by the spirit of responsibility and solidarity which is at the root of Article 16 and of the whole League of Nations.

166. While it appears wise to leave it to the lessons of experience to provide material for defining in future the provisions of Article 16, it must also be recognised that there would be a certain danger in fixing in an immutable form, the measures which might be taken in application of these texts.
Indeed, an interpretation providing hard and fast criteria for deciding whether there is resort to war or not might force the Council and the Members to declare that the conditions of Article 16 were present at a time when there was still room for doubt as to whether there had really been resort to war, and for hope that the mediation of the Council might stop the hostilities which had begun, and prevent the irrevocable operation of Article 16. We may recall the observations made in the chapter on Article 10 concerning the criteria to be taken as a basis in determining the aggressor.

Application of the Article.

167. We now come to the measures which can be taken to prepare the application of Article 16. A distinction must here be made between preparing the application of Articles 11 and 16. The action exercised under Article 11 aims at safeguarding the peace of nations ; it is conciliatory and pacifying in its object.
Article 16 is applied at a more advanced stage of the dispute. As M. de Brouckère's report justly says, it lays down terrible measures for the extreme case in which the pacific endeavours of the League finally fail before the criminal determination of a State resolved on war. Thus, to prepare the application of Article 11 is to prepare a pacific action, and to prepare the application of Article 16 is to prepare to take measures of extreme gravity. To prepare the Council's action under Article 11 is to prepare an action which it is hoped will be exerted in time and will be successful, while to prepare the execution of Article 16 is to prepare for action which it is hoped will never be required.·

168. Preparation of the application of Article 16 may be conceived in two different forms. The preparation might consist in special measures to be applied to given situations. Every eventuality would have to be considered. One might even go as far as to draw up plans of campaign for cases of aggression. On the other hand, preparation might also be general and might aim at creating a situation which would inspire confidence in the effectiveness of the League's organs and in the readiness of Members to perform their duty if the application of Article 16 became necessary. It is above all in the latter sense that preparations must be made for the application of the article. Unlike the special preparation, the general preparation does not involve the danger of arousing conflicts by imagining their existence.

169. The preparation of the military sanctions provided for in Article 16 does not seem likely to promote mutual confidence between the States Members of the League of Nations, if at the same time pacific procedure suitable for the settlement of all international disputes is not organised, and if there is not also a general agreement on the reduction and limitation of armaments.

170. In making preparations for the application of Article 11, that of Article 16 is also to a great extent prepared. This is easily understood if it is realised that the application of the measures provided for by Article 16 does not take place at the beginning of a dispute but only when it is proved that a serious crisis is no longer capable of a peaceful solution. The question of the application of Article 16 will therefore not come before the Council and the Members without the Council having first to deal with the conflict in virtue of Article 11 and similar articles. The application of the procedure of Article 11 will be for the Council the best preparation for the performance of its duties under Article 16. This procedure will enlighten it as to the attitude of the two parties, and supply it with valuable information which will enable it to give the Members of the League the guidance and the recommendations to which they are entitled.

171. It is not the Council which has the last word on the measures to be taken in execution of Article 16. It is for the Members, bearing constantly in mind their duty, to enforce respect

for the Covenant, to decide upon what measures they can take. To deal effectively with the aggressor, co-operation is essential. It is clear that, for this co-operation to succeed, it is most desirable that States should have the guidance, in regard to the general situation, of a weighty and authoritative opinion. As to military action against the aggressor, Article 16 itself instructs the Council to make recommendations to the Members. The provisional injunctions of 1921 added that if necessary it would be for the Council to recommend to the Members a plan for joint action co-ordinating the economic, commercial and financial measures to be taken. This is a valuable suggestion going beyond the provisional framework of the 1921 resolutions. The part assigned to the Council is in perfect harmony with the central position given to it by the Covenant.

172. For the recommendations it will have to make, the Council will need very full information on various points. In one of its resolutions of December 8th, 1926, the Council requested the Secretary-General to collect systematically precise information regarding the economic and financial relations of the various States with a view to a possible application of Article 16 of the Covenant, and to carry out this work in accordance with a plan to be submitted to the Council by the Secretary-General after consulting the technical organs of the League, including, if necessary, the Joint Commission. Correspondence has since passed between the Secretary-General and the Economic and Financial Committees of the League with regard to the plan to be drawn up.

In a letter dated October 13th, 1927 (see Appendix I), the Financial Committee informed the Secretary-General that it could not but feel that such a new form of enquiry might cause a misunderstanding of the purpose of the present work of collecting and publishing trade statistics and other economic information, which was undertaken in the general interests of scientific knowledge and practical economic purposes. The Committee thought it of great importance that this work should be continued and developed on its present lines and said that it would greatly regret any action which might restrict it or render it more difficult.

173. At the same time the Committee recognised that, apart from the duties falling upon the several States, the League might have a very important part to play in securing due co-ordination between the measures taken in the different countries, and that it was therefore desirable that, when the occasion arose, the League should have at its disposal both the information and expert advice and assistance which might be required in the circumstances peculiar to any particular crisis. In the Committee's opinion, these requirements could only be met by securing, as soon as the occasion arose, the expert assistance and information which the Member States were alone in a position to give.

174. In these circumstances, the Committee recommended that, apart from the development and extension of the League's work of collecting economic information on the present lines and for its present purpose, no new form of enquiry should be instituted. It recommended, however, that Member States should be asked, in addition to carrying out their specific obligations under Article 16, to undertake to place at the disposal of the League, when the need arose, the economic and financial information in their possession which was relevant to the particular crisis, and the advice and assistance of competent experts in order to help the League to secure due co-ordination between the measures taken by the different Member States.

175. The Economic Committee's opinion, which will be found in its letter to the Secretary-General of December 21st, 1927 (see Appendix II), is to the same effect. According to the authoritative opinion of these two Committees, the League of Nations should confine itself for the moment to collecting and publishing commercial statistics and other economic particulars which have already been compiled. If it should become necessary to apply Article 16, the Council would obtain the opinion of the economic and financial experts of the countries specially concerned in the sanctions, and would thus obtain the knowledge necessary for drawing up its recommendations.

176. We might now go into the details of the measures to be taken in the case provided for in Article 16. We may quote the first sentence of the tenth resolution of 1921 :

" It is not possible to decide beforehand, and in detail, the various measures of an economic, commercial and financial nature to be taken in each case where economic pressure is to be applied. "

Indeed, the variety of cases which might arise is such that it is impossible to settle in advance what measures will be possible and expedient. When the time comes, the Council will act with a full knowledge of the facts acquired by the action it will have taken in virtue of the Covenant during the development of the conflict.

There is therefore no question of drawing up a code of procedure for the application of Article 16.

It is possible, however, to formulate in a general manner a series of indications and recommendations capable of guiding the Council and the Members of the League without restricting the freedom of the League's organs to judge at any time the best line of action to take, and without diminishing or increasing the rights and duties of the Members under the Covenant. Indications of this kind will be found summarised in the conclusions at the end of this memorandum.

177. *Appendix 1 to Chapter IV.*

REPLY OF THE FINANCIAL COMMITTEE ON THE SYSTEMATIC COLLECTION OF INFORMATION.

The Committee considered very carefully the following resolution of the Council :

" The Council requests the Secretary-General :

" *(a)* To collect systematically precise information regarding the economic and financial relations of the various States, with a view to a possible application of Article 16 of the Covenant. This work will be carried out in accordance with a plan to be submitted to the Council by the Secretary-General after consulting the technical organisations of the League, including, if necessary, the Joint Commission. "

The Committee fully realises that it is essential that the provisions of Article 16 as to the severance of economic and financial relations should be enforced by Member States effectively and without delay, as soon as the necessity arises, and appreciates the importance of the part which the League's central organisation may play in securing this result.

The Committee cannot but feel, however, that such a new form of enquiry might cause a misunderstanding of the purposes of the present work of collecting and publishing trade statistics and other economic information which is undertaken in the general interests of scientific knowledge and practical economic purposes. The Committee thinks it of great importance that this work should be continued and developed on its present lines, and would greatly regret any action which might restrict it or render it more difficult.

At the same time the Committee recognises that, apart from the duties falling upon the several States, the League may have a very important part to play in securing due co-ordination between the measures taken in the different countries, and that it is therefore desirable that, when the occasion arises, the League should have at its disposal both the information and expert advice and assistance which may be required in the circumstances peculiar to any particular crisis. These requirements can, in the Committee's opinion, only be met by securing, as soon as the occasion arises, the expert assistance and information which the Member States are alone in a position to give.

In these circumstances, the Committee recommends that, apart from the development and extension of the League's work of collecting economic information on the present lines and for its present purpose, no new form of enquiry should be instituted. It recommends, however, that Member States should be asked, in addition to carrying out their specific obligations under Article 16, to undertake to place at the disposal of the League, when the need arises, the economic and financial information in their possession, which is relevant to the particular crisis, and the advice and assistance of competent experts in order to help the League to secure due co-ordination between the measures taken by the different Member States.

178. *Appendix 2 to Chapter IV.*

REPLY OF THE ECONOMIC COMMITTEE ON THE SYSTEMATIC COLLECTION OF INFORMATION.

In response to the request for an opinion as to the most expedient means whereby it may be possible

" to collect systematically precise information regarding the economic and financial relations of the various States, with a view to a possible application of Article 16 of the Covenant " ; the work to " be carried out in accordance with a plan to be submitted to the Council by the Secretary-General after consulting the technical organisations of the League, including, if necessary, the Joint Commission ",

the Economic Committee studied the question with the object of permitting as effective and speedy an application as possible of the provisions of Article 16 of the Covenant, relating to the severance of economic and financial relations.

In so doing it decided that it was necessary to differentiate between information of an international character which would be at the Council's permanent disposal and the information of a national character to which the Council should be able to call for in the event of the contingency mentioned in Article 16 arising, or for the purposes of preparatory studies or the institution of measures designed to meet such a contingency.

As regards the question of information of an international character, the Economic Committee is of opinion that it would not be expedient to contemplate collecting any information other than that which it already possesses.

With the information at its disposal, the Council will be able to estimate the resources for which any State is dependent on foreign help and those which it possesses within its own territory. It would be useless to attempt to rectify or supplement these data by a study of the plans of each country for remedying its dependence on foreign help or increasing its own resources in the contingency mentioned in Article 16 of the Covenant. As regards these national plans, which may in some cases be of assistance in interpreting international statistics, the Committee possesses no powers of investigation.

The Committee decided accordingly that the general international information, so far as the Committee has access to it, could not be considered of supreme value from the point of view of the contingencies contemplated by Article 16 or the studies connected therewith. For this purpose, the most valuable source of information is the national material, dealing, on the one hand, with the resources and requirements of each country and the means whereby it proposes to increase the first and supply the second, and, on the other, with the assistance which it hopes to obtain from abroad. The Economic Committee is of opinion therefore that every Government should be able at any moment to supply information of this nature, which might be used in the circumstances mentioned in Article 16 and for the purposes of the joint studies that the League organisations might decide to undertake in view of those circumstances.

The Committee desires to emphasise the fact that the national information should not only be available in writing but should, if necessary, be analysed, explained and substantiated by experts appointed in advance by each Government.

The Committee is convinced that the international statistical work in which it is engaged and the national information which it recommends should be collected, would enable the Secretariat of the League to comply with the obligations imposed on the League by the Covenant.

V. Communications of the League in Time of Emergency.

179. In the study of Article 11, in Chapter III, it has already been pointed out that the systematic preparation of the Council's action under this article has a political as well as a technical side. The latter includes the question of communications affecting the League in time of emergency.

180. The question of League communications in time of emergency is important not only for the application of Article 11, but also for that of other articles of the Covenant, in particular Articles 4, 10, 15, 16 and 17. The effectiveness of the action taken by the Council under these articles depends to a large extent on the rapidity with which the Council can assemble. The sooner the Council can meet the more rapid will be its intervention for the maintainance or restoration of peace. This is an important factor affecting security.

181. The last Assembly again stated categorically on this point that it is incumbent upon the Members of the League to facilitate the meeting of the Council in time of emergency by every available means in their power.

182. The rapid assembling of the Council, however, is not the only important point. Generally speaking, every effort should be made to ensure that the following steps are taken as rapidly as possible :

1. Appeal to the League from a Member of the League ;
2. Communication between the Secretary-General and the Members of the Council ;
3. Communication between the Secretary-General and the President of the Council ;
4. Communication between the President of the Council and the Secretary-General, and the States concerned ;
5. The assembling of the members of the Council at Geneva or in any other place;
6. The conveyance to the spot of the special missions despatched by the Council.

183. With the exception of the meeting of the Council and the despatch to the spot of instructions or missions, all these points are dependent on telegraphic or telephonic communications, by wire or wireless.

184. The importance of rapid communications was clearly shown during the frontier incident between Bulgaria and Greece. The Commission of Enquiry into this incident stated in its report that " the saving of a few minutes may prevent a catastrophe. In the present circumstances, which were exceedingly favourable — in that the President of the Council received a telephone message one hour after Bulgaria's appeal had been received by the Secretary-General — a military operation which might have had the most dangerous results was only just prevented ".

185. The question of communications was also raised by M. Paul-Boncour at the first session of the Preparatory Commission. He said that under certain circumstances rapidity of action was one of the essential conditions for the prevention of war. M. de Brouckère expressed a similar opinion when he said that whatever action was to be taken must be taken more rapidly than an army could be mobilised, an operation which was always carried out with the utmost speed.

186. The first enquiries undertaken, at the request of the Council, by the Advisory Committee on Communications and Transit have already resulted in the framing of definite proposals which have been approved by the Administrations concerned and which will enable the best use to be made of existing means of communication by rail as well as by water, by telegraph and telephone, etc.

187. The Council, however, desired to go a step further. On the Council's instructions, the Advisory Committee on Communications and Transit is already studying the possibility of establishing for the requirements of the League of Nations, particularly at times of emergency, independent means of communication which would be entirely at its disposal and therefore infinitely less likely to be affected by the disturbances which a crisis is bound to produce in the normal working of communications under the control of Governments.

188. The Transit Committee is therefore considering the possibility of securing for the League of Nations independent means of communication by air as well as the establishment of a radio-telegraphic station belonging to the League, which will enable it to communicate independently with the greatest possible number of its Members.

189. The Committee on Arbitration and Security is bound to concern itself with these questions. Any measures to increase the safety and speed of the communications necessary for the working of the League organs at times of emergency will strengthen general security. In particular, the Committee must, in cases of serious emergency, attach great importance to the possibility of safeguarding the independence of the League's means of communication.

190. The adoption of the measures contemplated will show in a practical and tangible manner that the Members of the League are determined that the League shall be an effective instrument for action, and will, in the eyes of all, be a striking demonstration of solidarity.

VI. STUDY OF THE SCHEME OF FINANCIAL ASSISTANCE TO BE GIVEN TO STATES THREATENED WITH AGGRESSION.

Introduction.

191. The resolution adopted by the Committee on Arbitration and Security at its first session defines the study which it desires to carry out as follows :

" Study of the scheme of financial assistance to be given to States threatened with aggression, and particularly of the preliminary points raised by the Financial Committee :

" *(a)* Study of the criteria by which aggression may be presumed and the procedure of the Council in this matter ;

" *(b)* Right of participation by States (the question of States not Members of the League). "

192. With regard to the scheme of financial assistance to be studied, the Assembly, at its eighth ordinary session, adopted the following resolution :

" The Assembly,

" Having taken note of the plan submitted to the Council by the Financial Committee with regard to the Finnish Government's proposal for ensuring financial aid to any State victim of aggression ;

" Being convinced of the need for a system of financial aid for contributing to the organisation of security, which is an indispensable preliminary to general disarmament :

" Requests the Council to continue and complete it with a view to its final adoption either by a Disarmament Conference or by a special Conference to be convened for the purpose.

" The Assembly suggests to the Council that it would be advisable to submit the plan referred to, and the documents relating to Article 16 prepared by the Legal Section of the Secretariat, the observations submitted by the several Governments and the Minutes of the discussions in the Third Committee on this subject, to the committee which it proposes should be appointed in pursuance of its resolution relative to arbitration, security and disarmament. "

193. The Council, at its forty-seventh session, referred the Assembly resolution through the Preparatory Commission for the Disarmament Conference to our Committee by the following resolution :

" The Council,

" Notes the Assembly's resolution of September 26th, 1927, concerning financial aid to States victims of aggression ;

" Forwards this resolution to the Preparatory Commission for communication to the committee which it is to appoint to study questions relating to arbitration and security;

" Authorises that committee to consult the Financial Committee whenever it thinks fit and, if necessary, to request the latter to make technical studies of the question ;

" Requests the Financial Committee to co-operate with the Committee on Arbitration and Security and the Preparatory Commission for the Disarmament Conference for the purposes mentioned above. "

194. The scheme proposed by the Financial Committee is in its general outline as follows :

The State which is the victim of aggression would be assisted by the League to obtain a loan on the money market in the ordinary way.

The assistance would take the form of a guarantee for the loan. This guarantee would be given by the States participating in the scheme, perhaps in the same proportions as their contributions to the League. The Convention establishing the scheme would fix a maximum limit for the guarantee. If this maximum were fixed at fifty million pounds, and if all the

Members of the League participated, each State would be called upon to guarantee the interest on and amortisation of a sum equal to about fifty times its annual contribution to the League. The signatories of the Convention would deposit general bonds of guarantee with the Secretary-General or the Trustees (who would be appointed by the Council). When a State which was a party to the Convention was attacked and asked for financial assistance under the terms of the Convention, the Council of the League would, on the advice of the Financial Committee, decide how and to what extent the request should be complied with, and would fix the amount of the loan.

For this purpose the signatories would exchange the general bonds for " specific bonds of guarantee " to the amount required, but not exceeding the total of their guarantees.

The " specific bonds of guarantee " would be drawn up in a form generally corresponding to that of the bonds deposited with the trustees for the Austrian Reconstruction Loan, and the procedure of their operation would be the same.

Should the attacked State default, the " specific bonds " would be presented to their signatories.

The Committee further proposes to strengthen the scheme by establishing a supplementary guarantee whereby a small number of signatories holding a very strong financial position would guarantee the signatories of the specific bonds for the entire amount. If necessary, they would temporarily furnish the funds required for the payments to be made.

Each Government signing the supplementary guarantee would undertake to facilitate the public issue, in its country, of loans floated under the Convention.

195. A detailed technical examination of the Financial Committee's scheme cannot be expected in this memorandum. Such an examination would be valueless without the assistance of the Financial Committee, which has already done work of very considerable practical importance in this matter. The Council has made provision for this co-operation ; the Security Committee will have to arrange to inaugurate it, either through a sub-committee or by any other method which seems suitable.

196. It should be remembered that the British representative on the Council stated that his Government approved the scheme outlined by the Financial Committee but could only accept it on two conditions, namely, that the scheme should form part of an adequate measure of general disarmament and that the principal States should also accept a satisfactory allotment of the obligations contained in the guarantee.

197. For the moment it seems sufficient to explain the two main points mentioned in the Committee's programme.

Study of the Criteria by which Aggression may be presumed and the Procedure of the Council in this Matter.

198. Under the Financial Committee's scheme, action on the part of each guarantor State is necessary before the scheme of assistance can operate for the benefit of a country which is the victim of aggression ; the general bonds of guarantee must be exchanged for specific bonds of guarantee. This is an important point. The Financial Committee proposes to make it a matter for the Council to decide whether the financial assistance in contemplation shall be given to an attacked State. Notwithstanding the deposit of the general bonds of guarantee, however, the Council will not have full and free disposal of the guarantee, but will require the concurrence of the States. The question then arises whether it will be possible in practice to introduce, side by side with the system of Article 16, under which each Member of the League is left to decide whether the Covenant has been broken, a different system for financial assistance. There arises at the same time the question whether the criteria of aggression should be studied separately in regard to the application of Article 16 and that of the scheme of financial assistance.

199. It is hardly to be supposed that, having arrived at a decision as to whether aggression within the meaning of Article 16 has taken place and who is the aggressor, any State will co-operate in giving financial assistance to a country which it cannot recognise as having been attacked. No State will lend financial assistance, even if enjoined to do so by the Council, to a State which it regards as the aggressor and against which it is applying economic or military sanctions. Still less can it be imagined that any State will voluntarily give military assistance to one of the belligerents and financial assistance to the other, simply because the criteria of aggression are different. It would seem necessary to establish a relation between the system of financial assistance and the application of Article 16. Whether the financial assistance contemplated in the Financial Committee's scheme constitutes the fulfilment of an obligation under Article 16 is a question that has already been discussed. As financial assistance under the Financial Committee's scheme will be governed by a special convention, the question of the relation in law between this assistance and the obligations embodied in Article 16 can be left open. The essential point, however, is that there must be a relation and concordance between the application of Article 16 by any Member and the provision of financial assistance by the same Member in the same conflict.

200. The position would be different if a system of financial assistance were adopted whereby from the outset the Council would have full and free disposal of the funds required to guarantee a loan for an attacked State. In that case, the decision as to the according of a guarantee could be left in the Council's hands. On the other hand, we may conclude from the Financial Committee's report that such a system would encounter technical difficulties ; and statements

which have been made both in the Council and in the Third Committee of the Eighth Assembly suggest that it is doubtful whether all States can be expected to agree to such a scheme.

201. The conclusion is that financial assistance should be so regulated as to ensure definite concordance between decisions taken under Article 16 and decisions regarding financial assistance. This object might be attained by mentioning, in the Convention on financial assistance, the cases in which Article 16 applies.

202. One reservation must, however, be made. Organised financial assistance presupposes the participation of a large number of States and supervision by the Council. Thus, although no State can be obliged to co-operate in assisting financially another State which in its opinion has not been attacked, it must always be remembered that a number of States may be prepared to lend their financial aid to a State which in their opinion has been attacked, and that nevertheless the concerted plan will not come into force, either because a number of other States do not admit that the *casus fœderis* has arisen, or because the Council itself has not taken the necessary decisions for setting in motion the plan for financial assistance.

With regard to the procedure to be followed by the Council, the remark which was made on the subject of criteria for the designation of the aggressor again applies. On this point also, financial assistance must be made to harmonise with the application of sanctions under Article 16.

203. Here, however, it should be pointed out that the Council may avail itself of the plan for financial assistance before Article 16 comes into play. By the time this article has to be applied, the efforts of the Council to maintain peace have failed. It is the preceding period, before the Covenant has been infringed, which is of far greater interest to the League. It is on this period — the fact cannot be stated too often — that the League should concentrate its efforts with a view to avoiding the dreaded event of the entry into operation of Article 16. In this period, too, the plan of financial assistance might already be brought into play and exercise a beneficial influence. Among the means of pressure which the Council might employ when taking action under the various articles of the Covenant, and particularly Article 11, for the prevention of war, not the least effective is the possibility of guaranteeing a loan to a party in case of attack.

204. The holding out of such a possibility, and if circumstances so required the making of actual promises, would be an affirmation of the solidarity on the part of the Members of the League with any State which might be attacked, and it would show beforehand that they were determined to maintain the principles of the Covenant by action if necessary. If a definite plan were prepared, the Council ought to be able to utilise it in this manner when taking action under Article 11.

Right of Countries to participate. (Question of States non-Members of the League.)

205. There is no reason why any Member of the League of Nations should be prevented from participating in the plan, provided it accedes to the Convention within a definite period.

206. The question of the participation of States non-Members of the League does not seem to be of any practical interest. It is hardly likely that a non-Member State would desire to enter into such close co-operation with the League. A country for which the protection offered by the League holds no particular attraction — possibly because it feels that it will never require such protection — will not desire to participate in the organisation of financial assistance. We do not, however, think that non-Member States should be generally excluded. The Convention might be open to States non-Members who would be admitted by special decision of the parties on a unanimous or a majority vote. It does not seem necessary to go into the details of this question at present.

VII. Conclusions.

207. It does not seem advisable to draw up a rigid and complete code of procedure for the League in times of emergency, and the present memorandum and its conclusions propose neither to extend nor to curtail the rights and duties of the Members of the League.

It is both feasible and desirable, however, to give some indication of the possibilities offered by the different articles of the Covenant and the way in which they may be applied, without expressing any opinion as to the particular methods which the infinite variety of possible cases may in practice require.

208. To ensure the effectiveness of the League's action in any eventuality under the articles of the Covenant and, in particular, under Articles 4, 10, 11 and 16, it is vitally important that the technical studies and preparations for improving the communications of the League's organs should be actively pushed forward.

209. The task of the League of Nations is to maintain peace ; to fulfil this task it must, above all, *prevent* war. The application of repressive measures, which cannot but have serious consequences, will only take place in extreme cases in which the preventive measures have unfortunately failed in their object.

210. With regard to the application of Article 11, the Report of the Committee of the Council, approved by the Assembly at its eighth ordinary session, is a valuable guide, to which the present memorandum adds a few new indications.

211. A hard-and-fast definition of the expressions " aggression " (Article 10), and " resort to war " (Article 16) would not be free from danger, since it might oblige the Council and the Members of the League to pronounce on a breach of the Covenant and apply sanctions at a time when it would still be preferable to refrain for the moment from measures of coercion. There would also be the risk that criteria might be taken which, in unforeseen circumstances, might lead to a State which was not in reality responsible for hostilities being described as an aggressor.

212. The preparation of the military sanctions provided for in Article 16 does not seem likely to promote mutual confidence between the States Members of the League of Nations unless at the same time various forms of pacific procedure suitable for the settlement of all international disputes are organised, and unless there is also a general agreement on the reduction and limitation of armaments.

213. In order to facilitate the application of Article 16 in case of need, it is necessary to make a full and conscientious use of the other articles of the Covenant and especially of Article 11. This article enables the Council to keep in touch with developments in a conflict and so to construct a basis for the decisions which it may be called upon to take under Article 16.

214. It would be desirable to put an end to the uncertainty consequent upon the fact that several amendments to Article 16, the majority dating from 1921, have not yet secured the necessary number of ratifications, either by securing their ratification in the near future or finally abandoning them.

215. It would be well that, in the event of resort to war, the Council should declare whether a breach of the Covenant has or has not taken place, and should state which of the two parties to the dispute has broken the Covenant.

216. In determining the aggressor the Council will find, among other factors helping it to form a judgment, a valuable indication in the extent to which and the manner in which the parties to the dispute have promoted the action previously taken by the Council in application of the articles of the Covenant, and especially of Article 11, to maintain peace.

217. Apart from the recommendations provided for in paragraph 2 of Article 16 concerning participation in military sanctions, it would be desirable for the Council in some cases to make recommendations to the Members regarding the application of the measures of economic pressure mentioned in the first paragraph of Article 16. In this eventuality, the Council could consult economic and financial experts in the countries specially concerned.

218. The study of the question of the financial assistance to be given to a State victim of an aggression should be pursued both from the technical and the political points of view. In carrying out this study, the possibility of providing assistance, even before Article 16 is applied, should be examined.

No. 2137. — GENERAL TREATY [1] FOR RENUNCIATION OF WAR AS AN INSTRUMENT OF NATIONAL POLICY. SIGNED AT PARIS AUGUST 27, 1928.

French and English official texts communicated by the President of the Council, Minister for Foreig Affairs of the French Republic and the Belgian Minister for Foreign Affairs. The registratio of this Treaty took place September 4, 1929.
This Treaty was transmitted to the Secretariat by the Department of State of the Government of th United States of America, August 9, 1929.

THE PRESIDENT OF THE GERMAN REICH, THE PRESIDENT OF THE UNITED STATES OF AMERICA HIS MAJESTY THE KING OF THE BELGIANS, THE PRESIDENT OF THE FRENCH REPUBLIC, HIS MAJESTY THE KING OF GREAT BRITAIN, IRELAND AND THE BRITISH DOMINIONS BEYOND THE SEAS, EMPEROI OF INDIA, HIS MAJESTY THE KING OF ITALY, HIS MAJESTY THE EMPEROR OF JAPAN, THE PRESIDEN OF THE REPUBLIC OF POLAND, THE PRESIDENT OF THE CZECHOSLOVAK REPUBLIC, deeply sensibl of their solemn duty to promote the welfare of mankind ;

Persuaded that the time has come when a frank renunciation of war as an instrument of nationa policy should be made to the end that the peaceful and friendly relations now existing betweer their peoples may be perpetuated ;

Convinced that all changes in their relations with one another should be sought only by pacific means and be the result of a peaceful and orderly process, and that any signatory Powe

---

[1] Ratifications deposited at Washington by all the States signatories, July 25, 1929.

Accessions :

Afghanistan	November 30, 1928	Lithuania	April 5, 192ᴄ
Abyssnia	November 28, 1928	Luxemburg	August 24, 192ᴄ
Albania	February 12, 1929	Mexico	November 26, 192ᴄ
Austria	December 31, 1928	The Netherlands	July 12, 192ᴄ
Bulgaria	July 22, 1929	Nicaragua	May 13, 192ᴄ
Chile	August 12, 1929	Norway	March 26, 192ᴄ
China	May 8, 1929	Panama	February 25, 192ᴄ
Costa Rica	October 1st, 1929	Paraguay	December 4, 192ᴄ
Cuba	March 13, 1929	Peru	July 23, 192ᴄ
Denmark	March 23, 1929	Persia	July 25, 192ᴄ
Free City of Danzig	September 11, 1929	Portugal	March 1st, 192ᴄ
Dominican Republic	December 12, 1928	Roumania	March 21, 192ᴄ
Egypt	May 9, 1929	Kingdom of the Serbs, Croats	
Estonia	April 26, 1929	and Slovenes	February 20, 192ᴄ
Finland	July 24, 1929	Siam	January 16, 192ᴄ
Greece	August 3, 1929	Spain	March 7, 192ᴄ
Guatemala	July 16, 1929	Sweden	April 12, 192ᴄ
Haiti	March 10, 1930	Switzerland	December 2, 192ᴄ
Honduras	August 5, 1929	Turkey	July 8, 192ᴄ
Hungary	July 22, 1929	Union of Soviet Socialist Re-	
Iceland	June 10, 1929	publics	September 27, 1928
Latvia	July 23, 1929	Venezuela	October 24, 192ᴄ
Liberia	February 23, 1929		

which shall hereafter seek to promote its national interests by resort to war should be denied the benefits furnished by this Treaty ;

Hopeful that, encouraged by their example, all the other nations of the world will join in this humane endeavour and by adhering to the present Treaty as soon as it comes into force bring their peoples within the scope of its beneficent provisions, thus uniting the civilized nations of the world in a common renunciation of war as an instrument of their national policy ;

Have decided to conclude a Treaty and for that purpose have appointed as their respective Plenipotentiaries :

THE PRESIDENT OF THE GERMAN REICH :

Dr. Gustav STRESEMANN, Minister for Foreign Affairs ;

THE PRESIDENT OF THE UNITED STATES OF AMERICA :

The Honorable Frank B. KELLOGG, Secretary of State ;

HIS MAJESTY THE KING OF THE BELGIANS :

Mr. Paul HYMANS, Minister for Foreign Affairs, Minister of State ;

THE PRESIDENT OF THE FRENCH REPUBLIC :

Mr. Aristide BRIAND, Minister for Foreign Affairs ;

HIS MAJESTY THE KING OF GREAT BRITAIN, IRELAND AND THE BRITISH DOMINIONS BEYOND THE SEAS, EMPEROR OF INDIA :

FOR GREAT BRITAIN AND NORTHERN IRELAND AND ALL PARTS OF THE BRITISH EMPIRE WHICH ARE NOT SEPARATE MEMBERS OF THE LEAGUE OF NATIONS :

The Right Honourable Lord CUSHENDUN, Chancellor of the Duchy of Lancaster, Acting Secretary of State for Foreign Affairs ;

FOR THE DOMINION OF CANADA :

The Right Honourable William Lyon MACKENZIE KING, Prime Minister and Minister for External Affairs ;

FOR THE COMMONWEALTH OF AUSTRALIA :

The Honourable Alexander John McLACHLAN, Member of the Executive Federal Council ;

FOR THE DOMINION OF NEW ZEALAND :

The Honourable Sir Christopher James PARR, High Commissioner for New Zealand in Great Britain ;

FOR THE UNION OF SOUTH AFRICA :

The Honourable Jacobus Stephanus SMIT, High Commissioner for the Union of South Africa in Great Britain ;

FOR THE IRISH FREE STATE :

Mr. William Thomas COSGRAVE, President of the Executive Council ;

FOR INDIA

The Right Honourable Lord CUSHENDUN, Chancellor of the Duchy of Lancaster, Acting Secretary of State for Foreign Affairs;

His Majesty the King of Italy :

Count Gaetano Manzoni, His Ambassador Extraordinary and Plenipotentiary at Paris ;

His Majesty the Emperor of Japan :

Count Uchida, Privy Councillor ;

he President of the Republic of Poland

Mr. A. Zaleski, Minister for Foreign Affairs ;

The President of the Czechoslovak Republic :

Dr. Eduard Beneš, Minister for Foreign Affairs ;

Who, having communicated to one another their full powers found in good and due form have agreed upon the following articles :

Article I.

The High Contracting Parties solemnly declare in the names of their respective peoples that they condemn recourse to war for the solution of international controvesies, and renounce it as an instrument of national policy in their relations with one another.

Article II.

The High Contracting Parties agree that the settlement or solution of all disputes or conflicts of whatever nature or of whatever origin they may be, which may arise among them, shall never be sought except by pacific means.

Article III.

The present Treaty shall be ratified by the High Contracting Parties named in the Preamble in accordance with their respective constitutional requirements, and shall take effect as between them as soon as all their several instruments of ratification shall have been deposited at Washington.

This Treaty shall, when it has come into effect as prescribed in the preceding paragraph, remain open as long as may be necessary for adherence by all the other Powers of the world. Every instrument evidencing the adherence of a Power shall be deposited at Washington and the Treaty shall immediately upon such deposit become effective as between the Power thus adhering and the other Powers parties hereto.

It shall be the duty of the Government of the United States to furnish each Government named in the Preamble and every Government subsequently adhering to this Treaty with a certified copy of the Treaty and of every instrument of ratification or adherence. It shall also be the duty of the Government of the United States telegraphically to notify such Governments immediately upon the deposit with it of each instrument of ratification or adherence.

En foi de quoi les plénipotentiaires respectifs ont signé le présent traité établi en langue française et anglaise, les deux textes ayant force égale, et y ont apposé leurs cachets.

Fait à Paris, le vingt-sept août mil neuf cent vingt-huit.

In faith whereof the respective Plenipotentiaries have signed this Treaty in the French and English languages both texts having equal force, and hereunto affix their seals.

Done at Paris, the twenty-seventh day of August in the year one thousand nine hundred and twenty-eight.

(L. S.)	(Signé)	Gustav STRESEMANN.
(L. S.)	(Signé)	Frank B. KELLOGG.
(L. S.)	(Signé)	Paul HYMANS.
(L. S.)	(Signé)	Aristide BRIAND.
(L. S.)	(Signé)	CUSHENDUN.
(L. S.)	(Signé)	W. L. MACKENZIE KING.
(L. S.)	(Signé)	A. J. McLACHLAN.
(L. S.)	(Signé)	C. J. PARR.
(L. S.)	(Signé)	J. S. SMIT.
(L. S.)	(Signé)	William Thomas COSGRAVE.
(L. S.)	(Signé)	CUSHENDUN.
(L. S.)	(Signé)	G. MANZONI.
(L. S.)	(Signé)	UCHIDA.
(L. S.)	(Signé)	Auguste ZALESKI.
(L. S.)	(Signé)	Dʳ. Edvard BENEŠ.

Copie certifiée conforme :

Le Ministre plénipotentiaire,
Chef du Service du Protocole :
   ˙P. de Fouquières.

DOCUMENT 8

PROPOSALS OF DELEGATIONS

Official No.: Conf. D. 56.

Geneva, February 5th, 1932.

PROPOSALS OF THE FRENCH DELEGATION.

The Government of the Republic, conscious of the gravity of the problem to be solved, is convinced that, in accordance with previous work of the League of Nations, the Conference should deal with this problem as a part of general policy.

This is all the more important since it meets at a time of economic and moral tension, at a time of general disturbance and uneasiness, when events emphasise the absolute necessity of a better organisation in a tormented world.

The Government of the Republic is anxious to honour the promise contained in its memorandum of July 15th, 1931, and to reply to the repeated appeals made by the League of Nations, notably in the resolution of the Assembly of 1927. It intends thus to fulfil a double duty.

It assumes that, on the basis of the draft Convention of 1930, action will be taken with the least possible delay.

Further, it presents herewith proposals for placing civil aviation and bombing aircraft, and also certain material of land and naval forces, at the disposal of the League of Nations [1]; for the creation of a preventive and repressive international force; for the political conditions upon which such measures depend; and, lastly, for new rules providing for the protection of civil population.

I. Proposals to Place Civil Aviation and Bombing Aircraft at the Disposal of the League of Nations.

The Government of the Republic proposes, in the first place, to the Conference a series of measures dealing with the newest arm of war, now increasing immoderately in size and technique with consequent disorganisation of prices and international competition—this war arm whose character is the most specifically offensive and the most threatening to civilians.

Bombing machines capable of carrying great loads and having a wide radius of action which enables them to conduct operations far within the territory of belligerent countries offer the aggressor a particularly cruel weapon for use against non-combatants. It is to such machines that the following provisions refer:

1. *Internationalisation of Civil Air Transport under a Regime to be organised by the League.*

This internationalisation, already studied by certain Governments for economic and financial reasons, would include:

(*a*) The undertaking by the Contracting parties not to permit their nationals to construct (with the exception of orders placed in accordance with the conditions fixed in paragraphs (*b*), (*c*) and (*d*) hereafter) or to employ machines capable of military use. The maximum unladen tonnage of authorised aircraft will be to this end and in accordance with the advice of their experts, limited by the Contracting parties to x tons for aeroplanes, x' for seaplanes and x'' cubic metres for dirigibles.

(*b*) The creation of an international civil air transport service entrusted to continental, inter-continental or inter-colonial organisations, to operate air transport under the auspices

---

[1] Or, in the case of the accession of States non-members of the League of Nations, of which several have taken part in the work of the Preparatory Commission, at the disposal of the international authority which would be constituted to ensure their co-operation.

of the League of Nations, which alone will have the right to build and to use machines of greater tonnage than that indicated in the preceding paragraph.

(c)   The right to create lines between the home country and colonial territories presenting particular interest for one or more of the Contracting parties, provided always that they undertake to bear the costs, if requested to do so by the League of Nations, and that they submit to the League for its approval the number, the type and the unladen tonnage of the machines to be used.

(d)   The fair distribution, according to their capacity, between the aviation industries of the different countries, of orders for material for international civil aviation, in accordance with conditions to be fixed in an annexed convention.

(e)   The exclusive, permanent and inalienable right for the League of Nations to requisition all machines for the International Civil Air Service.

(f)   The guarantee of the Contracting Parties not to place an embargo on machines belonging to the International Civil Air Service and not to sequestrate them, but to facilitate the League's right of requisition by all means in their power.

This internationalisation of civil aviation is the necessary condition of the proposals which follow.

2.   Limitation of Bombing Aircraft.

The problem to be solved has two aspects of equal importance.

On the one hand, it is necessary that, in order to carry out its preventive and, if need be, its repressive action against war, the League of Nations should dispose of a superiority in air strength.

On the other hand, it would be inadmissible for a State suffering from an air bombardment, in violation of the rules laid down in Chapter V below, not to retain the full use of all its air strength in order to reply to this flagrant act of aggression.

In order to reconcile these two necessities, the Government of the Republic proposes:

(a)   The contracting parties undertake not to retain, or not to build in the future for their military air forces, machines having an unladen tonnage exceeding a limit to be fixed by the contracting parties in consultation with their experts, at y tons for aeroplanes, y' tons for seaplanes and y'' cubic metres for dirigibles.

Machines of tonnage above this limit will be set aside for the constitution of an international military air force. Consequently, they will be transferred by those contracting parties who own them when the Convention comes into force, to the League of Nations which will decide where they have to be stationed and will organise the command of the International Air Force.

(b)   In the military air forces of the different States, two categories must be distinguished:

(1)   Machines which will be left, in all circumstances, at the disposal of the Military Air Forces, and the unladen tonnage of which will be decided by the contracting parties after consultation with their experts and will not exceed z tons for aeroplanes, z' tons for seaplanes and z'' cubic metres for dirigibles;

(2)   Machines the unladen tonnage of which comes within the limits y and z and which will conform with the rules of paragraph (c) below.

(c)   The inclusion of aeroplanes, the unladen tonnage of which comes between z and y tons, in the Air Forces they are entitled to possess, is only authorised to those contracting parties who undertake to place them at the disposal of the League in the eventuality of the application of Article 16 of the Covenant and of common action by the League of Nations. These machines will be permanently under the inspection of the League.

(d)   Any contracting party suffering from an air bombardment in violation of Chapter V below, on the sole condition that it notifies the League of Nations, will be entitled immediately to use all its air forces including those machines earmarked to be at the disposal of the League of Nations. The contracting party will also, ipso facto, be freed from its own obligations vis-à-vis the aggressor.

The above provisions, while ensuring to the League its superiority of air strength, result in limiting bombing aircraft as regards number, power and use.

II.   PROPOSALS TO PLACE CERTAIN MATERIAL OF LAND AND NAVAL FORCES AT THE DISPOSAL OF THE LEAGUE OF NATIONS.

The same problem arises in the case of certain land and naval material as arises in the case of bombing aircraft. The French delegation offers a similar solution — namely :

(a)   Only those Powers which undertake to place them at the disposal of the League of Nations in the event of the application of Article 16 of the Covenant and of common action by the League shall have the right to possess such materials;

· (b)   In the case of aggression contrary to the rules laid down in Chapter V of the present proposals, the said Powers, after notifying the League of Nations, will recover the full right to dispose of all such means of defence;

(c)   The material coming under the present section includes:

Batteries of heavy long-range artillery;
Capital ships carrying guns exceeding 8 inches or of a tonnage exceeding 10,000 (W.T.) tons;
Submarines with a tonnage exceeding n tons.

III. Creation of an International Force.

The object of the third French proposal is to set up on behalf of the League of Nations and apart from the measures provided in Chapters 1 and 2:

(1)   An international police force to prevent war;
(2)   A first contingent of coercionary forces to repress war and to bring immediate assistance to any State victim of aggression.

(a)   The police force will be permanently available with complete freedom of passage to occupy in times of emergency areas where a threat of war has arisen, and to assist the action of commissioners of the League of Nations on the spot, and also to contribute to all conservatory measures within the scope of the Convention to improve the Means of Preventing War and of Article 11 of the League Covenant.

This police force will be made up of contingents furnished by each of the contracting parties in a proportion to be determined.   France is prepared to contribute a mixed brigade, a light naval division and a mixed group of reconnaissance and fighter aircraft.

The League of Nations will arrange for the command of the international police force and will be entitled to inspect its component elements.

(b)   The first contingent of coercionary forces would, in conformity with the undertakings to be assumed by contracting parties, be made up of elements of strength varying according to the regions concerned.

These undertakings entered into by States towards the League of Nations would oblige them to come to the help of any State victim of agression with forces of definite strength constantly available.   The contracting parties would have the option of increasing this contribution on the recommendation of the Council of the League (Paragraph 2 of Article 16 of the Covenant) or, in the event of aggression, with a view to applying regional conventions of mutual assistance coming within the scope of the Covenant.

The undertakings of the various States would differ according to the place of the conflict— a conflict concerning another continent from that to which the State belongs; a conflict concerning the continent to which the State belongs; a conflict in which the aggressor has a common frontier with the contracting State.

France is prepared to undertake the following contributions:

In the case of a conflict outside Europe: a mixed brigade, a light naval division, a mixed group of aircraft, material for land warfare without *personnel*, and munitions;

For a conflict in Europe: a division of all arms, a naval division, a mixed group of aircraft, material for land warfare with *personnel*, and munitions;

For a conflict in Europe in which the aggressor has a common frontier with France the contingents provided for in the preceding paragraph and, in addition, forces, the strength of which would be decided in each case in agreement with the League.

As far as material for land warfare is concerned, the contracting parties which possess tanks or similar armoured implements, as well as heavy field artillery, undertake to contribute from them to the forces which will be placed at the disposal of the League under the conditions mentioned above.

In these various eventualities the undertakings of each State would only become operative if the forces thus placed at any moment at the disposal of the League reached a minimum total to be determined, and if there were equitable proportion between the contributions of the principal States.

IV. Protection of Civilian Populations.

In addition to the preceding provisions, the Government of the Republic proposes the adoption of the following rules which can be adopted unconditionally:

(a)   The use by aeroplanes and by land or naval artillery of projectiles which are specifically incendiary or which contain poison gases or bacteria is forbidden, whatever the objective.

(b)   Any bombardment either from the air or by artillery is forbidden at a distance of more than x kilometres from the front line in land warfare.   The only exceptions admitted to this rule concern the bombardment of air bases used by belligerents or of the emplacements of long-range artillery.

(c)   Along the coast air bombardment is forbidden behind a zone of a depth of x kilometres except on air bases and on batteries of artillery.   In this zone of x kilometres air bombardment is not permitted except under the conditions laid down by Convention IX of The Hague for naval artillery acting with or without preliminary warning according to the cases mentioned in Article 2 of the said Convention.

(*d*) The use of naval artillery will continue to be governed by the provisions of Convention IX of The Hague.

(*e*) Any flagrant violation of one of the rules stated in the present chapter will be regarded as *prima facie* evidence that the State guilty thereof has resorted to war within the meaning of Article 16 of the Covenant of the League of Nations.

V. Conditions for the Organisation of Peace.

The Government of the Republic is fully aware that the above proposals entail political measures, which alone permit and guarantee their successful operation.

It affirms once more that no substantial reduction of armaments can be brought about by empirical and technical means. Whoever desires the end—and the end is essential—must also desire the means. There must be a change of method; in future we must seek in common action that security which each nation has hithero endeavoured to obtain from its own force alone.

This is the very spirit of the Covenant. We must give vitality to its stipulations, which, ever since we began to discuss their application, have been constantly interpreted along the line of least resistance.

The present Conference offers the best opportunity that has ever occurred to make a definite choice between a League of Nations possessing executive authority and a League of Nations paralysed by the uncompromising attitude of national sovereignty. France has made her choice. She suggests that the other nations should make theirs.

The measures without which the above proposals would be ineffective and even unthinkable include amongst others compulsory arbitration; definition of the aggressor; guarantees as to the rapidity of the decision of the authority controlling the international force; the bringing of the action of that authority into conformity with international law, which is still insufficiently precise, but the permanent and contractual elements of which result from international treaties and pacts; and the international control of the execution of all agreements concerning armaments.

These provisions, in regard to which the French delegation reserves the right to make concrete proposals are an integral part of the enquiries carried out by the League of Nations during the last twelve years. All the elements of the necessary solution are brought together.

Such a solution would be not only an important step towards a general and contractual limitation of armaments and towards their reduction, but also a great advance in the organisation of peace.

As the proposed organisation would have to be general, the execution of the undertakings which the various Powers would declare themselves ready to accept will be held in suspense until the ratification of the final Convention by all the contracting parties.

The Government of the Republic furnished in its Memorandum of July 15th, 1931, and in the Annexes to that Memorandum precise details of the modification of its armaments and the reductions which it has already brought about of its own accord, in execution of Article 8 of the League Covenant, since it came into force and since the conclusion of the Locarno Agreements.

These reductions, which the political conditions based on the existing order of things have rendered possible to France, are a pledge of her determination not only to fix them by treaty, but also, once co-operation has taken the place of isolation, to endeavour to achieve further reductions on the lines of the present proposals and of the fundamental guarantees to peace which these proposals would ensure.

DOCUMENT 9

THIRTY-FIRST MEETING

Held on Monday, February 6th, 1933, at 3.30 p.m.

President : The Right Honourable A. HENDERSON.

61. PLAN FOR GENERAL DISARMAMENT AND THE ORGANISATION OF PEACE, SUBMITTED
BY THE FRENCH GOVERNMENT : GENERAL DISCUSSION OF THE MEMORANDUM BY THE FRENCH
DELEGATION DATED NOVEMBER 14TH, 1932 *(continuation)*.

M. POLITIS (Greece). — I cordially welcome the French plan[1] in principle on behalf of
the Greek Government, which accepts the plan in all its parts and is prepared to go as far as
the principal Powers are prepared to go in carrying it into effect. This attitude is based on a
deep-seated conviction that peace, in order to be lasting and beneficial, can only result from
the organisation of the international community. The firmer the international organisation,
the greater the safeguards of peace.

[1] Document Conf.D.146.

198

M. LITVINOFF (Union of Soviet Socialist Republics). — The French delegation has appealed to us to refrain from vague general remarks, but to make clear the attitude of each delegation to the French plan. I am in complete sympathy with this appeal and consider it thoroughly apposite. We are too fond of promising to study proposals without, however, really making a practical study of them or even considering them. The Conference has received any number of proposals, and we have spent a whole year, not on their discussion, but on their postponement, pigeonholing them for some future occasion, or putting them into cold storage in technical commissions. I can assure our French colleagues that the Soviet delegation, which has always spoken frankly and sincerely on all the questions brought before us here, will not now mince its words and will give a precise definition of its attitude. The French delegation has asked us to give " considered approval " or " exact criticism " of its proposals. I shall endeavour to give both.

The Soviet delegation has studied with the deepest interest the French proposals now under discussion, and I am happy to declare that some of them can be supported by it. While far from desiring to minimise their importance, I am, nevertheless, bound to remark that we are unable to find among them any new proposals for the reduction of armaments, or, if any such are to be found therein, they are made to depend strictly on the acceptance by the Conference of the French scheme for security. We are invited first to draw up definite premises which should enable us subsequently to discuss measures for the reduction of armaments. It may not be irrelevant to remind ourselves that, as long ago as 1927, at the fourth session of the Preparatory Commission, the French delegation, in the person of the present Minister for Foreign Affairs, M. Paul-Boncour, demanded that the Commission should investigate the problem of security before drawing up a draft disarmament convention. This proposal was supported by some other delegations and resulted in the creation of a special " Committee for Arbitration and Security ", which, in the course of two years, produced a series of proposals, and work was begun upon a draft convention for disarmament.

If I go back to this, it is in part for the purpose of paying due respect to the consistency and tenacity of the leaders of French politics. Now, however, whether because the proposals worked out by the Security Committee have failed to satisfy the French delegation, or because they have been rejected by other delegations, we are confronted by new French proposals for security. This means that, after four years of work on disarmament by the Preparatory Commission and in the second year of the Conference itself, we have been thrown back to the place we were five years ago and are compelled once more to leave the question of disarmament in the background and take up the problem of security. Let us hope this cycle will not repeat itself, and that we shall not find ourselves, at the end of another five years, back again where we now stand.

The Soviet delegation has repeatedly shown its attitude to the question of security, both in the Preparatory Commission and at the present Conference. It has not the slightest desire to ignore this problem, the enormous importance of which it thoroughly realises. We have always, however, been convinced, and still are convinced, that the best, if not the only, guarantee of security for all nations would be total disarmament, or at least the utmost possible reduction of armaments in the shortest possible period. We have always considered, and still consider, that the problem of security approached by any other method is so complex, and evokes such serious political questions and international differences, that it could hardly be solved fortuitously and in a short time, and that to take it up would mean to abandon all idea of disarmament for a very considerable period.

But apparently there is no escape from this problem, if only because it has been raised by a great and powerful State, whose representatives have declared that until it is solved they cannot undertake any obligations with regard to the reduction of armaments. If, therefore, we want to advance, and not just to go round and round, we shall have to consider with all seriousness the French proposals, and make up our minds whether there is any possibility of reaching an international agreement based upon these and other proposals which may be made on security by other delegations, proceeding subsequently to questions of disarmament, or whether such an agreement will prove impossible, in which case we shall have to admit that, owing to the attitude of some States, the whole problem of disarmament and security is insoluble and that it is not through international conferences that humanity will rid itself of the heavy burden of armaments and the scourge of war. In either case, some clarity will have been shed on the fate of the Conference.

In turning to the essence of the French memorandum, I feel bound to state that only its first chapter could affect all the States here represented. The other chapters seem to be intended only for members either of existing international organisations or of future voluntary organisations. Chapter II, for instance, has in view Members of the League of Nations only ; Chapter III—and, to a certain extent, Chapter V—European States only, and moreover those connected in a formal way with the League of Nations ; Chapter IV, signatories to the Washington Naval Agreement, and Mediterranean States, and these if they are ready to consider the decisions of the League of Nations binding for themselves. It is to be presumed that the authors of these chapters did not have in view the participation in the organisations proposed by them of the Soviet Union, which is situated on the continent of Asia as well as that of Europe, is not a Member of the League of Nations, and is not a signatory of the Washington Agreement.

It seems to me indubitable that, inasmuch as special and very serious obligations are to be imposed upon the participants of the proposed organisations, they are entitled to demand that these obligations should be extended at least to their nearest neighbours. Consequently, since the Soviet Union has not only European States upon its borders, but also Asiatic States, such as Japan, China and others, which are excluded in advance from the organisations proposed and thus exempted from the new obligations, it can hardly be expected that the Soviet Union itself should undertake these obligations. Further, the fulfilment of these obligations and the manner of their fulfilment are left entirely to the decisions of the Council of the League of Nations, which is further proof that this part of the French proposals is not meant to apply to the Soviet Union.

In the circumstances, the Soviet delegation sees no necessity to make at the present moment a detailed analysis of the proposals contained in Chapters II to V of the French memorandum ; the more so since it has already expressed its opinion on certain of these proposals, such as, for example, the internationalisation of armed forces, when put before the Disarmament Conference by M. Tardieu, then head of the French delegation. It nevertheless reserves to itself the right to revert to them, if and when the States for which they are intended show readiness to accept them.

As I have already pointed out, only the proposals contained in the first chapter of the French memorandum, dealing with the interpretation and considerable extension of the obligations undertaken by the signatories to the Briand-Kellogg Pact, may be considered as addressed to all the States here represented, including the Soviet Union. I am happy to be able to state that the Soviet delegation raises no objections to these proposals and would be ready to sign a convention embodying them. I venture, however, to make a few observations, in my opinion, of the utmost relevance.

I assume that, if we aim at the strengthening and extension of obligations under the Pact, we are bound at the same time to see to it that the obligations already undertaken remain in full force for all its signatories, and are not limited or minimised by those reservations made on their own account by certain States—reservations practically nullifying the whole Pact. These reservations, it is true, have no legal force, inasmuch as the other signatories to the Pact have not given their assent to them ; but, for all that, cases have been known of aggression being justified by reference to them. The Soviet delegation, therefore, will propose in due time that the States which have made these reservations should formally repudiate them, or that they should be deprived of all legal and moral force by an international agreement.

Further, the French proposals provide for certain international sanctions with regard to a State infringing the Pact—that is to say, a State found to be the aggressor in any armed conflict. This inevitably brings us to the questions : How is the aggressor to be determined, and who is to determine the aggressor ? Apparently we must either think about setting up a special international organ for this purpose, or invest a conference of all signatories to the Pact with the necessary judicial powers. In either case, the question of the impartiality of a decision on a matter of such vital importance for any State as its stigmatisation as an aggressor, and the application to it of international sanctions, is bound to arise. This question is of great interest to all States, but is of special interest to the State which I represent, and on this point more than any other, perfect frankness and mutual understanding are indispensable.

We represent the only country in the whole world which has altered its political system, created a perfectly new political system of Soviets and destroyed capitalism, and which is building up a new social order, while all the other States have preserved the capitalist regime. You are aware that the phenomenon of a Soviet socialist State was so distasteful to the whole capitalist world that, at the time, attempts were even made by way of intervention to restore capitalism in our country, or at least by way of dismemberment to reduce the dimensions of the new State.

These attempts were fruitless, and have not been renewed, but it cannot be said that the idea of fresh attempts has been completely abandoned. On the contrary, we know that it is still cherished in some countries by extremely influential politicians, leaders of great parties, former, future, and even present members of Governments, making a crusade against the Soviet Union almost the centre of their foreign policy, and for this purpose keeping up close organisational and financial connections with *émigrés*, adherents of the old Russian regime. It must be admitted, then, that the capitalist world as a whole has not yet completely reconciled itself to the existence of a country building up socialism, and this irreconcilability continues to give rise to hostility to such a country, hostility continually finding the most varied means of expression.

I will not weary you by enumerating all the many and various anti-Soviet campaigns which spring up from one year to another. I will merely remark that, taking into account all the States in both hemispheres, the majority have not as yet established normal relations with the Soviet Union—in other words, are applying a boycott against it, one of those very sanctions proposed to be applied in the future only against an aggressor.

In such circumstances it is permissible to enquire whether the Soviet Union may expect a fair attitude towards it and impartial decisions from any international organ, when such an organ consists exclusively of representatives of a capitalist world which is hostile to it, and may have a majority of representatives of the Governments of countries boycotting it. It seems to me there can be no two answers to this question, and, should anyone here doubt this, I would recommend him to imagine, for the sake of hypothesis, that his own State is the only capitalist country in the midst of countries which have established the Soviet system and are building up socialism, and I would ask him to tell us if he thinks his country would entrust the solution of questions vital to itself to an international organ consisting exclusively of representatives of the Governments of Soviet countries.

A moment's thought will show why the Soviet Union, as long as the present attitude to it lasts, cannot agree to acknowledge as binding upon itself the decisions of such international organisations as the Assembly or the Council of the League of Nations, existing international tribunals and arbitration courts, although by no means rejecting on principle the idea of international co-operation or arbitration. This question becomes acute for us every time there is talk of setting up international organs with judicial, controlling and similar functions. It is natural enough, in such circumstances, that we should demand a composition of these organs which should ensure for us the same measure of impartiality and fairness as is enjoyed by other States, and such a demand will have to be made by the Soviet delegation when, in consequence of the French proposals, the question of the establishment of such organs comes up for discussion. We do not think, however, that the fulfilment of this legitimate demand need meet with serious practical difficulties.

Whatever its composition, however, any international organ called upon to determine the aggressor would be bound to experience extraordinary difficulties in existing circumstances, if only from the simple fact that there is no universally acknowledged definition of aggression, and that, in practice as well as in theory, multitudinous discordance prevails on this point. This is demonstrated, among other things, by the reservations made when signing the Briand-

Kellogg Pact to which I have referred. What is the meaning of these reservations ? Do they not amount to the insistence of certain States on freedom of action, pact or no pact, in certain cases or in certain parts of the globe ? What these cases or localities are is left for each State to decide. What, it may be asked, are the guarantees that those very circumstances which have hitherto been made pretexts for war will not be regarded as such cases ? Experience has shown us that numerous and various circumstances have been used as justification for aggression, such as, the desire to exploit the natural riches of a given territory, the infringement of some international agreement, the measures taken by some State encroaching upon the material interest of another, the defence of nationals voluntarily residing at their own risk in a given country, the infringement of established privileges by some State, the outbreak of revolution or disorders, and so on. Such justifications for attack have been made, not in the Middle Ages, not in past centuries, but in quite recent times. And this practice has been enriched with new theories. There seems to be a tendency nowadays to justify attack by the actual or alleged chaotic condition of another State, by the extent of capital investments or by special interests in another State, by the allegation of absence of certain State attributes in another country, by strategical considerations, or by the desire to extend one country's line of self-defence well beyond its own frontiers. A theory has also lately been advanced justifying war as one method of ensuring peace. If such theories are widely spread and are taken into account by international arbiters, that is to say, by members of international tribunals, it may confidently be prophesied that an aggressor will never be found in any armed conflict, and that only mutually aggressive or mutually defensive parties will be established, or, worse still, the defensive party will be considered the aggressor, and *vice versa*.

You are aware that even tribunals acting on the basis of exact laws are not always able to pass just decisions. This is shown by the fact that different judicial authorities, acting on the basis of identical laws, in identical cases pass judgments which are not identical. How much less can it be expected that tribunals will pass fair decisions when they are not bound to obey any laws or guiding lines, and would not this be precisely the situation of an international organ obliged now to apply the Briand-Kellogg Pact ? And here it is a matter, not of the interests of individual citizens, but of those of States and of peoples.

It seems to us obvious that, if we wish to see in action the Briand-Kellogg Pact, together with the extension proposed by the French delegation, and to secure the minimum of authority, impartiality and confidence to the international organ to be called into life by these extensions, we shall have to give it instructions for its guidance, and that means, first of all, defining war and aggression and the distinction between aggression and defence, and once for all condemning those fallacious justifications of aggression with which the past has familiarised us. The Soviet delegation has endeavoured to embody the ideas I have just expounded in a draft declaration which it ventures to offer for your consideration.

DEFINITION OF " AGGRESSOR " : DRAFT DECLARATION. [1]

The General Commission

Considering that, in the interests of general security and in order to facilitate the attainment of an agreement for the maximum reduction of armaments, it is necessary, with the utmost precision, to define aggression, in order to remove any possibility of its justification ;

Recognising the principle of equal right of all States to independence, security and self-defence ;

Animated by the desire of ensuring to each nation, in the interests of general peace, the right of free development according to its own choice and at the rate that suits it best, and of safeguarding the security, independence and complete territorial inviolability of each State and its right to self-defence against attack or invasion from outside, but only within its own frontiers ; and

Anxious to provide the necessary guidance to the international organs which may be called upon to define the aggressor :

Declares :

1. The aggressor in an international conflict shall be considered that State which is the first to take any of the following actions :

(a) Declaration of war against another State ;

(b) The invasion by its armed forces of the territory of another State without declaration of war ;

---

[1] Document Conf.D/C.G.38.

(c) Bombarding the territory of another State by its land, naval or air forces or knowingly attacking the naval or air forces of another State ;

(d) The landing in, or introduction within the frontiers of, another State of land, naval or air forces without the permission of the Government of such a State, or the infringement of the conditions of such permission, particularly as regards the duration of sojourn or extension of area ;

(e) The establishment of a naval blockade of the coast or ports of another State.

2. No considerations whatsoever of a political, strategical or economic nature, including the desire to exploit natural riches or to obtain any sort of advantages or privileges on the territory of another State, no references to considerable capital investments or other special interests in a given State, or to the alleged absence of certain attributes of State organisation in the case of a given country, shall be accepted as justification of aggression as defined in Clause 1.

In particular, justification for attack cannot be based upon :

A. *The internal situation in a given State,* as, for instance :

(a) Political, economic or cultural backwardness of a given country ;

(b) Alleged mal-administration ;

(c) Possible danger to life or property of foreign residents ;

(d) Revolutionary or counter-revolutionary movement, civil war, disorders or strikes ;

(e) The establishment or maintenance in any State of any political, economic or social order.

B. *Any acts, laws, or regulations of a given State,* as, for instance :

(a) The infringement of international agreements ;

(b) The infringement of the commercial, concessional or other economic rights or interests of a given State or its citizens ;

(c) The rupture of diplomatic or economic relations ;

(d) Economic or financial boycott ;

(e) Repudiation of debts ;

(f) Non-admission or limitation of immigration, or restriction of rights or privileges of foreign residents ;

(g) The infringement of the privileges of official representatives of other States ;

(h) The refusal to allow armed forces transit to the territory of a third State ;

(i) Religious or anti-religious measures ;

(k) Frontier incidents.

3. In the case of the mobilisation or concentration of armed forces to a considerable extent in the vicinity of its frontiers, the State which such activities threaten may have recourse to diplomatic or other means for the peaceful solution of international controversies. It may at the same time take steps of a military nature, analogous to those described above, without, however, crossing the frontier.

* * *

The General Commission decides to embody the above principles in the Convention on security and disarmament, or in a special agreement to form an integral part of the said Convention.

* * *

In drawing up this document, I was by no means unaware of those discussions which have taken place in the League of Nations, and the difficulties with which attempts to define aggressive acts have met. I am, therefore, able to foresee all the objections and observations which might be made with regard to our document by lawyers or other experts, who will once again point out the impossibility of an absolute definition of aggression, the possibility of cases unforeseen by us, and—most important of all—the difficulty of establishing the original aggressor in the case of concentration of armed forces on either side of a frontier. I can reply in advance to these, that we make no pretensions to absolute definitions, since such are hardly possible or conceivable, and, moreover, in the great majority of cases known to us in history, if not in all cases of armed conflicts, the establishment of such factors as which side was the first to declare war or to commit a real act of aggression has presented no real difficulties, controversy only arising as to the legitimacy of the causes and justification for such aggression. I think the same thing may be said with regard to cases which have come before the League of Nations during the last few years. I admit, however, that the Soviet delegation itself attributes infinitely greater importance to the second clause in its declaration, in which will be found denunciation of instances of justification of aggression, both already known to us in history and capable of arising in the future, than to the other clauses.

I do not feel sure that, in the draft declaration I have just read to you, all conceivable justifications of war have been exhausted, and indeed this was not our purpose. In saying that no considerations whatsoever could justify attack on foreign territory, we cover also circumstances not specially mentioned in the declaration. We are ready to admit the imperfections of the document we are placing before you; we are ready to listen to your objections, to advance and accept amendments, additions and the like. It is not, however, details that matter, but the acceptance of the basic principles underlying this document. These principles consist in the acknowledgment of the inviolability of established and recognised frontiers for any State, great or small; the denial of any State's right to interfere in the affairs, development, legislation or administration of another. We ought to proclaim a " Charter of the Freedom of Nations " at this Conference. Only then will international agreements for the renunciation of war and for non-aggression acquire real significance, and inspire all States with the feeling of some degree of security. I say " some degree ", because we still insist that full security for all can only be ensured by total or the utmost possible disarmament.

Until and unless this is fulfilled, however, we shall endeavour to bring about solutions for what is known as the problem of security—solutions that cannot be made the object of diplomatic juggling, but will profit the smaller and weaker, and not only the stronger, countries.

You will realise that our proposals are not meant to compete with or be substituted for the French proposals, but are their logical extension. This is why we regard their consideration as desirable during the discussion of the French proposals

The Soviet Government, in placing its new proposals before you, is moved exclusively by those same aspirations which caused it at the time to propose total disarmament, and which are causing it to give such prominence in its foreign policy to the system of bilateral non-aggression pacts—aspirations for the utmost possible guarantees of world peace. I do not think there are any left to doubt the peaceable dispositions of the country I represent. It is true there are still sceptics and cynics who endeavour to minimise its significance by pointing out that the Soviet State requires peace for its socialist construction. We do not deny this; but do such people imply that it is only the Soviet State which can build itself up and develop in peaceful conditions, and that other conditions, not peaceful, are required for the development of capitalist States ? If any State giving evidence of peaceable disposition should explain that it requires peace for its own development, we for our part would not hold this against it. We gave every State represented here the opportunity to display such disposition by accepting our proposals for disarmament, and non-aggression pacts ; we give them this opportunity once more by our present proposals.

The PRESIDENT observed that, in the declaration which the Soviet representative had made, the latter had stated that he considered it desirable that the proposals he had put forward should be discussed during the discussion of the French plan. The President had, accordingly, requested the Secretariat to circulate the declaration at once, so that, if delegates wished to refer to it during the discussion of the French proposals, they would be in a position to do so.

M. DE ZULUETA (Spain). — From the very outset of our examination of the French disarmament plan, we are unable to free ourselves from the international political atmosphere in which it is submitted to us.

This plan is dictated by the noble aim of organising peace and so making disarmament a practical proposition. It assembles, so to speak, in a logical combination, the developments that have occurred since the League's foundation. It is designed to continue and complete the Geneva Covenant and the Pact of Paris ; and I do not think that I am being unduly pessimistic when I say that these two instruments are at present passing through the most serious crisis they have known.

While the world is struggling in the throes of an economic depression, grave international conflicts are putting our faith in the efficacy of treaties to the severest test. In the Far East, notwithstanding the endeavours which the Council and Assembly have been making since September 1931, and are still making, might is still the deciding factor. In the West, two peoples, united to one another, and to Spain as well, by ties of kinship, are openly employing force in defiance of the obligations they assumed under the League Covenant. There are other conflicts, too, poisoning the international atmosphere. In the East as in the West, for various reasons which it is not for me to discuss, we see methods of ensuring peace wrecked by the age-long tendency to resort to violence.

Those are the facts, and any policy which did not set out from a direct appreciation of them would be condemned to failure through lack of realism.

The Spanish Republic, which I represent, has testified to its sense of idealism in international matters ; but I wish to say in the clearest possible terms that its idealism is in fact only a clear-sighted realism—that is to say that, while Spain desires always to look afar

DOCUMENT 10

EIGHTH MEETING

Held on Friday, March 10th, 1933, at 3.30 p.m.

─────────

President : The Right Honourable A. HENDERSON.

─────────

10. DEFINITION OF AGGRESSION : DRAFT DECLARATION PROPOSED BY THE DELEGATION OF THE UNION OF SOVIET SOCIALIST REPUBLICS : [1] GENERAL DISCUSSION.

The PRESIDENT reminded the Commission of some of the previous studies undertaken by the League of Nations with regard to this question. It had first been considered in a report of the Temporary Mixed Commission in 1923. The Geneva Protocol of 1924 contained a whole article — Article 10 — dealing with the definition of aggression. In the report accompanying the Protocol, the Rapporteur, M. Politis, had stated that it was sufficient to say that " any State is the aggressor which resorts in any shape or form to force in violation of the engagements contracted by it either under the Covenant . . . or under the Protocol ". There was, lastly, the General Convention to improve the Means of preventing War, Articles 2 and 4 of which had a bearing on the same matter.

M. DOVGALEVSKY (Union of Soviet Socialist Republics) said that the principles underlying the attitude of the Soviet Government towards the interdependence of disarmament and security had been expounded fairly explicitly. He need only remind the Commission, therefore, that these principles could be expressed in two propositions :

    1. The maximum security can only be achieved by complete disarmament.

    2. In the absence of complete disarmament, the degree of security is determined by the extent of the reduction of armaments.

─────────

[1] Document Conf.D./C.G./P.V.38 (see also Minutes of the General Commission, Volume I, page 237).

The Soviet Government's original proposal,[1] which, it would be remembered, was for general and complete disarmament, was unfortunately not adopted by the Conference. Guided by the pacific aspirations of the labouring masses, the Soviet delegation had pursued its aim, which was to reduce the danger of war as far as possible and to lighten the burden of armaments that weighed most heavily on those very sections of the population that most eagerly desired peace and had the greatest hatred of war. That was why, after the failure of its proposal for total disarmament, the Soviet delegation, in the hope this time of obtaining the Conference's unanimous approval, had put forward its plan for a substantial reduction of armaments, and had declared its readiness to support any proposal for a real and extensive reduction of armaments going as far as possible in the direction desired by the Soviet Government.

The Soviet delegation maintained that attitude of principle. It had, however, always felt its duty to be to neglect nothing that might contribute towards the success of the Conference's work. In obedience to that idea, it could not overlook the fact that, if the Conference felt that disarmament must be preceded by security and was dependent upon security, it was faced with the alternative of defining and increasing security, thus making possible some reduction in armaments, or of declaring itself powerless and admitting the failure of several years' work. Having this in mind, the Soviet delegation had carefully studied the French proposal on security and had looked, in that proposal, for what was of interest to the States as a whole. As a result of its examination, it had once more noted the indisputable truth that no system of security against aggression could be complete and efficacious in the absence of a clear idea as to what constituted aggression.

Desiring that attention should, as soon as possible, be devoted to real disarmament, the Soviet delegation had placed before the Conference a draft definition of an aggressor.

The aim of this definition was therefore to place security on a sound basis. The Soviet delegation thought this definition should take the form of a declaration, universal in scope, either to be embodied in the future Convention on security and disarmament or to be the subject of a special agreement forming an integral part of that Convention.

Once the definition of the aggressor was accepted by all, and was consequently binding on all, it would serve as a guide for each State individually or for any group of States. It would also contribute, if not towards the complete avoidance of partial agreements between different groups of States, at any rate towards reducing considerably the danger of their assuming the character of alliances directed against third parties.

The Soviet declaration consisted, apart from its preamble, of two parts. The first part contained a positive definition of the acts constituting an aggression. The second part contained a list of circumstances which might not be invoked in its justification by a State guilty of the acts defined in the first part. Both parts were imbued with the common idea that all resort to force as a means for settling disputes between States must be considered as illegal. Both were therefore on the same plane as the " renunciation of the resort to force " that had been accepted by the Political Commission at its fifth meeting on March 2nd, in as far as it related to European States, though the Conference had still to make it universal.

The Soviet delegation reserved its right to discuss at a suitable moment and in detail each of the paragraphs forming the articles of the draft. One general remark might, however, be made at once with regard to Article 1. In particular, this article included among acts of aggression, in addition to the formal declaration of war, the various forms of hostility undertaken without a previous declaration of war. The prohibition to open hostilities without declaring war dated back to 1907. The third Hague Convention, in fact, at that time made it an international offence, whereas war as such was still considered perfectly legitimate. At the present moment, the fact that a formal declaration of war was prohibited internationally as an instrument of national policy provided yet another reason for making no difference, from the point of view of the idea of aggression, between war declared officially and de facto hostilities.

With regard to Article 2, in which were set out the circumstances that could never be invoked as an excuse for an act of aggression, the Soviet delegate desired to say that this list — which was perhaps incomplete — should, in his delegation's opinion, cover the most frequent causes of disputes and differences between States ; its aim was that no dispute of that kind should ever serve as a cause, pretext or justification for an aggression. The list contained in Article 2 of the draft could therefore be supplemented, if necessary, in accordance with the suggestions which would, he hoped, be made during the discussion.

Perhaps the following question would be asked — M. Dovgalevsky thought he had already perceived it in the speeches of certain delegates during the general discussion in the Political Commission during the last two meetings — Was not the proposed definition

---

[1] Document Conf.D.82 (Documents of the Conference, Volume I, page 124).

of the aggressor too complete ? Was not its detailed character likely to give it undue rigidity which would subsequently hamper those who were called upon to establish the aggressor ?

To this observation M. Dovgalevsky would reply that a full definition, a definition dealing with every conceivable aspect of aggression, would indeed be somewhat rigid. But the Soviet delegation had not only sought to provide a rigid formula ; it had desired to make it as rigid as possible. The definition and establishment of an act of aggression must leave as little opening as possible for subjective feelings and judgments. Still more, a complete definition must, as far as possible, exclude any possibility of subjective interpretation, and the more automatic the establishment of the aggressor, the better for the work of peace.

That was why the Soviet delegation, which would of course be willing to accept any amendment improving its definition, hoped that amendments would not be aimed at weakening the text in such a way as to decrease its value as an objective and sure basis for determining who was the aggressor.

M. Lo (China) observed that a discussion on the definition of the aggressor must necessarily precede any useful consideration of the closely related questions as to how the provisions of the articles concerning sanctions in the Covenant, the provisions in the Pact of Paris, and the contemplated pact on the non-recourse to force could be made effective. There seemed to be a certain amount of unreality in the Political Commission's efforts, an unreality which might have been born of a highly strung and recently disillusioned world consciousness, but which could not fail to have a disturbing effect on the present deliberations. The man in the street would inevitably ask what was the use of seeking a definition of the aggressor when actual aggression, having already been both generally and juridically ascertained, was suffered to go on at the very moment when the abstract question was being vehemently debated.

However that might be, the very fact that new efforts were being made to seek a definition of the aggressor constituted definite recognition of the necessity for reaching a reasonable agreement upon this all-important question. The existing state of things in the international situation, particularly in the Far East, emphasised the urgency of those endeavours. That, he imagined, was the spirit inspiring the Soviet delegation's very frank and comprehensive proposal, which did not, as M. Litvinoff had said, pretend to absolute definitions, since such were hardly possible or conceivable. The proposal also made a wise distinction between the establishment of such factors as which side was the first to declare war or to commit a real act of aggression — questions that were relatively easy to determine — and the legitimacy of the causes and justifications for such aggression, which might be highly controversial and which did not lend themselves to ascertainment by the existing international procedure. This distinction ought to bring home the fact that, in striving for international security, the Conference could not, on the pretext of the existing limitations, delay too long in the solution of pressing problems, but would have to be satisfied if a machinery were evolved which could serve more or less as a fire extinguisher, leaving the final assessment of responsibilities to the judges and, perhaps, the historians.

As an abstract definition couched in a single sentence was deemed impossible, the Soviet proposal had resorted to the enumeration of the characteristics of aggression. It must be admitted that, while the enumeration of concrete examples lent considerable reality to a hypothetical concept, there were always disadvantages to be found in an attempt to define by example. A legal mind would object on the ground that since, according to the old maxim, the mention of one thing excluded another, in any future and unpredicted case which did not come, apparently or *prima facie*, within one of the various categories, it could be plausibly argued that they did not apply to such a case. A State unwilling to assume onerous responsibilities for action against the aggressor would not fail to cite the words, in opposition to the attempt to define the aggressor, that such an attempt would " be a trap for the innocent and a sign-post for the guilty ".

In truth, however, definition by example, if not understood to be exhaustive, was better than a general and abstract statement of a set of circumstances. Opinions might differ as to the inclusion and exclusion of certain items in the list enumerated in the Soviet proposal. Most of the examples given were, nevertheless, satisfactory to the Chinese delegation. A few alleged fissures in the Covenant, the Pact of Paris, and general international law had been repaired. The character of war, in its actual as well as in its technical sense, had been fixed. A declaration of war was considered, emphatically, as not necessary to the creation of a juridical situation in a case where a State employing military measures denied the intention of waging war. Pacific blockade was denounced as aggression in the way it ought to be denounced. Political causes of justifications of aggression were properly excluded from the domain of law, in which only overt acts should form the subject of its regulation.

There would be very little disagreement as to the necessity of international efforts in the direction of the various problems raised in the Soviet list. If only a reasoned adjustment of these problems could have been achieved during the fifteen years since the great war, the extremely tense situation in the Far East might possibly have been averted and China might have been spared a tragic loss of blood and treasure. Failure resolutely to face these inevitable and challenging questions at the eleventh hour would no doubt presage future complications. The delegations would, indeed, be deemed to have failed in their duty.

In the discussion of the Soviet proposal, the fact must not be overlooked that an all-pervading and readily comprehensible principle had inspired perennial efforts for the collective control of conflicts. Such a principle was that of pacific settlement. Political exigency or opportunism had been its inveterate enemy, and lawyers had invented excuses for justifying deviations from such a principle and had looked in international instruments for loopholes which did not exist. There was, indeed, much food for thought in M. Rutgers' reference to the maxim, *summun jus, summa injuria*.

While there must, of course, be no relaxation of the endeavour to make the peace machinery perfect in its working, the imperfect state of the existing machinery must not be seized upon as an excuse for not making every effort to see to the execution of the peace-preserving instruments already in force. Much less should it be assumed that, because the existing machinery had to be perfected, it would be right to sit and wait for the stage of perfection and leave pending problems uncared for.

In order, therefore, to rally world public opinion, it could not be too strongly emphasised that any scheme to define the aggressor must take into account the alleged loopholes in international instruments, particularly those which had been demonstrated in the actualities of international life. Otherwise, the results achieved by the present discussions would be far removed from realities, and, as such, would be hardly able to withstand the impact of contemporary events. As peace-preserving devices, they would be found definitely wanting.

The same conclusion was inevitable if one definition of the aggressor were adopted for one part of the world and another for the rest. A yardstick of such importance must be of universal application.

The Soviet proposal, as an exposition of contemporary, as distinguished from merely theoretical, difficulties in the definition of the aggressor, was therefore deserving of the most careful and comprehensive discussion of which the Commission was capable. The Chinese delegation gave it its wholehearted support and hoped for its adoption.

M. LANGE (Norway) said he had been glad that the French delegate had proposed, at the end of the previous meeting, that the special Committee set up to study the plan of mutual assistance in Europe should defer its work. He believed that it would be extremely difficult to discuss that question without first being clear as to certain principles and possibilities which arose in the universal sphere, with a view to reaching that stage in the discussion at which all would be ready to express their views as to the proposals for the reduction of armaments. If the Commission had for some time confined itself to the European sphere, that was because one delegation — the United States delegation — had said that it would wait to see what attitude the European States would take with regard to the substantial reduction of armaments. That, therefore, was the Commission's object, and, in that respect, M. Lange entirely agreed with the Soviet delegate.

The Norwegian delegation had already expressed, during the general discussion on the French plan, its great sympathy towards the Soviet delegation's proposal for the definition of the aggressor. That proposal, which was opportune and extremely valuable, and contained elements deserving of the closest attention, would possibly have to be supplemented.

The President had observed, at the beginning of the meeting, that this was no new question in the international world. In particular, it had been studied during the discussion of the 1924 Protocol, which, if M. Lange was not mistaken, laid down, for the first time in an international document, the idea of presumptive evidence of aggression. That idea was of the greatest importance and had been taken up again in recent years during the discussion and preparation of the Convention to improve the Means of preventing War. In certain respects, therefore, the Soviet proposal would need supplementing.

M. Lange wondered whether, as M. Dovgalevsky had already said, the list appearing under No. 2 might not be too rigid and whether the formulas employed might not lead to some misunderstanding. He was no jurist, but, looking at the matter from the point of view of the man in the street, he wondered whether the list contained in Section B might not create the impression that the acts thus enumerated would receive some kind of recognition, if not as being legitimate, at any rate as being admissible. Such a result would certainly be undesirable. In this matter, however, the Commission must rely upon the wisdom of its jurists, and there was good reason to congratulate the Soviet delegation on the proposal and to recommend its close study.

Lastly, M. Lange was particularly glad to see in a document issued by the Soviet delegation a specific recognition of the need for international organs. That was a new development which was worth noting.

Count RACZYŃSKI (Poland) welcomed on behalf of the Polish delegation the Soviet initiative and viewed its proposal very sympathetically. On the one hand, that proposal was connected with the principles embodied in Article 10 of the League Covenant, and, on the other hand, took as a starting-point the principles embodied in Article 1 of the Pact of Non-Aggression which Poland had signed with the Soviet Government in July last, a pact that had been ratified and was in force.

The Polish delegate further desired to point out that this proposal covered only one part, undoubtedly an important part, of the system of security. It was an essential factor, but could only achieve its full significance when that system was established in its entirety and all the necessary consequences could be drawn from it.

The Polish delegation, moreover, thought it necessary to act prudently, and the vote taken at the Commission's previous meeting showed that prudence was, indeed, indispensable.

In conclusion, the Polish delegation considered that the Soviet proposal must be examined and given effect. No complete system of security could be established unless it included the very important ideas embodied in that proposal. Those ideas could, of course, be discussed and improved upon.

M. MASSIGLI (France) pointed out that the French delegation had already had an opportunity of expressing its sympathy with the Soviet proposal. He might therefore have refrained from speaking in the general discussion had he not thought it advisable to explain briefly in what spirit and for what reason his delegation was able to welcome the proposal. It believed that a definition of the aggressor was not, perhaps, in itself very important, and would form no more than an article in an encyclopædia. But it had nevertheless been very glad to read, in the Soviet proposal, a paragraph to which the Norwegian delegate had just referred and which read as follows:

" Anxious to provide the necessary guidance to the international organs which may be called upon to define the aggressor ".

The French delegation saw in this paragraph a starting-point, and it was that starting-point that it welcomed. It believed — and this was in accordance with the spirit of the French plan — that the Commission must in the first place set out to define the aggressor, in view of the consequences following upon such a definition. It was the international organs which would be responsible for drawing those consequences. The French delegation hoped the Soviet delegation would be able to follow it in that direction also.

The President had announced some days previously that a drafting committee would consider the details of the proposal. It was not necessary, therefore, for M. Massigli to dwell on any particular point in it. In his view, a declaration would not suffice, and some means must be found of embodying the principles underlying such a declaration in an article of the Convention.

Certain points in the positive definition of aggression might be open to discussion, and the Commission would not be surprised, he thought, to hear that he himself preferred the definition given in Chapter III, Section A, paragraph 3, of the French plan. [1]

Again, a negative list, such as that given in part 2 of the Soviet proposal might be thought to present more drawbacks than advantages, for no list was ever complete, and this might give rise to misunderstandings.

In conclusion, it might perhaps be found that part 3 of the Soviet proposal, which concerned the concentration of armed forces in the vicinity of a frontier, was not of such a nature as to cause the Commission to lose sight of a provision, to his mind preferable, to be found in the Convention to improve the Means of preventing War.

But these were only details, on which opinions might differ. They must be discussed and explained, and, in the circumstances, M. Massigli would confine himself to repeating that the French delegation approved the principle of the Soviet declaration and hoped that it would be studied as soon as possible in a small committee.

Mr. LESTER (Irish Free State) thought that a stage had been reached at which the old terminology regarding certain aspects of international affairs required to be revised. The absence of a declaration of war was no longer sufficient to make it possible to prevent the effects known as war, and for that reason he welcomed the Soviet delegation's proposal, which, he believed, would be found valuable in that it was necessary to have additional guidance on this fundamental question. He welcomed the proposal, particularly as it came from a State non-member of the League.

As to the text of the Soviet proposal, omissions from and additions to it — perhaps even very fundamental changes in regard to form — would probably be necessary before it could obtain any substantial agreement. He was not unaware of the legal difficulties and arguments which could be used against certain parts of the proposal, nor of the difficulties arising from what had been called the realities of each situation when a conflict between two States had occurred. Therefore, after a general discussion in the Political Commission, the best procedure might be to appoint a special committee to discuss the proposal or, better still, to have it discussed by a committee dealing with other related questions.

---

[1] Document Conf.D.146.

M. NADOLNY (Germany) assumed that the study of the question of the determination of the aggressor would, with other questions, be referred to a committee which would be not only a drafting committee but a committee of enquiry and drafting. He would therefore only make a few brief remarks.

As the President had already pointed out, the question of the determination of the aggressor was not a new problem. It had already been investigated and studied by the League of Nations. He would mention in this connection the work of the Special Committee of the Temporary Mixed Commission in 1923, M. de Brouckère's report of 1926 and the memoranda drawn up in 1928 by M. Politis and M. Rutgers for the Arbitration and Security Committee.

Since she had entered the League of Nations, Germany had taken part in the earlier work done with a view to setting the question of the aggressor, and the German delegation was to-day equally prepared to collaborate in studying the problem on the basis of the Soviet proposals and the French plan. Its motive in doing so would be the wish to contribute to the consolidation of world peace.

The great advantage of the Soviet proposal was that it laid down definite, concrete criteria for determining the aggressor. It was, he thought, very important to define, by means of as clear and objective criteria as possible, the rules which should govern the determination of the aggressor. That was an excellent suggestion which should undoubtedly be thoroughly studied. In doing so, it should not be forgotten that an agreement on the factors by which the aggressor could be determined was not only important from the standpoint of the exact measures to be taken against the aggressor, either under the Covenant of the League of Nations or in virtue of an understanding between the States signatory to the Paris Pact. There was still another aspect which the German delegation thought was of the utmost importance — namely, the preventive character of such international definition of the criteria for determining the aggressor.

He would point out that there was already one important precedent which should not be overlooked — namely, the General Convention to improve the Means of preventing War. Article 5 of that Convention provided that failure to comply with the Council's injunctions regarding the withdrawal of troops which had penetrated into the territory of another State or regarding the formation of a neutral zone would be considered as *prima facie* evidence that the party guilty thereof had resorted to war if war broke out as a result of its attitude. During the negotiations in connection with this Convention its preventive scope was particularly emphasised in several quarters. This aspect, therefore, should be constantly borne in mind by the delegations in examining the Soviet proposal.

A further advantage of the Soviet proposal, he thought, was that it had a universal basis. It would, in his view, be a serious mistake to think of laying down principles for determining the aggressor confined to a small group of countries, as that would lead to collisions and disputes with countries outside that group. International rules of such wide political scope should always have a universal basis. Naturally, there was nothing to prevent — and the Soviet delegation would certainly agree with him on that point — the rules thus laid down being used as a basis also for action taken under the League Covenant.

M. Nadolny added that the universal character of the Soviet proposal should also be reflected in the membership of the committee which would be asked to study it. Clearly, it would not be sufficient to appoint representatives of European countries only ; the committee should be composed of members representing every part of the world.

The German delegate did not intend to discuss the proposal in detail at the present time. He would only make one brief observation, in conclusion, on a point on which M. Dovgalevsky, moreover, had already spoken. He was referring to the doubts expressed by the Netherlands representative during the general discussion of the French plan about the advisability of laying down beforehand too rigid rules for determining the aggressor. M. Nadolny wondered whether rules of an automatic character would really be appropriate here. M. Dovgalevsky had, he agreed, been right in asking for as full a list as possible to be drawn up of the criteria of aggression, but M. Nadolny felt that the cases which might arise would be too numerous to be covered by an absolutely exhaustive definition. He had in mind mainly the fact that a dispute, in all its different phases, was frequently so complicated that rigid criteria for determining the aggressor would be insufficient : all the factors in the dispute should be considered and weighed as a whole. It would, he thought, be necessary in drawing up certain rules for the determination of the aggressor — and the Soviet proposal seemed to him to furnish a very valuable basis in this connection — to reach an agreement which would be sufficiently elastic to enable all the possibilities to be taken into account and all the methods of conciliation to be exhausted.

M. SCHMIDT (Estonia) agreed with many of the other delegations that the Soviet proposal was a very valuable contribution to the attempt to find a definition for the aggressor. The problem was one of very great practical importance, for it was highly desirable to establish as clear and definite a wording as was practically possible.

The Soviet proposal seemed to M. Schmidt to contain in this respect elements which were undoubtedly really valuable and he was therefore fully prepared to give it all the attention it deserved. As had already been said, the Soviet draft needed some rearrangement, but the questions involved would not, he hoped, be very difficult to solve. The Estonian delegate trusted, therefore, that the Commission's efforts in this connection would lead to a positive result which would represent a substantial advance in the sphere of present-day international law.

Mr. EDEN (United Kingdom) had listened with very great interest to the discussion on the Soviet delegation's very important proposals. The objective which it was sought to realise was not, of course, a new one. There had been many and important attempts to realise it in the past in the sphere of varied international activities, more especially among the Members of the League of Nations themselves.

The preamble to the Soviet proposal stated, "It is necessary, with the utmost precision, to define aggression, in order to remove any possibility of its justification". That was the problem, and with this object in view the Soviet definition laid down a series of rigid and automatic tests according to which the aggressor in any particular case was to be identified.

Mr. Eden considered that to this attempt the Commission was bound to bring some of the experience of the past, to which the German delegate had rightly alluded. The possibility of defining the aggressor had been fully discussed in the past, and the conclusion had always been that it was impossible to lay down any such rigid criteria of universal application, since it was impossible to foretell how they would work in particular sets of circumstances, and there was serious risk that their application might result, as in the quotation to which the Chinese delegate had referred, in the aggressee being pronounced to be the aggressor.

Without attempting in any way to go into the history of the matter in detail at the present stage, he might refer to the study of the question, which M. Nadolny had mentioned, in the report of the Third Committee of the fourth Assembly in 1923, and the documents printed with that report. One quotation from the conclusion reached by the Special Committee of the Temporary Mixed Commission which had considered the definition of a case of aggression had been that "under the conditions of modern warfare it would seem impossible to decide, even in theory, what constitutes an act of aggression". The quotation goes on : "It is clear, therefore, that no simple definition of aggression can be drawn up and that no simple test of when an act of aggression has actually taken place can be devised".

Reference had also been made to the very important report of M. Rutgers [1] on Article 10 of the Covenant, in which he stated :

"The question of acts which are evidence of aggression has already been the subject of the most exhaustive and careful study by the League of Nations and by many of its Members. These studies have led to different conclusions, and we are constrained to believe that any attempt to lay down rigid or absolute criteria in advance for determining the aggressor would be unlikely in existing circumstances to lead to any practical result."

There was one other aspect of this question of which those countries which were Members of the League must not be neglectful. It was absolutely essential for such States that any definition which might be considered should not be inconsistent with the situation resulting for Members of the League from the Covenant, and, for certain of the States Members of the League, from treaties to which they were already parties. At a first examination it seemed, at least, very uncertain whether the proposals under discussion did, in fact, comply with that condition.

Mr. Eden drew the Political Commission's attention to the foregoing considerations, not, of course, in any hostile sense, but because he thought that the Commission could start its work more clearly if it discussed the matter in the light of the very considerable efforts made in the past. That being so, he must say quite frankly that, in view of the abandonment of previous attempts to lay down very rigid and absolute criteria such as those set forth in the Soviet proposal, he hardly felt sanguine of the success of any endeavour to retain that proposal, at least in the form suggested in the present instance.

M. WESTMAN (Sweden) noted that the Soviet proposal, as M. Dovgalevsky had pointed out on several occasions, attempted to define the aggressor on the universal plane. That was a high and meritorious aspiration.

In the course of the studies undertaken at Geneva for many years, the advantages and risks of fixing in advance the criteria to be applied in defining as an aggressor a State that had broken its international obligations had been weighed. These discussions were recalled by the present debate.

---

[1] See *Official Journal*, May 1928, page 671.

The Swedish delegation would be very glad if, after this discussion, it were found possible to reach unanimous agreement on such a definition, which would be both clear and precise in theory, and thorough and efficacious in practice. As the Committee which was about to be appointed would probably have a fairly heavy task in connection with the problem of security submitted to it by the Political Commission, M. Westman would take advantage of the general discussion to add a few remarks.

One thing was certain — namely, that one of the bases on which subsequent measures for increasing security would be founded must be the improvement of the existing methods of defining the aggressor, which would, in fact, amount to making more and more automatic the system of sanctions. That idea was undoubtedly correct in principle.

If the rules at present in force were examined, it would be noted that they took, as a starting-point, the principle, which was difficult to justify, that each State must determine separately whether, in the event of a conflict, one of the parties was at fault; that was to say, each State must itself settle the problem of the aggressor.

At the moment, however, when the Commission was endeavouring to make the sanctions more automatic and efficacious, it was important to ensure that, as far as possible, these rules would be practicable and would bring about the fundamental condition of any system of sanctions, which was not to provoke but to prevent war. In this connection, it was desirable, in M. Westman's opinion, to note that nothing would be gained by adopting a stipulation under which, for example, the Council was required to specify the aggressor by a majority decision, the various States being bound, in consequence of such a decision, to take part in economic and military sanctions. It was very doubtful whether the adoption of such a stipulation would really strengthen security, for the reason that it would be rash to expect, having regard to the grim realities of international life, that such a rule would be faithfully and unflinchingly observed. The decision which a Government would have to take with regard to the application of sanctions was, and always would be, a serious matter, and must be strongly supported by public opinion. From this point of view, it was essential that the aggressor State should be compelled to disclose its intentions to the whole world. It was important that the Council's decision should have the character of a confirmation of acts already recognised and observed by the whole world. Proceeding from that idea, the Swedish delegation was prepared, so far as it was concerned, to confer on the Council more extensive powers with regard to all decisions to be taken with a view to disclosing the aggressor State and in order to place world public opinion in a position to make its influence felt.

The Spanish delegate had pointed out some days previously that there was an international Convention to improve the Means of preventing War. Several speakers — M. Lange, M. Massigli and M. Nadolny — had just referred to that very Convention, which was, indeed, based on the principles M. Westman had just mentioned.

During the preparatory work for the Convention, the Swedish delegate had recommended certain stipulations which, on several points, went further than those actually embodied in the Convention. The time had now come, in his view — in order, from this standpoint at least, to strengthen security — to extend the Council's powers when it was required to take the measures provided for in the Convention to improve the Means of preventing War. Thus the Commission might consider the adoption of a rule providing for decisions by a competent majority in the case of measures of that kind.

In the event of a threat of war, the Council should have the power, for example, to make investigations and to take measures of supervision of all kinds, to decide upon the establishment of neutral zones, to order the cessation of military preparations subject to the necessary supervision. Further, the Council should be invested with power to prohibit, by a majority vote, the exportation of arms and other war material to one or both States parties to the dispute. Also, after the beginning of hostilities, the Council should be empowered to order the above measures, to decide upon the evacuation of an occupied territory, and to prescribe an armistice. Should any State refuse to comply with the Council's decisions, the latter should be able to impose export prohibitions of a more special character, or to prescribe the declaration of a boycott of wider scope.

Whereas the Covenant of the League of Nations provided for the possibility of an immediate and general boycott, while at the same time conferring on each State the right to take a decision itself, the Commission should recommend a system whereby the Council would be entitled to take such decisions, while observing, however, that the measures recommended must be taken one after the other so as to act as psychological and economic methods of coercion.

M. YADA (Japan) said that his delegation had examined with great interest the Soviet draft declaration concerning the definition of aggression. It amounted to a list of deeds and acts which, in the Soviet delegation's opinion, might serve as criteria for the definition of the aggressor. The Japanese delegation would venture to ask whether it was really possible to designate an aggressor State in so automatic and mechanical a way as was proposed in the draft.

One speaker in the General Commission had said, among other things, in connection with the definition of aggression, that attention must also be paid to an aggressor guilty of an economic war, of a Customs war or of a financial war. Further, it had been said in the Political Commission itself that the decision, in the case of an armed conflict, as to whether there was aggression and who was the aggressor was always a complicated and delicate matter. To be able to pronounce on the aggressive or defensive attitude of the countries engaged in a dispute, account must necessarily be had to the whole group of problems forming the subject of the dispute. All that was entirely true. In recalling these points he had, of course, no intention of pointing out certain gaps or omissions in the Soviet draft. All that he wanted was that a fair and equitable formula should be found, one which would at the same time take into consideration the actual facts and have regard to all the aspects of human activity in the field of international relations, their complexity and their infinite variety.

M. Yada himself would frankly say that he felt quite incapable of juridical syntheses of that kind, especially as he realised that they involved very arduous and difficult work, for the solution of which the League had made the utmost endeavours since its origin down to the present day.

M. Künzl-Jizersky (Czechoslovakia), on behalf of the States of the *Petite Entente*, expressed their sympathy with the Soviet proposal concerning the definition of the aggressor. They regarded that definition as a valuable contribution to the working out of a real system of security. The three delegations considered that the question deserved most careful study. On points of detail they reserved their right to propose the necessary amendments, but, in principle, they would sincerely co-operate in the working out of an improved definition of the aggressor on the basis of M. Litvinoff's declaration.

Mr. Gibson (United States of America) observed that the Conference had raised a series of technical questions which, up to the present, it had been unable to solve, and which still barred the path to an agreement on the reduction of armaments. The discussion in the Political Commission, in its turn, had not failed to raise a question which had bothered all students of international relations ; for the definition of the aggressor had perhaps been more discussed than any other point in this whole field of thought. It seemed to him that the difficulty had always resided in the fact that any definition was by its nature limited. Thus there would always be ways of resorting to force which remained technically outside any definition that man in his finite wisdom could conceive, and conversely it was inconceivable that it should be possible to formulate an all-inclusive definition which would give assurance that it could be relied upon ultimately to meet any situation created by the infinitely complex interplay of human relationships.

Furthermore, he questioned the utility of a rigid definition, particularly one like that given under point 1 of the Soviet proposal, since conditions could readily be imagined in which even some of the acts listed would not in themselves necessarily constitute an act of aggression.

For practical reasons, it might perhaps be wiser to approach the problem from a somewhat different angle, and endeavour to examine the criteria which each Government would find helpful in any given case in reaching a decision regarding aggression. Such a method would perhaps be calculated to clear the thoughts of delegates on the subject, and it would avoid the danger of binding future action of which neither the cause nor the results could at present be foreseen.

Such were the queries which the United States delegation ventured to raise. The forthcoming discussion might, perhaps, clear them up, but at present the United States delegation questioned, in all sincerity, whether it was desirable and advisable to endeavour to put into words a problem which must in the final analysis be judged on the basis of more factors than could possibly be foreseen at the moment, and also on factors the relative evaluation of which would be different in each concrete case that would have to be decided.

M. di Soragna (Italy) associated himself with the previous speakers' expressions of gratitude to the Soviet delegation for the practical contribution it had made to the study of the problem of the definition of the aggressor. Whatever opinion might be held as to the nature of that problem, it was none the less one of the most important points in the international law of the present day and of the future. The Italian delegation would be happy to take part in the work of the technical and legal committee which would study the problem, and would contribute its entire store of knowledge of the relevant texts and facts with the utmost goodwill. From the experience gained during the discussions on this matter in the past few years, it did not seem to M. di Soragna that it would be possible to classify it with those questions of which it was possible to say, at the present stage, with some degree of exactitude that they would receive a definite solution covering both their general character and limits. The very interesting observations of Mr. Eden and Mr. Gibson seemed to warrant doubts on the subject. It was, however, in any case certain that any progress which was real and not merely apparent could only be eminently desirable. It would represent a notable contribution to the common stock of international law.

In M. di Soragna's view, the progress of the work and its success would be the better assured the wider and more universal the basis upon which the delegations co-operated in the Commission, and the less the work itself remained dependent on any idea of subordination to more or less restricted plans for international organisation.

The PRESIDENT thought that the discussion had reached the stage when a Committee might be appointed to deal with the question of the definition of aggression. He therefore suggested that this Committee, under the chairmanship of the Vice-President, M. Politis, should consist of the representatives of the following countries : Belgium, United Kingdom, Cuba, Denmark, Estonia, Finland, France, Germany, Hungary, Italy, Poland, Spain, Switzerland, Turkey, Union of Soviet Socialist Republics, United States of America and Yugoslavia.

The Committee would be instructed to consider all questions of security, and the President would suggest that it would be helpful if it would, in the first instance, consider the Soviet delegation's proposal and, if possible, submit to the Political Commission a report on the definition of aggression upon which the Committee had found agreement. After reporting on the definition of aggression, the Committee would then examine other questions relating to security — that was to say, the Belgian proposal [1] and the question of mutual assistance which had been discussed by the Commission at the preceding meetings.

The proposals of the President were adopted.

---

[1] Document Conf.D.,C.P.12.

DOCUMENT 11

Conf.D./C.G./108.   [1]
Conf.D./C.P./C.R.S./9[1]
Geneva, May 24th, 1933.

LEAGUE OF NATIONS
CONFERENCE FOR THE REDUCTION AND LIMITATION
OF ARMAMENTS
GENERAL COMMISSION

Report of the Committee on Security Questions.
(Rapporteur: M.N. Politis)

The Committee originally set up by the Political Commission on
March 10th, 1933, for the examination of the Soviet delegation's
proposal on the definition of the aggressor (Document Conf.D/C.G.
38) and of the Belgian delegation's proposal on the establishment of
the fact of aggression (Document Conf.D./C.P./12 was in addition
requested by the General Commission on April 28th, 1933, to deal
also with Article 6 of the Draft Convention submitted by the United
Kingdom.

The Committee was presided over by M.N. Politis, and consisted
of the following countries:

Belgium, Cuba, Denmark, Estonia, Finland, France, Germany, Hungary, Italy, Poland, Spain, Switzerland, Turkey, United Kingdom,
U.S.S.R., United States of America, Yugoslavia.

As regards the first two subjects, the Committee has drawn up
the attached Acts, the structure of which is explained in the present
report (Parts I and II).

As regards the third subject, certain delegations (Germany, Hungary, Italy) confined themselves to following the Committee's work
as observers. It was understood, moreover, that the draft European
Pact prepared by the Committee does not bind the Governments in   [2]
any way and is submitted to the General Commission as a basis of
discussion.

The texts prepared regarding the establishment of the fact of aggression (Part II) and the European Security Pact (Part III) are intended to constitute Annexes X and Y referred to in Article 6 of the
British draft Convention.

The Committee accordingly drew up a new text which would constitute Article 6 of the said draft and would refer to these annexes,

explaining their connection with the General Convention for the Reduction and Limitation of Armaments (Part IV).

PART I.
Definition of Aggressor.

1. The present Act (Annex I), conceived on the universal plane, aims at determining acts of aggression in a definite, practical and direct manner.

2. In the opinion of its supporters this method would constitute the foundation of any system of security envisaged by the Disarmament Conference by putting an end to doubts and controversies on the point whether States which resort to force have committed an aggression or not. States would thus be definitely informed in advance of what they could not do without being regarded as aggressors. Even in the absence of any intervention by an international organ, such a determination would be of some value. It would considerably strengthen the authority of the prohibition to resort to force by enabling public opinion and other States to judge with greater certainty whether this prohibition had been respected or not.

3. In the second place, in the event of international bodies being [3] called upon to determine in fact the aggressor in a given conflict, the existence of a precise definition of the notion which these bodies would have to apply would render the determination of the aggressor much easier and there would be less risk of an attempt to shield or excuse the aggressor for various political reasons without appearing to break the rule to be applied.

4. The Committee has drawn up a draft conceived on the universal plane. Certain members of the Committee, nevertheless, expressed doubts as to the possibility of achieving results on this plane, and accordingly some of them considered that before adopting definitions it would be well to know on what framework or to what States they would apply.

5. If the proposed definition was not universally accepted it would of course be compulsory only for the States who became parties to the present Act, and then only in their relations with one another. In such a case the international bodies would have to apply it to this extent only.

6. It should further be noted that the question of the definition of the aggressor and that of the sanctions to be taken against the aggressor, while of course closely connected, are nevertheless separate questions. The strictness of the definition of the aggressor does not necessarily lead to the automatic application of sanctions.

7.   Furthermore, criticisms of principle were directed against the method itself.

8.   Certain members of the Committee (Germany, Hungary, Italy,   [4] Spain, Switzerland, United Kingdom) showed a preference for an elastic definition of aggression, which would permit the international authorities to take all the circumstances into account, thus obviating the drawbacks of the application of rigid definitions which in certain cases might not be adaptable to the actual facts. What would be essential according to this view would be for the parties to the conflict to agree to submit the judgment of the facts in cases of alleged aggression to an international body.

9.   As regards cases in which the international body might have doubts, despite the definition given, two proposals were made. According to the first, the international body would have to resort to arbitration in order to settle the doubt as to the determination of the aggressor. According to the second the aggressor should be regarded as being the State which refused to cease hostilities and to withdraw its troops from the territory in which they should not be situated. Nevertheless, the majority of the Committee preferred to keep to the original proposals.

Article 1.

General Observations.

10. Article 1 enumerates limitatively five facts, each of which, by itself, would constitute an act of aggression. But, first of all, three points should be mentioned, two of which are clear from the actual text of Article 1.

11. (a) A reservation is made in regard to agreements in force between the parties.

12. This reservation has a double purpose. In the first place it   [5] aims at safeguarding the special provisions in existing agreements, which, in certain hypotheses, permit recourse to one of the acts considered in the present Act as acts of aggression. The chief example of such agreements is the Covenant of the League of Nations. Thus, in the case of States Members of the League of Nations, the measures prescribed by the Covenant which might be taken by States Members against other States would not constitute acts of aggression, even if they were covered by the definition of the five facts enumerated.

13. In the second place, this reservation aims at the possibility of reconciling the present Act with the Convention of September 26th, 1931, to Improve the Means of Preventing War. This reconciliation

gives satisfaction to some extent to those who might fear that the system laid down in the present Act is too rigid.

14. As regards the said Convention, mention must be made of two opposing observations submitted to the Committee but not accepted by the latter.

15. On the one hand the fear was expressed that the provisions of Articles 2 and 3 of this Convention, which contemplate the possibility of armed forces having entered the territory of a State in circumstances not giving rise to a state of war, might be rendered more difficult of application by the fact that the Act defining the aggressor regards invasion as an act of aggression.

16. The same apprehension was expressed in a more general manner as regards the application in similar cases of Article 11 of the Covenant of the League of Nations. [6]

17. On the other hand it was pointed out that the application of the said Convention should be subordinated to the Act defining aggression for States who were at the same time parties to that Act and parties to the above-mentioned Convention, so as not to weaken in any way the scope of that Act.

18. (b) It is clearly specified that the State which will be recognised as the aggressor is the first State which commits one of the acts of aggression. Thus, if the armed forces of one State invade the territory of another State, the latter State may declare war on the invading State or invade its territory in turn, without itself being regarded as an aggressor. The chronological order of the facts is decisive here.

19. (c) The question was raised before the Committee whether, if a State committed against another State an act constituting an aggression according to the definitions of Article 1, a third State might commit an act of the same nature against the first State without itself being regarded as an aggressor.

20. It appeared to the Committee that in view of the fact that the Act regarding the definition of the aggressor was on the lines of the Pact of Paris, it would be sufficient if reference were made in this respect to the principle laid down in the preamble of the said Pact, viz: "that any signatory Power which shall hereafter seek to promote its national interests by resort to war should be denied the benefits furnished by this Treaty."

Enumeration of the five facts constitutiong aggression. [7]
First Fact. - Declaration of War.

21. The Committee considered the question whether it was advis-

able to take the declaration of war as a criterion of aggression, or whether the acts of aggression enumerated below would not be sufficient to define it.

22. It appeared to it that the declaration of war should not be eliminated from the list of criteria of aggression. On the one hand, it is true, a declaration of war can occur before any act of hostility, and in this case it is the prelude to the hostilities which the declaring State will initiate or which the State on whom war is declared will be authorised to initiate. On the other hand, the Pact of Paris condemns resort to war and, as has been said, the Act defining the aggressor is regarded as an extension of the Pact of Paris.

Second fact. - Invasion of the territory of a State, even without declaration of war, by the armed forces of another State.

23. The act of invasion consitutes essentially an act of aggression, apart from any declaration of war.

By territory is here meant territory over which a State actually exercises authority.

Third fact. - Attack by land, naval or air forces of the territory of another State, of its vessels or of its aircraft.

24. This hypothesis is distinct from the previous one. The territory of the State attacked is not entered by armed forces but is subjected to artillery or rifle fire, air bombardment, etc.

25. As regards the vessels or aircraft of another State, no distinction has been made according to whether these vessels or aircraft belong to the armed forces of the State or are of a non-military character belonging either to the State or its nationals. [8]

Fourth fact. - Establishment of a naval blockade of the coasts or ports or another State.

26. In spite of the objections raised by certain members to the mention of this case, the Committee considered that, while a naval blockade did not necessarily lead to war, it was nevertheless an act applying material force in a limited but real manner against another State. Only the weakness of the State against which a naval blockade is established can deter it from retaliating by acts of war. In certain cases, this weakness might also induce it to submit to a mili-

tary invasion (see previous heading), which undoubtedly constitutes the most definite act of aggression.

Fifth fact. - Support given to armed bands which have invaded the territory of another State.

The Committee, of course, did not wish to regard as an act of aggression any incursion into the territory of a State by armed bands setting out from the territory of another country. In such a case aggression could only be the outcome of complicity by the State in furnishing its support to the armed bands or in failing to take the measures in its power to deprive them of help and protection. In certain cases (character of frontier districts, scarcity of population, etc.) the State may not be in a position to prevent or put a stop to the activities of these bands. In such a case it would not be regarded as responsible, provided it had taken the measures which were [9] in its power, to put down the activities of the armed bands. In each particular case, it will be necessary to determine in practice what these measures are.

28. Article 2.

The purpose of this article is to specify that acts of aggression, as defined in Article 1, cannot find excuse or justification in considerations of any kind whatever. In other words, these acts can only be justified by a State in the single hypothesis of that State having first been the victim of acts of this kind. Certain members made reservations regarding this article owing to its absolute character.

29. A special protocol (Annex II) has been drawn up which constitutes an annex to Article 2.

30. This Protocol, which forms an integral part of the act, simply aims at illustrating the scope of Article 2. It enumerates the principal cases in which States might have thought themselves authorised to resort to measures of force against another State under international law as it existed previously to the Pact of Paris and to the Covenant of the League of Nations. But it is evident that this enumeration cannot have the effect of in any way restricting the scope of the general formula of Article 2.

31. Furthermore, the Protocol takes care to specify that breaches of international law which would not justify the use against the State committing them of the measures of force defined as acts of aggression and enumerated in Article 1, cannot be legitimated by the Protocol. A State which complains of violations of international law will be entitled, in order to redress the wrongs which it claims to

have suffered, to have recourse to procedures of pacific settlement [10] and, if necessary, it may employ means of pressure, such as the breaking off of diplomatic, economic and other relations, which do not constitute measures of force.

32. The question of provocation was raised in the Committee. In this connection an explanation is called for. "Provocation" is either one of the acts of aggression defined in Article 1; in such case the State which has been the victim of such an act can obviously retaliate by acts of a similar nature and no difficulty arises. Or "provocation" consists in a breach of international law or in the unfriendly attitude of Governments or public opinion without the commission of an act of aggression. In such case the provocation cannot be regarded as an excuse.

33. Certain reservations were made with regard to the drafting of this Protocol.

34. Article 3.

There were no comments on this article. In any case it will be for the General Commission to decide whether the present Act will have the same period of validity as the Convention of which it will form part.

PART II.
ESTABLISHMENT OF THE FACT OF AGGRESSION.

35. The Committe unanimously adopted, subject to certain minor modifications, the Belgian delegation's draft regarding the creation of commissions for establishing the facts in the case of aggression or threatened aggression.

36. The U.S.S.R. delegation, however, declared that it would only [11] be able to declare its views on this Act when the problem of the definition of the aggressor had been settled.

* * * *

37. Three fundamental ideas dominate the draft.

38. 1) In the case of a crisis (whether a frontier has already been violated or whether a State feels it is under the imminent threat of aggression), it is highly desirable that there should be an impartial and immediate investigation of the facts likely to throw a light on the situation. Such investigations may be extremely valuable in guiding not only the international bodies which would have to give an opinion on the responsibilities involved in the conflict, but also public opinion, whose judgment can in such cases be decisive.

39. 2) To achieve their purpose investigations should be made forthwith without any formalities intervening to delay the operation

of the system. It is therefore essential that the moment the incident occurs the commission for establishing the facts should be already in existence, or could be constituted immediately to carry out its mission without delay.

40. 3) Care should be taken to eliminate the chief objection which might be encountered by the creation of commissions of this kind by studiously avoiding investing them with any powers which could be regarded as directly or indirectly of an inquisitorial nature.

41. The Commissions referred to are in no way instruments ma- [12] nipulated from outside or directed either by the League of Nations or any other international body. They are merely instruments put at the disposal of the Governments concerned. The latter are the sole judges as to whether they require to make use of their services and have the sole power of deciding what should be submitted to their investigations.

42. It should be pointed out in this connection that the commissions in question have no other duties but to establish the facts and they have no power whatever to express in this respect any legal opinion whatsoever.

* * * *

43. The texts which the Committee submits to the General Commission are, taken as a whole, sufficiently clear for comment to be unnecessary.

44. The following few brief observations may however be made:

45. 1) The Committee has expressed no opinion as to the place which should be allotted to the Act in the general body of Decisions which will finally be adopted by the Conference. It points out that the elasticity of the system is such as to make it adaptable to the most diverse combinations; it can be inserted just as well in a general as in a regional scheme.

46. 2) Article 2 lays down the conditions under which commissions for establishing the facts will be appointed. Each Government will select five members of its commission out of a list of ten names drawn up on request every five years by an international organisation. What should this organisation be? On this point the Committee felt it better not to express a definite opinion but to leave for later decision by the Conference the choice between the future Permanent [1] Disarmament Commission and the Council of the League of Nations.

47. One member of the Committee proposed that the Council should act for States Members of the League of Nations and the Permanent Disarmament Commission for the other States, but it seemed better to reserve the question entirely for the moment.

48. 3) Paragraph 2 of Article 2 reads: "It shall be permissible for it (each Government) to make this choice and if necessary to modify it until such time as the Commission is despatched." This rule adds to the elasticity of the system and makes it more practical. In adopting it the Committee had in mind certain conjunctures which might otherwise have raised difficulties in case a Government preferred, as the wording allows, to decide the membership of its own commission before the occurrence of any political crisis. It may happen that at the last moment one of the persons selected by it is unavailable owing to absence, sickness etc., or that as a result of his nationality or changes in international relations he no longer appears to that Government to offer the guarantees of impartiality and confidence which had led to his appointment. It seemed advisable to take account of these various possibilities and to allow the Government concerned to modify the membership of its commission. The option thus accorded lapses, of course, as soon as the Government applies to the chairman of the commission for the intervention of the latter.

49. 4) Some members of the Committee questioned whether it [14] would not be possible to extend the powers of commissions for establishing the facts and to provide for the possibility of the Permanent Disarmament Commission resorting to them in cases where it had to make local investigations.

50. This suggestion however was opposed by other members, and the Committee agreed to recognise that the question could not for the moment be examined.

51. Certain delegations reserved the right to raise this question when the chapter relating to supervision in the United Kingdom Draft Convention is discussed.

The continuation of the report will be distributed in Conf. D./C.G./108(a).

Draft Act relating to the definition of the aggressor.

The States ....
Deeming it necessary in the interest of the general security, to define aggression as specifically as possible in order to obviate any pretext whereby it might be justified;

And noting that all States have an equal right to independence, security, the defence of their territory and the free development of their institutions;

And desirous, in the interest of the general peace, to ensure to all peoples the inviolability of their territory;

And judging it expedient to establish the rules that are to be followed by the international bodies responsible for determining the aggressor:

Have agreed upon the following provisions:

Article 1.
The aggressor in an international conflict shall, subject to the agreements in force between the parties to the dispute, be considered to be that State which is the first to commit any of the following actions:

1) declaration of war upon another State;

2) invasion by its armed forces, with or without a declaration of war, of the territory of another State;

3) attack by its land, naval or air forces, with or without a declaration of war, on the territory, vessels or aircraft of another State;

4) naval blockade of the coasts or ports of another State;

5) provision of support to armed bands formed in its territory [16] which have invaded the territory of another State, or refusal, notwithstanding the request of the invaded State, to take in its own territory all the measures in its power to deprive those bands of all assistance or protection.

Article 2.
No political, military, economic or other considerations may serve as an excuse or justification for the aggression referred to in Article 1.

Article 3.
The present Act shall form an integral part of the General Convention for the Reduction and Limitation of Armaments.

ANNEX II.

Draft Protocol annexed to Article 2 of the Act relating to the Definition of the Aggressor.

The H.C.P. signatories of the act relating to the definition of the aggressor,

desiring, subject to the express reservation that the absolute validity of the rule laid down in Article 2 of that act shall be in no way restricted, to furnish certain indications for the guidance of the international bodies that may be called upon to determine the aggressor,

declare that no act of aggression within the meaning of Article 1 of that act can be justified on either of the following grounds among others:

A. The internal condition of a State.

e.g. its political, economic or social structure; alleged defects in its administration; disturbances due to strikes, revolutions, counter-revolutions or civil war.

B. The International conduct of a State.

e.g. the violation or threatened violation of the material or moral rights or interests of a foreign State or its nationals; the rupture of diplomatic or economic relations; economic or financial boycotts; disputes relating to economic, financial or other obligations towards foreign States; frontier incidents not forming any of the cases of aggression specified in Article 1.

The H.C.P. further agree to recognise that the present Protocol can never legitimate any violations of international law that may be implied in the circumstances comprised in the above list.

ANNEX III.

Act relating to the establishment of facts constituting aggression.

Article 1.

There shall be set up at the seat of the Government of each of the High Contracting Parties which may so request a Commission for Establishing the Facts, consisting of five members, constituted as follows:

Ever five years the Permanent Disarmament Commission (or: the Council of the League of Nations) shall establish, for each of the said High Contracting Parties, a list of 10 persons of different nationalities chosen from among the diplomatic agents and military, naval or air attaches accredited to the Government of such High Contracting Party. It shall further make provision in the interval for filling any vacancies that may occur in the personnel thus designated.

Each Government shall select from this list the five members of the Commission. It shall be permissible for it to make this choice and if necessary to modify it until such time as the Commission is despatched.

The Commission shall be presided over by those of its Members holding the highest diplomatic rank.

Article 2.

Any High Contracting Party which believes itself to be the victim of, or threatened with any aggression or violation of its territory shall have the option of calling upon the Commission to establish all the facts likely to throw light on the situation.

Article 3.

A High Contracting Party making use of this option must, immediately and by the most rapid means, notify the Secretary of the Permanent Disarmament Commission (or the Secretary-General of the League of Nations). The latter shall at once notify the High Contracting Party accused, in order that it may, should it so desire, have the facts established on its side by the Commission set up on its territory.

Article 4.

If the Commission considers it useful for the accomplishment of its task to verify certain facts other than those to which its attention has been drawn by the complainant Government, it shall inform the latter, which shall decide what action should be taken in this respect.

Article 5.

Any Commission before which a request for the establishment of facts has been laid shall, as soon as possible, make known to the Secretary of the Permanent Disarmament Commission and to the Secretary-General of the League of Nations, as also to the complainant Government, a detailed report, giving such evidence as it has been able to establish regarding the significance of the facts related therein and a statement of the conditions in which its mission has been carried out.

The Commission shall supply the Permanent Disarmament Commission and the Council of the League of Nations with any supplementary written or verbal explanations which it may be asked to give in this connection.

Article 6.

The decisions of the Commission for Establishing the Facts shall be taken by a majority vote, the members of the minority having the right to add to the report a note explaining the reasons for their disagreement.

Article 7.

The High Contracting Parties accept forthwith, on behalf of their diplomatic agents and military, naval and air attaches, any mission that may be entrusted to the latter in execution of the present Convention.

DOCUMENT 12

LEAGUE OF NATIONS.

Conf.D./C.G./108(a)
Conf.D./C.P./C.R.S./9(a)[1]

Geneva, May 25th, 1933.

CONFERENCE FOR THE REDUCTION AND
THE LIMITATION OF ARMAMENTS.

COMMITTEE ON SECURITY QUESTIONS

Draft Report on the work of the Committee on Security Questions.

M.N. POLITIS, Rapporteur.

PART THREE.

EUROPEAN SECURITY PACT.

52. - This Pact (Annex IV) consists of two separate chapters. The first is exclusively devoted to the obligation not to resort to war, and the second to the subject of mutual assistance.

53. - States will have the option of assuming the obligations provided for in both these chapters or of limiting their commitments to the obligations in Chapter I.

54. - The Pact is solely concerned with security in the strict sense of the term. Consequently, while its provisions contemplate various international conventions such as the Convention of September 26th, 1931 to Improve the Means of Preventing War, and the Financial Assistance Convention of October 20th, 1930, it makes no reference to the organisation of procedures for the pacific settlement of disputes, and hence does not mention the General Act of Arbitration of September 26th, 1928.

55. - The Committee's conception is that for the present this Pact, one of the main objects of which is to facilitate the development of mutual assistance, can only be in the nature of a regional agreement, if the accession of a sufficient number of countries is to be secured. The Committee contemplates the conclusion of such a Pact within a European frame-work. In the present circumstances [2]

it would appear that Chapter I should concern all the European countries parties to the Pact of Paris and Chapter II all the States of continental Europe.

Chapter I.

56. - This Chapter consists of two Articles. Its sole object is to prevent States from resorting to war, with or without a declaration.

It is not concerned with mutual assistance.

57. - Article 1 provides for the undertaking not to resort to force in any circumstances. It reproduces in full a text already approved by the Political Commission on March 3rd, 1933.

58. - Article 2 provides for the undertaking to accede to the General Convention to Improve the Means of Preventing War of September 26th, 1931.

59. - The Committee felt that the undertaking not to resort to force could usefully be supplemented by accession to the Convention of September 26th, 1931, which is calculated to enhance the efficacy of the action taken by the Council of the League of Nations to prevent the outbreak and development of an armed conflict.

60. - As the Convention of September 26th, 1931 is independent of the Convention for the Reduction and Limitation of Armaments and will come into force as soon as ratifications or accessions have been received, it has been specified that accessions given in virtue of Chapter I of the European Security Pact, which would itself form part of the Convention for the Reduction and Limitation of Armaments, would only take effect as from the entry into force of the Disarmament Convention.

61. - Various members of the Committee proposed the omission of Article 2 on the ground that it would not be advisable to establish [3] a compulsory connection between accession to the present Pact and accession to the Convention on the Means of Preventing War. In their view that Convention, which was concluded in 1931, no longer corresponds to the development of international law at the present time. Acts such as the unanimous acceptance by the Political Commission of the Conference of an undertaking not to resort to force, or President Roosevelt's recent message condemning among other practices the use of armed forces outside the national territory do not seem to be such as to authorise a distinction between an invasion and an act of aggression committed in violation of the Pact of Paris, which seems to be allowed by the Convention. Moreover, the maintenance of Article 2 would make it more difficult if not impossible for States not Members of the League to accede to Chapter I

This should be avoided, more especially since that Chapter contains the condemnation of resort to force.

62. - This Chapter originally contained an Article reproducing the provisions of the Act regarding the definition of the aggressor and the Act on the determination of aggression. It seems preferable to await the decisions taken on those two acts. In consequence the Article in question has been provisionally omitted.

Chapter II.
General Remarks.

63. 1. - This Chapter of the European Security Pact, which concerns the organisation of mutual assistance, is not designed to create in itself obligations upon States to provide mutual assistance. The Committee's intention is that it should simply increase the efficacy of the mutual assistance obligations established by other treaties, whether particular or general. It would thus serve to determine and strengthen the value of the assistance to be given, under Article 16 of the Covenant of the League, to a State victim of aggression.

64. - Several members of the Committee would have preferred [4] that the other conception be adopted - that of a treaty making assistance compulsory. Other delegations which would have preferred a treaty of that kind stated that such a treaty would at present stand little chance of securing a sufficient number of accessions, and they therefore thought that for the time being it was better to be content with the much more modest achievement aimed at by Chapter II.

65. - 2. The importance of Chapter II lies principally in the three following points:

66. - a) Determination of cases of aggression.

By reproducing certain clauses of the Act defining Aggression, the European Pact facilitates the decision as to the cases in which the assistance provided for by Article 16 of the Covenant of the League of Nations is due to the State to which it has been promised.

67. - b) Reinforcement of the system of sanctions in Article 16 of the Covenant of the League of Nations.

68. - This is secured in that the recommendation with regard to the effective military, naval or air force, to be made by the Council of the League under Article 16, paragraph 2 of the Covenant, instead of being merely optional, become obligatory when voted unanimously by the Members of the Council with the exception of the representatives of the parties involved in the conflict.

69. - On the other hand, the States signatories have the option

to determine in respect of which States, exclusively, they are assuming this obligation, as well as the nature and extent of the assistance they undertake to furnish.   [5]

70. - c) The necessary distinction between the conceptions of assistance and belligerency is established. Acts of assistance performed in application of Article 16 of the Covenant are not to be regarded as acts of war.

71. - 3. Relation between the provisions of Chapter II and the League Covenant.

The Committee has not thought it necessary to point out that the European Security Pact cannot affect the rights and duties of Members of the League under the Covenant; for the Convention for the Reduction and Limitation of Armaments will contain an article establishing that principle, and that article will apply to the European Security Pact, which will form an integral part of that Convention.

72. - Moreover, so far from weakening the Covenant, the European Security Pact - as has already been said - tends to strengthen it, by defining and amplifying certain of the obligations it involves.

73. - The question that might arise is how far Members of the League who are not parties to the European Security Pact would be affected by the provisions of that Pact which define and develop the obligations contained in certain Articles of the Covenant of the League of Nations.

74. - The Committee considered that the provisions of the European Security Pact could obviously only be applied in conflicts between States parties to that Pact. Nevertheless, in such cases the organs of the League of Nations and the other Members of the League would be called upon to apply them. The provisions proposed for Article 6, moreover, removes any doubt on this point.   [6]

* * * *

75. - Article 3. - This article indicates that, in accordance with the spirit of the Covenant of the League of Nations, the aim pursued by the European Pact is an essentially practical one. The purpose is, not to inflict a penalty properly so-called on an aggressor State, but to restore peace by putting a stop to aggression and settling its consequences.

76. - Article 4. - It has already been said that the European Pact does not itself create any obligation of assistance. Article 4 indicates the first case in which assistance is due. It is due in virtue of general or particular treaties concluded between the parties. These treaties must have been published by and registered with the Secretariat of the League of Nations. The Committee was not in favour of establishing a discrimination between treaties already con-

cluded and those that might be concluded in future, which are mentioned in Article 11. The purpose of the obligation in regard to publicity and registration is to permit of supervision over these treaties, which must obviously be in keeping with the requirements of Article 20 of the Covenant of the League of Nations.

77. - _Article 5_. - This article indicates the second case in which assistance is due, i.e. the assistance provided for by the Covenant of the League of Nations. This case has a wide application.

78. - _Article 6._ - This article reproduces, with a single change, the definition of the aggressor which is given in the Act regarding this definition (Part I).

79. - The fourth of the facts mentioned in that Act, namely the [7] establishment of a naval blockade of the coasts or ports of another State, has not been included. It was thought that this fact should not be regarded as in all cases involving the obligation to provide assistance.

80. - It should be noted that this article contains a reservation as regards the agreements in force between the parties - a reservation which was already included in the Act defining the aggressor. This reservation gave rise to observations in the Committee. It seemed likely to permit of the application of the European Pact being reconciled with that of the Convention of September 26th, 1931, on the Means of Preventing War; for, even in cases in which there might be obligations of assistance, the duty of the international organs would still be to prevent war. If, for example, an act of aggression by one State against another State has not in fact led to the creation of a state of war, the existence of obligations of assistance will clearly not have the effect of preventing a settlement which would conclude the conflict by putting an end to the aggression without a state of war having arisen and without assistance having come into play. With regard to this point attention must be drawn to the point of view of certain members of the Committee referred to in Chapter I.

81. - A proposal was also made to introduce here a certain element of elasticity, by making the assistance contingent upon the gravity of the facts, or by empowering the Council, by a majority vote, to bring the assistance to an end. The Committee did not adopt the suggestion.

82. - _Article 7._ Article 7 refers to the assistance furnished in virtue of Article 16 of the Covenant of the League of Nations. The first paragraph of Article 7 obliges States to carry out the recommendations referred to in Article 16, paragraph 2, when such re- [8] commendations have been adopted unanimously by the Members of

the Council other than the representatives of the Countries parties to the dispute.

83. - Apart from this, it in no way affects the system of Article 16 and does not restrict the freedom of the parties if the unanimity in question is not secured.

84. - The object of paragraphs 2 and 3 is to determine in advance the assistance which will be supplied both as regards the form and extent of the assistance. Thus, States will indicate to what State they would supply this assistance, and they will also indicate, in a table, their contribution, i.e. the material or the effectives, or both, which will represent their contribution. These two questions will be settled by negotiations.

85. - The purpose of paragraph 4 is to dissociate the notions of assistance and belligerence.

86. - Article 8. - This article, in its first paragrah, contemplates the possibility of assuming the obligations provided for in paragraphs 2 and 3 of article 7 after the entry into force of the European Pact. In the same way as the obligations entered into previously to the entry into force of the Pact will have necessitated negotiations, the obligations entered into subsequently will require an agreement between the signatories of Chapter II.

87. - The second paragraph lays down a similar procedure for the extension to another area of obligations already assumed.

88. - Article 9. - This article is inserted "pour mémoire". It relates to the hypothesis of material or effectives being placed at the disposal of the League of Nations. If this hypothesis should be realised, the necessary provisions would have to be drawn up and inserted in this article.

89. - Article 10. - This article places the parties to the Euro- [9] pean Security Pact under the obligation of acceding to the Convention on Financial Assistance of October 2nd, 1930.

90. - Article 11, - The purpose of this article is to introduce into the system of the Pact the treaties of mutual assistance which may be concluded in future. This provision is intended both to unify the practice of mutual assistance, while rendering it more effective, and to provide guarantees against possible deviations from the policy of assistance.

91. - Article 12. - This article indicates that States may accept the obligations of the two Chapters of the Pact, or of Chapter I only.

92. - Article 13. - The first paragraph of this article provides the possibility for all European States who may not have signed the Pact to accede thereto whenever they wish.

93. - In virtue of the second paragraph, which refers to Article 7 (paragraphs 2 and 3), a new acceding State must conclude agreements concerning the determination of the States to which assistance will be promised and concerning the nature and extent of this assistance.

Part IV.

94. - The purpose of the text drawn up by the Committee to replace the present text of Article 6 of the Draft Convention is to determine the legal position, with regard to the annexes to which it refers, of the States which are parties to the General Convention but not parties to the said annexes. It determines the effect of the European Security Pact in regard to the signatories of the general Convention. These clauses are sufficiently explicit, and call for no comment.

ANNEX Y

EUROPEAN SECURITY PACT.

Chapter I.

The High Contracting Parties (....) have agreed upon the following provisions:

Art. 1. Being desirous of promoting the cause of disarmament and with a view thereto of encouraging a spirit of mutual confidence among the nations of Europe by a declaration forbidding resort to force in the circumstances in which the Pact of Paris forbids any resort to war,

The High Contracting Parties solemnly reaffirm that they will in no circumstances resort among themselves to force as an instrument of national policy.

Art. 2. The High Contracting Parties undertake to accede, if they have not already done so, to the General Convention to Improve the Means of Preventing War, signed at Geneva on September 26th, 1931, such accession to take effect as from the date of the entry into force of the Convention for the Reduction and Limitation of Armaments.

Chapter II.

Recognising that it is important for the maintenance of peace and the success of the efforts they have undertaken for the reduction and limitation of armaments, that a State victim of aggression should receive prompt assistance, the High Contracting Parties have further agreed upon the following provisions:

Art. 3. The purpose of assistance is to bring about the cessation of the aggression and to ensure a just settlement of its consequences.

Art. 4. Assistance shall be due by any High Contracting Party having assumed the obligation to assist another under treaties published by and registered with the Secretariat of the League of Nations, in accordance with the conditions and procedure laid down in those treaties.

Art. 5. Assistance is also due in the cases indicated in the Covenant of the League of Nations.

Art. 6. A State shall be considered as having resorted to war within the meaning of Article 16 of the Covenant of the League of Nations, subject to the agreements in force between the parties in conflict, when it is the first to have committed one of the following acts:

    (1) declaration of war on another State;

    (2) invasion by its armed forces, even without declaration   [2] of war, of the territory of another State;

    (3) attack by its land, naval or air forces, even without declaration of war, on the territory, ships or aircraft of another State;

    (4) support given to armed bands which, having been formed in its territory have invaded the territory of another State, or refusal to take in its own territory, notwithstanding the request of the invaded State, all the measures in its power to deprive the said bands of all help or protection.

Art. 7. Each of the High Contracting Parties undertakes to participate immediately to the extent determined hereafter, in the execution of any recommendations which the Council of the League of Nations may make in pursuance of Article 16, paragraph 2, of the Covenant of the League, when such recommendations have been adopted unanimously, excluding the votes of the Parties to the dispute.

The assistance thus promised shall be due by a Contracting State to the Contracting States situated in a particular area. (This clause will be completed after negotiations on the subject).

This immediate assistance shall consist in the contributions specified in the table annexed to the present agreement. (The contents of this table will be settled after negotiations on the subject).

The High Contracting Parties undertake not to regard as acts of war acts performed with a view to providing this assistance.

Art. 8. If after the entry into force of the present pact a High Contracting Party which has not yet assumed an obligation within the meaning of paragraphs 2 and 3 of the preceding article desires to assume such obligation, it shall be allowed to do so by agreement between the States bound by the present Chapter.

Similarly, if a High Contracting Party desires to extend the obligation assumed by it in a given area to another area it shall be allowed to do so by agreement between the States bound by the present Chapter.

Art. 9. (Pour mémoire. Should material or effectives be placed at the disposal of the League of Nations, a clause would be inserted relating to the employment of these effectives and material for the assistance provided for in the present pact).

Art. 10. Such of the High Contracting Parties as are members of the League of Nations undertake to accede, if they have not already done so, to the Convention for Financial Assistance, signed at Geneva on October 2nd, 1930, such accession to take effect as from the date of the entry into force of the Convention for the Reduction and Limitation of Armaments.

Art. 11. Any treaty which may be concluded with a view to laying [3] down fresh obligations of assistance in case of aggression shall be included in the present pact after being published by and registered with the Secretariat of the League of Nations.

Art. 12. The High Contracting Parties shall state on signing the present pact whether their signatures apply

    a) to the pact as a whole (Chapter I and Chapter II)

    b) or only to the provisions of Chapter I.

Art. 13. European States which are not signatories of the present pact may accede to it under the same conditions. States bound by the obligations of Chapter II shall determine by common agreement with the State adhering to the said Chapter the methods of application of paragraphs 2 and 3 of Article 7.

Article 6 of the Convention.

The High Contracting Parties recognise that the provisions of Annex Y of the present Convention are likely to contribute to the maintenance of peace, and accordingly agree to base thereon any decisions which they may have to take, particularly in the Permanent Disarmament Commission, with a view to preventing any breach of the Pact of Paris by a Power which has signed Annex Y, determining the responsibility should such a breach occur and fixing the consequences.

The High Contracting Parties agree to refrain from any action which might hamper the application of the measures to be taken in the cases provided for by Articles IV, V and VI of Annex Y and not to recognise any de facto situation brought about by the breach of an international obligation on the part of a State recognised as the aggressor in application of the provisions of the said annex.

The High Contracting Parties Members of the League of Nations also undertake to comply with the provisions of Article VI of the said annex as regards the application of Article 16 of the Covenant of the League of Nations to the signatories of the said annex.

The High Contracting Parties Members of the League and signatories of the Convention for Financial Assistance signed at Geneva on October 2nd, 1932, likewise undertake to comply with the provisions of Article VI of the said annex as regards the application of that Convention.

119. Report of the Committee on Security Questions: Statement by M. Politis, Chairman of the Committee, as to the Position of the Work.

M. Politis (Greece), Chairman of the Committee on Security Questions, submitted to the General Commission the first two parts of the report of the Committee.[1] The Committee had been given three tasks. It had, first of all, to study the proposal of the Soviet delegation concerning the definition of the aggressor. Secondly, it had to deal with the Belgian delegation's proposals for determining the aggressor, and, lastly, under a recent decision of the General Commission, it had to study the European Security Pact proposed by the French delegation.

The two sections now communicated to the Commission covered the first two subjects, and for the moment M. Politis would confine himself to explaining the structure of the Act relating to the definition of the aggressor. Some such explanation was required, as it would enable the General Commission, which had only just received the report, to form an adequate idea of the work done by the Committee.

The Act relating to the definition of the aggressor, the text of which formed the first annex to the present report, had been intended, and still was intended by those who had

---

[1] Cf. document Conf.D./C.G.108.

proposed it, and also by the members of the Committee who had approved it, to constitute the foundation-stone of the security system which the General Commission was at present considering.

Its effect and its practical advantage would be that it warned States of the acts they must not commit if they did not wish to run the risk of being declared aggressors. Thanks to it, public opinion would be able, when a grave incident occurred in international relations, to form a judgment as to which State was responsible. Lastly, and above all, it would facilitate the work of the international organ called upon to determine the aggressor. Furthermore, when that organ had before it sufficiently definite rules to facilitate its task, it would be less tempted to incur the danger of excusing, on political grounds, the act of aggression which it was called upon to judge.

So much for the purpose and utility of this Act.

What was its sphere of action ? According to the Soviet proposal, which had been accepted by the majority of the Committee, the Act was conceived as of universal application. It was designed to become a general law for all States. Nevertheless, it went without saying that, should it fail to command the acceptance of all States, it would only be compulsory and its rules would only apply in relations between the States which had accepted it. The system embodied in the Act was marked by a certain strictness and that was its principal merit in the view of the Committee which had drawn it up. Its strictness resided in the fact that the cases which the contracting parties undertook to regard as acts of aggression were determined in a restrictive manner. This system had been criticised by certain members of the Committee, who regarded as a drawback what had appeared to the majority as an advantage. The former would have preferred the system to be more elastic, because circumstances might be very complex and the very rigidity of the system might hamper the action of the body responsible for determining the aggressor. The majority had considered that, between a rigid system and an elastic system which ran the risk of being marked by the drawbacks that experience, and particularly the studies made at the League, had only too clearly revealed, the preference must go to the rigid system embodied in the Act defining the aggressor, for its drawbacks were largely outweighed by the advantages which it was calculated to offer. Moreover, whatever might be the drawbacks of this system, it had appeared to the Committee that, in the interests of peace and as a guarantee of security, it had undoubted advantages over the more flexible system. As a matter of fact, the possible rigidity of the system embodied in the Act was likely to be mitigated to a certain extent by the fact that the Act was to be taken in combination with the 1931 Convention on the means of preventing war and also with the League Covenant itself.

It had indeed been found during the Committee's enquiry—although this conclusion had not met with unanimous support—that the operation of these different Acts would enable the body responsible for determining the aggressor—and hence for applying the rules laid down in the Act—to take into account the powers which it held under Article 11 if it were the League of Nations and, in the case of the application of the 1931 Convention, the special rules laid down in that Convention, which, taken as a whole, did after all permit of a certain elasticity in the application of the strict rules laid down in the Act.

Before entering upon an analysis of the provisions of the Act, three observations of a general character were required.

First, the rules laid down were subject to a reservation as to the agreements in force between the parties. This reservation had been made for two reasons : (a) to safeguard the special stipulations existing in agreements in force between the parties which might, in certain cases, permit of recourse to one of the acts considered in this document as acts of aggression. The most striking and general example was in the League Covenant itself, which contained a clause whereby the States Members of the League could, in certain specified cases, take steps which in themselves might be regarded as acts of aggression according to the definitions given in the Act, but which nevertheless had not this character, because they were legalised by the agreement binding the parties concerned ; (b) to make it possible to reconcile the present Act with the Convention of September 26th, 1931, on the means of preventing war. The Committee had thought it necessary to make a reservation as to the application of the Convention concurrently with the present Act, because the combination of these two texts might lead to a certain flexibility, thus lessening the rigid character of the system proposed.

Secondly, in the enumeration of the acts of aggression which M. Politis would describe later, the State which first committed one of the acts mentioned was declared the aggressor. Emphasis should be laid on the word " first ". It might very well be that, in the complicated circumstances of an international dispute, there might at one time or another have been committed by either party certain acts coming within the scope of the definition in the Act. The only way of having a clear view in so complicated a situation and so being able to apportion the responsibilities and finally to determine the aggressor was to observe the chronological order of events—namely, to ascertain who had been the first to begin to commit one of the forbidden acts—since, once it was proved that one of the parties had been the first to commit one of those acts, the attitude of the other party would immediately be seen to be that of legitimate defence and, by that fact alone, should be excluded from the conception of aggression.

The third general observation related to the position of third parties, which at first sight might appear somewhat doubtful. When a dispute arose between two countries and one of them was the first to commit one of the forbidden acts, and when it was, on that account, regarded as the aggressor, were third parties free, in respect of the aggressor, from the obligation in the Act whereby they were bound not to commit the acts described as acts of aggression ? The reply which was given to this question was very simple. It was linked up to the 'Pact of Paris, which laid down that, when one of the contracting parties had broken the Pact, the others were immediately released from the obligations they had assumed towards the party which had committed the first breach. The position in the present case was exactly the same, and the result was that third parties which had resorted to force and violent measures against the aggressor with the object of assisting the victim of the aggression were assured by this rule that they would not be regarded as aggressors.

The list of facts constituting aggression gave a restrictive enumeration of five cases of aggression.

The first was the declaration of war. It had been thought necessary to mention this case, although in itself it might not be a definite act of aggression, because, in fact, the declaration of war would be immediately followed by hostilities and it was manifest that the party which should bear the responsibility therefor was the party which had issued the declaration. But, in accordance with the observations which he had made previously, if the declaration were made after the commission of one of the forbidden acts had been established, it could not be held to be an act of aggression, because the responsibility would fall upon the party which had first committed one of the forbidden acts.

The second fact agreed to was the invasion of the territory of a State, even without a declaration of war, by the armed forces of another State. That was obviously the most characteristic case of all, and the Committee had carefully made clear in its report that by the term "territory" was meant the area of land over which a country actually exercised its authority. When a territory answering to that description was invaded by the armed forces of another country, the latter was committing a forbidden act ; it would be declared the aggressor and the invaded State would be the victim of the aggression.

The third fact was attack by land, naval or air forces of the territory of another State or of its vessels or of its aircraft. No comment was required on this point.

The fourth fact was the establishment of a naval blockade of the coasts or ports of another State. In this connection, certain objections had been raised in the Committee, but the latter had held that, if a naval blockade did not necessarily lead to war, it was nevertheless an act implying material force, in a limited but real manner, against another State and that, in most cases, only the weakness of the country subjected to the blockade prevented the blockade from being the initial act in the final rupture of peace and resort to hostilities. For that reason, the Committee had thought it right to include this case among the acts of aggression.

Lastly, there was a case which was in some ways a novelty, because it had never so far been recognised in studies on the subject. It was the case in which a country supported armed bands which set out from its own territory and invaded that of another country.

Such was the restrictive enumeration in Article 1 of the draft Act.

Article 2 laid down an extremely important rule which brought out the true character of the system. Article 2 said that no consideration of whatever kind, whether political, economic or financial, or other, could be advanced as excusing or justifying an illegitimate act if committed. A State which, having committed such an act, advanced an argument of that nature could not avoid condemnation as the aggressor.

The Soviet delegation had proposed that this article should be followed by a somewhat lengthy clause giving, by way of illustration, a number of the most probable cases in which considerations of any kind, if advanced in justification of the aggression, might be held to be invalid. The Committee had felt that to insert so long a list in the body of the clause itself would make the text too heavy. In a spirit of conciliation, however, it had agreed that there should be a special Protocol annexed to Article 2 giving a certain number of illustrations. That was the object of the Special Protocol in Annex II of the Committee's report.

Lastly there was a third article, which stated that it was the Committee's intention that the Act concerning the definition of the aggressor should be made an integral part of the Convention. The only point held over was that of the duration of the Act, because it was possible and natural that an Act of this nature, which was intended to establish a permanent international law, should be given a duration other than that of the General Convention for the Reduction and Limitation of Armaments, which was designed, by its very nature, to represent only the first stage and consequently was, in certain respects, of a provisional character and might have a limited duration.

Such was the general structure of the Act on the definition of the aggressor.

In conclusion, M. Politis, speaking at least on his own behalf—for he did not know whether he expressed the opinion of all his colleagues on the Committee—desired to add that he regarded this Act on the definition of the aggressor as an advance, and a very notable advance, in the long chain of work undertaken at Geneva for many years past. For ten years at least, a vain attempt had been made to devise suitable formulæ for crystallising this somewhat evasive idea of aggression. Success had not been achieved, apparently for two reasons. The first was that, hitherto, the determination of aggression had been closely bound up with the idea of sanctions and the application of Article 16 of the Covenant. In the present case, that consideration had been entirely dropped. The aggressor was defined and it was reserved for other instruments and other authorities entrusted with defining and applying the sanctions to decide whether all the cases indicated in the present document as acts of aggression should be taken into consideration for the purposes of the application of sanctions. The second factor which had hitherto blocked the success of the work for the definition of the aggressor was that, until the Conference had set to work, all arguments in connection with the term "aggressor" had referred solely to the definite case of war, and that was another difficulty, since the term " war " itself was difficult to define.

. Since the Pact of Paris had come into force, since the virtues inherent in it had become more apparent and since it had become gradually more manifest that to-day it was no longer possible, in the conscience of civilised man, to make a really practical distinction between what had previously been regarded as war and what modern men regarded as resort to force or the use of violence—ever since that time it had been seen that it was easier to arrive at a definition of the aggressor, because one of the difficulties which had prevented the elaboration of that definition had been jettisoned. The idea that a distinction should no longer be made between war in the strict sense of the term and resort to force had gained a striking success during the present Conference, and the unanimous adoption in March 1933 [1] by the Political Commission of its resolution in which resort to force was henceforth an act forbidden to all States constituted, in M. Politis' view, the greatest success which the Conference had hitherto achieved.

It was true that the resolution then taken applied to Europe only, but M. Politis did not think that he was mistaken in saying that, in the intention of the vast majority of the Conference, it had been voted in the sense of a general law applying to civilised mankind, which now desired that the use of force should give way to the application of pacific methods.

From the standpoint of the League's work, therefore, that was a very great success, and it was a point of some interest that the Conference owed it to one of the non-member States, the Union of Soviet Socialist Republics, whose delegation had courageously and with deep conviction submitted a text which had exercised an extraordinary attraction over those who had studied it, with the result that, finally, the Committee on Security Questions had succeeded in coming to a conclusion, notwithstanding all the difficulties it had encountered.

It was M. Politis' most agreeable duty to congratulate the Soviet delegation on the initiative it had taken, on the part it had played in the Security Committee and on the success it had finally achieved. It was with special pleasure that he paid this tribute to the Soviet delegation, since it demonstrated beyond all doubt that, when men rose above the contingencies of day-to-day politics and allowed themselves to be guided by the more general ideas which should lead the civilised world, it was found that, whether a country was a Member of the League or not, there was a community of ideals which was capable, with a little goodwill, of bringing to fruition the noblest and most difficult enterprises.

The PRESIDENT felt sure that the Commission would like him to express its very sincere thanks to M. Politis, Chairman of the Security Committee, for the report which he had presented and for the explanatory statement he had been good enough to make. Both the report and the explanatory statement would certainly assist the Commission very much when it began the discussion on the articles in Annex I.

241

SIXTY-NINTH MEETING

Held on Monday, May 29th, 1933, at 3.30 p.m.

President : The Right Honourable A. HENDERSON.

125. REPORT OF THE COMMITTEE ON SECURITY QUESTIONS [1] : DEFINITION OF THE AGGRESSOR
(*continuation*).

M. DE MADARIAGA (Spain) said that a few days previously [2] the Commission had heard the
Vice-President's statement on the problem of the definition of the aggressor, in the course of
which M. Politis had referred to the two theses which, in that matter as in all matters relating
to the League, brought face to face the Anglo-Saxon mentality and the so-called Latin mentality.
M. de Madariaga thought that there was clear evidence of this parallelism in the past history
of the question, because, the first time an attempt was made to define aggression—in a sub-
committee of the Temporary Mixed Commission, if he were not mistaken—the idea which
had occurred to all was that embodied in the most recent document on the question—the
declaration of the President of the United States of America .[3] It had been suggested that the
party crossing his own frontier was the aggressor. That idea of defining aggression as invasion
had been at once sharply rejected by all the military experts then assisting in the work
of disarmament, as, in their view, it was quite conceivable that there might be countries whose
frontiers were so unfavourably drawn that, even though they followed a fundamentally pacific
policy and had a fundamentally defensive military organisation, they might find themselves
obliged to take a military initiative in order not to be crushed by an essentially aggressive
country which was preparing an overwhelming attack. In view of the respective forces engaged,
the operations, once begun, would rapidly become disastrous for the first country. It was
that idea which had led, in the Temporary Mixed Commission, to an intervention by two
members who then represented, not Spain, but at all events Spanish thought, for, on that
Commission, the members did not represent their Governments. These two Spanish members
had put forward a proposal in which an endeavour was made, even at that time, to find a
more elastic, more fluid system for defining aggression. A purely automatic criterion was
avoided ; but an attempt was nevertheless made to give the system a certain degree of precision
by the adoption of preliminary undertakings, one of which was of a legal character : provision
was made for compulsory recourse to arbitration in any dispute, failing which there was
a presumption of aggression. Another undertaking was of a conservatory character : provision
was made for the adoption, by the Council, of conservatory measures and, should either of
the parties not accept those measures, there was again a presumption of aggression.
It was from this first idea that eventually, after the stage represented by the Treaty of
Mutual Assistance, there was born the idea of an automatic criterion which had been crystallised
in the Protocol, in which, as the General Commission would remember, the method of arbitration was so ingeniously devised that it led, as it were, mechanically to the definition of the
aggressor. But, for reasons that everyone knew, the Protocol had been dropped. Then, thanks
mainly to an extremely important proposal by the German delegation on the Preparatory
Commission, the Convention for strengthening the Means of preventing War had been drawn up.
In M. de Madariaga's opinion, that Convention had not received sufficient attention ; it
constituted, he thought, a fundamental idea, one of the most concrete, precise and useful
proposals that had ever been made in the course of the work in question.
The Spanish delegation on the Committee over which M. Politis had presided with such
conspicuous ability had taken up, with regard to the definition of the aggressor, an attitude
which M. de Madariaga would like to define more closely. It did not agree with the automatic
method advocated by the Soviet delegation, not because it was not in sympathy with that
method, but because it thought that it involved an excessive national individualism.
The automatic method had the very considerable advantage of eliminating the individual
responsibility of States in naming the aggressor. Everyone knew from experience how difficult
it was for one State to judge the conduct of another. Consequently, it was in every way desirable
that the decisions to be taken in the matter should be based on facts and not taken by persons
who, as far as they could, would always avoid the necessity of giving a decision in this matter.
He must point out, however, that the automatic method would certainly, by a process which
was not difficult to foresee, and several instances of which had already occurred in the brief
history of the League, give rise to all kinds of political artifices which would in many cases make
it possible to elude automatic criteria, however ingenious and rigid they might be, and would

---

[1] Document Conf.D./C.G.108.

[2] See Minutes of the sixty-third meeting of the General Commission, page 499.

[3] See Minutes of the fifty-ninth meeting of the General Commission, page 462.

enable States which were bent on doing so to commit certain acts contrary to international law without being caught, if that expression might be used. Moreover, it had the advantage that, if it compelled States to employ such artifices, that in itself was already a result. Possibly, in some cases, States might commit certain international acts which were not strictly to be commended, while at the same time avoiding being caught by the automatic method ; in most cases, however, that would probably prove impossible.

It was not, therefore, on account of definite opposition to the automatic method that the Spanish delegation had not been able to adopt a final attitude in this matter on the Security Committee ; it was rather because it saw in that method a tendency to weaken the organs of the League. M. de Madariaga had just said that the States, which, after all, constituted the self-working machinery of the League, avoided giving a definite decision ; but it was only inasmuch as States failed to assume their responsibilities that the organs of which they were members were enfeebled. He thought there was a serious danger of weakening the League's organs through the very fact that the States Members were enabled to avoid assuming their responsibilities.

In the method advocated by the Soviet delegation, M. de Madariaga thought he could perceive—and he asked that delegation's pardon for making the observation—a certain inconsistency between the spirit of Soviet policy in international affairs and that of Soviet policy in home affairs. Unless he was inadequately informed regarding it, Soviet national policy was not remarkable for an excess of individualism, whereas in its international policy, as instanced by this definition of the aggressor, there was a kind of exaltation of national liberty within the international community, since, whatever the faults of which that nation might be guilty, there was no possibility of bringing influence to bear upon it to discharge its responsibilities. True, in M. Politis's report there was a paragraph reserving the question for the international authorities, but M. de Madariaga agreed with the Soviet delegation that it would be desirable to strengthen very considerably the idea of opposing attempts by a State to take justice into its own hands when another country committed acts which were unjustifiable or caused it dissatisfaction. The Spanish delegation was opposed to such an anarchistic method. At the same time it wanted to strengthen the idea that the international authority must always intervene at the request of a State or even on the direct initiative of these collective organs ; for it was quite inadmissible that acts which, from the international point of view, were unjustifiable before the community of nations should go unpunished on account of a kind of exaltation of the individual liberty of the nations constituting the international society.

It must be realised, moreover, that, in applying the definition of aggression, whatever the method employed—elastic or rigid—the great difficulty was that the number of armaments was much too large, that these armaments were much too powerful and that it was much more difficult to approach a strongly armed nation than an unarmed one. That was the first great difficulty which would be experienced and which perhaps had already been experienced. The fact that a country was strongly armed did not warrant the hope that it would have the courage to pronounce against another strongly armed State if the latter were guilty of wrongful acts. Consequently, armaments were much less likely to protect the Covenant than to jeopardise it. That was the essential point, the theoretical truth of which was clear in itself but which experience was making clearer still. Moreover, despite the Covenant, there were still far too many cases of national policy insufficiently co-ordinated with the principles of the international policy of co-operation. Consequently, so long as this two-fold evolution towards disarmament and towards the co-ordination of national policy with an international policy of co-operation failed to make any great progress—whatever definition, rigid or elastic, were adopted—that definition would be in peril whenever serious and more or less automatic decisions had to be taken in regard to strongly armed countries.

In conclusion, M. de Madariaga would ask M. Politis to be good enough to explain a discrepancy between two documents, each of which represented his report. In the first, which had been distributed without a number, there was the following sentence :

" The act of invasion constitutes essentially an act of aggression apart from any declaration of war."

Then in document Conf.D./C.G.108 the same sentence was followed by the words :

" By territory is here meant territory over which a State actually exercises authority".

M. de Madariaga felt serious doubts as regards that last sentence, which, according to the interpretation given to it, might be harmless but might also be extremely dangerous.

He would also like to ask M. Politis whether, in the draft Protocol attached to the same document (Annex II), he would agree to add at the end of the last paragraph the words :

" in regard to which the victims could always appeal to the international courts".

Lastly, M. de Madariaga stated that, if the majority of the Commission was in favour of the automatic definition, the Spanish delegation, subject to the reservations it had just indicated, would have no objection to accepting it.

M. NADOLNY (Germany) had followed with the greatest interest the discussion on the Act relating to the definition of the aggressor. It was a problem which had occupied the League's organs for some years, but for which no solution acceptable to all had been found. Mr. Eden had already mentioned the report of the Mixed Commission drawn up in 1923. M. Nadolny would also refer to the Geneva Protocol of 1924, which had just been mentioned by M. de Madariaga. Opinions as to the best way of solving the problem were therefore divided, although it was generally recognised as highly desirable, in the interest of peace, that the problem of the definition of the aggressor should be settled by common agreement.

In his very interesting statement, M. Politis had already pointed out the two opposing tendencies towards rigidity and elasticity. In the Act now before the Commission, the system prescribed was of the fixed kind ; indeed, it might even be termed automatic. The fundamental objections which had been raised against rigidity in an international system for the definition of the aggressor were well known. Mr. Eden had explained them anew very clearly, so that it was almost impossible to throw any new light on that aspect of the problem.

M. Nadolny himself, desirous of elucidating the problem as a whole, might add a further consideration in regard to an aspect to which the German delegation had always attached great importance. In its opinion, the establishment of rules for the definition of the aggressor would be of great preventive value. M. de Madariaga had rightly emphasised that aspect of the problem.

As the report said, States would then be definitely informed in advance of what they could not do without being regarded as aggressors. Moreover, if no strict or rigid criteria were set up, the Council, or the international organ dealing with the question, would not be under the necessity of proceeding to establish the fact of an aggression, even in cases where it might be preferable to apply means of conciliation, which might prove ineffective from the moment when one of the parties to the conflict had been stigmatised as the aggressor.

The report already contained a certain element of elasticity, since it provided that acceptance of the Act, as drafted by the Committee, would not preclude the application of the Convention for developing the means of preventing war, which Convention provided preventive measures even if a State had committed acts regarded as determinant factors of aggression according to the draft relating to the definition of the aggressor. M. Nadolny thought that idea, which was very clearly set forth in the report, was not yet adequately expressed in the Act itself. It would have to be seen, therefore, whether the element of elasticity could not be strengthened and incorporated clearly and precisely in the actual text of the Act.

Further, he would like to add another consideration of a technical nature, which might be of particular interest to jurists. The Security Committee had submitted another draft—the European Pact of Security [1]—with a new text intended to replace Article 6 of the United Kingdom plan. That draft also contained a definition of the aggressor. In that case the aggressor was referred to as "the State which had resort to war", but the facts constituting the aggression were the same in both Acts. There was one exception, however—namely, that the wrongful acts did not include blockade. A State which established a blockade would therefore not be violating the Covenant ; and, according to the draft, that decision must be recognised, not only by the signatories of the European Pact, but by all the States represented at the Conference. But such a State, through having established a blockade, would have to be recognised as the aggressor under the other Act.

In addition to the two Acts to which he had just referred there were other proposals. There was the new text of Articles 1 to 3, submitted by the United Kingdom delegation and accompanied by the important statement of Mr. Norman Davis.[2] In Article 2 of that text it was stated that the object of the consultation provided for, in the event of a breach of the Paris Pact, between the League of Nations and States which were not Members of the League would be to determine which party or parties to the dispute " are to be held responsible ". Here, therefore, there was no mention of an aggressor or of a State having resort to war, but of the State responsible.

Then there were the proposals set forth in President Roosevelt's message, which referred to a general Convention of non-aggression combined with an undertaking by States not to allow their armed forces to cross their frontiers.

M. Nadolny therefore ventured to put the following question : Would it not be desirable and necessary to co-ordinate and reduce to a common denominator all the different projects and proposals among which the experts had the greatest difficulty in finding their way ? It would undoubtedly be of capital importance to lay down rules in such a way as to be intelligible to other people besides the legal advisers of delegations.

M. DI SORAGNA (Italy), realising the importance of the arguments submitted by a number of delegations which had met to discuss the definition of the aggressor, felt bound to indicate briefly the Italian delegation's position in the matter. That delegation largely shared the ideas, the preoccupations, the arguments and also the misgivings of the United Kingdom delegation, which had been so fully and exactly described by Mr. Eden at the meeting on

---

[1] Document Conf.D./C.G.108(a).
[2] See Minutes of the sixty-third meeting of the General Commission, pages 494 and 495.

May 25th. M. Dovgalevsky, who had spoken on the same day, had classed the various attitudes of his colleagues on the Committee in two categories. He had said that he could thank some of them for having helped him by their support and the others for having equally helped him by their objections. M. di Soragna had himself been present, and he wondered whether the Italian delegation could be classed in either of those categories, or whether it should not be included in a third class which had helped M. Dovgalevsky by remaining silent. Such an attitude could not surprise anyone who knew the position as regards Italian legal doctrine on the subject.

Mr. Eden had very rightly referred to the principle laid down by that great friend of peace, Lord Cecil. The Italian delegation could only refer to the teaching, the principles and the speeches of another distinguished statesman, one of the survivors of the great founders of the Covenant, M. Scialoja. He need only read a few sentences from a speech delivered by M. Scialoja at the eighth Assembly (ninth meeting, September 9th, 1927) :

" . . . when we speak of aggression, we are perfectly aware of what it means. We know that it means nothing at all. We realise the difficulty of formulating a definition of aggression, and the joint efforts of jurists, diplomats and politicians have so far failed to arrive at any acceptable definition of the term. Furthermore, a State which is resolved to coerce its neighbours by armed force will never be the apparent aggressor, for, however unskilled its diplomacy, it will always manage to make its neighbour begin the attack.

" Therefore, in our attempt to fix the responsibility for the aggression, we must not dwell too much on appearances. We must subject to a close scrutiny all those relations between the States concerned which have in the past given rise to differences. That is far from easy."

There was no need to explain this opinion further. Moreover, the United Kingdom delegation had told the Commission all that was necessary on the subject.

M. di Soragna added that he would have said no more if Mr. Eden's speech had not been followed by that of M. Politis. That distinguished jurist's remarks had been, as always, most noteworthy, but M. di Soragna felt bound to say that he had been entranced rather than persuaded, charmed rather than convinced. In M. Politis's statement he had noted the three or four points which formed its framework.

The first argument to consider was that of a reconciliation between two systems. M. Politis had already explained that, ever since the Covenant came into existence, two principles had confronted one another : the continental—or, as M. de Madariaga termed it, Latin—principle and the Anglo-Saxon principle. The spirit of logical synthesis on the one hand, and the spirit of empiricism on the other. On the one hand, codification, automatic action and, on the other, freedom, the enforcement of verdicts as a matter of judgment and not as absolute measures. M. Politis had said that the Committee felt it had done something to reconcile the two theories, and that the texts before the Commission might help to fuse them together. M. di Soragna must confess that he was not convinced.

The texts submitted contained a list which, to his mind, was as rigid and automatic as it could be. Such a list of cases of aggression left no room for appraising the circumstances accompanying the actions specified or the responsibility of those who committed them. That was already very far from the system formerly advocated and which was based on the idea of presumption, a fact which made the whole system more conciliatory in character. In this matter, M. di Soragna did not see that any headway had been made ; he would even say that the rigidity of the system was proved by the fact that it did not allow for provocation.

The judges were bound hand and foot. On the one hand, five quite specific cases were laid down. If any one of them occurred, even on a very small scale, full international action would immediately come into operation. On the other hand, no provision was made for a large number of other cases. They might be extremely serious cases. The injured party would be powerless and would have to rely on pacific procedure, which was not always very speedy. There was no need to quote examples. On the one hand, international action might be taken because a cottage had been burnt down ; on the other hand, one State might massacre the nationals of another for several days without the latter being able to do anything other than resort to pacific procedure. Those were, doubtless, exceptional cases, but the Commission would agree that a State might well ask with some anxiety whether it should subscribe to such onerous and rigorous undertakings, whether it could take the risk, by simply appending its signature to a document, of compromising so gravely what might be the primary interests of its nationals.

This procedure went far beyond the point reached in the establishment of rules of procedure in international and private law. The latter contained a conception of the responsibility of a party giving provocation. That conception was immensely important, so much so that provocation might completely cover the party which resented an insult. The present procedure might mean completely reversing the rôles. It was on the banks of the Tiber that the following sentence, which seemed to be one of the most divine of human judgments, had been uttered— " summum jus, summa injuria " (the rigour of the law is the height of oppression).

The Rapporteur had pointed out that the States concerned could sign the Act or not. He had said that, if States did not wish to sign, they should at least allow the others to enjoy the assurance of security given by the Act before them. A glance at the text was sufficient. Article 3 read :

" The present Act shall form an integral part of the General Convention for the Reduction and Limitation of Armaments."

M. di Soragna did not see how an integral part of the Convention could be excepted from the signature of a party to the General Convention. Furthermore, the Preamble said that the Act had been drawn up because it was deemed "expedient to establish the rules that are to be followed by the international bodies responsible for determining the aggressor". Nor did he see how it could be said that this Act would not bind States which did not sign it. They would even be bound to a very large extent. That was, in fact, the difficulty.

Of course, it might be said that States which did not sign bore no responsibility, either for the verdict or for the action to be taken. But that was absolutely impossible, since there would be an advisory body consisting of two kinds of members—those who proposed to apply the principle of the free hand, who would consider things as they were, take all details and circumstances into account in determining the consequences of the acts committed, and those who, on the contrary, had in their pockets the definition of the aggressor and had a ready-made decision in their minds. How could two such opposing conceptions be reconciled?

M. Politis had remarked that the subject was not a new one. There already existed many international instruments, concluded between several countries, which were based on special rules of law arising out of special agreements between those countries and were not open to others. Possibly. In some cases the Council might take such instruments into account, but the case before the Commission was quite a different one. The Act submitted to it contained no rules on special questions affecting only certain specific States. It contained rules relating to a problem of quite general character : the determination of the aggressor. A State could hardly risk having to accept a system under which it might, as a member of an international organisation, have to help in determining the party responsible for a dispute and to determine that responsibility, not on the basis of special rules, but on the basis of a general rule which it had not accepted.

In conclusion, the Italian delegation, which had already accepted the general plan of the United Kingdom, though, of course, without contemplating the possibility of the addition of an Act of this character and tenor, considered that this second factor was calculated to alter very substantially the structure of the plan which it had accepted in its original shape. It could not hide its feeling that this addition to the plan might arouse very serious anxiety and misgivings.

M. DE BARCZA (Hungary) supported the view of the delegations which had questioned the advisability of laying down beforehand too strict criteria for the determination of the aggressor and which had also emphasised the various drawbacks of a specific and absolute enumeration of the acts of aggression.

He wished to recall that, Hungary having been a member of the Committee on Security Questions which had drawn up the draft Act now before the General Commission, he had not omitted to tell that Committee that, in principle, his delegation preferred a general formula, one that was as elastic as possible, for the purposes of the definition required—if, of course, it was at all possible to find such a formula.

In explanation of his delegation's attitude, M. Barcza would merely refer to the arguments previously adduced in this connection by several delegations at the Political Commission's meeting on March 10th.[1] He therefore need only associate himself fully with the views on this matter expressed by the delegates of the United Kingdom, Germany and Italy at the General Commission's meetings on May 25th and to-day.

M. Wellington Koo (China) wished, on behalf of the Chinese delegation, to support the draft Act relating to the definition of the aggressor recommended by the Committee on Security Questions, to thank the Committee for the valuable fruits of its work as crystallised in its report and the two annexes, and to express his appreciation to its Chairman, M. Politis, for his brilliant explanatory statement.

In the Chinese delegation's opinion, the proposed Act provided a useful set of criteria for determining the aggressor. The lack at present of any agreed set of rules for the definition of the aggressor inevitably led to delay in arriving at an agreement. In the case of aggression, time was an important element, and delay usually worked in favour of the aggressor and to the detriment of the victim of aggression.

In the second place, an agreed definition of aggression served to increase the sense of security in that it might tend to deter and discourage aggression. It might be argued, as it, indeed, had been in the Commission, that the enumeration of certain acts as constituting aggression would not be very helpful or do much good, because human ingenuity, especially on the part of the more designing among the nations, would manœuvre its actions and so regulate its conduct as to be able to commit real acts of aggression without exposing itself to be considered as an aggressor by any of the tests proposed. In such a case, the ends of international justice as well as the purposes of world peace would be defeated, rather than promoted, by an explicit definition.

In the Chinese delegation's view it was better to have imperfect rules than to have none at all. The particular objection of some delegations could be met by making it clear that the list of acts enumerated as constituting aggression was not exhaustive. Thus there

---

[1] See Minutes of the eighth meeting of the Political Commission, pages 47 *et seq.*

might be added, for example, at the end of the introductory sentence, a clause to the effect that the aggressor was not only that State which was the first to commit any of the specified actions but also that State which committed any action which by the procedure of consultation provided in Article X of the Convention might be determined as constituting aggression. Such an addition would make it possible to have the advantage of elasticity to meet the countless possibilities of human ingenuity without depriving the world of the benefit of an agreed set of tests of international aggression.

For the same reasons, the Chinese delegation would support the adoption of the draft Protocol annexed to Article 2 of the Act. The Protocol gave a number of useful indications as illustrations for the guidance of international bodies that might be called upon to determine the aggressor. Thus, the grounds which it was proposed should be considered as unjustifiable grounds for aggression were just those which had heretofore given rise to interminable debates between the parties to past disputes and to divergent views among third parties, thereby causing a great deal of delay in arriving at a conclusion. The Chinese delegation believed that the proposed Protocol, if adopted, would greatly assist the interests of justice and peace and facilitate prompt decisions in any given crisis created by aggression.

In short, the Chinese delegation was of the view that it was highly desirable that the present Conference, devoted to the cause of disarmament and peace, should adopt certain rules to define aggression and to facilitate the determination of the aggressor in any given case. The very phrase "organisation of peace", which was the delegations' common object, implied that practical and concrete rules should be adopted wherever possible for the purpose of restraining and discouraging aggression between nations and promoting a general sense of security. It was only by such process that chaos in international life could be completely eliminated and a new international order firmly established.

M. Mikoff (Bulgaria) said the Bulgarian delegation had given the Act relating to the definition of the aggressor all the attention which such an important document merited. It was, indisputably, a great contribution to the solution of the problem of the determination of aggression, a problem which was one of the corner-stones in the edifice of peace.

In the eternal controversy referred to by M. Politis between the two kinds of mentality which were divided on this question—the mentality dominated by the need for rigid and strict rules and the mentality which liked to have an elastic system of law, vague in outline and becoming definite in form only in contact with experience—the Bulgarian delegation could only side with those who supported the second view.

The Bulgarian delegation was convinced that, while the rigidity of the criteria adopted might suit simple cases—and simple cases did not demand exact definitions—it might conflict with justice and leave the door open to abuse in complicated and difficult cases. There was even a risk that the application of any one of the five criteria enumerated in Article 1 of the Act might, in view of the special conditions prevailing in a particular area, give results the opposite of what was expected and the contrary of the object in view.

For these reasons, M. Mikoff fully agreed with those members who considered that the Act relating to the definition of the aggressor should not enumerate the facts constituting aggression, all of which, moreover, were by no means covered by the five points in Article 1, and that, as regarded aggression, full liberty to form a judgment should be left to the Council.

The Bulgarian Government could not accept the criteria for the automatic designation of the aggressor contained in Article 1 of the Act in question. It would be glad, however, to support any text giving a general definition of the act of aggression.

Colonel Beazley (India) said that, having regard to the distance which separated the country he represented from Geneva, it would be understood how it was that he had not received the views of the Government of India with regard to the contents of the extremely important document before the Commission. Lest, however, his silence should be interpreted as implying acceptance of the report and of the terms of the annexes thereto, he wished, on behalf of the delegation of India, to record a reservation in regard to the views which his Government might wish to express on a subsequent occasion with regard to the subject under discussion.

M. Paul-Boncour (France) had wished, notwithstanding the rather pressing duties which might have kept him in Paris, to attend the present meeting in order to support the laudable efforts—which might, he thought, lead to very satisfactory results—of the Committee on Security Questions and of M. Politis, its Rapporteur. The French delegation gave its full and unreserved support to the proposals made for defining the aggressor, and would support also those regarding the determination of the fact of aggression ; it had given and would give the same support to the inferences to be drawn therefrom as regarded both the Consultative Pact and a more specific Pact of Mutual Assistance. He trusted that those proposals would be accepted by the General Commission. Frankly, he felt obliged to say, even at this stage, that he feared they would not be so accepted ; he would very much regret it. It should be fully realised that this was one of the keystones, if not the chief keystone, of the edifice of mutual international security which the Conference was trying to build up.

Whether the question to be considered was the opening articles of the United Kingdom delegation proposal, as revised by it in the light of the United States declarations regarding the Consultative Pact and its enforcement, or the narrower Pact of Mutual Assistance, which would be the next problem to be discussed by the Commission, or even, it had to be said, the working of the Covenant in its present form, the definition and establishment of the fact of aggression constituted a basic principle without which nothing could be constructed. The Commission had just been reminded, it was true, of the difficulties which had for years been experienced and which had arisen in connection both with the definition of aggression and the establishment of the fact of aggression. The French delegation had never very clearly understood what difficulties could be raised.

The Italian delegate had just quoted the saying of an eminent countryman of his, with whom M. Paul-Boncour had often had the honour of sitting at the Council table or of pleading before the Permanent Court of International Justice at The Hague, and for whom he felt a very real intellectual admiration and friendship. Like all the members of the Commission, who had so often felt his charm, M. Paul-Boncour knew that M. Scialoja concealed under a kindly scepticism a very sound knowledge of the law. In the phrase quoted, M. Scialoja had said that everyone knew very well the meaning of aggression because no one could know what it meant. If M. Scialoja had meant to say that no concrete cases of aggression could be cited, that would have been going farther than seemed to be implied by many statements which M. Paul-Boncour had heard from the lips of M. Scialoja. He thought that M. Scialoja had in view that abstract definition of aggression for which so long a search had been made and which was very difficult to frame. The merit, however, of the Committee on Security Questions, the merit of the lucid spirit of its Rapporteur, was that they had substituted, for the comparative futility and uselessness of an abstract declaration, concrete cases of aggression and had substituted for the definition facts and an enumeration of those facts. War, like the devil when he was tempting St. Anthony, took the most varied and fanciful disguises. The wisdom of the proposals before the Commission was that they did not claim to be an exhaustive enumeration of the many forms which the ingenuity of anyone who wished to commit an aggression could assume. He ventured, however, to stress the fact that the problem was not whether those forms were all enumerated but whether those specified were indubitably facts of aggression.

If the list were considered, what room was there for doubt ? First fact : Declaration of war upon another State. That would doubtless be the least common occurrence ; since pacific procedure had come into existence and with its gradual development declarations of war in solemn and diplomatic form would be less important. There could therefore be no possible discussion on the first fact. Was there any possibility of discussion as regards the second : " Invasion by its armed forces, with or without a declaration of war,"—and the latter would almost always be the case—" of the territory of another State ". If the second fact were beyond discussion, how could there be any about the third, which only differed from the second in that the latter represented invasion properly so-called, penetration on a large scale far into the territory of another country, which was nevertheless the result of an " attack by its land, naval or air forces . . . on the territory, vessels or aircraft of another State ". The fifth fact, he thought, was very closely connected with the third and the second, in the sense that it covered a case which it was very necessary to cover, in view of the changes which had occurred, since the war, in the conception which could be held of armed forces—namely, the same invasion, the same kind of attack conducted not by regular forces but by armed bands which were shown to be supported by the State sending them into its neighbour's territory.

M. Paul-Boncour wished to point out that these four concrete facts were merely the expansion of a small, short but very clear sentence in President Roosevelt's message. He could not very well understand how anyone could object to the concrete proposals before the Commission and at the same time accept the message of President Roosevelt. President Roosevelt's message contained this decisive phrase : that the signatory Powers " . . . should individually agree that they will send no armed force of whatsoever nature across their frontiers." That was the same idea, put in another form, as appeared in the list proposed by the Committee, since, if there was to be invasion of or attack on the territory of another State, the regular or irregular troops would have to cross the frontiers of the country sending them. That was quite clear. What President Roosevelt's message lacked—and this was what the Committee had tried to do—was this : the same rules should be applied to navies and air forces. But M. Paul-Boncour considered that the list of facts proposed was the strict logical development of that essential passage in the message sent by President Roosevelt to the Heads of States.

The Italian delegate had just raised the objection that the Committee's list of facts of aggression was incomplete, that there might still be others. Undoubtedly, but that was an objection which had been anticipated by the Committee on Security Questions and M. Politis. The Committee had done the necessary additional work of stating the facts which could not be adduced as pretexts for justifying, under international law, aggression in the strict sense of the term and so defined. That had been necessary. Did that mean that such facts were themselves licit actions and that the State committing them should have no account to render to international justice because the Conference had adopted those concrete cases of aggression ? That was not so. M. Politis's report and the Protocol (Annex II) expressly said so ; that there was no justification under the law of nations for acts which were thus eliminated as legitimate pretexts for aggression. To make that objection was to forget that the Conference was trying to give the international organisation of which it formed a part the possibility of ascertaining clearly, speedily and without useless discussion, the fact of aggression and that, in the case of other facts which did not constitute the brutal and obvious act of aggression, but which were nevertheless contrary to international law, it was an international instance, the League of Nations, the Council, the Assembly or the body formed, according to the first three articles of the United Kingdom plan, by adding to the Council or the Assembly States signatories to the Convention, which would have to determine them. But the essential task carried out by the Committee and embodied in M. Politis's report was to give such future judgments a definite basis. How could a preference for elastic regulations and for greater latitude in deciding as to the aggressor be set up against that system ? M. Politis had said — so clearly that M. Paul-Boncour had almost nothing to add and was even embarrassed to have to repeat it — that that did not detract from the power of appreciation possessed by the body whose duty it would be, under the Consultative Pact or the Pact of Mutual Assistance or the League Covenant, to take a decision. The task of international law in all questions, literary rights, transit, etc., was to try, as had been done in private law, to give textual bases for the judgment of the court, so that the latter need not give unlimited play to its imagination but would have positive data to corroborate its own view.

Were those who would be asked to guarantee by international measures the security of all to be deprived of this basis, the initial Act, the essential Act ? If the Commission negatived the proposals of the Committee on Security Questions, M. Paul-Boncour confessed he would feel the deepest anxiety as to the outcome of the Commission's proceedings.

Colonel LANSKORONSKIS (Lithuania) said that Lithuania had a most profound belief in the supremacy of right over force and she believed in international justice. Concerned as she was for her own security, she lent her modest help to every attempt made to strengthen the organisation of peace and thereby her own security.

When the Commission had taken up the study of the Soviet draft, Lithuania had felt gratified that a decisive step was at last going to be taken.

Though the list of facts constituting an act of aggression did not perhaps cover all conceivable cases of aggression, the Lithuanian delegation at any rate thought that those mentioned left not the slightest doubt that they would be a violation of Lithuania's security. It was not the small States that engaged in provocation. They might certainly suffer from it and would then be forced to take legal steps through the League to secure justice. It was none the less true that the facts enumerated were really cases of aggression.

Lithuania gave her full and complete support to the draft now under discussion.

M. POLITIS (Greece), Chairman of the Committee on Security Questions, said that he might have refrained from speaking again in the discussion had he not wished, first, to thank those colleagues who had kindly supported the draft under discussion, and, secondly, to reply to some observations, in particular to a certain number of objections which had been put forward.

He agreed with M. de Madariaga on almost all the points he had mentioned, and felt with him that the cardinal merit of the draft was that it might have a preventive effect. On that point, he was glad to note the view of M. Nadolny and other speakers that the Committee's report did really possess that merit. He also agreed with M. de Madariaga in the emphasis which he had laid on the fact that application of the rules proposed should be entrusted to an international organ. That idea was suggested in the actual Preamble of the draft Act and might perhaps be more clearly stipulated were it not that Article 2 of the new text proposed last week by Sir John Simon indicated what body would be responsible for applying the general code of rules directly or indirectly included in the general Convention for the Reduction and Limitation of Armaments.

Article 2 stated that this organ, which would be the Council or Assembly of the League, with the addition of contracting States not members of the League, would, in the event of a breach of the rules, have to examine the situation and ultimately fix the responsibilities.

It was a very simple matter to give the explanation asked for by M. de Madariaga, of the sentence in paragraph 23 of the report. The idea of that sentence was not to justify unlawful occupation, but solely to protect peaceful possession against any act of force, even when the legal titles ·on which possession was founded might accidentally be open to dispute.

Lastly, referring to M. Madariaga's final request that, at the end of the Protocol annexed to Article 2 of the draft Act, it should be specified that breaches of the law of nations which were not justified therein should give the victim the possibility of appealing to an international instance, M. Politis took that for granted. What the Committee had wished to lay down here was that, if breaches of the law could not justify aggression, they were none the less open to condemnation. Obviously, the victim of those breaches could resort to pacific procedure. It could use all the pacific means in its power under treaty law. Was there any point in saying so ?

M. Politis left it to M. de Madariaga to decide. If the latter so wished, he need only submit an amendment, worded as he thought fit, which would be inserted in this final section of the Protocol annexed to Article 2.

To M. Nadolny, who had spoken of the desirability of explicit texts and the value of co-ordinating them, M. Politis replied that it would be impossible to find anyone more anxious than himself to introduce the greatest possible clarity into documents intended to govern international relations. M. Politis would nevertheless like to be quite clear as to the obscurities which, it was suggested, needed dissipating in the present case, because, though the two instruments—that now under consideration and that relating to European security—were not identical in their enumeration of acts of aggression, this was to be explained by the fact that their purpose was not precisely the same. The instrument under consideration enumerated acts of aggression in a general way without drawing any practical consequences, whereas, in the European Security Pact, such acts were enumerated with a definite practical end in view— namely, the application of such mutual assistance as would be prescribed. That being so, it was obvious that, though it had been possible to lengthen the list in the first Act because such a proceeding was without general importance and did not entail very definite practical results, in the second instrument, it had been necessary to limit the list and merely to include the most characteristic cases which, should they occur, would call for the application of mutual assistance in a more definite and more legitimate manner.

M. Nadolny had suggested that there was a further misunderstanding which had to be cleared up. The Commission, he suggested, was discussing aggression, whereas Article 2 of the new text proposed by the United Kingdom delegation spoke of responsibility. M. Politis took the view that " aggression " in the general sense of the term and " responsibility " within the meaning of Article 2 were exactly synonymous terms.

Lastly, as regards the possibility of taking into account the very interesting ideas—which M. Politis personally had welcomed with the keenest satisfaction—embodied in President Roosevelt's message and in Mr. Norman Davis's speech of May 22nd, M. Politis thought that, before an attempt could be made to co-ordinate the texts, it would be necessary to ascertain whether these ideas were intended to be given written and treaty form. Hitherto, the Committee had not been informed that such should be the case. If texts were submitted, such co-ordination would become indispensable and, as M. Politis would show at the conclusion of his remarks, he considered that such co-ordination would not present the slightest difficulty.

M. Politis now came to the objections raised by M. di Soragna. He asked to be allowed to dwell upon them at somewhat greater length, as he could not conceal the deep concern which they had caused him. In this case, it was no longer a question of different conceptions of the nature of law, but of a sharp, a radical disagreement as to the conception of the organisation of international relations, and more especially the organisation of peace. M. Politis was greatly flattered that his previous remarks had charmed M. di Soragna ; at the same time he was equally distressed at having failed to convince him. In the pacific battle being waged in the Commission, with its constant clash of arguments, the force of the latter was countered by another and, unlike other conflicts, in which success could be determined, in the Conference it was only third parties who could weigh the respective pros and cons and take a decision. For his own part, however, M. Politis was bound to say, no less frankly than M. di Soragna, that the latter had not merely failed to convince him, but, on the contrary, had strongly confirmed him in the views which he had expounded before the Commission on May 25th.

What had M. di Soragna said ? There were two points on which absolute clearness was essential. First of all, M. di Soragna had said that the fragility of the system proposed had been more especially demonstrated by the fact that it made no allowance for provocation. The latter, he maintained, played a very important part in the system of law. It played an important part in the national system, and must, in consequence, play an important part in the international system. On this point M. Politis could concur in what M. di Soragna had said, and he accepted the postulate that, in international relations, provocation should play the same part as in the relations between private individuals and between nations. M. Politis, however, hastened to add that, though he accepted this analogy, he was not prepared to agree that provocation should play a greater part in international relations than in municipal law. What precisely was the part played by provocation in municipal law ? To what extent could it absolve a crime, an infringement of the rules of conduct laid down by criminal law ? As far as he knew, there were only two possibilities.

In the first place, provocation constituted an act which placed the victim in a position of legitimate defence, in which case the act with which the victim was charged was condoned, by reason, however, not of the act of provocation itself, but of the situation which it had brought about—that was to say, the special situation known as legitimate defence. On this point, there was complete agreement. The situation was the same in international relations. M. Politis had made this clear on May 25th, [1] when he had dealt with the following problem : either provocation consisted of an act which had placed the victim in a position of legitimate defence, in which case the latter, through the very fact of being in such a position, could commit one of the prohibited acts without being considered an aggressor, or else provocation was not one of the prohibited acts, in which case aggression could not take place on any ground whatsoever, and, against such an act of provocation there remained no other remedy than the application of a pacific procedure to secure the vindication of the right infringed. There was, therefore, a complete analogy in private law ; when provocation resulted in a case of

---

[1] See Minutes of the sixty-fifth meeting of the General Commission, page 516.

legitimate defence, the act was condoned ; when it did not result in such an act of legitimate defence, there was no condonation. Provocation merely enabled the court to consider the case as an extenuating circumstance which, though reducing the penalty, could not entirely do away with it. In examining the instrument under consideration, moreover, this question of repression, this question of punishment did not arise, for, as M. Politis had frequently stated— and repeated a few moments ago in reply to M. Nadolny—the general Act defined aggression in general terms without dealing with the practical consequences. In this case, there was no question of repression, but when entering the sphere of sanctions and of assistance, within the terms of the European Pact of Assistance, provocation, interpreted as an extenuating circumstance, might then be taken into consideration with a view to delaying or modifying the award of mutual assistance. Accordingly the parallelism was complete, and it was not possible to leave open the door—against the closing of which M. di Soragna had protested in respect of cases in which pacific methods of procedure came to nought, or in which a country was faced with an obstinate refusal—and to condone in advance resort to force. M. Politis ventured, with all due respect, to point out to M. di Soragna that to accept the latter's line of argument would be tantamount to tearing up the Pact of Paris ; it would be equivalent to cancelling the extension of that Pact, which had been accepted by the General Commission in a unanimous resolution, whereby recourse to force had been assimilated to recourse to war. What was the meaning of the expressions " prohibit recourse to force " and " prohibit recourse to war" ? They meant, as Article II of the Pact of Paris indicated, that the States undertook that in no circumstance would they employ other means than pacific forms of procedure for settling their disputes, so that, if provocation were to play any part, it could only be the part which it played in private law. If, however, it were desired to extend this idea of provocation in order to justify the use of force in international relations, that meant a very profound difference of opinion as regards the manner in which international relations were conceived. The arguments just put forward belonged, in M. Politis's opinion, to the past. He claimed that the conception which he was maintaining existed already in the texts adopted, and was in harmony with the object at which the civilised world was aiming in organising peace.

The same remarks applied to the other observation with which M. di Soragna had supported the view expressed by Mr. Eden a few days previously. M. di Soragna had said : " We are asked to accept or not to accept. Obviously, everyone is free to act as he thinks fit. We are told, however, that we have no right to prevent those who would like to sign this instrument from doing so." And M. di Soragna had gone on to observe : " But what would be the position of these third States ? What would be their position in this international organism of which they are members, when they are called upon to apply rules to which certain States only have agreed? You would be placing them in an impossible position ; you would be causing them indirectly to assume the very obligations which they are not prepared to assume." On the previous occasion, M. Politis, replying to Mr. Eden's remark, had quoted the example of the Pact of Locarno and had claimed that it proved that third States might find themselves in a similar position and that that position had hitherto given rise to no objection. He now received the answer : " Yes, but the Pact of Locarno lays down special rules, whereas the rules under discussion are of a general character. The comparison therefore does not hold and consequently cannot be used as an argument."

Did that really justify so clear-cut a distinction ? It was contended that, in the present case, the rules were of a general character. In what sense ? In character they were general rules, but they remained special rules in so far as they were only accepted by certain parties. And if immediate agreement were impossible that was because there was too strong a tendency, in accordance with the time-honoured principles which had so far governed the world, to consider that international organs were composed of States exercising their sovereign rights uncontrolled and as arbitrarily as they wished. It had not yet become sufficiently the custom to take the view that, as their name indicated, international organs were actually organs—that was to say, entities entrusted with the exercise of a public function. If, therefore, two countries had concluded, within the limits authorised by general law, special Conventions which, though binding upon themselves, did not bind third parties, and if the application of the rules thus established gave rise to a discussion before the international organ, it appeared to M. Politis an anachronism to say : " How do you expect the members of the international organism, who are not contracting parties, to be able to apply these rules ? " M. Politis was aware that the evolution of law had not yet reached this stage, but it was approaching it. Think of what took place in the municipal courts when the two parties were bound by a contract which the civil code of every country in the world regarded as the law of the parties. Was the judge entitled to say that, as a third party to this contract, he had no concern in the matter ? It was more or less in the same way that the international organ and the members of which it consisted would have to act in the present case. They had to apply rules accepted by certain parties and to apply them solely in the relations between those parties. The argument that, as States—not as members of the organism, but as States—they had not accepted these rules was an objection which could not, in M. Politis's opinion, be regarded as valid, from the point of view of the application of the system proposed. The consideration raised was therefore not really relevant, and it was, M. Politis thought, for that reason that it had failed to convince him. Was it desired to re-open the question of the Pact of Locarno and say that, if the rules had a special instead of a general character, they could not be applied by the third party members of an international organism ? If that were the case, M. Politis would venture to point out that, after the conclusion of the Locarno Agreements, the 1926 Assembly had, by a unanimous vote, recommended all Members of the League to take example by these Agreements and imitate them in any other regions where their application might be possible. That was more or less what the Commission was engaged in doing, and it was fortunate in having the co-operation of States which were not members of the League.

Even from the special point of view of the relations of States Members of the League with each other, the argument did not hold and, if the votes of the League had any value, M. Politis would emphasise the fact that, in 1926, the League Assembly had recommended that the Locarno Agreements be imitated wherever possible.

In conclusion, M. Politis noted with satisfaction that the great majority of the Commission had pronounced in favour of the draft Act ; on a few formal points, it might require certain amendments or additions. Any delegation which so desired was free to make suggestions in this respect, so that they could be examined in due course. It was with all the greater regret that M. Politis noted that, on the other hand, a certain number of the delegations were not prepared to accept the draft instrument, not merely in so far as they themselves were concerned, but even as regarded the others ; they were not prepared to agree to this draft instrument becoming a general law open to any country which was willing to accept it. On this point, M. Politis's views harmonised with those just expressed by M. Paul-Boncour ; he observed that President Roosevelt's message proposed a fourth measure, and M. Paul-Boncour had pointed out a few moments ago that this measure summed up the majority of the cases enumerated in the Act which the Commission was discussing. M. Politis would further remind the Commission that, in his speech on May 22nd, Mr. Norman Davis, in commenting on this fourth measure, had said that it contained the elements of a definition, and that some day it might perhaps be possible to arrive at a clear and explicit definition of aggression. He had added that the clearest and most accurate definition of an aggressor was a State the armed forces of which were found in foreign territory in violation of treaties.

It was for the General Commission, which had applauded Mr. Norman Davis's speech, which had enthusiastically supported President Roosevelt's message, to decide whether it was prepared to prove its consistency by accepting the conclusions which the Committee had drawn from these data and embodied in the Act under consideration, or whether it wished to contradict itself by refusing to accept that instrument.

The PRESIDENT summed up the position in which the Commission found itself as the result of the two days' discussion on the question of aggression.

It was quite clear that two very distinct lines of thought had run through the discussion. There were those who did not desire to lay down any definition of a rigid character and those who wished to accept something on the lines of the report presented by the Vice-President. The President thought, further, that he had noticed in M. de Madariaga's speech something more in the nature of a centre position, and there were one or two suggestions made by the Spanish delegate which might be very carefully considered.

It had been suggested that the Commission should try to close the discussion, but the President was afraid that that was quite impossible, and he would point out that the invitation extended by the Chairman of the Committee on Security Questions towards the close of his speech should be acted upon. He suggested accordingly that Mr. Eden, who had taken a very definite position on one side, M. Dovgalevsky, who had taken a definite position on the other and who had been responsible for the first motion introduced seeking to provide a definition of aggression, and perhaps, M. de Madariaga, might consult with M. Politis ; the President could not help thinking that if that were done it might be possible, without destroying the work of the Committee, to get something through on the lines of its report, but not quite so rigid as the present wording. At any rate, the President would like to see that suggestion tried before the question of aggression was discussed a second time, as he hoped it would be not more than a few days hence.

If that were agreed, the question would arise what business should be taken at the next meeting. The part of the report at present under discussion contained a third annex which set out provisions of an optional character. There had been no criticism of this part of the report, and the President proposed that the Commission should take it as the first business for its next meeting and, in view of its optional character, dispose of it speedily. The Commission might then take Part III of the report dealing with the very important question of a European Security Pact. [1]

The President strongly hoped that the Commission would follow the plan he had suggested, as it would enable the Vice-President to have the conversations in view and, if possible, to bring forward some arrangement on which general agreement might be obtained. That procedure would, he believed, expedite the Commission's work.

M. DOVGALEVSKY (Union of Soviet Socialist Republics) observed that the President had just proposed that a further effort be made to reconcile the two conflicting trends of thought revealed at the meetings of the Committee and General Commission respectively. To be frank, M. Dovgalevsky was not optimistic as to the possibility of reaching a satisfactory result. Nevertheless, he did not wish it to be said that they had shrunk from a last attempt. It was for that reason that he would not oppose the President's proposal. He asked, however, that the General Commission should allow a period of three or four days for this attempt at reconciliation, in order that the question might immediately come up again before the Commission, which could then proceed to take a vote.

[1] Document Conf.D./C.G.108(a).

Mr. EDEN (United Kingdom) felt he need hardly say that he gladly agreed to the President's suggestion that the delegates mentioned should do their best, under the skilful chairmanship of the Vice-President, to find some method of overcoming the difficulty in which the General Commission clearly found itself. The United Kingdom delegation would be happy to do all it could to that end. He would have thought that the correct place for the proposal as to the definition of the aggressor was its present position (end of Part I) in the draft Convention. It would not, he considered, be right to take individual items from the draft Convention and give them an earlier second reading. The Commission should complete the first reading of the whole draft Convention and then have the second reading as originally arranged. He would regret to see any part of the draft given preferential treatment, since, if that were done, each delegation would be apt to have its own preferences.

M. NADOLNY (Germany) was in complete agreement with Mr. Eden. He thought that the latter's remarks might give satisfaction to M. Dovgalevsky; it would thus be possible to discuss and settle this question before the second reading.

M. DOVGALEVSKY (Union of Soviet Socialist Republics) said that when he had originally put forward his proposal, he had not thought it necessary to state the arguments in its support ; now, however, he desired to do so.
The Soviet proposal relative to the definition of the aggressor had been laid before the Conference at the beginning of February, as a motion entirely independent of the draft Convention which the Conference was at present discussing. That was why the procedure applied to the definition of the aggressor had been different from that adopted in the case of the United Kingdom draft, and M. Dovgalevsky was asking that it be continued. He therefore maintained his proposal that three or four days be allotted for the negotiations. If M. Nadolny wished to have this period somewhat extended—to a week, for example—M. Dovgalevsky would not object, but he asked the General Commission to name a period, on the expiry of which the draft Act on the definition of the aggressor would again come before the Commission for general discussion.

The PRESIDENT did not think it possible to discuss the matter any further at the moment. More than one speaker had said that the Commission could not begin to give preferential treatment. He would, however, suggest a means of meeting M. Dovgalevsky. It was that there should be fewer and shorter speeches on the second part of the Convention —i.e., Parts IV and V—upon which the Commission would soon be starting. These two parts had already been through the Drafting Committee and the Bureau, and should not therefore require very much time. Part III could not be completed until it was known what the remainder of the Convention would be. That meant that, in a very few days, the Commission would begin the second reading of Part I. There were at present three articles in Part I to which there were no amendments, and the fourth article would depend upon the results of the consultations in question. It would therefore be far better if M. Dovgalevsky would accept the position suggested by the President, who could assure the Soviet delegate that everything would be done to finish Parts IV and V as soon as possible, after which the Commission would begin the second reading of Part I, when votes would have to be taken on all questions on which amendments had been submitted.

Count RACZYŃSKI (Poland) apologised for making suggestions after the President had done so. He nevertheless considered that, after the brilliant speeches to which they had listened, the members of the Commission would have little doubt that the question under discussion was something in the nature of a preliminary question and that it would be necessary for them to face their responsibilities and decide for or against. After the speeches to which they had listened, he considered that such a discussion would be essential and extremely valuable before the debate on Part I of the United Kingdom draft. There was also a technical reason : the Soviet proposal had been submitted as long ago as February ; it had therefore preceded the United Kingdom plan. In considering that the discussion should take place, Count Raczyński was, however, actuated rather by reasons of principle than by any formal reasons.

Mr. EDEN (United Kingdom) pointed out that the Commission was working on a basis which had been generally approved by itself and that basis was the draft Convention. The Commission was discussing the subject because of the desire, with which, naturally, he did not in any way quarrel, of the Security Committee to place the definition of the aggressor in a special position in the draft Convention. He would have thought that the normal place for further discussion was in the proposed place in the draft Convention. He would regret any departure from the basis which the General Commission had accepted, since it might lead to confusion later.

The PRESIDENT noted that Mr. Eden had supported the statement which he, the President, had put forward in the interests of the work in hand, and, in view of the explanations that had been given, he hoped M. Dovgalevsky and his supporter, Count Raczyński, would not press their suggestion to a division. It would create a rather unfavourable impression if the Commission could not agree upon a little matter of procedure in the way which the President had suggested, a way which he hoped might lead to a peaceful settlement of the differences between the two parties, which had been revealed in the discussion.

M. DOVGALEVSKY (Union of Soviet Socialist Republics) acceded to the President's request, but nevertheless reserved his right to raise again the question of the immediate examination of the proposal regarding the definition of the aggressor in the course of the first reading of the United Kingdom plan if the conversations were unduly protracted.

The PRESIDENT said that if M. Dovgalevsky did not hold out too hard when the Vice-President was carrying on his negotiations, it would probably be possible to get all the sooner a settlement of the question satisfactory to the Soviet delegation. He thought, therefore, that, on that understanding, the Commission might adjourn.

----

[1] TRADUCTION. — TRANSLATION.

No. 3391. — CONVENTION [2] FOR THE DEFINITION OF AGGRESSION. SIGNED AT LONDON, JULY 3RD, 1933.

French official text communicated by the Roumanian Envoy Extraordinary and Minister Plenipotentiary accredited to the League of Nations, by the Minister for Foreign Affairs of Turkey, and by the Permanent Delegate of Finland accredited to the League of Nations. The registration of this Convention took place March 29th, 1934.

HIS MAJESTY THE KING OF ROUMANIA, THE PRESIDENT OF THE ESTONIAN REPUBLIC, THE PRESIDENT OF THE LATVIAN REPUBLIC, THE PRESIDENT OF THE POLISH REPUBLIC, THE PRESIDENT OF THE TURKISH REPUBLIC, THE CENTRAL EXECUTIVE COMMITTEE OF THE UNION OF SOVIET SOCIALIST REPUBLICS, HIS IMPERIAL MAJESTY THE SHAH OF PERSIA, AND HIS MAJESTY THE KING OF AFGHANISTAN;

Being desirous of consolidating the peaceful relations existing between their countries;

Mindful of the fact that the Briand-Kellogg Pact, of which they are signatories, prohibits all aggression;

Deeming it necessary, in the interests of the general security, to define aggression as specifically as possible, in order to obviate any pretext whereby it might be justified;

And noting that all States have an equal right to independence, security, the defence of their territories, and the free development of their institutions;

And desirous, in the interest of the general peace, to ensure to all peoples the inviolability of the territory of their countries;

And judging it expedient, in the interest of the general peace, to bring into force, as between their countries, precise rules defining aggression, until such time as those rules shall become universal;

---

[1] Traduit par le Secrétariat de la Société des Nations, à titre d'information.

[1] Translated by the Secretariat of the League of Nations, for information.

[2] *Deposit of ratifications in Moscow:*

ROUMANIA	October 16th, 1933.
POLAND	October 16th, 1933.
UNION OF SOVIET SOCIALIST REPUBLICS	October 16th, 1933.
AFGHANISTAN	October 20th, 1933.
PERSIA	November 16th, 1933
LATVIA	December 4th, 1933.
ESTONIA	December 4th, 1933.
TURKEY	March 23rd, 1934.

Accession:

FINLAND	January 31st, 1934.

Have decided, with the aforesaid objects, to conclude the present Convention, and have duly authorised for the purpose :

HIS MAJESTY THE KING OF ROUMANIA :

M. Nicholas TITULESCU, Minister for Foreign Affairs ;

THE PRESIDENT OF THE ESTONIAN REPUBLIC :

Dr. Oskar KALLAS, Envoy Extraordinary and Minister Plenipotentiary in London ;

THE PRESIDENT OF THE LATVIAN REPUBLIC :

M. Waldemaras SALNAIS, Minister for Foreign Affairs ;

THE PRESIDENT OF THE POLISH REPUBLIC :

M. Edouard RACZYNSKI, Permanent Delegate to the League of Nations, Envoy Extraordinary and Minister Plenipotentiary ;

THE PRESIDENT OF THE TURKISH REPUBLIC :

Tevfik RÜŞTÜ Bey, Minister for Foreign Affairs ;

THE CENTRAL EXECUTIVE COMMITTEE OF THE UNION OF SOVIET SOCIALIST REPUBLICS:

M. Maxime LITVINOFF, People's Commissary for Foreign Affairs ;

HIS IMPERIAL MAJESTY THE SHAH OF PERSIA :

Fatollah Khan NOURY ESFANDIARY, Chargé d'Affaires in London ;

HIS MAJESTY THE KING OF AFGHANISTAN :

Ali MOHAMMED Khan, Minister of Education;

Who have agreed on the following provisions :

Article I.

Each of the High Contracting Parties undertakes to accept in its relations with each of the other Parties, from the date of the entry into force of the present Convention, the definition of aggression as explained in the report dated May 24th, 1933, of the Committee on Security Questions (Politis report) to the Conference for the Reduction and Limitation of Armaments, which report was made in consequence of the proposal of the Soviet delegation.

Article II.

Accordingly, the aggressor in an international conflict shall, subject to the agreements in force between the parties to the dispute, be considered to be that State which is the first to commit any of the following actions :

(1) Declaration of war upon another State ;

(2) Invasion by its armed forces, with or without a declaration of war, of the territory of another State ;

(3) Attack by its land, naval or air forces, with or without a declaration of war, on the territory, vessels or aircraft of another State ;

(4) Naval blockade of the coasts or ports of another State ;

(5) Provision of support to armed bands formed in its territory which have invaded the territory of another State, or refusal, notwithstanding the request of the invaded State, to take, in its own territory, all the measures in its power to deprive those bands of all assistance or protection.

Article III.

No political, military, economic or other considerations may serve as an excuse or justification for the aggression referred to in Article II. (For examples, see Annex.)

Article IV.

The present Convention shall be ratified by each of the High Contracting Parties in accordance with its laws.

The instruments of ratification shall be deposited by each of the High Contracting Parties with the Government of the Union of Soviet Socialist Republics.

As soon as the instruments of ratification have been deposited by two of the High Contracting Parties, the present Convention shall come into force as between those two Parties. The Convention shall come into force as regards each of the other High Contracting Parties when it deposits its instruments of ratification.

Each deposit of instruments of ratification shall immediately be notified by the Government of the Union of Soviet Socialist Republics to all the signatories of the present Convention.

Article V.

The present Convention has been signed in eight copies, of which each of the High Contracting Parties has received one.

In faith whereof the above-named Plenipotentiaries have signed the present Convention and have thereto affixed their seals.

Done in London, July 3rd, 1933.

(L. S.)	(Signed)	N. TITULESCU.
(L. S.)	(Signed)	O. KALLAS.
(L. S.)	(Signed)	Waldemaras SALNAIS.
(L. S.)	(Signed)	E. RACZYNSKI.
(L. S.)	(Signed)	Tevfik RÜŞTÜ.
(L. S.)	(Signed)	Maxime LITVINOFF.
(L. S.)	(Signed)	Ali MOHAMMED Khan.
(L. S.)	(Signed)	F. NOURY ESFANDIARY.

ANNEX

TO ARTICLE III OF THE CONVENTION RELATING TO THE DEFINITION OF AGGRESSION.

The High Contracting Parties signatories of the Convention relating to the definition o aggression,

Desiring, subject to the express reservation that the absolute validity of the rule laid down in Article III of that Convention shall be in no way restricted, to furnish certain indications fo determining the aggressor,

Declare that no act of aggression within the meaning of Article II of that Convention can be justified on either of the following grounds, among others :

A. *The internal condition of a State :*

E.g., its political, economic or social structure ; alleged defects in its administration disturbances due to strikes, revolutions, counter-revolutions, or civil war.

B. *The international conduct of a State :*

E.g., the violation or threatened violation of the material or moral rights or interests of a foreign State or its nationals ; the rupture of diplomatic or economic relations ; economic o financial boycotts ; disputes relating to economic, financial or other obligations towards foreign States ; frontier incidents not forming any of the cases of aggression specified in Article II.

The High Contracting Parties further agree to recognise that the present Convention can never legitimate any violations of international law that may be implied in the circumstance comprised in the above list.

(L. S.)	*(Signed)*	N. TITULESCU.
(L. S.)	*(Signed)*	O. KALLAS.
(L. S.)	*(Signed)*	Waldemaras SALNAIS.
(L. S.)	*(Signed)*	E. RACZYNSKI.
(L. S.)	*(Signed)*	Tevfik RÜŞTÜ.
(L. S.)	*(Signed)*	Maxime LITVINOFF.
(L. S.)	*(Signed)*	Ali MOHAMMED Khan.
(L. S.)	*(Signed)*	F. NOURY ESFANDIARY.

PROTOCOL OF SIGNATURE.

It is hereby agreed between the High Contracting Parties that should one or more of the other States immediately adjacent to the Union of Soviet Socialist Republics accede in the future to the present Convention, the said accession shall confer on the State or States in question the same rights and shall impose on them the same obligations as those conferred and imposed on the ordinary signatories.

Done at London on July 3rd, 1933.   *(Signed)*   Maxime LITVINOFF.

S. SALNAIS.

N. TITULESCO.

Ali MOHAMMAD.

F. NOURY ESFANDIARY.

O. KALLAS.

E. RACZYNSKI.

T. RÜŞTÜ.

[1] TRADUCTION. — TRANSLATION.

No. 3414. — CONVENTION [2] FOR THE DEFINITION OF AGGRESSION BETWEEN ROUMANIA, THE UNION OF SOVIET SOCIALIST REPUBLICS, CZECHOSLOVAKIA, TURKEY AND YUGOSLAVIA. SIGNED AT LONDON, JULY 4TH, 1933.

French official text communicated by the President of the Permanent Council of the Little Entente and by the Turkish Minister for Foreign Affairs. The registration of this Convention took place April 26th, 1934.

THE PRESIDENT OF THE REPUBLIC OF CZECHOSLOVAKIA, HIS MAJESTY THE KING OF ROUMANIA, THE PRESIDENT OF THE REPUBLIC OF TURKEY, THE CENTRAL EXECUTIVE COMMITTEE OF THE UNION OF SOVIET SOCIALIST REPUBLICS and HIS MAJESTY THE KING OF YUGOSLAVIA;

Being desirous of consolidating the peaceful relations existing between their countries ;

Mindful of the fact that the Briand-Kellogg Pact, of which they are signatories, prohibits all aggression ;

Deeming it necessary, in the interest of the general security, to define aggression as specifically as possible in order to obviate any pretext whereby it might be justified ;

Noting that all States have an equal right to independence, security, the defence of their territories and the free development of their institutions ;

Desirous, in the interest of the general peace, to ensure to all peoples the inviolability of the territory of their countries ;

Judging it expedient, in the interest of the general peace, to bring into force, as between their countries, precise rules defining aggression, until such time as those rules shall become universal ;

Have decided, with these objects, to conclude the present Convention and have duly authorised for the purpose :

THE PRESIDENT OF THE REPUBLIC OF CZECHOSLOVAKIA :

     M. Jan Garrigue MASARYK, Envoy Extraordinary and Minister Plenipotentiary in London ;

HIS MAJESTY THE KING OF ROUMANIA :

     M. Nicolas TITULESCU, Minister for Foreign Affairs ;

---

[1] Traduit par le Secrétariat de la Société des Nations, à titre d'information.

[1] Translated by the Secretariat of the League of Nations, for information.

[2] *Ratifications deposited in Moscow :*

ROUMANIA	
UNION OF SOVIET SOCIALIST REPUBLICS	February 17th, 1934.
CZECHOSLOVAKIA	
YUGOSLAVIA	
TURKEY	March 23rd, 1934.

Came into force February 17th, 1934..

THE PRESIDENT OF THE REPUBLIC OF TURKEY :

Mehmet MUNIR Bey, Ambassador Extraordinary and Plenipotentiary in London ;

THE CENTRAL EXECUTIVE COMMITTEE OF THE UNION OF SOVIET SOCIALIST REPUBLICS :

M. Maxime LITVINOFF, People's Commissary for Foreign Affairs ;

HIS MAJESTY THE KING OF YUGOSLAVIA :

Dr. Georges DIOURITCH, Envoy Extraordinary and Minister Plenipotentiary in London;

Who have agreed upon the following provisions :

Article I.

Each of the High Contracting Parties undertakes to accept in its relations with each of the other Parties, from the date of the entry into force of the present Convention, the definition of aggression as explained in the Report, dated May 24th, 1933, of the Committee on Security Questions (Politis Report) to the Conference for the Reduction and Limitation of Armaments, which Report was made in consequence of the Soviet delegation's proposal.

Article II.

Accordingly, the aggressor in an international conflict shall, subject to the agreements in force between the Parties to the dispute, be considered to be that State which is the first to commit any of the following actions :

1. Declaration of war upon another State ;

2. Invasion by its armed forces, with or without a declaration of war, of the territory of another State ;

3. Attack by its land, naval or air forces, with or without a declaration of war, on the territory, vessels or aircraft of another State ;

4. Naval blockade of the coasts or ports of another State ;

5. Provision of support to armed bands formed in its territory which have invaded the territory of another State, or refusal, notwithstanding the request of the invaded State, to take, in its own territory, all the measures in its power to deprive those bands of all assistance or protection.

Article III.

No political, military, economic or other consideration may serve as an excuse or justification or the aggression referred to in Article II. (For examples, see Annex.)

Article IV.

The present Convention is open for the accession of all other nations. Accession shall confer he same rights and impose the same obligations as initial signature. Such accession shall be otified to the Government of the Union of Soviet Socialist Republics, which shall forthwith inform he other signatories.

Article V.

The present Convention shall be ratified by each of the High Contracting Parties in conformity with its laws.

The instruments of ratification shall be deposited by each of the High Contracting Parties with the Government of the Union of Soviet Socialist Republics.

As soon as the instruments of ratification have been deposited by two of the High Contracting Parties, the present Convention shall come into force as between those two Parties. It shall come into force as regards all the other High Contracting Parties according as the latter deposit in their turn their instruments of ratification.

Each deposit of instruments of ratification shall immediately be notified by the Government of the Union of Soviet Socialist Republics to all the signatories of the present Convention.

Article VI.

The present Convention has been signed in five copies, of which each of the High Contracting Parties has received one.

In faith whereof the above-mentioned Plenipotentiaries have signed the present Convention and have thereto affixed their seals.

Done in London, July 4th, 1933.

(L. S.) Jan MASARYK.
(L. S.) N. TITULESCU.
(L. S.) Mehmet MÜNIR.
(L. S.) Maxime LITVINOFF.
(L. S.) G. DIOURITCH.

ANNEX

TO ARTICLE III OF THE CONVENTION RELATING TO THE DEFINITION OF AGGRESSION.

The High Contracting Parties signatories of the Convention relating to the definition of aggression,

Desiring, subject to the express reservation that the absolute validity of the rule laid down in Article III of that Convention shall be in no way restricted, to furnish certain indications for determining the aggressor,

Declare that no act of aggression within the meaning of Article II of that Convention can be justified on either of the following grounds, among others :

A. *The internal condition of a State,*

for example :

its political, economic or social structure ; alleged defects in its administration ; disturbances due to strikes, revolutions, counter-revolutions or civil war.

B. *The international conduct of a State,*

for example :

the violation or threatened violation of the material or moral rights or interests of a foreign State or its nationals ; the rupture of diplomatic or economic relations ; economic or financial boycotts ; disputes relating to economic, financial or other obligations towards foreign States ; frontier incidents not forming any of the cases of aggression specified in Article II.

The High Contracting Parties further agree to recognise that the present Convention can never legitimate any violations of international law that may be implied in the circumstances comprised in the above list.

(L. S.) Jan MASARYK.

(L. S.) N. TITULESCU.

(L. S.) Mehmet MÜNIR.

(L. S.) Maxime LITVINOFF.

(L. S.) G. DIOURITCH.

[1] TRADUCTION. — TRANSLATION.

No. 3405. — CONVENTION [2] BETWEEN LITHUANIA AND THE UNION OF SOVIET SOCIALIST REPUBLICS FOR THE DEFINITION OF AGGRESSION. SIGNED AT LONDON, JULY 5TH, 1933.

French official text communicated by the Lithuanian Minister for Foreign Affairs. The registration of this Convention took place April 16th, 1934.

THE PRESIDENT OF THE REPUBLIC OF LITHUANIA and THE CENTRAL EXECUTIVE COMMITTEE OF THE UNION OF SOVIET SOCIALIST REPUBLICS;

Being desirous of consolidating the peaceful relations existing between their countries ;

Mindful of the fact that the Briand-Kellogg Pact [3], of which they are signatories, and likewise the Pact [4] of Non-Aggression concluded between them at Moscow on September 28th, 1926, prohibit all aggression ;

Deeming it necessary, in the interest of the general security, to define aggression as specifically as possible, in order to obviate any pretext whereby it might be justified ;

And noting that all States have an equal right to independence, security, the defence of their territories and the free development of their institutions ;

And desirous, in the interest of the general peace, to ensure to all peoples the inviolability of the territory of their countries ;

And judging it expedient, in the interest of the general peace, to bring into force as between their countries precise rules defining aggression, until such time as those rules shall become universal ;

Have decided, with the aforesaid objects, to conclude the present Convention and have duly authorised for that purpose :

THE PRESIDENT OF THE REPUBLIC OF LITHUANIA :

     M. Vaclovas SIDZIKAUSKAS, Envoy Extraordinary and Minister Plenipotentiary in London ;

THE CENTRAL EXECUTIVE COMMITTEE OF THE UNION OF SOVIET SOCIALIST REPUBLICS :

     M. Maxime LITVINOFF, People's Commissary for Foreign Affairs;

Who have agreed upon the following provisions :

Article 1.

Each of the High Contracting Parties undertakes to accept in its relations with the other Party, from the date of the entry into force of the present Convention, the definition of aggression framed

---

[1] Traduit par le Secrétariat de la Société des Nations, à titre d'information.

[1] Translated by the Secretariat of the League of Nations, for information.

[2] The exchange of ratifications took place at Moscow, December 14th, 1933.

[3] Vol. XCIV, page 57; and Vol. CXXXIV, page 411, of this Series.

[4] Volume LX, page 145, of this Series.

by the Committee on Security Questions of the Conference for the Reduction and Limitation of Armaments, following on the Soviet delegation's proposal.

Article 2.

Accordingly, the aggressor in an international conflict shall, subject to the agreements in force between the parties to the dispute, be considered to be that State which is the first to commit any of the following actions :

(1) Declaration of war upon another State ;

(2) Invasion by its armed forces, with or without a declaration of war, of the territory of another State ;

(3) Attack by its land, naval or air forces, with or without a declaration of war, on the territory, vessels or aircraft of another State ;

(4) Naval blockade of the coasts or ports of another State ;

(5) Provision of support to armed bands formed in its territory which have invaded the territory of another State, or refusal, notwithstanding the request of the invaded State, to take in its own territory all the measures in its power to deprive those bands of all assistance or protection.

Article 3.

No political, military, economic or other considerations may serve as an excuse or justification for the aggression referred to in Article 2 (for examples, see Annex).

Article 4.

The present Convention shall be ratified by the High Contracting Parties in conformity with their national laws.

It shall come into force immediately after the exchange of the instruments of ratification, which shall take place at Moscow.

In faith whereof the above-mentioned Plenipotentiaries have signed the present Convention and have thereto affixed their seals.

Done in London in two copies, in French, July 5th, one thousand nine hundred and thirty-three.

(s) Vaclovas SIDZIKAUSKAS.

(s) Maxime LITVINOFF.

ANNEX

TO ARTICLE 3 OF THE CONVENTION RELATING TO THE DEFINITION OF AGGRESSION.

The High Contracting Parties signatories of the Convention relating to the definition of aggression,

Desiring, subject to the express reservation that the absolute validity of the rule laid down in Article 3 of that Convention shall be in no way restricted, to furnish certain indications for determining the aggressor,

Declare that no act of aggression within the meaning of Article 2 of that Convention can be justified on either of the following grounds, among others :

A. *The internal condition of a State :*

E.g., its political, economic or social structure ; alleged defects in its administration ; disturbances due to strikes, revolutions, counter-revolutions or civil war.

B. *The international conduct of a State :*

E.g., the violation or threatened violation of the material or moral rights or interests of a foreign State or its nationals ; the rupture of diplomatic or economic relations ; economic or financial boycotts ; disputes relating to economic, financial or other obligations towards foreign States ; frontier incidents not forming any of the cases of aggression specified in Article 2.

The High Contracting Parties further agree to recognise that the present Convention can never legitimate any violations of international law that may be implied in the circumstances comprised in the above list.

(s) V. SIDZIKAUSKAS.
(s) Maxime LITVINOFF.

[1] TRADUCTION. — TRANSLATION.

No. 4402. — TREATY[2] OF NON-AGGRESSION BETWEEN THE KINGDOM OF AFGHANISTAN, THE KINGDOM OF IRAQ, THE EMPIRE OF IRAN AND THE REPUBLIC OF TURKEY. SIGNED AT TEHERAN, JULY 8TH, 1937.

French official text communicated by the Minister for Foreign Affairs of Iran. The registration of this Treaty took place July 19th, 1938.

PREAMBLE.

HIS IMPERIAL MAJESTY THE SHAHINSHAH OF IRAN,
HIS MAJESTY THE KING OF AFGHANISTAN,
HIS MAJESTY THE KING OF IRAQ,
THE PRESIDENT OF THE REPUBLIC OF TURKEY ;
Being desirous of contributing by every means in their power to the maintenance of friendly and harmonious relations between them ;
Actuated by the common purpose of ensuring peace and security in the Near East by means of additional guarantees within the framework of the Covenant of the League of Nations, and of thus contributing to general peace ; and
Deeply conscious of their obligations under the Treaty[3] for Renunciation of War, signed at Paris on August 27th, 1928, and of the other treaties to which they are parties, all of which are in harmony with the Covenant of the League of Nations and the Treaty for Renunciation of War ;
Have decided to conclude the present Treaty and have for that purpose appointed :

HIS IMPERIAL MAJESTY THE SHAHINSHAH OF IRAN :

His Excellency Monsieur Enayatollah SAMIY, Minister for Foreign Affairs of Iran ;

HIS MAJESTY THE KING OF AFGHANISTAN :

His Excellency Monsieur FAIZ MOHAMMAD Khan, Minister for Foreign Affairs of Afghanistan ;

HIS MAJESTY THE KING OF IRAQ :

His Excellency Dr. NADJI-AL-ASIL, Minister for Foreign Affairs of Iraq ;

THE PRESIDENT OF THE REPUBLIC OF TURKEY :

His Excellency Dr. Tevfik RUSTU ARAS, Minister for Foreign Affairs of Turkey ;

---

[1] Traduit par le Secrétariat de la Société des Nations, à titre d'information.   [1] Translated by the Secretariat of the League of Nations, for information.

[2] The ratifications were deposited at Teheran, June 25th, 1938.

[3] Vol. XCIV, page 57 ; Vol. CXXXIV, page 411 ; Vol. CLII, page 298 ; and Vol. CLX, page 354, of this Series.

Who, having exchanged their full powers, found in good and due form, have agreed upon the following provisions :

Article 1.

The High Contracting Parties undertake to pursue a policy of complete abstention from any interference in each other's internal affairs.

Article 2.

The High Contracting Parties expressly undertake to respect the inviolability of their common frontiers.

Article 3.

The High Contracting Parties agree to consult together in all international disputes affecting their common interests.

Article 4.

Each of the High Contracting Parties undertakes in no event to resort, whether singly or jointly with one or more third Powers, to any act of aggression directed against any other of the Contracting Parties.

The following shall be deemed to be acts of aggression :

    1. Declaration of war ;

    2. Invasion by the armed forces of one State, with or without a declaration of war, of the territory of another State ;

    3. An attack by the land, naval or air forces of one State, with or without a declaration of war, on the territory, vessels or aircraft of another State ;

    4. Directly or indirectly aiding or assisting an aggressor.

The following shall not constitute acts of aggression :

    1. The exercise of the right of legitimate self-defence, that is to say, resistance to an act of aggression as defined above ;

    2. Action under Article 16 of the Covenant of the League of Nations ;

    3. Action in pursuance of a decision of the Assembly or Council of the League of Nations, or under Article 15, paragraph 7, of the Covenant of the League of Nations, provided always that in the latter case such action is directed against the State which was the first to attack ;

    4. Action to assist a State subjected to attack, invasion or recourse to war by another of the High Contracting Parties, in violation of the Treaty for Renunciation of War signed in Paris on August 27th, 1928.

Article 5.

Should one of the High Contracting Parties consider that a breach of Article 4 of the present Treaty has been or is about to be committed, he shall at once bring the matter before the Council of the League of Nations.

The foregoing provision shall not affect the right of such High Contracting Party to take any steps which, in the circumstances, he may deem necessary.

Article 6.

Should one of the High Contracting Parties commit an aggression against a third Power, any other High Contracting Party may denounce the present Treaty, without notice, as towards the aggressor.

Article 7.

Each of the High Contracting Parties undertakes to prevent, within his respective frontiers, the formation or activities of armed bands, associations or organisations to subvert the established institutions, or disturb the order or security of any part, whether situated on the frontier or elsewhere, of the territory of another Party, or to change the constitutional system of such other Party.

Article 8.

The High Contracting Parties, having already recognised, in the General Treaty for Renunciation of War of August 27th, 1928, that the settlement or solution of all disputes or conflicts, whatever their nature or origin, which may arise among them, shall never be sought by other than pacific means, reaffirm that principle and undertake to rely upon such modes of procedure as have been or shall be established between the High Contracting Parties in that respect.

Article 9.

No Articles of the present Treaty shall be considered as in any way diminishing the obligations assumed by each of the High Contracting Parties under the Covenant of the League of Nations.

Article 10.

The present Treaty, drawn up in the French language and signed in quadruplicate, one copy having, as they severally recognise, been delivered to each of the High Contracting Parties, is concluded for a period of five years.

On the expiry of that period, and failing its denunciation, with six months' notice, by one of the High Contracting Parties, the Treaty shall be deemed to be renewed for successive periods of five years, until its denunciation with six months' notice by one or more of the High Contracting Parties. On its denunciation as towards one of the Parties, the Treaty shall nevertheless remain in force as between the others.

The present Treaty shall be ratified by each of the High Contracting Parties in accordance with its Constitution, and registered at the League of Nations by the Secretary-General, who shall be requested to bring it to the knowledge of the other Members of the League.

The instruments of ratification shall be deposited by each of the High Contracting Parties with the Iranian Government.

On the deposit of instruments of ratification by two of the High Contracting Parties, the present Treaty shall at once come into force as between those two Parties. It shall come into force as regards the third and fourth Parties respectively on the deposit of their instruments of ratification.

On the deposit of each instrument of ratification, the Government of Iran shall immediately notify all the signatories of the present Treaty.

Done at the Palace of Saad-Abad (Teheran), on the eighth day of July, one thousand nine hundred and thirty-seven.

Enayatollah SAMIY, *Minister for Foreign Affairs* *of Iran.*	FAIZ MOHAMMAD Khan, *Minister for Foreign Affairs* *of Afghanistan.*
Dr. NADJI-AL-ASIL, *Minister for Foreign Affairs* *of Iraq.*	Dr. Tevfik RUSTU ARAS, *Minister for Foreign Affairs* *of Turkey.*

DOCUMENT 16

| 107th Session of the Council | | |
| Second Meeting (14/XII/1939) | *League of Nations — Official Journal* | NOVEMBER-DECEMBER 1939 |

4178. **Appeal by the Finnish Government.**

The PRESIDENT. — The Assembly has to-day adopted, in virtue of Article 15 of the Covenant, its report on the appeal by the Finnish Government. At the end of this report, there are two resolutions, the second containing a recommendation by the Assembly to the Council. I should like to remind you of the text of this second resolution:

" Whereas, notwithstanding an invitation extended to it on two occasions, the Union of Soviet Socialist Republics has refused to be present at the examination of its dispute with Finland before the Council and the Assembly;

" And whereas, by thus refusing to recognise the duty of the Council and the Assembly as regards the execution of Article 15 of the Covenant, it has failed to observe one of the League's most essential covenants for the safeguarding of peace and the security of nations;

" And whereas it has vainly attempted to justify its refusal on the ground of the relations which it has established with an alleged Government which is neither *de jure* nor *de facto* the Government recognised by the people of Finland in accordance with the free working of their institutions;

" And whereas the Union of Soviet Socialist Republics has not merely violated a covenant of the League, but has by its own action placed itself outside the Covenant;

" And whereas the Council is competent under Article 16 of the Covenant to consider what consequences should follow from this situation:

" Recommends the Council to pronounce upon the question."

As, in this second resolution, the Assembly has stated that the Union of Soviet Socialist Republics has not merely violated a covenant of the League but has by its own action placed itself outside the Covenant, and as it has recommended the Council to pronounce upon the question, I would remind you of the provisions of Article 16, paragraph 4:

" Any Member of the League which has violated any covenant of the League may be declared to be no longer a Member of the League by vote of the Council concurred in by the representatives of all the other Members of the League represented thereon."

505

Article 16, paragraph 4, of the Covenant, which I have just read to you, provides for a vote by the Members of the League represented on the Council. I accordingly submit for the Council's approval the following draft resolution:

" The Council,

" Having taken cognisance of the resolution adopted by the Assembly on December 14th, 1939, regarding the appeal of the Finnish Government;

" 1. Associates itself with the condemnation by the Assembly of the action of the Union of Soviet Socialist Republics against the Finnish State; and

" 2. For the reasons set forth in the resolution of the Assembly,

" In virtue of Article 16, paragraph 4, of the Covenant,

" Finds, that, by its act, the Union of Soviet Socialist Republics has placed itself outside the League of Nations. It follows that the Union of Soviet Socialist Republics is no longer a Member of the League."

I now invite you to discuss this draft resolution.

M. POLYCHRONIADIS. — Before I make a statement, there is a duty which I am in honour bound to discharge. I am particularly proud that it should have fallen to me to express the profound admiration and respectful sympathy which Greece feels for the noble Finnish people. I wish to pay a tribute to the heroic effort being made by a valiant nation struggling for liberty and independence, a nation which is distinguished both by its efforts in peaceful labour and by the degree of culture to which it has attained.

Having thus made my country's attitude quite clear, I have the honour, acting on instructions received from my Government, to state that I shall abstain from voting in regard to that part of the resolution according to which the Union of Soviet Socialist Republics has placed itself outside the League of Nations. My abstention relates, in particular, to point 2 of the resolution —that is to say, the passage extending from the words " For the reasons . . ." to the end.

M. GAVRILOVITCH. — On behalf of Yugoslavia, and acting on instructions from my Government, I beg to inform the Council that when the vote is taken I shall abstain, and more particularly with regard to point 2 of the resolution.

M. HOLSTI. — I should like to make it quite clear that in her opinion Finland cannot sit as a judge in a matter brought by her before the Council. I shall therefore abstain from voting, in order that any decision taken by the Council may retain a wholly impartial character.

M. PAUL-BONCOUR. — I think, indeed I hope, that none of our colleagues will have misunderstood the reasons for the extreme discretion that France, like the United Kingdom, has observed in the course of this debate.

It is, however, in defence of the principles which you are yourselves defending, the principles upon which our institution is founded, and in the name of which you are about to take a grave decision, that we have risen up and are now making war.

But we have been mindful of the hospitality extended to us by a State whose humanity towards our prisoners and wounded during two wars—the second of which might surely have been thought to be the last—we have not forgotten and shall never forget. We have been anxious to respect the position of States Members of the League, most of which have so far been able to preserve their neutrality in the present conflict. We, for our part, do not violate either territories or consciences.

Now, however, the Assembly, in conformity with the provisions of the Covenant, has passed on to the Council the heaviest share of responsibility for the decision that is to be taken. The Council is preparing to assume that responsibility, and France, as a Member of the Council, is about to do the same. I think it would be held strange if she did so in silence.

France is here, although she has many other preoccupations, because, whatever States might be involved, she has always answered " present " when it was necessary to defend principles of which I may fairly say that, had they been defended a little sooner and a little more firmly, we should not perhaps be having to defend them to-day, at the price of immense material sacrifices and of the personal sacrifices of the whole younger generation massed on our frontiers, by tearing an entire nation away from its peaceful labours and mobilising it to wage a war that it will continue to the end, until the causes that led to it have ceased to exist.

France is here to impose by her vote a sanction, in the most categorical and painful form, for the breach of the Covenant brought about by the violation of the territory and sovereignty of free and democratic Finland, by an associated State which we were accustomed of late years to see in the front rank of the defenders of those principles in whose name we are constrained to pass judgment upon it to-day.

But I should be failing in my duty to the great country that I have the honour to represent here if I did not say to you that, as we see it, this condemnation would not have its full meaning or its full scope if the aggression that has led to it were not shown to be closely and indisputably linked with all those previous aggressions that have made it possible.

I cannot, I could not, condemn Russia in the text of a resolution without remembering, for my own part, that another condemnation is in process of execution, and is being executed by our allies and ourselves by force of arms.

I could not have spoken of Finland, I could not have paid homage to that country, and promised it all the assistance we can give, so far as our own necessities allow, without at the same time paying homage to the other victims—Austria, Czecho-Slovakia 'and Poland—the echo of whose sufferings you have heard this morning; indeed, it would have been incomprehensible for that echo not to be heard in this discussion.

And so you see that, beyond the present aggression on which alone we have to pronounce to-day, that truth appears which lies at the very foundation of the League of Nations, which is the reason of its existence, and to which it must return—indeed, it is already doing so, as witness the speed and the plainness of our decisions in the present conflict—if it wishes that the great hope that must emerge from this new conflict shall still bear its name: collective security, indivisible collective security.

I seem to remember—not in irony, but with real grief—that it was M. Litvinoff who, here and in the Assembly, so often dwelt upon the indivisible character of collective security. He it was who most persistently propagated that conception, and who deduced its consequences in the definition of the aggressor—the clearest and completest of all the definitions that resulted from labours in which I had too large a share to forget them—which was signed in London by Russia and her neighbours.

It is in the name of that very definition of aggression, which covered everything, even, alas, the circumstances and methods of the present case; it is in order to associate myself, on behalf of my country, with this somewhat tardy awakening of the universal conscience which it is for the League of Nations to turn to account to prevent the list of victims from lengthening, that, without absolving the first and chief author of the present European upheaval, without forgetting the previous aggressions that have made this new aggression possible, I shall vote for the resolution which is submitted to the Council.

Mr. BUTLER. — We have all heard with pleasure the declaration made by M. Paul-Boncour. The League has its own traditions and we are fortunate on this occasion to be inspired by a speech from one who has known the League so long. His speech has placed in its right perspective the act of aggression on Finland which we have met here to consider. The French representative has alluded to the conflict in which his country and mine are comrades in arms, fighting in defence of the principles for which the Covenant was founded. Our responsibilities in meeting here and in the Assembly have been two-fold—first, to answer the appeal for help made by a fellow Member of the League who has been brutally attacked by another Member and, secondly, to maintain and ensure the continuance of the standards of international morality in which we believe and upon which our whole policy is founded.

These responsibilities have already been in a large measure discharged by the Assembly. But the Council has now to perform a duty which is laid upon it by the Covenant. Once the issue which we have to decide has been raised—and you will all remember the manner in which it was raised—the Council has in my view no alternative but to accept the resolution before it. Our decision seems to follow inevitably from the actions of the Soviet Government and from the resolutions of the Assembly, which have so well summarised the discussions before the Special Committee appointed to consider this matter.

The Council is not, in my view, in a position to reach any other decision without stultifying itself and compromising those principles of which it is the guardian. I should like to endorse the words which M. Paul-Boncour used about the re-awakening and the new life which we have evidenced here at this meeting of the Council. Should we fail to discharge the duty laid upon us by the Assembly, the whole world will doubt the reality of our convictions, and the structure which in the present world crisis we are striving to maintain will be dangerously shaken.

Let me now trespass upon your time by making a few general observations. The struggle in which we in the United Kingdom are now engaged has not been on the agenda of our meeting. But His Majesty's Government in the United Kingdom and the French Government had already communicated to all Members of the League through the Secretary-General a statement of the reasons for which they had been obliged to take up arms. As I said in my speech to the Assembly, this present attack which we have been considering follows directly upon previous acts of a similar nature. The movement of world opinion, the moral and material support which has been given to the Finnish cause, is due in a large measure to sympathy and admiration for the Finnish nation. But the strength of the general feeling in the world derives also from the realisation that another blow is being struck at the foundations on which the existence of all of us as independent nations is founded. It appears to us a blow not only against our independence but against those national institutions which we have so patiently evolved within our own boundaries. Wild movements have been loosed which seem to threaten the life of free peoples.

When we discussed last autumn the question of the application of the principles of the Covenant, it was unanimously agreed that recourse to war against a Member of the League, whether immediately affecting any other Member or not, was a matter of concern to the whole League and would not be considered to be a matter to which the Members are entitled to adopt an attitude of indifference. The majority of States Members then declared that they were not

507

bound to apply automatically the measures which the Covenant provides. This view has been generally accepted by the Assembly in considering the Finnish appeal. A full allowance would therefore seem to have been made for the individual views of particular States. But we have to recognise that the issues arising out of recent acts of aggression in Europe are essentially the same, even though they have not all been formally brought before this tribunal. It must not be thought that any one of them can be viewed in isolation.

Many States maintain an attitude of neutrality in the major struggle for freedom which is now being waged. We understand and respect this attitude; but the implications of the present struggle must be clear to all who are inspired by the principles of the Covenant. It is in the light of these general considerations which I have just enunciated that our own attitude at the present meeting has been decided, and necessarily so.

We have not been inspired by prejudice or by vindictive designs. We are unable to depart from the moral position we have long since taken up. In the present circumstances, heavy burdens are laid upon individual Members of the League, and it is difficult for the latter to perform all those tasks which its founders intended. Here at Geneva we are called upon to play a difficult part; but the principles of the Covenant remain and their observance is in the best interests of international society. We do not cling to them out of some old-fashioned belief or desire that the world should never be changed; we adhere to them because they form the best and only inspiration upon which an international order can be based. These principles are now being challenged, and this challenge gives us the opportunity to prove their worth. It will be our duty, in our generation, to make the principles which unite us here prevail.

Dr. WELLINGTON KOO. — In conformity with my declaration in the Assembly this morning, and in the absence of final instructions from my Government, I shall abstain from the vote to be taken on the resolution before the Council.

The PRESIDENT. — The Council will take note of the statements that have just been made and, as abstentions do not count in establishing unanimity, if there are no other observations I shall take it that the draft resolution has been adopted.

The resolution was adopted.

4179. Close of the Session.

The PRESIDENT. — The Council of the League of Nations, at a moment the gravity of which cannot be overemphasised, has assumed its responsibilities in defence of the principles of which it is the guardian.

" Such principles demand respect for corresponding rights to independence, to life and to the possibility of continuous development in the paths of civilisation; they demand, further, fidelity to compacts agreed upon and sanctioned in conformity with the principles of the law of nations.

" The indispensable presupposition, without doubt, of all peaceful intercourse between nations, and the very soul of the juridical relations in force among them, is mutual trust; the expectation and conviction that each party will respect its plighted word; the certainty that both sides are convinced that better is wisdom than weapons of war, and are ready to enter into discussion and to avoid recourse to force or to threats of force in case of delays, hindrances, changes or disputes, because all these things can be the result, not of bad will, but of changed circumstances and of genuine conflicts of interests . . . But to consider treaties on principle as ephemeral and tacitly to assume the authority of rescinding them unilaterally when they are no longer to one's advantage would be to abolish all mutual trust among States."

The words I have just quoted are taken from the Encyclical Summi Pontificatus, recently issued by His Holiness Pius XII, in which he appealed to the world conscience. I am sure that no words of mine could add anything to this solemn affirmation of the principles which must be respected if nations are to live at peace with one another, and which are in fact the very principles that are embodied in the Covenant of the League of Nations.

M. PAUL-BONCOUR. — Mr. President, I desire, in the first place, to congratulate you on the wise and deeply moving words with which you have closed so serious a discussion: your quotation adds to the loftiness of your pronouncement. I should like to thank you also for the way in which you have presided over this meeting, and in saying that I am sure I shall be voicing the wishes of all present.

Mr. BUTLER. — I should like to support the words of M. Paul-Boncour in thanking our President and to thank also the Secretary-General.

The PRESIDENT. — I am deeply moved by what the representatives of France and the United Kingdom have been good enough to say, and I should like to thank them very sincerely.

I declare closed the hundred-and-seventh session of the Council.

XV. STATEMENT MADE IN THE SPECIAL COMMITTEE ON DECEMBER 13TH, 1939, BY HIS EXCELLENCY M. NIETO CABALLERO, DELEGATE OF COLOMBIA

Finland's appeal raises a moral question, on which Colombia has no hesitation, and which requires that the Assembly declare that Finland has been the victim of unjust and unprovoked aggression on the part of the U.S.S.R.

According to the principles of the Covenant, that declaration should be followed by a demand for the withdrawal of the invading Soviet troops from Finnish territory, in order that the aggression may be brought to an end and that the dispute may be submitted to the procedures provided for in the Covenant.

Colombia is anxious that the establishment of the aggression and the designation of the aggressor should be couched in strong, clear, unambiguous terms, so that the final resolution may produce the desired effects.

To demand *a priori* the expulsion of the U.S.S.R. from the League of Nations, which would require a unanimous vote of the Council, would perhaps be a mistake, inasmuch as the U.S.S.R. would in that case be released from the obligations imposed by the Covenant and would be placed outside the scope of the Covenant by a binding decision of the Members of the League —which would make it easier for the U.S.S.R. to achieve its aims, and would afford it an opportunity of committing further crimes.

Expulsion, the fourth and last possibility contemplated in Article 16, which defines sanctions, should be looked upon as a last resort, and should not be the first measure adopted, before the procedure prescribed by the Covenant has been exhausted.

Colombia feels as profound an indignation as any other country, and would not desire to be less severe than any other Member of the League in applying the punitive clauses of the Covenant; but, at the same time, she is anxious that the immense dangers that might be involved for other countries by a hasty decision should be carefully borne in mind. The moral and legal problem is the same for all, but the geographical position is different. In the unexampled complexity of the present juncture in international affairs, Colombia will act with equal firmness and tact, leaving not the slightest room for doubting her loyal support for Finland and Finland's cause.

A.46.1939.VII.

Geneva, December 13th, 1939.

XVI. REPORT OF THE ASSEMBLY, PROVIDED FOR IN ARTICLE 15, PARAGRAPHS 4 AND 10, OF THE COVENANT, SUBMITTED BY THE SPECIAL COMMITTEE OF THE ASSEMBLY

INTRODUCTION

The first duty of the Assembly, which is seized in virtue of Article 15 of the Covenant, is to endeavour " to effect a settlement of the dispute " referred to it.

531

The Government of the U.S.S.R. having announced that it had decided not to send representatives to the Assembly, the following telegram was despatched to Moscow on December 11th after the first meeting of the Committee set up by the Assembly:

" The Committee set up by the Assembly, which is seized in virtue of Article 15 of the Covenant, addresses an urgent appeal to the Government of the U.S.S.R. and to the Finnish Government to cease hostilities and open immediate negotiations under the mediation of the Assembly with a view to restoring peace. Finland, which is present, accepts. Should be grateful if you would inform me before to-morrow (Tuesday) evening if the Government of the U.S.S.R. is prepared to accept this appeal and cease hostilities forthwith."

The Government of the U.S.S.R. replied on December 12th as follows:

" The Government of the U.S.S.R. thanks you, Monsieur le Président, for kind invitation to take part in discussion of the Finnish question. At the same time, the Government of the U.S.S.R. begs to inform you that it cannot accept this invitation for the reasons set out in the telegram of December 5th from the Commissariat for Foreign Affairs sent in reply to Monsieur Avenol's communication." [1]

In view of the absence of a delegation of the Government of the U.S.S.R. and as a result of the examination of the reasons it adduces in explanation of that absence, it is unfortunately clear that to attempt at the present time to obtain the cessation of hostilities and the restoration of normal peaceful relations between Finland and the U.S.S.R. through mediation and conciliation would be fruitless.

The Assembly has therefore the duty of publishing the report provided for in the Covenant " containing a statement of the facts of the dispute and the recommendations which are deemed just and proper in regard thereto ".

A.

To establish the circumstances of the dispute, the Assembly has had before it the documents furnished by the Finnish delegation. As the Secretary-General has been apprised of the views of the Soviet Government only through the brief telegram from M. Molotov dated December 4th, 1939, it has been thought desirable, in order to ensure the impartiality of this statement, to refer to the official documents published in the *communiqués* of the Tass Agency.

Below will be found a statement of the undisputed facts that emerge from the Finnish and Soviet documents and, in the case of disputed points, the versions given by both Governments.

The Moscow Negotiations between Finland and the U.S.S.R. (October 12th-November 13th, 1939).

1. On October 5th, the Finnish Government was invited by the Soviet Government to exchange views on political questions. Finland decided to accept the invitation and send delegates to Moscow.

2. In the circumstances, the news that the Soviet Government had invited the Finnish Government to negotiate with it made a certain impression, not only in Finland, but in many other countries.

On October 11th, just as the Finnish delegation was arriving in Moscow, President Roosevelt sent a personal message to M. Kalinin, President of the Presidium of the Supreme Soviet, expressing " the earnest hope that the Soviet Union will make no demands on Finland which are inconsistent with the maintenance and development of amicable and peaceful relations between the two countries and the independence of each ".

The Soviet Government replied on October 12th: " I think I should remind you, Mr. President, that the independence of the Finnish Republic as a State was recognised spontaneously by the Soviet Government on December 31st, 1917, and that the sovereignty of Finland is guaranteed by the Treaty of Peace between the R.S.F.S.R. and Finland signed on October 14th, 1920. The above-mentioned acts on the part of the Soviet Government determined the fundamental principles of the relations between the Soviet Union and Finland. It is in accordance with those principles that the present negotiations between the Soviet Government and the Finnish Government are being conducted. Notwithstanding the tendencious versions put about by some who evidently have not the peace of Europe at heart, the sole object of the negotiations in question is to establish closer relations between the Soviet Union and Finland and to strengthen the friendly co-operation between the two countries, in order to ensure the security of the Soviet Union and that of Finland."

3. The Finno-Soviet negotiations opened on October 12th.

The Soviet Government proposed to the Finnish Government the conclusion of a pact of mutual assistance on the same lines as those it had lately concluded with other Baltic States. Finland pointed out that the conclusion of such a pact would be inconsistent with her policy of strict neutrality.

The Soviet Government withdrew this first proposal. Making reference to the safety of the U.S.S.R., and more particularly of Leningrad, it then put forward proposals involving the cession of Finnish territories to the Soviet Union (leasing of the port of Hanko and, in exchange for other

---

[1] See VII, page 512.

territories in Soviet Karelia, cession of certain islands in the Gulf of Finland and of part of the Isthmus of Karelia, to the north of Leningrad, and cession of the western part of the Rybachi Peninsula, on the Arctic Ocean).

At the moment when negotiations were broken off (November 13th), the Finnish Government had announced that it was prepared to make various concessions to meet the wishes of the Soviet Government. Nevertheless, " having regard to the international situation of Finland, her policy of absolute neutrality, and her firm resolve to remain outside any group of great Powers and to hold aloof from any wars and conflicts between them ", the Finnish Government could not " consent to the cession of Hanko or any islands situated in the immediate proximity of the Finnish mainland as military bases to any foreign Power ".[1]

Nor had the two Governments been able to agree upon the extent of the Finnish territories which should be ceded to the U.S.S.R. in exchange for certain compensations offered by the latter in Soviet Karelia. The difference of opinion concerned the frontier-line which the Soviet Government wished to obtain in the Isthmus of Karelia, to the north of Leningrad.

The Finnish Government considers that it took due account of the desire that the Government of the U.S.S.R. might have to increase the security of Leningrad, that it accepted the proposals made to it so far as practicable possibilities allowed, and that it went as far as it could with proper regard to its own independence, security and neutrality. When, on November 3rd, it submitted its counter-proposals, it pointed out that " the concessions which Finland agrees to make to the U.S.S.R. in order to improve neighbourly relations and ensure peace represent a very heavy sacrifice for the Finnish people, as they affect an area which has been inhabited by a Finnish population since very ancient date and which, for centuries, has formed part of Finland's political territory." [2]

The point of view of the Soviet Government, as expressed in a declaration which the Tass Agency was " authorised " to make on November 11th, is that the Finns not merely showed no inclination to accept the minimum proposals of the U.S.S.R., but, on the contrary, increased their " irreconcilability ". The Tass Agency's statement adds that the Finns had increased the number of their divisions in the neighbourhood of Leningrad from two or three to seven, thus " giving proof of their intransigent spirit ".

4. On November 13th, the Finno-Soviet negotiations were broken off. The Finnish Government stated that its delegates were returning to Helsinki for fresh instructions. It also wished to discuss the question with Parliament. It was convinced that with good-will it would be possible to find a solution satisfactory to both parties. In any case, as regards its attitude to the U.S.S.R., the Finnish Government " was still anxious to bring the matter to a successful conclusion ".

The Mainila Incident: the Soviet Government demands the Withdrawal of the Finnish Troops.

5. On November 26th, the first incident occurred on the frontier in the Isthmus of Karelia.

According to the Soviet version, Finnish artillery suddenly opened fire on Soviet troops near the village of Mainila. Seven shots were fired. There were 4 killed and 9 wounded on the Soviet side. The Soviet troops, however, having received strict orders not to give way to provocation, refrained from retaliating.

According to the Finnish version, the Finnish frontier guard observed the seven gunshots mentioned, which were fired, not from the Finnish, but from the Soviet side. It may have been " an accident which occurred in the course of firing practice ".[3]

6. By a note of the same date (November 26th), the People's Commissar for Foreign Affairs informed the Finnish Minister at Moscow of the incident, and concluded in these terms:

" In bringing the foregoing to your knowledge, the Soviet Government considers it desirable to stress the fact that, during the recent negotiations with MM. Tanner and Paasikivi, it had directed their attention to the danger resulting from the concentration of large regular forces in the immediate proximity of the frontier near Leningrad. In consequence of the provocative firing on the Soviet troops from Finnish territory, the Soviet Government is obliged to declare now that the concentration of Finnish troops in the vicinity of Leningrad not only constitutes a menace to Leningrad, but is, in fact, an act hostile to the Union of Soviet Socialist Republics which has already resulted in aggression against the Soviet troops and caused casualties. The Government of the Union of Soviet Socialist Republics has no intention of exaggerating the importance of this revolting act committed by troops belonging to the Finnish Army—owing perhaps to a lack of proper guidance on the part of their superiors—but it desires that revolting acts of this nature shall not be committed in future. In consequence, the Government of the Union of Soviet Socialist Republics, while protesting energetically against what has happened, proposes that the Finnish Government should, without delay, withdraw its troops on the Karelian Isthmus from the frontier to a distance of 20 to 25 kilometres and thus preclude all possibility of a repetition of provocative acts ".[4]

7. On November 27th, the Finnish Minister, on the basis of the findings of the enquiry carried out by his Government, " rejected the protest " of the Soviet Government in connection with the Mainila incident, and stated that the alleged hostile act had not been committed by Finland.

Referring to the passage in the Soviet Government's note which alluded to the danger resulting from the concentration of regular forces in the immediate proximity of the frontier near Leningrad, the Minister pointed out that, on the Finnish side, it was principally troops belonging

[1] See IX, paper 8, page 525.
[2] See IX, paper 5, page 521.
[3] See IX, paper 11, page 526.
[4] See IX, paper 10, page 526.

533

to the frontier guard who were stationed there, and that there were no guns in that area whose range would reach beyond the frontier.

With reference to the Soviet proposal for the withdrawal of troops, the Finnish Government, although there were " no concrete grounds " for such withdrawal, was prepared to open conversations with a view to a mutual withdrawal to a certain distance from the frontier.

Lastly, in order that full light might be thrown on the Mainila incident, the Finnish Government proposed that the frontier commissioners of the two countries on the Karelian Isthmus should be instructed to carry out a joint enquiry, in conformity with the Convention of September 24th, 1928.[1]

The U.S.S.R. declares itself no longer bound by the Pact of Non-aggression.

8. The Soviet Government's reply, dated November 28th,[2] opened with these words: " The Finnish Government's reply to the note from the Government of the Union of Soviet Socialist Republics, dated November 26th, 1939, is a document which reflects the deep-rooted hostility of the Finnish Government towards the Union of Soviet Socialist Republics and is the cause of extreme tension in the relations between the two countries."

The Finnish version of the Mainila incident " can be explained only by a desire to mislead public opinion and make light of those casualties ".

The refusal to withdraw the Finnish " troops who committed this hostile act ", and the demand for the simultaneous withdrawal of the Finnish and Soviet troops in accordance with the formal principle of the equality of the parties revealed the hostile desire to expose Leningrad to danger. While the Soviet troops did not constitute a menace to Finland's vital centres, which were hundreds of kilometres away, the Finnish troops constituted a direct menace to Leningrad, a vital centre of the U.S.S.R. The withdrawal of the Soviet troops by 25 kilometres would mean posting them in the suburbs of Leningrad. The Soviet Government's proposal for the withdrawal of the Finnish troops by 20 to 25 kilometres represented a minimum, since it was not designed to create equality of situation as between the Finnish and Soviet troops, but simply to attenuate the existing disproportion. If the Finnish Government refused to accept that minimum proposal, that meant that its intention was that Leningrad should remain under a direct threat from its troops.

The concentration of a large number of Finnish regular troops near Leningrad was a hostile act against the U.S.S.R., and was incompatible with the Pact of Non-aggression concluded between the two countries.

The Soviet Government's note concluded in the following terms:

" The refusal of the Finnish Government, after the criminal gunfire directed against the Soviet troops, to withdraw its own troops to a distance of 20 to 25 kilometres shows that the Government is desirous of persisting in its hostile attitude towards the Union of Soviet Socialist Republics, that it has no intention of complying with the provisions of the Treaty of Non-aggression and that it has decided to keep Leningrad under a perpetual menace.

"The Government of the Union of Soviet Socialist Republics cannot, however, admit that one of the Parties should be allowed to violate the Treaty of Non-aggression, while the other Party respects it. In consequence, the Government of the Union of Soviet Socialist Republics is obliged to state that it considers itself, as from to-day, released from the obligations ensuing from the Treaty of Non-aggression concluded between the Union of Soviet Socialist Republics and Finland, obligations which are being systematically violated by the Finnish Government."

9. On the same day, November 28th, according to a telegram from the Tass Agency dated the 29th, a frontier incident took place between two patrols in the neighbourhood of the Isthmus of Karelia. In consequence of this incident, the Soviet Government announced that it had strengthened the protection of the frontier in that sector. The Soviet General Staff also reported two other frontier incidents on the same day.

10. On this question of frontier incidents, the responsibility for which is attributed by the Soviet *communiqués* to the Finnish troops, the Finnish Government points out that, " even during the negotiations at Moscow, the air forces of the U.S.S.R. committed several violations of the territorial integrity of Finland. Between October 10th and November 14th, some thirty such violations were recorded. Finland drew the attention of the U.S.S.R. to this fact through the diplomatic channel, but she was careful not to exaggerate its importance, so as to avoid tension and also in order to facilitate the negotiations then in progress.

With regard to the frontier incidents that took place in the last days of November, she denies the Soviet accusations, and points out that the Finnish troops and frontier guards had been withdrawn to a stated distance from the frontier.[3]

11. November 29th was marked by the following events:

(a) *Reply from the Finnish Government to the Note of November 28th, by which M. Molotov rejected the Finnish Proposal for the Mutual Withdrawal of Troops and declared that the U.S.S.R. was thenceforward released from the Obligations of the Pact of Non-aggression.*

The Finnish Government regarded the denunciation of that Treaty as unjustified. Under the 1934 Protocol, the Treaty was to remain in force without the possibility of denunciation until the end of 1945.

[1] See IX, paper 11, page 526. The exchange of notes referred to by the Finnish Government is published in the *Treaty Series* of the League of Nations, Vol. LXXXII, page 64. See below, B (3), page 537.
[2] See IX, paper 12, page 527.
[3] See IX, paper 1, page 517.

534

Article 5 of the Treaty provided that the procedure of conciliation should be applied in the case of a dispute concerning the question whether the mutual undertaking as to non-aggression had or had not been violated.

The Finnish Government accordingly proposed that a conciliation commission should be summoned. Alternatively, it stated that it was prepared to submit the settlement of the dispute to neutral arbitration.

It was also prepared to come to an understanding with the Government of the U.S.S.R. concerning the withdrawal of the defence troops on the Karelian Isthmus, with the exception of the units of frontier guards and Customs officials, to a distance from Leningrad such that it could no longer be claimed that they threatened the security of that town.[1]

(b) *Rupture of Relations between Finland and the U.S.S.R.*

In its statement, the Finnish Government explains that this note could not be handed to the Soviet Government because its telegraphic transmission was delayed in Soviet territory and because in the meantime the Finnish Minister was sent for at midnight to the Commissariat for Foreign Affairs and informed that the U.S.S.R. no longer proposed to maintain diplomatic relations with Finland.

The rupture of relations was stated to be due to the fact that the Government of the U.S.S.R. could no longer tolerate "attacks on the Soviet troops by the Finnish troops", which were continuing not only on the Karelian Isthmus but also in other frontier regions.

(c) *M. Molotov's Speech.*

At the moment when the Finnish Minister was notified of the rupture of relations, M. Molotov delivered a broadcast speech, in which he said: [2]

"The hostile policy that the present Finnish Government is pursuing towards our country obliges us to take immediate steps to ensure the external security of the State. . . . From such a Government and from its mad military clique there is nothing now to be expected but fresh violent provocations. . . . The Soviet Government has come to the conclusion that it can no longer maintain normal relations with the Finnish Government, and for that reason it has thought it necessary to recall its political and economic representatives immediately from Finland."

The President of the Council of People's Commissars then proceeded to deny the "ill-intentioned calumnies" of the foreign Press hostile to the U.S.S.R. The Soviet Government had no intention of taking and annexing Finnish territory and, had Finland's policy towards it been friendly, would have been prepared to discuss in a favourable sense even such questions as that of the union of the Karelian people living in the principal districts of the present Soviet Karelia with the nearly-related Finnish people in a single independent Finnish State. Nor had the Government of the U.S.S.R. any intention of infringing the independence of Finland or of interfering in her domestic and foreign affairs.

"We regard Finland", he said, "whatever may be the regime in existence there, as an independent State, sovereign in all its domestic and foreign policy. We are most anxious that the Finnish people should itself decide its internal and external affairs as it thinks best. The peoples of the U.S.S.R. did all that was necessary in the past to create an independent Finland. In the future, too, the peoples of our country are ready to help the Finnish people to secure its free and independent development.

"Nor has the U.S.S.R. any intention of injuring in any degree the interests of other States in Finland. The question of the relations between Finland and other States is entirely one for Finland herself, and not a matter in which the U.S.S.R. considers that it has any right to interfere. The object of the steps we are taking is solely to ensure the security of the U.S.S.R., and particularly of Leningrad, with its 3½ million inhabitants. In the present atmosphere, raised to white heat by the war, we cannot allow the solution of this vital and urgent problem to depend upon the ill-will of those who at present govern Finland. That problem must be solved by the efforts of the U.S.S.R. itself, in friendly co-operation with the Finnish people. We are sure that a favourable solution of this problem of the security of Leningrad will lay the foundations of an indissoluble friendship between the U.S.S.R. and Finland."

Soviet Troops cross the Frontier.

12. On November 30th, at 8 a.m., the troops of the Leningrad military area crossed the frontier on the Isthmus of Karelia and in several other regions. The order had been given by the High Command of the Red Army, on account, according to the Tass Agency's *communiqué*, of "fresh armed provocations on the part of the Finnish military clique".

According to the same *communiqué*, these provocations had taken place during the night at various points on the frontier. While Soviet troops were entering Finland, Soviet aircraft "dropped bombs on the aerodromes at Viipuri and Helsinki".

The Finnish Government gives a different version of these events; the Soviet troops crossed the frontier as early as the evening of November 29th, near Pummanki, on the Rybachi Peninsula, and on the morning of the 30th, while the Soviet troops were crossing the frontier at various

---

[1] See IX, paper 14, page 528.
[2] The full text of the speech is appended to the present report, page 541.

535

points, Soviet aircraft bombed not merely the aerodromes but the towns of Helsinki and Viipuri, as well as several other places.[1]

13. On December 2nd, the Tass Agency announced that " M. Kuusinen, President of the Popular Government and Minister for Foreign Affairs of Finland, has addressed an official declaration to the Presidium of the Supreme Soviet of the U.S.S.R. concerning the formation of the Popular Government of Finland and has proposed to establish diplomatic relations between the 'Democratic Republic of Finland' and the Soviet Union. The Presidium of the Supreme Soviet of the U.S.S.R. has decided to recognise the Popular Government of Finland and to establish diplomatic relations between the U.S.S.R. and the 'Democratic Republic of Finland' ".

The Finnish Government points out that the reference is to a " puppet government " set up by the U.S.S.R. in the village of Terijoki, near the frontier. It is composed of Finnish communists, most of whom took refuge in Soviet territory after the civil war of 1918.[2]

14. Since that date, while the Soviet Government maintains diplomatic relations and has concluded a " pact of mutual assistance and friendship " with this " popular government ", whose powers are limited to the portion of Finnish territory occupied by the Soviet troops, the Finnish Government, reconstituted on the basis of the national union of all parties, and still recognised by all the Powers except the U.S.S.R., is directing the Finnish nation's resistance to the Soviet forces.

Offers of Good Offices and Offers of Negotiations subsequent to the Outbreak of Hostilities.

15. A few hours after the entry of the Soviet troops into Finland, the diplomatic representatives of the United States at Helsinki and at Moscow communicated to the Finnish and Soviet Governments the text of a statement made on the previous day by the United States Secretary of State. According to this statement, the United States Government, " without in any way becoming involved in the merits of the dispute and limiting its interest to the solution of the dispute by peaceful processes only . . . would, if agreeable to both Parties, gladly extend its good offices ".

This offer was accepted by Finland alone.

The Soviet Government also rejected, on December 4th, a Finnish proposal transmitted by the Minister of Sweden at Moscow for the opening of fresh negotiations with a view to an agreement. The Soviet Government replied that it only recognised the " Popular Government of the Republic of Finland ".

16. The existence of this " Popular Government " was also one of the reasons given by the Soviet Government for its refusal to sit on the Council or in the Assembly if they examined Finland's appeal.

* * *

B.

The facts set forth above have to be considered in relation to the legal situation arising from the commitments by which the two countries are bound.

Since the recognition of the independence and sovereignty of the Finnish State, the latter has concluded with the U.S.S.R. a number of treaties. Moreover, both States are Parties to the Pact of Paris of 1928 and the Convention of 1933 defining the aggressor, and both are Members of the League of Nations.

(1) The Treaty of Peace signed at Dorpat on October 14th, 1920, between Finland and the Russian Socialist Federal Soviet Republic recalls in its Preamble that in 1917 Finland was proclaimed an independent State and that Russia had recognised the independence and sovereignty of the Finnish State within the frontiers of the Grand-Duchy of Finland. This Treaty fixes, *inter alia*, the frontier " between the States of Russia and Finland ", the limit of the territorial waters of the contracting Powers, the military neutralisation of certain Finnish islands in the Gulf of Finland, etc.

(2) As regards the territorial frontier between the two States from Lake Ladoga to the Arctic Ocean, the Republic of Finland and the Russian Socialist Federal Soviet Republic signed at Helsinki on June 1st, 1922, a Convention regarding measures taken in order to ensure peace at the frontier. This Convention established and delimited a zone on both sides of and along the frontier. Each of the two contracting Parties undertook, *inter alia*, with a view to ensuring the inviolability of the frontier, not to maintain within the limits of its zone armed forces other than the regular military units or groups belonging to the regular frontier guard, whose total strength might not exceed 2,500 men on either side. The distribution of the armed forces in the frontier zones was to be carried out under the supervision of each country, which was to communicate to

---

[1] See IX, paper 1, page 518.
[2] See VIII, page 514, and IX, paper 1, page 518.

536

the other Party information regarding such distribution. The establishment of organisations in the frontier zones for the avowed purpose of preparing, encouraging or supporting attacks on the territory of the other Party was unconditionally prohibited. The Russo-Finnish Central Mixed Commission was to have the duty of supervising the carrying-out of the provisions of the Convention; it was to act through the Frontier Sub-Commissions and Local Supervisory Committees.

(3) As regards the frontier on the Karelian Isthmus, the two Governments exchanged at Helsinki on September 24th, 1928, notes whereby Finland and the Union of Soviet Socialist Republics each appointed a frontier commissioner in order to prevent the occurrence of local incidents on the common frontier on that Isthmus or to facilitate their prompt settlement. The frontier commissioners of the two Parties were to deal jointly with frontier incidents, including cases where shots had been fired from the territory of one of the Parties at persons belonging to the frontier guard, or at other persons, or into the territory of the other Party. When such incidents occurred, the commissioners were to take appropriate measures to settle them in the easiest and quickest way. Incidents regarding which the commissioners were unable to agree were to be dealt with through diplomatic channels.

(4) Under the General Pact for the Renunciation of War dated August 27th, 1928 (Paris Pact), the Parties solemnly declared in the names of their respective peoples that they condemned recourse to war for the solution of international controversies and renounced it as an instrument of national policy in their relations with one another. They further agreed that the settlement or solution of all disputes or conflicts of whatever nature or whatever origin they might be, which might arise among them, should never be sought except by pacific means.

(5) Desirous " of confirming and completing the General Pact of August 27th, 1928, for the Renunciation of War ", the Union of Soviet Socialist Republics and Finland signed at Helsinki on January 21st, 1932, a Treaty of Non-aggression and Pacific Settlement of Disputes. Under the terms of Article 1 of this Treaty, the " High Contracting Parties mutually guarantee the inviolability of the existing frontiers between the Union of Soviet Socialist Republics and the Republic of Finland, as fixed by the Treaty of Peace concluded at Dorpat on October 14th, 1920, which shall remain the firm foundation of their relations, and reciprocally undertake to refrain from any act of aggression directed against each other. Any act of violence attacking the integrity and inviolability of the territory or the political independence of the other High Contracting Party shall be regarded as an act of aggression, even if it is committed without declaration of war and avoids warlike manifestations ". A " Protocol to Article 1 " maintains fully in force " the Agreement of June 1st, 1922, regarding Measures ensuring the inviolability of the Frontiers ". Under Article 5, the High Contracting Parties declare that they will always endeavour to settle in a spirit of justice any disputes of whatever nature or origin which may arise between them, and will resort exclusively to pacific means of settling such disputes. For this purpose, the High Contracting Parties undertake to submit any disputes which may arise between them after the signature of the Treaty, and which it may not have been possible to settle through diplomatic proceedings within a reasonable time, to a procedure of conciliation before a joint conciliation commission. Conciliation procedure shall also be applied in the event of any dispute as to the application or interpretation of a convention concluded between the High Contracting Parties, and particularly the question whether the mutual undertaking as to non-aggression has or has not been violated.

In the Protocol of Signature, the High Contracting Parties declare that subsequent denunciation of the Treaty before its termination or annulment shall neither cancel nor restrict the undertakings arising from the Pact for the Renunciation of War signed at Paris on August 27th, 1928.

(6) The Conciliation Commission provided for in Article 5 of the Treaty of Non-aggression of January 21st, 1932, was set up by a Convention signed at Helsinki on April 22nd, 1932.

(7) Finland acceded on January 31st, 1934, to the Convention for the Definition of Aggression concluded in London on July 3rd, 1933, between the Union of Soviet Socialist Republics and various other Powers immediately adjacent to it. In the Preamble to that Convention, the parties declare that they deem it necessary, in the interest of the general security, to define aggression as specifically as possible in order to obviate any pretext whereby it might be justified; they note that all States have an equal right to independence, security, the defence of their territories and the free development of their institutions.

Under Article I, each of the High Contracting Parties undertakes to accept in its relations with each of the other Parties, ... " the definition of aggression as explained in the report dated May 24th, 1933, of the Committee on Security Questions (Politis Report) to the Conference for the Reduction and Limitation of Armaments, which report was made in consequence of the Soviet delegation's proposal".

Under Article II, the aggressor in an armed conflict shall, subject to the agreements in force between the parties to the dispute, be considered to be that State which is the first to commit any of the following actions:

. . . .

(2) Invasion by its armed forces, with or without a declaration of war, of the territory of another State;

(3) Attack by its land, naval, or air forces, with or without a declaration of war, on the territory, vessels or aircraft of another State;

(4) Naval blockade of the coast or ports of another State.

537

Article III stipulates that no political, military, economic or other consideration may serve as an excuse or justification for the aggression referred to in Article II. Under the terms of the Annex to this Article III, the High Contracting Parties, desiring, " subject to the express reservation that the absolute validity of the rule laid down in Article III . . . shall be in no way restricted ", to furnish certain indications for determining the aggressor, declare that no act of aggression within the meaning of Article II of the Convention can be justified on either of the following grounds:

A. — The internal condition of a State: *e.g.*, its political, economic or social structure; alleged defects in its administration; disturbances due to strikes, revolutions, counter-revolutions, or civil war.

B. — The international conduct of a State: *e.g.*, the violation or threatened violation of the material or moral rights or interests of a foreign State or its nationals; the rupture of diplomatic or economic relations; . . . frontier incidents not forming any of the cases of aggression specified in Article II.

The accession of Finland to this Convention for the Definition of Aggression was given in virtue of the attached Protocol of Signature dated July 3rd, 1933, which reads as follows:

" It is hereby agreed between the High Contracting Parties that, should one or more of the other States immediately adjacent to the Union of Soviet Socialist Republics accede in the future to the present Convention, the said accession shall confer on the State or States in question the same rights and shall impose on them the same obligations as those conferred and imposed on the ordinary signatories."

(8) The Treaty of Non-aggression and Pacific Settlement of Disputes concluded between Finland and the U.S.S.R. on January 21st, 1932, was extended to December 31st, 1945, by a Protocol signed at Moscow on April 7th, 1934.

(9) By Article 12 of the Covenant of the League of Nations, the Members of the League agree that, if there should arise between them any dispute likely to lead to a rupture, they will submit the matter either to arbitration or judicial settlement or to enquiry by the Council, and they agree in no case to resort to war until three months after the award by the arbitrators or the judicial decision or the report by the Council.

* * *

C.

If the attitude and the acts of the two Governments in the course of the last few weeks are considered with reference to international commitments, the conclusions reached are as follows:

I. In the course of the various stages of the dispute the Finnish Government has not rejected any peaceful procedure.

(1) It agreed to enter into direct negotiations with the Soviet Government, although the invitation it received from that Government at the beginning of October contained no explanation of the nature or scope of the negotiations contemplated.
In the course of those negotiations, although it was entitled to invoke the treaties it had signed with the Union of Soviet Socialist Republics to reject any proposal infringing the territorial integrity of Finland, it agreed to contemplate cessions of territory, and when it received the Soviet proposals, it submitted counter-proposals which, in its opinion, went as far as it was possible for it to go.

(2) When the dispute arose regarding the Mainila incident, the Finnish Government proposed that the frontier commissioners of the two countries should jointly proceed to carry out an enquiry, as provided for in the above-mentioned Exchange of Notes dated September 24th, 1928.

(3) Faced with the denunciation by the Union of Soviet Socialist Republics of the Non-aggression Treaty of January 21st, 1932—the denunciation being based on the accusation that Finland had systematically violated that Treaty—the Finnish Government, in a note which, owing to the rupture of diplomatic relations by the Union of Soviet Socialist Republics, it was not possible to hand over at Moscow in time, asked for the application of the conciliation procedure laid down by that Treaty for cases of a dispute as to whether the mutual non-aggression undertaking had been violated.

(4) In the same note (which could not be handed in at Moscow) the Finnish Government proposed the convening of a conciliation commission or, alternatively, neutral arbitration.

(5) When requested by the Soviet Government on November 26th to remove its frontier troops on the Isthmus of Karelia forthwith to a distance of 20-25 kilometres, the Finnish Government replied that it was ready to enter into negotiations for a reciprocal withdrawal to a certain distance from the frontier.

The Soviet Government having made it known that its proposal regarding the withdrawal of Finnish troops to a distance of 20-25 kilometres was a minimum proposal, the Finnish Government, in its note of November 29th, which could not be handed to the Soviet Government, declared itself ready to come to an agreement with the latter for the removal of the defence troops on the Karelian Isthmus, except frontier guards and Customs officials, to a distance from Leningrad such that they could no longer be held to menace the security of that city.

(6) After the outbreak of hostilities, the Finnish Government accepted the offer of good offices made by the United States Government.

(7) On December 3rd, the Finnish Government referred the matter to the Council of the League of Nations under Articles 11 and 15 of the Covenant.

On December 4th, it vainly endeavoured to transmit to the Soviet Government, through the Minister of Sweden at Moscow, a proposal for the opening of fresh negotiations for an agreement.

II. The attitude and acts of the Government of the Union of Soviet Socialist Republics, on the other hand, have been incompatible with the commitments entered into by that country.

(1) In the course of the negotiations at Moscow with the Finnish Government, it made to that Government proposals for cessions of territory. It stated that these proposals "represented its minimum conditions, its attitude having been dictated by the fundamental security requirements of the Soviet Union and, particularly, of the city of Leningrad ".[1]

Under the terms of Article 1 of the Treaty of Non-aggression of January 21st, 1932, the two countries had, however, undertaken mutually to guarantee the inviolability of the existing frontiers as fixed by the Treaty of Peace concluded at Dorpat on October 14th, 1920, which was to remain the firm foundation of their relations.

(2) After the Mainila incident, the Soviet Government insisted on the unilateral withdrawal of the Finnish frontier troops on the Karelian Isthmus to a distance of 20 to 25 kilometres. It made no reply to the Finnish Government's proposal that the commissioners of the two countries should be instructed to carry out a joint enquiry as provided for in the Exchange of Notes of September 24th, 1928.

(3) The Soviet Government interpreted the Finnish Government's refusal to accept immediately a unilateral withdrawal of its forces for 20-25 kilometres as indicating the wish of the latter Government to keep Leningrad under a constant menace. On the ground that the Finnish Government was systematically violating the Treaty of Non-aggression, the Soviet Government declared that it regarded itself as released from the undertakings assumed by it under that Treaty. The Treaty in question, which had been prolonged by the Protocol of April 7th, 1934, until December 31st, 1945, laid down, however, that a procedure of conciliation would be applied in the event of any dispute on the question whether the mutual undertakings as to non-aggression had or had not been violated.

(4) Even if one of the Parties could, without first resorting to the conciliation procedure, have declared that the Treaty of Non-aggression no longer existed because the other Party had violated it, the Protocol of Signature of January 21st, 1932, declares that subsequent denunciation of this Treaty before its termination shall neither cancel nor restrict the undertakings arising from the Pact for the Renunciation of War signed on August 27th, 1928, which the Treaty of Non-aggression between Finland and the Union of Soviet Socialist Republics was intended to confirm and complete.

(5) The invasion of Finland by the land forces and the bombardments carried out by the naval and air forces of Soviet Russia are incompatible with the Pact for the Renunciation of War of August 27th, 1928, and with the provisions of Article 12 of the Covenant of the League of Nations.

(6) It is impossible to argue that the operations of the Soviet forces in Finland do not constitute resort to war within the meaning of the Pact of Paris or Article 12 of the Covenant of the League of Nations.

Finland and the Union of Soviet Socialist Republics are bound by the Convention for the Definition of Aggression signed at London on July 3rd, 1933. According to Article II of this Convention, the aggressor in an armed conflict shall be considered to be that State which is the first to invade by its armed forces, with or without a declaration of war, the territory of another State or to attack by its land, naval or air forces, with or without a declaration of war, the territory, vessels or aircraft of another State.

Under the terms of Article III " no political, military, economic or other consideration may serve as an excuse or justification for the aggression referred to in Article II ".

The order to enter Finland was given to the Soviet troops on the ground of " further armed provocation ". The reference was to frontier incidents or alleged frontier incidents. In the Annex, however, to Article II of the Convention, it is declared that no act of aggression within the meaning of Article II of the Convention can be justified by frontier incidents not forming any of the cases of aggression specified in Article II.

(7) After having broken off diplomatic relations with the Finnish Government and rejected the good offices of the United States Government, the Soviet Government refused to send representatives to the Council or Assembly, on the ground that it was not in a state of war with

---

[1] See IX, paper 4, page 521.

539

Finland and was not threatening the Finnish people with war. This affirmation was based, *inter alia*, on the fact that the Soviet Government maintained peaceful relations with the " Democratic Republic of Finland " and that it had signed with the latter, a Pact of Assistance and Friendship " settling all the questions which the Soviet Government had fruitlessly discussed with the delegates of the former Finnish Government, now divested of its power ".

The so-called " former Finnish Government " is the regular Government of the Republic of Finland. It is composed of all the important parties in the Parliament, whose unanimous confidence it enjoys. The Parliament is freely elected by the Finnish people. The last elections took place in July of this year. The Government is thus based on respect for democratic institutions.

The Soviet Government invokes in support of its attitude the relations which it maintains with a so-called government of its own creation which cannot, either *de jure* or *de facto*, be regarded as the Government of the Republic of Finland. That fact therefore cannot serve the Soviet Government as justification for its refusal to follow, for the settlement of its dispute with Finland, the procedure laid down in Article 15 of the Covenant of the League of Nations.

Furthermore, in so refusing, the Soviet Government is failing to observe its obligation to respect the sovereignty and independence of Finland, and is also directly contravening the very definite obligations laid down in the Convention for the Definition of Aggression, which it signed and in the preparation of which it took a decisive part.

The whole object of this Convention, indeed, is to ensure that no political, military, economic or other consideration shall serve as an excuse or justification for aggression. The Annex to Article III specifies that aggression cannot be justified either by the international conduct of a State, for example: the violation or threatened violation of the material or moral rights or interests of a foreign State; or by the internal condition of a State, for example: its political, economic or social structure; alleged defects in its administration; disturbances due to strikes, revolutions, counter-revolutions or civil war.

* * *

It follows from these findings that the Soviet Government has violated, not only its special political agreements with Finland, but also Article 12 of the Covenant of the League of Nations and the Pact of Paris.

RESOLUTION

The Assembly:

I

Whereas, by the aggression which it has committed against Finland, the Union of Soviet Socialist Republics has failed to observe not only its special political agreements with Finland but also Article 12 of the Covenant of the League of Nations and the Pact of Paris;

And whereas, immediately before committing that aggression, it denounced, without legal justification, the Treaty of Non-aggression which it had concluded with Finland in 1932, and which was to remain in force until the end of 1945:

Solemnly condemns the action taken by the Union of Soviet Socialist Republics against the State of Finland;

Urgently appeals to every Member of the League to provide Finland with such material and humanitarian assistance as may be in its power and to refrain from any action which might weaken Finland's power of resistance;

Authorises the Secretary-General to lend the aid of his technical services in the organisation of the aforesaid assistance to Finland;

And likewise authorises the Secretary-General, in virtue of the Assembly resolution of October 4th, 1937, to consult non-member States with a view to possible co-operation.

Ii

Whereas, notwithstanding an invitation extended to it on two occasions, the Union of Soviet Socialist Republics has refused to be present at the examination of its dispute with Finland before the Council and the Assembly;

And whereas, by thus refusing to recognise the duty of the Council and the Assembly as regards the execution of Article 15 of the Covenant, it has failed to observe one of the League's most essential covenants for the safeguarding of peace and the security of nations;

And whereas it has vainly attempted to justify its refusal on the ground of the relations which it has established with an alleged Government which is neither *de jure* nor *de facto* the Government recognised by the people of Finland in accordance with the free working of their institutions;

540

And whereas the Union of Soviet Socialist Republics has not merely violated a covenant of the League, but has by its own action placed itself outside the Covenant;

And whereas the Council is competent under Article 16 of the Covenant to consider what consequences should follow from this situation:

Recommends the Council to pronounce upon the question.

Appendix

PRESS COMMUNIQUÉ — TASS AGENCY

Moscow, November 30th. — On November 29th, at midnight, Molotov, President of the Council of People's Commissars, People's Commissar for Foreign Affairs of the U.S.S.R., broadcast the following speech:

" Men and women, citizens of the Soviet Union, the hostile policy pursued by the present Finnish Government towards our country obliges us to take immediate steps to ensure the external security of the State. As you know, during these last two months, the Soviet Government has patiently carried on negotiations with the Finnish Government on proposals which, in the present alarming international situation, it regarded as an indispensable minimum to ensure the safety of the country, and particularly that of Leningrad. During those negotiations, the Finnish Government has adopted an uncompromising and hostile attitude towards our country. Instead of amicably seeking a basis of agreement, those who at present govern Finland, out of deference to the foreign imperialists who stir up hatred against the Soviet Union, have followed a different path. Despite all our concessions, the negotiations have led to no result. Now we see the consequences. During the last few days, on the frontier between the U.S.S.R. and Finland, the Finnish military clique has begun to indulge in revolting provocations, not stopping short of artillery fire upon our troops near Leningrad, which has caused serious casualties among the Red troops.

" The attempts made by our Government to prevent the renewal of these provocations by means of practical proposals addressed to the Finnish Government have not merely met with no support but have again been countered by the hostile policy of the governing circles in Finland. As you have learnt from the Soviet Government's note of yesterday, they have replied to our proposals by a hostile refusal, by an insolent denial of the facts, by an attitude of mockery towards the casualties we have suffered, and by an unconcealed desire to continue to hold Leningrad under the direct threat of their troops. All this has definitely shown that the present Finnish Government, embarrassed by its anti-Soviet connections with the imperialists, is unwilling to maintain normal relations with the U.S.S.R. It continues to adopt a hostile position towards our country and will take no heed of the stipulations of the Treaty of Non-aggression concluded between the two countries, being anxious to keep our glorious Leningrad under a military menace. From such a Government and from its insensate military clique nothing is now to be expected but fresh insolent provocations.

" For this reason, the Soviet Government was compelled yesterday to declare that it now considered itself released from the engagements which it had undertaken under the Treaty of Non-aggression concluded between the U.S.S.R. and Finland and which had been irresponsibly violated by the Finnish Government. In view of the fresh attacks made by Finnish troops against Soviet troops on the Soviet-Finnish frontier, the Government now finds itself compelled to take new decisions. The Government can no longer tolerate the situation created, for which the Finnish Government is entirely responsible. The Soviet Government has come to the conclusion that it could no longer maintain normal relations with the Finnish Government, and for this reason has found it necessary to recall immediately its political and economic representatives from Finland. Simultaneously, the Government gave the order to the Supreme Command of the Red Army and Navy to be prepared for all eventualities and to take immediate steps to cope with any new attacks on the part of the Finnish military clique. . . .

DOCUMENTS

PART TWO

THE AFTERMATH OF WORLD WAR II

THE DUMBARTON OAKS PROPOSALS
FOR A GENERAL INTERNATIONAL ORGANIZATION

There should be established an international organization under the title of The United Nations, the Charter of which should contain provisions necessary to give effect to the proposals which follow.

1	*Chapter I. Purposes*
2	The purposes of the Organization should be:
3	1. To maintain international peace and security; and to
4	that end to take effective collective measures for the pre-
5	vention and removal of threats to the peace and the suppres-
6	sion of acts of aggression or other breaches of the peace, and
7	to bring about by peaceful means adjustment or settlement
8	of international disputes which may lead to a breach of the
9	peace;
10	2. To develop friendly relations among nations and to
11	take other appropriate measures to strengthen universal
12	peace;
13	3. To achieve international cooperation in the solution
14	of international economic, social and other humanitarian
15	problems; and
16	4. To afford a center for harmonizing the actions of
17	nations in the achievement of these common ends.

1 *Chapter II. Principles*

2 In pursuit of the purposes mentioned in Chapter I the

3 Organization and its members should act in accordance with

4 the following principles:

5 1. The Organization is based on the principle of the

6 sovereign equality of all peace-loving states.

7 2. All members of the Organization undertake, in order

8 to ensure to all of them the rights and benefits resulting from

9 membership in the Organization, to fulfill the obligations

10 assumed by them in accordance with the Charter.

11 3. All members of the Organization shall settle their dis-

12 putes by peaceful means in such a manner that international

13 peace and security are not endangered.

14 4. All members of the Organization shall refrain in their

15 international relations from the threat or use of force in any.

16 manner inconsistent with the purposes of the Organization.

17 5. All members of the Organization shall give every

18 assistance to the Organization in any action undertaken by

19 it in accordance with the provisions of the Charter.

20 6. All members of the Organization shall refrain from

21 giving assistance to any state against which preventive or

22 enforcement action is being undertaken by the Organization.

23 The Organization should ensure that states not members

1 of the Organization act in accordance with these principles

2 so far as may be necessary for the maintenance of inter-

3 national peace and security.

4 *Chapter III. Membership*

5 1. Membership of the Organization should be open to all

6 peace-loving states.

7 *Chapter IV. Principal Organs*

8 1. The Organization should have as its principal organs:

9 a. A General Assembly;

10 b. A Security Council;

11 c. An international court of justice; and

12 d. A Secretariat.

13 2. The Organization should have such subsidiary agen-

14 cies as may be found necessary.

15 *Chapter V. The General Assembly*

16 SECTION A. COMPOSITION. All members of the Or-

17 ganization should be members of the General Assembly and

18 should have a number of representatives to be specified in

19 the Charter.

20 SECTION B. FUNCTIONS AND POWERS. 1. The Gen-

21 eral Assembly should have the right to consider the general

22 principles of cooperation in the maintenance of international

23 peace and security, including the principles governing dis-

1 armament and the regulation of armaments; to discuss any

2 questions relating to the maintenance of international peace

3 and security brought before it by any member or members

4 of the Organization or by the Security Council; and to make

5 recommendations with regard to any such principles or

6 questions. Any such questions on which action is necessary

7 should be referred to the Security Council by the General

8 Assembly either before or after discussion. The General

9 Assembly should not on its own initiative make recom-

10 mendations on any matter relating to the maintenance of

11 international peace and security which is being dealt with

12 by the Security Council.

13   2. The General Assembly should be empowered to admit

14 new members to the Organization upon recommendation of

15 the Security Council.

16   3. The General Assembly should, upon recommendation

17 of the Security Council, be empowered to suspend from

18 the exercise of any rights or privileges of membership any

19 member of the Organization against which preventive or

20 enforcement action shall have been taken by the Security

21 Council. The exercise of the rights and privileges thus

22 suspended may be restored by decision of the Security

23 Council. The General Assembly should be empowered, upon

1 recommendation of the Security Council, to expel from the
2 Organization any member of the Organization which per-
3 sistently violates the principles contained in the Charter.

4   4. The General Assembly should elect the non-perma-
5 nent members of the Security Council and the members of
6 the Economic and Social Council provided for in Chapter
7 IX. It should be empowered to elect, upon recommendation
8 of the Security Council, the Secretary-General of the Or-
9 ganization. It should perform such functions in relation
10 to the election of the judges of the international court of
11 justice as may be conferred upon it by the statute of the
12 court.

13   5. The General Assembly should apportion the expenses
14 among the members of the Organization and should be
15 empowered to approve the budgets of the Organization.

16   6. The General Assembly should initiate studies and
17 make recommendations for the purpose of promoting inter-
18 national cooperation in political, economic and social fields
19 and of adjusting situations likely to impair the general
20 welfare.

21   7. The General Assembly should make recommenda-
22 tions for the coordination of the policies of international
23 economic, social, and other specialized agencies brought into

1 relation with the Organization in accordance with agree-

2 ments between such agencies and the Organization.

3   8. The General Assembly should receive and consider

4 annual and special reports from the Security Council and

5 reports from other bodies of the Organization.

6   SECTION C. VOTING. 1. Each member of the Organ-

7 ization should have one vote in the General Assembly.

8   2. Important decisions of the General Assembly, in-

9 cluding recommendations with respect to the maintenance

10 of international peace and security; election of members of

11 the Security Council; election of members of the Economic

12 and Social Council; admission of members, suspension of

13 the exercise of the rights and privileges of members, and

14 expulsion of members; and budgetary questions, should be

15 made by a two-thirds majority of those present and voting.

16 On other questions, including the determination of additional

17 categories of questions to be decided by a two-thirds ma-

18 jority, the decisions of the General Assembly should be made

19 by a simple majority vote.

20   SECTION D. PROCEDURE. 1. The General Assembly

21 should meet in regular annual sessions and in such special

22 sessions as occasion may require.

1   2. The General Assembly should adopt its own rules of

2   procedure and elect its President for each session.

3   3. The General Assembly should be empowered to set

4   up such bodies and agencies as it may deem necessary for the

5   performance of its functions.

6   *Chapter VI. The Security Council*

7   SECTION A. COMPOSITION. The Security Council should

8   consist of one representative of each of eleven members of the

9   Organization. Representatives of the United States of

.10   America, the United Kingdom of Great Britain and

11   Northern Ireland, the Union of Soviet Socialist Re-

12   publics, the Republic of China, and, in due course, France,

13   should have permanent seats. The General Assembly should

14   elect six states to fill the non-permanent seats. These six

15   states should be elected for a term of two years, three retir-

16   ing each year. They should not be immediately eligible for

17   reelection. In the first election of the non-permanent mem-

18   bers three should be chosen by the General Assembly for

19   one-year terms and three for two-year terms.

20   SECTION B. PRINCIPAL FUNCTIONS AND POWERS. 1. In

21   order to ensure prompt and effective action by the Organi-

22   zation, members of the Organization should by the Charter

23   confer on the Security Council primary responsibility for

1 the maintenance of international peace and security and

2 should agree that in carrying out these duties under this re-

3 sponsibility it should act on their behalf.

4   2. In discharging these duties the Security Council

5 should act in accordance with the purposes and principles

6 of the Organization.

7   3. The specific powers conferred on the Security Coun-

8 cil in order to carry out these duties are laid down in

9 Chapter VIII.

10   4. All members of the Organization should obligate

11 themselves to accept the decisions of the Security Council

12 and to carry them out in accordance with the provisions

13 of the Charter.

14   5. In order to promote the establishment and mainte-

15 nance of international peace and security with the least di-

16 version of the world's human and economic resources for

17 armaments, the Security Council, with the assistance of the

18 Military Staff Committee referred to in Chapter VIII,

19 Section B, paragraph 9, should have the responsibility for

20 formulating plans for the establishment of a system of

21 regulation of armaments for submission to the members of

22 the Organization.

1   [Here follows the text of Section C as proposed at

2 the Crimea Conference:]

3   SECTION C. VOTING. 1. Each member of the Security

4 Council should have one vote.

5   2. Decisions of the Security Council on procedural mat-

6 ters should be made by an affirmative vote of seven members.

7   3. Decisions of the Security Council on all other matters

8 should be made by an affirmative vote f seven members

9 including the concurring votes of the permanent members;

10 provided that, in decisions under Chapter VIII, Section A,

11 and under the second sentence of Paragraph 1 of Chapter

12 VIII, Section C, a party to a dispute should abstain from

13 voting.

14   SECTION D. PROCEDURE. 1. The Security Council

15 should be so organized as to be able to function continuously

16 and each state member of the Security Council should be

17 permanently represented at the headquarters of the Organiza-

18 tion. It may hold meetings at such other places as in its

19 judgment may best facilitate its work. There should be

20 periodic meetings at which each state member of the Security

21 Council could if it so desired be represented by a member of

22 the government or some other special representative.

1   2. The Security Council should be empowered to set up

2 such bodies or agencies as it may deem necessary for the

3 performance of its functions including regional subcommittees

4 of the Military Staff Committee.

5   3. The Security Council should adopt its own rules of

6 procedure, including the method of selecting its President.

7   4. Any member of the Organization should participate in

8 the discussion of any question brought before the Security

9 Council whenever the Security Council considers that the

10 interests of that member of the Organization are specially

11 affected.

12   5. Any member of the Organization not having a seat

13 on the Security Council and any state not a member of the

14 Organization, if it is a party to a dispute under consideration

15 by the Security Council, should be invited to participate in

16 the discussion relating to the dispute.

17   *Chapter VII. An International Court of Justice*

18   1. There should be an international court of justice which

19 should constitute the principal judicial organ of the Organ-

20 ization.

21   2. The court should be constituted and. should function

22 in accordance with a statute which should be annexed to and

23 be a part of the Charter of the Organization.

1 3. The statute of the court of international justice should

2 be either (a) the Statute of the Permanent Court of Inter-

3 national Justice, continued in force with such modifications

4 as may be desirable or (b) a new statute in the preparation

5 of which the Statute of the Permanent Court of International

6 Justice should be used as a basis.

7 4. All members of the Organization should *ipso facto*

8 be parties to the statute of the international court of justice.

9 5. Conditions under which states not members of the

10 Organization may become parties to the statute of the inter-

11 national court of justice should be determined in each case

12 by the General Assembly upon recommendation of the

13 Security Council.

14 *Chapter VIII. Arrangements for the Maintenance of Inter-*

15 *national Peace and Security Including Prevention and*

16 *Suppression of Aggression*

17 SECTION A. PACIFIC SETTLEMENT OF DISPUTES.

18 1. The Security Council should be empowered to investigate

19 any dispute, or any situation which may lead to inter-

20 national friction or give rise to a dispute, in order to deter-

21 mine whether its continuance is likely to endanger the

22 maintenance of international peace and security.

23 2. Any state, whether member of the Organization or

1 not, may bring any such dispute or situation to the attention

2 of the General Assembly or of the Security Council.

3   3. The parties to any dispute the continuance of which

4 is likely to endanger the maintenance of international peace

5 and security should obligate themselves, first of all, to seek

6 a solution by negotiation, mediation, conciliation, arbitration

7 or judicial settlement, or other peaceful means of their own

8 choice. The Security Council should call upon the parties

9 to settle their dispute by such means.

10   4. If, nevertheless, parties to a dispute of the nature

11 referred to in paragraph 3 above fail to settle it by the

12 means indicated in that paragraph, they should obligate

13 themselves to refer it to the Security Council. The Se-

14 curity Council should in each case decide whether or not

15 the continuance of the particular dispute is in fact likely

16 to endanger the maintenance of international peace and

17 security, and, accordingly, whether the Security Council

18 should deal with the dispute, and, if so, whether it should

19 take action under paragraph 5.

20   5. The Security Council should be empowered, at any

21 stage of a dispute of the nature referred to in paragraph

22 3 above, to recommend appropriate procedures or methods

23 of adjustment.

1   6. Justiciable disputes should normally be referred to
2 the international court of justice. The Security Council
3 should be empowered to refer to the court, for advice, legal
4 questions connected with other disputes.

5   7. The provisions of paragraph 1 to 6 of Section A
6 should not apply to situations or disputes arising out of
7 matters which by international law are solely within the
8 domestic jurisdiction of the state concerned.

9   SECTION B. DETERMINATION OF THREATS TO THE
10 PEACE OR ACTS OF AGGRESSION AND ACTION WITH
11 RESPECT THERETO. 1. Should the Security Council deem
12 that a failure to settle a dispute in accordance with proce-
13 dures indicated in paragraph 3 of Section A, or in accordance
14 with its recommendations made under paragraph 5 of Sec-
15 tion A, constitutes a threat to the maintenance of inter-
16 national peace and security, it should take any measures
17 necessary for the maintenance of international peace and
18 security in accordance with the purposes and principles of
19 the Organization.

20   2. In general the Security Council should determine the
21 existence of any threat to the peace, breach of the peace or
22 act of aggression and should make recommendations or

1 decide upon the measures to be taken to maintain or restore

2 peace and security.

3   3. The Security Council should be empowered to de-

4 termine what diplomatic, economic, or other measures not

5 involving the use of armed force should be employed to give

6 effect to its decisions, and to call upon members of the

7 Organization to apply such measures. Such measures may

8 include complete or partial interruption of rail, sea, air,

9 postal, telegraphic, radio and other means of communication

10 and the severance of diplomatic and economic relations.

11   4. Should the Security Council consider such measures

12 to be inadequate, it should be empowered to take such action

13 by air, naval or land forces as may be necessary to main-

14 tain or restore international peace and security. Such ac-

15 tion may include demonstrations, blockade and other

16 operations by air, sea or land forces of members of the

17 Organization.

18   5. In order that all members of the Organization should

19 contribute to the maintenance of international peace and

20 security, they should undertake to make available to the

21 Security Council, on its call and in accordance with a special

22 agreement or agreements concluded among themselves,

23 armed forces, facilities and assistance necessary for the pur-

1 pose of maintaining international peace and security. Such

2 agreement or agreements should govern the numbers and

3 types of forces and the nature of the facilities and assistance

4 to be provided. The special agreement or agreements

5 should be negotiated as soon as possible and should in each

6 case be subject to approval by the Security Council and to

7 ratification by the signatory states in accordance with their

8 constitutional processes.

9   6. In order to enable urgent military measures to be

10 taken by the Organization there should be held immediately

11 available by the members of the Organization national air

12 force contingents for combined international enforcement

13 action. The strength and degree of readiness of these con-

14 tingents and plans for their combined action should be deter-

15 mined by the Security Council with the assistance of the Mili-

16 tary Staff Committee within the limits laid down in the

17 special agreement or agreements referred to in paragraph 5

18 above.

19   7. The action required to carry out the decisions of the

20 Security Council for the maintenance of international peace

21 and security should be taken by all the members of the Organ-

22 ization in cooperation or by some of them as the Security

23 Council may determine. This undertaking should be carried

1 out by the members of the Organization by their own action

2 and through action of the appropriate specialized organiza-

3 tions and agencies of which they are members.

4   8. Plans for the application of armed force should be

5 made by the Security Council with the assistance of the Mili-

6 tary Staff Committee referred to in paragraph 9 below.

7   9. There should be established a Military Staff Commit-

8 tee the functions of which should be to advise and assist the

9 Security Council on all questions relating to the Security

10 Council's military requirements for the maintenance of inter-

11 national peace and security, to the employment and command

12 of forces placed at its disposal, to the regulation of armaments,

13 and to possible disarmament. It should be responsible under

14 the Security Council for the strategic direction of any armed

15 forces placed at the disposal of the Security Council. The

16 Committee should be composed of the Chiefs of Staff of the

17 permanent members of the Security Council or their repre-

18 sentatives. Any member of the Organization not perma-

19 nently represented on the Committee should be invited by

20 the Committee to be associated with it when the efficient dis-

21 charge of the Committee's responsibilities requires that such a

22 state should participate in its work. Questions of command

23 of forces should be worked out subsequently.

1   10. The members of the Organization should join in
2   affording mutual assistance in carrying out the measures
3   decided upon by the Security Council.

4   11. Any state, whether a member of the Organiza-
5   tion or not, which finds itself confronted with special eco-
6   nomic problems arising from the carrying out of measures
7   which have been decided upon by the Security Council
8   should have the right to consult the Security Council in
9   regard to a solution of those problems.

10 SECTION C. REGIONAL ARRANGEMENTS. 1. Nothing
11 in the Charter should preclude the existence of regional
12 arrangements or agencies for dealing with such matters
13 relating to the maintenance of international peace and
14 security as are appropriate for regional action, provided such
15 arrangements or agencies and their activities are consistent
16 with the purposes and principles of the Organization. The
17 Security Council should encourage settlement of local dis-
18 putes through such regional arrangements or by such re-
19 gional agencies, either on the initiative of the states
20 concerned or by reference from the Security Council.

21 2. The Security Council should, where appropriate,
22 utilize such arrangements or agencies for enforcement action

1   under its authority, but no enforcement action should be

2   taken under regional arrangements or by regional agencies

3   without the authorization of the Security Council.

4   3. The Security Council should at all times be kept

5   fully informed of activities undertaken or in contemplation

6   under regional arrangements or by regional agencies for

7   the maintenance of international peace and security.

8   *Chapter IX. Arrangements for International Economic and*

9   *Social Cooperation*

10   SECTION A. PURPOSE AND RELATIONSHIPS. 1. With

11   a view to the creation of conditions of stability and well-being

12   which are necessary for peaceful and friendly relations among

13   nations, the Organization should facilitate solutions of inter-

14   national economic, social and other humanitarian problems

15   and promote respect for human rights and fundamental free-

16   doms. Responsibility for the discharge of this function should

17   be vested in the General Assembly and, under the authority

18   of the General Assembly, in an Economic and Social Council.

19   2. The various specialized economic, social and other

20   organizations and agencies would have responsibilities in their

21   respective fields as defined in their statutes. Each such or-

22   ganization or agency should be brought into relationship with

23   the Organization on terms to be determined by agreement

1   between the Economic and Social Council and the appropriate

2   authorities of the specialized organization or agency, subject

3   to approval by the General Assembly.

4   SECTION B. COMPOSITION AND VOTING. The Economic

5   and Social Council should consist of representatives of eighteen

6   members of the Organization. The states to be represented

7   for this purpose should be elected by the General Assembly

8   for terms of three years. Each such state should have one

9   representative, who should have one vote. Decisions of the

10   Economic and Social Council should be taken by simple

11   majority vote of those present and voting.

12   SECTION C. FUNCTIONS AND POWERS OF THE ECO-

13   NOMIC AND SOCIAL COUNCIL. 1. The Economic and

14   Social Council should be empowered:

15   a. to carry out, within the scope of its functions,.

16   recommendations of the General Assembly;

17   b. to make recommendations, on its own initiative,

18   with respect to international economic, social and other

19   humanitarian matters;

20   c. to receive and consider reports from the eco-

21   nomic, social and other organizations or agencies brought

22   into relationship with the Organization, and to co-

1 ordinate their activities through consultations with, and

2 recommendations to, such organizations or agencies;

3   d. to examine the administrative budgets of such

4 specialized organizations or agencies with a view to

5 making recommendations to the organizations or agen-

6 cies concerned;

7   e. to enable the Secretary-General to provide in-

8 formation to the Security Council;

9   f. to assist the Security Council upon its request;

10 and

11   g. to perform such other functions within the gen-

12 eral scope of its competence as may be assigned to it by

13 the General Assembly.

14 SECTION D. ORGANIZATION AND PROCEDURE. 1. The

15 Economic and Social Council should set up an economic

16 commission, a social commission, and such other commis-

17 sions as may be required. These commissions should con-

18 sist of experts. There should be a permanent staff which

19 should constitute a part of the Secretariat of the Organ-

20 ization.

21   2. The Economic and Social Council should make suit-

22 able arrangements for representatives of the specialized

23 organizations or agencies to participate without vote in its

1 deliberations and in those of the commissions established
2 by it.

3   3. The Economic and Social Council should adopt its
4 own rules of procedure and the method of selecting its
5 President.

6   *Chapter X. The Secretariat*

7   1. There should be a Secretariat comprising a Secre-
8 tary-General and such staff as may be required. The
9 Secretary-General should be the chief administrative officer
10 of the Organization. He should be elected by the General
11 Assembly, on recommendation of the Security Council,
12 for such term and under such conditions as are specified in
13 the Charter.

14   2. The Secretary-General should act in that capacity
15 in all meetings of the General Assembly, of the Security
16 Council, and of the Economic and Social Council and should
17 make an annual report to the General Assembly on the work
18 of the Organization.

19   3. The Secretary-General should have the right to bring
20 to the attention of the Security Council any matter which
21 in his opinion may threaten international peace and security.

22   *Chapter XI. Amendments*

23   Amendments should come into force for all members of

1 the Organization, when they have been adopted by a vote

2 of two-thirds of the members of the General Assembly and

3 ratified in accordance with their respective constitutional

4 processes by the members of the Organization having per-

5 manent membership on the Security Council and by a

6 majority of the other members of the Organization.

7 *Chapter XII. Transitional Arrangements*

8 1. Pending the coming into force of the special agree-

9 ment or agreements referred to in Chapter VIII, Section B,

10 paragraph 5, and in accordance with the provisions of para-

11 graph 5 of the Four-Nation Declaration, signed at Moscow,

12 October 30, 1943, the states parties to that Declaration

13 should consult with one another and as occasion arises with

14 other members of the Organization with a view to such joint

15 action on behalf of the Organization as may be necessary for

16 the purpose of maintaining international peace and security.

17 2. No provision of the Charter should preclude action

18 taken or authorized in relation to enemy states as a result of

19 the present war by the Governments having responsibility for

20 such action.

DOCUMENT 17 (b)

The United Nations Conference
on International Organization

RESTRICTED   [466]
Doc. 2 (English)
G/14(b)
May 1, 1945

GENERAL

Observations of the Czechoslovak Government
on the Dumbarton Oaks Proposals

The Government of the Czechoslovak Republic is in full agreement with the statement of the Crimea Conference that the earliest
possible establishment of a general international organization for
the maintenance of peace and security is essential, both to prevent
aggression and to remove the political, economic, and social causes
of war through the close and continuing collaboration of all peace-
loving peoples. The Dumbarton Oaks Proposals certainly constitute
an excellent basis for the deliberations of the forthcoming San Francisco Conference; and the Czechoslovak Government expresses its
heartiest thanks to the Powers whose representatives have accomplished such valuable preparatory work. These Proposals, together
with observations and suggestions presented by other Governments,
will enable the Conference to deal thoroughly with all aspects of the
problems involved and to achieve results which will be beneficial
to the future collaboration of all peace-loving States.

Moved by the sincerest desire to contribute to the success of
the Conference, the Czechoslovak Government submits the following
observations and suggestions.

I

The Dumbarton Oaks Proposals are dominated by the idea that
the maintenance of international peace and security can best be secured by a single organ capable of rapid deliberation and swift decision. They therefore place primary responsibility in this respect
on the Security Council and invest it with the widest powers. Chapter VI (B) (2) states only that "the Security Council shall act in accordance with the purposes and principles of the Organization".
Chapters I and II which enumerate these purposes and principles
are, therefore, of the utmost importance and the Conference will
certainly submit their contents to a very exhaustive and careful examination.

The Czechoslovak Government agrees that the new Organization should possess the widest powers and should retain sufficient flexibility to be capable of organic growth and of mastering any situation that may arise. Past experience has proved sufficiently that rigidity and over-elaborate definitions may not always produce the desired results. Nevertheless, there are, in the opinion of the Czechoslovak Government, certain fundamental principles which should be expressly included in the Charter of the new Organization. The discussions at the Conference will reveal the general feeling of the delegations on this important subject. It seems to the Czechoslovak Government that these principles should at least include, in addition to those already mentioned in Chapters I and II of the Proposals, the observation of international law and of treaty obligations; and, further, respect for the territorial integrity and political independence of States-members.

Should the Security Council come to the conclusion that international peace and security can be maintained only by measures not in conformity with these fundamental principles, and especially by territorial changes, the matter should be laid before the Assembly. At the request of any party to the dispute, the question shall also be laid before the Assembly. In these cases the Assembly should decide by a two-thirds majority vote.

The council shall always have the right and the duty to take all conservatory measures necessary for the maintenance of peace and security.

II

Chapter VIII (A) refers to the pacific settlement of disputes. The Czechoslovak Government is of the opinion that this very important Chapter deserves several observations:

1) It is certainly desirable and necessary that for this preventive action the Security Council should be given as much power as possible. The Czechoslovak Government understands, however, that the Council should intervene only when, and after, all other means of pacific settlement convened beforehand or agreed ad hoc by the parties, have been exhausted. Paragraphs (3) and (4) seem to justify this interpretation. Paragraph (3) stipulates that the parties should obligate themselves, first of all, to seek a solution by negotiation, mediation, conciliation, arbitration, or judicial settlement, or other peaceful means of their choice. And paragraph (4) binds the parties to refer their dispute to the Council only if settlement by other means has failed. But paragraph (5) may create some confusion, because it gives to the Council the right to intervene at any stage of the dispute. It is true that according to paragraph (1) this

intervention is to be limited to the determination "whether the continuance of the dispute is likely to endanger the maintenance of international peace and security". What is the meaning of this restriction? Is it to be understood that while a special procedure is [468] in progress the Council should limit its intervention to the recommendation of conservatory measures proper to the elimination of any threat to peace and security? The Czechoslovak Government would advocate this interpretation. The main issue of the dispute should be settled, first of all, by the special procedures and the Council should undertake such a settlement only when, and if, the parties fail to find a solution by the special means indicated. The wording of paragraph (5) should, therefore, be redrafted in order to make clear the different nature of the intervention of the Council during, and after, the special procedures.

2) The Czechoslovak Government notes with satisfaction that all the provisions of Chapter VIII (A) refer only to disputes "likely to endanger the maintenance of international peace and security". This seems a reasonable and necessary limitation. The obligation of the Council to examine, in each case, whether a dispute falls within this category, will prevent, it is hoped, any attempt to encumber the Council with minor affairs, or to misuse it by presenting it with artificial claims and disputes.

3) The role to be given to the International Court of Justice seems, to the Czechoslovak Government, a matter of far-reaching importance. The Court has certainly proved a very valuable institution and its activity should be not only maintained but developed and extended as far as possible. Paragraph (6) provides that "justifiable disputes should normally be referred to the International Court of Justice". It is suggested that the word "normally" should be omitted. If there are any doubts whether a given dispute is "justifiable" or not, the Court itself should decide by a preliminary statement. The reference to the Court by the Council of "legal questions connected with other disputes" should be regarded as a matter or procedure.

4) Paragraph (7) stipulates that the Council should not deal with matters which, by international law, are solely within the domestic jurisdiction of the State concerned. This provision is certainly well-founded and will be welcomed particularly by smaller States. They will rightly see in it an important guarantee against the possibility of interference in their internal questions. If there is a difference of opinion as to whether a given question falls within the domestic jurisdiction, it should be considered a judicial dispute and therefore referred for decision to the International Court of Justice.

The Czechoslovak Government welcomes particularly the Proposals contained in Chapter VIII (B) relating to the "determination of threats to the peace or acts of aggression, and action in respect thereto,". In addition to the preventive action of Chapter VIII (A), [469 here is the second pillar of the whole edifice. The authors of Dumbarton Oaks, having in mind the bitter experience of the past, have endeavored to construct it of solid material. They propose to give to the Council as much power as possible. Paragraph (2) provides rightly that the Council should be able not only to make "recommendations" but to "decide" upon measures to be taken to maintain or restore peace and security. Here again, the drafting is very general and no precision is given, so that the Council will be practically free to take any measure which it might consider necessary. This complete freedom certainly has the advantage of enabling the Council to adapt its action to any situation. Yet it remains a question whether this absence of any rule of conduct will still be of advantage when the case seems absolutely clear, and when only the application of previously defined rules would seem to guarantee action sufficiently swift to prevent an unscrupulous aggressor from creating, in his own favor, a situation the redress of which may prove very lengthy and very difficult. In the past, the Czechoslovak Government has concluded with several other Governments a Convention for the definition of the term "aggressor". Article 2 of this Convention had the following text:

"The aggressor in an international conflict shall, subject to the arrangements in force between the parties to the dispute, be considered to be that State which is the first to commit any of the following actions:

1). Declaration of war upon another State;
2). Invasion by its armed forces, with or without declaration of war, of the territory of another State;
3). Attack by its land, naval, or air-forces, with or without declaration of war, on the territory, vessels, or aircraft of another State;
4). Naval-blockade of the coasts or ports of another State;
5). Provision of support to armed bands formed in its territory which have invaded the territory of another State, or refusal, notwithstanding the request of the invaded State, to take in its own territory all the

measures in its power to deprive these bands of
all assistance or protection."

IV

Chapter VIII (C) concerning regional arrangements will prove
very useful for the promotion and the strengthening of international
peace and security. The needs of certain regions may be different
and peculiar, involving situations which can best be handled by regional conventions and agencies. It seems clear, however, that it
will be absolutely necessary to ensure the compatibility of such conventions by placing them within the general framework of the World
Organization. Dumbarton Oaks provides rightly that they should be
"consistent with the purposes and principles of the Organization".
It stipulates further that "no enforcement action should be taken under regional arrangements or by regional agencies without the authorization of the Security Council". The Czechoslovak Government
considers that such authorization should be given in advance and as
a general rule for cases of immediate danger where the suspension
of any coercive action until the intervention of the Security Council
may cause irremediable delays. The measures taken in these cases
could be submitted subsequently for approval to the Council.

V

The arrangements for International Economic and Social Co-operation (Chapter IX), and in particular the creation of a special Economic and Social Council, deserve the fullest approval. Future
peace and security depend in an ever-increasing measure on general
economic and social progress, which can be attained only by constant and friendly international interchange and collaboration. Before this war, and even during hostilities, numerous international
organizations and agencies have done valuable work in this respect.
It seems very important to bring them all together and to create a
new central organ with sufficient authority for general direction and
co-ordination. The countries which suffered most from enemy occupation or from the progress of hostilities will be among the most
anxious to share in this economic and social collaboration. They
face a difficult and dangerous period of transition and re-adaptation.
The new central organ may prove very useful in bringing about the
speedy return to normal and acceptable conditions throughout the
world.

VI

Chapter X gives to the new Secretary-General the important
right and duty of bringing to the attention of the Security Council
any matter which, in his opinion, may threaten international peace
and security. This may be very useful in situations where Govern-

ments may hesitate to take action because of diplomatic or other considerations. The Secretary-General and his chief advisers will therefore bear a heavy responsibility.

The choice of this personnel will certainly be affected with the utmost care and caution. There is, however, every reason to believe that the best men will be available. Experience has proved that whatever may have been the causes of the failures and disappointments of recent international institutions, they were certainly not due to the personnel. The staff of international organizations have shown in general a high degree of efficiency and moral standing. They have been valuable promoters of that true international spirit and solidarity which must be of the greatest advantage to any new organization.

April 25, 1945

[471

The United Nations Conference
on International Organization

Doc. 2 (ENGLISH)
G/14 (r)
May 5, 1945

[577]

GENERAL

PROPOSALS OF THE DELEGATION OF THE REPUBLIC OF BOLIVIA FOR THE ORGANIZATION OF A SYSTEM OF PEACE AND SECURITY

1. The Government of the Republic of Bolivia considers that the establishment of a lasting and just peace is founded on three postulates:

   a) The guaranty of a system of world security.

   b) The organization of a mechanism for international justice.

   c) The economic and social well-being of the great masses of the people

2. The great powers, who have borne the greatest sacrifices in this war and have brought about by their efforts its victorious conclusion, have the greatest responsibility in the maintenance of peace and of the system of world security. The duties of the great powers to remain watchful, added to their ability to take expedient defensive action in cases of threats to the peace, is therefore the principal guaranty of the system of security, especially for those countries which cannot insure this security by means of their own military and economic resources.

In virtue of the foregoing, the existence of a Security Council with permanent seats for the great powers deserves the unreserved support of the Government of Bolivia, particularly insofar as concerns the breadth of powers which will permit them to settle rapidly the disputes which might arise among members of the international community.

3. The system of security, to be effective, requires the cooperation of all the nations participating in the International Organization. The extension of the duties and rights of the International Organization to all sovereign states, in order to make them universal, would contribute to the efficacy of the system. In virtue of this, the sovereign states which at present are not members of the community of United Nations might be admitted to the Organization by means of a formal agreement which would bind them to the following: [578]

   a) Submission to the principles, purposes, and duties of the Organization.

b)   Repudiation of the use of force as an instrument of international policy.
c)   Compliance with the specific conditions determined by
the Organization for their admission.

4. World security is founded on the principle that a mere attempt
at aggression is a policy contrary to good understanding, good neigh-
borliness, and the purposes of lasting peace. This principle can be
put into practice only if all nations, great and small, admit that an
act of violence on their part should be immediately countered by
collective measures.

To achieve this end, there must exist, in the Charter of the Organization, a double and reciprocal guaranty among its members :
the first, concerning the territorial inviolability of the states, the
legal validity of acquisitions of territory which may originate in acts
of force or other means of compulsion not being recognized; and the
second, concerning respect for the political independence of the
states and the right which they possess to develop freely in their internal life, without the intervention of any other state.

As soon as the attitude of one state toward the guaranties expressed above affects the peaceful existence of another, displaying
symptoms which foreshadow an act of aggression, the machinery of
collective action should immediately be put into motion.

5. The efficacy of the security machinery is directly related to
the need of designating the aggression as such and defining what is
meant by "aggressor state", a point which should be considered in
the Charter of the General Organization. A previous definition of
typically aggressive acts is absolutely essential in order that states
composing the international community may recognize what they
should avoid in their international conduct so as not to give occasion
for collective sanctions.

It is a foregone conclusion, in this connection, that an act of armed   [5
invasion typifies aggression by form, and should dictate the adoption
of immediate sanctions without the need of previous consultation.

The definition of an aggressor is characterized by the commission of any one of the following acts :

a) Invasion, by armed force, of a foreign territory.
b) Declaration of war.
c) An attack by land, sea, or air forces.
d) Aid lent to armed bands for the purposes of invasion
e) The intervention of a state in the internal or external policy
of another.
f) Refusal to submit the cause of belligerence to the procedures
of peaceful solution.

314

g) Refusal to comply with a decision pronounced by a court of international justice.

6. The extension of the powers of the Security Council to all controversies that might arise between member states of the Organization and between the latter and nonmember states eliminates paragraph 7 of Section A of Chapter VIII of the Dumbarton Oaks Proposals which, by distinguishing matters that according to international law fall solely within the jurisdiction of a state, limits the effectiveness of the system of general security. In the opinion of the Government of Bolivia, no conflict should be excluded from the cognizance of the principal organs listed in the Dumbarton Oaks Proposals if it cannot be settled by agreement of the parties involved.

From this point of view, all disputes of a political nature between two or more states should be referred to the Security Council for settlement by means of the procedures of investigation and conciliation as far as possible, and all litigation of a juridical nature should be submitted to the International Court of Justice.

7. Concerning military measures, the Military Staff Committee contemplated in paragraph 9 of Section B of Chapter VIII should be composed of the Chiefs of Staff of all the United Nations, or their [580] representatives, by means of the creation of regional military organizations dependent on the Military Staff Committee in matters of advice and policy.

8. The purposes of the general International Organization should assure the rule of justice and law in international relations. Unless states submit completely to juridical norms, international justice cannot be attained; without an international justice duly organized and efficiently administered, lasting peace cannot be assured in the world.

9. For the application of justice among nations, the constitutional Charter of the Organization should specify clearly the means of eliminating evidently unjust situations which may exist or might arise in spite of the noble purposes which inspired the action of the United Nations in the present war.

10. The maintenance of a peaceful good-neighborliness among states depends on the adoption of regular procedures for the adoption or adjustment of international agreements on the enforcement of which a better order in the community of nations depends.

When international agreements create unjust situations, or maintain a state of affairs which is onerous to one of the parties, and when its prolonged existence can endanger harmony among the members of the community of nations, it should be deemed necessary to eliminate such situations.

Such coordinated planning is not inconsistent with respect for and faithful fulfilment of international treaties, which is the norm of juridical tradition and has deserved, does deserve, and will deserve at all times the fullest support of the Republic of Bolivia in its international conduct.

The lasting nature of international instruments regulating the harmonious life of states, however, is not consistent with the development of new circumstances and new conditions which may differ fundamentally from those which gave rise to the agreements. Hence they should continually be perfected in the light of the evolution of conditions created by the dynamics of history.

These readjustments are necessary to strengthen the spirit of [58] cooperation among countries.

Any international treaty which implicitly carries the clause "rebus sic stantibus" can be revised by agreement of the parties; and only when such an agreement is impossible and there exists a grave threat to international peace and harmony, should the mode of revision be decided by the International Court in all that concerns juridical questions, and by the Security Council in cases of a political nature which are not susceptible to settlement of a juridical nature.

The Security Council should then be able to propose the application of procedures of investigation and conciliation for a satisfactory readjustment.

11. The International Court of Justice provided for in Chapter VII of the Dumbarton Oaks Proposals should be organized on the basic principles of the Statute of the Permanent Court of the Hague, with modifications necessary for the due effectiveness of its judicial action. This Court should have universal jurisdication and competence in all disputes of a juridical nature which may arise in the life of international relations.

Decisions pronounced by the said Court should be of a binding nature for the parties, none of them being able to refuse compliance under penalty of being designated an aggressor state.

Besides its judicial functions, the Court should also have those of advising on legal matters both the International Organization and its member states.

12. The Government of Bolivia considers that the maintenance of permanent peace and the development of international good-neighborliness depend on insuring positive conditions of well-being for the great masses of the peoples represented in the future Organization, by means of the raising of the standard of living in the less favored nations, the protection of the international rights of man, the perfecting of social security, the provision of material opportunities

for work, and the solution of problems of health, population, and others of the same nature.

PROPOSALS CONCERNING THE DUMBARTON OAKS PROPOSAL   [582]

In view of the preceding considerations, the Bolivian Delegation has the honor to submit for consideration to the United Nations Conference on International Organization, the following proposed additions and amendments to the Dumbarton Oaks Proposals :

Chapter I. Purposes

1. To maintain international peace and security, under the rule of justice; and to that end to take effective collective measures for the prevention and removal of threats to the peace, as well as to suppress all threats or acts of aggression and to bring about by peaceful means the settlement of international situations and disputes.

2. To develop friendly relations among nations and to take appropriate measures to strengthen universal peace, in conformity with the provisions stated in the preceding paragraph.

Chapter II. Principles

1. The Organization is based on the principles of the sovereign equality of all states which pursue peace and justice in relations between member states.

3. All members of the Organization shall be bound to settle their disputes by peaceful means in such a manner that international peace, security, and justice are not endangered.

4. All members of the Organization shall refrain in their international relations from the threat or use of force in any manner inconsistent with the purposes of the Organization. All threats or acts of violence committed by any state to the detriment of any other state shall be considered as acts of aggression committed against all the other members of the Organization.

5. All members of the Organization shall guarantee to each other that the inviolability of their territories shall be respected, and shall not grant any legal recognition to territorial acquisitions which may have been obtained through the use of force or of other   [583] means of coercion. They shall likewise offer to each other the same guarantees concerning respect for their political independence and the right for each to develop freely without the intervention of other states in its internal or external affairs.

317

6. All members of the Organization agree that any threat or act of violence committed by one state to the detriment of another, in defiance of the above-mentioned guaranties, will suffice to qualify that state as an aggressor and for the immediate adoption of the collective security measures contemplated for the maintenance of international peace and harmony.

Chapter III. Membership

1. Membership of the Organization should be open to all sovereign states. States which are not at the moment members of the Organization shall be able to enter it by means of a formal undertaking to respect the principles, purposes, and duties contained in the Charter, to repudiate the use of force as an instrument of national policy and to comply with the special conditions set by the Organization for their admission.

Chapter V. The General Assembly

Section B. 1. The General Assembly should have the right to consider the general principles of cooperation in the maintenance of international peace, security, and justice.

Chapter VII. An International Court of Justice

3. The Statute of the International Court of Justice shall be based on the existing Statute of the Permanent Court of International Justice, which is appended as an annex to this Covenant, with the amendments which may be made to them. The decisions of this Court shall be of a binding and final nature in all disputes of a juridical nature which it may not have been possible to solve by other peaceful means. All states which refuse to comply with these decisions shall be declared aggressor states.

Chapter VIII. Arrangements for the Maintenance of International Peace and Security Including Prevention and Suppression of Aggression.

[58

Section A. 1. The Security Council should be empowered to investigate any dispute or situation which may lead to international friction or give rise to a dispute, and to propose the means which it considers necessary and to determine the measures which will be chosen in order to prevent the continued existence of the dispute or situation from endangering international peace, security, and justice.

2. The Security Council shall recommend the revision of all international treaties or agreements whose continued existence would endanger a good understanding between states or would destroy international harmony. Where the agreement of the parties concerned cannot be obtained, the Security Council shall decide on the expediency of the said revision and shall promote the use of the peaceful means provided for in paragraph 3.

2. Any state, whether member of the Organization or not, may bring any such dispute, situation, or agreement of the sort indicated in the preceding paragraphs to the attention of the General Assembly or of the Security Council.

3. The parties to any dispute the continuance of which is likely to endanger the maintenance of international peace, security, and justice should obligate themselves, first of all, to seek a solution by direct negotiation, investigation, and conciliation, in matters of a political nature, or by judicial settlement in disputes of a juridical nature, or by other peaceful means of their own choice.

7. Paragraph 7 of Section A of Chapter VIII of the Dumbarton Oaks Proposals should be suppressed.

Section B. 2. In general the Security Council should determine the existence of any threat to the peace, breach of the peace, or act of aggression and should make recommendations or decide on the measures to be taken to maintain or restore peace and security. If the nature of the acts investigated entails designating a state as an aggressor as indicated in the following paragraph, these measures should be applied immediately by collective action.

3. A state shall be designated an aggressor if it has committed [585] any of the following acts to the detriment of another state.
a) Invasion of another state's territory by armed forces.
b) Declaration of war.
c) Attack by land, sea, or air forces, with or without declaration of war, on another state's territory, shipping, or aircraft.
d) Support given to armed bands for the purpose of invasion.
e) Intervention in another state's internal or foreign affairs.
f) Refusal to submit the matter which has caused a dispute to the peaceful means provided for its settlement.
g) Refusal to comply with a judicial decision lawfully pronounced by an International Court.

9. The Committee should be composed of the Chiefs of Staff of the permanent members of the Security Council or their representatives, but this should not be construed as excluding the possibility of its being expanded to include the Chiefs of Staff, or their representatives, of all members of the Organization, by the creation of subsidi-

319

ary military organs in the geographical areas of their respective nationalities, to act in an advisory capacity.

Section C. 1. Nothing in the Charter of the Organization should preclude the existence of regional systems, arrangements, or agencies which might co-operate in dealing with such matters relating to the maintenance of international peace, security, and justice, provided that the activities of such regional systems, arrangements or agencies are consistent with the purposes and principles of the Organization. The Security Council should encourage settlement of local disputes through such regional systems, arrangements or agencies, and should not overlook the adoption of such means as it may consider appropriate for the maintenance of world peace or the suppression of an act of aggression. [5

2. The Security Council should, where appropriate, utilize the cooperation of such regional systems, arrangements, or agencies, for enforcement action under its authority. In no case should such regional systems, arrangements, or agencies be able to adopt measures of sanction, whether economic or military, without the expressed authority of the Security Council.

Chapter IX. Social and Economic Problems

Section B. The Economic and Social Council should consist of representatives of eighteen members of the Organization. The states which should be represented for this purpose should be elected by the General Assembly for terms of three years. Each state should have one representative, who should have one vote. Decisions of the Economic and Social Council should be taken by simple majority vote of those present and voting. A procedure should be established to give adequate representation in the Economic and Social Council to the organized labor of the world.

Section C.

    b. to make recommendations, on its own initiative, with respect to international economic and social matters, preferably relative to insuring the well-being of the populations of the member states of the Organization and the solution of humanitarian problems of an international nature.

    c. to achieve concerted action destined to promote the economic development, the industrialization, and the raising of the standard of living of the less favored nations as well as the protection of the international rights of men, the perfecting of social security and the provision of the material opportunities for work, the solution of problems of health and population and others of a similar nature.

DOCUMENT 17 (d)

The United Nations Conference
on International Organization

[53

Doc. 2 (ENGLISH)
G/14 (k)
May 5, 1945

GENERAL

PROPOSED AMENDMENTS TO THE
DUMBARTON OAKS PROPOSALS
SUBMITTED BY THE PHILIPPINE DELEGATION

(NOTE -- For purposes of clarity and convenience, all in-
sertions in and additions to the text are underlined while
words and line proposed for deletion are crossed out. All
page and line numbers refer to those of the printed Text of
the Dumbarton Oaks Proposals, Document 1, G/1.)

PAGE 1. Chapter I. Purposes

10   2. To develop friendly relations and the spirit of
            brotherhood and racial equality among nations and to
11   take other appropriate measures to strengthen universal
12   peace;

II

PAGE 1. Chapter I. Purposes

13   3. To achieve international cooperation in the solution
14   of international economic, cultural, social and other humani-
            tarian
15   problems; and

III

PAGE 2 Chapter II. Principles

2   In pursuit of the purposes mentioned in Chapter I the
3   Organization and its members should act in accordance with

the principles declared in the Atlantic Charter and with
4   the following principles:

IV

PAGE 2. <u>Chapter II. Principles</u>

5
6   1. The Organization is based on the principle of the sovereign equality of all peace-loving <u>and law-abiding</u> ~~states~~ <u>nations.</u>

PAGE 3. <u>Chapter III. Membership</u>

5   ~~1. Membership of the Organization should be open to all~~
6 ~~peace-loving states.~~
5   <u>The members of the Organization should be:</u>
6   <u>1. The original signatories to this Charter;</u>
     <u>2. Any other peace-loving and law-abiding nation which</u> <u>may hereafter be admitted in accordance with the provisions of</u> <u>this Charter.</u>

VI

PAGE 3. Chapter V. <u>The General Assembly</u>

16   SECTION A. COMPOSITION. All members of the Or-
17 ganization should be members of the General Assembly and <u>each</u>
18 should have ~~a number of representatives to be specified in~~ <u>one</u> <u>representative therein.</u>
19 ~~the Charter.~~

VII

PAGE 4. <u>Chapter V. The General Assembly</u>, SECTION B.
        FUNCTIONS AND POWERS. 1.

8 Assembly either before or after discussion. ~~The General~~
9 ~~Assembly should not on its own initiative make recom-~~
10 ~~mendations on any matter relating to the maintenance of~~
11 ~~international peace and security which is being dealt with~~
12 ~~by the Security Council.~~

VIII

PAGE 6. <u>Chapter V. The General Assembly</u>, SECTION B.
FUNCTIONS AND POWERS.

3   8. The General Assembly should receive and consider
4 annual and special reports from the Security Council and
5 reports from other bodies of the Organization.
     9. <u>The General Assembly should be vested with the
legislative authority to enact rules of international law
which should become effective and binding upon the members</u>   [5:
<u>of the Organization after such rules have been approved
by a majority vote of the Security Council. Should the
Security Council fail to act on any of such rules within
a period of thirty (30) days after submission thereof to
the Security Council, the same should become effective
and binding as if approved by the Security Council. In
the exercise of this legislative authority the General
Assembly may codify the existing rules of international
law with such changes as the Assembly may deem proper.</u>

PAGE 7. Chapter VI. The Security Council, SECTION A.
COMPOSITION

7   SECTION A. COMPOSITION. The Security Council should
8 consist of one representative of each of eleven members of the
9 Organization. Representatives of the United States of
10 America, the United Kingdom of Great Britain and
11 Northern Ireland, the Union of Soviet Socialist Re-
12 publics, the Republic of China, and, in due course, France,
13 should have permanent seats. The General Assembly should
14 ~~elect six states to fill the non-permanent seats. These six~~
<u>elect the six representatives to fill the non-permanent
seats on the basis of geographical regions, each region
to be entitled to one representative. These geographical
regions should be: (1) North and Central America,
(2) South America, (3) Europe, (4) Africa, (5) Western
Asia, and (6) Western Pacific Community. The General
Assembly should determine the nations that should be
included in each geographical region. These six</u>

15 states representatives should be elected for a term of two
    years, three retir-
16 ing each year. They should not be immediately eligible for
17 reelection. In the first election of the non-permanent mem-
18 bers three should be chosen by the General Assembly for
19 one-year terms and three for two-year terms.

X

PAGE 9. Chapter VI. The Security Council, SECTION C.
         VOTING:

7   3. Decisions of the Security Council on all other matters
8   should be made by an affirmative vote of seven members
9   including the concurring votes of the permanent members;
        3. Decisions of the Security Council on all other matters
    should be made by an affirmative vote of a majority of the
    permanent members and a majority of the non-permanent mem-
    bers, voting separately;
10   provided that, in decisions under Chapter VIII, Section A,   [538]
11 and under the second sentence of Paragraph 1 of Chapter
12 VIII, Section C, a party to a dispute should abstain from
13 voting.

XI

PAGE 9. Chapter VI. The Security Council, SECTION C.
         VOTING. 3.

13 voting. In all decisions involving the use of armed forces
    to maintain peace, an affirmative vote of four-fifths (4/5)
    of the permanent members and three-fourths (3/4) of the non-
    permanent members of the Security Council should be required.

XII

PAGE 10. Chapter VII. An International Court of Justice

21   2. The court should be constituted and should function
22 in accordance with a statute which should be annexed to an
23 be a part of the Charter of the Organization - ; provided,
    however, that the court should have compulsory jurisdiction.

1 decide upon the measures to be taken to maintain or restore
2 peace and security. Any nation should be considered as threatening the peace or as an aggressor, if it should be the first party to commit any of the following acts: (1) To declare war against another nation; (2) To invade or attack, with or without declaration of war, the territory, public vessel, or public aircraft of another nation; (3) To subject another nation to a naval, land or air blockade; and (4) To interfere with the internal affairs of another nation by supplying arms, ammunition, money or other forms of aid to any armed band, faction or group, or by establishing agencies in that nation to conduct propaganda subversive of the institutions of that nation.

15 forces placed at the disposal of the Security Council. The
16 Committee should be composed of the Chiefs of Staff of all the
17 permanent members of the Security Council or their repre-

18 sentatives. Any member of the Organization not perma-
19 ~~nently~~ represented on the Committee should be invited by

XVI

PAGE 18. Chapter IX. Arrangements for International Economic and Social Cooperation, SECTION A.
PURPOSE AND RELATIONSHIPS.

10   SECTION A. PURPOSE AND RELATIONSHIPS. 1. With
11 a view to the creation of conditions of stability and well-being
12 which are necessary for peaceful and firendly relations among
13 nations, the Organization should facilitate solutions of inter-
14 national economic, cultural, social and other humanitarian
problems

XVII

PAGE 18. Chapter IX. Arrangements for International Economic and Social Cooperation, SECTION A.
PURPOSE AND RELATIONSHIPS. 2.

19   2. The various specialized economic, cultural, social
and other
20 organizations and agencies would have responsibilities in their
21 respective fields as defined in their statutes. Each such or-

XVIII

PAGE 19. Chapter IX. Arrangements for International Economic and Social Cooperation, SECTION B.
COMPOSITION AND VOTING.

The United Nations Conference   Doc. 2 (ENGLISH
on International Organization   G/14 (i)
                                             May 4, 1945

GENERAL

AMENDMENTS TO DUMBARTON OAKS PROPOSALS SUPPLEMENTED BY THE TEXTS ADOPTED AT YALTA, SUBMITTED BY THE GREEK DELEGATION, MAY 3, 1945

In his opening speech, delivered to the Plenary Session of the Conference on April 28, Mr. John Sofianopoulos, Chairman of the Greek Delegation, informed the Conference of his Government's observations in respect of the principles and procedures embodied in the Dumbarton Oaks and the Yalta proposals.

He reserved the right of the Delegation to table specific amendments with the competent organs of the Conference.

In accordance with the rules of procedure adopted by the Conference, the Greek Delegation now has the honor to request the Secretary General of the Conference to submit to the latter for its consideration and eventual adoption the following amendments :

-1-

CHAPTER I and II

Purposes and Principles of the Organization

In Paragraph 1, of Chapter I, to add after the words "To maintain international peace and security" the words: "with due respect for contractual obligations and the generally accepted principles of international law, justice and morality."

The Greek Delegation believes that the adoption of the above amendment would dispel misgivings in the implementation of Chapter VIII. In particular, the last words of paragraph 1 of Section B of that Chapter are vaguely reminiscent of the policy that was followed in the sad pre-war years of "peace at any price," and need clarification by rendering unequivocal the principles and purposes of the organization.

CHAPTER V, SECTION B   [532]

At the end of paragraph 8 to add the words: "It shall be open to the Assembly to make recommendations on any question that is under consideration or has already been treated by the Security Council."

This would involve the deletion of the last part of paragraph 1, Section B of Chapter V.

In the opinion of the Greek Delegation, the role assigned to the Assembly appears to be unimportant in comparison with the powers possessed by the Security Council, and should be rendered more important in extent and depth, since all the members of the organization are represented in the Assembly.

-3-

CHAPTER VI, SECTION C

As at present, with the Yalta text on voting unmodified, the code of international conduct that would emerge from the San Francisco Conference would create a positive right in favor of the potential law-breaker and to the detriment of his victim, since, through the exercise by any one of the permanent members of the power of veto, the Security Council might be debarred from probing into the determination of the existence of an act of aggression. The Greek Delegation reserves to itself the right to support one of the several amendments already tabled by other Delegations with a view to obviating this drawback. Moreover, they propose the insertion between paragraphs 2 and 3 of the texts elaborated at Yalta of a new paragraph 3, reading as follows:

Paragraph 3: "Recommendations by the Security Council under paragraph 2 of Section B of Chapter VIII should be made by an affirmative vote of seven members."

The original paragraph 3 would thus become paragraph 4.

-4-

CHAPTER VIII, SECTION A, PARAGRAPH 5

To add to paragraph 5 the following words: "Should no adjustment be reached and should such failure be considered by the Security Council to be a threat to the peace of the world, the Council [533] should determine by an affirmative vote of seven members the existence of a threat to the peace."

-5-

CHAPTER VIII, SECTION A, PARAGRAPH 7

At the end of paragraph 7 the following words to be added: "It should be left to the Permanent Court at the request of a party to decide whether or no such situation or dispute arises out of matters that, under international law, fall within the domestic jurisdiction of the state concerned."

CHAPTER VIII, SECTION B, PARAGRAPH 2

At the end of paragraph 2 to add the following words: "In particular, in the event of a dispute between two or more countries, other than permanent members of the Security Council, the latter should take decisions by an affirmative vote of seven members in the determination of the existence of a breach of the peace or of an act of aggression."

The United Nations Conference   Doc. 2 (ENGLISH)
on International Organization   G/29
                                       May 5, 1945

GENERAL

AMENDMENTS PROPOSED BY THE GOVERNMENTS OF THE UNITED STATES, THE UNITED KINGDOM, THE SOVIET UNION, AND CHINA

The Delegations of the four Governments which participated in the Dumbarton Oaks Conversations, the United States, the United Kingdom, the Soviet Union, and China, have consulted together concerning amendments to the Dumbarton Oaks Proposals which each of them desired to submit. The proposed amendments on which the four find themselves in agreement are submitted to the Conference as joint proposals. Such further amendments as each of these Governments may wish to propose will be presented separately.

(Note: Amendments are indicated by underscoring added passages and striking out deleted passages.)

CHAPTER I. PURPOSES

1. To maintain international peace and security; and to that end to take effective collective measures for the prevention and removal of threats to the peace and the suppression of acts of aggression or other breaches of the peace, and to bring about by peaceful means, and with due regard for principles of justice and international law, adjustment or settlement of international disputes which may lead to a breach of the peace.

2. To develop friendly relations among nations based on respect for the principle of equal rights and self-determination of peoples and to take other appropriate measures to strengthen universal peace;

3. To achieve international cooperation in the solution of international economic, social, cultural and other humanitarian problems and promotion and encouragement of respect for human rights and for fundamental freedoms for all without distinction as to race, lan-   [623] guage, religion or sex; and

CHAPTER II.   PRINCIPLES

1. The Organization is based on the principle of the sovereign equality of all ~~peace-loving states~~ its members.

3. All members of the Organization shall settle their international disputes by peaceful means in such a manner that international peace and security are not endangered.

New paragraph to be added following paragraph 6, to take the place of paragraph 7 of Chapter VIII, Section A, which would be deleted:

Nothing contained in this Charter shall authorize the Organization to intervene in matters which are essentially within the domestic jurisdiction of the State concerned or shall require the members to submit such matters to settlement under this Charter; but this principle shall not prejudice the application of Chapter VIII, Section B.

CHAPTER V.   THE GENERAL ASSEMBLY
Section B.   Functions and Powers

6. The General Assembly should initiate studies and make recommendations for the purpose of promoting internatioanl cooperation in political, economic, and social and cultural fields to assist in the realization of human rights and basic freedoms for all, without distinction as to race, language, religion or sex and also for the encouragement of the development of international law ~~and of adjusting situations likely to impair the general welfare~~.

New paragraph to follow paragraph 7:

The General Assembly should examine the administrative budgets of such specialized agencies with a view to making recommendations to the agencies concerned.

CHAPTER VI.   THE SECURITY COUNCIL
Section A.   Composition

The Security Council should consist of one representative of each of eleven members of the Organization. Representatives of the United States of America, the United Kingdom of Great Britain and Northern Ireland, the Union of Soviet Socialist Republics, the Republic of China, and, in due course, France, should have permanent seats. The General Assembly should elect six states to fill the non-permanent seats, due regard being specially paid in the first instance to the contribution of members of the Organization towards

[62

the maintenance of international peace and security and towards the other purposes of the Organization, and also to equitable geographical distribution. These six states should be elected for a term of two years, three retiring each year. They should not be immediately eligible for reelection. In the first election of the non-permanent members three should be chosen by the General Assembly for one-year terms and three for two-year terms.

Section D. Procedure

2. The Security Council should be empowered to set up such bodies or agencies as it may deem necessary for the performance of its functions. ~~including regional sub-committees of the Military Staff Committee.~~

5. Any member of the Organization not having a seat on the Security Council and any state not a member of the Organization, if it is a party to a dispute under consideration by the Security Council, should be invited to participate in the discussion relating to the dispute. In the case of a non-member the Security Council should lay down such conditions as it may deem just for the participation of such a non-member.

CHAPTER VII. AN INTERNATIONAL COURT OF JUSTICE

The provisions of Chapter VII of the Dumbarton Oaks Proposals should be adjusted to bring it into conformity with the recommendations of Commission IV in light of the report of the Jurists Committee.

CHAPTER VIII. ARRANGEMENTS FOR THE MAINTENANCE OF INTERNATIONAL PEACE AND SECURITY INCLUDING PREVENTION AND SUPPRESSION OF AGGRESSION

Section A. Pacific Settlement of Disputes

The following new paragraph should be inserted before Paragraph 1 of Section A of Chapter VIII:

Without prejudice to the provisions of paragraphs 1-5 below, the Security Council should be empowered, if all the parties so request, to make recommendations to the parties to any dispute with a view to its settlement in accordance with the principles laid down in Chapter II, Paragraph 3.

2. Any state, whether member of the Organization or not, may bring any such dispute or situation to the attention of the General

Assembly or of the Security Council. In the case of a non-member, [6
it should be required to accept, for the purposes of such dispute,
the obligations of pacific settlement provided in the Charter.

4. If, nevertheless, parties to a dispute of the nature referred
to in paragraph 3 above fail to settle it by the means indicated in
that paragraph, they should obligate themselves to refer it to the
Security Council. ~~The~~ If the Security Council ~~should in each case
decide whether or not~~ deems that the continuance of the particular
dispute is in fact likely to endanger the maintenance of international
peace and security, ~~and, accordingly, whether the Security Council
should deal with the dispute, and, if so, whether it should take action under paragraph 5~~ it shall decide whether to take action under
paragraph 5 or whether itself to recommend such terms of settlement as it may consider appropriate.

7. ~~The provisions of paragraph 1 to 6 of Section A should not
apply to situations or disputes arising out of matters which by in-
ational law are solely within the domestic jurisdiction of the state
concerned.~~

    (Note: This paragraph would be replaced by the new paragraph
    proposed for addition following paragraph 6, Chapter II, Prin-
    ciples.)

Section B. Determination of Threats to the Peace or Acts of Aggression and Action with Respect Thereto

1. Should the Security Council deem that a failure to settle a
dispute in accordance with procedures indicated in paragraph 3 of
Section A, or in accordance with its recommendations made under
paragraphs 4 or 5 of Section A, constitutes a threat to the maintenance of international peace and security, it should take any measures necessary for the maintenance of international peace and security in accordance with the purposes and principles of the Organization.

2. In general the Security Council should determine the existence of any threat to the peace, breach of the peace or act of aggression and should make recommendations or decide upon the
measures set forth in paragraphs 3 and 4 of this Section to be taken
to maintain or restore peace and security.

Insert the following paragraph between paragraphs 2 and 3:

Before making the recommendations or deciding upon the
measures for the maintenance or restoration of peace and security
in accordance with the provisions of paragraph 2, the Security Council may call upon the parties concerned to comply with such provisional measures as it may deem necessary or desirable in order to
prevent an aggravation of the situation. Such provisional measures
should be without prejudice to the rights, claims or position of the
parties concerned. Failure to comply with such provisional measures should be duly taken account of by the Security Council.

9. There should be established a Military Staff Committee
the functions of which should be to advise and assist the Security
Council on all questions relating to the Security Council's military
requirements for the maintenance of international peace and security, to the employment and command of forces placed at its disposal,
to the regulation of armaments, and to possible disarmament. It
should be responsible under the Security Council for the strategic
direction of any armed forces placed at the disposal of the Security
Council. The Committee should be composed of the Chiefs of Staff
of the permanent members of the Security Council or their representatives. Any member of the Organization not permanently represented on the Committee should be invited by the Committee to be
associated with it when the efficient discharge of the Committee's
responsibilities requires that such a state should participate in its
work. Questions of command of forces should be worked out subsequently. The Military Staff Committee, with the authorization of the
Security Council, may establish regional subcommittees of the Military Staff Committee.

CHAPTER IX. ARRANGEMENTS FOR INTERNATIONAL ECONOMIC AND SOCIAL COOPERATION

Section A. Purposes and Relationships

1. With a view to the creation of conditions of stability and
well-being which are necessary for peaceful and friendly relations am
among nations based on respect for the principle of equal rights and
self-determination of peoples, the Organization should facilitate solutions of international economic, social, cultural, and other humanitarian problems and promote respect for human rights and for
fundamental freedoms for all without distinction as to race, language, religion or sex. Responsibility for the discharge of this
function should be vested in the General Assembly, in an Economic
and Social Council.

335

1. The Economic and Social Council should be empowered:

Insert after paragraph a, new paragraph as follows:

To make recommendations for promoting respect for
human rights and fundamental freedoms;

b. To make recommendations, on its own initiative with
respect to international economic, social, cultural
and other humanitarian matters;

c. To receive and consider reports from the economic,
social, cultural and other organizations or agencies
brought into relationship with the Organization, and
to coordinate their activities through consultations
with, and recommendations to such organizations or
agencies;

Section D.   Organization and Procedure

1. The Economic and Social Council should set up ~~an economic commission, a social commission and such other commissions as may be required~~ commissions in the fields of economic
activity, social activity, cultural activity, promotion of human
rights and any other field within the competence of the Council.
These commissions should consist of experts. There should be a
permanent staff which should constitute a part of the Secretariat of
the Organization.

CHAPTER X. THE SECRETARIAT

1. There should be a Secretariat comprising a Secretary-
General, four deputies and such staff as may be required. ~~The
Secretary General should be the chief administrative officer of the
Organization. He should be elected by the General Assembly, on
recommendation of the Security Council, for such term and under
such conditions as are specified in the Charter.~~ The Secretary-General and his deputies should be elected by the General Assembly on
recommendation of the Security Council for a period of three years,
and the Secretary-General should be eligible for re-election. The

Secretary-General should be the chief administrative officer of the Organization.

4. In the performance of their duties, the Secretary-General and the staff should be responsible only to the Organization. Their responsibilities should be exclusively international in character, and they should not seek or receive instructions in regard to the discharge thereof from any authority external to the Organization. The members should undertake fully to respect the international character of the responsibilities of the Secretariat and not to seek to influence any of their nationals in the discharge of such responsibilities.

[628]

CHAPTER XI. AMENDMENTS

1. The present Charter comes into force after its ratification in accordance with their respective constitutional processes by the members of the Organization having permanent seats on the Security Council and by a majority of the other members of the Organization.

> Note: The existing text of Chapter XI would become paragraph 2.

2. A general conference of the members of the United Nations may be held at a date and place to be fixed by a three-fourths vote of the General Assembly with the concurrence of the Security Council voting in accordance with the provisions of Chapter VI, Section C, paragraph 2, for the purpose of reviewing the Charter. Each member shall have one vote in the Conference. Any alterations of the Charter recommended by a two-thirds vote of the Conference shall take effect when ratified in accordance with their respective constitutional processes by the members of the Organization having permanent membership on the Security Council and by a majority of the other members of the Organization.

DOCUMENT 17 (g)

RESTRICTED
Doc. 289 (ENGLISH)
III/3/11
May 13, 1945

Texts of Dumbarton Oaks Proposals, Amendments

of Sponsoring Powers, and Amendment Submitted

by Other Participating Governments, Relating

to Chapter VIII B and XII.

Committee 3   Enforcement Arrangements

338

TEXT OF DUMBARTON OAKS PROPOSALS AND OF AMENDMENTS PRESENTED BY THE FOUR SPONSORING POWERS

Chapter VIII, Section B, Paragrah 1

1. Should the Security Council deem that a failure to settle a dispute in accordance with procedures indicated in paragraph 3 of Section A, or in accordance with its recommendations made under paragraph 5 of Section A, constitutes a threat to the maintenance of international peace and security, it should take any measures necessary for the maintenance of international peace and security in accordance with the purposes and principles of the Organization.

Amendment Proposed by Sponsoring Powers

1. Should the Security Council

Australia

1. Should the Security Council deem that a failure to settle a dispute in accordance with the procedures indicated in paragraph 3 of Section A, or in accordance with its recommendations made under paragraph 5 of Section A, constitutes a threat to the maintenance of international peace and security, it shall, in accordance with the purposes and principles of the United Nations, lay down just terms for the settlement of the dispute, and take any measures necessary for carrying out that settlement and for maintaining international peace and security. (Doc. 2, G/14 (1) p. 9)

Chile

1. Should the Security Council believe that failure to settle a dispute in accordance with procedures indicated in paragraph 3 of Section A above, or in accordance with its recommendations under paragraph 5 of the said Section A, constitutes a threat to the maintenance of international peace and security, it should take any measures necessary for the maintenance of international peace and security which are in accord with the purposes, principles and Charter of the Organization.
(The phrase "purposes and principles of the Organization" is amended

339

to "purposes, principles and Charter of the Organization"). (Doc. 2, G/7 (i) p. 7)

Mexico

1. Should the Security Council or the General Assembly deem that a failure to settle a dispute in accordance with procedures indicated in paragraph 3 of Section A, or in accordance with its recommendations made under paragraph 5 of Section A, constitutes a threat to the maintenance of international peace and security, the Security Council should take any measures necessary for the maintenance of international peace and security in accordance with the purposes and principles of the organization. (Doc. 2, G/7 (1) pp. 12-13)

deem that a failure to settle a dispute in accordance with procedures indicated in paragraph 3 of Section A, or in accordance with its recommendations made under paragraphs 4 or 5 of Section A, constitutes a threat to the maintenance of international peace and security, it should take any measures necessary for the maintenance of international peace and security in accordance with the purposes and principles of the Organization.

Netherlands

1. Should the Security Council under paragraph 8 of Section A deter-mine the existence of a threat to the maintenance of international peace and security, it should take any measures necessary for the maintenance of international peace and security in accordance with the purposes and principles of the Organization. (Doc. 2 G/7 (j) (1), p. 5)

Turkey
(To be added to paragraph 1)

At all events, the Council will lend its assistance to any party to a dispute who has agreed to submit to judicial settlement and to the deci-sion of the court, if required. (Doc. 2 G/7 (e)(1) p. 2)

Australia

(No paragraph after paragraph 2)

(3) If a situation calling for preventive or enforcement action under paragraph (1) or paragraph (2) above has arisen out of a matter which by international law is solely within the domestic jurisdiction of the State concerned, the Security Council shall not make any recommenda-tion or decision which would curtail that State's lawful freedom of ac-tion, but shall take, in accordance with this Section, whatever preven-tive or enforcement action is necessary to maintain or restore interna-

Chapter VIII, Section B, Para-graph 2

2. In general the Security Coun-cil should determine the existence of any threat to the peace, broach of the peace or act of aggression and should make recommendations or decide upon the measures to be taken to maintain or restore peace and security.

341

tional peace and security. (Doc. 2 G/14 (1) pp. 9-10)

Bolivia

2. In general the Security Council should determine the existence of any threat to the peace, breach of the peace, or act of aggression and should make recommendations or decide on the measures to be taken to maintain or restore peace and security. If the nature of the acts investigated entails designating a state as an aggressor as indicated in the following paragraph, these measures should be applied immediately by collective action.

3. A state shall be designated an aggressor if it has committed any of the following acts to the detriment of another state.

a) Invasion of another state's territory by armed forces.

b) Declaration of war.

c) Attack by land, sea, or air forces, with or without declaration of war, on another state's territory, shipping, or aircraft.

d) Support given to armed bands for the purpose of invasion.

e) Intervention in another state's internal or foreign affairs.

f) Refusal to submit the matter which has caused a dispute to the peaceful means provided for its settlement.

g) Refusal to comply with a judicial decision lawfully pronounced by an International Court. (Doc. 2 G/14 (r), pp. 8-9)

Amendment Proposed by Sponsoring Powers

2. In general the Security Council should determine the existence of any threat to the peace, breach of the peace or act of aggression and should make recommendations or decide upon the measures set forth in paragraphs 3 and 4 of this Section to be taken to maintain or restore peace and security.

(Insert the following paragraph between paragraphs 2 and 3)

Before making the recommendations or deciding upon the measures for the maintenance or restoration of peace and security in accordance with the provisions of paragraph 2, the Security Council may call upon the parties con-

342

cerned to comply with such provisional measures as it may deem necessary or desirable in order to prevent an aggravation of the situation. Such provisional measures should be without prejudice to the rights, claims or position of the parties concerned. Failure to comply with such provisional measures should be duly taken account of by the Security Council.

Ethiopia
(To be added as an additional sentence)
So long as a dispute is subject to the procedure of paragraphs 3, 4 and 5 of the present Section the parties to the dispute shall resort to no measures of a military character and the Security Council shall take such measures or action as it shall find necessary to ensure the fulfilment of this obligation. (Doc. 2 G/14 (n), p. 3)

Greece
(To be added at the end of paragraph 2)
In particular, in the event of a dispute between two or more countries, other than permanent members of the Security Council, the latter should take decisions by an affirmative vote of seven members in the determination of the existence of a breach of the peace or of an act of aggression. (Doc. 2, G/14 (i) p. 3)

Mexico
2. The Security Council or the General Assembly, should determine the existence of any threat to the peace, breach of the peace or act of aggression and should make recommendations or decide upon the measures to be taken to maintain or restore peace and security. (Doc. 2 G/7 (c)(1) p. 13)

Netherlands
2. Should the Security Council in general under paragraph 9 of Section A determine the existence of any threat to the peace, breach of the

peace or act of aggression, it should decide upon the measures to be taken to maintain or restore peace and security. (Doc. 2 G/7 (j)(1) p.5)

Philippine Commonwealth
(Add the following sentence at the end of the paragraph)

Any nation should be considered as threatening the peace or as an aggressor, if it should be the first party to commit any of the following acts: (1) To invade or attack, with or without declaration of war, the territory, public vessel, or public aircraft of another nation; (2) To declare war against another nation; (3) To subject another nation to a naval, land or air blockade; and (4) To interfere with the internal affairs of another nation by supplying arms, ammunition, money or other forms of aid to any armed band, faction or group, or by establishing agencies in that nation to conduct propaganda subversive of the institutions of that nation. (Doc. 2 G/14 (k) p. 4)

Mexico
3. The Security Council, after prior decision of the General Assembly, should be empowered to determine what diplomatic, economic, or other measures not involving the use of armed forces should be employed to give effect to its decisions, and to call upon members of the Organization to apply such measures. (Doc. 2 G/7 (c) (1) p. 13)

Chapter VIII, Section B, Paragraph 3
3. The Security Council should be empowered to determine what diplomatic, economic, or other measures not involving the use of armed force should be employed to give effect to its decisions, and to call upon members . . .

The United Nations Conference
on International Organization

RESTRICTED
Doc. 442 (ENGLISH)
III/3/20
May 19, 1945

COMMISSION III   Security Council

Committee 3   Enforcement Arrangements

SUMMARY REPORT OF NINTH MEETING OF COMMITTEE III/3

Veterans Building, Room 223, May 18, 1945, 10:30 a. m.

The Chairman opened the ninth meeting of the Committee at 10:45 a.m.

1.   Discussion: Designation of Aggression

The Secretary read the proposed amendments to Chapter VIII, Section B, paragraph 2, by Bolivia (Doc. 2, G/14 (r), pp. 8, 9) and by the Philippine Commonwealth (Doc 2, G/14 (k), p.4).

The Bolivian Delegate made the following motion:

"that the Security Council should intervene immediately when one or all of the circumstances listed
in the Bolivian amendment present themselves, and
that the establishment of the list of circumstances
be referred to a Subcommittee."

The motion was seconded by Delegates from Uruguay and Mexico.

Delegates from Bolivia, Colombia, Egypt, Ethiopia, Guatemala, Honduras, Iran, Mexico, New Zealand, and Uruguay gave the following arguments in support of the motion. It should be known beforehand what acts would constitute aggression and, consequently, what acts would be subject to sanctions. The Council's work would be facilitated if a definite list were written in the Charter. The seven cir- cumstances listed would provide for automatic Council action in these cases. The list was not intended as a de- finitive one nor as one which would prohibit the Council from acting in other cases.

In certain instances there could be no doubt of ag- gression. Assurance is desirable that the Council would act in these circumstances. The Charter should contain a state- ment of principle, at least, to the effect that aggression would not be tolerated, even though an exact definition were not given. The proposed four-government amendment to be added after paragraph 2 constitutes a partial definition of aggression and should be expanded. (Doc. 2, G/29. pp.4, 5) The Organization must bind itself to oppose lawless force by lawful forces in certain cases where action should be obligatory. No one could doubt the necessity for action in the event of the first three Bolivian circumstances. If one vote on the Security Council could prevent action, then it would be essential to have a list of circumstances when Council action would be automatic.

It was suggested that reference might profitably be made to the terms of the treaty between Afghanistan, Iraq, Iran, and the U.S.S.R.

Delegates from Czechoslovakia, the Netherlands, Norway, Paraguay, the Union of South Africa, the United Kingdom, and the United States of American opposed the motion on the following grounds. It would be impossible to enumerate all the acts that constitute aggression. Prior definition would be difficult whereas recognition of an act after it had been committed would be simple. The tendency, in the case of an incomplete list, would be to exclude the omitted acts from consideration. Any attempt to make Council action automatic would be dangerous for it might force premature application of sanctions. The safest course would be to give the Council discretion to decide when an act of aggression had been performed. The six nonpermanent members of the Council could veto action in such circumstances.

It was further suggested that refusal of a state to comply with the judicial decision of an international court, point (g) of the Bolivian amendment, had been improperly included in list of acts of aggression. Adequate provision for the detection of aggression had been made in the Charter in Chapter VIII Section A, where states were obligated to follow peaceful procedures for settlement of disputes. There was no one kind of act, defined as an act of aggression, which in conceivable circumstances might not be a legitimate act of self-defense. Even with reference to the first item of the Bolivian list, invasion by armed force, it might be difficult to determine th invader if there had been provocation on one side which forced action by the other. Furthermore, within the list there were several points which would require definition, e.g. when "intervention" was to be considered aggression.

*The United Nations Conference
on International Organization*

RESTRICTED
Doc. 502 (ENGLISH)
III/3/22
May 23, 1945

COMMISSION III   Security Council

Committee 3   Enforcement Arrangements

SUMMARY REPORT OF TENTH MEETING OF COMMITTEE III/3

Veterans Building, Room 223, May 21, 1945, 8:50 p.m.

The Chairman opened the tenth meeting of the Committee at 8:50 p.m.

1. Discussion: Definition of Aggression

Discussion continued on the pending Bolivian motion to make more explicit reference to certain acts of aggression in the Charter.

The Delegate from the Philippine Commonwealth, in supporting the Bolivian motion, requested that the first sentence of the proposed Philippine amendment be revised as follows:

> "Any nation should be considered as threatening
> the peace or as an aggressor, if it should be the first
> party to commit any of the following acts, among others..."
> (Doc. 2, G/14 (k), p.4)

The revision is to insert the words "among others".

Delegates from Bolivia, Egypt, the Philippine Commonwealth and Uruguay spoke in favor of the motion. Delegates from the Byelorussian S.S.R., Chile, France, and the U.S.S.R. spoke against the motion.

At the request of the Bolivian Delegate the following statement is incorporated in the record:

> "The Delegation of Bolivia, in proposing an amendment to provide criteria for determining an aggressor, had in mind the desirability of facilitating the action of the Security Council, through the determination of certain acts of an aggressive nature which, since they provide objective tests, might permit the application of immediate repressive measures for the maintenance of peace and security. It consequently maintains that

the failure to specify such cases detracts from the
effectiveness and celerity of the system of world
security for the urgent and timely repression of aggression."

A proposal to turn the question over to some other body
of the international organization, perhaps the Committee of
Jurists, for further consideration, was ruled out of order.

Decision: The Bolivian motion was defeated by a vote
of 22 to 12.

2. Announcements

The Delegate from Greece withdrew his proposed amendment
to paragraph 2, Section B, Chapter VIII, for reference to the
appropriate Committee concerned with voting.

The Chairman announced that the agenda for the next
meeting would include consideration of the Subcommittee draft
amending paragraphs 1 and 2 of Chapter VIII, Section B. (Doc.
478, III/3/B/1, May 21, 1945.)

The meeting was adjourned at 10:45 p.m.

The United Nations Conference
on International Organization

RESTRICTED
Doc. 881 (ENGLISH)
III/3/46
June 10, 1945

COMMISSION III   Security Council
    Committee 3   Enforcement Arrangements

REPORT OF MR. PAUL-BONCOUR, RAPPORTEUR, ON CHAPTER VIII, SECTION B

Committee 3 of the Third Commission has been charged with the task of redrafting the provisions included in Chapter VIII, Section B, and Chapter XII of the Dumbarton Oaks Proposals.

These provisions have been under consideration by this Committee at meetings held since May 4 under the chairmanship of Mr. Camilo Ponce Enriquez, Minister of Foreign Affairs of Ecuador. It gives me especial pleasure to acknowledge the great credit which is due him for his helpful leadership of the Committee's discussions.

In the course of its first meetings, the Committee was faced by a multiplicity of amendments referring to a single idea, though expressed at times in different paragraphs. It decided to study the various amendments in the systematic order which I had suggested for their classification in my preliminary report.

It is, therefore, in the order thus set forth, that I shall report on the deliberations to which these amendments gave rise.

I. ROLE OF THE SECURITY COUNCIL

An initial category of amendments proposed by the various powers referred to the procedure contemplated in Section B of Chapter VIII for the determination of the existence of threats to the peace or of acts of aggression, and of the role of the Security Council in this procedure.

A. Participation by the Assembly or   [503]
    Enlargement of the Council

A general discussion was first entered into on the proposal

to supplement the action of the Security Council by participation of the Assembly in decisions relative to enforcement measures or to provide for the particiaption of states not members of the Council in decisions relative to such measures.

The majority of the powers that expressed their opinion on these two proposals emphasized in the first place that the Council included a majority of members elected by the Assembly, in which all the powers of the international Organization originally reside. For this reason, the Security Council must be granted full confidence since, aside from the question of the unanimity of the permanent members, it expresses, in the final analysis, only the opinions of the Assembly.

They then stated that the application of enforcement measures, in order to be effective, must above all be swift; they recognized in general that it is impossible to conceive of swift and effective action if the decision of the Council must be submitted to ratification by the Assembly, or if the measures applied by the Council are susceptible of revision by the Assembly. This, moreover, would be contrary to the basic idea of the Organization, which contemplated a differentiation between the functions of the Council and those of the Assembly.

Under these conditions, the Committee formally declared itself, by several votes, against intervention by the Assembly in this procedure.

Nevertheless, retaining the idea expressed by a Canadian amendment, a subcommittee was constituted to find a compromise formula which, while taking into account the major consideration that the action of the Security Council should be neither weakened nor delayed, might nevertheless associate states not represented in the Council with decisions concerning the utilization of the forces which they place at the disposal of the Organization.

At the meeting of June 2, the Committee approved the following text of a new paragraph to be inserted between paragraphs 5 and 6 of Section B of Chapter VIII:

"When a decision to use force has been taken
by the Security Council, it shall, before calling
upon any member not represented on it to provide
armed forces in fulfillment of its obligations
under the preceding paragraph, invite such member,
if it so request, to send a representative to participate in the decisions of the Security Council concerning the employment of contingents of its armed
forces."

This supplementary paragraph takes into account the concern very vigorously expressed by many powers that the military
forces put at the disposition of the Security Council by the special
agreements might be used without the contributing nation having had
a voice in the Council meetings where it is decided to use these
forces. Henceforth, every member not represented on the Council
may participate, with the right of voting, in the deliberations of the
Council when it is a question of the utilization of its armed forces.
To repeat a well chosen expression of the Delegate of the Netherlands, the principle of "no military action without representation"
was accepted by the Committee.

This decision is of such a nature as to reassure, in large
measure, the middle and small powers, which might otherwise
have feared that they were giving carte blanche to the Council in
the particularly serious domain of the utilization of their military
forces outside their national frontiers.

It has not appeared possible to extend the conception of ad
hoc representation on the Council to include those instances wherein the latter discusses, not the utilization of armed forces, but rather the use of facilities and assistance to be furnished by a state
not a member of the Council. As a matter of fact, it was recognized that the adoption of such a formula might unduly increase the
number of Council members and delay its decisions.

Furthermore, the desire to take into consideration the well-
founded observations of the Egyptian Delegation on this subject led
the Committee to approve the explanations furnished by the Delegations of Great Britain, the U.S.S.R., France, and Greece. Accordingly, it was recognized that the question "of facilities and assistance" was already covered by the special agreements contemplated
in paragraph 5, Section B, Chapter VIII. Paragraph 9 of the said
chapter contemplates, on the other hand, that a state not represented on the Military Staff Committee should be invited to be associated with it should be need arise. Finally, paragraph 4 of Section
D, Chapter VI, formally provides for the participation in the Council discussions of any member of the Organization whose interests
may be particularly affected.

In the light of these assurances, which covered its point of
view, the Delegation of Egypt withdrew its amendment.

B. Limitations on the Council's Freedom of Action

A number of amendments referring to paragraphs 1 and 2

were directed at limiting the very great freedom which, in the Dumbarton Oaks Proposals, is left to the Council in determining what action, if any, to take.

Some of these amendments were designed to make more precise the Council's obligation to act in accordance with the purposes and principles of the Organization and the provisions of the Charter. The Committee considered that, since such specifications were already stated in Chapter VI defining the powers of the Council, it was unnecessary to make special mention of them in the present chapter.

The Committee similarly put aside a proposal which would have obligated the Council to aid any party submitting to judicial settlement. It believed that this unduly restricted the Council's freedom of action and that cases might arise where a party refusing to submit to a judicial settlement might not necessarily be at fault.

C.   Determination of Acts of Aggression

A more protracted discussion developed in the Committee on the possible insertion in paragraph 2, Section B, Chapter VIII, of the determination of acts of aggression.

Various amendments proposed on this subject recalled the definitions written into a number of treaties concluded before this war but did not claim to specify all cases of aggression. They proposed a list of eventualities in which intervention by the Council would be automatic. At the same time they would have left to the Council the power to determine the other cases in which it should likewise intervene.

Although this proposition evoked considerable support, it nevertheless became clear to a majority of the Committee that a preliminary definition of aggression went beyond the possibilities of this Conference and the purpose of the Charter. The progress of the technique of modern warfare renders very difficult the definition of all cases of aggression. It may be noted that, the list of such cases being necessarily incomplete, the Council would have a tendency to consider of less importance the acts not mentioned therein; those omissions would encourage the aggressor to distort the definition or might delay action by the Council. Furthermore, in the other cases listed, automatic action by the Council might bring about a premature application of enforcement measures.

The Committee therefore decided to adhere to the text drawn up at Dumbarton Oaks and to leave to the Council the entire decision as to what constitutes a threat to peace, a breach of the peace, or an act of aggression.

An amendment which would have called upon the Council to
have recourse to provisional measures before applying enforcement
measures, and another amendment specifying the enforcement meas-   [506]
ures to be taken, revealed the lack of precision of the term "measures" used in paragraphs 1 and 2, Section B, Chapter VIII, of the
Dumbarton Oaks Proposals. An explanation was also requested as
to the meaning of the word "recommendations" in the same text.
A drafting Subcommittee was charged with the work of proposing a
rewording of these texts, taking into account the various amendments presented.

In the work of redrafting the texts by the Subcommittee,
every effort was made to distinguish between the cases of threats to
the peace in paragraph 1 in which cases the Security Council would
have latitude to judge whether it should or should not apply enforcement measures, and the cases in paragraph 2 where the Council,
having found that a breach of the peace or the act of aggression had
occurred, should be obliged to decide upon the application of enforcement measures. The Committee believed that this distinction, which
had the merit of clarity, might endanger the Council's free discretion as proposed in the text of Dumbarton Oaks. Too rigid a distinction between threats to the peace and attempts against the peace,
or acts of aggression, appeared to the Committee to be in contradiction with the previous decision to avoid a definition of aggression
and with the general spirit of the Charter.

Under these circumstances a motion, inspired by a desire
to follow more faithfully the original text, was made by China. This
motion, which omits paragraph 1 of the Dumbarton Oaks Proposals
and constitutes a new paragraph 2 of the amendment concerning provisional measures, reads as follows:

(1) The Security Council should determine the existence of any threat to the peace, breach of the
peace, or act of aggression, and should make recommendations or decide upon the measures set forth in
paragraphs 3 and 4 of this Section to be taken to
maintain or restore peace and security.

(2) Before making recommendations or deciding upon
the measures for the maintenance or restoration
of peace and security in accordance with the provisions of paragraph 1, the Security Council may

call upon the parties concerned to comply with
such provisional measures as it may deem necessary
or desirable in order to prevent an aggravation
of the situation. Such provisional measures
should be without prejudice to the rights, claims,
or position of the parties concerned. Failure
to comply with such provisional measures should
be duly taken account of by the Security Council.

The new paragraph 1 which reproduces in effect the provi- [507]
sions of the former paragraph 2 of the Dumbarton Oaks Proposals
leaves to the Security Council the task of determining the existence
of any threat to the peace, breach of the peace, or act of aggression.
According to the circumstances the Security Council should make
recommendations and decide upon the enforcement measures to be
taken as set forth in this Chapter. It may also initially call upon
the parties concerned to comply with provisional measures (paragraph 2).

I would nevertheless be contrary to the opinion generally expressed within the Committee to imagine that the very great latitude
thus left to the Council should retard its action or diminish its effectiveness.

This is what Senator Rolin, the Belgian Representative, desired to emphasize by withdrawing in the name of the drafting sub-
comittee the draft proposed by that subcommittee. Therefore, according to his request it was decided that the new text should be interpreted in accordance with the scope of the following observations,
the inclusion of which in the report was unanimously approved by
the committee.

(1) "In using the word 'recommendations' in Section B,
as already found in paragraph 5, Section A, the
Committee has intended to show that the action of
the Council so far as it relates to the peaceful
settlement of a dispute or the situations giving
rise to a threat of war, a breach of the peace, or
aggression, should be considered as governed by
the provisions contained in Section A. Under such
an hypothesis, the Council would in reality pursue
simultaneously two distinct actions, one having for
its object the settlement of the dispute or the
difficulty, and the other, the enforcement or provisional measures, each of which is governed by an
appropriate section in Chapter VIII."

(2) "It is the Committee's view that the power given
to the Council under paragraphs 1 and 2 not to
resort to the measures contemplated in paragraphs
3 and 4, or to resort to them only after having
sought to maintain or restore peace by inviting
the parties to consent to certain conservatory
measures, refers above all to the presumption of
a threat of war. The Committee is unanimous in
the belief that, on the contrary, in the case of
flagrant aggression imperiling the existence of a
member of the Organization, enforcement measures
should be taken without delay, and to the full
extent required by circumstances, except that the
Council should at the same time endeavor to persuade the aggressor to abandon its venture, by the
means contemplated in Section A and by prescribing
conservatory measures."

In addition, assurance was sought by the Canadian Delega-   [508]
tion that members would not be required to provide forces in excess of those which had already been promised in the special agreements mentioned in paragraph 5. This interpretation was forthcoming from the Delegate of the United Kingdom, speaking on behalf of the sponsoring governments.

It was after reconsideration of the above observations that
the Committee finally approved the new text by a vote of 35 to 1.

II. MECHANISM OF ENFORCEMENT MEASURES

A second category of amendments proposed by various powers refers to the actual mechanism of application of enforcement
measures.

A. Economic Measures and other Non-Military Measures

After an exchange of views concerning financial measures
and the compatibility of obligations resulting from paragraph 3,
Section B, with other obligations deriving from treaties, the Committee adopted paragraph 3, Section B, Chapter VIII, or the Dumbarton Oaks Proposals.

B. Military Measures

The Committee turned then to consider military enforcement
measures. In the first place, an amendment presented by the Norwegian Delegation, to provide that the Security Council may "take

355

over on behalf of the Organization the administration of any territory of which the continued administration by the state in possession is found to constitute a threat to the peace", was withdrawn, after it had been indicated that such a reference to a particular procedure could be interpreted as restrictive and of such nature as to limit te the field of application of measures at the disposition of the Council.

The Committee adopted by unanimous vote the text of paragraph 4 of the Dumbarton Oaks Proposals, which gives to the Council the power, when diplomatic, economic, or other measures are considered by the Council to be inadequate, to undertake such aerial, naval, or other operations as may be necessary to maintain or restore international peace and security.

One cannot overemphasize the importance of this unanimous vote, which renders sacred the obligation of all states to participate in the operations.

The principle of enforcement measures of a military nature [509 being thus established, the Committee proceeded to a study of the methods of applying these measures.

1.   National Contingents and Special Agreements

It will be recalled that the Dumbarton Oaks Proposals contemplated that the force put at the disposition of the Security Council should take the form of national contingents furnished by the members according to the special agreements to be negotiated subsequently. These contingents would be put into action in accordance with the plans of a Military Staff Committee. Furthermore, the special agreements should specifiy the number and type of forces as well as the facilities and assistance to be furnished in each case. Finally, it was contemplated that national air force contingents should be held at the immediate disposition of the Security Council.

We have classified in two categories the amendments relative to this part of the Dumbarton Oaks Proposals, by distinguishing between those which concern the organization and the composition of the national contingents, on the one hand, and those which refer to special agreements, on the other.

In reality, it soon became evident that all these amendments were closely connected and that a comprehensive solution was necessary.

This solution was found in a new draft of paragraph 5. Proposed by the Representative of France in the name of the four sponsoring governments, France, and Australia, this text was unanimously approved by the Committee which considered that it incorporated the substance of the amendments presented and of the ob-

servations formulated during the discussion. The text of the new
paragraph 5 is as follows:

"In order that all members of the Organization should contribute to the maintenance of international peace and security, they should undertake
to make available to the Security Council, on its
call and in accordance with a special agreement or
agreements, armed forces, assistance and facilities
including rights of passage necessary for the purpose
of maintaining international peace and security.
Such agreement or agreements should govern the
numbers and types of forces, their degree of readiness and general location, and the nature of the
facilities and assistance to be provided. The
special agreement or agreements should be negotiated
as soon as possible on the initiative of the   [510]
Security Council and concluded between the
Security Council and member states or between
the Security Council and groups of member states.
All such agreements should be subject to ratification by the signatory states in accordance
with their constitutional processes."

Contents of the Special Agreements. One of the criticisms
made of the Dumbarton Oaks Proposals was its lack of precision
concerning the content of the special agreements. In this respect,
the new text contains some specifications of great interest.

Taking into consideration the desire expressed by France,
the right of passage is specifically mentioned in the text as one of
the "facilities" to be furnished by the member states, although this
mention is not intended to exclude the granting of other facilities.
The Committee agreed to this inclusion in the light of the precedent
contained in the Covenant of the League of Nations, but with the conviction that this important international obligation should not be violated or disregarded as has occurred too often in the past.

The next text of paragraph 5 specifies, on the other hand,
that the special agreements should fix the degree of readiness and
general location of the forces. It thus incorporates the substance
of the amendments introduced by France to paragraphs 5 and 6 concerning the period within which forces must be made available and
the zones of occupation of the military contingents.

Agreements Concluded With the Council. Another very serious criticism of the Dumbarton Oaks Proposals made by the Delegations of Australia, New Zealand, and India related to the excessive

357

latitude allowed member states with respect to the conclusion of the special agreements. The obligation imposed upon them was not specific; the consent of the Security Council was presented as a simple formality, to such an extent that one might ask if, in reality, such agreements would ever be concluded and if they would fulfil their objective.

The new text of paragraph 5 remedies these defects inasmuch as it provides:

in the first place, that the special agreements
will be concluded on the initiative of the Council.
The latter may, should the occasion arise, counter-
act any dilatory action on the part of a member not
anxious to conclude a special agreement;
in the second place, that the special agreements
shall be concluded between the Security Council and
members or groups of members.

Inasmuch as the Council, as such, will be a party in all cases to the special agreements, it may demand that the agreements be formulated in such a manner that they effectively fulfil the aims stipulated for them in the Charter.

This in no way excludes the possibility of the conclusion of special agreements to which several members would be parties. Mention is made, in fact, in the new text of "groups of members" which may be mutually bound by special agreements but on the express condition that the Council itself be included among the signatories and that it would not be satisfied with merely giving its approval.

The progress made on the text of paragraph 5 was considered so satisfactory that it permitted the unanimous adoption without modification of paragraphs 6 and 7 of the Dumbarton Oaks Proposals.

Air Force Contingents. In the light of the explanations furnished on the subject of paragraph 5, it became apparent that the mention in paragraph 6 of national air force contingents to be held immediately available to the Organization could not in any way be considered as restrictive. The mention in paragraph 5 of the "Number and types of forces, their degree of readiness and general location" covers, in reality, military contingents in their entirety, and there is absolutely no question of limiting them to the air force contingents. If air force contingents are mentioned in paragraph 6, it is solely for the purpose of supplementary precision, without the general scope of paragraph 5 being in any way restricted.

Under these conditions Australia and France, taking into account these explanations, withdrew the amendments which they had presented in regard to the use of "mixed contingents" or of "forces of all arms".

Paragraph 7. A worthy desire for precision led the Delegation of Chile to ask that it be indicated in paragraph 7 that members of the Organization, in the application of military measures, should act as may be determined by the Security Council and in accordance with the agreements mentioned in paragraph 5. The explanations offered during the discussion of the new paragraph 5 and the fact that such a definition concerning military measures might be interpreted as relieving the member states of their obligations relative [512] to diplomatic, economic, or other measures led the Delegation of Chile to withdraw its amendment.

Paragraphs 6, 7, and 8 -- the latter serving only as an introduction to paragraph 9 -- were therefore adopted unanimously.

Military Staff Committee. Paragraph 9 of the Dumbarton Oaks Proposals concerning the Military Staff Committee, which is to advise and help the Security Council concerning its military needs, gave rise to an interesting debate.

The Committee unanimously approved an amendment to the effect that the Military Staff Committee should have power to establish regional subcommittees of the Military Staff Committee with the authorization of the Security Council. The Committee further provided that regional staff subcommittees should be constituted only after consultation with regional agencies.

As regards the actual composition of the Military Staff Committee, after having considered various proposals to increase the number of states eligible for representation, the Committee recognized the need for the membership on the Staff Committee to be limited. The Dumbarton Oaks Proposals quite rightly intended an organ composed of a small number of representatives; strategic plans and a means of putting them into effect cannot be formulated in discussions among too large a number of people responsible for them. The explanations given both as regards consultation between the international Committee and the national military staff of any country called upon to provide armed forces, and as regards the role of strategic direction rather than that of military command assigned to the international Military Staff Committee were deemed satisfactory by the Committee.

The Committee therefore unanimously adopted paragraph 9 with the additions just mentioned.

The Delegate of the Netherlands furthermore requested that this report should mention the explanation given by the Delegate of

359

Great Britain to the effect that in his personal opinion the Military Staff Committee should reply to any written or verbal questions raised by members of the Organization which are not represented on this Committee.

Economic Problems of Enforcement Action, In conclusion, [513 having heard various explanations on the subject of mutual assistance between states in the application of the measures determined by the Security Council and having noted the legitimate concern expressed by South Africa that the expenses of enforcement action carried out against a guilty state should fall upon that state, the Committee declared itself satisfied with the provisions of paragraphs 10 and 11.

A desire moreover was expressed that the Organization should, in the future, seek to promote a system aiming at the fairest possible distribution of expenses incurred as a result of enforcement action.

Having duly noted the explanations and suggestions given, the Committee unanimously adopted paragraphs 10 and 11 of the Dumbarton Oaks Proposals without change.

Your Committee has thus accomplished the difficult task which was entrusted to it and which was destined to establish what might justly be considered the keystone of the peace structure which we are in the process of building. As I said in my preliminary report, this part of the Proposals of Dumbarton Oaks constitutes, in effect, from the point of view of security, definite and considerable progress over measures adopted previously and especially over the Covenant of the League of Nations.

Its authors have taken into consideration the experience gained in the course of the twenty years which preceded this war and have adopted some concepts which, allow me to remind you, France has the honor of having advocated since 1919 with Léon Bourgeois, well remembered by those of his Geneva colleagues whom I have had the great pleasure of seeing again here, and which I did not cease to defend in the discussions of the League of Nations.

Military assistance, in case of aggression, ceases to be a "recommendation" made to member states; it becomes for us an "obligation" which none can shirk.

If these proposals are adopted, the international Organization will cease to be unarmed in the face of violence; a collective force the size, the degree of preparedness, the composition, and the general location of which will be determined beforehand will have been placed at the disposal of the Council to carry out these decisions.

Here is a great historic development in the accomplishment [514] of which it will be the honor of the members of Committee 3 of Commission III to have collaborated. May I be allowed, in concluding, to thank them for the zeal and unceasing application they have shown in the course of long and earnest discussions, a testimony of the will for peace and international solidarity which animates all of us here.

IV. American Draft of Definitive Proposal, Presented to Foreign Ministers at San Francisco, April 1945

Note: At the time of President Roosevelt's death in April 1945, Judge Samuel Rosenman was in Europe representing the President and endeavoring to obtain agreement by the United Kingdom to proceed with the trial of war criminals in general conformity with the plan outlined in the Yalta proposal. Under President Truman's direction Judge Rosenman continued these efforts at San Francisco at the time of the United Nations Conference on International Organization. Representatives of the State, War, and Justice Departments, in conference with Justice Jackson, had reduced the proposal to a draft protocol which Judge Rosenman, accompanied by representatives of the three Departments, took to San Francisco. At San Francisco minor revisions were made of the draft and, as revised, it was delivered to Foreign Ministers Eden of the United Kingdom, Molotov of the Union of Soviet Socialist Republics, and Bidault of the Provisional Government of France. This was the first submission of a proposed agreement by the United States and was the basis on which the Foreign Ministers accepted, in principle, the plan for trial.

No action was taken at San Francisco other than informal discussions held between May 2 and May 10. These resulted in acceptance by the four Governments of the following general principles: first, trial of the major war criminals rather than political disposition; second, return of criminals whose crimes had fixed geographic localization to the countries where their crimes were committed; third, an international military tribunal to hear the cases of the major war criminals; and fourth, a committee of four representatives or chiefs of counsel to prepare and manage the prosecutions, one to represent each of the four Governments, the United Kingdom, the French Republic, the Union of Soviet Socialist Republics, and the United States. It was agreed that after the San Francisco Conference, and probably at Washington, meetings of representatives would be held to formulate definitive agreements.

The draft of the proposed protocol as submitted at San Francisco follows:

22

EXECUTIVE AGREEMENT

PARTIES

1. This Executive Agreement is entered into by the Governments of the Union of Soviet Socialist Republics, the United States of America, the United Kingdom of Great Britain and Northern Ireland, and the Provisional Government of the French Republic, acting by their respective duly authorized representatives, on their own behalf and on behalf of any other members of the United Nations who shall adhere to this Agreement as hereinbelow provided.

2. All members of the United Nations shall be invited by the Government of the United Kingdom, acting on behalf of the other signatories hereto, to adhere to this Agreement. Such adherence shall in each case be notified to the Government of the United Kingdom which shall promptly inform the other parties to this Agreement.

3. For convenience, (*a*) the four signatories will sometimes be referred to as "the Signatories," (*b*) the members of the United Nations adhering hereto as provided in the preceding Article will sometimes be referred to as "the Adherents," and (*c*) the Signatories and all Adherents will sometimes be collectively referred to as "the parties to this Agreement."

POLICY AND PURPOSE

4. The United Nations have on various occasions pledged themselves that those responsible for the atrocities and crimes committed by the Axis Powers or any officer or agent thereof shall not escape punishment. These atrocities and crimes include those which will be charged as provided in Article 6 of this Agreement.

5. The United Kingdom, the United States, and the Soviet Union in the Declaration issued at Moscow November 1, 1943 stated:

(1) that those German officers and men who have been responsible for or have taken a consenting part in these atrocities "will be sent back to the countries in which their abominable deeds were done in order that they may be judged and punished according to the laws of these liberated countries and of the free governments which will be erected therein"; and

(2) that the above declaration was "without prejudice to the case of major criminals, whose offenses have no particular geographical localization and who will be punished by joint decision of the Governments of the Allies".

This Agreement is entered into in order to establish the necessary measures for bringing to justice the major criminals referred to above, their principal agents and accessories, and all other offenders who are not sent back for trial to the countries in which their atrocities and crimes were committed.

DECLARATION REGARDING THE CRIMINAL ACTS TO BE CHARGED

6. The parties to this Agreement agree to bring to trial, in the names of their respective peoples, the persons referred to in Article 5 for their responsibility for the following criminal acts:

a. Violation of the customs and rules of warfare.

b. Invasion by force or threat of force of other countries in violation of international law or treaties.

c. Initiation of war in violation of international law or treaties.

d. Launching a war of aggression.

e. Recourse to war as an instrument of national policy or for the solution of international controversies.

7. This declaration shall also include the right to charge and try defendants under this Agreement for violations of law other than those recited above, including but not limited to atrocities and crimes committed in violation of the domestic law of any Axis Power or satellite or of any of the United Nations.

DECLARATION REGARDING ACCESSORIAL LIABILITY

8. In any trial of charges pursuant to this Agreement, the prosecution may invoke where applicable and the tribunal before which the charges are tried shall recognize and apply the general rule of liability that those who participate in the formulation and execution of a criminal plan involving multiple crimes are liable for each of the offenses committed and responsible for the acts of each other.

DECLARATION REGARDING DEFENSES

9. No indictment, statement of charges, or other document of arraignment shall be deemed legally insufficient which charges violation of law as set forth in this Agreement.

10. The parties to this Agreement declare that any defense based upon the fact that the accused is or was the head or purported head or other principal official of a state is legally inadmissible, and will not be entertained by any tribunal before which charges brought pursuant to this Agreement are tried.

11. The fact that a defendant acted pursuant to order of a superior or government sanction shall not constitute an absolute defense but may be considered either in defense or in mitigation of punishment if the tribunal before which the charges are being tried determines that justice so requires.

DUE PROCESS FOR DEFENDANTS

12. In order to insure fair trial for defendants charged with crime pursuant to this Agreement, it is declared that the following is required in order to constitute due process in their behalf:

a. Reasonable notice shall be given to the defendants of the charges against them and of the opportunity to defend. Such notice may be actual or constructive. Any tribunal before which charges are tried pursuant to this Agreement shall have the right to determine what constitutes reasonable notice in any given instance.

b. The defendants physically present before the tribunal (*a*) will be furnished with copies, translated into their own language, of any indictment, statement of charges or other document of arraignment upon which they are being tried, and (*b*) will be given fair opportunity to be heard in their defense personally and by counsel. The tribunal shall determine to what extent proceedings against defendants may be taken without their presence.

c. Organizations, official or unofficial, may be charged pursuant to this Agreement with criminal acts or with complicity therein by producing before the tribunal and putting on trial such of their number as the tribunal may determine to be fairly representative of the group or organization in question.

d. Upon conviction of an organization hereunder, the tribunal shall make written findings and enter written judgment finding and adjudicating the charges against such organization and the representative members on trial. Such findings and judgment shall be given full faith and credit with respect to the criminal purposes and activities of the organization in any subsequent trial hereunder of a person charged with criminal liability through membership in such organization. Upon proof of such membership the burden shall be upon the defendant to establish any circumstances relating to his membership or participation therein which are relevant either in defense or in mitigation.

EVIDENCE AND PROCEDURE

13. Tribunals established pursuant to this Agreement shall adopt and apply, to the greatest extent possible expeditious and non-technical procedures.

14. Such tribunals shall (*a*) admit any evidence which in their opinion has probative value, (*b*) confine trials strictly to an expeditious hearing of the issues raised by the charges, (*c*) disallow action by defendants the effect of which will be to cause unreasonable delay or the introduction of irrelevant issues or evidence, and (*d*) employ with all possible liberality simplifications of proof, such as but not limited to: requiring defendants to make proffers of proof; taking judicial notice of facts of common knowledge; and utilizing reasonable presumptions

TRIBUNALS

15. There shall be set up one or more military tribunals, hereinafter referred to for convenience as "International Military Tribunal,"

which shall have jurisdiction to try the leaders of the European Axis powers and their principal agents and accessories. Each International Military Tribunal shall consist of four members and four alternates, to be appointed as follows: One member and one alternate each by the representatives of the Control Council for Germany of the Soviet Union, the United States, the United Kingdom, and France. The alternate, so far as practicable, shall be present at the sessions of the tribunal.

16. In the event of the death or incapacity of any member of an International Military Tribunal, his alternate shall sit in his stead, and the nation of which he is a citizen shall forthwith appoint another alternate. Three members of the Tribunal shall constitute a quorum, and all actions and decisions shall be taken by majority vote of the members of the Tribunal at any time sitting, except that sentence of death shall not be imposed on the vote of less than three members.

17. An International Military Tribunal may sit in any zone in Germany, Austria or Italy or in any other country with the consent of such country. It shall have the power to summon witnesses and to compel their attendance, to require the production of documents, to administer oaths, to appoint special masters and other officers, to hold hearings, and generally to exercise in a manner not inconsistent with the provisions of this Agreement plenary judicial authority with respect to the trial of charges brought pursuant to this Agreement.

18. An International Military Tribunal shall have the power to establish its own rules of procedure, which shall be not inconsistent with the provisions of this Agreement.

19. Occupation courts or other tribunals may be set up by the Signatories or any of them for the trial of offenders other than those tried before an International Military Tribunal who are not sent back for trial to the countries in which their atrocities and crimes were committed, including offenders charged with criminal liability through membership in any group or organization as provided in Article 12 (d) of this Agreement.

PUNISHMENT

20. Defendants brought to trial before an International Military Tribunal as provided in this Agreement shall, upon conviction, suffer death or such other punishment as shall be determined by the Tribunal before which they are tried and approved by the Control Council acting by majority vote. The Control Council, by such vote, may approve, reduce, or otherwise alter the sentences determined by the Tribunal, but may not increase the severity thereof.

21. The sentences, when and as approved by the Control Council, shall be carried into execution in accordance with the written orders of the Control Council.

PREPARATION OF CHARGES AND PROSECUTION

22. At the earliest possible time the Soviet Union, the United States, the United Kingdom and France shall each designate a representative, and such representatives acting as a group shall prepare the charges pursuant to Article 6 hereof and shall institute and conduct the prosecution. Such representatives shall also prepare and recommend to the Control Council plans for the prosecution and trial of persons charged with liability pursuant to Article 12 (*d*) through membership in organizations found criminal by an International Military Tribunal.

23. The representatives shall also be charged with:

(*a*) recommending to appropriate governmental authorities agreements and measures supplemental to or in addition to this Agreement, necessary or appropriate to accomplish the objectives thereof, and

(*b*) the maintenance of liaison among and with the appropriate military and civil agencies, authorities and commissions of or representing any of the United Nations with respect to the matters dealt with in this Agreement.

EMOLUMENTS AND EXPENSES

24. The emoluments and expenses of those members of the International Military Tribunal designated by the respective Signatories as provided in Article 15 of this Agreement and of the representatives provided for in Article 22 of this Agreement, shall be borne by the respective Signatories by whom they have been appointed.

25. The emoluments and expenses of the staffs for the International Military Tribunal and the representatives and incidental expenses, such as rent, heat, light, stationery and printing shall be borne in equal shares by the Signatories.

26. The emoluments and expenses of those occupation courts and tribunals established as provided in Article 19 of this Agreement shall be justly apportioned between the Signatories concerned and any participating Adherents as may be agreed between them.

Done at _____ this the _____ day of _____ 1945.

42

VIII. Report to the President by Mr. Justice Jackson, June 6, 1945

Note: Upon his return from Europe, Mr. Justice Jackson made a report to the President. It was released to the press by the White House with a statement of the President's approval and was widely published throughout Europe as well as in the United States. This report was accepted by other governments as an official statement of the position of the United States and as such was placed before all of the delegations to the London Conference. It follows:

June 6, 1945.

THE PRESIDENT,
The White House,
Washington, D. C.

MY DEAR MR. PRESIDENT:

I have the honor to report accomplishments during the month since you named me as Chief of Counsel for the United States in prosecuting the principal Axis War Criminals. In brief, I have selected staffs from the several services, departments and agencies concerned; worked out a plan for preparation, briefing, and trial of the cases; allocated the work among the several agencies; instructed those engaged in collecting or processing evidence; visited the European theater to expedite the examination of captured documents, and the interrogation of witnesses and prisoners; coordinated our preparation of the main case with preparation by Judge Advocates of many cases not included in my responsibilities; and arranged cooperation and mutual assistance with the United Nations War Crimes Commission and with Counsel appointed to represent the United Kingdom in the joint prosecution.

IV.

The legal position which the United States will maintain, being thus based on the common sense of justice, is relatively simple and non-technical. We must not permit it to be complicated or obscured by sterile legalisms developed in the age of imperialism to make war respectable.

Doubtless what appeals to men of good will and common sense as the crime which comprehends all lesser crimes, is the crime of making unjustifiable war. War necessarily is a calculated series of killings, of destructions of property, of oppressions. Such acts unquestionably would be criminal except that International Law throws a mantle of protection around acts which otherwise would be crimes, when committed in pursuit of legitimate warfare. In this they are distinguished from the same acts in the pursuit of piracy or brigandage which have been considered punishable wherever and by whomever the guilty are caught. But International Law as taught in the Nineteenth and the early part of the Twentieth Century generally declared that war-making was not illegal and is no crime at law. Summarized by a standard authority, its attitude was that "both parties to every war are regarded as being in an identical legal position, and consequently as being possessed of equal rights." This, however, was a departure from the doctrine taught by Grotius, the father of International Law, that there is a distinction between the just and the unjust war—the war of defense and the war of aggression.

International Law is more than a scholarly collection of abstract and immutable principles. It is an outgrowth of treaties or agreements between nations and of accepted customs. But every custom has its origin in some single act, and every agreement has to be initiated by the action of some state. Unless we are prepared to abandon every principle of growth for International Law, we cannot deny that our own day has its right to institute customs and to conclude agreements that will themselves become sources of a newer and strengthened International Law. International Law is not capable of development by legislation, for there is no continuously sitting international legislature. Innovations and revisions in International Law are brought about by the action of governments designed to meet a change in circumstances. It grows, as did the Common-law, through decisions reached from time to time in adapting settled principles to new situations. Hence I am not disturbed by the lack of precedent for the inquiry we propose to conduct. After the shock to civilization of the last World War, however, a marked reversion to the earlier and sounder doctrines of International Law took place. By the time the Nazis came to power it was thoroughly established that launching an aggressive war or the institution of war by treachery was illegal and that the defense of legitimate warfare was no longer available to those who engaged in such an enterprise. It is high time that we act on the juridical principle that aggressive war-making is illegal and criminal.

The reestablishment of the principle of unjustifiable war is traceable in many steps. One of the most significant is the Briand-Kellogg Pact of 1928, by which Germany, Italy and Japan, in common with ourselves and practically all the nations of the world, renounced war as an instrument of national policy, bound themselves to seek the settlement of disputes only by pacific means, and condemned recourse to war for the solution of international controversies. Unless this Pact altered the legal status of wars of aggression, it has no meaning at all and comes close to being an act of deception. In 1932, Mr. Stimson, as Secretary of State, gave voice to the American concept of its effect. He said, "War between nations was renounced by the signatories of the Briand-Kellogg Treaty. This means that it has become illegal throughout practically the entire world. It is no longer to be the source and subject of rights. It is no longer to be the principle around which the duties, the conduct, and the rights of nations revolve. It is an illegal thing. . . . By that very act, we have made obsolete many legal precedents and have given the legal profession the task of re-examining many of its codes and treaties."

This Pact constitutes only one in a series of acts which have reversed the viewpoint that all war is legal and have brought International Law into harmony with the common sense of mankind, that unjustifiable war is a crime. Without attempting an exhaustive catalogue, we may mention the Geneva Protocol of 1924 for the Pacific Settlement of International Disputes, signed by the representatives of forty-eight governments, which declared that "a war of aggression consti-

tutes . . . an international crime". The Eighth Assembly of the
League of Nations in 1927, on unanimous resolution of the representatives of forty-eight member nations, including Germany, declared
that a war of aggression constitutes an international crime. At the
Sixth Pan-American Conference of 1928, the twenty-one American
Republics unanimously adopted a resolution stating that "war of aggression constitutes an international crime against the human species."

The United States is vitally interested in recognizing the principle
that treaties renouncing war have juridical as well as political meaning. We relied upon the Briand-Kellogg Pact and made it the cornerstone of our national policy. We neglected our armaments and
our war machine in reliance upon it. All violations of it, wherever
started, menace our peace as we now have good reason to know. An
attack on the foundations of international relations cannot be regarded
as anything less than a crime against the international community,
which may properly vindicate the integrity of its fundamental compacts by punishing aggressors. We therefore propose to charge that
a war of aggression is a crime, and that modern International Law has
abolished the defense that those who incite or wage it are engaged in
legitimate business. Thus may the forces of the law be mobilized
on the side of peace.

Any legal position asserted on behalf of the United States will have
considerable significance in the future evolution of International Law.
In untroubled times, progress toward an effective rule of law in the
international community is slow indeed. Inertia rests more heavily
upon the society of nations than upon any other society. Now we
stand at one of those rare moments when the thought and institutions
and habits of the world have been shaken by the impact of world war
on the lives of countless millions. Such occasions rarely come and
quickly pass. We are put under a heavy responsibility to see that our
behavior during this unsettled period will direct the world's thought
toward a firmer enforcement of the laws of international conduct, so
as to make war less attractive to those who have governments and the
destinies of peoples in their power.

XXV. Draft of Agreement and Charter, Reported by Drafting Subcommittee, July 11, 1945

AGREEMENT by the Governments of the UNITED KINGDOM OF GREAT BRITAIN AND NORTHERN IRELAND, of the UNITED STATES OF AMERICA, of the Provisional Government of the FRENCH REPUBLIC and of the UNION OF SOVIET SOCIALIST REPUBLICS for the Prosecution and Punishment of the Major EUROPEAN AXIS WAR CRIMINALS

WHEREAS the United Nations have from time to time made declarations of their intention that War Criminals shall be brought to justice;

AND WHEREAS the Moscow Declaration of the 30th October, 1943 on German atrocities in Occupied Europe stated that those German officers and men and members of the Nazi Party who have been responsible for or have taken a consenting part in atrocities and crimes "will be sent back to the countries in which their abominable deeds were done in order that they may be judged and punished according to the laws of these liberated countries and of the free Governments that will be created therein";

AND WHEREAS this Declaration was stated to be "without prejudice to the case of major criminals, whose offences have no particular geographical location and who will be punished by the joint decision of the Governments of the Allies";

NOW THEREFORE the Governments of the United Kingdom of Great Britain and Northern Ireland, of the United States of America, of the Provisional Government of the French Republic and of the Union of Soviet Socialist Republics (hereinafter called "the Signatories") acting in the interests of all the United Nations and by their representatives duly authorized thereto have concluded this following Agreement.

Article 1.

There shall be established after consultation with the Control Council of Germany an International Military Tribunal for the trial of war criminals whose offences have no particular geographical location

194

whether they be accused individually or as representative members of organisations or groups or in both capacities.

Article 2.

The constitution, jurisdiction and functions of the International Military Tribunal shall be those set out in the Charter annexed to this Agreement, which Charter shall form an integral part of this Agreement.

Article 3.

Each of the Signatories shall take the necessary steps to make available for the investigation of the charges and trial the major war criminals detained by them who are to be tried by the International Military Tribunal. The signatories shall also use their best endeavours to make available for investigation of the charges against and the trial before the International Military Tribunal such of the major war criminals as are not in the territories of any of the Signatories themselves.

Article 4.

Each of the Signatories shall establish procedure governing the return of persons charged with offences who, in accordance with the Moscow Declaration, are to be tried at the scenes of their crimes.

Article 5.

Any Government of the United Nations may accede to this Agreement by notice given through the diplomatic channel to the Government of the United Kingdom, who shall inform the other Signatory and acceding Governments of each such accession.

Article 6.

Nothing in this Agreement shall prejudice the jurisdiction or the powers of any national or occupation court established or to be established in any Allied territory or Germany for the trial of war criminals.

Article 7.

This Agreement shall come into force on the day of signature and shall remain in force for the period of one year and shall continue thereafter, subject to the right of any Signatory or any acceding Government, to give, through the diplomatic channel, one month's notice of intention to terminate it.

IN WITNESS WHEREOF the Undersigned Plenipotentiaries have signed the present agreement [and have affixed thereto their seals].

DONE in quadruplicate in   this   day of

1945 in English, French and Russian, each text to have equal authenticity.

> For the Government of the United Kingdom of Great Britain and Northern Ireland
>
> --
>
> For the Government of the United States of America
>
> --
>
> For the Provisional Government of the French Republic
>
> --
>
> For the Government of the Union of Soviet Socialist Republics
>
> --

Charter

CONSTITUTION OF THE INTERNATIONAL MILITARY TRIBUNAL

1. In pursuance of the Agreement dated   there shall be established an International Military Tribunal (hereinafter called "the Tribunal") for the just and prompt trial and punishment of the major war criminals of the European Axis Powers.

2. The Tribunal shall consist of four members, each with an alternate. One member and one alternate shall be appointed by each of the Signatories. The alternates shall, so far as they are able, be present at all sessions of the Tribunal. In case of illness of any member of the Tribunal or his incapacity for some other reason to fulfil his functions, his alternate shall take his place.

3. Neither the Tribunal, its members nor their alternates can be challenged by the prosecution or by the defendants or their counsel. Each Signatory may replace its member of the Tribunal or his alternate for reasons of health or for other good reasons.

4. The presence of all four members of the Tribunal or their alternates shall be necessary to constitute the quorum.

If a session of the Tribunal is taking place on the territory of one of the four Signatories, the representative of that Signatory on the Tribunal shall preside. In other cases, the members of the Tribunal shall, before any trial begins, agree among themselves upon the selection from their number of a president, and the president shall hold office during that trial, or as may otherwise be agreed by a vote of not less than three members. The principle of rotation of presidency for successive trials is agreed.

Save as aforesaid the Tribunal shall take decisions by a simple majority vote and in case the votes are evenly divided, the vote of the president shall be decisive; provided always that convictions and sentences shall only be imposed by affirmative votes of at least three members of the Tribunal.

5. The Tribunal may, in case of need and depending on the number of the matters to be tried, sit in one or more Chambers or Divisions, and the establishment, functions, and procedure of each Chamber or Division shall be identical, and shall be governed by this Charter.

JURISDICTION AND GENERAL PRINCIPLES

6. The following acts shall be considered criminal violations of International Law and shall come within the jurisdiction of the Tribunal:

(a) Violations of the laws, rules or customs of war. Such violations shall include murder and ill-treatment of prisoners of war; atrocities against and violence towards civil populations; the deportation of such populations for the purpose of slave labour; the wanton destruction of towns and villages; and plunder; as well as other violations of the laws, rules and the customs of war.

(b) Launching a war of aggression.

(c) [Invasion or threat of invasion of or] initiation of war against other countries in breach of treaties, agreements or assurances between nations or otherwise in violation of International Law.

(d) [Entering into a common plan or enterprise aimed at domination over other nations, which plan or enterprise involved or was reasonably calculated to involve or in its execution did involve the use of unlawful means for its accomplishment, including any or all of the acts set out in sub-paragraphs (a) to (c) above or the use of a combination of such unlawful means with other means.]

(e) Atrocities and persecutions and deportations on political, racial or religious grounds [in pursuance of a common plan or enterprise referred to in sub-paragraph (d) hereof, whether or not in violation of the domestic law of the country where perpetrated.]

7. The official position of defendants, whether as heads of State or responsible officials in various Departments, shall not be considered as freeing them from responsibility or mitigating punishment.

8. The fact that the defendant acted pursuant to order of a superior or to Government sanction shall not free him from responsibility but may be considered in mitigation of punishment if the Tribunal determines that justice so requires.

9. Organizers, instigators and accomplices who participated in the formulation or execution of a common criminal plan or in the perpetration of individual crimes are equally responsible with other participants in the crimes.

10. At the trial of any individual member of any group or organiza-

tion, the Tribunal may declare (in connection with any act of which the individual may be convicted) that the group or organization of which the individual was a member was a criminal organization.

11. In cases where a group or organization is declared criminal by the Tribunal, the competent national authorities of any Signatory have the right to bring individuals to trial for membership therein before national, military or occupation courts. In any such case the criminal nature of the group or organization is considered proved and shall not be questioned.

12. Any person may be charged before a national, military or occupation court, referred to in Article 11, with a crime other than of membership in a criminal group or organization and such court may, after convicting him, impose upon him punishment independent of and additional to the punishment imposed by the Tribunal for participation in the criminal activities of such group or organization.

13. The Tribunal shall have the right to take proceedings against a person charged with crimes set out in Article 6 of this Charter in his absence if he should be in hiding or if the Tribunal, for other reasons, finds it necessary, in the interests of justice, to conduct the hearing in his absence.

14. The Tribunal shall draw up rules for its procedure. These rules shall not be inconsistent with the provisions of this Charter.

COMMITTEE FOR THE INVESTIGATION AND PROSECUTION OF MAJOR WAR CRIMINALS

15. Each Signatory shall appoint a Chief Prosecutor.

1. The Chief Prosecutors shall act as a committee for the following purposes:

(*a*) Co-ordination of the individual work of each of the Chief Prosecutors and his staff.

(*b*) The final designation of the defendants to be tried by the Tribunal.

(*c*) The approval of the indictment and of the documents to be submitted therewith.

(*d*) The lodgement of the indictment and the accompanying documents with the Tribunal.

(*e*) The drawing up and recommending to the Tribunal for their approval of draft rules of procedure contemplated by Article 14. The Tribunal shall have power to accept, with or without amendments, or to reject the rules so recommended.

The committee shall act in all the above matters by a majority vote and shall appoint a Chairman as may be convenient and in accordance with the principle of rotation.

XXIX. Amendments Proposed by American Delegation, July 16, 1945

MEMORANDUM to Conference of Representatives of the UNION OF SOVIET SOCIALIST REPUBLICS, the UNITED KINGDOM, the UNITED STATES OF AMERICA and the Provisional Government of FRANCE, Submitted by the UNITED STATES To Accompany Suggested AMENDMENTS to the Draft of the CHARTER Prepared by the DRAFTING COMMITTEE

1. It is suggested that there be added at the end of Article 10 a proviso reading as follows:

"provided notice deemed reasonable by the Tribunal is given all members of the organization and any such members desiring to be heard as witnesses regarding the criminal character of such organization are afforded an opportunity to be heard in such manner as the Tribunal deems fair and just."

2. It is suggested that there be added as a parenthesis after subparagraph (*b*) of Article 6 the following:

"(An invasion of another country in the absence of an attack upon, invasion of, or declaration of war against such country shall for purposes of this Agreement constitute the launching of a war of aggression)."

3. It is suggested that there be added as subparagraph 3 of Article 15 the following:

"Any Chief Prosecutor may (1) bring to trial before such International Military Tribunal any person in the custody of his Government or of any Government which consents to the trial of such person, and any group or organization, representative members of which are in the custody of his Government, if, in his judgment such person, group, or organization has committed any criminal violation of International Law defined in Article 12 hereof; and (2) introduce any evidence which in his judgment has probative value relevant to the issues raised by the charges being tried."

244

Mr. Justice Jackson. I want to say I am entirely in sympathy with the purpose of the Soviet Delegation in suggesting this sentence, although I could not be happy at the use of the sentence as it is. I think we should give a little thought to whether this purpose can be accomplished by some other means. There is a very real danger of this trial being used, or of an attempt being made to use it, for propaganda purposes, and I should like to make a suggestion as to what seems to me a weakness in the original American proposal that would help overcome this difficulty. It seems to me that the chief way in which the Germans can use this forum as a means for disseminating propaganda is by accusing other countries of various acts which they will say led them to make war defensively. That would be ruled out of this case if we could find and adopt proper language which would define what we mean when we charge a war of aggression. Language has been used in a number of treaties which defines aggression and limits it in such a way that it would prevent their making these counteraccusations which would take lots of time and cause lots of trouble. It seems to me that, if we make a study of treaties which have defined "war of aggression", we can confine our charge against them to a physical act of attack—and that is the crime, the attack. We might consider one or two definitions used heretofore.

Sir David Maxwell Fyfe. In preparation for paragraph 6.

Mr. Justice Jackson. Yes, I think it should go in paragraph 6, but it limits the possibility of propaganda. For example, here is a definition used in the treaty signed at London on July 3, 1933, by Afghanistan, Estonia, Latvia, Persia, Poland, Rumania, Turkey and the U.S.S.R., which was apparently worked out with great care:

"Article II. Accordingly, the aggressor in an international conflict shall, subject to the agreements in force between the Parties to the dispute, be considered to be that State which is the first to commit any of the following actions:

"1. Declaration of war upon another State;

"2. Invasion by its armed forces, with or without a declaration of war, of the territory of another State;

"3. Attack by its land, naval or air forces, with or without a declaration of war, on the territory, vessels or aircraft of another State;

"4. Naval blockade of the coasts or ports of another State;

"5. Provision of support to armed bands formed in its territory which have invaded the territory of another State, or refusal, notwithstanding the request of the invaded State, to take, in its own territory, all the measures in its power to deprive those bands of all assistance or protection.

"ARTICLE III. No political, military, economic or other consideration may serve as an excuse or justification for the aggression referred to in Article II. (For examples, see Annex.)"

These definitions would foreclose what they are apt to attempt because they are going to say for propaganda purposes, "It is true we made an attack, but there are political and economic situations which were our justifications." And that may have to be litigated. There are other treaties which we could consult for perhaps other definitions. We will try to get them all together and think it would be helpful.

SIR DAVID MAXWELL FYFE. I am very grateful to Mr. Justice Jackson and am sure it will be helpful to have them to consider.

Has anyone anything on 18 (c)? Then 19 or 20.

XXXV. Draft Article on Definition of "Crimes", Submitted by French Delegation, July 19, 1945

Note: On July 19, 1945, the French Delegation submitted a draft of article 6 on the definition of "crimes", together with their own translation of it into English, as follows:

[Translation]

DRAFT ARTICLE ON THE DEFINITION OF CRIMES

The Tribunal will have jurisdiction to try any person who has, in any capacity whatsoever, directed the preparation and conduct of:

i) the policy of aggression against, and of domination over, other nations, carried out by the European Axis Powers in breach of treaties and in violation of international law;

ii) the policy of atrocities and persecutions against civilian populations;

iii) the war, launched and waged contrary to the laws and customs of international law;

and who is responsible for the violations of international law, the laws of humanity and the dictates of the public conscience, committed by the armed forces and civilian authorities in the service of those enemy Powers.

293

XXXVI. Definition of "Aggression," Suggested by American Delegation as Basis of Discussion, July 19, 1945

DEFINITION OF AGGRESSION SUGGESTED FOR CONSIDERATION WITH ARTICLE 6

An aggressor, for the purposes of this Article, is that state which is the first to commit any of the following actions:

(1) Declaration of war upon another state;
(2) Invasion by its armed forces, with or without a declaration of war, of the territory of another state;
(3) Attack by its land, naval, or air forces, with or without a declaration of war, on the territory, vessels, or aircraft of another state;
(4) Naval blockade of the coasts or ports of another state;
(5) Provision of support to armed bands formed in its territory which have invaded the territory of another state, or refusal, notwithstanding the request of the invaded state, to take in its own territory, all the measures in its power to deprive those bands of all assistance or protection.

No political, military, economic or other considerations shall serve as an excuse or justification for such actions; but exercise of the right of legitimate self-defense, that is to say, resistance to an act of aggression, or action to assist a state which has been subjected to aggression, shall not constitute a war of aggression.

294

XXXVII. Minutes of Conference Session of July 19, 1945

Sir David Maxwell Fyfe called the Conference to order and called attention to a draft article on the definition of crimes proposed by the French Delegation [XXXV], and a definition of aggression suggested by the American Delegation for consideration in connection with the definition of crimes [XXXVI].

SIR DAVID MAXWELL FYFE. Perhaps the French Delegation will be good enough to explain their suggestion of definitions.

PROFESSOR GROS. It is hard to add anything to the actual draft. The intention is the same as those of others who have proposed drafts of article 6. Our objections to the definitions so far proposed are that the statute of the International Tribunal will stand as a landmark which will be examined for many years to come, and we want to try to avoid any criticisms.

We do not consider as a criminal violation the launching of a war of aggression. If we declare war a criminal act of individuals, we are going farther than the actual law. We think that in the next years any state which will launch a war of aggression will bear criminal responsibility morally and politically; but on the basis of international law as it stands today, we do not believe these conclusions are right. Where a state would launch a war of aggression and not conduct that war according to rules of international law, it would be desirable to punish them as criminals, but it would not be criminal for only launching a war of aggression.

We do not want criticism in later years of punishing something that was not actually criminal, such as launching a war of aggression. The judges would be in a very difficult position if we insist on that fact. The subject was often up for discussion in the League of Nations. It is said very often that a war of aggression is an international crime, as a consequence of which it is the obligation of the aggressor to repair the damages caused by his actions. But there is no criminal sanction. It implies only an obligation to repair damage. We think it will turn out that nobody can say that launching a war of aggression is an international crime—you are actually inventing the sanction. The subject was studied by Professor Trainin in his book. He tries to construct the idea of an international crime. He recognized that international

295

law, as it now stands, does not make it punishable. The effort to make war of aggression an international crime is still tentative.

If, instead of making a declaration of international law which is not certain, we use our draft, we will avoid that difficulty and get the same results. We are not declaring a new principle of international law. We are just declaring we are going to punish those responsible for criminal acts. We do not go beyond what is traditional with most lawyers as to acts that were crimes even before the effort to make a war of aggression a war crime. The judges that will sit on the Tribunal will be lawyers, and they will be watched by all countries and will try to judge fairly and impartially. We attempt to avoid any discussion between the judges on the subject that we are trying to put in the draft.

Sir David Maxwell Fyfe. Do we gather that what you are saying is objectionable is the words in the draft "shall be considered criminal violations of International Law"?

Professor Gros. Yes. We start from something that is not in doubt—that the conduct of a war in violation of international law is a crime—and from that we build a case. The responsibility goes up to the perpetrator and instigator.

Sir David Maxwell Fyfe. Just one other point. Is your number i), referring to "policy of aggression against, and of domination over", intended to be the equivalent of the common plan to wage a war of aggression in violation of international law? Had you in mind the common plan or great design?

Professor Gros. We tried to cover exactly the same ideas but to build from a different basis. The previous drafts of article 6 start from the top and say what will be a criminal violation of international law. On the contrary, we start from the bottom, say that there have been indisputable crimes and go up the line of responsibility to the instigator of the war. It is difficult for me to discuss this very delicate point in another language. It seems to me that the previous drafts amount only to a declaration by four people, while in our definition you have a reminder that this policy is criminal because it is carried out in violation of treaties and of international law.

Sir David Maxwell Fyfe. We have a conception of conspiracy in our law and would like to know whether you have it too. Take arson, for which there is no criminal sanction and which has its only remedy in reparations, as you mention. But the conspiracy to commit such arson in English law is a criminal act.

Professor Gros. No, we do not have that conception of conspiracy. We would have to make new law.

Sir David Maxwell Fyfe. For you in America, a conspiracy to commit a tort is a crime?

Mr. Justice Jackson. Sometimes, but by virtue of statutes. Except in a very few States we do not have common-law crimes, but only statutory ones.

SIR DAVID MAXWELL FYFE. The question comes to this: whether it is right or desirable to accept the position that a war of aggression is a crime. It seems to be agreed that it is. The fundamental difficulty is the lack of sanction. More strictly it may be said that it is accepted as a crime without declared punishment or any declared sanction against it.

PROFESSOR GROS. It may be a crime to launch a war of aggression on the part of a state that does so, but that does not imply the commission of criminal acts by individual people who have launched a war. When you say that a state which launches a war has committed a crime, you do not imply that the members of that state are criminals.

SIR DAVID MAXWELL FYFE. Don't you imply that the people who have actually been personally responsible for launching the war have committed a crime?

PROFESSOR GROS. We think that would be morally and politically desirable but that it is not international law.

SIR DAVID MAXWELL FYFE. You see the distinction in my mind. To look at it as a crime of the state only may include people who have very little real responsibility for it. But, if you can show that the war has been the result of the actions of 15 or 20 people, it is a difficult conception that those people are not responsible for their own acts when it is admitted that they result in an international crime.

PROFESSOR GROS. That certainly is what we would wish. But I would like you to note one thing that is important because it will be used as a precedent. I refer to the report to the Peace Conference in 1919. It certainly was the state of the law in 1919 that the acts which brought about a war would not be charged against officers or made the subject of procedure before a tribunal. And the Germans will take for a precedent what is still worse for our object—the report of James Brown Scott and Robert Lansing to show that we have no legal basis to say that launching a war of aggression shows criminal responsibility of the people who launched that war.

But, if you define their crimes according to their practical results, if you show that the Germans have been breaking treaties and as a result of that have annexed populations, run concentration camps, and violated international law by criminal acts against people, what you will condemn are those acts which in fact are criminal in all legislation, and you will condemn them for having directed those acts. I would not object at all to those same words in the charter if they were designed as a precedent for any government for the future. My difficulty is that this charter is not made to declare new international law; it is made to punish war criminals and the basis must be a safe one. Naturally, we would be open to modifications of our draft.

GENERAL NIKITCHENKO. The definition of "war criminals" was set forth in the Moscow and Crimea declarations, and it is our opinion we should act on those declarations. If we turn once again to the terms of the Moscow declaration, we see that apparently the conception of what is a war criminal is quite clear. But the difficulty is in trying to confine this definition to a legal formula which would form the basis of a trial of these war criminals. In my opinion we should not try to draw up this definition for the future. The critics will try to find any inconsistencies and any points that are not clear and to turn these points against those who draw up the definition in the charter. In my opinion our task should be to form the basis for the trial not of any criminals who may commit international crimes in the future but of those who have already done so. I refer to the beginning of the Moscow declaration in which it is stated that Great Britain, the United States, and the Soviet Union have received from various sources evidences of atrocities, murders, cold-blooded mass executions which are being committed by Hitler's armed forces in many countries captured by them. For these crimes the Nazis should be punished. By our formula we should not give those who committed criminal acts the possibility of considering themselves political criminals. If we were to try to set forth in detail the various crimes committed by the Nazis, we might very well make a mistake. It is quite impossible to give an exhaustive list of the crimes. If, on the other hand, we should confine ourselves to a few matters, that too would not be right. Therefore we should work out a formula which would make it possible to bring to trial and punish those who have committed all the various atrocities. At the same time we should not, of course, confine ourselves to persons who have actually committed the crimes but should also especially reach those who organized or conspired them. From our point of view the form of article 6, as it has been formulated by the direction of the committee, is not agreeable thus. It gives a very wide field of interpretation to acts which in one case might be an international crime and in another case might not be so. That is why from our point of view the formula proposed by the French Delegation is better—first of all, because it provides not for the responsibility of states or any social organisms but for the responsibility of persons; secondly, because the crimes are set forth in such a manner that they are turned only against those who have committed the crimes.

We did not submit a text of our own, not only not to provoke a fresh discussion, but in order to be able to come to an agreement quickly. We are ready to support the formula submitted by the French Delegation, that is, we would be in a position to recommend it to our Government.

Mr. Justice Jackson. Well, I am in agreement with a great deal that Professor Gros and General Nikitchenko have said. This is a most difficult subject and a most important one, not only for today but for time to come. However, if we look only to the past with our action, it will be of little importance to the future. We have no interest in any particular formula so long as it accomplishes the purpose of giving some real moral meaning to the principles that underlie any prosecution. I agree entirely that the formula should look, as General Nikitchenko says, to the responsibility of persons, rather than of states, and think the formula as stated is defective in that respect.

We have given a great deal of thought—not only the men of my staff but other eminent American scholars—to this subject of the crime of making war. I must say that sentiment in the United States and the better world opinion have greatly changed since Mr. James Brown Scott and Secretary Lansing announced their views as to criminal responsibility for the first World War. I have no expectation that any rule we could formulate would avoid the criticism of some scholars of international law, for a good many of them since 1918—in language that was used about others—have learned nothing and have forgotten nothing. But I don't think we can take the 1918 view on matters of war and peace. At least in the United States we have moved far from it with such measures as lend-lease and neutrality. As I have understood Professor Trainin's book, which I have read carefully in the effort to understand the Soviet views, I gather that his view comes very close to the view which we entertain in the United States. Our attitude as a nation, in a number of transactions, was based on the proposition that this was an illegal war from the moment that it was started, and that therefore, without losing our rights as neutrals or nonbelligerents, it was our right to extend aid to the nations under illegal attack, and the lend-lease program, the exchange of bases for destroyers, and much of American policy was based squarely on the proposition that a war of aggression is outlawed.

I was obliged to pass on a good deal of American activity in the period just preceding the war, as Attorney General, and I stated the position quite clearly that our view was that this was an illegal war of aggression in violation of the Briand-Kellogg pact and other applicable treaties. And I notice that the latest issue of Oppenheim on International Law, just out, says that my Havana speech, which some of you have read, was a sound view of international law, although it was criticized in my own country at the time. Therefore, our view is that this isn't merely a case of showing that these Nazi Hitlerite people failed to be gentlemen in war; it is a matter of their having designed an illegal attack on the international peace, which to our mind is a criminal offense by common-law tests, at least, and the other atrocities were all preparatory to it or done in execution of it.

Now the difficulty, as I see it, is that there is no prescribed sanction, no criminal penalty, provided for that kind of what we may call "common law" crime of violation of international law. Neither is there a criminal sanction or penalty prescribed for the other violations of international law which the French draft considers to be punishable. In other words, we have no statute which states any penalties or individual responsibilities for any offenses under whatever formula we attempt to arraign them.

To be specific: The language of the French draft, I am fearful, does not cover just the same things that our draft covers. If it did, I should be quite happy to accept the formula. In subparagraph (1) for example, to be punishable the policy of aggression must be carried out, as I read the statement, both in breach of treaties and in violation of international law. That we think would leave open to argument before the court whether this policy of aggression is in violation of present international law, and brings up at the trial all of the questions that our statute ought to settle. If that read "in breach of treaties *or* violation" of international law, we would have much less difficulty with it.

PROFESSOR GROS. If you will read the French text, which I am afraid was somewhat difficult to translate into English, that covers your point. We say in violation of international law and treaties, but international law is composed of treaties. To violate a treaty is to violate international law. So if you want to say "or" instead of "and", we do not object at all. Aggression is certainly the same if you breach a special treaty or if you just invade your neighbor—it is the same condemnable policy.

MR. JUSTICE JACKSON. The other doubt that I have is whether this draft sufficiently and explicitly embodies the common plan or conspiracy idea which is necessary to reach a great many of the equally guilty persons against whom evidence of specific violent acts may be lacking although there is ample proof that they participated in the common plan or enterprise or conspiracy. I think that if those points could be clarified, so that we don't leave them in doubt, we might be able to work out from this an acceptable basis. I do like the brevity of the French version. But I again repeat that in connection with this we should attempt to make some provision as to what constitutes aggression, in which I think all of the American proposals were defective. Otherwise we may get into litigation over whether what we call a policy of aggression was in fact a policy of long-range self-defense. That is the point which I suggested the other day and is one on which I would like to present this written proposal to this group [XXXVI]. Would it be a good thing to consider that now or later?

PROFESSOR GROS. I think to embody the common-plan theory would be easy. It is only a question of drafting. We thought of putting the word "planned", but it is difficult. It would have "or the plan of", but as it refers to conduct—

SIR DAVID MAXWELL FYFE. It occurred to me you could do it in either of two ways. In the beginning "and took part in a plan to further", or the policy of aggression could be put in a more concrete form by "conduct of a plan to achieve aggression against". What is in my mind is getting a man like Ribbentrop or Ley. It would be a great pity if we failed to get Ribbentrop or Ley or Streicher. Now I want words that will leave no doubt that men who have originated the plan or taken part in the early stages of the plan are going to be within the jurisdiction of the Tribunal. I do not want any argument that Ribbentrop did not direct the preparation because he merely was overborne by Hitler, or any nonsense of that kind.

GENERAL NIKITCHENKO. Will Professor Gros excuse me if I try to amend his draft? In my opinion, in the Russian the word "policy" is not quite enough to mean actually the carrying out of a wide plan of aggression or domination over other nations, and in my opinion Ribbentrop, Ley, and others can say that they do not come under that.

PROFESSOR GROS. "Policy" is the widest term we can use.

SIR DAVID MAXWELL FYFE. Our difficulty is that "policy" is rather a loose word in English and is inclined to be used by people when they want to get out of expressing a concrete meaning. I should have to consider that a little. With the idea which Professor Gros initiated and General Nikitchenko supported I am in entire agreement. That is what we want to draft in order to do as inclusive a job as we can.

MR. JUSTICE JACKSON. May I ask one question more on the French draft? Could the "and" in the last paragraph be "or"? You could drop both "and who" and thus eliminate the issue that seems to lurk in the definition.

PROFESSOR GROS. In fact we put under that responsibility everything that has been committed in detail, and they are responsible because they are the instigators of the plan. It puts the charge of every detail on them.

MR. JUSTICE JACKSON. If you are embodying our concept of conspiracy in that language, my difficulty is that an American judge would not be certain to recognize it in that dress.

PROFESSOR GROS. We imply that all people who have planned invasions and atrocities are responsible for all the atrocities which have been committed in execution of that plan. They are the instigators of the crimes.

MR. JUSTICE JACKSON. Well, I think that clarifies a point that was troublesome in my mind, and I think in the Attorney General's mind, about this, and we do seem close together in our ultimate meaning.

PROFESSOR GROS. Mrs. Mackenzie suggests we might put "and who is therefore responsible". That would be acceptable.

Shall we return to Mr. Justice Jackson's proposal to define aggression?

MR. JUSTICE JACKSON. On the aggression point, what we did was to look at some of the treaties which have been made on that subject and try to draft something in line with what has been accepted before. I have here a draft of a proposed provision. That is a draft from what was used in one treaty to which the Soviet Union was a party. There is another treaty of nonaggression that was the subject of a great deal of consideration, and I call attention to the other treaty, the London nonaggression treaty of July 4, 1933, the language of which is followed closely. The point is that we take the actual attack, actual invasion, as constituting the aggression, and we cut off arguments that there wasn't an "attack" because invasion really was in defense against political or economic measures. Now Germany will undoubtedly contend, if we don't put this in, that this wasn't a war of aggression although it looked like it. They will say that in reality they were defending against encirclement or other remote menaces. Then you are in the whole political argument of who was doing what to whom in Europe before 1939.

I think we should not litigate the cause of the war but should hold this case within the issue as to who first made an attack, without allowing trial as to any motive that involved only economic or political considerations.

This language is not suggested as perfect, but I think the idea of defining "aggressor" is very important and that we shall have to face it at some point in this prosecution. We either have to define it now, in which case it will end argument at the trial, or define it at the trial, in which case it will be the subject of an argument in which the Germans will participate; and it seems to me that it is much better that we face it now and preclude all of that argument.

SIR DAVID MAXWELL FYFE. I wonder whether it would meet our purposes if, on the explanation of Professor Gros, the French draft is accepted as a basis in essentials covering our purpose. Then I think I would be happier myself if after "directed" is inserted a combination of some such words as "or took part in a plan to further". I would suggest that, if we accept that as a basis, including some such words again referring to the substance of a plan, Professor Gros and Mr. Clyde and Mr. Troyanovsky could act as an unofficial drafting committee on that point, and they might present us with a final copy which we would consider.

GENERAL NIKITCHENKO. On the point of the Jackson proposal as to the definition of "aggressor", this question has been frequently discussed at various conferences and meetings, and it seems to us it does not enter into the competence of this commission to do so; in trying to punish persons guilty, we should base ourselves on the definitions entered in the various previous documents.

I do not quite share the fears expressed by Mr. Justice Jackson that this would provoke an argument in court between prosecutors and defense because the Tribunal would always be in a position to put a stop to irrelevant matters. The Tribunal would not be competent to judge really what kind of war was launched by the defendants; neither would it go into the question of the causes of war. If we try to enter a definition of aggression into the charter, that we would not be competent to do, as the Tribunal would not be competent to do so. It would really be up to the United Nations or the security organization which has already been established to go into questions of that sort. There is an international court forming part of the U.N.'s organization which would pass judgment on conflicts and arguments between the different states. The task of the Tribunal is to try war criminals who have committed certain criminal acts.

SIR DAVID MAXWELL FYFE. I would like General Nikitchenko to help me on this. If we accept the French draft, that one of the crimes which the Tribunal will try is directing the preparation and policy of aggression, would not the Tribunal have to decide whether and why the policy charged is a policy of aggression? I would like to know how he would envision this being carried out.

GENERAL NIKITCHENKO. The policy which has been carried out by the Axis powers has been defined as an aggressive policy in the various documents of the Allied nations and of all the United Nations, and the Tribunal would really not need to go into that.

MR. JUSTICE JACKSON. If we are to proceed on that basis, why do we need a trial at all?

GENERAL NIKITCHENKO. The fact that the Nazi leaders are criminals has already been established The task of the Tribunal is only to determine the measure of guilt of each particular person and mete out the necessary punishment—the sentences.

SIR DAVID MAXWELL FYFE. To take an actual case, one that involves my country and one in which the Soviet Union and the United States are not involved at all—take Norway for example—you see there you have a clear aggressive attack by the Germans on Norway. But we have information that they are going to say that it was done in anticipation of measures which they claim we were about to take to prevent the Norwegians from assisting the Germans by the supply of iron—that is the sort of point. If we are going to introduce Norway —and we might want to for the atrocities in Norway—I think we are rather opening the door for trouble if there is no definition. That is a concrete point about which I am worried.

GENERAL NIKITCHENKO. Would a question of that sort really come up before the Tribunal? The Tribunal would not concern itself with questions like that—why Germany attacked Norway—but take it as granted.

SIR DAVID MAXWELL FYFE. I don't think the defense will take it as granted. It is going to be difficult. If you charge Ribbentrop as having "directed the conducting of the policy of aggression" against other nations, one of them probably Norway, and he says there was no policy of aggression, can you keep that issue away from the Tribunal?

GENERAL NIKITCHENKO. Of course a question like that might come up, but we should pass judgment on the whole policy of Germany and not on individual acts taken apart from the whole. There might be other acts in this war which were taken in self-defense, but here we should take it as the general policy of Germany.

PROFESSOR GROS. I think that is also our view of the question. I hope we get the inside story of the Nazis and are able to prove that they had maps in 1934 covering Norway as northern territory for German colonization. If so, it would shut the door to the German lawyers. The German plan should not be judged only in 1939 and 1940. It will be presented by the Chiefs of Counsel since 1933. I have no inside knowledge of the German archives but think we could find plenty to establish their intention much before the war. The question by Mr. Justice Jackson is, what aggression would be considered criminal by the Tribunal? I wonder whether we are in a position to choose the definition which should be up before the Tribunal. First, there are plenty of documents in actual international law defining aggression, and they will be used by the court; and second, if we put in an agreement on that text, it will be an anticipation of what will be adopted by the United Nations. Thus, if the new one differed from ours on this point, we would be in difficulty. Perhaps we could agree on a companion text which would be sent by us to our governments. We would make a note of this text or any text which may be adopted and say we consider this would be a useful definition for the court; but it would not be on the same level as the rest of the agreement, to try to avoid the difficulties mentioned by Mr. Nikitchenko. It might even be only one of the rules suggested to the Tribunal. The Tribunal will look into all those declarations and treaties.

MR. JUSTICE JACKSON. But the fear I have, and the fear which I take it is shared to some extent at least by the Attorney-General, is that this problem will come up at the trial as it seems certain to do. Some vague idea that Germany was defending herself against some remote menace is the line of defense taken by apologists for

Germany in all countries. Certainly an American judge will then say, "Why did not you fellows define aggression when drawing up the agreement? It is not a clearly defined term of art—we find no body of law that clearly defines it." The treaties that I have cited use different language and sometimes with quite different meaning, and I am sure that an American judge would say that, if you charge a man with making aggressive war, it is his privilege to show that the war he made was not aggressive, and it is his privilege to show, in defense or in mitigation, provocation, threats, economic strangulation, and that sort of thing. It might be that from the point of view of the application of Continental law you would not have that difficulty. But, you see, you would have here two judges brought up in the common-law tradition, and I would be greatly surprised if they would not say that the charge of aggression could be met by any evidence showing that the purpose was ultimately defensive, if we do not define aggression in such a way that it excludes resort to war to redress economic or political disadvantages or threats of encirclement, et cetera.

PROFESSOR GROS. I may be overconfident, but it is confidence in you. If the prosecution presents its case on that policy of aggression, there will be no necessity of defining aggression. If you begin by making a definition of aggression in this agreement, you will have to define other things—launching of war contrary to international law—and you will have to define what you call the laws of humanity and the dictates of the public conscience. When you begin clarifying, if you go to the full length of it, you will have 340 articles. In contrast, if you will leave it in the American way of dealing with international law, you leave it to the judge to consult the sources. And even if you give that definition, it is controversial. It remains controversial because, if you give the definition which is now proposed, your judge may discuss and disagree with that definition; so you run the same danger.

SIR DAVID MAXWELL FYFE. Professor Gros, it comes to this: that your argument is bound to admit the possibility of an argument at the trial on what is aggression. We have three choices: first, leave aggression out, which does not appeal to us because it is the essence of our complaint against the Germans; second, have political argument; third, define aggression. I am merely trying to clarify it. You really would run the risk of having a long trial.

PROFESSOR GROS. We had a great trial at the end of the last century—the Dreyfus case. The French court's president said always when there was a difficulty that such a question could not be raised; you must settle our difficulty in the court.

MR. JUSTICE JACKSON. I really think that this trial, if it should get into an argument over the political and economic causes of this war, could do infinite harm, both in Europe, which I don't know well, and in America, which I know fairly well. If we should have a prolonged controversy over whether Germany invaded Norway a few jumps ahead of a British invasion of Norway, or whether France in declaring war was the real aggressor, this trial can do infinite harm for those countries with the people of the United States. And the same is true of our Russian relationships. The Germans will certainly accuse all three of our European Allies of adopting policies which forced them to war. The reason I say that is that captured documents which we have always made that claim—that Germany would be forced into war. They admit they were planning war, but the captured documents of the Foreign Office that I have examined all come down to the claim, "We have no way out; we must fight; we are encircled; we are being strangled to death." Now, if the question comes up, what is a judge to do about it? I would say that, before one is judged guilty of being an aggressor, we must not only let him deny it, but say we will hear his case. I am quite sure a British or American judge would say to a defendant, "You may prove your claim", unless we had something like this which says, "No political, military, or other considerations excuse going to war". In other words, states have got to settle their grievances peacefully. I am afraid there is great risk in omitting this, and I see no risk in putting it in. It may be criticized, but I see no such risk in putting it in as in leaving it out. We did not think it necessary originally, but more recently we have.

SIR DAVID MAXWELL FYFE. There is one point that Mr. Clyde suggested, and it is worth exploring because it is a difficult point. He points out that in the French draft after "aggression" you have the words "and of domination over". Now, in fact, every country that was the subject of aggression was the subject of domination. If I might just remind you, there were Austria, Czechoslovakia, Denmark, Russia—the plan was to dominate Russia—Yugoslavia, Belgium, and Holland. Aggression was succeeded by domination, and in the case of Russia there was an attempt to dominate which failed. Mr. Clyde suggests also that we limit it to "the domination of others"—that we say in the charter everything we wanted.

PROFESSOR GROS. I think ultimately we must face the facts that difficulty exists now and that we have to try to have a fair trial. The question is whether one deals with it as you suggest by putting it in writing now or by leaving it to the judges. I do not object to the idea of trying to find a solution, but what I mean is that the text in itself should not be equivalent to the charge, "No, you cannot say that." For public opinion there is always a certain difficulty in shutting out a defense.

MR. JUSTICE JACKSON. I had not thought of it in just that way. It seems to me that it is quite a proper thing to be said as a matter of law in advance of a trial that an attack by one upon another is not justified by political or economic considerations. Just as we would say in advance of a trial for assault that an attack of one person upon another would not be justified by the fact that there were political or economic advantages in doing it, that one must not pursue his political or economic aims by that method. And that is what I understand to be the substance of the Kellogg-Briand pact, the whole nonaggression policy, and of nonaggression treaties, that the states renounce the right to pursue those advantages by attack upon each other. And from the point of view of the sentiment of the world and the average man, I think that is a very important consideration and one that it is quite justifiable to embody in our statement of the law of the case to be applied by the court. I think that is the law; I think that ought to be the law; and I think that if we could make it clear in the instrument it would avoid a great deal of controversy.

PROFESSOR GROS. Could I make a suggestion? What is stopping us practically is that this is a definition of aggression and we do not see a possibility of adopting between our four delegations a definition of aggression. But if in that agreement we refer the Tribunal to the existing definition of aggression—which is a complete text—the declaration of the League of Nations of 1927, signed by Germany, Italy, and Japan, by way of denouncing war, we have a solid basis in international law defining war of aggression. If we say that the Tribunal will refer to those two pacts and to any other convention defining aggression that will give them the possibility of choosing their definition, they will have to do that. Do you not think that, if we just put in three lines referring the Tribunal to the definition of those texts, it would be enough? [Here Professor Gros read from the Kellogg-Briand pact.] It covers political, military, and economic situations; so there you have a part of your definition. The pact condemns international war, and the declaration of 1927, which they signed, condemns it too.

MR. JUSTICE JACKSON. You would prefer just a general reference to it, or would there be any objection to using language that the court should apply the principle of that treaty to which Germany was a party? Would you find any objection to that?

PROFESSOR GROS. No, none at all.

MR. JUSTICE JACKSON. That treaty was the pact of Paris of 1928 (Kellogg-Briand) and the 1927 resolution by the Assembly of the League of Nations. Germany, Italy, and Japan were there. Perhaps we could work out some reference covering what we have in mind. I think it is very important here.

PROFESSOR GROS. I do not see any harm in referring to pacts signed by Germany, because they will be referred to by the Tribunal.

SIR DAVID MAXWELL FYFE. I should be glad to accept that as a compromise between the two views.

GENERAL NIKITCHENKO. I wish to repeat it is not part of our task to try to work out a definition of aggression because, however perfect or good our definition would be, it would not be binding to the defendants, and they might question it. If such an argument does crop up, it would be up to the Chief Prosecutors, who would be very competent to parry any arguments that the defendants or counsel might put up. As far as I know, although I have not studied in detail the United Nations Charter adopted in San Francisco, even there there was no attempt to define aggression as such. If the San Francisco Conference did not do that, the more reason I think that this commission, or I personally, am not competent to work out a definition.

SIR DAVID MAXWELL FYFE. I wonder whether it would meet that point and give us the assistance we want if we were to put in quite briefly as the policy of aggression the policy defined, for example, by the Kellogg-Briand pact and the declaration of the United Nations. That would give a pointer without defining it. That would not be tying us to defining it but would be showing us the sort of aggression at which we were aiming.

PROFESSOR GROS. I cannot see any difficulty. It is only the position of the treaties, and it should be said that it is only an example, because there are other treaties.

GENERAL NIKITCHENKO. Wouldn't it be rather disrespectful to the members of the Tribunal to point out to them the treaties which we should expect them to know or at least to study?

MR. JUSTICE JACKSON. I do not think so. We don't usually assume that a judge knows any specific laws in my country and require counsel to file a brief on nearly every point.

SIR DAVID MAXWELL FYFE. I do suggest that that would really give us reasonable basis of compromise; it would indicate to the Tribunal where they ought to look and what they ought to see, which, though I haven't been in Mr. Justice Jackson's high judicial position, I think would help without offense. On the other hand, we would not be falling into the position which General Nikitchenko and Professor Gros have envisaged of trying to decide a problem which the United Nations organization has not yet tackled.

PROFESSOR GROS. It was implied that—if Mr. Justice Jackson thinks it will give satisfaction, particularly to public opinion—materially it is in the text of the treaties.

MR. JUSTICE JACKSON. Really I do not think it concerns me very much. That is probably one thing we Americans would not get in at all at the trial. It concerns European powers rather than ourselves. I should hate to see a political controversy at this trial, which will be widely reported, and the suggestion really comes to mind because of the Soviet suggestion that we should eliminate propaganda. I do not think we can eliminate what may be propaganda if it also is relevant to issues we ourselves raise in the case. But I should think we could so limit the crime charged in this case that it would not be necessary to worry about propaganda. It is an entirely different thing trying to define aggression for the United Nations organization as a future policy and solving it as a juridical policy. This Tribunal will have to act on the subject, and the United Nations organization does not. Political definition seems to me much more difficult than judicial definition. Either we or the court have got to define this concept on which we predicate a charge of crime.

SIR DAVID MAXWELL FYFE. Then I revert to my original suggestion: If we take the French draft as the basis, perhaps Professor Gros could discuss it with Mr. Clyde and Mr. Troyanovsky on the question of wording, and we might meet tomorrow afternoon after our pleasant interlude as guests of General Nikitchenko [see note following] and see whether we have the form to suit us.

GENERAL NIKITCHENKO. As for this reference, would it not be better to refer to some more recent declarations—say, for instance, the policy of aggression condemned by the United Nations organization?

PROFESSOR GROS. The reason for referring to the Kellogg-Briand pact is that it was signed by Germany.

SIR DAVID MAXWELL FYFE. Perhaps, if you could find a good modern one to add to them, it would do no harm. Perhaps you could turn that over in your mind—a very short one, but I think it would be necessary.

The draft of article 15 [XXXVIII] was circulated, and the Conference adjourned.

Note: On Friday, July 20, 1945, all delegations were guests of the Soviet Delegation at a luncheon at the Savoy Hotel in London. At that time the Soviet Delegation advised that they would not be able to go on the trip to Nürnberg on the following day. Justice Jackson offered to change the date to any time that would be agreeable to them. They said, however, that a change of date would not make any difference to them. On consultation with the Attorney-General and Judge Falco it was decided that the remaining delegations should proceed to Nürnberg nevertheless.

On July 21, 1945, the British Delegation and the French Delegation, together with the American Delegation and staff, flew to Nürnberg, inspected the Palace of Justice and the prison, as well as hotel facilities, billeting, and other features entering into the desirability of the selection of that city as the place for the trial.

LII. Revised Definition of "Crimes", Prepared by British Delegation and Accepted by French Delegation, July 28, 1945

Note: On July 26, 1945, Mr. Justice Jackson flew to Potsdam, where a conference of heads of state was in session, for consultation with Secretary of State Byrnes concerning the progress and prospects of the London Conference and its relation to questions that had arisen at Potsdam. While he was at Potsdam, the results of the British elections were announced. The Churchill government, in which Sir David Maxwell Fyfe was Attorney-General, was superseded. This foreshadowed changes in the British representation at the London Conference. Upon his return to London on July 28, 1945, Mr. Justice Jackson resumed informal conferences with Sir Thomas Barnes, Treasury-Solicitor, whose position would not be affected by the change of government. Sir Thomas delivered the following revised definition of "crimes", prepared by him, with the explanation that he had obtained French acceptance of it but that the Soviet Delegation had rejected it. The definition was as follows:

26th July, 1945.
4 p. m.

For the purpose of the trials before the Tribunal established by the Agreement referred to in Article 1 hereof, the following acts or designs or attempts at any of them shall be deemed to be crimes coming within the jurisdiction of the Tribunal:

(*a*) Violations of the laws, rules and customs of war. Such violations shall include but shall not be limited to murder and ill-treatment of prisoners of war, atrocities against civilian populations of occupied countries and the deportation of such populations to slave labour, wanton destruction of towns and villages, and plunder.

(*b*) Atrocities against civilian populations other than those referred to in paragraph (*a*). These include but are not limited to murder and ill-treatment of civilians and deportations of civilians to slave labour and persecution on political, racial or religious grounds committed in pursuance of the common plan or conspiracy referred to in paragraph (*d*) below.

(*c*) Initiation of war of aggression against other nations, or initia-

390

tion of war in violation of treaties, agreements or assurances or
otherwise in violation of international law.

(d) Entering into a common plan or conspiracy aimed at domination over other nations, which plan or conspiracy involved or
was reasonably likely to involve in its execution all or any of
the above crimes.

Any person who is proved to have in any capacity directed or
participated in the initiation of war or in the said plan or conspiracy referred to in paragraphs (c) and (d) hereof shall be personally answerable for each and every violation or atrocity referred
to in paragraphs (a) or (b) above committed in furtherance of
such war as aforesaid, or in pursuance of the said plan or conspiracy.

LIII. Revised Definition of "Crimes", Prepared by British Delegation To Meet Views of Soviet Delegation, July 28, 1945

Note: On July 28, 1945, Sir Thomas Barnes delivered to Justice Jackson a further redraft which he had prepared in an endeavor to meet the Soviet views. He explained that the Soviet Delegation had agreed to this definition and had insisted on this form. The document follows:

27th July, 1945.
12:15 p. m.

For the purpose of the trials of the major war criminals of the European Axis Powers before the Tribunal established by the Agreement referred to in Article 1 hereof, the following acts or designs or attempts at any of them shall be deemed to be crimes coming within the jurisdiction of the Tribunal:

(*a*) Initiation of a war of aggression or participating in the waging of war or preparing for war in violation of treaties, agreements or assurances or participating in a common plan or conspiracy aimed at the domination of one nation over other nations and carried out by the European Axis Powers.

(*b*) Violations of the laws, rules and customs of war. Such violations shall include murder and ill-treatment of prisoners of war, atrocities against civilian populations of occupied countries and the deportation of such populations to slave labour, wanton destruction of towns and villages, and plunder.

(*c*) Atrocities against civilian populations other than those referred to in paragraph (*b*). These include murder and ill-treatment of civilians and deportations of civilians to slave labour and persecution on political, racial or religious grounds committed in pursuance of the common plan or conspiracy referred to in paragraph (*a*) above.

Any person who is proved to have in any capacity directed or participated in the war or in the plan or conspiracy referred to in paragraph (*a*) above shall be personally answerable for each and every violation or atrocity referred to in paragraphs (*b*) or (*c*) above committed in furtherance of such war, or in pursuance of such plan or conspiracy, by the forces and authorities, whether armed, civilian or otherwise, in the service of any of the European Axis Powers.

392

LIV. Revised Definition of "Crimes", Submitted by American Delegation, July 30, 1945

The Tribunal established by the Agreement referred to in Article 1 hereof shall have power and jurisdiction to hear, try and determine charges of crime against only those who acted in aid of the European Axis Powers.

The following acts, designs, or attempts at any of them, shall be deemed to be crimes coming within its jurisdiction:

(*a*) Initiation of a war of aggression; or initiation of a war in violation of treaties, agreements or assurances, or otherwise in violation of International Law; or participating in a common plan or conspiracy aimed at the domination of one nation over other nations to be carried out by means of any such war.

(*b*) Violations of the laws, rules or customs of war. Such violations shall include but are not limited to murder and ill-treatment of prisoners of war; atrocities against civilian populations of occupied countries; the deportation of such populations to slave labour; wanton destruction of towns and villages; and plunder or spoliation.

(*c*) Atrocities against civilian populations other than those referred to in paragraph (*b*). These include but are not limited to murder and ill-treatment of civilians and deportations of civilians to slave labour or persecution on political, racial or religious grounds committed in any country, at any time, in pursuance of the common plan or conspiracy referred to in paragraph (*a*) above.

Any person who is proved to have in any capacity directed or participated in the plan or conspiracy referred to in paragraph (*a*) above shall be personally answerable for each and every violation or atrocity referred to in paragraphs (*b*) or (*c*) above committed in furtherance of such plan or conspiracy, by forces and authorities, whether armed, civilian or otherwise.

393

LV. Notes on Proposed Definition of "Crimes", Submitted by American Delegation, July 31, 1945

1. The jurisdiction of this Tribunal, of course, is limited to trial of those of the European Axis Powers. The definition of a crime cannot, however, be made to depend on which nation commits the act. I am not willing to charge as a crime against a German official acts which would not be crimes if committed by officials of the United States. I think no one will respect any conviction that rests on such a legal foundation. The draft attached suggests changes which would meet those objections.

2. In (a) "participating in the waging of the war" makes one guilty of the crime. This would make the entire soldiery, conscript and volunteer, and numerous civilians guilty. It comes close to making the entire German people guilty by definition. As I have explained, the guilt we should reach is not that of numberless little people of no consequence or influence, but of those who planned and whipped up the war. I suggest words which would accomplish this change.

3. Both (b) and (c) begin with general statements and go on to more specific items. It should be made clear that these specific statements do not limit the general ones. Destruction, as well as plunder, should be specified or we fail to reach such conduct as opening dykes to flood lands with salt water, etc.

4. In (c) we should insert words to make clear that we are reaching persecution, etc. of Jews and others in Germany as well as outside of it, and before as well as after commencement of the war.

5. The objection of Note 1 applies to "participated in the war" in the last paragraph in that as it stands at present it seems to render the entire draft meaningless. It may be interpreted as meaning that a person guilty under (a) shall not be answerable unless he is also guilty under (b) and (c), and that a person guilty of crimes under (b) and (c) shall not be answerable unless the crimes are committed in connection with the planning or the initiation of aggressive war. This, of course, would largely render all three paragraphs futile.

I attach a draft intended to overcome what we regard as defects.

Respectfully submitted,

ROBERT H. JACKSON

394

LVI. Revision of Definition of "Crimes", Submitted by American Delegation, July 31, 1945

ARTICLE 6. DEFINITION OF CRIMES

The Tribunal established by the Agreement referred to in Article 1 hereof shall have power and jurisdiction to try and determine charges of crime against individuals who and organizations which acted in aid of the European Axis Powers and to impose punishments on those found guilty.

The following acts, or any of them, are crimes coming within its jurisdiction for which there shall be individual responsibility:

(*a*) THE CRIME OF WAR, namely, planning, preparation, initiation or waging of a war of aggression, or a war in violation of any international treaty, agreement, or assurance, or in particular, of the General Treaty for the Renunciation of War, or participation in a common plan or conspiracy for the accomplishment of any of the foregoing;

(*b*) WAR CRIMES, namely, violations of the laws or customs of war. Such violations shall include, but not be limited to, murder, ill-treatment or deportation of civilian population of or in occupied territory; murder or ill-treatment of prisoners of war or persons on the seas; killing of hostages; sinking of merchant vessels in disregard of international law; attack upon hospital ships; plunder of public or private property; wanton destruction of cities, towns or villages; devastation not justified by military necessity.

(*c*) CRIMES AGAINST HUMANITY, namely, murder extermination, enslavement, deportation, and other inhumane acts committed against any civilian population, before or during the war, or persecutions on political, racial, religious grounds, in furtherance of or in connection with any crime within the jurisdiction of the International Tribunal, whether or not in violation of the domestic law of the country where perpetrated.

Leaders, organizers, instigators and accomplices participating in the formulation or execution of a common plan or conspiracy to commit any of the foregoing crimes are responsible for all acts performed by any persons in furtherance of such plan.

International law shall include treaties, agreements, and assurances between nations, and the principles of the law of nations, as they result from the usages established among civilized peoples, from the laws of humanity, and from the dictates of the public conscience.

395

LORD CHANCELLOR. Very well. Let that be altered. Now, gentlemen, we have got article 6. Shall we start it or leave off here? It would be very good if we could finish it. I shall have to leave in about 15 minutes.

MR. JUSTICE JACKSON. Perhaps in 15 minutes we might get something to think about.

LORD CHANCELLOR. All right. Mr. Justice Jackson, you might tell us the difficulties in regard to article 6 which you have set out.

MR. JUSTICE JACKSON. I think our difficulties were set forth in memoranda [LV]. Our difficulties with the draft which had been approved by the British and Soviet Delegations are before the delegates, and I have submitted an alternative which meets our criticism [LVI]. Perhaps it would save time, since everyone is probably familiar with those, if we would hear the criticisms of our counterproposal, or the criticisms of our criticisms.

LORD CHANCELLOR. May I suggest that we look at your draft and take the first sentence first of all? So this is what the new draft says: "The Tribunal established by the Agreement referred to in Article 1 hereof shall have power and jurisdiction to try and determine charges of crime against individuals who and organizations which acted in aid

415

of the European Axis Powers and to impose punishment on those found guilty."

GENERAL NIKITCHENKO. As for the body of this article, paragraphs (a), (b), and (c), we have only one or two very minor drafting objections. But as for the first paragraph, we think that it could be made more precise. It seems to us that these words, "acted in aid", are rather indefinite and liable to misunderstanding. We might not reach the actual persons who organized and carried out the crimes, and that is why we would propose to follow this formula for the first paragraph: "The Tribunal established by the Agreement referred to in Article 1 hereof for the trial and punishment of the major war criminals of the European Axis countries shall have the power to try and punish persons who, acting in the interests of the European Axis Powers, whether as individuals or as members of organizations, committed any of the following crimes." Then we could repeat, "The following—"

LORD CHANCELLOR. I would be prepared to accept that.

MR. JUSTICE JACKSON. It sounds all right to me.

JUDGE FALCO. We agree.

LORD CHANCELLOR. Paragraphs (a), (b), and (c)—what alterations do you want?

GENERAL NIKITCHENKO. In all three articles we propose to leave out the headings, "The Crime of War" and other titles. The crime of war is, to be more precise, "the crime against peace", and we think the titles complicate things. We could just say "planning, initiating", et cetera, and then also say not of "any" international, but of "war in violation of international treaties".

LORD CHANCELLOR. Leave out "any" and—?

MR. TROYANOVSKY. And leave the general treaty for the renunciation of war.

LORD CHANCELLOR. I thought it rather convenient to have it in, but I don't think it matters a bit.

GENERAL NIKITCHENKO. We don't think that of great importance either.

PROFESSOR TRAININ. We think that from a theoretical point of view these titles are welcome, but to put them in a law would perhaps make it too vague.

MR. JUSTICE JACKSON. I think it is a very convenient designation. I may say it was suggested to me by an eminent scholar of international law. It would be a very convenient classification, and I think it would help the public understanding of what the difference is.

LORD CHANCELLOR. I think Professor Trainin's book treats aggression not as the crime of war but as a crime against peace, and I do think that if you do have a nomenclature it would be well to have a nomenclature that comes from his book, and instead of calling it "crime of war", call it "crime against peace". I myself prefer to keep the nomenclature but to substitute for the "crime of war" the "crime against peace".

GENERAL NIKITCHENKO. We have no objections to that. Take out the word "any" and the reference to the general treaty.

LORD CHANCELLOR. That is all right with me.

MR. JUSTICE JACKSON. I don't think that is very serious impairment of the definition.

LORD CHANCELLOR. Then let us take (b).

GENERAL NIKITCHENKO. In this paragraph the words "but not be limited to" in our translation are very strange. I think they should be dropped and we should add "or deportation".

MR. JUSTICE JACKSON. The difficulty is in our rules for interpretation of statutes, and you will have at least one judge on the Tribunal who is accustomed to that interpretation. If you name a general category and then go on to specify, you are limited to your specifications. I would be quite willing to have it in translation in any way it makes sense to you, but I think it is quite important that you do make clear that the specifications are not the only things that you are reaching, because some of these crimes are quite unique and are not covered perhaps by general definition. Now, the deportation to slave labor—The reason I dropped "deportation to slave labor" was that there are other deportations that are just as objectionable as slave labor from my point of view, for example, deportations to compulsory prostitution, deportations just to get people out of the way to take their land, or deportations to concentration camps. It seemed to me that we limited the deportations. I would be quite willing to say "deportation to slave labor or for any other purpose".

GENERAL NIKITCHENKO. The words "but not be limited to" are not very important really to us. If you don't mind, we could drop them and I would in our translation say "and other crimes". As for your suggestion, "to slave labor and for any other purposes", that is all right.

LORD CHANCELLOR. I am afraid I must go to rehearse my part in the proceedings of the House of Lords at the opening of Parliament. Would you like to go on? You are so near agreement. If you want me to come again, I could be available this afternoon about 5: 30 or tomorrow at 2: 30; or perhaps, if the Attorney-General could go on representing us, you could get finished here.

The Lord Chancellor left and Sir David Maxwell Fyfe took the chair.

LX. Agreement and Charter, August 8, 1945

AGREEMENT by the Government of the UNITED STATES OF AMERICA, the Provisional Government of the FRENCH REPUBLIC, the Government of the UNITED KINGDOM OF GREAT BRITAIN AND NORTHERN IRELAND and the Government of the UNION of SOVIET SOCIALIST REPUPLICS for the Prosecution and Punishment of the MAJOR WAR CRIMINALS of the EUROPEAN AXIS

WHEREAS the United Nations have from time to time made declarations of their intention that War Criminals shall be brought to justice;

AND WHEREAS the Moscow Declaration of the 30th October 1943 on German atrocities in Occupied Europe stated that those German Officers and men and members of the Nazi Party who have been responsible for or have taken a consenting part in atrocities and crimes will be sent back to the countries in which their abominable deeds were done in order that they may be judged and punished according to the laws of these liberated countries and of the free Governments that will be created therein;

AND WHEREAS this Declaration was stated to be without prejudice to the case of major criminals whose offenses have no particular geographical location and who will be punished by the joint decision of the Governments of the Allies;

Now THEREFORE the Government of the United States of America, the Provisional Government of the French Republic, the Government of the United Kingdom of Great Britain and Northern Ireland and the Government of the Union of Soviet Socialist Republics (hereinafter called "the Signatories") acting in the interests of all the United Nations and by their representatives duly authorized thereto have concluded this Agreement.

Article 1. There shall be established after consultation with the Control Council for Germany an International Military Tribunal for the trial of war criminals whose offenses have no particular geographical location whether they be accused individually or in their capacity as members of organizations or groups or in both capacities.

Article 2. The constitution, jurisdiction and functions of the International Military Tribunal shall be those set out in the Charter annexed to this Agreement, which Charter shall form an integral part of this Agreement.

Article 3.   Each of the Signatories shall take the necessary steps to make available for the investigation of the charges and trial the major war criminals detained by them who are to be tried by the International Military Tribunal.   The Signatories shall also use their best endeavors to make available for investigation of the charges against and the trial before the International Military Tribunal such of the major war criminals as are not in the territories of any of the Signatories.

Article 4.   Nothing in this Agreement shall prejudice the provisions established by the Moscow Declaration concerning the return of war criminals to the countries where they committed their crimes.

Article 5.   Any Government of the United Nations may adhere to this Agreement by notice given through the diplomatic channel to the Government of the United Kingdom, who shall inform the other signatory and adhering Governments of each such adherence.

Article 6.   Nothing in this Agreement shall prejudice the jurisdiction or the powers of any national or occupation court established or to be established in any allied territory or in Germany for the trial of war criminals.

Article 7.   This Agreement shall come into force on the day of signature and shall remain in force for the period of one year and shall continue thereafter, subject to the right of any Signatory to give, through the diplomatic channel, one month's notice of intention to terminate it.   Such termination shall not prejudice any proceedings already taken or any findings already made in pursuance of this Agreement.

IN WITNESS WHEREOF the Undersigned have signed the present Agreement.

DONE in quadruplicate in London this 8th day of August 1945 each in English, French and Russian, and each text to have equal authenticity.

For the Government of the United States of America
ROBERT H. JACKSON

For the Provisional Government of the French Republic
ROBERT FALCO

For the Government of the United Kingdom of Great Britain and Northern Ireland
JOWITT C.

For the Government of the Union of Soviet Socialist Republics
I. NIKITCHENKO
A. TRAININ

Charter of the International Military Tribunal

I. CONSTITUTION OF THE INTERNATIONAL MILITARY TRIBUNAL

Article 1. In pursuance of the Agreement signed on the 8th day of August 1945 by the Government of the United States of America, the Provisional Government of the French Republic, the Government of the United Kingdom of Great Britain and Northern Ireland and the Government of the Union of Soviet Socialist Republics, there shall be established an International Military Tribunal (hereinafter called "the Tribunal") for the just and prompt trial and punishment of the major war criminals of the European Axis.

Article 2. The Tribunal shall consist of four members, each with an alternate. One member and one alternate shall be appointed by each of the Signatories. The alternates shall, so far as they are able, be present at all sessions of the Tribunal. In case of illness of any member of the Tribunal or his incapacity for some other reason to fulfill his functions, his alternate shall take his place.

Article 3. Neither the Tribunal, its members nor their alternates can be challenged by the prosecution, or by the Defendants or their Counsel. Each Signatory may replace its member of the Tribunal or his alternate for reasons of health or for other good reasons, except that no replacement may take place during a Trial, other than by an alternate.

Article 4.

(*a*) The presence of all four members of the Tribunal or the alternate for any absent member shall be necessary to constitute the quorum.

(*b*) The members of the Tribunal shall, before any trial begins, agree among themselves upon the selection from their number of a President, and the President shall hold office during that trial, or as may otherwise be agreed by a vote of not less than three members. The principle of rotation of presidency for successive trials is agreed. If, however, a session of the Tribunal takes place on the territory of one of the four Signatories, the representative of that Signatory on the Tribunal shall preside.

(*c*) Save as aforesaid the Tribunal shall take decisions by a majority vote and in case the votes are evenly divided, the vote of the President shall be decisive: provided always that convictions and sentences shall only be imposed by affirmative votes of at least three members of the Tribunal.

Article 5. In case of need and depending on the number of the matters to be tried, other Tribunals may be set up; and the establishment, functions, and procedure of each Tribunal shall be identical, and shall be governed by this Charter.

II. JURISDICTION AND GENERAL PRINCIPLES

Article 6. The Tribunal established by the Agreement referred to in Article 1 hereof for the trial and punishment of the major war criminals of the European Axis countries shall have the power to try and punish persons who, acting in the interests of the European Axis countries, whether as individuals or as members of organizations, committed any of the following crimes.

The following acts, or any of them, are crimes coming within the jurisdiction of the Tribunal for which there shall be individual responsibility:

(a) CRIMES AGAINST PEACE: namely, planning, preparation, initiation or waging of a war of aggression, or a war in violation of international treaties, agreements or assurances, or participation in a common plan or conspiracy for the accomplishment of any of the foregoing;

(b) WAR CRIMES: namely, violations of the laws or customs of war. Such violations shall include, but not be limited to, murder, ill-treatment or deportation to slave labor or for any other purpose of civilian population of or in occupied territory, murder or ill-treatment of prisoners of war or persons on the seas, killing of hostages, plunder of public or private property, wanton destruction of cities, towns or villages, or devastation not justified by military necessity;

(c) CRIMES AGAINST HUMANITY: namely, murder, extermination, enslavement, deportation, and other inhumane acts committed against any civilian population, before or during the war; or persecutions on political, racial or religious grounds in execution of or in connection with any crime within the jurisdiction of the Tribunal, whether or not in violation of the domestic law of the country where perpetrated.[1]

Leaders, organizers, instigators and accomplices participating in the formulation or execution of a common plan or conspiracy to commit any of the foregoing crimes are responsible for all acts performed by any persons in execution of such plan.

Article 7. The official position of defendants, whether as Heads of

---

[1] See protocol [LXI] for correction of this paragraph.

State or responsible officials in Government Departments, shall not be considered as freeing them from responsibility or mitigating punishment.

Article 8. The fact that the Defendant acted pursuant to order of his Government or of a superior shall not free him from responsibility, but may be considered in mitigation of punishment if the Tribunal determines that justice so requires.

Article 9. At the trial of any individual member of any group or organization the Tribunal may declare (in connection with any act of which the individual may be convicted) that the group or organization of which the individual was a member was a criminal organization.

After receipt of the Indictment the Tribunal shall give such notice as it thinks fit that the prosecution intends to ask the Tribunal to make such declaration and any member of the organization will be entitled to apply to the Tribunal for leave to be heard by the Tribunal upon the question of the criminal character of the organization. The Tribunal shall have power to allow or reject the application. If the application is allowed, the Tribunal may direct in what manner the applicants shall be represented and heard.

Article 10. In cases where a group or organization is declared criminal by the Tribunal, the competent national authority of any Signatory shall have the right to bring individuals to trial for membership therein before national, military or occupation courts. In any such case the criminal nature of the group or organization is considered proved and shall not be questioned.

Article 11. Any person convicted by the Tribunal may be charged before a national, military or occupation court, referred to in Article 10 of this Charter, with a crime other than of membership in a criminal group or organization and such court may, after convicting him, impose upon him punishment independent of and additional to the punishment imposed by the Tribunal for participation in the criminal activities of such group or organization.

Article 12. The Tribunal shall have the right to take proceedings against a person charged with crimes set out in Article 6 of this Charter in his absence, if he has not been found or if the Tribunal, for any reason, finds it necessary, in the interests of justice, to conduct the hearing in his absence.

Article 13. The Tribunal shall draw up rules for its procedure. These rules shall not be inconsistent with the provisions of this Charter.

III. COMMITTEE FOR THE INVESTIGATION AND PROSECUTION OF MAJOR WAR CRIMINALS

Article 14. Each Signatory shall appoint a Chief Prosecutor for the investigation of the charges against and the prosecution of major war criminals.

The Chief Prosecutors shall act as a committee for the following purposes:

(a) to agree upon a plan of the individual work of each of the Chief Prosecutors and his staff,

(b) to settle the final designation of major war criminals to be tried by the Tribunal,

(c) to approve the Indictment and the documents to be submitted therewith,

(d) to lodge the Indictment and the accompanying documents with the Tribunal,

(e) to draw up and recommend to the Tribunal for its approval draft rules of procedure, contemplated by Article 13 of this Charter. The Tribunal shall have power to accept, with or without amendments, or to reject, the rules so recommended.

The Committee shall act in all the above matters by a majority vote and shall appoint a Chairman as may be convenient and in accordance with the principle of rotation: provided that if there is an equal division of vote concerning the designation of a Defendant to be tried by the Tribunal, or the crimes with which he shall be charged, that proposal will be adopted which was made by the party which proposed that the particular Defendant be tried, or the particular charges be preferred against him.

Article 15. The Chief Prosecutors shall individually, and acting in collaboration with one another, also undertake the following duties:

(a) investigation, collection and production before or at the Trial of all necessary evidence,

(b) the preparation of the Indictment for approval by the Committee in accordance with paragraph (c) of Article 14 hereof,

(c) the preliminary examination of all necessary witnesses and of the Defendants,

(d) to act as prosecutor at the Trial,

(e) to appoint representatives to carry out such duties as may be assigned to them,

(f) to undertake such other matters as may appear necessary to them for the purposes of the preparation for and conduct of the Trial.

It is understood that no witness or Defendant detained by any Signatory shall be taken out of the possession of that Signatory without its assent.

IV. FAIR TRIAL FOR DEFENDANTS

Article 16. In order to ensure fair trial for the Defendants, the following procedure shall be followed:

(a) The Indictment shall include full particulars specifying in detail the charges against the Defendants. A copy of the Indictment and of all the documents lodged with the Indictment, translated into a language which he understands, shall be furnished to the Defendant at a reasonable time before the Trial.

(b) During any preliminary examination or trial of a Defendant he shall have the right to give any explanation relevant to the charges made against him.

(c) A preliminary examination of a Defendant and his Trial shall be conducted in, or translated into, a language which the Defendant understands.

(d) A defendant shall have the right to conduct his own defense before the Tribunal or to have the assistance of Counsel.

(e) A defendant shall have the right through himself or through his Counsel to present evidence at the Trial in support of his defense, and to cross-examine any witness called by the Prosecution.

V. POWERS OF THE TRIBUNAL AND CONDUCT OF THE TRIAL

Article 17. The Tribunal shall have the power

(a) to summon witnesses to the Trial and to require their attendance and testimony and to put questions to them,

(b) to interrogate any Defendant,

(c) to require the production of documents and other evidentiary material,

(d) to administer oaths to witnesses,

(e) to appoint officers for the carrying out of any task designated by the Tribunal including the power to have evidence taken on commission.

Article 18. The Tribunal shall

(a) confine the Trial strictly to an expeditious hearing of the issues raised by the charges,

(b) take strict measures to prevent any action which will cause unreasonable delay, and rule out irrelevant issues and statements of any kind whatsoever, (*c*) deal summarily with any contumacy, imposing appropriate punishment, including exclusion of any Defendant or his Counsel from some or all further proceedings, but without prejudice to the determination of the charges.

Article 19.   The Tribunal shall not be bound by technical rules of evidence.   It shall adopt and apply to the greatest possible extent expeditious and non-technical procedure, and shall admit any evidence which it deems to have probative value.

Article 20. The Tribunal may require to be informed of the nature of any evidence before it is offered so that it may rule upon the relevance thereof.

Article 21.   The Tribunal shall not require proof of facts of common knowledge but shall take judicial notice thereof.   It shall also take judicial notice of official governmental documents and reports of the United Nations, including the acts and documents of the committees set up in the various allied countries for the investigation of war crimes, and the records and findings of military or other Tribunals of any of the United Nations.

Article 22.   The permanent seat of the Tribunal shall be in Berlin. The first meetings of the members of the Tribunal and of the Chief Prosecutors shall be held at Berlin in a place to be designated by the Control Council for Germany.   The first trial shall be held at Nuremberg, and any subsequent trials shall be held at such places as the Tribunal may decide.

Article 23.   One or more of the Chief Prosecutors may take part in the prosecution at each Trial.   The function of any Chief Prosecutor may be discharged by him personally, or by any person or persons authorized by him.

The function of Counsel for a Defendant may be discharged at the Defendant's request by any Counsel professionally qualified to conduct cases before the Courts of his own country, or by any other person who may be specially authorized thereto by the Tribunal.

Article 24.   The proceedings at the Trial shall take the following course:

(*a*) The Indictment shall be read in court.
(*b*) The Tribunal shall ask each Defendant whether he pleads "guilty" or "not guilty".
(*c*) The prosecution shall make an opening statement.
(*d*) The Tribunal shall ask the prosecution and the defense what evidence (if any) they wish to submit to the Tribunal, and the Tribunal shall rule upon the admissibility of any such evidence.

(*e*) The witnesses for the Prosecution shall be examined and after that the witnesses for the Defense. Thereafter such rebutting evidence as may be held by the Tribunal to be admissible shall be called by either the Prosecution or the Defense.

(*f*) The Tribunal may put any question to any witness and to any Defendant, at any time.

(*g*) The Prosecution and the Defense shall interrogate and may cross-examine any witnesses and any Defendant who gives testimony.

(*h*) The Defense shall address the court.

(*i*) The Prosecution shall address the court.

(*j*) Each Defendant may make a statement to the Tribunal.

(*k*) The Tribunal shall deliver judgment and pronounce sentence.

Article 25. All official documents shall be produced, and all court proceedings conducted, in English, French and Russian, and in the language of the Defendant. So much of the record and of the proceedings may also be translated into the language of any country in which the Tribunal is sitting, as the Tribunal considers desirable in the interests of justice and public opinion.

VI. JUDGMENT AND SENTENCE

Article 26. The judgment of the Tribunal as to the guilt or the innocence of any Defendant shall give the reasons on which it is based, and shall be final and not subject to review.

Article 27. The Tribunal shall have the right to impose upon a Defendant, on conviction, death or such other punishment as shall be determined by it to be just.

Article 28. In addition to any punishment imposed by it, the Tribunal shall have the right to deprive the convicted person of any stolen property and order its delivery to the Control Council for Germany.

Article 29. In case of guilt, sentences shall be carried out in accordance with the orders of the Control Council for Germany, which may at any time reduce or otherwise alter the sentences, but may not increase the severity thereof. If the Control Council for Germany, after any Defendant has been convicted and sentenced, discovers fresh evidence which, in its opinion, would found a fresh charge against him, the Council shall report accordingly to the Committee established under Article 14 hereof, for such action as they may consider proper, having regard to the interests of justice.

VII. EXPENSES

Article 30. The expenses of the Tribunal and of the Trials, shall be charged by the Signatories against the funds allotted for maintenance of the Control Council for Germany.

DOCUMENT 19 (a)

Chapter III

INTERNATIONAL MILITARY TRIBUNAL, INDICTMENT NUMBER I.

THE UNITED STATES OF AMERICA, THE FRENCH RE-
PUBLIC, THE UNITED KINGDOM OF GREAT BRITAIN
AND NORTHERN IRELAND, AND THE UNION OF SOVIET
SOCIALIST REPUBLICS

— AGAINST —

HERMANN WILHELM GOERING, RUDOLF HESS, JOACHIM
von RIBBENTROP, ROBERT LEY, WILHELM KEITEL,
ERNST KALTENBRUNNER, ALFRED ROSENBERG, HANS
FRANK, WILHELM FRICK, JULIUS STREICHER, WALTER
FUNK, HJALMAR SCHACHT, GUSTAV KRUPP von BOHLEN
UND HALBACH, KARL DOENITZ, ERICH RAEDER, BALDUR
von SCHIRACH, FRITZ SAUCKEL, ALFRED JODL, MARTIN
BORMANN, FRANZ von PAPEN, ARTUR SEYSS-INQUART,
ALBERT SPEER, CONSTANTIN von NEURATH, AND HANS
FRITZSCHE, INDIVIDUALLY AND AS MEMBERS OF ANY OF THE
FOLLOWING GROUPS OR ORGANISATIONS TO WHICH THEY RE-
SPECTIVELY BELONGED, NAMELY: DIE REICHSREGIERUNG
(REICH CABINET); DAS KORPS DER POLITISCHEN
LEITER DER NATIONALSOZIALISTISCHEN DEUTSCHEN
ARBEITERPARTEI (LEADERSHIP CORPS OF THE NAZI
PARTY); DIE SCHUTZSTAFFELN DER NATIONALSOZIAL-
ISTISCHEN DEUTSCHEN ARBEITERPARTEI (COMMONLY
KNOWN AS THE "SS") AND INCLUDING DIE SICHERHEITS-
DIENST (COMMONLY KNOWN AS THE "SD"); DIE GEHEIME
STAATSPOLIZEI (SECRET STATE POLICE, COMMONLY
KNOWN AS THE "GESTAPO"); DIE STURMABTEILUNGEN
DER N.S.D.A.P. (COMMONLY KNOWN AS THE "SA") AND THE
GENERAL STAFF AND HIGH COMMAND OF THE GERMAN
ARMED FORCES ALL AS DEFINED IN APPENDIX B.

Defendants

CHAPTER III

INDICTMENT

I.

The United States of America, the French Republic, the United Kingdom of Great Britain and Northern Ireland and the Union of Soviet Socialist Republics by the undersigned, Robert H. Jackson, Francois de Menthon, Hartley Shawcross and R. A. Rudenko, duly appointed to represent their respective Governments in the investigation of the charges against and the prosecution of the major war criminals, pursuant to the Agreement of London dated 8th August, 1945, and the Charter of this Tribunal annexed thereto, hereby accuse as guilty, in the respects hereinafter set forth, of Crimes against Peace, War Crimes, and Crimes against Humanity, and of a Common Plan or Conspiracy to commit those Crimes, all as defined in the Charter of the Tribunal, and accordingly name as defendants in this cause and as indicted on the counts hereinafter set out: HERMANN WILHELM GOERING, RUDOLF HESS, JOACHIM von RIBBENTROP, ROBERT LEY, WILHELM KEITEL, ERNST KALTENBRUNNER, ALFRED ROSENBERG, HANS FRANK, WILHELM FRICK, JULIUS STREICHER, WALTER FUNK, HJALMAR SCHACHT, GUSTAV KRUPP von BOHLEN UND HALBACH, KARL DOENITZ, ERICH RAEDER, BALDUR von SCHIRACH, FRITZ SAUCKEL, ALFRED JODL, MARTIN BORMANN, FRANZ von PAPEN, ARTUR SEYSS-INQUART, ALBERT SPEER, CONSTANTIN von NEURATH AND HANS FRITZSCHE, individually and as members of any of the Groups or Organizations next hereinafter named.

II.

The following are named as Groups or Organizations (since dissolved) which should be declared criminal by reason of their aims and the means used for the accomplishment thereof and in connection with the conviction of such of the named defendants as were members thereof: DIE REICHSREGIERUNG (REICH CABINET); DAS KORPS DER POLITISCHEN LEITER DER NATIONALSOZIALISTISCHEN DEUTSCHEN ARBEITERPARTEI (LEADERSHIP CORPS OF THE NAZI PARTY); DIE SCHUTZSTAFFELN DER NATIONALSOZIALISTISCHEN DEUTSCHEN ARBEITERPARTEI (commonly known as the "SS") and including DIE SICHERHEITSDIENST (commonly known as the "SD"); DIE GEHEIME STAATSPOLIZEI (SECRET STATE POLICE, commonly known as the "GESTAPO"); DIE STURMABTEILUNGEN DER N.S.D.A.P. (commonly known as the "SA"); and the GENERAL STAFF and HIGH COMMAND of the GERMAN ARMED FORCES. The identity and membership of the Groups or Organizations referred to in the foregoing titles are hereinafter in Appendix B more particularly defined.

(E) THE ACQUIRING OF TOTALITARIAN CONTROL IN GERMANY: ECONOMIC; AND THE ECONOMIC PLANNING AND MOBILIZATION FOR AGGRESSIVE WAR

Having gained political power the conspirators organized Germany's economy to give effect to their political aims.

1. In order to eliminate the possibility of resistance in the economic sphere, they deprived labour of its rights of free industrial and political association as particularized in paragraph *(D)* 3 *(c)* (1) herein.

2. They used organizations of German business as instruments of economic mobilization for war.

CHAPTER III

3. They directed Germany's economy towards preparation and equipment of the military machine. To this end they directed finance, capital investment, and foreign trade.

4. The Nazi conspirators, and in particular the industrialists among them, embarked upon a huge re-armament programme and set out to produce and develop huge quantities of materials of war and to create a powerful military potential.

5. With the object of carrying through the preparation for war the Nazi conspirators set up a series of administrative agencies and authorities. For example, in 1936 they established for this purpose the office of the Four Year Plan with the defendant GOERING as Plenipotentiary, vesting it with overriding control over Germany's economy. Furthermore, on 28th August, 1939, immediately before launching their aggression against Poland, they appointed the defendant FUNK Plenipotentiary for Economics; and on 30th August, 1939, they set up the Ministerial Council for the Defence of the Reich to act as a War Cabinet.

(F) UTILIZATION OF NAZI CONTROL FOR FOREIGN AGGRESSION

1. *Status of the conspiracy by the middle of 1933 and projected plans.*

By the middle of the year 1933 the Nazi conspirators, having acquired governmental control over Germany, were in a position to enter upon further and more detailed planning with particular relationship to foreign policy. Their plan was to re-arm and to re-occupy and fortify the Rhineland, in violation of the Treaty of Versailles and other treaties, in order to acquire military strength and political bargaining power to be used against other nations.

2. The Nazi conspirators decided that for their purpose the Treaty of Versailles must definitely be abrogated and specific plans were made by them and put into operation by 7th March, 1936, all of which opened the way for the major aggressive steps to follow, as hereinafter set forth. In the execution of this phase of the conspiracy the Nazi conspirators did the following acts:

    (a) They led Germany to enter upon a course of secret re-armament from 1933 to March, 1935, including the training of military personnel and the production of munitions of war, and the building of an air force.

    (b) On 14th October, 1933, they led Germany to leave the International Disarmament Conference and the League of Nations.

    (c) On 10th March, 1935, the defendant GOERING announced that Germany was building a military air force.

(d) On 16th March, 1935, the Nazi conspirators promulgated a law for universal military service, in which they stated the peace-time strength of the German Army would be fixed at 500,000 men.

(e) On 21st May, 1935, they falsely announced to the world, with intent to deceive and allay fears of aggressive intentions, that they would respect the territorial limitations of the Versailles Treaty and comply with the Locarno Pacts.

(f) On 7th March, 1936, they reoccupied and fortified the Rhineland, in violation of the Treaty of Versailles and the Rhine Pact of Locarno of 16th October, 1925, and falsely announced to the world that "we have no territorial demands to make in Europe."

3. *Aggressive action against Austria and Czechoslovakia*

(a) *The 1936-1938 phase of the plan: planning for the assault on Austria and Czechoslovakia*

The Nazi conspirators next entered upon the specific planning for the acquisition of Austria and Czechoslovakia, realizing it would be necessary, for military reasons, first to seize Austria before assaulting Czechoslovakia. On 21st May, 1935, in a speech to the Reichstag, Hitler stated that: "Germany neither intends nor wishes to interfere in the internal affairs of Austria, to annex Austria or to conclude an Anschluss." On 1st May, 1936, within two months after the re-occupation of the Rhineland, Hitler stated: "The lie goes forth again that Germany tomorrow or the day after will fall upon Austria or Czechoslovakia." Thereafter, the Nazi conspirators caused a treaty to be entered into between Austria and Germany on 11th July, 1936, Article 1 of which stated that "The German Government recognizes the full sovereignty of the Federated State of Austria in the spirit of the pronouncements of the German Fuehrer and Chancellor of 21st May, 1935." Meanwhile, plans for aggression in violation of that treaty were being made. By the autumn of 1937, all noteworthy opposition within the Reich had been crushed. Military preparation for the Austrian action was virtually concluded. An influen-

CHAPTER III

tial group of the Nazi conspirators met with Hitler on 5th November, 1937, to review the situation. It was reaffirmed that Nazi Germany must have "Lebensraum" in central Europe. It was recognized that such conquest would probably meet resistance which would have to be crushed by force and that their decision might lead to a general war, but this prospect was discounted as a risk worth taking. There emerged from this meeting three possible plans for the conquest of Austria and Czechoslovakia. Which of the three was to be used was to depend upon the developments in the political and military situation in Europe. It was contemplated that the conquest of Austria and Czechoslovakia would, through compulsory emigration of 2,000,000 persons from Czechoslovakia and 1,000,000 persons from Austria, provide additional food to the Reich for 5,000,000 to 6,000,000 people, strengthen it militarily by providing shorter and better frontiers, and make possible the constituting of new armies up to about twelve divisions. Thus, the aim of the plan against Austria and Czechoslovakia was conceived of not as an end to itself but as a preparatory measure toward the next aggressive steps in the Nazi conspiracy.

(b) *The execution of the plan to invade Austria: November, 1937, to March, 1938*

Hitler on 8th February, 1938, called Chancellor Schuschnigg to a conference at Berchtesgaden. At the meeting of 12th February, 1938, under threat of invasion, Schuschnigg yielded a promise of amnesty to imprisoned Nazis and appointment of Nazis to ministerial posts. He agreed to remain silent until Hitler's 20th February speech in which Austria's independence was to be reaffirmed, but Hitler in his speech, instead of affirming Austrian independence, declared himself protector of all Germans. Meanwhile, subversive activities of Nazis in Austria increased. Schuschnigg on 9th March, 1938, announced a plebiscite for the following Sunday on the question of Austrian independence. On 11th March Hitler sent an ultimatum, demanding that the plebiscite be called off or that Germany would invade Austria. Later the same day a second ultimatum threatened invasion unless Schuschnigg should resign in three hours.

Schuschnigg resigned. The defendant SEYSS-IN-QUART, who was appointed Chancellor, immediately invited Hitler to send German troops into Austria to "preserve order." The invasion began on 12th March, 1938. On 13th March, Hitler by proclamation assumed office as Chief of State of Austria and took command of its armed forces. By a law of the same date Austria was annexed to Germany.

(c) *The execution of the plan to invade Czechoslovakia: April,* 1938, *to March,* 1939

1. Simultaneously with their annexation of Austria the Nazi conspirators gave false assurances to the Czechoslovak Government that they would not attack that country. But within a month they met to plan specific ways and means of attacking Czechoslovakia, and to revise, in the light of the acquisition of Austria, the previous plans for aggression against Czechoslovakia.

2. On 21st April, 1938, the Nazi conspirators met and prepared to launch an attack on Czechoslovakia not later than 1st October, 1938. They planned specifically to create an "incident" to "justify" the attack. They decided to launch a military attack only after a period of diplomatic squabbling which, growing more serious, would lead to the excuse for war, or, in the alternative, to unleash a lightning attack as a result of an "incident" of their own creation. Consideration was given to assassinating the German Ambassador at Prague to create the requisite incident. From and after 21st April, 1938, the Nazi conspirators caused to be prepared detailed and precise military plans designed to carry out such an attack at any opportune moment and calculated to overcome all Czechoslovak resistance within four days, thus presenting the world with a fait accompli, and so forestalling outside resistance. Throughout the months of May, June, July, August and September, these plans were made more specific and detailed, and by 3rd September, 1938, it was decided that all troops were to be ready for action on 28th September, 1938.

3. Throughout this same period, the Nazi conspirators were agitating the minorities question in Czechoslovakia, and particularly in the Sudetenland, leading to a diplomatic crisis in August and September, 1938.

CHAPTER III

After the Nazi conspirators threatened war, the United Kingdom and France concluded a pact with Germany and Italy at Munich on 29th September, 1938, involving the cession of the Sudetenland by Czechoslovakia to Germany. Czechoslovakia was required to acquiesce. On 1st October, 1938, German troops occupied the Sudetenland.

4. On 15th March, 1939, contrary to the provisions of the Munich Pact itself, the Nazi conspirators caused the completion of their plan by seizing and occupying the major part of Czechoslovakia not ceded to Germany by the Munich Pact.

4. *Formulation of the plan to attack Poland: preparation and initiation of aggressive war: March, 1939, to September, 1939*

(*a*) With these aggressions successfully consummated, the conspirators had obtained much desired resources and bases and were ready to undertake further aggressions by means of war. Following assurances to the world of peaceful intentions, an influential group of the conspirators met on 23rd May, 1939, to consider the further implementation of their plan. The situation was reviewed and it was observed that "the past six years have been put to good use and all measures have been taken in correct sequence and in accordance with our aims"; that the national-political unity of the Germans had been substantially achieved; and that further successes could not be achieved without war and bloodshed. It was decided nevertheless next to attack Poland at the first suitable opportunity. It was admitted that the questions concerning Danzig which they had agitated with Poland were not true questions, but rather that the question was one of aggressive expansion for food and "Lebensraum." It was recognized that Poland would fight if attacked and that a repetition of the Nazi success against Czechoslovakia without war could not be expected. Accordingly, it was determined that the problem was to isolate Poland and, if possible, prevent a simultaous conflict with the Western Powers. Nevertheless, it was agreed that England was an enemy to their aspirations, and that war with England and her ally France must eventually result, and therefore that in that war every attempt must be made to overwhelm England with a "Blitzkrieg." It was thereupon determined immediately to prepare detailed plans for an attack on Poland at the first suitable opportunity and thereafter for an attack on England and France, together with plans for the simultaneous occupation by armed force of air bases in the Netherlands and Belgium.

(b) Accordingly, after having denounced the German-Polish Pact of 1934 on false grounds, the Nazi conspirators proceeded to stir up the Danzig issue to prepare frontier "incidents" to "justify" the attack, and to make demands for the cession of Polish territory. Upon refusal by Poland to yield, they caused German armed forces to invade Poland on 1st September, 1939, thus precipitating war also with the United Kingdom and France.

5. *Expansion of the war into a general war of aggression: planning and execution of attacks on Denmark, Norway, Belgium, The Netherlands, Luxembourg, Yugoslavia, and Greece: 1939 to April, 1941*

Thus the aggressive war prepared for by the Nazi conspirators through their attacks on Austria and Czechoslovakia was actively launched by their attack on Poland, in violation of the terms of the Briand-Kellogg Pact, 1928. After the total defeat of Poland, in order to facilitate the carrying out of their military operations against France and the United Kingdom, the Nazi conspirators made active preparations for an extension of the war in Europe. In accordance with those plans, they caused the German armed forces to invade Denmark and Norway on 9th April, 1940; Belgium, the Netherlands and Luxembourg on 10th May, 1940; Yugoslavia and Greece on 6th April, 1941. All these invasions had been specifically planned in advance.

6. *German invasion on June 22nd, 1941, of the U.S.S.R. territory in violation of Non-Aggression Pact of 23rd August, 1939*

On June 22nd, 1941, the Nazi conspirators deceitfully denounced the Non-Aggression Pact between Germany and the U.S.S.R. and without any declaration of war invaded Soviet territory thereby beginning a War of Aggression against the U.S.S.R. From the first day of launching their attack on Soviet territory

CHAPTER III

the Nazi conspirators, in accordance with their detailed plans, began to carry out the destruction of cities, towns and villages, the demolition of factories, collective farms, electric stations and railroads, the robbery and barbaric devastation of the natural cultural institutions of the peoples of the U.S.S.R., the devastation of museums, churches, historic monuments. The mass deportation of the Soviet citizens for slave labor to Germany, as well as the annihilation of old people, women and children, especially Belo-Russians and Ukrainians. The extermination of Jews committed throughout the territory of the Soviet Union.

The above mentioned criminal offenses were perpetrated by the German troops in accordance with the orders of the Nazi Government and the General Staff and High Command of the German armed forces.

7. *Collaboration with Italy and Japan and aggressive war against the United States: November, 1936, to December, 1941*

After the initiation of the Nazi wars of aggression the Nazi conspirators brought about a German-Italian-Japanese ten-year military-economic alliance signed at Berlin on 27th September, 1940. This agreement, representing a strengthening of the bonds among those three nations established by the earlier but more limited pact of 25th November, 1936, stated: "The Governments of Germany, Italy and Japan, considering it as a condition precedent of any lasting peace that all nations of the world be given each its own proper place, have decided to stand by and co-operate with one another in regard of their efforts in Greater East Asia and regions of Europe respectively wherein it is their prime purpose to establish and maintain a new order of things calculated to promote the mutual prosperity and welfare of the peoples concerned." The Nazi conspirators conceived that Japanese aggression would weaken and handicap those nations with whom they were at war, and those with whom they contemplated war. Accordingly, the Nazi conspirators exhorted Japan to seek "a new order of things." Taking advantage of the wars of aggression then being waged by the Nazi conspirators, Japan commenced an attack on 7th December, 1941, against the United States of America at Pearl Harbor and the Philippines, and against the British Commonwealth of Nations, French Indo-China and the Netherlands in the southwest Pacific. Germany declared war against the United States on 11th December, 1941.

(G) War Crimes and Crimes against Humanity committed in the course of executing the conspiracy for which the conspirators are responsible

1. Beginning with the initiation of the aggressive war on 1st September, 1939, and throughout its extension into wars involving almost the entire world, the Nazi conspirators carried out their common plan or conspiracy to wage war in ruthless and complete disregard and violation of the laws and customs of war. In the course of executing the common plan or conspiracy there were committed the War Crimes detailed hereinafter in Count Three of this Indictment.

2. Beginning with the initiation of their plan to seize and retain total control of the German State, and thereafter throughout their utilization of that control for foreign aggression, the Nazi conspirators carried out their common plan or conspiracy in ruthless and complete disregard and violation of the laws of humanity. In the course of executing the common plan or conspiracy there were committed the Crimes against Humanity detailed hereinafter in Count Four of this Indictment.

3. By reason of all the foregoing, the defendants with divers other persons are guilty of a common plan or conspiracy for the accomplishment of Crimes against Peace; of a conspiracy to commit Crimes against Humanity in the course of preparation for war and in the course of prosecution of war; and of a conspiracy to commit War Crimes not only against the armed forces of their enemies but also against non-belligerent civilian populations.

(H) Individual, group and organization responsibility for the offense stated in Count One

Reference is hereby made to Appendix A of this Indictment for a statement of the responsibility of the individual defendants for the offense set forth in this Count One of the Indictment. Reference is hereby made to Appendix B of this Indictment for a statement of the responsibility of the groups and organizations named herein as criminal groups and organizations for the offense set forth in this Count One of the Indictment.

COUNT TWO—CRIMES AGAINST PEACE
(Charter, Article 6 (a))

V. Statement of the Offense

All the defendants with divers other persons, during a period of years preceding 8th May, 1945, participated in the planning,

CHAPTER III

preparation, initiation and waging of wars of aggression, which were also wars in violation of international treaties, agreements and assurances.

VI. Particulars of the wars planned, prepared, initialed and waged

(*A*) The wars referred to in the Statement of Offense in this Count Two of the Indictment and the dates of their initiation were the following: against Poland, 1st September, 1939; against the United Kingdom and France, 3rd September, 1939; against Denmark and Norway, 9th April, 1940; against Belgium, the Netherlands and Luxembourg, 10th May, 1940; against Yugoslavia and Greece, 6th April, 1941; against the U.S.S.R., 22nd June, 1941; and against the United States of America, 11th December, 1941.

(*B*) Reference is hereby made to Count One of the Indictment for the allegations charging that these wars were wars of aggression on the part of the defendants.

(*C*) Reference is hereby made to Appendix C annexed to this Indictment for a statement of particulars of the charges of violations of international treaties, agreements and assurances caused by the defendants in the course of planning, preparing and initiating these wars.

VII. Individual, group and organization responsibility for the offense stated in Count Two

Reference is hereby made to Appendix A of this Indictment for a statement of the responsibility of the individual defendants for the offense set forth in this Count Two of the Indictment. Reference is hereby made to Appendix B of this Indictment for a statement of the responsibility of the groups and organizations named herein as criminal groups and organizations for the offense set forth in this Count Two of the Indictment.

APPENDIX C

Charges and Particulars of Violations of International Treaties, Agreements and Assurances Caused by the Defendants in the Course of Planning, Preparing and Initiating the Wars

I

CHARGE: *Violation of the Convention for the Pacific Settlement of International Disputes signed at The Hague, 29 July, 1899.*

PARTICULARS: In that Germany did, by force and arms, on the dates specified in Column 1, invade the territory of the sovereigns specified in Column 2, respectively, without first having attempted to settle its disputes with said sovereigns by pacific means.

Column 1	*Column 2*
6 April 1941	Kingdom of Greece
6 April 1941	Kingdom of Yugolsavia

CHAPTER III

II

CHARGE: *Violation of the Convention for the Pacific Settlement of International Disputes signed at The Hague, 18 October 1907.*

PARTICULARS: In that Germany did, on or about the dates specified in Column 1, by force of arms invade the territory of the sovereigns specified in Column 2, respectively, without having first attempted to settle its dispute with said sovereigns by pacific means.

Column 1	*Column 2*
1 September 1939	Republic of Poland
9 April 1940	Kingdom of Norway
9 April 1940	Kingdom of Denmark
10 May 1940	Grand-Duchy of Luxembourg
10 May 1940	Kingdom of Belgium
10 May 1940	Kingdom of the Netherlands
22 June 1941	Union of Soviet Socialist Republics

III

CHARGE: *Violation of Hague Convention III Relative to the Opening of Hostilities, signed 18 October 1907.*

PARTICULARS: In that Germany did, on or about the dates specified in Column 1, commence hostilities against the countries specified in Column 2, respectively, without previous warning in the form of a reasoned declaration of war or an ultimatum with conditional declaration of war.

Column 1	*Column 2*
1 September 1939	Republic of Poland
9 April 1940	Kingdom of Norway
9 April 1940	Kingdom of Denmark
10 May 1940	Kingdom of Belgium
10 May 1940	Kingdom of the Netherlands
10 May 1940	Grand-Duchy of Luxembourg
22 June 1941	Union of Soviet Socialist Republics

IV

CHARGE: *Violation of Hague Convention V Respecting the Rights and Duties of Neutral Powers and Persons in Case of War on Land, signed 18 October 1907.*

PARTICULARS: In that Germany did, on or about the dates specified in Column 1, by force and arms of its military forces, cross into, invade, and occupy the territories of the sovereigns specified in Column 2, respectively, then and thereby violating the neutrality of said sovereigns.

Column 1	Column 2
9 April 1940	Kingdom of Norway
9 April 1940	Kingdom of Denmark
10 May 1940	Grand-Duchy of Luxembourg
10 May 1940	Kingdom of Belgium
10 May 1940	Kingdom of the Netherlands
22 June 1941	Union of Soviet Socialist Republics

V

CHARGE: *Violation of the Treaty of Peace between the Allied and Associated Powers and Germany, signed at Versailles, 28 June 1919, known as the Versailles Treaty.*

PARTICULARS: (1) In that Germany did, on and after 7 March 1936, maintain and assemble armed forces and maintain and construct military fortifications in the demilitarized zone of the Rhineland in violation of the provisions of Articles 42 to 44 of the Treaty of Versailles.

(2) In that Germany did, on or about 13 March 1938, annex Austria into the German Reich in violation of the provisions of Article 80 of the Treaty of Versailles.

(3) In that Germany did, on or about 22 March 1939, incorporate the district of Memel into the German Reich in violation of the provisions of Article 99 of the Treaty of Versailles.

(4) In that Germany did, on or about 1 September 1939, incorporate the Free City of Danzig into the German Reich in violation of the provisions of Article 100 of the Treaty of Versailles.

(5) In that Germany did, on or about 16 March 1939, incorporate the provinces of Bohemia and Moravia, formerly part of Czechoslovakia, into the German Reich in violation of the provisions of Article 81 of the Treaty of Versailles.

(6) In that Germany did, at various times in March 1935 and thereafter, repudiate various parts of Part V, Military, Naval and Air Clauses of the Treaty of Versailles, by creating an air force, by use of compulsory military service, by increasing the size of the army beyond treaty limits, and by increasing the size of the navy beyond treaty limits.

VI

CHARGE: *Violation of the Treaty between the United States and Germany Restoring Friendly Relations, signed at Berlin, 25 August 1921.*

CHAPTER III

PARTICULARS: In that Germany did, at various times in March 1935 and thereafter, repudiate various parts of Part V, Military, Naval and Air Clauses of the Treaty Between the United States and Germany Restoring Friendly Relations by creating an air force, by use of compulsory military service, by increasing the size of the army beyond treaty limits, and by increasing the size of the navy beyond treaty limits.

VII

CHARGE: *Violation of the Treaty of Mutual Guarantee between Germany, Belgium, France, Great Britain and Italy, done at Locarno, 16 October 1925.*

PARTICULARS: (1) In that Germany did, on or about 7 March 1936, unlawfully send armed forces into the Rhineland demilitarized zone of Germany, in violation of Article 1 of the Treaty of Mutual Guarantee.

(2) In that Germany did, on or about March 1936, and thereafter, unlawfully maintain armed forces in the Rhineland demilitarized zone of Germany, in violation of Article 1 of the Treaty of Mutual Guarantee.

(3) In that Germany did, on or about 7 March 1936, and thereafter, unlawfully construct and maintain fortifications in the Rhineland demilitarized zone of Germany, in violation of Article 1 of the Treaty of Mutual Guarantee.

(4) In that Germany did, on or about 10 May 1940, unlawfully attack and invade Belgium, in violation of Article 2 of the Treaty of Mutual Guarantee.

(5) In that Germany did, on or about 10 May 1940, unlawfully attack and invade Belgium, without first having attempted to settle its dispute with Belgium by peaceful means, in violation of Article 3 of the Treaty of Mutual Guarantee.

VIII

CHARGE: *Violation of the Arbitration Treaty between Germany and Czechoslovakia, done at Locarno, 16 October 1925.*

PARTICULARS: In that Germany did, on or about 15 March 1939, unlawfully by duress and threats of military might force Czechoslovakia to deliver the destiny of Czechoslovakia and its inhabitants into the hands of the Fuehrer and Reichschancellor of Germany without having attempted to settle its dispute with Czechoslovakia by peaceful means.

IX

CHARGE: *Violation of the Arbitration Convention between Germany and Belgium, done at Locarno, 16 October 1925.*

PARTICULARS: In that Germany did, on or about 10 May 1940, unlawfully attack and invade Belgium without first having attempted to settle its dispute with Belgium by peaceful means.

X

CHARGE: *Violation of the Arbitration Treaty between Germany and Poland, done at Locarno, 16 October 1925.*

PARTICULARS: In that Germany did, on or about 1 September 1939, unlawfully attack and invade Poland without first having attempted to settle its dispute with Poland by peaceful means.

XI

CHARGE: *Violation of Convention of Arbitration and Conciliation entered into between Germany and the Netherlands on 20 May 1926.*

PARTICULARS: In that Germany, without warning and notwithstanding its solemn covenant to settle by peaceful means all disputes of any nature whatever which might arise between it and the Netherlands which were not capable of settlement by diplomacy and which had not been referred by mutual agreement to the Permanent Court of International Justice, did, on or about 10 May 1940, with a Military force, attack, invade, and occupy the Netherlands, thereby violating its neutrality and territorial integrity and destroying its sovereign independence.

XII

CHARGE: *Violation of Convention of Arbitration and Conciliation entered into between Germany and Denmark on 2 June 1926.*

PARTICULARS: In that Germany, without warning, and notwithstanding its solemn covenant to settle by peaceful means all disputes of any nature whatever which might arise between it and Denmark which were not capable of settlement by diplomacy and which had not been referred by mutual agreement to the Permanent Court of International Justice, did, on or about 9 April, 1940, with a Military Force, attack, invade, and occupy Denmark, thereby violating its neutrality and territorial integrity and destroying its sovereign independence.

XIII

CHARGE: *Violation of Treaty between Germany and other Powers providing for Renunciation of War as an Instrument of*

CHAPTER III

National Policy, signed at Paris 27 August 1928, known as the Kellogg-Briand Pact.

PARTICULARS: In that Germany did, on or about the dates specified in Column 1, with a military force, attack the sovereigns specified in Column 2, respectively, and resort to war against such sovereigns, in violation of its solemn declaration condemning recourse to war for the solution of international controversies, its solemn renunciation of war as an instrument of national policy in its relations with such sovereigns, and its solemn covenant that settlement or solution of all disputes or conflicts of whatever nature or origin arising between it and such sovereigns should never be sought except by pacific means.

Column 1	Column 2
1 September 1939	Republic of Poland
9 April 1940	Kingdom of Norway
9 April 1940	Kingdom of Denmark
10 May 1940	Kingdom of Belgium
10 May 1940	Grand-Duchy of Luxembourg
10 May 1940	Kingdom of the Netherlands
6 April 1941	Kingdom of Greece
6 April 1941	Kingdom of Yugoslavia
22 June 1941	Union of Soviet Socialist Republics
11 December 1941	United States of America

XIV

CHARGE: *Violation of Treaty of Arbitration and Conciliation entered into between Germany and Luxembourg on 11 September 1929.*

PARTICULARS: In that Germany, without warning, and notwithstanding its solemn covenant to settle by peaceful means all disputes which might arise between it and Luxembourg which were not capable of settlement by diplomacy, did, on or about 10 May 1940, with a military force, attack, invade, and occupy Luxembourg, thereby violating its neutrality and territorial integrity and destroying its sovereign independence.

XV

CHARGE: *Violation of the Declaration of Non-Aggression entered into between Germany and Poland on 26 January 1934.*

PARTICULARS: In that Germany proceeding to the application of force for the purpose of reaching a decision did, on or about 1 September 1939, at various places along the German-Polish frontier employ military forces to attack, invade and commit other acts of aggression against Poland.

XVI

CHARGE: *Violation of German Assurance given on 21 May 1935 that the Inviolability and Integrity of the Federal State of Austria would be Recognized.*

PARTICULARS: In that Germany did, on or about 12 March 1938, at various points and places along the German-Austrian frontier, with a military force and in violation of its solemn declaration and assurance, invade and annex to Germany the territory of the Federal State of Austria.

XVII

CHARGE: *Violation of Austro-German Agreement of 11 July 1936.*

PARTICULARS: In that Germany during the period from 12 February 1938 to 13 March 1938 did by duress and various aggressive acts, including the use of military force, cause the Federal State of Austria to yield up its sovereignty to the German State in violation of Germany's agreement to recognize the full sovereignty of the Federal State of Austria.

XVIII

CHARGE: *Violation of German Assurances given on 30 January 1937, 28 April 1939, 26 August 1939 and 6 October 1939 to Respect the Neutrality and Territorial Inviolability of the Netherlands.*

PARTICULARS: In that Germany, without warning, and without recourse to peaceful means of settling any considered differences did, on or about 10 May 1940, with a military force and in violation of its solemn assurances, invade, occupy, and attempt to subjugate the sovereign territory of the Netherlands.

XIX

CHARGE: *Violation of German Assurances given on 30 January 1937, 13 October 1937, 28 April 1939, 26 August 1939 and 6 October 1939 to Respect the Neutrality and Territorial Integrity and Inviolability of Belgium.*

PARTICULARS: In that Germany, without warning, did on or about 10 May 1940, with a military force and in violation of its solemn assurances and declarations, attack, invade, and occupy the sovereign territory of Belgium.

XX

CHARGE: *Violation of Assurances given on 11 March 1938 and 26 September 1938 to Czechoslovakia.*

PARTICULARS: In that Germany, on or about 15 March

CHAPTER III

1939 did, by establishing a Protectorate of Bohemia and Moravia under duress and by the threat of force, violate the assurance given on 11 March 1938 to respect the territorial integrity of the Czechoslovak Republic and the assurance given on 26 September 1938 that, if the so-called Sudeten territories were ceded to Germany, no further German territorial claims on Czechoslovakia would be made.

XXI

CHARGE: *Violation of the Munich Agreement and Annexes of 29 September 1938.*

PARTICULARS: (1) In that Germany on or about 15 March 1939, did by duress and the threat of military intervention force the Republic of Czechoslovakia to deliver the destiny of the Czech people and country into the hands of the Fuehrer of the German Reich.

(2) In that Germany refused and failed to join in an international guarantee of the new boundaries of the Czechoslovakia state as provided for in Annex No. 1 to the Munich Agreement.

XXII

CHARGE: *Violation of the Solemn Assurance of Germany given on 3 September 1939, 28 April 1939 and 6 October 1939 that they would not violate the Independence or Sovereignty of the Kingdom of Norway.*

PARTICULARS: In that Germany, without warning did, on or about 9 April 1940, with its military and naval forces attack, invade and commit other acts of aggression against the Kingdom of Norway.

XXIII

CHARGE: *Violation of German Assurances given on 28 April 1939 and 26 August 1939 to Respect the Neutrality and Territorial Inviolability of Luxembourg.*

PARTICULARS: In that Germany, without warning, and without recourse to peaceful means of settling any considered differences, did, on or about 10 May 1940, with a military force and in violation of the solemn assurances, invade, occupy, and absorb into Germany the sovereign territory of Luxembourg.

XXIV

CHARGE: *Violation of the Treaty of Non-Aggression between Germany and Denmark signed at Berlin 31 May 1939.*

PARTICULARS: In that Germany, without prior warning did, on or about 9 April 1940, with its military forces attack, invade and commit other acts of aggression against the Kingdom of Denmark.

XXV

CHARGE: *Violation of Treaty of Non-Aggression entered into between Germany and U.S.S.R. on 23 August 1939.*

PARTICULARS: (1) In that Germany did, on or about 22 June 1941, employ military forces to attack and commit acts of aggression against the U.S.S.R.

(2) In that Germany without warning or recourse to a friendly exchange of views or arbitration did, on or about 22 June 1941, employ military forces to attack and commit acts of aggression against the U.S.S.R.

XXVI

CHARGE: *Violation of German Assurance given on 6 October 1939 to Respect the Neutrality and Territorial Integrity of Yugoslavia.*

PARTICULARS: In that Germany, without prior warning did, on or about 6 April 1941, with its military forces attack, invade and commit other acts of aggression against the Kingdom of Yugoslavia.

DOCUMENT 19 (b)

Chapter V

OPENING ADDRESS FOR THE UNITED STATES

The following address, opening the American case under Count I of the Indictment, was delivered by Justice Robert H. Jackson, Chief of Counsel for the United States, before the Tribunal on 21 November 1945:

May it please Your Honors,

The privilege of opening the first trial in history for crimes against the peace of the world imposes a grave responsibility. The wrongs which we seek to condemn and punish have been so calculated, so malignant and so devastating, that civilization cannot tolerate their being ignored because it cannot survive their being repeated. ᵼ That four great nations, flushed with victory and stung with injury stay the hand of vengeance and voluntarily submit their captive enemies to the judgment of the law is one of the most significant tributes that Power ever has paid to Reason.

This tribunal, while it is novel and experimental, is not the product of abstract speculations nor is it created to vindicate legalistic theories. This inquest represents the practical effort of four of the most mighty of nations, with the support of seventeen more, to utilize International Law to meet the greatest menace of our times—aggressive war. The common sense of mankind demands that law shall not stop with the punishment of petty crimes by little people. It must also reach men who possess themselves of great power and make deliberate and concerted use of it to set in motion evils which leave no home in the world untouched. It is a cause of this magnitude that the United Nations will lay before Your Honors.

In the prisoners' dock sit twenty-odd broken men. Reproached by the humiliation of those they have led almost as bitterly as by the desolation of those they have attacked, their personal capacity for evil is forever past. It is hard now to perceive in these miserable men as captives the power by which as Nazi leaders they once dominated much of the world and terrified most of it. Merely as individuals, their fate is of little consequence to the world.

What makes this inquest significant is that those prisoners represent sinister influence that will lurk in the world long after their bodies have returned to dust. They are living symbols of racial hatreds, of terrorism and violence, and of the arrogance and cruelty of power. They are symbols of fierce nationalisms and militarism, of intrigue and war-making which have embroiled Europe generation after generation, crushing its manhood, destroying its homes, and impoverishing its life. They have so identified them-selves with the philosophies they conceived and with the forces they directed that any tenderness to them is a victory and an en-couragement to all the evils which are attached to their names. Civilization can afford no compromise with the social forces which would gain renewed strength if we deal ambiguously or inde-cisively with the men in whom those forces now precariously sur-vive.

What these men stand for we will patiently and temperately disclose. We will give you undeniable proofs of incredible events. The catalogue of crimes will omit nothing that could be conceived by a pathological pride, cruelty, and lust for power. These men created in Germany, under the *Fuehrerprinzip,* a National Social-ist despotism equalled only by the dynasties of the ancient East. They took from the German people all those dignities and free-doms that we hold natural and inalienable rights in every human being. The people were compensated by inflaming and gratifying hatreds toward those who were marked as "scape-goats." Against their opponents, including Jews, Catholics, and free labor the Nazis directed such a campaign of arrogance, brutality, and an-nihilation as the world has not witnessed since the pre-Christian ages. They excited the German ambition to be a "master race," which of course implies serfdom for others. They led their people on a mad gamble for domination. They diverted social energies and resources to the creation of what they thought to be an in-vincible war machine. They overran their neighbors. To sustain the "master race " in its war making, they enslaved millions of human beings and brought them into Germany, where these hap-less creatures now wander as "displaced persons". At length bes-tiality and bad faith reached such excess that they aroused the sleeping strength of imperiled civilization. Its united efforts have ground the German war machine to fragments. But the struggle has left Europe a liberated yet prostrate land where a demoralized society struggles to survive. These are the fruits of the sinister forces that sit with these defendants in the prisoners' dock.

In justice to the nations and the men associated in this prose-cution, I must remind you of certain difficulties which may leave their mark on this case. Never before in legal history has an ef-fort been made to bring within the scope of a single litigation the developments of a decade, covering a whole Continent, and in-volving a score of nations, countless individuals, and innumerable events. Despite the magnitude of the task, the world has de-manded immediate action. This demand has had to be met, though perhaps at the cost of finished craftsmanship. In my country,

CHAPTER V

established courts, following familiar procedures, applying well thumbed precedents, and dealing with the legal consequences of local and limited events seldom commence a trial within a year of the event in litigation. Yet less than eight months ago today the courtroom in which you sit was an enemy fortress in the hands of German SS troops. Less than eight months ago nearly all our witnesses and documents were in enemy hands. The law had not been codified, no procedure had been established, no Tribunal was in existence, no usable courthouse stood here, none of the hundreds of tons of official German documents had been examined, no prosecuting staff had been assembled, nearly all the present defendants were at large, and the four prosecuting powers had not yet joined in common cause to try them. I should be the last to deny that the case may well suffer from incomplete researches and quite likely will not be the example of professional work which any of the prosecuting nations would normally wish to sponsor. It is, however, a completely adequate case to the judgment we shall ask you to render, and its full development we shall be obliged to leave to historians.

Before I discuss particulars of evidence, some general considerations which may affect the credit of this trial in the eyes of the world should be candidly faced. There is a dramatic disparity between the circumstances of the accusers and of the accused that might discredit our work if we should falter, in even minor matters, in being fair and temperate.

Unfortunately, the nature of these crimes is such that both prosecution and judgment must be by victor nations over vanquished foes. The worldwide scope of the aggressions carried out by these men has left but few real neutrals. Either the victors must judge the vanquished or we must leave the defeated to judge themselves. After the First World War, we learned the futility of the latter course. The former high station of these defendants, the notoriety of their acts, and the adaptability of their conduct to provoke retaliation make it hard to distinguish between the demand for a just and measured retribution, and the unthinking cry for vengeance which arises from the anguish of war. It is our task, so far as humanly possible, to draw the line between the two. We must never forget that the record on which we judge these defendants today is the record on which history will judge us tomorrow. To pass these defendants a poisoned chalice is to put it to our own lips as well. We must summon such detachment and intellectual integrity to our task that this trial will commend itself to posterity as fulfilling humanity's aspirations to do justice.

At the very outset, let us dispose of the contention that to put

THE LAW OF THE CASE

The end of the war and capture of these prisoners presented the victorious Allies with the question whether there is any legal responsibility on high-ranking men for acts which I have described. Must such wrongs either be ignored or redressed in hot blood? Is there no standard in the law for a deliberate and reasoned judgment on such conduct?

The Charter of this Tribunal evidences a faith that the law is not only to govern the conduct of little men, but that even rulers are, as Lord Chief Justice Coke put it to King James, "under God and the law." The United States believed that the law long has afforded standards by which a juridical hearing could be conducted to make sure that we punish only the right men and for the right reasons. Following the instructions of the late President Roosevelt and the decision of the Yalta conference, President Truman directed representatives of the United States to formulate a proposed International Agreement, which was submitted during the San Francisco Conference to Foreign Ministers of the United Kingdom, the Soviet Union, and the Provisional Government of France. With many modifications, that proposal has become the Charter of this Tribunal.

But the Agreement which sets up the standards by which these prisoners are to be judged does not express the views of the signatory nations alone. Other nations with diverse but highly respected systems of jurisprudence also have signified adherence to it. These are Belgium, The Netherlands, Denmark, Norway, Czechoslovakia, Luxembourg, Poland, Greece, Yugoslavia, Ethiopia, Australia, Haiti, Honduras, Panama, New Zealand, Venezuela, and India. You judge, therefore, under an organic act which represents the wisdom, the sense of justice, and the will of twenty-one governments, representing an overwhelming majority of all civilized people.

The Charter by which this Tribunal has its being embodies certain legal concepts which are inseparable from its jurisdiction and which must govern its decision. These, as I have said, also are conditions attached to the grant of any hearing to defendants. The validity of the provisions of the Charter is conclusive upon us all whether we have accepted the duty of judging or of prosecuting under it, as well as upon the defendants, who can point to no other law which gives them a right to be heard at all. My able and experienced colleagues believe, as do I, that it will contribute to the expedition and clarity of this trial if I expound briefly the application of the legal philosophy of the Charter to the facts I have recited.

While this declaration of the law by the Charter is final, it may be contended that the prisoners on trial are entitled to have it applied to their conduct only most charitably if at all. It may be said that this is new law, not authoritatively declared at the time they did the acts it condemns, and that this declaration of the law has taken them by surprise.

I cannot, of course, deny that these men are surprised that this is the law; they really are surprised that there is any such thing as law. These defendants did not rely on any law at all. Their program ignored and defied all law. That this is so will appear from many acts and statements, of which I cite but a few. In the Fuehrer's speech to all military commanders on November 23, 1939, he reminded them that at the moment Germany had a pact with Russia, but declared, "Agreements are to be kept only as long as they serve a certain purpose." Later on in the same speech he announced, "A violation of the neutrality of Holland

CHAPTER V

and Belgium will be of no importance." (*789–PS*). A Top Secret document, entitled "Warfare as a Problem of Organization," dispatched by the Chief of the High Command to all Commanders on April 19, 1938, declared that "the normal rules of war toward neutrals may be considered to apply on the basis whether operation of rules will create greater advantages or disadvantages for belligerents." (*L–211*). And from the files of the German Navy Staff, we have a "Memorandum on Intensified Naval War," dated October 15, 1939, which begins by stating a desire to comply with International Law. "However," it continues, "if decisive successes are expected from any measure considered as a war necessity, it must be carried through even if it is not in agreement with international law." (*UK–65*). International Law, natural law, German law, any law at all was to these men simply a propaganda device to be invoked when it helped and to be ignored when it would condemn what they wanted to do. That men may be protected in relying upon the law at the time they act is the reason we find laws of retrospective operation unjust. But these men cannot bring themselves within the reason of the rule which in some systems of jurisprudence prohibits *ex post facto* laws. They cannot show that they ever relied upon International Law in any state or paid it the slightest regard.

The Third Count of the Indictment is based on the definition of war crimes contained in the Charter. I have outlined to you the systematic course of conduct toward civilian populations and combat forces which violates international conventions to which Germany was a party. Of the criminal nature of these acts at least, the defendants had, as we shall show, clear knowledge. Accordingly, they took pains to conceal their violations. It will appear that the defendants Keitel and Jodl were informed by official legal advisors that the orders to brand Russian prisoners of war, to shackle British prisoners of war, and to execute commando prisoners were clear violations of International Law. Nevertheless, these orders were put into effect. The same is true of orders issued for the assassination of General Giraud and General Weygand, which failed to be executed only because of a ruse on the part of Admiral Canaris, who was himself later executed for his part in the plot to take Hitler's life on July 20, 1944 (*Affidavit A*).

The Fourth Count of the Indictment is based on crimes against humanity. Chief among these are mass killings of countless human beings in cold blood. Does it take these men by surprise that murder is treated as a crime?

The First and Second Counts of the Indictment add to these

crimes the crime of plotting and waging wars of aggression and wars in violation of nine treaties to which Germany was a party. There was a time, in fact I think the time of the first World War, when it could not have been said that war-inciting or war-making was a crime in law, however reprehensible in morals.

Of course, it was under the law of all civilized peoples a crime for one man with his bare knuckles to assault another. How did it come that multiplying this crime by a million, and adding fire arms to bare knuckles, made a legally innocent act? The doctrine was that one could not be regarded as criminal for committing the usual violent acts in the conduct of legitimate warfare. The age of imperialistic expansion during the Eighteenth and Nineteenth Centuries added the foul doctrine, contrary to the teachings of early Christian and International Law scholars such as Grotius, that all wars are to be regarded as legitimate wars. The sum of these two doctrines was to give war making a complete immunity from accountability to law.

This was intolerable for an age that called itself civilized. Plain people, with their earthly common sense, revolted at such fictions and legalisms so contrary to ethical principles and demanded checks on war immunity. Statesmen and international lawyers at first cautiously responded by adopting rules of warfare designed to make the conduct of war more civilized. The effort was to set legal limits to the violence that could be done to civilian populations and to combatants as well.

The common sense of men after the First World War demanded, however, that the law's condemnation of war reach deeper, and that the law condemn not merely uncivilized ways of waging war, but also the waging in any way of uncivilized wars —wars of agression. The world's statesmen again went only as far as they were forced to go. Their efforts were timid and cautious and often less explicit than we might have hoped. But the 1920's did outlaw aggressive war.

The reestablishment of the principle that there are unjust wars and that unjust wars are illegal is traceable in many steps. One of the most significant is the Briand-Kellogg Pact of 1928, by which Germany, Italy, and Japan, in common with practically all the nations of the world, renounced war as an instrument of national policy, bound themselves to seek the settlement of disputes only by pacific means, and condemned recourse to war for the solution of international controversies. This pact altered the legal status of a war of aggression. As Mr. Stimson, the United States Secretary of State put it in 1932, such a war "is no longer to be the source and subject of rights. It is no longer

CHAPTER V

to be the principle around which the duties, the conduct, and the rights of nations revolve. It is an illegal thing. * * * By that very act, we have made obsolete many legal precedents and have given the legal profession the task of reexamining many of its codes and treaties."

The Geneva Protocol of 1924 for the Pacific Settlement of International Disputes, signed by the representatives of forty-eight governments, declared that "a war of aggression constitutes * * * an international crime." The Eighth Assembly of the League of Nations in 1927, on unanimous resolution of the representatives of forty-eight member nations, including Germany, declared that a war of aggression constitutes an international crime. At the Sixth Pan-American Conference of 1928, the twenty-one American Republics unanimously adopted a resolution stating that "war of aggression constitutes an international crime against the human species."

A failure of these Nazis to heed, or to understand the force and meaning of this evolution in the legal thought of the world is not a defense or a mitigation. If anything, it aggravates their offense and makes it the more mandatory that the law they have flouted be vindicated by juridical application to their lawless conduct. Indeed, by their own law—had they heeded any law— these principles were binding on these defendants. Article 4 of the Weimar Constitution provided that "The generally accepted rules of international law are to be considered as binding integral parts of the law of the German Reich." (*2050–PS*). Can there be any doubt that the outlawry of aggressive war was one of the "generally accepted rules of international law" in 1939?

Any resort to war—to any kind of a war—is a resort to means that are inherently criminal. War inevitably is a course of killings, assaults, deprivations of liberty, and destruction of property. An honestly defensive war is, of course, legal and saves those lawfully conducting it from criminality. But inherently criminal acts cannot be defended by showing that those who committed them were engaged in a war, when war itself is illegal. The very minimum legal consequence of the treaties making aggressive wars illegal is to strip those who incite or wage them of every defense the law ever gave, and to leave warmakers subject to judgment by the usually accepted principles of the law of crimes.

But if it be thought that the Charter, whose declarations concededly bind us all, does contain new law I still do not shrink from demanding its strict application by this Tribunal. The rule of law in the world, flouted by the lawlessness incited by these defendants, had to be restored at the cost to my country of over a million casualties, not to mention those of other nations. I cannot subscribe to the perverted reasoning that society may advance and strengthen the rule of law by the expenditure of morally innocent lives but that progress in the law may never be made at the price of morally guilty lives.

It is true, of course, that we have no judicial precedent for the Charter. But International Law is more than a scholarly collection of abstract and immutable principles. It is an outgrowth of treaties and agreements between nations and of accepted customs. Yet every custom has its origin in some single act, and every agreement has to be initiated by the action of some state. Unless we are prepared to abandon every principle of growth for International Law, we cannot deny that our own day has the right to institute customs and to conclude agreements that will themselves become sources of a newer and strengthened International Law. International Law is not capable of development by the normal processes of legislation for there is no continuing international legislative authority. Innovations and revisions in International Law are brought about by the action of governments designed to meet a change in circumstances. It grows, as did the Common Law, through decisions reached from time to time in adapting settled principles to new situations. The fact is that when the law evolves by the case method, as did the Common Law and as International Law must do if it is to advance at all, it advances at the expense of those who wrongly guessed the law and learned too late their error. The law, so far as International Law can be decreed, had been clearly pronounced when these acts took place. Hence, I am not disturbed by the lack of judicial precedent for the inquiry we propose to conduct.

The events I have earlier recited clearly fall within the standards of crimes, set out in the Charter, whose perpetrators this Tribunal is convened to judge and punish fittingly. The standards for war crimes and crimes against humanity are too familiar to need comment. There are, however, certain novel problems in applying other precepts of the Charter which I should call to your attention.

THE CRIME AGAINST PEACE

A basic provision of the Charter is that to plan, prepare, initiate, or wage a war of aggression, or a war in violation of international treaties, agreements, and assurances, or to conspire or participate in a common plan to do so is a crime.

CHAPTER V

It is perhaps a weakness in this Charter that it fails itself to define a war of aggression. Abstractly, the subject is full of difficulty and all kinds of troublesome hypothetical cases can be conjured up. It is a subject which, if the defense should be permitted to go afield beyond the very narrow charge in the Indictment, would prolong the trial and involve the Tribunal in insoluble political issues. But so far as the question can properly be involved in this case, the issue is one of no novelty and is one on which legal opinion has well crystalized.

One of the most authoritative sources of International Law on this subject is the Convention for the Definition of Aggression signed at London on July 3, 1933 by Roumania, Estonia, Latvia, Poland, Turkey, The Soviet Union, Persia, and Afghanistan. The subject has also been considered by international committees and by commentators whose views are entitled to the greatest respect. It had been little discussed prior to the First World War but has received much attention as International Law has evolved its outlawry of aggressive war. In the light of these materials of International Law, and so far as relevant to the evidence in this case, I suggest that an "aggressor" is generally held to be that state which is the first to commit any of the following actions:

(1) Declaration of war upon another State;

(2) Invasion by its armed forces, with or without a declaration war, of the territory of another State;

(3) Attack by its land, naval, or air forces, with or without a declaration of war, on the territory, vessels, or aircraft of another State;

(4) Provision of support to armed bands formed in the territory of another State, or refusal, notwithstanding the request of the invaded State, to take in its own territory, all the measures in its power to deprive those bands of all assistance or protection.

And I further suggest that it is the general view that no political, military, economic or other considerations shall serve as an excuse or justification for such actions; but exercise of the right of legitimate self-defense, that is to say, resistance to an act of aggression, or action to assist a State which has been subjected to aggression, shall not constitute a war of aggression.

It is upon such an understanding of the law that our evidence of a conspiracy to provoke and wage an aggressive war is prepared and presented. By this test each of the series of wars begun by these Nazi leaders was unambiguously aggressive.

It is important to the duration and scope of this trial that we bear in mind the difference between our charge that this war was one of aggression and a position that Germany had no grievances. We are not inquiring into the conditions which contributed to causing this war. They are for history to unravel. It is no part of our task to vindicate the European *status quo* as of 1933, or as of any other date. The United States does not desire to enter into discussion of the complicated pre-war currents of European politics, and it hopes this trial will not be protracted by their consideration. The remote causations avowed are too insincere and inconsistent, too complicated and doctrinaire to be the subject of profitable inquiry in this trial. A familiar example is to be found in the *Lebensraum* slogan, which summarized the contention that Germany needed more living space as a justification for expansion. At the same time that the Nazis were demanding more space for the German people, they were demanding more German people to occupy space. Every known means to increase the birth rate, legitimate and illegitimate, was utilized. *Lebensraum* represented a vicious circle of demand—from neighbors more space, and from Germans more progeny. We do not need to investigate the verity of doctrines which led to constantly expanding circles of aggression. It is the plot and the act of aggression which we charge to be crimes.

Our position is that whatever grievances a nation may have, however objectionable it finds the *status quo*, aggressive warfare is an illegal means for settling those grievances or for altering those conditions. It may be that the Germany of the 1920's and 1930's faced desperate problems, problems that would have warranted the boldest measures short of war. All other methods—persuasion, propaganda, economic competition, diplomacy—were open to an aggrieved country, but aggressive warfare was outlawed. These defendants did make aggressive war, a war in violation of treaties. They did attack and invade their neighbors in order to effectuate a foreign policy which they knew could not be accomplished by measures short of war. And that is as far as we accuse or propose to inquire.

THE RESPONSIBILITY OF THIS TRIBUNAL

To apply the sanctions of the law to those whose conduct is found criminal by the standards I have outlined, is the responsibility committed to this Tribunal. It is the first court ever to undertake the difficult task of overcoming the confusion of many tongues and the conflicting concepts of just procedure among divers systems of law, so as to reach a common judgment. The tasks of all of us are such as to make heavy demands on patience and good will. Although the need for prompt action has admittedly resulted in imperfect work on the part of the prosecution, four great nations bring you their hurriedly assembled contributions of evidence. What remains undiscovered we can only guess. We could, with witnesses' testimony, prolong the recitals of crime for years—but to what avail? We shall rest the case when we have offered what seems convincing and adequate proof of the crimes charged without unnecessary cumulation of evidence. We doubt very much whether it will be seriously denied that the crimes I have outlined took place. The effort will undoubtedly be to mitigate or escape personal responsibility.

Among the nations which unite in accusing these defendants the United States is perhaps in a position to be the most dispassionate, for, having sustained the least injury, it is perhaps the least animated by vengeance. Our American cities have not been bombed by day and night, by humans and by robots. It is not our temples that have been laid in ruins. Our countrymen have not had their homes destroyed over their heads. The menace of Nazi aggression, except to those in actual service, has seemed less personal and immediate to us than to European peoples. But while the United States is not first in rancor, it is not second in determination that the forces of law and order be made equal to the task of dealing with such international lawlessness as I have recited here.

Twice in my lifetime, the United States has sent its young manhood across the Atlantic, drained its resources, and burdened itself with debt to help defeat Germany. But the real hope and faith that has sustained the American people in these great efforts was that victory for ourselves and our Allies would lay the basis for an ordered international relationship in Europe and would end the centuries of strife on this embattled continent.

Twice we have held back in the early stages of European conflict in the belief that it might be confined to a purely European affair. In the United States, we have tried to build an economy without armament, a system of government without militarism, and a society where men are not regimented for war. This purpose, we know now, can never be realized if the world periodically is to be embroiled in war. The United States cannot, generation after generation, throw its youth or its resources onto the battlefields of Europe to redress the lack of balance between Germany's strength and that of her enemies, and to keep the battles from our shores.

The American dream of a peace and plenty economy, as well as the hopes of other nations, can never be fulfilled if those nations are involved in a war every generation so vast and devastating as to crush the generation that fights and burden the generation that follows. But experience has shown that wars are no longer local. All modern wars become world wars eventually. And none of the big nations at least can stay out. If we cannot stay out of wars, our only hope is to prevent wars.

I am too well aware of the weaknesses of juridical action alone

CHAPTER V

to contend that in itself your decision under this Charter can prevent future wars. Judicial action always comes after the event. Wars are started only on the theory and in the confidence that they can be won. Personal punishment, to be suffered only in the event the war is lost, will probably not be a sufficient deterrent to prevent a war where the warmakers feel the chances of defeat to be negligible.

But the ultimate step in avoiding periodic wars, which are inevitable in a system of international lawlessness, is to make statesmen responsible to law. And let me make clear that while this law is first applied against German aggressors, the law includes, and if it is to serve a useful purpose it must condemn aggression by any other nations, including those which sit here now in judgment. We are able to do away with domestic tyranny and violence and aggression by those in power against the rights of their own people only when we make all men answerable to the law. This trial represents mankind's desperate effort to apply the discipline of the law to statesmen who have used their powers of state to attack the foundations of the world's peace and to commit aggressions against the rights of their neighbors.

The usefulness of this effort to do justice is not to be measured by considering the law or your judgment in isolation. This trial is part of the great effort to make the peace more secure. One step in this direction is the United Nations organization, which may take joint political action to prevent war if possible, and joint military action to insure that any nation which starts a war will lose it. This Charter and this trial, implementing the Kellogg-Briand Pact, constitute another step in the same direction —juridical action of a kind to ensure that those who start a war will pay for it personally.

While the defendants and the prosecutors stand before you as individuals, it is not the triumph of either group alone that is committed to your judgment. Above all personalities there are anonymous and impersonal forces whose conflict makes up much of human history. It is yours to throw the strength of the law back of either the one or the other of these forces for at least another generation. What are the real forces that are contending before you?

No charity can disguise the fact that the forces which these defendants represent, the forces that would advantage and delight in their acquittal, are the darkest and most sinister forces in society—dictatorship and oppression, malevolence and passion, militarism and lawlessness. By their fruits we best know them. Their acts have bathed the world in blood and set civilization back a century. They have subjected their European neighbors to every outrage and torture, every spoliation and deprivation that insolence, cruelty, and greed could inflict. They have brought the German people to the lowest pitch of wretchedness, from which they can entertain no hope of early deliverance. They have stirred hatreds and incited domestic violence on every continent. These are the things that stand in the dock shoulder to shoulder with these prisoners.

The real complaining party at your bar is Civilization. In all our countries it is still a struggling and imperfect thing. It does not plead that the United States, or any other country, has been blameless of the conditions which made the German people easy victims to the blandishments and intimidations of the Nazi conspirators.

But it points to the dreadful sequence of aggressions and crimes I have recited, it points to the weariness of flesh, the exhaustion of resources, and the destruction of all that was beautiful or useful in so much of the world, and to greater potentialities for destruction in the days to come. It is not necessary among the ruins of this ancient and beautiful city, with untold members of its civilian inhabitants still buried in its rubble, to argue the proposition that to start or wage an aggressive war has the moral qualities of the worst of crimes. The refuge of the defendants can be only their hope that International Law will lag so far behind the moral sense of mankind that conduct which is crime in the moral sense must be regarded as innocent in law.

Civilization asks whether law is so laggard as to be utterly helpless to deal with crimes of this magnitude by criminals of this order of importance. It does not expect that you can make war impossible. It does expect that your juridical action will put the forces of International Law, its precepts, its prohibitions and, most of all, its sanctions, on the side of peace, so that men and women of good will in all countries may have "leave to live by no man's leave, underneath the law."

III. THE COMMON PLAN OF CONSPIRACY AND AGGRESSIVE WAR

The Tribunal now turns to the consideration of the crimes against peace charged in the indictment. Count one of the indictment charges the defendants with conspiring or having a common plan to commit crimes against peace. Count two of the indictment charges the defendants with committing specific crimes against peace by planning, preparing, initiating, and waging wars of aggression against a number of other States. It will be convenient to consider the question of the existence of a common plan and the question of aggressive war together, and to deal later in this judgment with the question of the individual responsibility of the defendants.

The charges in the indictment that the defendants planned and waged aggressive wars are charges of the utmost gravity. War is essentially an evil thing. Its consequences are not confined to the belligerent states alone, but affect the whole world.

To initiate a war of aggression, therefore, is not only an international crime; it is the supreme international crime differing only from other war crimes in that it contains within itself the accumulated evil of the whole.

The first acts of aggression referred to in the indictment are the seizure of Austria and Czechoslovakia; and the first war of aggression charged in the indictment is the war against Poland begun on the 1st September 1939.

Before examining that charge it is necessary to look more closely at some of the events which preceded these acts of aggression. The war against Poland did not come suddenly out of an otherwise clear sky; the evidence has made it plain that this war of aggression, as well as the seizure of Austria and Czechoslovakia, was premeditated and carefully prepared, and was not undertaken until the moment was thought opportune for it to be carried through as a definite part of the preordained scheme and plan.

For the aggressive designs of the Nazi Government were not accidents arising out of the immediate political situation in Europe and the world; they were a deliberate and essential part of Nazi foreign policy.

From the beginning, the National Socialist movement claimed that its object was to unite the German people in the consciousness of their mission and destiny, based on inherent qualities of race, and under the guidance of the Fuehrer.

For its achievement, two things were deemed to be essential: The disruption of the European order as it had existed since the Treaty

16

of Versailles, and the creation of a Greater Germany beyond the frontiers of 1914. This necessarily involved the seizure of foreign territories.

War was seen to be inevitable, or at the very least, highly probable, if these purposes were to be accomplished. The German people, therefore, with all their resources, were to be organized as a great political-military army, schooled to obey without question any policy decreed by the State.

(A) Preparation for Aggression

In "Mein Kampf" Hitler had made this view quite plain. It must be remembered that "Mein Kampf" was no mere private diary in which the secret thoughts of Hitler were set down. Its contents were rather proclaimed from the house tops. It was used in the schools and universities and among the Hitler Youth, in the SS and the SA, and among the German people generally, even down to the presentation of an official copy to all newly married people. By the year 1945 over 6½ million copies had been circulated. The general contents are well known. Over and over again Hitler asserted his belief in the necessity of force as the means of solving international problems, as in the following quotation:

> "The soil on which we now live was not a gift bestowed by Heaven on our forefathers. They had to conquer it by risking their lives. So also in the future, our people will not obtain territory, and therewith the means of existence, as a favor from any other people, but will have to win it by the power of a triumphant sword."

"Mein Kampf" contains many such passages, and the extolling of force as an instrument of foreign policy is openly proclaimed.

The precise objectives of this policy of force are also set forth in detail. The very first page of the book asserts that "German-Austria must be restored to the great German Motherland," not on economic grounds, but because "people of the same blood should be in the same Reich."

The restoration of the German frontiers of 1914 is declared to be wholly insufficient, and if Germany is to exist at all, it must be as a world power with the necessary territorial magnitude.

"Mein Kampf" is quite explicit in stating where the increased territory is to be found:

> "Therefore we National Socialists have purposely drawn a line through the line of conduct followed by prewar Germany in foreign policy. We put an end to the perpetual Germanic march towards the south and west of Europe, and turn our eyes towards the lands of the east. We finally put a stop to the colonial and

17

trade policy of the prewar times, and pass over to the territorial policy of the future.

"But when we speak of new territory in Europe today, we must think principally of Russia and the border states subject to her."

"Mein Kampf" is not to be regarded as a mere literary exercise, nor as an inflexible policy or plan incapable of modification.

Its importance lies in the unmistakable attitude of aggression revealed throughout its pages.

(B) The Planning of Aggression

Evidence from captured documents has revealed that Hitler held four secret meetings to which the Tribunal proposes to make special reference because of the light they shed upon the question of the common plan and aggressive war.

These meetings took place on the 5th November 1937, the 23d of May 1939, the 22d of August 1939, and the 23d of November 1939.

At these meetings important declarations were made by Hitler as to his purposes, which are quite unmistakable in their terms.

The documents which record what took place at these meetings have been subject to some criticism at the hands of defending counsel.

Their essential authenticity is not denied, but it is said, for example, that they do not propose to be verbatim transcripts of the speeches they record, that the document dealing with the meeting on the 5th November 1937, was dated 5 days after the meeting had taken place, and that the two documents dealing with the meeting of August 22, 1939 differ from one another, and are unsigned.

Making the fullest allowance for criticism of this kind, the Tribunal is of the opinion that the documents are documents of the highest value, and that their authenticity and substantial truth are established.

They are obviously careful records of the events they describe, and they have been preserved as such in the archives of the German Government, from whose custody they were captured. Such documents could never be dismissed as inventions, nor even as inaccurate or distorted; they plainly record events which actually took place.

(C) Conferences of the 23rd November 1939 and 5th November 1937

It will perhaps be useful to deal first of all with the meeting of the 23d November 1939, when Hitler called his supreme commanders together. A record was made of what was said, by one of these present. At the date of the meeting, Austria and Czechoslovakia had been incorporated into the German Reich, Poland had been conquered by the German armies, and the war with Great Britain and France was still in its static phase. The moment was opportune for a review of past events. Hitler informed the commanders that the purpose of the con-

18

454

ference was to give them an idea of the world of his thoughts, and to tell them his decision. He thereupon reviewed his political task since 1919, and referred to the secession of Germany from the League of Nations, the denunciation of the Disarmament Conference, the order for rearmament, the introduction of compulsory armed service, the occupation of the Rhineland, the seizure of Austria, and the action against Czechoslovakia. He stated:

"One year later, Austria came; this step also was considered doubtful. It brought about a considerable reinforcement of the Reich. The next step was Bohemia, Moravia, and Poland. This step also was not possible to accomplish in one campaign. First of all, the western fortification had to be finished. It was not possible to reach the goal in one effort. It was clear to me from the first moment that I could not be satisfied with the Sudeten German territory. That was only a partial solution. The decision to march into Bohemia was made. Then followed the erection of the Protectorate and with that the basis for the action against Poland was laid, but I wasn't quite clear at that time whether I should start first against the east and then in the west or vice versa . . . Basically I did not organize the armed forces in order not to strike. The decision to strike was always in me. Earlier or later I wanted to solve the problem. Under pressure it was decided that the east was to be attacked first."

This address, reviewing past events and reaffirming the aggressive intentions present from the beginning, puts beyond any question of doubt the character of the actions against Austria and Czechoslovakia, and the war against Poland.

For they had all been accomplished according to plan; and the nature of that plan must now be examined in a little more detail.

At the meeting of the 23d November 1939, Hitler was looking back to things accomplished; at the earlier meetings now to be considered, he was looking forward, and revealing his plans to his confederates. The comparison is instructive.

The meeting held at the Reich Chancellery in Berlin on the 5th November 1937 was attended by Lieutenant Colonel Hossbach, Hitler's personal adjutant, who compiled a long note of the proceedings, which he dated the 10th November 1937 and signed.

The persons present were Hitler, and the defendants Goering, von Neurath, and Raeder, in their capacities as Commander in Chief of the Luftwaffe, Reich Foreign Minister, and Commander in Chief of the Navy respectively, General von Blomberg, Minister of War, and General von Fritsch, the Commander in Chief of the Army.

Hitler began by saying that the subject of the conference was of such high importance that in other States it would have taken place before the Cabinet. He went on to say that the subject matter of

19

his speech was the result of his detailed deliberations, and of his experiences during his 4½ years of government. He requested that the statements he was about to make should be looked upon in the case of his death as his last will and testament. Hitler's main theme was the problem of living space, and he discussed various possible solutions, only to set them aside. He then said that the seizure of living space on the continent of Europe was therefore necessary, expressing himself in these words:

"It is not a case of conquering people but of conquering agriculturally useful space. It would also be more to the purpose to seek raw material producing territory in Europe directly adjoining the Reich and not overseas, and this solution would have to be brought into effect for one or two generations . . . The history of all times—Roman Empire, British Empire—has proved that every space expansion can only be effected by breaking resistance and taking risks. Even set-backs are unavoidable; neither formerly nor today has space been found without an owner; the attacker always comes up against the proprietor."

He concluded with this observation:

"The question for Germany is where the greatest possible conquest could be made at the lowest cost."

Nothing could indicate more plainly the aggressive intentions of Hitler, and the events which soon followed showed the reality of his purpose. It is impossible to accept the contention that Hitler did not actually mean war; for after pointing out that Germany might expect the opposition of England and France, and analyzing the strength and the weakness of those powers in particular situations, he continued:

"The German question can be solved only by way of force, and this is never without risk . . . If we place the decision to apply force with risk at the head of the following expositions, then we are left to reply to the questions 'when' and 'how'. In this regard we have to decide upon three different cases."

The first of these three cases set forth a hypothetical international situation, in which he would take action not later than 1943 to 1945, saying:

"If the Fuehrer is still living then it will be his irrevocable decision to solve the German space problem not later than 1943 to 1945. The necessity for action before 1943 to 1945 will come under consideration in cases 2 and 3."

The second and third cases to which Hitler referred show the plain intention to seize Austria and Czechoslovakia, and in this connection Hitler said:

20

456

"For the improvement of our military-political position, it must be our first aim in every case of entanglement by war to conquer Czechoslovakia and Austria simultaneously in order to remove any threat from the flanks in case of a possible advance westwards."

He further added:

"The annexation of the two States to Germany militarily and politically would constitute a considerable relief, owing to shorter and better frontiers, the freeing of fighting personnel for other purposes, and the possibility or reconstituting new armies up to a strength of about twelve divisions."

This decision to seize Austria and Czechoslovakia was discussed in some detail; the action was to be taken as soon as a favorable opportunity presented itself.

The military strength which Germany had been building up since 1933 was now to be directed at the two specific countries, Austria and Czechoslovakia.

The defendant Goering testified that he did not believe at that time that Hitler actually meant to attack Austria and Czechoslovakia, and that the purpose of the conference was only to put pressure on von Fritsch to speed up the rearmament of the Army.

The defendant Raeder testified that neither he, nor von Fritsch, nor von Blomberg, believed that Hitler actually meant war, a conviction which the defendant Raeder claims that he held up to the 22d August 1939. The basis of this conviction was his hope that Hitler would obtain a "political solution" of Germany's problems. But all that this means, when examined, is the belief that Germany's position would be so good, and Germany's armed might so overwhelming, that the territory desired could be obtained without fighting for it. It must be remembered too that Hitler's declared intention with regard to Austria was actually carried out within a little over 4 months from the date of the meeting, and within less than a year the first portion of Czechoslovakia was absorbed, and Bohemia and Moravia a few months later. If any doubts had existed in the minds of any of his hearers in November 1937, after March of 1939 there could no longer be any question that Hitler was in deadly earnest in his decision to resort to war. The Tribunal is satisfied that Lieutenant Colonel Hossbach's account of the meeting is substantially correct, and that those present knew that Austria and Czechoslovakia would be annexed by Germany at the first possible opportunity.

(D) THE SEIZURE OF AUSTRIA

The invasion of Austria was a premeditated aggressive step in furthering the plan to wage aggressive wars against other countries.

21

As a result Germany's flank was protected, that of Czechoslovakia being greatly weakened. The first step had been taken in the seizure of "Lebensraum"; many new divisions of trained fighting men had been acquired; and with the seizure of foreign exchange reserves the rearmament program had been greatly strengthened.

On the 21st May 1935 Hitler announced in the Reichstag that Germany did not intend either to attack Austria or to interfere in her internal affairs. On the 1st May 1936 he publicly coupled Czechoslovakia with Austria in his avowal of peaceful intentions; and so late as the 11th July 1936 he recognized by treaty the full sovereignty of Austria.

Austria was in fact seized by Germany in the month of March 1938. For a number of years before that date the National Socialists in Germany had been cooperating with the National Socialists of Austria with the ultimate object of incorporating Austria into the German Reich. The Putsch of July 25, 1934, which resulted in the assassination of Chancellor Dollfuss, had the seizure of Austria as its object; but the Putsch failed, with the consequence that the National Socialist Party was outlawed in Austria. On the 11th July 1936 an agreement was entered into between the two countries, article 1 of which stated:

> "The German Government recognizes the full sovereignty of the Federated State of Austria in the spirit of the pronouncements of the German Fuehrer and Chancellor of the 21st May 1935."

Article 2 declared:

> "Each of the two Governments regards the inner political order (including the question of Austrian National Socialism) obtaining in the other country as an internal affair of the other country, upon which it will exercise neither direct nor indirect influence."

The National Socialist movement in Austria, however, continued its illegal activities under cover of secrecy; and the National Socialists of Germany gave the party active support. The resulting "incidents" were seized upon by the German National Socialists as an excuse for interfering in Austrian affairs. After the conference of the 5th November 1937 these "incidents" rapidly multiplied. The relationship between the two countries steadily worsened, and finally the Austrian Chancellor Schuschnigg was persuaded by the defendant von Papen and others to seek a conference with Hitler, which took place at Berchtesgaden on the 12th February 1938. The defendant Keitel was present at the conference, and Dr. Schuschnigg was threatened by Hitler with an immediate invasion of Austria. Schuschnigg finally agreed to grant a political amnesty to various Nazis convicted of crime, and to appoint the Nazi Seyss-Inquart as Minister of the Interior and Security with control of the police. On the 9th March

22

1938, in an attempt to preserve the independence of his country, Dr. Schuschnigg decided to hold a plebescite on the question of Austrian independence, which was fixed for the 13th March 1938. Hitler, 2 days later, sent an ultimatum to Schuschnigg that the plebescite must be withdrawn. In the afternoon and evening of the 11th March 1938 the defendant Goering made a series of demands upon the Austrian Government, each backed up by the threat of invasion. After Schuschnigg had agreed to the cancellation of the plebiscite another demand was put forward that Schuschnigg must resign, and that the defendant Seyss-Inquart should be appointed Chancellor. In consequence Schuschnigg resigned, and President Miklas, after at first refusing to appoint Seyss-Inquart as Chancellor, gave way and appointed him.

Meanwhile Hitler had given the final order for the German troops to cross the border at dawn on the 12th of March and instructed Seyss-Inquart to use formations of Austrian National Socialists to depose Miklas and to seize control of the Austrian Government. After the order to march had been given to the German troops, Goering telephoned the German Embassy in Vienna and dictated a telegram in which he wished Seyss-Inquart to send to Hitler to justify the military action which had already been ordered. It was:

"The provisional Austrian Government, which, after the dismissal of the Schuschnigg Government, considers its task to establish peace and order in Austria, sends to the German Government the urgent request to support it in its task and to help it to prevent bloodshed. For this purpose it asks the German Government to send German troops as soon as possible."

Keppler, an official of the German Embassy, replied:

"Well, SA and SS are marching through the streets, but everything is quiet."

After some further discussion, Goering stated:

"Please show him (Seyss-Inquart) the text of the telegram, and do tell him that we are asking him—well, he doesn't even have to send the telegram. All he needs to do is to say 'Agreed'."

Seyss-Inquart never sent the telegram; he never even telegraphed, "Agreed."

It appears that as soon as he was appointed Chancellor, some time after 10 p. m., he called Keppler and told him to call up Hitler and transmit his protests against the occupation. This action outraged the defendant Goering, because "it would disturb the rest of the Fuehrer, who wanted to go to Austria the next day." At 11:15 p. m. an official in the Ministry of Propaganda in Berlin telephoned the German Embassy in Vienna and was told by Keppler: "Tell the General Field Marshal that Seyss-Inquart agrees."

23

At daybreak on the 12th March 1938, German troops marched into Austria, and met with no resistance. It was announced in the German press that Seyss-Inquart had been appointed the successor to Schuschnigg, and the telegram which Goering had suggested, but which was never sent, was quoted to show that Seyss-Inquart had requested the presence of German troops to prevent disorder. On the 13th March 1938, a law was passed for the reunion of Austria in the German Reich. Seyss-Inquart demanded that President Miklas should sign this law, but he refused to do so, and resigned his office. He was succeeded by Seyss-Inquart, who signed the law in the name of Austria. This law was then adopted as a law of the Reich by a Reich Cabinet decree issued the same day, and signed by Hitler and the defendants Goering, Frick, von Ribbentrop, and Hess.

It was contended before the Tribunal that the annexation of Austria was justified by the strong desire expressed in many quarters for the union of Austria and Germany; that there were many matters in common between the two peoples that made this union desirable; and that in the result the object was achieved without bloodshed.

These matters, even if true, are really immaterial, for the facts plainly prove that the methods employed to achieve the object were those of an aggressor. The ultimate factor was the armed might of Germany ready to be used if any resistance was encountered. Moreover, none of these considerations appear from the Hossbach account of the meetings of the 5th November 1937, to have been the motives which actuated Hitler; on the contrary, all the emphasis is there laid on the advantage to be gained by Germany in her military strength by the annexation of Austria.

(E) The Seizure of Czechoslovakia

The conference of the 5th November 1937, made it quite plain that the seizure of Czechoslovakia by Germany had been definitely decided upon. The only question remaining was the selection of the suitable moment to do it. On the 4th March 1938, the defendant von Ribbentrop wrote to the defendant Keitel with regard to a suggestion made to von Ribbentrop by the Hungarian Ambassador in Berlin, that possible war aims against Czechoslovakia should be discussed between the German and Hungarian armies. In the course of this letter von Ribbentrop said:

> "I have many doubts about such negotiations. In case we should discuss with Hungary possible war.aims against Czechoslovakia, the danger exists that other parties as well would be informed about this."

On the 11th March 1938, Goering made two separate statements to M. Mastny, the Czechoslovak Minister in Berlin, assuring him that

24

the developments then taking place in Austria would in no way have any detrimental influence on the relations between the German Reich and Czechoslovakia, and emphasized the continued earnest endeavor on the part of the Germans to improve those mutual relations. On the 12th March, Goering asked M. Mastny to call on him, and repeated these assurances.

This design to keep Czechoslovakia quiet whilst Austria was absorbed was a typical maneuver on the part of the defendant Goering, which he was to repeat later in the case of Poland, when he made the most strenuous efforts to isolate Poland in the impending struggle. On the same day, the 12th March, the defendant von Neurath spoke with M. Mastny, and assured him on behalf of Hitler that Germany still considered herself bound by the German-Czechoslovak arbitration convention concluded at Locarno in October 1925.

The evidence shows that after the occupation of Austria by the German Army on the 12th March, and the annexation of Austria on the 13th March, Conrad Henlein, who was the leader of the Sudeten German Party in Czechoslovakia, saw Hitler in Berlin on the 28th March. On the following day, at a conference in Berlin, when von Ribbentrop was present with Henlein, the general situation was discussed, and later the defendant Jodl recorded in his diary:

> "After the annexation of Austria the Fuehrer mentions that there is no hurry to solve the Czech question, because Austria has to be digested first. Nevertheless, preparations for Case Gruen (that is, the plan against Czechoslovakia) will have to be carried out energetically; they will have to be newly prepared on the basis of the changed strategic position because of the annexation of Austria."

On the 21st April 1938, a discussion took place between Hitler and the defendant Keitel with regard to "Case Gruen", showing quite clearly that the preparations for the attack on Czechoslovakia were being fully considered. On the 28th May 1938, Hitler ordered that preparations should be made for military action against Czechoslovakia by the 2d October, and from then onwards the plan to invade Czechoslovakia was constantly under review. On the 30th May 1938 a directive signed by Hitler declared his "unalterable decision to smash Czechoslovakia by military action in the near future."

In June 1938, as appears from a captured document taken from the files of the SD in Berlin, an elaborate plan for the employment of the SD in Czechoslovakia had been proposed. This plan provided that "the SD follow, if possible, immediately after the leading troops, and take upon themselves the duties similar to their tasks in Germany . . ."

Gestapo officials were assigned to cooperate with the SD in certain operations. Special agents were to be trained beforehand to prevent

25

461

sabotage, and these agents were to be notified "before the attack in due time . . . in order to give them the possibility to hide themselves, avoid arrest and deportation . . ."

"At the beginning, guerilla or partisan warfare is to be expected, therefore weapons are necessary . . ."

Files of information were to be compiled with notations as follows: "To arrest" . . . "To liquidate" . . . "To confiscate" . . . "To deprive of passport", etc.

The plan provided for the temporary division of the country into larger and smaller territorial units, and considered various "suggestions", as they were termed, for the incorporation into the German Reich of the inhabitants and districts of Czechoslovakia. The final "suggestion" included the whole country, together with Slovakia and Carpathian Russia, with a population of nearly 15 millions.

The plan was modified in some respects in September after the Munich Conference, but the fact that the plan existed in such exact detail and was couched in such war-like language indicated a calculated design to resort to force.

On the 31st August 1938, Hitler approved a memorandum by Jodl dated 24th August 1938, concerning the timing of the order for the invasion of Czechoslovakia and the question of defense measures. This memorandum contained the following:

"Operation Gruen will be set in motion by means of an 'incident' in Czechoslovakia, which will give Germany provocation for military intervention. The fixing of the *exact time* for this incident is of the utmost importance."

These facts demonstrate that the occupation of Czechoslovakia had been planned in detail long before the Munich conference.

In the month of September 1938, the conferences and talks with military leaders continued. In view of the extraordinarily critical situation which had arisen, the British Prime Minister, Mr. Chamberlain, flew to Munich and then went to Berchtesgaden to see Hitler. On the 22d September Mr. Chamberlain met Hitler for further discussions at Bad Godesberg. On the 26th September 1938, Hitler said in a speech in Berlin, with reference to his conversation:

"I assured him, moreover, and I repeat it here, that when this problem is solved there will be no more territorial problems for Germany in Europe; and I further assured him that from the moment when Czechoslovakia solves its other problems, that is to say, when the Czechs have come to an arrangement with their other minorities, peacefully and without oppression, I will be no longer interested in the Czech State, and that as far as I am concerned I will guarantee it. We don't want any Czechs."

26

On the 29th September 1938, after a conference between Hitler and Mussolini and the British and French Prime Ministers in Munich, the Munich Pact was signed, by which Czechoslovakia was required to acquiesce in the cession of the Sudetenland to Germany. The "piece of paper" which the British Prime Minister brought back to London, signed by himself and Hitler, expressed the hope that for the future Britain and Germany might live without war. That Hitler never intended to adhere to the Munich Agreement is shown by the fact that a little later he asked the defendant Keitel for information with regard to the military force which in his opinion would be required to break all Czech resistance in Bohemia and Moravia. Keitel gave his reply on the 11th October 1938. On the 21st October 1938, a directive was issued by Hitler, and countersigned by the defendant Keitel, to the armed forces on their future tasks, which stated:

> "Liquidation of the remainder of Czechoslovakia. It must be possible to smash at any time the remainder of Czechoslovakia if her policy should become hostile towards Germany."

On the 14th March 1939, the Czech President Hacha and his Foreign Minister Chvalkovsky came to Berlin at the suggestion of Hitler, and attended a meeting at which the defendants von Ribbentrop, Goering, and Keitel were present, with others. The proposal was made to Hacha that if he would sign an agreement consenting to the incorporation of the Czech people in the German Reich at once Bohemia and Moravia would be saved from destruction. He was informed that German troops had already received orders to march and that any resistance would be broken with physical force. The defendant Goering added the threat that he would destroy Prague completely from the air. Faced by this dreadful alternative, Hacha and his Foreign Minister put their signature to the necessary agreement at 4:30 in the morning, and Hitler and Ribbentrop signed on behalf of Germany.

On the 15th March, German troops occupied Bohemia and Moravia, and on the 16th March the German decree was issued incorporating Bohemia and Moravia into the Reich as a protectorate, and this decree was signed by the defendants von Ribbentrop and Frick.

(F) The Aggression Against Poland

By March 1939 the plan to annex Austria and Czechoslovakia, which had been discussed by Hitler at the meeting of the 5th November 1937, had been accomplished. The time had now come for the German leaders to consider further acts of aggression, made more possible of attainment because of that accomplishment.

On the 23d May 1939, a meeting was held in Hitler's study in the new Reich Chancellery in Berlin. Hitler announced his decision to attack Poland and gave his reasons, and discussed the effect the deci-

27

sion might have on other countries. In point of time, this was the second of the important meetings to which reference has already been made, and in order to appreciate the full significance of what was said and done, it is necessary to state shortly some of the main events in the history of German-Polish relations.

As long ago as the year 1925 an Arbitration Treaty between Germany and Poland had been made at Locarno, providing for the settlement of all disputes between the two countries. On the 26th January 1934, a German-Polish declaration of nonaggression was made, signed on behalf of the German Government by the defendant von Neurath. On the 30th January 1934, and again on the 30th January 1937, Hitler made speeches in the Reichstag in which he expressed his view that Poland and Germany could work together in harmony and peace. On the 20th February 1938, Hitler made a third speech in the Reichstag in the course of which he said with regard to Poland:

> "And so the way to a friendly understanding has been successfully paved, an understanding which, beginning with Danzig, has today, in spite of the attempts of certain mischief makers, succeeded in finally taking the poison out of the relations between Germany and Poland and transforming them into a sincere, friendly cooperation. Relying on her friendships, Germany will not leave a stone unturned to save that ideal which provides the foundation for the task which is ahead of us—peace."

On the 26th September 1938, in the middle of the crisis over the Sudetenland, Hitler made the speech in Berlin which has already been quoted, and announced that he had informed the British Prime Minister that when the Czechoslovakian problem was solved there would be no more territorial problems for Germany in Europe. Nevertheless, on the 24th November of the same year, an OKW directive was issued to the German armed forces to make preparations for an attack upon Danzig; it stated:

> "The Fuehrer has ordered: (1) Preparations are also to be made to enable the Free State of Danzig to be occupied by German troops by surprise."

In spite of having ordered military preparations for the occupation of Danzig, Hitler, on the 30th January 1939, said in a speech in the Reichstag:

> "During the troubled months of the past year, the friendship between Germany and Poland has been one of the reassuring factors in the political life of Europe."

Five days previously, on the 25th January 1939, von Ribbentrop said in the course of a speech in Warsaw:

> "Thus Poland and Germany can look forward to the future with full confidence in the solid basis of their mutual relations."

28

Following the occupation of Bohemia and Moravia by Germany on the 15th March 1939, which was a flagrant breach of the Munich Agreement, Great Britain gave an assurance to Poland on the 31st March 1939, that in the event of any action which clearly threatened Polish independence, and which the Polish Government accordingly considered it vital to resist with their national forces, Great Britain would feel itself bound at once to lend Poland all the support in its power. The French Government took the same stand. It is interesting to note in this connection, that one of the arguments frequently presented by the defense in the present case is that the defendants were induced to think that their conduct was not in breach of international law by the acquiescence of other powers. The declarations of Great Britain and France showed, at least, that this view could be held no longer.

On the 3d April 1939, a revised OKW directive was issued to the armed forces, which after referring to the question of Danzig made reference to Fall Weiss (the military code name for the German invasion of Poland) and stated:

"The Fuehrer has added the following directions to Fall Weiss: (1) Preparations must be made in such a way that the operation can be carried out at any time from the 1st September 1939 onwards. (2) The High Command of the Armed Forces has been directed to draw up a precise timetable for Fall Weiss and to arrange by conferences the synchronized timings between the three branches of the Armed Forces."

On the 11th April 1939, a further directive was signed by Hitler and issued to the armed forces, and in one of the annexes to that document the words occur:

"Quarrels with Poland should be avoided. Should Poland, however, adopt a threatening attitude toward Germany, 'a final settlement' will be necessary, notwithstanding the pact with Poland. The aim is then to destroy Polish military strength, and to create in the east a situation which satisfies the requirements of defense. The Free State of Danzig will be incorporated into Germany at the outbreak of the conflict at the latest. Policy aims at limiting the war to Poland, and this is considered possible in view of the internal crisis in France, and British restraint as a result of this."

In spite of the contents of those two directives, Hitler made a speech in the Reichstag on the 28th April 1939, in which, after describing the Polish Government's alleged rejection of an offer he had made with regard to Danzig and the Polish Corridor, he stated:

"I have regretted greatly this incomprehensible attitude of the Polish Government, but that alone is not the decisive fact;

29

the worst is that now Poland like Czechoslovakia a year ago believes, under the pressure of a lying international campaign, that it must call up its troops, although Germany on her part has not called up a single man, and had not thought of proceeding in any way against Poland. . . . The intention to attack on the part of Germany which was merely invented by the international Press . . ."

It was 4 weeks after making this speech that Hitler, on the 23d May 1939, held the important military conference to which reference has already been made. Among the persons present were the defendants Goering, Raeder, and Keitel. The adjutant on duty that day was Lieutenant Colonel Schmundt, and he made a record of what happened, certifying it with his signature as a correct record.

The purpose of the meeting was to enable Hitler to inform the heads of the armed forces and their staffs of his views on the political situation and his future aims. After analyzing the political situation and reviewing the course of events since 1933, Hitler announced his decision to attack Poland. He admitted that the quarrel with Poland over Danzig was not the reason for this attack, but the necessity for Germany to enlarge her living space and secure her food supplies. He said:

"The solution of the problem demands courage. The principle by which one evades solving the problem by adapting oneself to circumstances is inadmissible. Circumstances must rather be adapted to needs. This is impossible without invasion of foreign states or attacks upon foreign property."

Later in his address he added:

"There is therefore no question of sparing Poland, and we are left with the decision to attack Poland at the first suitable opportunity. We cannot expect a repetition of the Czech affair. There will be war. Our task is to isolate Poland. The success of the isolation will be decisive. . . . The isolation of Poland is a matter of skillful politics."

Lieutenant Colonel Schmundt's record of the meeting reveals that Hitler fully realized the possibility of Great Britain and France coming to Poland's assistance. If, therefore, the isolation of Poland could not be achieved, Hitler was of the opinion that Germany should attack Great Britain and France first, or at any rate should concentrate primarily on the war in the West, in order to defeat Great Britain and France quickly, or at least to destroy their effectiveness. Nevertheless, Hitler stressed that war with England and France would be a life and death struggle, which might last a long time, and that preparations must be made accordingly.

30

During the weeks which followed this conference, other meetings were held and directives were issued in preparation for the war. The defendant von Ribbentrop was sent to Moscow to negotiate a non-aggression pact with the Soviet Union.

On the 22d August 1939 there took place the important meeting of that day, to which reference has already been made. The prosecution have put in evidence two unsigned captured documents which appear to be records made of this meeting by persons who were present. The first document is headed: "The Fuehrer's speech to the Commanders in Chief on the 22nd August 1939 . . ." The purpose of the speech was to announce the decision to make war on Poland at once, and Hitler began by saying:

"It was clear to me that a conflict with Poland had to come sooner or later. I had already made this decision in the spring, but I thought that I would first turn against the West in a few years, and only afterwards against the East . . . I wanted to establish an acceptable relationship with Poland in order to fight first against the West. But this plan, which was agreeable to me, could not be executed since essential points have changed. It became clear to me that Poland would attack us in case of a conflict with the West."

Hitler then went on to explain why he had decided that the most favorable moment had arrived for starting the war. "Now," said Hitler, "Poland is in the position in which I wanted her . . . I am only afraid that at the last moment some Schweinhund will make a proposal for mediation . . . A beginning has been made for the destruction of England's hegemony."

This document closely resembles one of the documents put in evidence on behalf of the defendant Raeder. This latter document consists of a summary of the same speech, compiled on the day it was made, by one Admiral Boehm, from notes he had taken during the meeting. In substance it says that the moment had arrived to settle the dispute with Poland by military invasion, that although a conflict between Germany and the West was unavoidable in the long run, the likelihood of Great Britain and France coming to Poland's assistance was not great, and that even if a war in the West should come about, the first aim should be the crushing of the Polish military strength. It also contains a statement by Hitler that an appropriate propaganda reason for invading Poland would be given, the truth or falsehood of which was unimportant, since "the Right lies in Victory."

The second unsigned document put in evidence by the prosecution is headed: "Second Speech by the Fuehrer on the 22d August 1939," and it is in the form of notes of the main points made by Hitler. Some of these are as follows:

31

"Everybody shall have to make a point of it that we were determined from the beginning to fight the Western Powers. Struggle for life or death . . . destruction of Poland in the foreground. The aim is elimination of living forces, not the arrival at a certain line. Even if war should break out in the West, the destruction of Poland shall be the primary objective. I shall give a propagandist cause for starting the war—never mind whether it be plausible or not. The victor shall not be asked later on whether we told the truth or not. In starting and making a war, not the Right is what matters, but Victory . . . The start will be ordered probably by Saturday morning." (That is to say, the 26th August.)

In spite of it being described as a second speech, there are sufficient points of similarity with the two previously mentioned documents to make it appear very probable that this is an account of the same speech, not as detailed as the other two, but in substance the same.

These three documents establish that the final decision as to the date of Poland's destruction, which had been agreed upon and planned earlier in the year, was reached by Hitler shortly before the 22d August 1939. They also show that although he hoped to be able to avoid having to fight Great Britain and France as well, he fully realized that there was a risk of this happening, but it was a risk which he was determined to take.

The events of the last days of August confirm this determination. On the 22d August 1939, the same day as the speech just referred to, the British Prime Minister wrote a letter to Hitler, in which he said:

"Having thus made our position perfectly clear, I wish to repeat to you my conviction that war between our two peoples would be the greatest calamity that could occur."

On the 23d August, Hitler replied:

"The question of the treatment of European problems on a peaceful basis is not a decision which rests with Germany, but primarily on those who since the crime committed by the Versailles Dictate have stubbornly and consistently opposed any peaceful revision. Only after a change of spirit on the part of the responsible Powers can there be any real change in the relationship between England and Germany."

There followed a number of appeals to Hitler to refrain from forcing the Polish issue to the point of war. These were from President Roosevelt on the 24th and 25th August; from His Holiness the Pope on the 24th and 31st August; and from M. Daladier, the Prime Minister of France, on the 26th August. All these appeals fell on deaf ears.

32

On the 25th August, Great Britain signed a pact of mutual assistance with Poland, which reinforced the understanding she had given to Poland earlier in the year. This coupled with the news of Mussolini's unwillingness to enter the war on Germany's side, made Hitler hesitate for a moment. The invasion of Poland, which was timed to start on the 26th August, was postponed until a further attempt had been made to persuade Great Britain not to intervene. Hitler offered to enter into a comprehensive agreement with Great Britain, once the Polish question had been settled. In reply to this, Great Britain made a countersuggestion for the settlement of the Polish dispute by negotiation. On the 29th August, Hitler informed the British Ambassador that the German Government, though skeptical as to the result, would be prepared to enter into direct negotiations with a Polish emissary, provided he arrived in Berlin with plenipotentiary powers by midnight for the following day, August 30. The Polish Government were informed of this, but with the example of Schuschnigg and Hacha before them, they decided not to send such an emissary. At midnight on the 30th August the defendant von Ribbentrop read to the British Ambassador at top speed a document containing the first precise formulation of the German demands against Poland. He refused, however, to give the Ambassador a copy of this, and stated that in any case it was too late now, since no Polish plenipotentiary had arrived.

In the opinion of the Tribunal, the manner in which these negotiations were conducted by Hitler and von Ribbentrop showed that they were not entered into in good faith or with any desire to maintain peace, but solely in the attempt to prevent Great Britain and France from honoring their obligations to Poland.

Parallel with these negotiations were the unsuccessful attempts made by Goering to effect the isolation of Poland by persuading Great Britain not to stand by her pledged word, through the services of one Birger Dahlerus, a Swede. Dahlerus, who was called as a witness by Goering, had a considerable knowledge of England and of things English, and in July 1939 was anxious to bring about a better understanding between England and Germany, in the hope of preventing a war between the two countries. He got into contact with Goering as well as with official circles in London, and during the latter part of August, Goering used him as an unofficial intermediary to try and deter the British Government from their opposition to Germany's intentions toward Poland. Dahlerus, of course, had no knowledge at the time of the decision which Hitler had secretly announced on the 22d August, nor of the German military directives for the attack on Poland which were already in existence. As he admitted in his evidence, it was not until the 26th September, after the conquest of Poland was virtually complete, that he first realized that Goering's aim all along had been to get Great Britain's consent to Germany's seizure of Poland.

33

After all attempts to persuade Germany to agree to a settlement of her dispute with Poland on a reasonable basis had failed, Hitler, on the 31st August, issued his final directive, in which he announced that the attack on Poland would start in the early morning of the 1st September, and gave instructions as to what action would be taken if Great Britain and France should enter the war in defense of Poland.

In the opinion of the Tribunal, the events of the days immediately preceding the 1st September 1939, demonstrate the determination of Hitler and his associates to carry out the declared intention of invading Poland at all costs, despite appeals from every quarter. With the ever increasing evidence before him that this intention would lead to war with Great Britain and France as well, Hitler was resolved not to depart from the course he had set for himself. The Tribunal is fully satisfied by the evidence that the war initiated by Germany against Poland on the 1st September 1939, was most plainly an aggressive war, which was to develop in due course into a war which embraced almost the whole world, and resulted in the commission of countless crimes, both against the laws and customs of war, and against humanity.

(G) The Invasion of Denmark and Norway

The aggressive war against Poland was but the beginning. The aggression of Nazi Germany quickly spread from country to country. In point of time the first two countries to suffer were Denmark and Norway.

On the 31st May 1939, a treaty of nonaggression was made between Germany and Denmark, and signed by the defendant von Ribbentrop. It was there solemnly stated that the parties to the treaty were "firmly resolved to maintain peace between Denmark and Germany under all circumstances." Nevertheless, Germany invaded Denmark on the 9th April 1940.

On the 2d September 1939, after the outbreak of war with Poland, Germany sent a solemn assurance to Norway in these terms:

"The German Reich Government is determined in view of the friendly relations which exist between Norway and Germany, under no circumstance to prejudice the inviolability and integrity of Norway, and to respect the territory of the Norwegian State. In making this declaration the Reich Government naturally expects, on its side, that Norway will observe an unimpeachable neutrality towards the Reich and will not tolerate any breaches of Norwegian neutrality by any third party which might occur. Should the attitude of the Royal Norwegian Government differ from this so that any such breach of neutrality by a third party occurs, the Reich Government would then obviously be compelled to safeguard the interests of the Reich in such a way as the resulting situation might dictate."

On the 9th April 1940, in pursuance of her plan of campaign, Norway was invaded by Germany.

The idea of attacking Norway originated, it appears, with the defendants Raeder and Rosenberg. On the 3d October 1939, Raeder prepared a memorandum on the subject of "gaining bases in Norway," and amongst the questions discussed was the question: "Can bases be gained by military force against Norway's will, if it is impossible to carry this out without fighting?" Despite this fact, 3 days later, further assurances were given to Norway by Germany, which stated:

"Germany has never had any conflicts of interest or even points of controversy with the Northern States and neither has she any today."

Three days later again, the defendant Doenitz prepared a memorandum on the same subject, namely, bases in Norway, and suggested the establishment of a base in Trondheim with an alternative of supplying fuel in Narvik. At the same time the defendant Raeder was in correspondence with Admiral Karls, who pointed out to him the importance of an occupation of the Norwegian coast by Germany. On the 10th October, Raeder reported to Hitler the disadvantages to Germany which an occupation by the British would have. In the months of October and November Raeder continued to work on the possible occupation of Norway, in conjunction with the "Rosenberg Organization." The "Rosenberg Organization" was the Foreign Affairs Bureau of the NSDAP, and Rosenberg as Reichsleiter was in charge of it. Early in December, Quisling, the notorious Norwegian traitor, visited Berlin and was seen by the defendants Rosenberg and Raeder. He put forward a plan for a *coup d'etat* in Norway. On the 12th December, the defendant Raeder and the naval staff, together with the defendants Keitel and Jodl, had a conference with Hitler, when Raeder reported on his interview with Quisling, and set out Quisling's views. On the 16th December, Hitler himself interviewed Quisling on all these matters. In the report of the activities of the Foreign Affairs Bureau of the NSDAP for the years 1933-43, under the heading of "Political preparations for the military occupation of Norway," it is stated that at the interview with Quisling, Hitler said that he would prefer a neutral attitude on the part of Norway as well as the whole of Scandinavia, as he did not desire to extend the theater of war, or to draw other nations into the conflict. If the enemy attempted to extend the war he would be compelled to guard himself against that undertaking. He promised Quisling financial support, and assigned to a special military staff the examination of the military questions involved.

35

On the 27th January 1940, a memorandum was prepared by the defendant Keitel regarding the plans for the invasion of Norway. On the 28th February 1940, the defendant Jodl entered in his diary:

"I proposed first to the Chief of OKW and then to the Fuehrer that 'Case Yellow' (that is the operation against the Netherlands) and Weser Exercise (that is the operation against Norway and Denmark) must be prepared in such a way that they will be independent of one another as regards both time and forces employed."

On the 1st March, Hitler issued a directive regarding the Weser Exercise which contained the words:

"The development of the situation in Scandinavia requires the making of all preparations for the occupation of Denmark and Norway by a part of the German Armed Forces. This operation should prevent British encroachment on Scandinavia and the Baltic; further, it should guarantee our ore base in Sweden and give our Navy and Air Force a wider start line against Britain . . . The crossing of the Danish border and the landings in Norway must take place simultaneously . . . It is most important that the Scandinavian States as well as the Western opponents should be taken by surprise by our measures."

On the 24th March the naval operation orders for the Weser Exercise were issued, and on the 30th March the defendant Doenitz as Commander in Chief of U-boats issued his operational order for the occupation of Denmark and Norway. On the 9th April 1940, the German forces invaded Norway and Denmark.

From this narrative it is clear that as early as October 1939 the question of invading Norway was under consideration. The defense that has been made here is that Germany was compelled to attack Norway to forestall an Allied invasion, and her action was therefore preventive.

It must be remembered that preventive action in foreign territory is justified only in case of "an instant and overwhelming necessity for self-defense, leaving no choice of means and no moment of deliberation." (The Caroline Case, Moores Digest of International Law, Vol. II, p. 412.) How widely the view was held in influential German circles that the Allies intended to occupy Norway cannot be determined with exactitude. Quisling asserted that the Allies would intervene in Norway with the tacit consent of the Norwegian Government. The German Legation at Oslo disagreed with this view, although the Naval Attaché at that Legation shared it.

The War Diary of the German Naval Operations Staff for January 13, 1940, stated that the Chief of the Naval Operations Staff thought that the most favorable solution would be the maintenance of the

36

neutrality of Norway, but he harbored the firm conviction that England intended to occupy Norway in the near future, relying on the tacit agreement of the Norwegian Government.

The directive of Hitler issued on March 1, 1940, for the attack on Denmark and Norway stated that the operation "should prevent British encroachment on Scandinavia and the Baltic."

It is, however, to be remembered that the defendant Raeder's memorandum of the 3d October 1939 makes no reference to forestalling the Allies, but is based upon "the aim of improving our strategical and operational position."

The memorandum itself is headed "Gaining of Bases in Norway." The same observation applies *mutatis mutandis* to the memorandum of the defendant Doenitz of October 9, 1939.

Furthermore, on the 13th March the defendant Jodl recorded in his diary:

> "Fuehrer does not give order yet for 'W' (Weser Exercise). He is still looking for an excuse." (Justification?)

On the 14th March 1940 he again wrote:

> "Fuehrer has not yet decided what reason to give for 'Weser Exercise'."

On the 21st March 1940 he recorded the misgivings of Task Force XXI about the long interval between taking up readiness positions and the close of the diplomatic negotiations, and added:

> "Fuehrer rejects any earlier negotiations, as otherwise calls for help go out to England and America. If resistance is put up, it must be ruthlessly broken."

On April 2d he records that all the preparations are completed; on April 4th the Naval Operational Order was issued; and on the 9th April the invasion was begun.

From all this it is clear that when the plans for an attack on Norway were being made they were not made for the purpose of forestalling an imminent Allied landing, but, at the most, that they might prevent an Allied occupation at some future date.

When the final orders for the German invasion of Norway were given, the diary of the Naval Operations Staff for March 23, 1940, records:

> "A mass encroachment by the English into Norwegian territorial waters . . . is not to be expected at the present time."

And Admiral Assmann's entry for March 26 says:

> "British landing in Norway not considered serious."

Documents which were subsequently captured by the Germans are relied on to show that the Allied plan to occupy harbors and airports in western Norway was a definite plan, although in all points considerably behind the German plans under which the invasion was actually carried out. These documents indicate that an altered plan had been finally agreed upon on March 20, 1940, that a convoy should leave England on April 5, and that mining in Norwegian waters would begin the same day; and that on April 5 the sailing time had been postponed until April 8. But these plans were not the cause of the German invasion of Norway. Norway was occupied by Germany to afford her bases from which a more effective attack on England and France might be made, pursuant to plans prepared long in advance of the Allied plans which are now relied on to support the argument of self-defense.

It was further argued that Germany alone could decide, in accordance with the reservations made by many of the Signatory Powers at the time of the conclusion of the Kellogg-Briand Pact, whether preventive action was a necessity, and that in making her decision her judgment was conclusive. But whether action taken under the claim of self-defense was in fact aggressive or defensive must ultimately be subject to investigation and adjudication if international law is ever to be enforced.

No suggestion is made by the defendants that there was any plan by any belligerent, other than Germany, to occupy Denmark. No excuse for that aggression has ever been offered.

As the German armies entered Norway and Denmark, German memoranda were handed to the Norwegian and Danish Governments which gave the assurance that the German troops did not come as enemies, that they did not intend to make use of the points occupied by German troops as bases for operations against England, as long as they were not forced to do so by measures taken by England and France, and that they had come to protect the North against the proposed occupation of Norwegian strong points by English-French forces.

The memoranda added that Germany had no intention of infringing upon the territorial integrity and political independence of the Kingdom of Norway then or in the future. Nevertheless, on the 3d of June 1940, a German naval memorandum discussed the use to be made of Norway and Denmark, and put forward one solution for consideration, that the territories of Denmark and Norway acquired during the course of the war should continue to be occupied and organized so that they could in the future be considered as German possessions.

In the light of all the available evidence it is impossible to accept the contention that the invasions of Denmark and Norway were defensive, and in the opinion of the Tribunal they were acts of aggressive war.

(H) The Invasion of Belgium, the Netherlands and Luxemburg

The plan to seize Belgium and the Netherlands was considered in August 1938, when the attack on Czechoslovakia was being formulated, and the possibility of war with France and England was contemplated. The advantage to Germany of being able to use these countries for their own purposes, particularly as air bases in the war against England and France, was emphasized. In May of 1939, when Hitler made his irrevocable decision to attack Poland, and foresaw the possibility at least of a war with England and France in consequence, he told his military commanders:

"Dutch and Belgian air bases must be occupied . . . Declarations of neutrality must be ignored."

On 22 August in the same year, he told his military commanders that England and France, in his opinion, would not "violate the neutrality of these countries." At the same time he assured Belgium and Holland and Luxemburg that he would respect their neutrality; and on the 6th October 1939, after the Polish campaign, he repeated this assurance. On the 7th October General von Brauchitsch directed Army Group B to prepare "for the immediate invasion of Dutch and Belgian territory, if the political situation so demands." In a series of orders, which were signed by the defendants Keitel and Jodl, the attack was fixed for the 10th November 1939, but it was postponed from time to time until May of 1940 on account of weather conditions and transport problems.

At the conference on the 23d November 1939, Hitler said:

"We have an Achilles heel: The Ruhr. The progress of the war depends on the possession of the Ruhr. If England and France push through Belgium and Holland into the Ruhr, we shall be in the greatest danger . . . Certainly England and France will assume the offensive against Germany when they are armed. England and France have means of pressure to bring Belgium and Holland to request English and French help. In Belgium and Holland the sympathies are all for France and England . . . If the French army marches into Belgium in order to attack us, it will be too late for us. We must anticipate them . . . We shall sow the English coast with mines which cannot be cleared. This mine warfare with the Luftwaffe demands a different starting point. England cannot live without its imports. We can feed ourselves. The permanent sowing of mines on the English coasts will bring England to her knees. However, this can only occur if we have occupied Belgium and Holland . . . My decision is unchangeable; I shall attack France and England at the most favorable and quickest moment. Breach of the neutrality of Belgium and Holland is meaningless. No one will question that

39

when we have won. We shall not bring about the breach of neutrality as idiotically as it was in 1914. If we do not break the neutrality, then England and France will. ˙ Without attack, the war is not to be ended victoriously."

On the 10th May 1940 the German forces invaded the Netherlands, Belgium, and Luxemburg. On the same day the German Ambassadors handed to the Netherlands and Belgian Governments a memorandum alleging that the British and French armies, with the consent of Belgium and Holland, were planning to march through those countries to attack the Ruhr, and justifying the invasion on these grounds. Germany, however, assured the Netherlands and Belgium that their integrity and their possessions would be respected. A similar memorandum was delivered to Luxemburg on the same date.

There is no evidence before the Tribunal to justify the contention that the Netherlands, Belgium, and Luxemburg were invaded by Germany because their occupation had been planned by England and France. British and French staffs had been cooperating in making certain plans for military operations in the Low Countries, but the purpose of this planning was to defend these countries in the event of a German attack.

The invasion of Belgium, Holland, and Luxemburg was entirely without justification.

It was carried out in pursuance of policies long considered and prepared, and was plainly an act of aggressive war. The resolve to invade was made without any other consideration than the advancement of the aggressive policies of Germany.

(I) The Aggression Against Yugoslavia and Greece

On the 12th August 1939, Hitler had a conversation with Ciano and the defendant von Ribbentrop at Obersalzberg. He said then:

"Generally speaking, the best thing to happen would be for the neutrals to be liquidated one after the other. This process could be carried out more easily if on every occasion one partner of the Axis covered the other while it was dealing with the uncertain neutral. Italy might well regard Yugoslavia as a neutral of this kind."

This observation was made only 2 months after Hitler had given assurances to Yugoslavia that he would regard her frontier as final and inviolable. On the occasion of the visit to Germany of the Prince Regent of Yugoslavia on 1 June 1939, Hitler had said in a public speech:

"The firmly established reliable relationship of Germany to Yugoslavia, now that owing to historical events we have become neighbors with common boundaries fixed for all time, will not only guarantee lasting peace between our two peoples and countries, but can also represent an element of calm to our nerve-racked continent. This peace is the goal of all who are disposed to perform really constructive work."

On the 6th October 1939, Germany repeated these assurances to Yugoslavia, after Hitler and von Ribbentrop had unsuccessfully tried to persuade Italy to enter the war on the side of Germany by attacking Yugoslavia. On the 28th October 1940, Italy invaded Greece, but the military operations met with no success. In November, Hitler wrote to Mussolini with regard to the invasion of Greece, and the extension of the war in Balkans, and pointed out that no military operations could take place in the Balkans before the following March, and therefore Yugoslavia must if at all possible be won over by other means, and in other ways. But on the 12th November 1940, Hitler issued a directive for the prosecution of the war, and it included the words:

"The Balkans: The Commander-in-Chief of the Army will make preparations for occupying the Greek mainland north of the Aegean Sea, in case of need entering through Bulgaria."

On the 13th December he issued a directive concerning the operation "Marita," the code name for the invasion of Greece, in which he stated:

"1. The result of the battles in Albania is not yet decisive. Because of a dangerous situation in Albania, it is doubly necessary that the British endeavor be foiled to create air bases under the protection of a Balkan front, which would be dangerous above all to Italy as to the Rumanian oil fields.

"2. My plan therefore is (a) to form a slowly increasing task force in Southern Rumania within the next month, (b) after the setting in of favorable weather, probably in March, to send a task force for the occupation of the Aegean north coast by way of Bulgaria and if necessary to occupy the entire Greek mainland."

On the 20th January 1941, at a meeting between Hitler and Mussolini, at which the defendants von Ribbentrop, Keitel, Jodl, and others were present, Hitler stated:

"The massing of troops in Rumania serves a threefold purpose:
(a) An operation against Greece;
(b) Protection of Bulgaria against Russia and Turkey;
(c) Safeguarding the guarantee to Rumania . . . It is desirable that this deployment be completed without interference from the enemy. Therefore, disclose the game as late as possible. The tendency will be to cross the Danube at the last possible moment, and to line up for attack at the earliest possible moment."

41

On the 19th February 1941, an OKW directive regarding the operation "Marita" stated:

> "On the 18th February the Fuehrer made the following decision regarding the carrying out of Operation Marita: The following dates are envisaged: Commencement of building bridge, 28th February; Crossing of the Danube, 2d March."

On the 3d March 1941, British troops landed in Greece to assist the Greeks to resist the Italians; and on the 18th March, at a meeting between Hitler and the defendant Raeder, at which the defendants Keitel and Jodl were also present, the defendant Raeder asked for confirmation that the "whole of Greece will have to be occupied, even in the event of a peaceful settlement," to which Hitler replied, "The complete occupation is a prerequisite of any settlement."

On the 25th March, on the occasion of the adherence of Yugoslavia to the Tripartite Pact at a meeting in Vienna, the defendant von Ribbentrop, on behalf of the German Government, confirmed the determination of Germany to respect the sovereignty and territorial integrity of Yugoslavia at all times. On the 26th March the Yugoslav Ministers, who had adhered to the Tripartite Pact, were removed from office by a *coup d'etat* in Belgrade on their return from Vienna, and the new Government repudiated the pact. Thereupon on 27 March, at a conference in Berlin with the High Command at which the defendants Goering, Keitel, and Jodl were present, and the defendant von Ribbentrop part of the time, Hitler stated that Yugoslavia was an uncertain factor in regard to the contemplated attack on Greece, and even more so with regard to the attack upon Russia which was to be conducted later on. Hitler announced that he was determined, without waiting for possible loyalty declarations of the new Government, to make all preparations in order to destroy Yugoslavia militarily and as a national unit. He stated that he would act with "unmerciful harshness."

On the 6th April, German forces invaded Greece and Yugoslavia without warning, and Belgrade was bombed by the Luftwaffe. So swift was this particular invasion that there had not been time to establish any "incidents" as a usual preliminary, or to find and publish any adequate "political" explanations. As the attack was starting on the 6th April, Hitler proclaimed to the German people that this attack was necessary because the British forces in Greece (who were helping the Greeks to defend themselves against the Italians) represented a British attempt to extend the war to the Balkans.

It is clear from this narrative that aggressive war against Greece and Yugoslavia had long been in contemplation, certainly as early as August of 1939. The fact that Great Britain had come to the assistance of the Greeks, and might thereafter be in a position to inflict great damage upon German interests was made the occasion for the occupation of both countries.

(J) THE AGGRESSIVE WAR AGAINST THE UNION OF SOVIET SOCIALIST REPUBLICS

On the 23d August 1939, Germany signed the nonaggression pact with the Union of Soviet Socialist Republics.

The evidence has shown unmistakably that the Soviet Union on their part conformed to the terms of this pact; indeed the German Government itself had been assured of this by the highest German sources. Thus, the German Ambassador in Moscow informed his Government that the Soviet Union would go to war only if attacked by Germany, and this statement is recorded in the German War Diary under the date of June 6; 1941.

Nevertheless, as early as the late summer of 1940, Germany began to make preparations for an attack on the USSR, in spite of the nonaggression pact. This operation was secretly planned under the code name "Case Barbarossa," and the former Field Marshal Paulus testified that on the 3d September 1940, when he joined the German General Staff, he continued developing "Case Barbarossa," which was finally completed at the beginning of November 1940; and that even then, the German General Staff had no information that the Soviet Union was preparing for war.

On the 18th of December 1940, Hitler issued directive No. 21, initialled by Keitel and Jodl, which called for the completion of all preparations connected with the realization of "Case Barbarossa" by the 15th May 1941. This directive stated:

> "The German armed forces must be prepared to crush Soviet Russia in a quick campaign before the end of the war against England . . . Great caution has to be exercised that the intention of an attack will not be recognized."

Before the directive of the 18th December had been made, the defendant Goering had informed General Thomas, chief of the Office of War Economy of the OKW, of the plan, and General Thomas made surveys of the economic possibilities of the USSR including its raw materials, its power and transport system, and its capacity to produce arms.

In accordance with these surveys, an economic staff for the Eastern territories with many military-economic units (inspectorates, commandos, groups) was created under the supervision of the defendant Goering. In conjunction with the military command, these units were to achieve the most complete and efficient economic exploitation of the occupied territories in the interest of Germany.

43

The framework of the future political and economic organization of the occupied territories was designed by the defendant Rosenberg over a period of 3 months, after conferences with and assistance by the defendants Keitel, Jodl, Raeder, Funk, Goering, von Ribbentrop, and Frick or their representatives. It was made the subject of a most detailed report immediately after the invasion.

These plans outlined the destruction of the Soviet Union as an independent State, and its partition, the creation of so-called Reich Commissariats, and the conversion of Esthonia, Latvia, Byelorussia, and other territories into German colonies.

At the same time Germany drew Hungary, Rumania, and Finland into the war against the USSR. In December 1940, Hungary agreed to participate on the promise of Germany that she should have certain territories at the expense of Yugoslavia.

In May 1941 a final agreement was concluded with Antonescu, the Prime Minister of Rumania, regarding the attack on the USSR, in which Germany promised to Rumania, Bessarabia, northern Bukovina and the right to occupy Soviet territory up to the Dnieper.

On the 22d June 1941, without any declaration of war, Germany invaded Soviet territory in accordance with the plans so long made.

The evidence which has been given before this Tribunal proves that Germany had the design carefully thought out, to crush the USSR as a political and military power, so that Germany might expand to the east according to her own desire. In "Mein Kampf," Hitler had written:

> "If new territory were to be acquired in Europe, it must have been mainly at Russia's cost, and once again the new German Empire should have set out on its march along the same road as was formerly trodden by the Teutonic Knights, this time to acquire soil for the German plough by means of the German sword and thus provide the nation with its daily bread."

But there was a more immediate purpose, and in one of the memoranda of the OKW, that immediate purpose was stated to be to feed the German armies from Soviet territory in the third year of the war, even if "as a result many millions of people will be starved to death if we take out of the country the things necessary for us."

The final aims of the attack on the Soviet Union were formulated at a conference with Hitler on July 16, 1941, in which the defendants Goering, Keitel, Rosenberg, and Bormann participated:

> "There can be no talk of the creation of a military power west of the Urals, even if we should have to fight 100 years to achieve this . . . All the Baltic regions must become part of the Reich. The Crimea and adjoining regions (North of the Crimea) must likewise be incorporated into the Reich. The region of the

44

Volga as well as the Baku district must likewise be incorporated into the Reich.   The Finns want Eastern Karelia.   However, in view of the large deposits of nickel, the Kola peninsula must be ceded to Germany."

It was contended for the defendants that the attack upon the USSR was justified because the Soviet Union was contemplating an attack upon Germany, and making preparations to that end.   It is impossible to believe that this view was ever honestly entertained.

The plans for the economic exploitation of the USSR, for the removal of masses of the population, for the murder of commissars and political leaders, were all part of the carefully prepared scheme launched on the 22d June without warning of any kind, and without the shadow of legal excuse.   It was plain aggression.

(K) War Against the United States

Four days after the attack launched by the Japanese on the United States fleet in Pearl Harbor on December 7, 1941, Germany declared war on the United States.

The Tripartite Pact between Germany, Italy, and Japan, had been signed on the 27th September 1940, and from that date until the attack upon the USSR the defendant von Ribbentrop, with other defendants, was endeavoring to induce Japan to attack British possessions in the Far East.   This, it was thought, would hasten England's defeat, and keep the United States out of the war.

The possibility of a direct attack on the United States was considered and discussed as a matter for the future.   Major von Falkenstein, the Luftwaffe liaison officer with the Operations Staff of the OKW, summarizing military problems which needed discussion in Berlin in October of 1940, spoke of the possibility "of the prosecution of the war against America at a later date".   It is clear, too, that the German policy of keeping America out of the war, if possible, did not prevent Germany promising support to Japan even against the United States.   On the 4th April 1941, Hitler told Matsuoka, the Japanese Foreign Minister, in the presence of the defendant von Ribbentrop, that Germany would "strike without delay" if a Japanese attack on Singapore should lead to war between Japan and the United States. The next day von Ribbentrop himself urged Matsuoka to bring Japan into the war.

On the 28th November 1941, 10 days before the attack on Pearl Harbor, von Ribbentrop encouraged Japan, through her Ambassador in Berlin, to attack Great Britain and the United States, and stated that should Japan become engaged in a war with the United States, Germany would join the war immediately.   A few days later, Japanese representatives told Germany and Italy that Japan was preparing to attack the United States, and asked for their support. Germany and Italy agreed to do this, although in the Tripartite Pact, Italy and Germany had undertaken to assist Japan only if she were attacked. When the assault on Pearl Harbor did take place, the defendant von Ribbentrop is reported to have been "overjoyed," and later, at a ceremony in Berlin, when a German medal was awarded to Oshima, the Japanese Ambassador, Hitler indicated his approval of the tactics which the Japanese had adopted of negotiating with the United States as long as possible, and then striking hard without any declaration of war.

Although it is true that Hitler and his colleagues originally did not consider that a war with the United States would be beneficial to their interest, it is apparent that in the course of 1941 that view was revised, and Japan was given every encouragement to adopt a policy which would almost certainly bring the United States into the war. And when Japan attacked the United States fleet in Pearl Harbor and thus made aggressive war against the United States, the Nazi Government caused Germany to enter that war at once on the side of Japan by declaring war themselves on the United States.

IV. VIOLATIONS OF INTERNATIONAL TREATIES

The Charter defines as a crime the planning or waging of war that is a war of aggression or a war in violation of international treaties. The Tribunal has decided that certain of the defendants planned and waged aggressive wars against 10 nations, and were therefore guilty of this series of crimes. This makes it unnecessary to discuss the subject in further detail, or even to consider at any length the extent to which these aggressive wars were also "wars in violation of international treaties, agreements, or assurances." These treaties are set out in appendix C of the indictment. Those of principal importance are the following:

(A) HAGUE CONVENTIONS

In the 1899 Convention the signatory powers agreed: "before an appeal to arms . . . to have recourse, as far as circumstances allow, to the good offices or mediation of one or more friendly powers." A similar clause was inserted in the Convention for Pacific Settlement of International Disputes of 1907. In the accompanying Convention Relative to Opening of Hostilities, article I contains this far more specific language:

> "The Contracting Powers recognize that hostilities between them must not commence without a previous and explicit warning, in the form of either a declaration of war, giving reasons, or an ultimatum with a conditional declaration of war."

Germany was a party to these conventions.

46

(B) Versailles Treaty

Breaches of certain provisions of the Versailles Treaty are also relied on by the prosecution—not to fortify the left bank of the Rhine (art. 42–44); to "respect strictly the independence of Austria" (art. 80); renunciation of any rights in Memel (art. 99) and the Free City of Danzig (art. 100); the recognition of the independence of the Czecho-Slovak State; and the Military, Naval, and Air Clauses against German rearmament found in part V. There is no doubt that action was taken by the German Government contrary to all these provisions, the details of which are set out in appendix C. With regard to the Treaty of Versailles, the matters relied on are:

1. The violation of articles 42 to 44 in respect of the demilitarized zone of the Rhineland.

2. The annexation of Austria on the 13th March 1938, in violation of article 80.

3. The incorporation of the district of Memel on the 22d March 1939, in violation of article 99.

4. The incorporation of the Free City of Danzig on the 1st September 1939, in violation of article 100.

5. The incorporation of the provinces of Bohemia and Moravia on the 16th March 1939, in violation of article 81.

6. The repudiation of the military naval and air clauses of the treaty, in or about March of 1935.

On the 21st May 1935, Germany announced that, whilst renouncing the disarmament clauses of the treaty, she would still respect the territorial limitations, and would comply with the Locarno Pact. (With regard to the first five breaches alleged, therefore, the Tribunal finds the allegation proved.)

(C) Treaties of Mutual Guarantee, Arbitration, and Non-Aggression

It is unnecessary to discuss in any detail the various treaties entered into by Germany with other powers. Treaties of Mutual Guarantee were signed by Germany at Locarno in 1925, with Belgium, France, Great Britain, and Italy, assuring the maintenance of the territorial status quo. Arbitration treaties were also executed by Germany at Locarno with Czechoslovakia, Belgium, and Poland.

Article I of the latter treaty is typical, providing:

> "All disputes of every kind between Germany and Poland . . . which it may not be possible to settle amicably by the normal methods of diplomacy, shall be submitted for decision to an arbitral tribunal . . ."

Conventions of arbitration and conciliation were entered into between Germany, the Netherlands, and Denmark in 1926; and be-

47

tween Germany and Luxemburg in 1929. Nonaggression treaties were executed by Germany with Denmark and Russia in 1939.

(D) Kellogg-Briand Pact

The Pact of Paris was signed on the 27th August 1928 by Germany, the United States, Belgium, France, Great Britain, Italy, Japan, Poland, and other countries; and subsequently by other powers. The Tribunal has made full reference to the nature of this Pact and its legal effect in another part of this judgment. It is therefore not necessary to discuss the matter further here, save to state that in the opinion of the Tribunal this pact was violated by Germany in all the cases of aggressive war charged in the indictment. It is to be noted that on the 26th January 1934, Germany signed a Declaration for the Maintenance of Permanent Peace with Poland, which was explicitly based on the Pact of Paris, and in which the use of force was outlawed for a period of 10 years.

The Tribunal does not find it necessary to consider any of the other treaties referred to in the appendix, or the repeated agreements and assurances of her peaceful intentions entered into by Germany.

(E) The Law of the Charter

The jurisdiction of the Tribunal is defined in the Agreement and Charter, and the crimes coming within the jurisdiction of the Tribunal, for which there shall be individual responsibility, are set out in Article 6. The law of the Charter is decisive, and binding upon the Tribunal.

The making of the Charter was the exercise of the sovereign legislative power by the countries to which the German Reich unconditionally surrendered; and the undoubted right of these countries to legislate for the occupied territories has been recognized by the civilized world. The Charter is not an arbitrary exercise of power on the part of the victorious nations, but in the view of the Tribunal, as will be shown, it is the expression of international law existing at the time of its creation; and to that extent is itself a contribution to international law.

The Signatory Powers created this Tribunal, defined the law it was to administer, and made regulations for the proper conduct of the trial. In doing so, they have done together what any one of them might have done singly; for it is not to be doubted that any nation has the right thus to set up special courts to administer law. With regard to the constitution of the court, all that the defendants are entitled to ask is to receive a fair trial on the facts and law.

The Charter makes the planning or waging of a war of aggression or a war in violation of international treaties a crime; and it is therefore not strictly necessary to consider whether and to what extent

48

aggressive war was a crime before the execution of the London Agreement. But in view of the great importance of the questions of law involved, the Tribunal has heard full argument from the prosecution and the defense, and will express its view on the matter.

It was urged on behalf of the defendants that a fundamental principle of all law—international and domestic—is that there can be no punishment of crime without a preexisting law. *"Nullum crimen sine lege, nulla poena sine lege."* It was submitted that *ex post facto* punishment is abhorrent to the law of all civilized nations, that no sovereign power had made aggressive war a crime at the time the alleged criminal acts were committed, that no statute had defined aggressive war, that no penalty had been fixed for its commission, and no court had been created to try and punish offenders.

In the first place, it is to be observed that the maxim *nullum crimen sine lege* is not a limitation of sovereignty, but is in general a principle of justice. To assert that it is unjust to punish those who in defiance of treaties and assurances have attacked neighboring states without warning is obviously untrue, for in such circumstances the attacker must know that he is doing wrong, and so far from it being unjust to punish him, it would be unjust if his wrong were allowed to go unpunished. Occupying the positions they did in the government of Germany, the defendants, or at least some of them must have known of the treaties signed by Germany, outlawing recourse to war for the settlement of international disputes; they must have known that they were acting in defiance of all international law when in complete deliberation they carried out their designs of invasion and aggression. On this view of the case alone, it would appear that the maxim has no application to the present facts.

This view is strongly reinforced by a consideration of the state of international law in 1939, so far as aggressive war is concerned. The General Treaty for the Renunciation of War of August 27, 1928, more generally known as the Pact of Paris or the Kellogg-Briand Pact, was binding on 63 nations, including Germany, Italy, and Japan at the outbreak of war in 1939. In the preamble, the signatories declared that they were—

"Deeply sensible of their solemn duty to promote the welfare of mankind; persuaded that the time has come when a frank renunciation of war as an instrument of national policy should be made to the end that the peaceful and friendly relations now existing between their peoples should be perpetuated . . . all changes in their relations with one another should be sought only by pacific means . . . thus uniting civilized nations of the world in a common renunciation of war as an instrument of their national policy . . ."

The first two articles are as follows:

"ARTICLE I. The High Contracting Parties solemnly declare in the names of their respective peoples that they condemn recourse to war for the solution of international controversies and renounce it as an instrument of national policy in their relations to one another."

"ARTICLE II. The High Contracting Parties agree that the settlement or solution of all disputes or conflicts of whatever nature or of whatever origin they may be, which may arise among them, shall never be sought except by pacific means."

The question is, what was the legal effect of this pact? The nations who signed the pact or adhered to it unconditionally condemned recourse to war for the future as an instrument of policy, and expressly renounced it. After the signing of the pact, any nation resorting to war as an instrument of national policy breaks the pact. In the opinion of the Tribunal, the solemn renunciation of war as an instrument of national policy necessarily involves the proposition that such a war is illegal in international law; and that those who plan and wage such a war, with its inevitable and terrible consequences, are committing a crime in so doing. War for the solution of international controversies undertaken as an instrument of national policy certainly includes a war of aggression, and such a war is therefore outlawed by the pact. As Mr. Henry L. Stimson, then Secretary of State of the United States, said in 1932:

"War between nations was renounced by the signatories of the Kellogg-Briand Treaty. This means that it has become throughout practically the entire world . . . an illegal thing. Hereafter, when engaged in armed conflict, either one or both of them must be termed violators of this general treaty law. . . We denounce them as law breakers."

But it is argued that the pact does not expressly enact that such wars are crimes, or set up courts to try those who make such wars. To that extent the same is true with regard to the laws of war contained in the Hague Convention. The Hague Convention of 1907 prohibited resort to certain methods of waging war. These included the inhumane treatment of prisoners, the employment of poisoned weapons, the improper use of flags of truce, and similar matters. Many of these prohibitions had been enforced long before the date of the Convention; but since 1907 they have certainly been crimes, punishable as offenses against the laws of war; yet the Hague Convention nowhere designates such practices as criminal, nor is any sentence prescribed, nor any mention made of a court to try and punish offenders. For many years past, however, military tribunals have tried and punished individuals guilty of violating the rules of land war-

50

fare laid down by this Convention. In the opinion of the Tribunal, those who wage aggressive war are doing that which is equally illegal, and of much greater moment than a breach of one of the rules of the Hague Convention. In interpreting the words of the pact, it must be remembered that international law is not the product of an international legislature, and that such international agreements as the Pact of Paris have to deal with general principles of law, and not with administrative matters of procedure. The law of war is to be found not only in treaties, but in the customs and practices of states which gradually obtained universal recognition, and from the general principles of justice applied by jurists and practiced by military courts. This law is not static, but by continual adaptation follows the needs of a changing world. Indeed, in many cases treaties do no more than express and define for more accurate reference the principles of law already existing.

The view which the Tribunal takes of the true interpretation of the pact is supported by the international history which preceded it. In the year 1923 the draft of a Treaty of Mutual Assistance was sponsored by the League of Nations. In Article I the treaty declared "that aggressive war is an international crime," and that the parties would "undertake that no one of them will be guilty of its commission." The draft treaty was submitted to twenty-nine states, about half of whom were in favor of accepting the text. The principal objection appeared to be in the difficulty of defining the acts which would constitute "aggression," rather than any doubt as to the criminality of aggressive war. The preamble to the League of Nations 1924 Protocol for the Pacific Settlement of International Disputes, ("Geneva Protocol"), after "recognising the solidarity of the members of the international community," declared that "a war of aggression constitutes a violation of this solidarity and is an international crime." It went on to declare that the contracting parties were "desirous of facilitating the complete application of the system provided in the Covenant of the League of Nations for the pacific settlement of disputes between the states and of ensuring the repression of international crimes." The Protocol was recommended to the members of the League of Nations by a unanimous resolution in the Assembly of the 48 members of the League. These members included Italy and Japan, but Germany was not then a member of the League.

Although the Protocol was never ratified, it was signed by the leading statesmen of the world, representing the vast majority of the civilized States and peoples, and may be regarded as strong evidence of the intention to brand aggressive war as an international crime.

At the meeting of the Assembly of the League of Nations on the 24th September 1927, all the delegations then present (including the Ger-

51

man, the Italian, and the Japanese), unanimously adopted a declaration concerning wars of aggression. The preamble to the declaration stated:

"The Assembly: Recognizing the solidarity which unites the community of nations;

Being inspired by a firm desire for the maintenance of general peace;

Being convinced that a war of aggression can never serve as a means of settling international disputes, and is in consequence an international crime   *   *   *."

The unanimous resolution of the 18th February 1928, of 21 American republics at the sixth (Havana) Pan-American Conference, declared that "war of aggression constitutes an international crime against the human species."

All these expressions of opinion, and others that could be cited, so solemnly made, reinforce the construction which the Tribunal placed upon the Pact of Paris, that resort to a war of aggression is not merely illegal, but is criminal. The prohibition of aggressive war demanded by the conscience of the world, finds its expression in the series of Pacts and Treaties to which the Tribunal has just referred.

It is also important to remember that Article 227 of the Treaty of Versailles provided for the constitution of a special tribunal, composed of representatives of five of the Allied and Associated Powers which had been belligerents in the First World War opposed to Germany, to try the former German Emperor "for a supreme offence against international morality and the sanctity of treaties." The purpose of this trial was expressed to be "to vindicate the solemn obligations of international undertakings, and the validity of international morality." In Article 228 of the Treaty, the German Government expressly recognized the right of the Allied Powers "to bring before military tribunals persons accused of having committed acts in violation of the laws and customs of war."

It was submitted that international law is concerned with the actions of sovereign States, and provides no punishment for individuals; and further, that where the act in question is an act of State, those who carry it out are not personally responsible, but are protected by the doctrine of the sovereignty of the State. In the opinion of the Tribunal, both these submissions must be rejected. That international law imposes duties and liabilities upon individuals as well as upon states has long been recognized. In the recent case of **Ex parte Quirin** (1942 317 U. S. 1), before the Supreme Court of the United States, persons were charged during the war with landing in the United States for purposes of spying and sabotage. The late Chief Justice Stone, speaking for the court, said:

"From the very beginning of its history this Court has applied the law of war as including that part of the law of nations which prescribes for the conduct of war, the status, rights, and duties of enemy nations as well as enemy individuals."

He went on to give a list of cases tried by the courts, where individual offenders were charged with offences against the laws of nations, and particularly the laws of war. Many other authorities could be cited, but enough has been said to show that individuals can be punished for violations of international law. Crimes against international law are committed by men, not by abstract entities, and only by punishing individuals who commit such crimes can the provisions of international law be enforced.

The provisions of Article 228 of the Treaty of Versailles already referred to illustrate and enforce this view of individual responsibility.

The principle of international law, which under certain circumstances, protects the representatives of a State, cannot be applied to acts which are condemned as criminal by international law. The authors of these acts cannot shelter themselves behind their official position in order to be freed from punishment in appropriate proceedings. Article 7 of the Charter expressly declares:

"The official position of defendants, whether as heads of State, or responsible officials in government departments, shall not be considered as freeing them from responsibility, or mitigating punishment."

On the other hand the very essence of the Charter is that individuals have international duties which transcend the national obligations of obedience imposed by the individual State. He who violates the laws of war cannot obtain immunity while acting in pursuance of the authority of the State if the State in authorizing action moves outside its competence under international law.

It was also submitted on behalf of most of these defendants that in doing what they did they were acting under the orders of Hitler, and therefore cannot be held responsible for the acts committed by them in carrying out these orders. The Charter specifically provides in Article 8:

"The fact that the defendant acted pursuant to order of his Government or of a superior shall not free him from responsibility, but may be considered in mitigation of punishment."

The provisions of this Article are in conformity with the law of all nations. That a soldier was ordered to kill or torture in violation of the international law of war has never been recognized as a defense to such acts of brutality, though, as the Charter here provides, the order may be urged in mitigation of the punishment. The true test, which

53

is found in varying degrees in the criminal law of most nations, is not the existence of the order, but whether moral choice was in fact possible.

V. THE LAW AS TO THE COMMON PLAN OR CONSPIRACY

In the previous recital of the facts relating to aggressive war, it is clear that planning and preparation had been carried out in the most systematic way at every stage of the history.

Planning and preparation are essential to the making of war. In the opinion of the Tribunal aggressive war is a crime under international law. The Charter defines this offense as planning, preparation, initiation, or waging of a war of aggression "or participation in a common plan or conspiracy for the accomplishment . . . of the foregoing." The indictment follows this distinction. Count one charges the common plan or conspiracy. Count two charges the planning and waging of war. The same evidence has been introduced to support both counts. We shall therefore discuss both counts together, as they are in substance the same. The defendants have been charged under both counts, and their guilt under each count must be determined.

The "common plan or conspiracy" charged in the indictment covers 25 years, from the formation of the Nazi Party in 1919 to the end of the war in 1945. The party is spoken of as "the instrument of cohesion among the defendants" for carrying out the purposes of the conspiracy—the overthrowing of the Treaty of Versailles, acquiring territory lost by Germany in the last war and "lebensraum" in Europe, by the use, if necessary, of armed force, of aggressive war. The "seizure of power" by the Nazis, the use of terror, the destruction of trade unions, the attack on Christian teaching and on churches, the persecution of the Jews, the regimentation of youth—all these are said to be steps deliberately taken to carry out the common plan. It found expression, so it is alleged, in secret rearmament, the withdrawal by Germany from the Disarmament Conference and the League of Nations, universal military service, and seizure of the Rhineland. Finally, according to the indictment, aggressive action was planned and carried out against Austria and Czechoslovakia in 1936–38, followed by the planning and waging of war against Poland; and, successively, against ten other countries.

The prosecution says, in effect, that any significant participation in the affairs of the Nazi Party or government is evidence of a participation in a conspiracy that is in itself criminal. Conspiracy is not defined in the Charter. But in the opinion of the Tribunal the conspiracy must be clearly outlined in its criminal purpose. It must not be too far removed from the time of decision and of action. The planning, to be criminal, must not rest merely on the declarations of a party pro-

II. JURISDICTIONAL BASIS OF THE TWELVE SUBSEQUENT WAR CRIMES TRIALS AT NUERNBERG

A. Introduction

Twelve war crimes trials were held in Nuernberg, subsequent to the trial before the International Military Tribunal. These trials were held under the authority of Allied Control Council Law No. 10 (subsec. B), which stated in its preamble that its purpose was "to give effect to the terms of the Moscow Declaration of 30 October 1943 and the London Agreement of 8 August 1945, and the Charter issued pursuant thereto, and in order to establish a uniform legal basis in Germany for the prosecution of war criminals and other similar offenders, other than those dealt with by the International Military Tribunal." Control Council Law No. 10 further provided that "Each occupying authority, within its Zone of occupation" should have the right to arrest and bring to trial persons suspected of having committed a crime, and that "The tribunal by which persons charged with offenses hereunder shall be tried and the rules of procedure thereof shall be determined or designated by each Zone Commander for his respective Zone."

In the United States Zone of Occupation, the Military Governor made provisions for the further trials of war criminals by Ordinance No. 7 of Military Government for Germany, United States Zone (subsec. C), and it was this ordinance which determined the basic procedure of the 12 Nuernberg trials under Control Council Law No. 10. Ordinance No. 7 was issued on 18 October 1946. Several of its articles were amended on 17 February 1947 by Ordinance No. 11 (subsec. D).

B. Allied Control Council Law No. 10, 20 December 1945

CONTROL COUNCIL LAW No. 10

PUNISHMENT OF PERSONS GUILTY OF WAR CRIMES, CRIMES AGAINST PEACE AND AGAINST HUMANITY

In order to give effect to the terms of the Moscow Declaration of 30 October 1943 and the London Agreement of 8 August 1945,[1] and the Charter issued pursuant thereto[2] and in order to establish a uniform legal basis in Germany for the prosecution of war criminals and other similar offenders, other than those dealt

---

[1] Reproduced in section I B.
[2] Reproduced in section I C.

with by the International Military Tribunal, the Control Council enacts as follows:

Article I

The Moscow Declaration of 30 October 1943 "Concerning Responsibility of Hitlerites for Committed Atrocities" and the London Agreement of 8 August 1945 "Concerning Prosecution and Punishment of Major War Criminals of the European Axis" are made integral parts of this Law. Adherence to the provisions of the London Agreement by any of the United Nations, as provided for in Article V of that Agreement, shall not entitle such Nation to participate or interfere in the operation of this Law within the Control Council area of authority in Germany.

Article II

1. Each of the following acts is recognized as a crime:

(a) *Crimes against Peace.* Initiation of invasions of other countries and wars of aggression in violation of international laws and treaties, including but not limited to planning, preparation, initiation or waging a war of aggression, or a war of violation of international treaties, agreements or assurances, or participation in a common plan or conspiracy for the accomplishment of any of the foregoing.

(b) *War Crimes.* Atrocities or offences against persons or property, constituting violations of the laws or customs of war, including but not limited to, murder, ill treatment or deportation to slave labour or for any other purpose, of civilian population from occupied territory, murder or ill treatment of prisoners of war or persons on the seas, killing of hostages, plunder of public or private property, wanton destruction of cities, towns or villages, or devastation not justified by military necessity.

(c) *Crimes against Humanity.* Atrocities and offences, including but not limited to murder, extermination, enslavement, deportation, imprisonment, torture, rape, or other inhumane acts committed against any civilian population, or persecutions on political, racial or religious grounds whether or not in violation of the domestic laws of the country where perpetrated.

(d) Membership in categories of a criminal group or organization declared criminal by the International Military Tribunal.

2. Any person without regard to nationality or the capacity in which he acted, is deemed to have committed a crime as defined in paragraph 1 of this Article, if he was (a) a principal or (b) was an accessory to the commission of any such crime or ordered or abetted the same or (c) took a consenting part therein or (d) was connected with plans or enterprises involving its commission or (e) was a member of any organization or group connected with

24

the commission of any such crime or (f) with reference to paragraph 1 (a), if he held a high political, civil or military (including General Staff) position in Germany or in one of its Allies, cobelligerents or satellites or held high position in the financial, industrial or economic life of any such country.

3. Any person found guilty of any of the Crimes above mentioned may upon conviction be punished as shall be determined by the tribunal to be just. Such punishment may consist of one or more of the following:

(a) Death.

(b) Imprisonment for life or a term of years, with or without hard labour.

(c) Fine, and imprisonment with or without hard labour, in lieu thereof.

(d) Forfeiture of property.

(e) Restitution of property wrongfully acquired.

(f) Deprivation of some or all civil rights.

Any property declared to be forfeited or the restitution of which is ordered by the Tribunal shall be delivered to the Control Council for Germany, which shall decide on its disposal.

4. (a) The official position of any person, whether as Head of State or as a responsible official in a Government Department, does not free him from responsibility for a crime or entitle him to mitigation of punishment.

(b) The fact that any person acted pursuant to the order of his Government or of a superior does not free him from responsibility for a crime, but may be considered in mitigation.

5. In any trial or prosecution for a crime herein referred to, the accused shall not be entitled to the benefits of any statute of limitation in respect of the period from 30 January 1933 to 1 July 1945, nor shall any immunity, pardon or amnesty granted under the Nazi regime be admitted as a bar to trial or punishment.

Article III

1. Each occupying authority, within its Zone of occupation,

(a) shall have the right to cause persons within such Zones suspected of having committed a crime, including those charged with crime by one of the United Nations, to be arrested and shall take under control the property, real and personal, owned or controlled by the said persons, pending decisions as to its eventual disposition.

(b) shall report to the Legal Directorate the names of all suspected criminals, the reasons for and the places of their detention, if they are detained, and the names and location of witnesses.

(c) shall take appropriate measures to see that witnesses and evidence will be available when required.

25

(*d*) shall have the right to cause all persons so arrested and charged, and not delivered to another authority as herein provided, or released, to be brought to trial before an appropriate tribunal. Such tribunal may, in the case of crimes committed by persons of German citizenship or nationality against other persons of German citizenship or nationality, or stateless persons, be a German Court, if authorized by the occupying authorities.

2. The tribunal by which persons charged with offenses hereunder shall be tried and the rules and procedure thereof shall be determined or designated by each Zone Commander for his respective Zone. Nothing herein is intended to, or shall impair or limit the jurisdiction or power of any court or tribunal now or hereafter established in any Zone by the Commander thereof, or of the International Military Tribunal established by the London Agreement of 8 August 1945.

3. Persons wanted for trial by an International Military Tribunal will not be tried without the consent of the Committee of Chief Prosecutors. Each Zone Commander will deliver such persons who are within his Zone to that committee upon request and will make witnesses and evidence available to it.

4. Persons known to be wanted for trial in another Zone or outside Germany will not be tried prior to decision under Article IV unless the fact of their apprehension has been reported in accordance with Section 1 (*b*) of this Article, three months have elapsed thereafter, and no request for delivery of the type contemplated by Article IV has been received by the Zone Commander concerned.

5. The execution of death sentences may be deferred by not to exceed one month after the sentence has become final when the Zone Commander concerned has reason to believe that the testimony of those under sentence would be of value in the investigation and trial of crimes within or without his Zone.

6. Each Zone Commander will cause such effect to be given to the judgments of courts of competent jurisdiction, with respect to the property taken under his control pursuant hereto, as he may deem proper in the interest of justice.

Article IV
1. When any person in a Zone in Germany is alleged to have committed a crime, as defined in Article II, in a country other than Germany or in another Zone, the government of that nation or the Commander of the latter Zone, as the case may be, may request the Commander of the Zone in which the person is located for his arrest and delivery for trial to the country or Zone in which the crime was committed. Such request for delivery shall be granted

by the Commander receiving it unless he believes such person is wanted for trial or as a witness by an International Military Tribunal, or in Germany, or in a nation other than the one making the request, or the Commander is not satisfied that delivery should be made, in any of which cases he shall have the right to forward the said request to the Legal Directorate of the Allied Control Authority. A similar procedure shall apply to witnesses, material exhibits and other forms of evidence.

2. The Legal Directorate shall consider all requests referred to it, and shall determine the same in accordance with the following principles, its determination to be communicated to the Zone Commander.

(a) A person wanted for trial or as a witness by an International Military Tribunal shall not be delivered for trial or required to give evidence outside Germany, as the case may be, except upon approval of the Committee of Chief Prosecutors acting under the London Agreement of 8 August 1945.

(b) A person wanted for trial by several authorities (other than an International Military Tribunal) shall be disposed of in accordance with the following priorities:

(1) If wanted for trial in the Zone in which he is, he should not be delivered unless arrangements are made for his return after trial elsewhere;

(2) If wanted for trial in a Zone other than that in which he is, he should be delivered to that Zone in preference to delivery outside Germany unless arrangements are made for his return to that Zone after trial elsewhere;

(3) If wanted for trial outside Germany by two or more of the United Nations, of one of which he is a citizen, that one should have priority;

(4) If wanted for trial outside Germany by several countries, not all of which are United Nations, United Nations should have priority;

(5) If wanted for trial outside Germany by two or more of the United Nations, then, subject to Article IV 2 (b) (3) above, that which has the most serious charges against him, which are moreover supported by evidence, should have priority.

Article V

The delivery, under Article IV of this Law, of persons for trial shall be made on demands of the Governments or Zone Commanders in such a manner that the delivery of criminals to one jurisdiction will not become the means of defeating or unnecessarily delaying the carrying out of justice in another place. If within six months the delivered person has not been convicted by

27

the Court of the zone or country to which he has been delivered, then such person shall be returned upon demand of the Commander of the Zone where the person was located prior to delivery. Done at Berlin, 20 December 1945.

JOSEPH T. MCNARNEY
General

B. L. MONTGOMERY
Field Marshal

L. KOELTZ
Général de Corps d'Armée
for P. KOENIG
Général d'Armée

G. ZHUKOV
Marshal of the Soviet Union

"THE MINISTRIES CASE"

MILITARY TRIBUNAL IV

Case 11

THE UNITED STATES OF AMERICA

—against—

ERNST VON WEIZSAECKER, GUSTAV ADOLF STEENGRACHT VON MOYLAND, WILHELM KEPPLER, ERNST WILHELM BOHLE, ERNST WOERMANN, KARL RITTER, OTTO VON ERDMANNSDORFF, EDMUND VEESENMAYER, HANS HEINRICH LAMMERS, WILHELM STUCKART, RICHARD WALTHER DARRÉ, OTTO MEISSNER, OTTO DIETRICH, GOTTLOB BERGER, WALTER SCHELLENBERG, LUTZ SCHWERIN VON KROSIGK, EMIL PUHL, KARL RASCHE, PAUL KOERNER, PAUL PLEIGER, and HANS KEHRL, *Defendants*

B. JUDGMENT[1]

INTRODUCTION

On 18 November 1947,[2] an indictment against the above-named defendants was filed with the Secretary General of the United States Military Tribunals at Nuernberg. Generally stated, said indictment, consisting of eight counts, charged the defendants with having committed crimes against peace, war crimes, crimes against humanity, and with having participated in a common plan and conspiracy to commit crimes against peace, all as defined in Control Council Law No. 10, duly enacted by the Allied Control Council on 20 December 1945.

Several, but not all, of the defendants are charged under each of the counts of the indictment. The applicable provisions of Control Council Law No. 10 will hereinafter be referred to and set forth as they relate to each count of the indictment when such counts are reached for discussion and decision.

The indictment was served upon all of the defendants in the German language, more than 30 days before arraignment of the defendants thereunder. On 19 December 1947 the case was assigned to this Tribunal for trial by the Supervisory Committee of Presiding Judges of the United States Military Tribunals in Germany, in conformity with Article V of Military Government Ordinance No. 7, as amended, this Tribunal theretofore having been duly established and constituted, pursuant to said Ordinance No. 7, which ordinance was promulgated by the United States Military Governor of the United States Occupation Zone of Germany on 18 October 1946. The arraignment of the defendants took place on 20 December 1947, at which time all defendants pleaded "Not Guilty" to the charges in the indictment.

Throughout the trial of this case, all of the defendants were represented by German counsel of their own choice. One defendant requested that he also be allowed to retain American counsel to represent him. The request was granted.

The presentation of evidence in the case was commenced on 7 January 1948. Final arguments before the Tribunal were concluded on 18 November 1948. The transcript record of the case consists of 28,085 pages. In addition thereto, the prosecution and

---

[1] The judgment was read in open Court on 11–13 April 1949 and is recorded in the mimeographed transcript, pages 28086–28803. Just before the reading of the judgment, Presiding Judge Christianson said "The Tribunal will file the original of such judgment with the Secretary General, and the original copy as filed shall constitute the official judgment record of this case." (Tr. p. 28086.) The judgment as reproduced herein is taken from the record copy filed with the Secretary General.

[2] The indictment was signed by the United States Chief of Counsel for War Crimes on 15 November 1947, but it was not filed until 18 November 1947.

314

the defense together introduced in evidence 9,067 documentary exhibits, totaling over 39,000 pages. Generally accepted technical rules of evidence were not adhered to during the trial, and any evidence that, in the opinion of the Tribunal, had probative value was admitted when offered by either the prosecution or the defense. This practice was in accord with that followed by the International Military Tribunal, and as subsequently thereto provided in Article VII of the hereinbefore referred to Military Government Ordinance No. 7. In the interest of expedition the Tribunal, following the practice adopted by the International Military Tribunal, appointed court commissioners to assist in taking both oral and documentary evidence, but many of the principal witnesses and all of the defendants who testified were heard before the Tribunal itself.

In order that any relevant documentary defense evidence of which the defendants had knowledge or which they believed existed might be made available to the defense, the Tribunal in response to various defense motions uniformly ordered that the persons or agencies having possession or custody of such evidence make same available to the defense. This was even true with respect to documentary evidence in possession of the prosecution. Moreover, at the request of a number of the defendants, the Tribunal appointed a German research analyst, of the defendants' choice, for the purpose of making a search of files of the former Reich government, located in the Document Center in Berlin, under Allied control. Such research analyst spent many months in Berlin in this search for defense evidence. The same research expert was further authorized by this Tribunal to visit London for the purpose of research in behalf of the defendants and was, in fact, so engaged for a number of weeks with the cooperation of British authorities. Other representatives were likewise authorized to make search of former Reich government files in Berlin.

In arriving at the conclusions hereinafter reached with respect to the charges against the defendants as contained in the indictment, the Tribunal has undeviatingly adhered to the proposition that a defendant is presumed innocent until proved guilty beyond a reasonable doubt.

During the course of the trial, a motion was made in behalf of all defendants charged in count four of the indictment that said count be stricken. The motion was granted and a formal order in the matter made and filed by the Tribunal.*

During the trial from time to time motions were also made in behalf of individual defendants to dismiss counts of the indict-

---

* The defense motion, the argumentation on the motion, and the Tribunal's order are reproduced in section VIII, Volume XIII, this series.

315

ment relating to them on the ground that the Tribunal was without jurisdiction to try the defendants on such counts and on the further ground that the evidence adduced by the prosecution was insufficient to sustain the charges. Such motions were denied without prejudice, except in three instances where charges in certain counts of the indictment were dismissed with respect to certain defendants because of a failure of proof. Specific attention to the charges thus dismissed and the defendants affected thereby will be given when the charges involved in such dismissals are reached in the ensuing discussion of the individual counts of the indictment. Like attention will be called to instances wherein the prosecution, during the trial, withdrew certain charges against certain of the defendants.

In the final arguments and briefs of the defendants, the contention that this Tribunal is without jurisdiction in this matter was renewed. In this connection, attention is directed to the fact that a number of United States Military Tribunals of precisely the same type and origin as this one have heretofore had their jurisdiction questioned on similar grounds in the course of their trial of cases involving offenses defined in Control Counsel Law No. 10. (Flick, et al., Case 5; List, et al., Case 7; and Ohlendorf, et al., Case 9.*) The statements made in the judgments of such cases in the course of disposing of the attacks made on the jurisdiction of such Tribunals, we deem to be conclusive answers to the challenge here made to this Tribunal's jurisdiction, and we accordingly reject the contention of the defendants that these proceedings should be dismissed because of the Tribunal's lack of jurisdiction.

The record, including briefs of counsel all of which the Court has considered and examined, amounts to approximately 79,000 pages. The evidence of this case presents a factual story of practically every phase of activity of the Nazi Party and of the Third Reich, whether political, economic, industrial, financial, or military.

Hundreds of captured official documents were offered, received, and considered which were unavailable at the trial before the International Military Tribunal (sometimes herein referred to as the IMT), and which were not offered in any of the previous cases before United States Military Tribunals, and the record here presents, more fully and completely than in any other case, the story of the rise of the Nazi regime, its programs, and its acts.

The Tribunal has had the aid of and here desires to express its appreciation and gratitude for the skill, learning, and meticu-

---

* Volumes VI, XI, and IV, respectively, this series.

316

lous care with which counsel for the prosecution and defense have presented their case.

Notwithstanding the provisions in Article X of Ordinance No. 7, that the determination of the International Military Tribunal that invasions, aggressive acts, aggressive wars, crimes, atrocities, and inhumane acts were planned or occurred, shall be binding on the Tribunals established thereunder and cannot be questioned except insofar as the participation therein and knowledge thereof of any particular person may be concerned, we have permitted the defense to offer evidence upon all these matters. In so doing we have not considered this article to be a limitation on the right of the Tribunal to consider any evidence which may lead to a just determination of the facts. If in this we have erred, it is an error which we do not regret, as we are firmly convinced that courts of justice must always remain open to the ascertainment of the truth and that every defendant must be accorded an opportunity to present the facts.

Before considering the questions of law and fact which are here involved, we deem it proper to state the nature of these trials, the basis on which they rest, and the standards by which these defendants should be judged.

These Tribunals were not organized and do not sit for the purpose of wreaking vengeance upon the conquered. Was such the purpose, the power existed to use the firing squad, the scaffold, or the prison camp without taking the time and putting forth labor which have been so freely expended on them, and the Allied Powers would have copied the methods which were too often used during the Third Reich. We may not, in justice, apply to these defendants because they are Germans standards of duty and responsibility which are not equally applicable to the officials of the Allied Powers and to those of all nations. Nor should Germans be convicted for acts or conducts which, if committed by Americans, British, French, or Russians would not subject them to legal trial and conviction. Both care and caution must be exercised not to prescribe or apply a yardstick to these defendants which cannot and should not be applied to others, irrespective of whether they are nationals of the victor or of the vanquished.

The defendants here are charged with violation of international law, and our task is: first, to ascertain and determine what it is; second, whether the defendants have infringed these principles.

International law is not statutory. It is in part defined by and described in treaties and covenants among the powers of the world. Nevertheless, much of it consists of practices, principles, and standards which have become developed over the years and have found general acceptance among the civilized powers of the world. It has grown and expanded as the concepts of international right and wrong have grown. It has never been suggested that it has been codified, or that its boundaries have been specifically defined, or that specific sanctions have been prescribed for violations of it. The various Hague and Geneva Conventions, the Constitution and the Charter of the League of Nations, and the Kellogg-Briand treaties have given definitive shape to limited fields of international law. It can be said that insofar as certain acts are prohibited or permitted by these treaties or covenants, a codification exists and specific rules of conduct prescribed. It does not follow however that they are exclusive, and assuredly it cannot be said that they cover or pretend to cover the entire field of international law.

In determining whether the action of a nation is in accordance with or violates international law, resort may be had not only to those treaties and covenants, but to treatises on the subject and to the principles which lie beneath and back of these treaties, covenants, and learned treatises; and we need not hesitate, after having determined what they are, to apply them to new or different situations. It is by this very means that all legal codes, civil or criminal, have developed.

Aggressive wars and invasions.—The question, therefore, is whether or not the London Charter and Control Council Law No. 10 define new offenses or whether they are but definitive statements of preexisting international law. That monarchs and states, at least those who considered themselves civilized, have for centuries recognized that aggressive wars and invasions violated the law of nations is evident from the fact that invariably he who started his troops on the march or his fleets over the seas to wage war has endeavored to explain and justify the act by asserting that there was no desire or intent to infringe upon the lawful rights of the attacked nation or to engage in cold-blooded conquest, but on the contrary that the hostile acts became necessary because of the enemy's disregard of its obligations; that it had violated treaties; that it held provinces or cities which in fact belonged to the attacker; or that it had mistreated or discriminated against his peaceful citizens.

Often these justifications and excuses were offered with cynical disregard of the truth. Nevertheless, it was felt necessary that an excuse and justification be offered for the attack to the end the attacker might not be regarded by other nations as acting in wanton disregard of international duty and responsibility. From Caesar to Hitler the same practice has been followed. It was used by Napoleon, was adopted by Frederick the Great, by Philip II of Spain, by Edward I of England, by Louis XIV of

318

France, and by the powers who seized lands which they desired to colonize and make their own. Every and all of the attackers followed the same time-worn practice. The white, the blue, the yellow, the black, and the red books had only one purpose, namely, to justify that which was otherwise unjustifiable.

But if aggressive invasions and wars were lawful and did not constitute a breach of international law and duty, why take the trouble to explain and justify? Why inform neutral nations that the war was inevitable and excusable and based on high notions of morality, if aggressive war was not essentially wrong and a breach of international law? The answer to this is obvious. The initiation of wars and invasions with their attendant horror and suffering has for centuries been universally recognized by all civilized nations as wrong, to be resorted to only as a last resort to remedy wrongs already or imminently to be inflicted. We hold that aggressive wars and invasions have, since time immemorial, been a violation of international law, even though specific sanctions were not provided.

The Kellogg-Briand Pact not only recognized that aggressive wars and invasions were in violation of international law, but proceeded to take the next step, namely, to condemn recourse to war (otherwise justifiable for the solution of international controversies), to renounce it as an instrumentality of national policy, and to provide for the settlement of all disputes or conflicts by pacific means. Thus war as a means of enforcing lawful claims and demands became unlawful. The right of self-defense, of course, was naturally preserved, but only because if resistance was not immediately offered, a nation would be overrun and conquered before it could obtain the judgment of any international authority that it was justified in resisting attack.

The preamble of the treaty [General Pact for the Renunciation of War] provides that the nations declare their conviction—

"* * * that any signatory power which shall hereafter seek to promote its national interests by resort to war should be denied the benefits furnished by this treaty."

Quincy Wright, Professor of International Law, University of Chicago, in January 1933 (American Journal of International Law, vol. 21, No. 1, 23 January 1933), reviewed the Pact and the conclusions put upon, and the implications arising from, its provisions by the leading statesmen of that time. He quotes Secretary Stimson as follows:

"Under the former concept of international law, when a conflict occurred it was usually deemed the concern only of the parties to the conflict * * *. But now, under the covenant and

319

the Kellogg-Briand Pact, the conflict becomes of legal concern to everybody connected with the treaty. All steps taken to enforce the treaty must be adjudged by this new situation. As was said by M. Briand, quoting the words of President Coolidge: 'An act of war in any part of the world is an act that injures the interests of my country.'

"The world has learned that great lesson and the execution of the Kellogg-Briand Treaty codified it."

Professor Wright continues—

"Furthermore, the suggestion that the obligation is not legal because it is unprovided with sanctions has carried no more weight. Many treaties have no specific sanctions but insofar as they create obligations under international law, those obligations are covered by the sanctions of all international law * * *.

"In his exposition of the treaty, Secretary Kellogg pointed out 'there can be no question, as a matter of law, that the violation of a multilateral antiwar treaty through resort to war by one party thereto would automatically release the other parties from their obligations to the treaty-breaking states. Any express recognition of this principle of law is wholly unnecessary * * *.'

"These changes in international law consequent upon the existence of war, arise from the following propositions:

"1. A Party to the Pact responsible for initiating a state of war (a primary belligerent) will have violated the rights of all the parties to the Pact and will have lost all title to its benefits from non-participating states as well as from its enemies.

"2. A Party to the Pact involved in a state of war but not responsible for initiating it (a secondary belligerent) will not have violated the Pact and consequently will continue entitled to its benefits not only from nonparticipating states but also from its enemies.

"3. The other Parties to the Pact, nonparticipating in the war or 'partial,' while free to keep out of the war, will have suffered a legal injury through the outbreak of war, and though bound to extend the full benefits of the traditional international law of neutrality as well as the benefits of the Pact to the secondary belligerent will be free to deny these benefits to the primary belligerent."

It is to be noted that these views were expressed long before the seizure of power by Hitler and the Nazi Party, and years before the occurrence of the acts of aggression here charged, and are contemporaneous conclusions regarding the intent, meaning, and scope of the Treaty.

320

Is there personal responsibility for those who plan, prepare, and initiate aggressive wars and invasions? The defendants have ably and earnestly urged that heads of states and officials thereof cannot be held personally responsible for initiating or waging aggressive wars and invasions because no penalty had been previously prescribed for such acts. History, however, reveals that this view is fallacious. Frederick the Great was summoned by the Imperial Council to appear at Regensburg and answer, under threat of banishment, for his alleged breach of the public peace in invading Saxony.

When Napoleon, in alleged violation of his international agreement, sailed from Elba to regain by force the Imperial Crown of France, the nations of Europe, including many German princes in solemn conclave, denounced him, outlawing him as an enemy and disturber of the peace, mustered their armies, and on the battlefield of Waterloo, enforced their decree, and applied the sentence by banishing him to St. Helena. By these actions they recognized and declared that personal punishment could be properly inflicted upon a head of state who violated an international agreement and resorted to aggressive war.

But even if history furnished no examples, we would have no hesitation in holding that those who prepare, plan, or initiate aggressive invasions, and wage aggressive wars; and those who knowingly participate therein are subject to trial, and if convicted, to punishment.

By the Kellogg-Briand Treaty, Germany as well as practically every other civilized country of the world, renounced war as an instrumentality of governmental policy. The treaty was entered into for the benefit of all. It recognized the fact that once war breaks out, no one can foresee how far or to what extent the flames will spread, and that in this rapidly shrinking world it affects the interest of all.

No one would question the right of any signatory to use its armed forces to halt the violator in his tracks and to rescue the country attacked. Nor would there be any question but that when this was successfully accomplished sanctions could be applied against the guilty nation. Why then can they not be applied to the individuals by whose decisions, cooperation, and implementation the unlawful war or invasion was initiated and waged? Must the punishment always fall on those who were not personally responsible? May the humble citizen who knew nothing of the reasons for his country's action, who may have been utterly deceived by its propaganda, be subject to death or wounds in battle, held as a prisoner of war, see his home destroyed by artillery or from the air, be compelled to see his wife and family suffer

321

privations and hardships; may the owners and workers in industry see it destroyed, their merchant fleets sunk, the mariners drowned or interned; may indemnities result which must be derived from the taxes paid by the ignorant and the innocent; may all this occur and those who were actually responsible escape?

The only rationale which would sustain the concept that the responsible shall escape while the innocent public suffers, is a result of the old theory that "the King can do no wrong," and that "war is the sport of Kings."

We may point out further that the [Hague and] Geneva Conventions relating to rules of land warfare and the treatment of prisoners of war provide no punishment for the individuals who violate those rules, but it cannot be questioned that he who murders a prisoner of war is liable to punishment.

To permit such immunity is to shroud international law in a mist of unreality. We reject it and hold that those who plan, prepare, initiate, and wage aggressive wars and invasions, and those who knowingly, consciously, and responsibly participate therein violate international law and may be tried, convicted, and punished for their acts.

The "Tu Quoque" Doctrine.—The defendants have offered testimony and supported it by official documents which tend to establish that the Union of Soviet Socialist Republics entered into a treaty with Germany in August 1939, which contains secret clauses whereby not only did Russia consent to Hitler's invasion of Poland, but at least tacitly agreed to send its own armed forces against that nation, and by it could demand and obtain its share of the loot, and was given a free hand to swallow the little Baltic states with whom it had then existing nonaggression treaties. The defense asserts that Russia, being itself an aggressor and an accomplice to Hitler's aggression, was a party and an accomplice to at least one of the aggressions charged in this indictment, namely, that against Poland, and therefore was legally inhibited from signing the London Charter and enacting Control Council Law No. 10, and consequently both the Charter and Law are invalid, and no prosecution can be maintained under them.

The justifications, if any, which the Soviet Union may claim to have had for its actions in this respect were not represented to this Tribunal. But if we assume, *arguendo*, that Russia's action was wholly untenable and its guilt as deep as that of the Third Reich, nevertheless, this cannot in law avail the defendants or lessen the guilt of those of the Third Reich who were themselves responsible. Neither the London Charter nor Control Council Law No. 10 did more than declare existing international law regarding aggressive wars and invasions. The Charter and

322

Control Council Law No. 10 merely defined what offenses against international law should be the subject of judicial inquiry, formed the International Military Tribunal, and authorized the signatory powers to set up additional tribunals to try those charged with committing crimes against peace, war crimes, and crimes against humanity.

But even if it were true that the London Charter and Control Council Law No. 10 are legislative acts, making that a crime which before was not so recognized, would the defense argument be valid? It has never been suggested that a law duly passed becomes ineffective when it transpires that one of the legislators whose vote enacted it was himself guilty of the same practice or that he himself intended, in the future, to violate the law.

COUNT ONE—CRIMES AGAINST PEACE

The defendants von Weizsaecker, Keppler, Bohle, Woermann, Ritter, von Erdmannsdorff, Veesenmayer, Lammers, Stuckart, Darré, Meissner, Dietrich, Berger, Schellenberg, Schwerin von Krosigk, Koerner, and Pleiger are charged with having participated in the initiation of invasions of other countries and wars of aggression, including but not limited to planning, preparation, initiation, and waging of wars of aggression in violation of international treaties, agreements, and assurances. The invasions and wars referred to and the dates of their initiation are alleged to have been as follows:

```
Austria _____12 March  1938
Czechoslovakia_____1 October 1938 and 15 March 1939
Poland _____1 September 1939
United Kingdom and France_____3 September 1939
Denmark and Norway_____9 April 1940
Belgium, Netherlands, and Luxembourg_____10 May 1940
Yugoslavia and Greece_____6 April 1941
Union of Soviet Socialist Republics_____22 June 1941
United States of America_____11 December 1941
```

The prosecution dismissed this count as to the defendants Bohle, von Erdmannsdorff, and Meissner.

Notwithstanding the fact that the International Military Tribunal and several of these Tribunals have decided that the Third Reich was guilty of aggressive wars and invasions, we have reexamined this question because of the claim made by the defense that newly discovered evidence reveals that Germany was not the aggressor. It should be made clear, however, that this defense is not submitted by all of the defendants. For example, the defendant von Weizsaecker freely admits that these acts were aggressions.

323

The argument is based on the alleged injustices and harsh terms of the Versailles Treaty, which it is claimed was imposed upon Germany by force; that agreements made under duress are not binding, and in attempting to rid itself of the bonds thus thrust upon it, Germany was compelled to use force and in so doing cannot be judged an aggressor. Unless the defense has sufficient legal merit necessitating our so doing, a review of the treaty and the reasons which underlie it and its terms, with a view to determining the accuracy of these claims, would expand our opinion beyond permissible limits. In our opinion, however, there is no substance to the defense, irrespective of the question whether the treaty was just or whether it was imposed by duress.

We deem it unnecessary to determine either the truth of these claims or whether one upon whom the victor by force of arms has imposed a treaty on unjust or unduly harsh terms may therefore reject the treaty and, by force of arms, attempt to regain that which it believes has been wrongfully wrested from it.

If, *arguendo*, both propositions were conceded, nevertheless, both are irrelevant to the question confronting us here. In any event the time must arrive when a given status, irrespective of the means whereby it came into being, must be considered as fixed, at least so far as a resort to an aggressive means of correction is concerned.

When Hitler solemnly informed the world that so far as territorial questions were concerned Germany had no claims, and by means of solemn treaty assured Austria, France, Czechoslovakia, and Poland that he had no territorial demands to be made upon them, and when he entered into treaties of peace and non-aggression with them, the status of repose and fixation was reached. These assurances were given and these treaties entered into when there could be no claim of existing compulsion. Thereafter aggressive acts against the territories of these nations became breaches of international law, prohibited by the provisions of the Kellogg-Briand Treaty to which Germany had become a voluntary signatory.

No German could thereafter look upon war or invasion to recover part or all of the territories of which Germany had been deprived by the Treaty of Versailles as other than aggressive. To excuse aggressive acts after these treaties and assurances took place is merely to assert that no treaty and no assurance by Germany is binding and that the pledged word of Germany is valueless. It is therefore particularly unfortunate both for the present and future of the German people that such a defense should be raised as it tends to create doubt when, if at all, the

324

nations of the world can place reliance upon German international obligations.

Czechoslovakia.—On 16 October 1929, Germany entered into a treaty with Czechoslovakia, Article I of part 1 of which provides that all disputes of any kind between Germany and Czechoslovakia, which it may not be possible to settle amicably by normal means of diplomacy, should be submitted for decision either to an arbitral tribunal or to a permanent court of international justice, and it was agreed that the disputes referred to include those mentioned in Article XIII of the Covenant of the League of Nations.

On 11 and 12 March 1938 the Hitler government reassured Czechoslovakia that the developments in Austria would in no way have any detrimental influence upon the relations of the German Reich and that state, emphasizing the continued earnest endeavor on the part of Germany to improve those mutual relations. The Czechs were so assured by Goering who gave his "word of honor" and by von Neurath, then Foreign Minister, who officially assured the Czech Minister Mastny, on behalf of Hitler, that Germany still considered herself bound by the German-Czech Arbitration Convention concluded at Locarno in October 1925. Von Mackensen of the Foreign Office gave further assurances that the clarification of the Austrian situation would tend to improve German-Czechoslovakian relations.

Austria.—On 21 May 1935, Germany assured Austria that it neither intended nor wished to intervene in the domestic affairs of that state, or annex, or attach that country to her. On 11 July 1936 Hitler entered into an agreement with Austria containing among other things the provision that the German Government recognized the full sovereignty of the Federal State of Austria and in the sense of the pronouncement of the German Leader and Chancellor of 21 May 1935.

By the Treaty of Versailles, Article 40, Germany acknowledged and agreed to respect strictly the independence of Austria within the boundaries which might be fixed in the treaty between the states and the principal Allied and Associated Powers, and further agreed that this independence should be inalienable except by the consent of the Council of the League of Nations.

Poland.—On 16 October 1925 Germany, at Locarno, entered into a treaty with Poland which recited that the contracting parties were equally resolved to maintain peace between them by assuring the peaceful settlement of differences which might arise between the two countries, and declared that respect for the rights established by treaty or resulting from the law of nations was obligatory for international tribunals, that the rights of a state

325

could not be modified save with its consent, and that all disputes of every kind between Germany and Poland, which it was not possible to settle amicably by normal methods of diplomacy, should be submitted for decision either to an arbitral tribunal or to an international court of justice.

On 26 January 1934 Germany and Poland signed a nonaggression pact which provided, among other things, that under no circumstances would either party proceed to use force for the purpose of settling disputes.

On 7 March 1936 Hitler announced: "We have no territorial demands to make in Europe." On 20 February 1938 Hitler in a speech said (2357–PS) :[1]

"* * * in our relations with the state with which we had had perhaps the greatest differences not only has there been a *detente*, but in the course of years there has been a constant improvement in relations * * *. The Polish state respects the national conditions in this state and both the city of Danzig and Germany respect Polish rights. And so the way to an understanding has been successfully paved, an understanding which, beginning with Danzig, has today in spite of the attempts of many mischief-makers finally succeeded in taking the poison out of the relations of Germany and Poland and transforming them into a sincere and friendly cooperation."

On 26 September 1938, Hitler said (TC–73 (42)) :[2]

"In Poland there ruled not a democracy, but a man, and with him I succeeded in precisely 12 months in coming to an agreement which, for 10 years, to begin with, entirely removed the danger of conflict. We are all convinced that this agreement will bring lasting pacification."

On 24 November 1938 Keitel issued orders based on Hitler's instructions of 21 October that preparations be made to enable German troops to occupy the Free City of Danzig by surprise.

Denmark and Norway.—On 31 May 1939 Germany and Denmark entered into a nonaggression pact in which they agreed that (TC–24, Pros. Ex. 202)—

"* * * in no case * * * [shall either country] resort to war or any other use of force, one against the other."

On 28 August 1939 the defendant von Weizsaecker assured the Danish Minister of Germany's intention to abide by the terms of this pact.

---

[1] This document was introduced in evidence in the IMT trial as Exhibit GB–30, and the German text is reproduced in part in Trial of the Major War Criminals, op. cit., volume XXX, pages 285 and following.

[2] This document is reproduced in part in Nazi Conspiracy and Aggression (U.S. Government Printing Office, Washington, 1946), volume VIII, page 482.

326

On 2 September 1939 Germany assured Norway that in view of the friendly relations existing between them, it would under no circumstances prejudice the inviolability or neutrality of Norway, and on 6 October 1939 Germany again assured Norway that it had never had any conflicts of interest or even points of controversy with the northern states, "and neither has she any today," and that Sweden and Norway had both been offered nonaggression pacts and refused them solely because they did not feel themselves threatened in any way.

Belgium.—On 13 January 1937 Hitler stated that Germany had "and here I repeat, solemnly" given assurances time and again that, for instance, between Germany and France there cannot be any humanly conceivable points of controversy; that the German Government had given the assurance to Belgium and Holland that it was prepared to recognize and guarantee the inviolability of those territories. This was reiterated on 26 August 1939 and was against renewed on 6 October of that year. At that very time, by Hitler's order, the chiefs of the German Army were engaged in planning and preparing the invasions of these countries.

Yugoslavia.—On 28 April 1938 the German Government, through the defendant von Weizsaecker, stated that having become reunited with Austria, it would consider the frontiers of Italy, Yugoslavia, Estonia, Lichtenstein, and Hungary as inviolable, and that the Yugoslavian Government had been informed by authoritative German circles that Germany policy had no aims beyond Austria, and that the Yugoslavian frontier would, in no case, be assaulted. When in September 1939 Heeren, Minister to Yugoslavia, reported that there was increased anxiety there over Germany's military intentions and requested that some kind of announcement be made to alleviate local fears, the defendant von Weizsaecker replied that in view of Hitler's recent speech dcelaring that Germany's boundaries to the west and south were final, it would not appear necessary to say more unless new occasions for reissuing reassuring communiques to Yugoslavia should arise.

On 6 October 1939 Hitler gave Yugoslavia the following assurance (*TC–43, Pros. Ex. 262*):

> "After the completion of the Anschluss I informed Yugoslavia that from now on the boundaries with this country would also be an inviolable one, and that we only desire to live in friendship and peace with her."

What reliance could be placed on German pledges is revealed by the minutes of the Hitler-Ciano meeting of 12 August 1939 where Hitler stated (*1871–PS, Pros. Ex. 260*):

327

"Generally speaking, it would be best to liquidate the pseudo-neutrals, one after another. This is fairly easily done if the Axis partner protects the rear of the other who is just finishing off one of the uncertain neutrals and vice versa. Italy might consider Yugoslavia such an uncertain neutral."

Russia.—On 23 August 1939 Germany entered into a non-aggression treaty with Russia, providing for arbitral commissions in case of any dispute, and on the same day entered into a secret protocol with the Soviet Union that in the event of a territorial and political rearrangement in the areas belonging to Latvia, Estonia, and Lithuania, the northern boundaries of Lithuania should represent the boundaries of spheres of influence between Germany and Russia, and that the spheres of Germany and Russia in Poland should be bound by the rivers Narew, Vistula, and San, and declared Germany's complete political disinterest in the Soviet claims in Bessarabia.

On 28 September 1939 Germany and the Soviet Union entered into a boundary and friendship agreement which divided Poland between them and fixed their mutual boundaries, and on the same date entered in a secret supplementary protocol which amended that of 23 August putting the Lithuanian state within the sphere of Soviet influence and Lublin and parts of Warsaw in the German sphere.

On the same day the two nations entered into a further agreement declaring that Germany and Russia would direct their common efforts jointly, and with other friendly powers if occasion arises, toward putting an end to the war between Germany and England and France, and that if these efforts remained fruitless, this failure would demonstrate the fact that England and France were responsible for the conditions of the war, and Germany and Russia would engage in mutual consultations with regard to necessary measures.

Such were the treaties. Nevertheless, as was found by the International Military Tribunal, as early as the late summer of 1940 Germany began to make preparations for an attack on the Soviets in spite of the nonaggression pact.

The German Ambassador in Moscow reported that the Soviet Union would go to war only if attacked. Russia had fulfilled not only its obligations under the political treaty, but those arising out of the commercial treaty.

The claim now made that Russia intended to attack Germany is without foundation. It expressed concern over the large German troop concentrations in Rumania which were of such size that the German explanation that they were intended to prevent the British from establishing a Salonikian front was obviously

328

false, but there is no substantial evidence that Russia intended to attack Germany; its concern was that it might become the attacked.

In addition to all speeches, assurances, and treaties Germany nad signed the Kellogg-Briand Pact, which not only prescribed aggressive wars between nations, but abandoned war as an instrument of governmental policy and substituted conciliation and arbitration for it. One of its most important and far-reaching provisions was that it implicitly authorized the other nations of the world to take such measures as they might deem proper or necessary to punish the transgressor. In short, it placed the aggressor outside the society of nations. The Kellogg-Briand Pact, however, did not attempt to either prohibit or limit the right of self-defense, but it is implicit, both in its word and spirit, that he who violates the treaty is subject to disciplinary action on the part of the other signatories and that he who initiates aggressive war loses the right to claim self-defense against those who seek to enforce the Treaty. This was merely the embodiment in international law of a long-established principle of criminal law:* "* * * there can be no self-defense against self-defense."

The indictment charges that German aggression started with the forcible annexation of Austria. It is not urged that this action arose because of any fear of aggression by that state, or that it had planned or proposed to join any other state in any aggressive action against Germany. That Hitler planned to seize both Austria and Czechoslovakia without regard to the wishes of those people is clear from his statements made at the famous secret conferences of 5 November 1937 and 23 November 1939.

The Austro-Hungarian Empire was dissolved at the end of the First World War, and by the Treaty of Versailles [St. Germain] Austria became an independent and sovereign state. At that time, and at least during most of the time of the Weimar Republic, there was a strong desire on the part of Austria to join Germany.

Notwithstanding attempts to conceal ultimate objectives and palpable deceptive disclaimers by official Germany and by the Nazi Party of any desire to interfere in Austrian affairs, it became obvious that by fair means or foul the Hitler regime intended and proceeded to subsidize, direct, and control the Austrian members of the Party, and that these efforts were directed toward the annexation of the country. No agreement was made which was not violated; none were made with any intention to

---

* Wharton's Criminal Law (12th Edition, Lawyer's Cooperative Publishing Company, Rochester, N. Y., 1932), volume I, page 180.

abide by them; and the same technique of propaganda, coercion, and violence was followed in Austria which had been successful in Germany. In the latter stages when it was felt that the plum was ripe and about to fall, and when the possible intervention of other powers still existed, a purported repudiation of Austrian radicals was put forth, not because of disapproval of what they were doing, but to camouflage the program.

While it is now asserted that an overwhelming majority of Austrians accepted and were enraptured by the Anschluss, neither Hitler nor his crew could contain themselves to await what they now term was the inevitable, nor run the hazard of a plebiscite, but Seyss-Inquart was forced on Schuschnigg and made Minister of the Interior where he could control the police, and finally an ultimatum was served on the Austrian Government, and the troops marched in. But before a German soldier crossed the border, armed bands of National Socialist SA and SS units under German control and orders and leaders had taken possession of the city of Vienna, seized the reins of government, and ousted the leaders of the Austrian state and placed them under guard.

In view of the size of the German Army, the disproportion in manpower and military resources, no hope of successful resistance existed. Austria fell without a struggle and the Anschluss was accomplished. It was followed by the proscription, persecution, and internment in concentration camps of those who had resisted the Nazi movement, and the policy there pursued was identical with those which had followed the seizure of power in Germany.

That the invasion was aggressive and that Hitler followed a campaign of deceit, threats, and coercion is beyond question. The whole story is one of duplicity and overwhelming force. It was a part of a program declared to his own circle, and was the first step in the well-conceived and carefully planned campaign of aggression; Austria first, Czechoslovakia second, and Poland third, while visions of the further aggressive aggrandizement were dangled before the eyes of the German leaders. Neither these acts nor the invasion by German armed forces can be said to be pacific means or a peaceful and orderly process within the meaning of the preamble of the Kellogg-Briand Pact, and violated both its letter and spirit.

It must be borne in mind that the term "invasion" connotes and implies the use of force. In the instant cases the force used was military force. In the course of construction of this definition, we certainly may consider the word "invasion" in its usually accepted sense. We may assume that the enacting author-

330

ities also used the term in a like sense. In Webster's Unabridged Dictionary, we find the following definition of invasion:

"Invasion.—1. Act of invading, especially a warlike or hostile entrance into the possessions or domains of another; the incursion of an army for conquest or plunder."

The evidence with respect to both Austria and Czechoslovakia indicates that the invasions were hostile and aggressive. An invasion of this character is clearly such an act of war as is tantamount to, and may be treated as, a declaration of war. It is not reasonable to assume that an act of war, in the nature of an invasion, whereby conquest and plunder are achieved without resistance, is to be given more favorable consideration than a similar invasion which may have met with some military resistance. The fact that the aggressor was here able to so overawe the invaded countries, does not detract in the slightest from the enormity of the aggression, in reality perpetrated. The invader here employed an act of war. This act of war was an instrument of national policy. Tribunal V in Case 12 (the High Command case)* in the course of its judgment said:

"As a preliminary to that we deem it necessary to give a brief consideration to the nature and characteristics of war. We need not attempt a definition that is all inclusive and all exclusive. It is sufficient to say that war is the exerting of violence by one state or politically organized body, against another. In other words, it is the implementation of a political policy by means of violence. Wars are contests by force between political units but the policy that brings about their initiation is made and the actual waging of them is done by individuals. What we have said thus far is equally applicable to a just as to an unjust war, to the initiation of an aggressive and, therefore, criminal war, as to the waging of defensive and, therefore, legitimate war against criminal aggression. The point we stress is that war activity is the implementation of a predetermined national policy.

"*Likewise, an invasion of one state by another is the implementation of the national policy of the invading state by force even though the invaded state, due to fear or a sense of the futility of resistance in the face of superior force, adopts a policy of non-resistance and thus prevents the occurrence of any actual combat.*" [Emphasis added.]

We hold that the invasion of Austria was aggressive and a crime against peace within the meaning of Control Council Law No. 10.

---

* United States *vs.* Wilhelm von Leeb, et al., Volumes X and XI, this series.

331

We have already quoted Hitler's words as to his plans regarding the Czechoslovakian state. The objectives were fixed but the tactics of accomplishment were elastic and depended upon the necessities and conveniences of time and circumstance. This was no more than the distinction between military strategy and tactics. Strategy is the over-all plan which does not vary. Tactics are the techniques of action which adjust themselves to the circumstances of weather, terrain, supply, and resistance. The Nazi plans to destroy the Czech state remained constant. But where, when, and how to strike depended upon circumstances as they arose.

The evidence establishes beyond all question or doubt that Germany, under Hitler, never made a promise which it intended to keep, that it promised anything and everything whenever it thought promises would lull suspicion, and promised peace on the eve of initiating war.

When in 1938 Germany invaded Austria it was in no danger from that state or its neighbors. When it had swallowed the Austrian Federal State, Germany moved against Czechoslovakia, using the question of the Sudeten Germans as a mere excuse for its demands at Munich. It completed its organization of and assumed even greater control over Henlein and his party, which it had secretly organized and subsidized, and directed him to reject any Czech efforts of composition and compromise and to constantly increase his demands.

At Munich it put forth demands for the annexation of the Sudetenland when theretofore it had not suggested it. Its Foreign Office had instructed its representatives to inform Lord Runciman that unless his report regarding the Sudeten question was favorable to the German wishes, dire international results would follow. After Munich it promised and declared that it had no further ideas of aggression against the remnants of the Czech state when, at the very moment, those plans were in existence, and were ready to be matured. It fomented, subsidized, and supported the Slovakian movement for independence in the face of its assurance of friendship with the Czechs. When Tiso seemed to hesitate, Hitler made it clear that unless this action was taken he would lose interest in the Slovakians. He summoned the aged and ill Hacha to Berlin and threatened his country with war and the destruction of its ancient capital, Prague, by aerial warfare. He started his armed forces on the march into Bohemia and Moravia before he had coerced Hacha into submission.

The announcement that its relations with Poland were excellent and that peace was assured came when plans for the invasion of Poland were already decided upon. It made nonaggression

332

pacts, gave assurances to Denmark and Norway, at a time when the question of occupying these countries for the purpose of obtaining bases was being considered. It assured Holland, Belgium, and Luxembourg that it would respect their neutrality when it had already planned to violate it and only awaited a propitious moment so to do.

When Germany fomented and subsidized the Henlein Sudeten movement, it knew that Czechoslovakia desired peace and not war. It used the technique of agent provocateur, both in Czechoslovakia and again in Poland, to create incidents upon which it could seize as an excuse for military action.

Hitler's aggression against Russia was not induced by fear of attack, but because Russia had material resources for which Hitler hankered. How, at that time, any country could have had the slightest faith in Germany's word is beyond comprehension.

The record is one of abyssmal duplicity which carried in its train death, suffering, and loss to practically every people in the world; it brought ruin to Germany and a world-wide distrust in the ability of its people to govern themselves as a peace-loving and useful nation. Because of this record the road back is long and arduous and beset with difficulty.

The attempt, which had been made to create the fiction and fable that the Third Reich acted in self-defense and was justified in its acts toward its neighbors, has no foundation and is, in fact, a disservice to the German people. We believe it is an effort to lay the ground work for a resurgence of the ideology which brought untold suffering to the world and ruin to the German nation.

Until the seizure of power, the Western World, on the whole, looked with sympathy and satisfaction on the efforts of the German people to regain the place in the family of nations to which it was entitled, and which it had lost. They suspected, even if they did not know, that Germany, from the very day that it signed the Versailles Treaty, had secretly violated its terms as to disarmament. But while suspicion of Germany's good faith existed in some circles, a strong hope and faith prevailed that the German nation would achieve a free and prosperous society.

It was the Nazi regime and its ready acceptance by the German people which brought the world to arms in defense against an ideology and a dictator whose programs and aims knew no bounds.

After having relied upon Germany's pledge at Munich and found it worthless, having observed the increasing demands upon and its intransigence toward Poland, it is not surprising that France and England found it necessary to enter into a treaty of assistance with Poland, and there is neither fact nor substance to the contention that that treaty gave Poland a blank check. Germany was so informed by France and England, as were the Poles.

No justification can, or has been, offered for the invasion of Denmark, other than the pseudo one of military necessity. The Danes had maintained their neutrality and had given no offense to Germany. It was helpless and resistance hopeless as the gallant but futile resistance of the Palace Guards indicated. But as we shall hereafter discuss, military necessity is never available to an aggressor as a defense for invading the rights of a neutral.

Norway.—The defense insists that the invasion of Norway was justified because of French and British plans to land expeditionary forces there, in violation of Norwegian neutrality, and, therefore, Germany acted in self-defense. We may repeat the statement that having initiated aggressive wars, which brought England and France to the aid of the Poles, Germany forfeited the right to claim self-defense, but there are other and cogent facts which make this defense unavailable.

Long before the discovery of alleged British and French plans, and before any such plans existed, the Third Reich commenced to support and subsidize Quisling and his movement for the purpose of gaining control of the Norwegian Government and therefore of Norway. It made no inquiry whether Norway could or would protect its neutrality against Britain and France, and the German official documents disclose that it avoided such an approach and kept its plans secret because of the fear that the other neutral powers would intervene and institute discussions directed toward maintaining Norwegian neutrality and preventing that country from becoming a theatre of war. Finally the desirability of obtaining air and other bases in Norway was a motivating factor for the invasion and this was pointed out by Raeder and Doenitz as early as 3 October 1939.

We hold that the invasion of Norway was aggressive, that the war which Germany initiated and waged there was without lawful justification or excuse and is a crime under international law and Control Council Law No. 10.

Luxembourg.—No justification or excuse is offered regarding the invasion of Luxembourg other than military convenience. No claim is made that Luxembourg had in any way violated its neutrality. In fact, it had not. The German invasion was aggressive, without legal justification or excuse.

Belgium and the Netherlands.—That both of these nations were pathetically eager to avoid being drawn into the holocaust is established beyond doubt. That they had every reason to be dis-

334

trustful of Germany's word is equally clear. The testimony offered by the defense discloses that when the Third Reich assured the Low Countries that it intended to, and would, observe its treaty obligations and had no hostile intentions, the intention to invade had already been determined upon and was only awaiting a favorable moment.

An attempt has been made to assert that the invasion of Belgium was justified because of conversations between the French and Belgian military staffs. The Belgian Government had been apprehensive for many months that Germany would use its territory as a means to attack the French flank. German preparations to invade Belgium had been matured long since and were hardly a secret. Belgium was properly concerned regarding her defense and possible aid if she were invaded, and her conversations with the French and English were addressed to this alone. Hitler's attack was without justification or excuse and constituted a crime against peace. As to Holland, there is even less ground for justification and excuse.

Yugoslavia and Greece.—Germany's Axis partner, Italy, initiated an aggressive attack against Greece which the defense does not attempt to justify, but asserts that this was undertaken without previous consultations or agreement with Hitler. This appears to be true. But Germany had been advised by its representatives in Rome of the imminence of the attack and its Foreign Office knew of Greek apprehensions regarding the same, and it intentionally displayed alleged ignorance and refused to take any action to prevent it. The German excuse for the attack on Greece is that England had landed certain troop elements in aid of Greece's defense against Italy and that as a matter of self-defense Germany was compelled to intervene, but an aggressor may not loose the dogs of war and thereafter plead self-defense.

The only justification offered for the German invasion of Yugoslavia is the *coup d'état* which overthrew the government which had signed the Anti-Comintern Pact, and the fear that Yugoslavia would remain neutral only until such time as it might join the ranks of Germany's enemies.

The unquestioned fact is that every country, and particularly those which lay along or near German boundaries, was fully aware that German actions in Austria, Czechoslovakia, and Poland were aggressive and unjustified, and that in attacking and invading, Hitler had broken not only the provisions of the Kellogg-Briand Pact, but the pledges which he had given to those countries; each fully disapproved of Germany's action and the question which lay in their minds was where the next blow would fall. We think there is no doubt whatsoever that every country in Europe, except

335

its Axis partners, hoped for German defeat as the one insurance for its own safety, but such hopes cannot justify the German action against them.

The claim of self-defense is without merit. That doctrine is never available either to individuals or nations who are aggressors. The robber or the murderer cannot claim self-defense, in attacking the police to avoid arrest or those who, he fears, disapprove of his criminal conduct and hope that he will be apprehended and brought to justice.

The invasion of Austria, the invasion of Bohemia and Moravia, and the attack on Poland were in violation of international law and in each case, by resorting to armed force, Germany violated the Kellogg-Briand Pact. It thereby became an international outlaw and every peaceable nation had the right to oppose it without itself becoming an aggressor, to help the attacked and join with those who had previously come to the aid of the victim. The doctrine of self-defense and military necessity was never available to Germany as a matter of international law, in view of its prior violations of that law.

United States of America.—That the United States abandoned a neutral attitude toward Germany long before Germany declared war is without question. It hoped for Germany's defeat, gave aid and support to Great Britain and to the governments of the countries which Germany had overrun. Its entire course of conduct for over a year before 11 December 1941 was wholly inconsistent with neutrality and that it had no intention of permitting Germany's victory, even though this led to hostilities, became increasingly apparent. However, in so doing, the United States did not become an aggressor; it was acting within its international rights in hampering and hindering with the intention of insuring the defeat of the nation which had wrongfully, without excuse, and in violation of its treaties and obligations embarked on a coldly calculated program of aggression and war. But such intent, purpose, and action does not remove the aggressive character of the German declaration of war of 11 December 1941.

A nation which engages in aggressive war invites the other nations of the world to take measures, including force, to halt the invasion and to punish the aggressor, and if by reason thereof the aggressor declares war on a third nation, the original aggression carries over and gives the character of aggression to the second and succeeding wars.

We hold that the invasions and wars described in paragraph two of the indictment against Austria, Czechoslovakia, Poland, the United Kingdom and France, Denmark and Norway, Belgium, the Netherlands, and Luxembourg, Yugoslavia and Greece,

336

the Union of Soviet Socialist Republics, and the United States of America were unlawful and aggressive, violated international law, and were crimes within the definition of the London Charter and Control Council Law No. 10.

Our task is to determine which, if any, of the defendants, knowing there was an intent to so initiate and wage aggressive war, consciously participated in either plans, preparations, initiations of those wars, or so knowing, participated or aided in carrying them on. Obviously, no man may be condemned for fighting in what he believes is the defense of his native land, even though his belief be mistaken. Nor can he be expected to undertake an independent investigation to determine whether or not the cause for which he fights is the result of an aggressive act of his own government. One can be guilty only where knowledge of aggression in fact exists, and it is not sufficient that he have suspicions that the war is aggressive.

Any other test of guilt would involve a standard of conduct both impracticable and unjust.

Criminal responsibility.—Article II, paragraph 2, of Control Council Law No. 10, provides that—

"Any person without regard to nationality or the capacity in which he acted, is deemed to have committed a crime as defined in paragraph 1 of this Article, if he was (*a*) a principal or (*b*) was an accessory to the commission of any such crime or ordered or abetted the same or (*c*) took a consenting part therein * * *."

Therefore, all those who were either principals or accessories before or after the fact, are criminally responsible, although the degree of criminal responsibility may vary in accordance with the nature of his acts.

Under the provisions of paragraph 4 (*b*), Article II—

"The fact that any person acted pursuant to the order of his government or of a superior does not free him from responsibility for a crime, but may be considered in mitigation."

In the realm of the ordinary criminal law, one who conceals the fact that a crime has been committed or gives false testimony as to the facts for the purpose of giving some advantage to the perpetrator, not on account of fear but for the sake of an advantage to the accused, is an accessory after the fact. Under English criminal law, one who destroys or suppresses evidence of a crime or manufactures evidence tending to prove the felon's innocence is likewise an accessory after the fact.*

---

* American Jurisprudence (Bancroft-Whitney Co., San Francisco, Calif., Lawyers' Cooperative Publishing Co., Rochester, N. Y., 1938), Criminal Law, volume 14, paragraphs 103 and 104, pages 837 and 838.

337

Charter of the International Military Tribunal for the Far East[1]

I.

CONSTITUTION OF TRIBUNAL

Article 1. Tribunal Established. The International Military Tribunal for the Far East is hereby established for the just and prompt trial and punishment of the major war criminals in the Far East. The permanent seat of the Tribunal is in Tokyo.

Article 2. Members. The Tribunal shall consist of not less than six members nor more than eleven members, appointed by the Supreme Commander for the Allied Powers from the names submitted by the Signatories to the Instrument of Surrender, India, and the Commonwealth of the Philippines.

Article 3. Officers and Secretariat.

(a) *President.* The Supreme Commander for the Allied Powers shall appoint a Member to be President of the Tribunal.

(b) *Secretariat.*

(1) The Secretariat of the Tribunal shall be composed of a General Secretary to be appointed by the Supreme Commander for the Allied Powers and such assistant secretaries, clerks, interpreters, and other personnel as may be necessary.

(2) The General Secretary shall organize and direct the work of the Secretariat.

(3) The Secretariat shall receive all documents addressed to the Tribunal, maintain the records of the Tribunal, provide necessary clerical services to the Tribunal and its Members, and perform such other duties as may be designated by the Tribunal.

---

[1] The Charter was approved by the Supreme Commander for the Allied Powers on Jan. 19, 1946; it was amended by order of the Supreme Commander, General Headquarters, APO 500, Apr. 26, 1946, General Orders No. 20. The amendments have been incorporated herewith.

39

Article 4. Convening and Quorum, Voting and Absence.

(a) *Convening and Quorum.* When as many as six members of the Tribunal are present, they may convene the Tribunal in formal session. The presence of a majority of all members shall be necessary to constitute a quorum.

(b) *Voting.* All decisions and judgments of this Tribunal, including convictions and sentences, shall be by a majority vote of those Members of the Tribunal present. In case the votes are evenly divided, the vote of the President shall be decisive.

(c) *Absence.* If a member at any time is absent and afterwards is able to be present, he shall take part in all subsequent proceedings; unless he declares in open court that he is disqualified by reason of insufficient familiarity with the proceedings which took place in his absence.

II.

JURISDICTION AND GENERAL PROVISIONS

Article 5. Jurisdiction Over Persons and Offenses. The Tribunal shall have the power to try and punish Far Eastern war criminals who as individuals or as members of organizations are charged with offenses which include Crimes against Peace.

The following acts, or any of them, are crimes coming within the jurisdiction of the Tribunal for which there shall be individual responsibility:

(a) *Crimes against Peace:* Namely, the planning, preparation, initiation or waging of a declared or undeclared war of aggression, or a war in violation of international law, treaties, agreements or assurances, or participation in a common plan or conspiracy for the accomplishment of any of the foregoing;

(b) *Conventional War Crimes:* Namely, violations of the laws or customs of war;

(c) *Crimes against Humanity:* Namely, murder, extermination, enslavement, deportation, and other inhumane acts committed against any civilian population, before or during the war, or persecutions on political or racial grounds in execution of or in connection with any crime within the jurisdiction of the Tribunal, whether or not in violation of the domestic law of the country where perpetrated. Leaders, organizers, instigators and accomplices participating in the formulation or execution of a common plan or conspiracy to commit any of the foregoing crimes are responsible for all acts performed by any person in execution of such plan.

Article 6. Responsibility of Accused. Neither the official position, at any time, of an accused, nor the fact that an accused acted pursuant to order of his government or of a superior shall, of itself, be sufficient to free such accused from responsibility for any crime with which he is

40

charged, but such circumstances may be considered in mitigation of punishment if the Tribunal determines that justice so requires.

Article 7. Rules of Procedure. The Tribunal may draft and amend rules of procedure consistent with the fundamental provisions of this Charter.

Article 8. Counsel.

(*a*) *Chief of Counsel.* The Chief of Counsel designated by the Supreme Commander for the Allied Powers is responsible for the investigation and prosecution of charges against war criminals within the jurisdiction of this Tribunal, and will render such legal assistance to the Supreme Commander as is appropriate.

(*b*) *Associate Counsel.* Any United Nation with which Japan has been at war may appoint an Associate Counsel to assist the Chief of Counsel.

III.

FAIR TRIAL FOR ACCUSED

Article 9. Procedure for Fair Trial. In order to insure fair trial for the accused the following procedure shall be followed:

(*a*) *Indictment.* The indictment shall consist of a plain, concise, and adequate statement of each offense charged. Each accused shall be furnished, in adequate time for defense, a copy of the indictment, including any amendment, and of this Charter, in a language understood by the accused.

(*b*) *Language.* The trial and related proceedings shall be conducted in English and in the language of the accused. Translations of documents and other papers shall be provided as needed and requested.

(*c*) *Counsel for Accused.* Each accused shall have the right to be represented by counsel of his own selection, subject to the disapproval of such counsel at any time by the Tribunal. The accused shall file with the General Secretary of the Tribunal the name of his counsel. If an accused is not represented by counsel and in open court requests the appointment of counsel, the Tribunal shall designate counsel for him. In the absence of such request the Tribunal may appoint counsel for an accused if in its judgment such appointment is necessary to provide for a fair trial.

(*d*) *Evidence for Defense.* An accused shall have the right, through himself or through his counsel (but not through both), to conduct his defense, including the right to examine any witness, subject to such reasonable restrictions as the Tribunal may determine.

(*e*) *Production of Evidence for the Defense.* An accused may apply in writing to the Tribunal for the production of witnesses or of documents. The application shall state where the witness or document is thought to be located. It shall also state the facts proposed to be proved by the witness of the document and the relevancy of such

41

facts to the defense. If the Tribunal grants the application the Tribunal shall be given such aid in obtaining production of the evidence as the circumstances require.

Article 10. Applications and Motions before Trial. All motions, applications, or other requests addressed to the Tribunal prior to the commencement of trial shall be made in writing and filed with the General Secretary of the Tribunal for action by the Tribunal.

IV.

POWERS OF TRIBUNAL AND CONDUCT OF TRIAL

Article 11. Powers. The Tribunal shall have the power

(a) To summon witnesses to the trial, to require them to attend and testify, and to question them,

(b) To interrogate each accused and to permit comment on his refusal to answer any question,

(c) To require the production of documents and other evidentiary material,

(d) To require of each witness an oath, affirmation, or such declaration as is customary in the country of the witness, and to administer oaths,

(e) To appoint officers for the carrying out of any task designated by the Tribunal, including the power to have evidence taken on commission.

Article 12. Conduct of Trial. The Tribunal shall

(a) Confine the trial strictly to an expeditious hearing of the issues raised by the charges,

(b) Take strict measures to prevent any action which would cause any unreasonable delay and rule out irrelevant issues and statements of any kind whatsoever,

(c) Provide for the maintenance of order at the trial and deal summarily with any contumacy, imposing appropriate punishment, including exclusion of any accused or his counsel from some or all further proceedings, but without prejudice to the determination of the charges,

(d) Determine the mental and physical capacity of any accused to proceed to trial.

Article 13. Evidence.

(a) *Admissibility.* The Tribunal shall not be bound by technical rules of evidence. It shall adopt and apply to the greatest possible extent expeditious and non-technical procedure, and shall admit any evidence which it deems to have probative value. All purported admissions or statements of the accused are admissible.

(b) *Relevance.* The Tribunal may require to be informed of the nature of any evidence before it is offered in order to rule upon the relevance.

42

(c) *Specific evidence admissible.* In particular, and without limiting in any way the scope of the foregoing general rules, the following evidence may be admitted:

(1) A document, regardless of its security classification and without proof of its issuance or signature, which appears to the Tribunal to have been signed or issued by any officer, department, agency or member of the armed forces of any government.

(2) A report which appears to the Tribunal to have been signed or issued by the International Red Cross or a member thereof, or by a doctor of medicine or any medical service personnel, or by an investigator or intelligence officer, or by any other person who appears to the Tribunal to have personal knowledge of the matters contained in the report.

(3) An affidavit, deposition or other signed statement.

(4) A diary, letter or other document, including sworn or unsworn statements which appear to the Tribunal to contain information relating to the charge.

(5) A copy of a document or other secondary evidence of its contents, if the original is not immediately available.

(d) *Judicial Notice.* The Tribunal shall neither require proof of facts of common knowledge, nor of the authenticity of official government documents and reports of any nation nor of the proceedings, records, and findings of military or other agencies of any of the United Nations.

(e) *Records, Exhibits and Documents.* The transcript of the proceedings, and exhibits and documents submitted to the Tribunal, will be filed with the General Secretary of the Tribunal and will constitute part of the Record.

Article 14. Place of Trial. The first trial will be held at Tokyo and any subsequent trials will be held at such places as the Tribunal decides.

Article 15. Course of Trial Proceedings. The proceedings at the Trial will take the following course:

(a) The indictment will be read in court unless the reading is waived by all accused.

(b) The Tribunal will ask each accused whether he pleads "guilty" or "not guilty."

(c) The prosecution and each accused (by counsel only, if represented) may make a concise opening statement.

(d) The prosecution and defense may offer evidence and the admissibility of the same shall be determined by the Tribunal.

(e) The prosecution and each accused (by counsel only, if represented) may examine each witness and each accused who gives testimony.

(f) Accused (by counsel only, if represented) may address the Tribunal.

43

(*g*) The prosecution may address the Tribunal.

(*h*) The Tribunal will deliver judgment and pronounce sentence.

V.

JUDGMENT AND SENTENCE

Article 16. Penalty. The Tribunal shall have the power to impose upon an accused, on conviction, death or such other punishment as shall be determined by it to be just.

Article 17. Judgment and Review. The judgment will be announced in open court and will give the reasons on which it is based. The record of the trial will be transmitted directly to the Supreme Commander for the Allied Powers for his action thereon. A sentence will be carried out in accordance with the order of the Supreme Commander for the Allied Powers, who may at any time reduce or otherwise alter the sentence except to increase its severity.

By command of General MacArthur:

RICHARD J. MARSHALL
*Major General, General Staff
Corps, Chief of Staff.*

OFFICIAL:

B M FITCH
Brigadier General, AGD,
Adjutant General.

44

International Military Tribunal for the Far East

NO. 1.

THE UNITED STATES OF AMERICA, THE REPUBLIC OF CHINA, THE UNITED KINGDOM OF GREAT BRITAIN AND NORTHERN IRELAND, THE UNION OF SOVIET SOCIALIST REPUBLICS, THE COMMONWEALTH OF AUSTRALIA, CANADA, THE REPUBLIC OF FRANCE, THE KINGDOM OF THE NETHERLANDS, NEW ZEALAND, INDIA, AND THE COMMONWEALTH OF THE PHILIPPINES.

-AGAINST-

ARAKI, Sadao; DOHIHARA, Kenji; HASHIMOTO, Kingoro; HATA, Shunroku; HIRANUMA, Kiichiro; HIROTA, Koki; HOSHINO, Naoki; ITAGAKI, Seishiro; KAYA, Okinori; KIDO, Koichi; KIMURA, Heitaro; KOISO, Kuniaki; MATSUI, Iwane; MATSUOKA, Yosuke; MINAMI, Jiro; MUTO, Akira; NAGANO, Osami; OKA, Takasumi; OKAWA, Shumei; OSHIMA, Hiroshi; SATO, Kenryo; SHIGEMITSU, Mamoru; SHIMADA, Shigetaro; SHIRATORI, Toshio; SUZUKI, Teiichi; TOGO, Shigenori; TOJO, Hideki; UMEZU, Yoshijiro.

Accused.

INDICTMENT[1]

In the years hereinafter referred to in this Indictment the internal and foreign policies of Japan were dominated and directed by a criminal, militaristic clique, and such policies were the cause of serious world troubles, aggressive wars, and great damage to the interests of peace-loving peoples, as well as to the interests of the Japanese people themselves.

The mind of the Japanese people was systematically poisoned with harmful ideas of the alleged racial superiority of the Japanese over

---

[1] Certain changes in style have been made in this printing of the Indictment and its appendixes by agreement between the Tribunal, the International Prosecution Section, and the Defense Panel.

45

other peoples of Asia and even of the whole world. Such parliamentary institutions as existed in Japan were used as implements for widespread aggression, and a system similar to those then established by Hitler and the Nazi party in Germany and by the Fascist party in Italy was introduced. The economic and financial resources of Japan were to a large extent mobilized for war aims, to the detriment of the welfare of the Japanese people.

A conspiracy among the accused, joined in by the rulers of other aggressive countries, namely, Nazi Germany and Fascist Italy, was entered into. The main objects of this conspiracy was to secure the domination and exploitation by the aggressive States of the rest of the world, and to this end to commit, or encourage the commission of crimes against peace, war crimes, and crimes against humanity as defined in the Charter of this Tribunal, thus threatening and injuring the basic principles of liberty and respect for the human personality.

In the promotion and accomplishment of that scheme, these accused, taking advantage of their power and their official positions and their own personal prestige and influence, intended to and did plan, prepare, initiate, or wage aggressive war against the United States of America, the Republic of China, the United Kingdom of Great Britain and Northern Ireland, the Union of Soviet Socialist Republics, the Commonwealth of Australia, Canada, the Republic of France, the Kingdom of the Netherlands, New Zealand, India, the Commonwealth of the Philippines, and other peaceful nations, in violation of international law, as well as in violation of sacred treaty commitments, obligations and assurances. In furtherance of such scheme the accused contemplated and carried out the violation of recognized customs and conventions of war by murdering, maiming and ill-treating prisoners of war, civilian internees, and persons on the high seas, denying them adequate food, shelter, clothing, medical care, or other appropriate attention, forcing them to labour under inhumane conditions, and subjecting them to indignities; the exploitation to Japan's benefit of the manpower and economic resources of the vanquished nations; the plundering of public and private property; the wanton destruction of cities, towns and villages beyond any justification of military necessity; the perpetration of mass murder, rape, pillage, brigandage, torture, and other barbaric cruelties upon the helpless civilian population of the over-run countries; the increase of the influence and control of the military and naval groups over Japanese government officials and agencies; the psychological preparation of Japanese public opinion for aggressive warfare by establishing so-called Assistance Societies, by teaching nationalistic policies of expansion, by disseminating war propaganda, and by exercising strict control over the press and radio; the setting up of "puppet" governments

46

in conquered countries; and the conclusion of military alliances with Germany and Italy to enhance by military might Japan's programme of expansion.

Therefore, the above named Nations by their undersigned representatives, duly appointed to represent their respective Governments in the investigation of the charges against and the prosecution of the Major War Criminals, pursuant to the Potsdam Declaration of the 20th July, 1945, and the Instrument of Surrender of the 2nd September, 1945, and the Charter of the Tribunal, promulgated by the Supreme Commander for the Allied Powers on 19th January, 1946 and amended 26th April, 1946, hereby accuse as guilty, in the respects hereinafter set forth, of Crimes against Peace, War Crimes, and Crimes against Humanity, and of Common Plans or Conspiracies to commit those Crimes, all as defined in the Charter of the Tribunal, and accordingly name as the accused in this cause and as indicted on the Counts hereinafter set out in which their names respectively appear, all the above-named individuals.

GROUP ONE: *CRIMES AGAINST PEACE*

The following counts charge Crimes against Peace, being acts for which it is charged that each of the persons named are individually responsible in accordance with Article 5 and particularly Article 5 (a) of the Charter of the International Military Tribunal for the Far East, and in accordance with International Law.

Count 1

All the accused together with other persons, between the 1st January, 1928, and the 2nd September, 1945, participated as leaders, organisers, instigators, or accomplices in the formulation or execution of a common plan or conspiracy, and are responsible for all acts performed by any person in execution of such plan.

The object of such plan or conspiracy was that Japan should secure the military, naval, political and economic domination of East Asia and of the Pacific and Indian Oceans, and of all countries bordering thereon and islands therein, and for that purpose they conspired that Japan should alone or in combination with other countries having similar objects, or who could be induced or coerced to join therein, wage declared or undeclared war or wars of aggression, and war or wars in violation of international law, treaties, agreements and assurances, against any country or countries which might oppose that purpose.

The whole of the Particulars in Appendix A, of the Treaty Articles in Appendix B, and of the Assurances in Appendix C, relate to this Count.

Count 2

All the accused together with other persons, between the 1st January, 1928, and the 2nd September, 1945, participated as leaders, organisers, instigators, or accomplices in the formulation or execution of a common plan or conspiracy and are responsible for all acts performed by any person in execution of such plan.

The object of such plan or conspiracy was that Japan should secure the military, naval, political and economic domination of the provinces of Liaoning, Kirin, Heilungkiang and Jehol, being parts of the Republic of China, either directly or by establishing a separate state under the control of Japan, and for that purpose they conspired that Japan should wage declared or undeclared war or wars of aggression, and war or wars in violation of international law, treaties, agreements and assurances, against the Republic of China.

The whole of the Particulars in Appendix A; the following Treaty Articles in Appendix B: Nos. 1 to 6 inclusive, 8 to 14 inclusive, 22 to 30 inclusive, 32 to 35 inclusive; and the following Assurances in appendix C: Nos. 1 to 8 inclusive, relate to this Count.

Count 3

All the accused together with other persons, between the 1st January, 1928, and the 2nd September, 1945, participated as leaders, organisers, instigators, or accomplices in the formulation or execution of a common plan or conspiracy, and are responsible for all acts performed by any person in execution of such plan.

The object of such plan or conspiracy was that Japan should secure the military, naval, political and economic domination of the Republic of China, either directly or by establishing a separate state or states under the control of Japan, and for that purpose they conspired that Japan should wage declared or undeclared war or wars of aggression, and war or wars in violation of international law, treaties, agreements and assurances, against the Republic of China.

The whole of the Particulars in Appendix A, and the same Treaty Articles and Assurances as in Count 2, relate to this Count.

Count 4

All the accused together with other persons, between the 1st January, 1928, and the 2nd September, 1945, participated as leaders, organisers, instigators, or accomplices in the formulation or execution of a common plan or conspiracy, and are responsible for all acts performed by any person in execution of such plan.

The object of such plan or conspiracy was that Japan should secure the military, naval, political and economic domination of East Asia and of the Pacific and Indian Oceans, and of all countries bordering thereon and islands therein, and for that purpose they conspired

48

that Japan should alone or in combination with other countries having similar objects, or who could be induced or coerced to join therein, wage declared or undeclared war or wars of aggression, and war or wars in violation of international law, treaties, agreements and assurances, against the United States of America, the British Commonwealth of Nations (which expression wherever used in this Indictment includes the United Kingdom of Great Britain and Northern Ireland, the Commonwealth of Australia, Canada, New Zealand, South Africa, India, Burma, the Malay States, and all other parts of the British Empire not separately represented in the League of Nations), the Republic of France, the Kingdom of the Netherlands, the Republic of China, the Republic of Portugal, the Kingdom of Thailand (Siam), the Commonwealth of the Philippines, and the Union of Soviet Socialist Republics, or such of them as might oppose that purpose.

The whole of the Particulars in Appendix A, of the Treaty Articles in Appendix B, and of the Assurances in Appendix C, relate to this Count.

Count 5

All the accused together with other persons, between the 1st January, 1928, and the 2nd September, 1945, participated as leaders, organisers, instigators, or accomplices in the formulation or execution of a common plan or conspiracy, and are responsible for all acts performed by any person in execution of such plan.

The object of such plan or conspiracy was that Germany, Italy and Japan should secure the military, naval, political and economic domination of the whole world, each having special domination in its own sphere, the sphere of Japan covering East Asia, the Pacific and Indian Oceans and all countries bordering thereon and islands therein, and for that purpose they conspired that Germany, Italy, and Japan should mutually assist one another to wage declared or undeclared war or wars of aggression, and war or wars in violation of international law, treaties, agreements and assurances, against any countries which might oppose that purpose, and particularly against the United States of America, the British Commonwealth of Nations, the Republic of France, the Kingdom of the Netherlands, the Republic of China, the Republic of Portugal, the Kingdom of Thailand (Siam), the Commonwealth of the Philippines, and the Union of Soviet Socialist Republics.

The whole of the Particulars in Appendix A, of the Treaty Articles in Appendix B, and of the Assurances in Appendix C, relate to this Count.

Count 6

All the accused, between the 1st January, 1928, and the 2nd September, 1945, planned and prepared a war of aggression and a

49

war in violation of international law, treaties, agreements and assurances, against the Republic of China.

The following Sections of the Particulars in Appendix A: Nos. 1 to 6 inclusive, and the same Treaty Articles and Assurances as in Count 2, relate to this Count

Count 7

All the accused, between the 1st January, 1928, and the 2nd September, 1945, planned and prepared a war of aggression and a war in violation of international law, treaties, agreements and assurances, against the United States of America.

The following Sections of the Particulars in Appendix A: Nos. 3, 4, 5, 6, 7, 9, and 10; the following Treaty Articles in Appendix B: Nos. 1 to 10 inclusive, 17 to 19 inclusive, 22 to 35, inclusive and 37; and the whole of the Assurances in Appendix C, relate to this Count.

Count 8

All the accused, between the 1st January, 1928, and the 2nd September, 1945, planned and prepared a war of aggression and a war in violation of international law, treaties, agreements and assurances, against the United Kingdom of Great Britain and Northern Ireland and all parts of the British Commonwealth of Nations not the subject of separate counts in this Indictment.

The following Sections of the Particulars in Appendix A: Nos. 3, 4, 5, 6, 7, 9, and 10; the following Treaty Articles in Appendix B: Nos. 1, 2, 5, 10 to 19 inclusive, 22 to 30 inclusive, 32 to 35 inclusive, 37 and 38; and the whole of the Assurances in Appendix C, relate to this Count.

Count 9

All the accused, between the 1st January, 1928, and the 2nd September, 1945, planned and prepared a war of aggression and a war in violation of international law, treaties, agreements and assurances, against the Commonwealth of Australia.

The same Sections of the Particulars in Appendix A, and the same Treaty Articles and Assurances as in Count 8, relate to this Count.

Count 10

All the accused, between the 1st January, 1928, and the 2nd September, 1945, planned and prepared a war of aggression and a war in violation of international law, treaties, agreements and assurances, against New Zealand.

The same Sections of the Particulars in Appendix A, and the same Treaty Articles and Assurances as in Count 8, relate to this Count.

Count 11

All the accused, between the 1st January, 1928, and the 2nd September, 1945, planned and prepared a war of aggression and a war in

50

violation of international law, treaties, agreements and assurances, against Canada.

The same Sections of the Particulars in Appendix A, and the same Treaty Articles and Assurances as in Count 8, relate to this Count.

Count 12

All the accused, between the 1st January, 1928, and the 2nd September, 1945, planned and prepared a war of aggression and a war in violation of international law, treaties, agreements and assurances, against India.

The same Sections of the Particulars in Appendix A, and the same Treaty Articles and Assurances as in Count 8, relate to this Count.

Count 13

All the accused, between the 1st January, 1928, and the 2nd September, 1945, planned and prepared a war of aggression and a war in violation of international law, treaties, agreements and assurances, against the Commonwealth of the Philippines.

The same Sections of the Particulars in Appendix A, and the same Treaty Articles and Assurances as in Count 7, relate to this Count.

Count 14

All the accused, between the 1st January, 1928, and the 2nd September, 1945, planned and prepared a war of aggression and a war in violation of international law, treaties, agreements and assurances, against the Kingdom of the Netherlands.

The following Sections of the Particulars in Appendix A: Nos. 3, 4, 5, 6, 7, 9, and 10; the following Treaty Articles in Appendix B: Nos. 1 to 5 inclusive, 10 to 18 inclusive, 20, 22 to 30 inclusive, 32 to 35 inclusive, 37 and 38; and the following Assurances in Appendix C: Nos. 10 to 15 inclusive, relate to this Count.

Count 15

All the accused, between the 1st January, 1928, and the 2nd, September, 1945, planned and prepared a war of aggression and a war in violation of international law, treaties, agreements and assurances, against the Republic of France.

The following Sections of the Particulars in Appendix A: Nos. 2, 3, 4, 5, 6, 7, 9, and 10; the following Treaty Articles in Appendix B: Nos. 1 to 5 inclusive, 10 to 19 inclusive, 22 to 30 inclusive, and 32 to 38 inclusive; and the following Assurances in Appendix C: Nos. 14 and 15, relate to this Count.

Count 16

All the accused, between the 1st January, 1928, and the 2nd September, 1945, planned and prepared a war of aggression and a war in

51

violation of international law, treaties, agreements and assurances against the Kingdom of Thailand.

The following Sections of the Particulars in Appendix A: Nos. 2, 3, 4, 5, 6, 7, 9, and 10; and the following Treaty Articles in Appendix B: Nos. 3, 4, 5, 10 and 32 to 38 inclusive, relate to this Count.

Count 17

All the accused, between the 1st January, 1928, and the 2nd September, 1945, planned and prepared a war of aggression and a war in violation of international law, treaties, agreements and assurances, against the Union of Soviet Socialist Republics.

The following Sections of the Particulars in Appendix A: Nos. 1 to 8 inclusive; the following Treaty Articles in Appendix B: Nos. 1 to 5 inclusive, 10 to 18 inclusive, 32 to 35 inclusive, 39 to 47 inclusive, and Assurance No. 13 in Appendix C, relate to this Count.

Count 18

The accused ARAKI, DOHIHARA, HASHIMOTO, HIRANUMA, ITAGAKI, KOISO, MINAMI, OKAWA, SHIGEMITSU, TOJO and UMEZU, on or about the 18th September, 1931, initiated a war of aggression and a war in violation of international law, treaties, agreements and assurances, against the Republic of China.

Section 1 of the Particulars in Appendix A; and the following Treaty Articles in Appendix B: Nos. 1 to 5 inclusive, 11 to 14 inclusive, 22, 23, 25, 30, 40 to 43 inclusive, relate to this Count.

Count 19

The accused ARAKI, DOHIHARA, HASHIMOTO, HATA, HIRANUMA, HIROTA, HOSHINO, ITAGAKI, KAYA, KIDO, MATSUI, MUTO, SUZUKI, TOJO and UMEZU, on or about the 7th July, 1937, initiated a war of aggression and a war in violation of international law, treaties, agreements and assurances, against the Republic of China.

Section 2 of the Particulars in Appendix A; the same Treaty Articles as in Count 18, and the following Assurances in Appendix C: Nos. 3, 4 and 5, relate to this Count.

Count 20

The accused DOHIHARA, HIRANUMA, HIROTA, HOSHINO, KAYA, KIDO, KIMURA, MUTO, NAGANO, OKA, OSHIMA, SATO, SHIMADA, SUZUKI, TOGO and TOJO, on or about the 7th December, 1941, initiated a war of aggression and a war in violation of international law, treaties, agreements and assurances, against the United States of America.

Section 9 of the Particulars in Appendix A; the following Treaty Articles in Appendix B: Nos. 1 to 9 inclusive, 19, 22 to 30 inclusive,

52

33, 34 and 37; and the whole of the Assurances in Appendix C, relate to this Count.

Count 21

The same accused as in Count 20, on or about the 7th December, 1941, initiated a war of aggression and a war in violation of international law, treaties, agreements and assurances, against the Commonwealth of the Philippines.

The same Particulars, Treaty Articles and Assurances as in Count 20, relate to this Count.

Count 22

The same accused as in Count 20, on or about the 7th December, 1941, initiated a war of aggression and a war in violation of international law, treaties, agreements and assurances, against the British Commonwealth of Nations.

Section 9 of the Particulars in Appendix A; the following Treaty Articles in Appendix B: Nos. 1 to 5 inclusive, 19, 22 to 30 inclusive, 33 and 37; and the whole of the Assurances in Appendix C, relate to this Count.

Count 23

The accused ARAKI, DOHIHARA, HIRANUMA, HIROTA, HOSHINO, ITAGAKI, KIDO, MATSUOKA, MUTO, NAGANO, SHIGEMITSU and TOJO, on or about the 22nd September, 1940, initiated a war of aggression and a war in violation of international law, treaties, agreements and assurances, against the Republic of France.

The same Particulars, Treaty Articles and Assurances as in Count 15, relate to this Count.

Count 24

The same accused as in Count 20, on or about the 7th December, 1941, initiated a war of aggression and a war in violation of international law, treaties, agreements and assurances, against the Kingdom of Thailand.

Section 7 of the Particulars in Appendix A, and the following Treaty Articles in Appendix B: Nos. 1 to 5 inclusive, 33, 34, 36, 37 and 38, relate to this Count.

Count 25

The accused ARAKI, DOHIHARA, HATA, HIRANUMA, HIROTA, HOSHINO, ITAGAKI, KIDO, MATSUOKA, MATSUI, SHIGEMITSU, SUZUKI and TOGO, during July and August, 1938, initiated a war of aggression and a war in violation of international law, treaties, agreements and assurances, by attacking the Union of Soviet Socialist Republics in the area of Lake Khasan.

The same Particulars, Treaty Articles and Assurances as in Count 17, relate to this Count.

53

Count 26

The accused ARAKI, DOHIHARA, HATA, HIRANUMA, ITAGAKI, KIDO, KOISO, MATSUI, MATSUOKA, MUTO, SUZUKI, TOGO, TOJO and UMEZU, during the summer of 1939, initiated a war of aggression and a war in violation of international law, treaties, agreements and assurances, by attacking the territory of the Mongolian People's Republic in the area of the Khackhin-Gol River.

The same Particulars, Treaty Articles and Assurances as in Count 17, relate to this Count.

Count 27

All the accused, between the 18th September, 1931, and the 2nd September, 1945, waged a war of aggression and a war in violation of international law, treaties, agreements and assurances, against the Republic of China.

The same Particulars, Treaty Articles and Assurances as in Count 2, relate to this Count.

Count 28

All the accused, between the 7th July, 1937, and the 2nd September, 1945, waged a war of aggression and a war in violation of international law, treaties, agreements and assurances, against the Republic of China.

The same Particulars, Treaty Articles and Assurances as in Count 2, relate to this Count.

Count 29

All the accused, between the 7th December, 1941, and the 2nd September, 1945, waged a war of aggression and a war in violation of international law, treaties, agreements and assurances, against the United States of America.

The following Sections of the Particulars in Appendix A: Nos. 4 to 10 inclusive; and the same Treaty Articles and Assurances as in Count 20, relate to this Count.

Count 30

All the accused, between the 7th December, 1941, and the 2nd September, 1945, waged a war of aggression and a war in violation of international law, treaties agreements and assurances, against the Commonwealth of the Philippines.

The same Particulars, Treaty Articles and Assurances as in Count 29, relate to this Count.

Count 31

All the accused, between the 7th December, 1941, and the 2nd September, 1945, waged a war of aggression and a war in violation of

54

international law, treaties, agreements and assurances, against the British Commonwealth of Nations.

The following Sections of the Particulars in Appendix A: Nos. 4 to 10 inclusive; and the same Treaty Articles and Assurances as in Count 22, relate to this Count.

Count 32

All the accused, between the 7th December, 1941, and the 2nd September, 1945, waged a war of aggression and a war in violation of international law, treaties, agreements and assurances, against the Kingdom of the Netherlands.

The same Particulars, Treaty Articles and Assurances as in Count 14, relate to this Count.

Count 33

The accused ARAKI, DOHIHARA, HIRANUMA, HIROTA, HOSHINO, ITAGAKI, KIDO, MATSUOKA, MUTO, NAGANO, SHIGEMITSU and TOJO, on and after the 22nd September, 1940, waged a war of aggression and a war in violation of international law, treaties, agreements and assurances, against the Republic of France.

The same Particulars, Treaty Articles and Assurances as in Count 15, relate to this Count.

Count 34

All the accused, between the 7th December, 1941, and the 2nd September, 1945, waged a war of aggression and a war in violation of international law, treaties, agreements, and assurances, against the Kingdom of Thailand.

The same Particulars and Treaty Articles as in Count 24, relate to this Count.

Count 35

The same accused as in Count 25, during the summer of 1938, waged a war of aggression and a war in violation of international law, treaties, agreements and assurances, against the Union of Soviet Socialist Republics.

The same Particulars, Treaty Articles and Assurances as in Count 17, relate to this Count.

Count 36

The same accused as in Count 26, during the summer of 1939, waged a war of aggression and a war in violation of international law, treaties, agreements and assurances against the Mongolian People's Republic and the Union of Soviet Socialist Republics.

The same Particulars, Treaty Articles and Assurances as in Count 17, relate to this Count.

DOCUMENT 24
INTERNATIONAL MILITARY TRIBUNAL
FOR THE FAR EAST

THE UNITED STATES OF AMERICA, THE REPUBLIC OF CHINA,
THE UNITED KINGDOM OF GREAT BRITAIN AND NORTHERN
IRELAND, THE UNION OF SOVIET SOCIALIST REPUBLICS, THE
COMMONWEALTH OF AUSTRALIA, CANADA, THE REPUBLIC OF
FRANCE, THE KINGDOM OF THE NETHERLANDS, NEW ZEALAND,
INDIA, AND THE COMMONWEALTH OF THE PHILIPPINES.

AGAINST

ARAKI, Sadao, DOHIHARA, Kenji, HASHIMOTO, Kingoro, HATA,
Shunroku, HIRANUMA, Kiichiro, HIROTA, Koki, HOSHINO, Naoki,
ITAGAKI, Seishiro, KAYA, Okinori, KIDO, Koichi, KIMURA,
Heitaro, KOISO, Kuniaki, MATSUI, Iwane, MATSUOKA, Yosuke,
MINAMI, Jiro, MUTO, Akira, NAGANO, Osami, OKA, Takasumi,
OKAWA, Shumei, OSHIMA, Hiroshi, SATO, Kenryo, SHIGEMITSU,
Mamoru, SHIMADA, Shigetaro, SHIRATORI, Toshio, SUZUKI,
Teiichi, TOGO, Shigenori, TOJO, Hideki, UMEZU, Yoshijiro.

JUDGMENT

The Judgment of the Tribunal was delivered on the 4th through
12th days of November 1948.

PART A - CHAPTER I
Establishment and Proceedings of the Tribunal

The Tribunal was established in virtue of and to implement the
Cairo Declaration of the 1st of December, 1943, the Declaration
of Potsdam of the 26th of July, 1945, the Instrument of Surrender
of the 2nd of September, 1945, and the Moscow Conference of the
26th of December, 1945.

The Cairo Declaration was made by the President of the United
States of America, the President of the National Government of the
Republic of China, and the Prime Minister of Great Britain. It
reads as follows:

"The several military missions have agreed upon future military
operations against Japan. The Three Great Allies expressed their
resolve to bring unrelenting pressure against their brutal enemies
by sea, land, and air. This pressure is already rising.

"The Three Great Allies are fighting this war to restrain and
punish the aggression of Japan. They covet no gain for themselves

and have no thought of territorial expansion. It is their purpose that Japan shall be stripped of all the islands in the Pacific which she has seized or occupied since the beginning of the first World War in 1914, and that all the territories Japan has stolen from the Chinese, such as Manchuria, Formosa, and the Pescadores, shall be restored to the Republic of China. Japan will also be expelled from all other territories which she has taken by violence and greed. The aforesaid Three Great Powers, mindful of the enslavement of the people of Korea, are determined that in due course Korea shall become free and independent.

"With these objects in view the three Allies, in harmony with those of the United Nations at war with Japan, will continue to persevere in the serious and prolonged operations necessary to procure the unconditional surrender of Japan."

The Declaration of Potsdam (Annex No. A-1) was made by the President of the United States of America, the President of the National Government of the Republic of China, and the Prime Minister of Great Britain and later adhered to by the Union of Soviet Socialist Republics. Its principal relevant provisions are:

"Japan shall be given an opportunity to end "this war."

"There must be eliminated for all time the authority and influence of those who have deceived and misled the people of Japan into embarking on world conquest, for we insist that a new order of peace, security and justice will be impossible until irresponsible militarism is driven from the world."

"The terms of the Cairo Declaration shall be carried out and Japanese sovereignty shall be limited to the islands of Honshu, Hokkaido, Kyushu, Shikoku and such minor islands as we determine."

"We do not intend that the Japanese people shall be enslaved as a race or destroyed as a nation, but stern justice shall be meted out to all war criminals including those who have visited cruelties upon our prisoners."

The Instrument of Surrender (Annex No. A-2) was signed on behalf of the Emperor and Government of Japan and on behalf of the nine Allied Powers. It contains inter alia the following proclamation, undertaking, and order:

"We hereby proclaim the unconditional surrender to the Allied Powers of the Japanese Imperial General Headquarters and all Japanese armed forces and all armed forces under Japanese control whereever situated."

"We hereby undertake for the Emperor, the Japanese Government, and their successors, to carry out the provisions of the Potsdam

Declaration in good faith, and to issue whatever orders and take whatever action may be required by the Supreme Commander for the Allied Powers or by any other designated representatives of the Allied Powers for the purpose of giving effect to the Declaration."

"The authority of the Emperor and the Japanese Government to rule the State shall be subject to the Supreme Commander for the Allied Powers who will take such steps as he deems proper to effectuate these terms of surrender. We hereby command all civil, military, and naval officials to obey and enforce all proclamations, orders, and directives deemed by the Supreme Commander for the Allied Powers to be proper to effectuate this surrender and issued by him or under his authority."

By the Moscow Conference (Annex No. A-3) it was agreed by and between the Governments of the United States of America, Great Britain, and the Union of Soviet Socialist Republics with the concurrence of China that:

"The Supreme Commander shall issue all orders for the implementation of the Terms of Surrender, the occupation and control of Japan and directives supplementary thereto."

Acting on this authority on the 19th day of January, 1946, General MacArthur, the Supreme Commander for the Allied Powers, by Special Proclamation established the Tribunal for "the trial of those persons charged individually or as members of organizations or in both capacities with offences which include crime against peace." (Annex No. A-4) The constitution, jurisdiction, and functions of the Tribunal were by the Proclamation declared to be those set forth in the Charter of the Tribunal approved by the Supreme Commander on the same day. Before the opening of the Trial the Charter was amended in several respects. (A copy of the Charter as amended will be found in Annex No. A-5).

On the 15th day of February, 1946, the Supreme Commander issued an Order appointing the nine members of the Tribunal nominated respectively by each of the Allied Powers. This Order also provides that "the responsibilities, powers, and duties of the Members of the Tribunal are set forth in the Charter thereof...."

By one of the amendments to the Charter the maximum number of members was increased from nine to eleven to permit the appointment of members nominated by India and the Commonwealth of the Philippines. By subsequent Orders the present members from the United States and France were appointed to succeed the original appointees who resigned and the members from India and the Philippines were appointed.

Pursuant to the provisions of Article 9(c) of the Charter each of the accused before the opening of the Trial appointed counsel of his own choice to represent him; each accused being represented by American and Japanese counsel.

On the 29th of April, 1946, an indictment, which had previously been served on the accused in conformity with the rules of procedure adopted by the Tribunal, was lodged with the Tribunal.

The Indictment (Annex No. A-6) is long, containing fifty-five counts charging twenty-eight accused with Crimes against Peace, Conventional War Crimes, and Crimes against Humanity during the period from the 1st of January, 1928, to the 2nd of September, 1945.

It may be summarized as follows:

In Count 1 all accused are charged with conspiring as leaders, organisers, instigators or accomplices between 1st January 1928 and 2nd September 1945 to have Japan, either alone or with other countries, wage wars of aggression against any country or countries which might oppose her purpose of securing the military, naval, political and economic domination of East Asia and of the Pacific and Indian oceans and their adjoining countries and neighbouring islands.

Count 2 charges all accused with conspiring throught the same period to have Japan wage aggressive war against China to secure complete domination of the Chinese provinces of Liaoning, Kirin, Heilungkiang, and Jehol (Manchuria).

Count 3 charges all accused with conspiracy over the same period to have Japan wage aggressive war against China to secure complete domination of China.

Count 4 charges all accused with conspiring to have Japan, alone or with other countries, wage aggressive war against the United States, the British Commonwealth, France, the Netherlands, China, Portugal, Thailand, the Philippines and the Union of Soviet Socialist Republics to secure the complete domination of East Asia and the Pacific and Indian Oceans and their adjoining countries and neighbouring islands.

Count 5 charges all accused with conspiring with Germany and Italy to have Japan, Germany and Italy mutually assist each other in aggressive warfare against any country which might oppose them for the purpose of having these three nations acquire complete domination of the entire world, each having special domination in its own sphere, Japan's sphere to cover East Asia and the Pacific and Indian Oceans.

Counts 6 to 17 charge all accused except SHIRATORI with having planned and prepared aggressive war against named countries.

Counts 18 to 26 charge all accused with initiating aggressive war against named countries.

542

Counts 27 to 36 charge all accused with waging aggressive war against named countries.

Count 37 charges certain accused with conspiring to murder members of the armed forces and civilians of the United States, the Philippines, the British Commonwealth, the Netherlands and Thailand by initiating unlawful hostilities against those countries in breach of the Hague Convention No. III of 18th October 1907.

Count 38 charges the same accused with conspiring to murder the soldiers and civilians by initiating hostilities in violation of the agreement between the United States and Japan of 30th November 1908, the Treaty between Britain, France, Japan and the United States of 13th December 1921, the Pact of Paris of 27th August 1928, and the Treaty of Unity between Thailand and Japan of 12th June 1940.

Counts 39 to 43 charge the same accused with the commission on 7th and 8th December 1941 of murder at Pearl Harbour (Count 39) Kohta Behru (Count 40) Hong Kong (Count 41) on board H.M.S. PETREL at Shanghai (Count 42) and at Davao (Count 43).

Count 44 charges all accused with conspiring to murder on a wholesale scale prisoners of war and civilians in Japan's power.

Counts 45 to 50 charge certain accused with the murder of disarmed soldiers and civilians at Nanking (Count 45) Canton (Count 46) Hankow (Count 47) Changsha (Count 48) Hengyang (Count 49) and Kweilin and Luchow (Count 50).

Count 51 charges certain accused with the murder of members of the armed forces of Mongolia and the Soviet Union in the Khalkin-Gol River area in 1939.

Count 52 charges certain accused with the murder of members of the armed forces of the Soviet Union in the Lake Khasan area in July and August 1938.

Counts 53 and 54 charge all the accused except OKAWA and SHIRATORI with having conspired to order, authorize or permit the various Japanese Theatre Commanders, the officials of the War Ministry and local camp and labour unit officials to frequently and habitually commit breaches of the laws and customs of war against the armed forces, prisoners of war, and civilian internees of complaining powers and to have the Government of Japan abstain from taking adequate steps to secure the observance and prevent breaches of the laws and customs of war.

Count 55 charges the same accused with having recklessly disregarded their legal duty by virture of their offices to take adequate steps to secure the observance and prevent breaches of the laws and customs of war.

There are five appendices to the Indictment:

Appendix A summarises the principal matters and events upon which the counts are based.

Appendix B is a list of Treaty Articles.

Appendix C specifies the assurances Japan is alleged to have broken.

Appendix D contains the laws and customs of war alleged to have been infringed.

Appendix E is a partial statement of the facts with respect to the alleged individual responsibility of the accused.

These appendices are included in Annex A-6.

* * * *

PART A -- CHAPTER II
THE LAW
(a) JURISDICTION OF THE TRIBUNAL

In our opinion the law of the Charter is decisive and binding on the Tribunal. This is a special tribunal set up by the Supreme Commander under authority conferred on him by the Allied Powers. It derives its jurisdiction from the Charter. In this trial its members have no jurisdiction except such as is to be found in the Charter. The Order of the Supreme Commander, which appointed the members of the Tribunal, states: "The responsibilities, powers, and duties of the members of the Tribunal are set forth in the Charter thereof..." In the result, the members of the Tribunal, being otherwise wholly without power in respect to the trial of the accused, have been empowered by the documents, which constituted the Tribunal and appointed them as members, to try the accused but subject always to the duty and responsibility of applying to the trial the law set forth in the Charter.

The foregoing expression of opinion is not to be taken as supporting the view, if such view be held, that the Allied Powers or any victor nations have the right under international law in providing for the trial and punishment of war criminals to enact or promulgate laws or vest in their tribunals powers in conflicts with recognised international law or rules or principles thereof. In the exercise of their right to create tribunals for such a purpose and in conferring powers upon such tribunals belligerent powers may act only within the limits of international law.

The substantial grounds of the defence challenge to the jurisdiction of the Tribunal to hear and adjudicate upon the charges contained in the Indictment are the following:

(1) The Allied Powers acting through the Supreme Commander

have no authority to include in the Charter of the Tribunal and to designate as justiciable "Crimes against Peace" (Article 5(a));

(2) Aggressive war is not per se illegal and the Pact of Paris of 1928 renouncing war as an instrument of national policy does not enlarge the meaning of war crimes nor constitute war a crime;

(3) War is the act of a nation for which there is no individual responsibility under international law;

(4) The provisions of the Charter are "ex post facto" legislation and therefore illegal;

(5) The Instrument of Surrender which provides that the Declaration of Potsdam will be given effect imposes the condition that Conventional War Crimes as recognised by international law at the date of the Declaration (26 July, 1945) would be the only crimes prosecuted;

(6) Killings in the course of belligerent operations except in so far as they constitute violations of the rules of warfare or the laws and customs of war are the normal incidents of war and are not murder;

(7) Several of the accused being prisoners of war are triable by court martial as provided by the Geneva Convention 1929 and not by this Tribunal.

Since the law of the Charter is decisive and binding upon it this Tribunal is formally bound to reject the first four of the above seven contentions advanced for the Defence but in view of the great importance of the questions of law involved the Tribunal will record its opinion on these questions.

After this Tribunal had in May 1946 dismissed the defence motions and upheld the validity of its Charter and its jurisdiction thereunder, stating that the reasons for this decision would be given later, the International Military Tribunal sitting at Nuremberg delivered its verdicts on the first of October 1946. That Tribunal expressed inter alia the following opinions:

"The Charter is not an arbitrary exercise of power on the part of the victorious nations but is the expression of international law existing at the time of its creation;"

"The question is what was the legal effect of this pact (Pact of Paris August 27, 1928)? The Nations who signed the pact or adhered to it unconditionally condemned recourse to war for the future as an instrument of policy and expressly renounced it. After the signing of the pact any nation resorting to war as an instrument of national policy breaks the pact. In the opinion of the Tribunal, the solemn renunciation of war as an instrument of national policy necessarily involves the proposition that such a war is illegal in international law; and that those who plan and wage such a war, with its inevitable and terrible consequences, are committing a crime in so doing."

"The principle of international law which under certain circumstances protects the representative of a state cannot be applied to acts which are condemned as criminal by international law. The authors of these acts cannot shelter themselves behind their official position in order to be freed from punishment in appropriate proceedings."

"The maxim 'nullum crimen sine lege' is not a limitation of sovereignty but is in general a principle of justice. To assert that it is unjust to punish those who in defiance of treaties and assurances have attacked neighbouring states without warning is obviously untrue for in such circumstances the attacker must know that he is doing wrong, and so far from it being unjust to punish him, it would be unjust if his wrong were allowed to go unpunished."

"The Charter specifically provides... 'the fact that a defendant acted pursuant to order of his Government or of a superior shall not free him from responsibility but may be considered in mitigation of punishment.' This provision is in conformity with the laws of all nations... The true test which is found in varying degrees in the criminal law of most nations is not the existence of the order but whether moral choice was in fact possible."

With the foregoing opinions of the Nuremberg Tribunal and the reasoning by which they are reached this Tribunal is in complete accord. They embody complete answers to the first four of the grounds urged by the defence as set forth above. In view of the fact that in all material respects the Charters of this Tribunal and the Nuremberg Tribunal are identical, this Tribunal prefers to express its unqualified adherence to the relevant opinions of the Nuremberg Tribunal rather than by reasoning the matters anew in somewhat different language to open the door to controversy by way of conflicting interpretations of the two statements of opinions.

The fifth ground of the Defence challenge to the Tribunal's jurisdiction is that under the Instrument of Surrender and the Declaration of Potsdam the only crimes for which it was contemplated that proceedings would be taken, being the only war crimes recognized by international law at the date of the Declaration of Potsdam, are Conventional War Crimes as mentioned in Article 5(b) of the Charter.

Aggressive war was a crime at international law long prior to the date of the Declaration of Potsdam, and there is no ground for the limited interpretation of the Charter which the defense seek to give it.

A special argument was advanced that in any event the Japanese Government, when they agreed to accept the terms of the Instrument of Surrender, did not in fact understand that those Japanese who were alleged to be responsible for the war would be prosecuted.

There is no basis in fact for this argument. It has been established to the satisfaction of the Tribunal that before the signature of the Instrument of Surrender the point in question had been considered by the Japanese Government and the then members of the Government, who advised the acceptance of the terms of the Instrument of Surrender, anticipated that those alleged to be responsible for the war would be put on trial. As early as the 10th of August, 1945, three weeks before the signing of the Instrument of Surrender, the Emperor said to the accused KIDO, "I could not bear the sight ...of those responsible for the war being punished...but I think now is the time to bear the unbearable."

The sixth contention for the Defence; namely, that relating to the charges which allege the commission of murder will be discussed at a later point.

The seventh of these contentions is made on behalf of the four accused who surrendered as prisoners of war -- ITAGAKI, KIMURA, MUTO and SATO. The submission made on their behalf is that they, being former members of the armed forces of Japan and prisoners of war, are triable as such by court martial under the articles of the Geneva Convention of 1929 relating to prisoners of war, particularly Articles 60 and 63, and not by a tribunal constituted otherwise than under that Convention. This very point was decided by the Supreme Court of the United States of America in the Yamashita case. The late Chief Justice Stone, delivering the judgment for the majority of the Court said: "We think it clear from the context of these recited provisions that Part 3 and Article 63, which it contains, apply only to judicial proceedings directed against a prisoner of war for offences committed while a prisoner of war. Section V gives no indication that this part was designated to deal with offences other than those referred to in Parts 1 and 2 of Chapter 3." With that conclusion and the reasoning by which it is reached the Tribunal respectfully agrees.

The challenge to the jurisdiction of the Tribunal wholly fails.
. . .

CONCLUSIONS

It remains to consider the contention advanced on behalf of the defendants that Japan's acts of aggression against France, her attack against the Netherlands, and her attacks on Great Britain and the United States of America were justifiable measures of self-defence. It is argued that these Powers took such measures to restrict the economy of Japan that she had no way of preserving the welfare and properity of her nationals but to go to war.

The measures which were taken by these Powers to restrict Japanese trade were taken in an entirely justifiable attempt to induce Japan to depart from a course of aggression on which she had long been embarked and upon which she had determined to continue. Thus the United States of America gave notice to terminate the Treaty of Commerce and Navigation with Japan on 26th July 1939 after Japan had seized Manchuria and a large part of the rest of China and when the existence of the treaty had long ceased to induce Japan to respect the rights and interests of the nationals of the United States in China. It was given in order that some other means might be tried to induce Japan to respect these rights. Thereafter the successive embargoes which were imposed on the export of materials to Japan were imposed as it became clearer and clearer that Japan had determined to attack the territories and interests of the Powers. They were imposed in an attempt to induce Japan to depart from the aggressive policy on which she had determined and in order that the Powers might no longer supply Japan with the materials to wage war upon them. In some cases, as for example in the case of the embargo on the export of oil from the United States of America to Japan, these measures were also taken in order to build up the supplies which were needed by the nations who were resisting the aggressors. The argument is indeed merely a repetition of Japanese propaganda issued at the time she was preparing for her wars of aggression. It is not easy to have patience with its lengthy repetition at this date when documents are at length available which demonstrate that Japan's decision to expand to the North, to the West and to the South at the expense of her neighbors was taken long before any economic measures were directed against her and was never departed from. The evidence clearly establishes contrary to the contention of the defense that the acts of aggression against France, and the attacks on Britain, the United States of America and the Netherlands were prompted by the desire to deprive China of any aid in the struggle she was waging against Japan's aggression and to secure for Japan the possessions of her neighbors in the South.

548

The Tribunal is of opinion that the leaders of Japan in the years 1940 and 1941 planned to wage wars of aggression against France in French Indo-China. They had determined to demand that France cede to Japan the right to station troops and the right to air bases and naval bases in French Indo-China, and they had prepared to use force against France if their demands were not granted. They did make such demands upon France under threat that they would use force to obtain them, if that should prove necessary. In her then situation France was compelled to yield to the threat of force and granted the demands.

The Tribunal also finds that a war of aggression was waged against the Republic of France. The occupation by Japanese troops of portions of French Indo-China, which Japan had forced France to accept, did not remain peaceful. As the war situation, particularly in the Philippines, turned against Japan the Japanese Supreme War Council in February 1945 decided to submit the following demands to the Governor of French Indo-China: (1) that all French troops and armed police be placed under Japanese command, and (2) that all means of communication and transportation necessary for military action be placed under Japanese control. These demands were presented to the Governor of French Indo-China on 9th March 1945 in the form of an ultimatum backed by the threat of military action. He was given two hours to refuse or accept. He refused, and the Japanese proceeded to enforce their demands by military action. French troops and military police resisted the attempt to disarm them. There was fighting in Hanoi, Saigon, Phnom-Penh, Nhatrang, and towards the Northern frontier. We quote the official Japanese account, "In the Northern frontiers the Japanese had considerable losses. The Japanese army proceeded to suppress French detachments in remote places and contingents which had fled to the mountains. In a month public order was re-established except in remote places". The Japanese Supreme War Council had decided that, if Japan's demands were refused and military action was taken to enforce them, "the two countries will not be considered as at war". This Tribunal finds that Japanese actions at that time constituted the waging of a war of aggression against the Republic of France.

The Tribunal is further of opinion that the attacks which Japan launched on 7th December 1941 against Britain, the United States of America and the Netherlands were wars of aggression. They were unprovoked attacks, prompted by the desire to seize the possessions of these nations. Whatever may be the difficulty of stating a com-

549

prehensive definition of "a war of aggression", attacks made with the above motive cannot but be characterised as wars of aggression.

It was argued on behalf of the defendants that, in as much as the Netherlands took the initiative in declaring war on Japan, the war which followed cannot be described as a war of aggression by Japan. The facts are that Japan had long planned to secure for herself a dominant position in the economy of the Netherlands East Indies by negotiation or by force of arms if negotiation failed. By the middle of 1941 it was apparent that the Netherlands would not yield to the Japanese demands. The leaders of Japan then planned and completed all the preparations for invading and seizing the Netherlands East Indies. The orders issued to the Japanese army for this invasion have not been recovered, but the orders issued to the Japanese navy on 5th November 1941 have been adduced in evidence. This is the Combined Fleet Operations Order No. 1 already referred to. The expected enemies are stated to be the United States, Great Britain and the Netherlands. The order states that the day for the outbreak of war will be given in an Imperial General Headquarters order, and that after 0000 hours on that day a state of war will exist and the Japanese forces will commence operations according to the plan. The order of Imperial General Headquarters was issued on 10th November and it fixed 8th December (Tokyo time), 7th December (Washington time) as the date on which a state of war would exist and operations would commence according to the plan. In the very first stage of the operations so to be commenced it is stated that the Southern Area Force will annihilate enemy fleets in the Philippines, British Malaya and the Netherlands East Indies area. There is no evidence that the above order was ever recalled or altered in respect to the above particulars. In these circumstances we find in fact that orders declaring the existence of a state of war and for the execution of a war of aggression by Japan against the Netherlands were in effect from the early morning of 7th December 1941. The fact that the Netherlands, being fully apprised of the imminence of the attack, in self defence declared war against Japan on 8th December and thus officially recognised the existence of a state of war which had been begun by Japan cannot change that war from a war of aggression on the part of Japan into something other than that. In fact Japan did not declare war against the Netherlands until 11th January 1942 when her troops landed in the Netherlands East Indies. The Imperial Conference of 1st December 1941 decided that "Japan will open hostilities against the United States, Great Britain and the Netherlands." Despite this decision to open hostilities against the Netherlands, and despite the fact that orders for the execution of hostilities against the Netherlands were already in effect, TOJO announced to the Privy Council on 8th December (Tokyo time) when they passed the Bill making a formal declaration of war against the United States of America and Britain that war would not be declared on the Netherlands in view of future strategic convenience. The reason for this was not satisfactorily explained in evidence. The Tribunal is inclined to the view that it was dictated by the policy decided in October 1940 for the purpose of giving as little time as possible for the Dutch to destroy oil wells. It has no bearing, however, on the fact that Japan launched a war of aggression against the Netherlands.

The position of Thailand is special. The evidence bearing upon the entry of Japanese troops into Thailand is meagre to a fault. It is clear that there was complicity between the Japanese leaders and the leaders of Thailand in the years 1939 and 1940 when Japan forced herself on France as mediator in the dispute as to the border between French Indo-China and Thailand. There is no evidence that the position of complicity and confidence between Japan and Thailand, which was then achieved, was altered before December 1941. It is proved that the Japanese leaders planned to secure a peaceful passage for their troops through Thailand into Malaya by agreement with Thailand. They did not wish to approach Thailand for such an agreement until the moment when they were about to attack Malaya, lest the news of the imminence of that attack should leak out. The Japanese troops marched through the territory of Thailand unopposed on 7th December 1941 (Washington time). The only evidence the prosecution has adduced as to the circumstances of that march is (1) a statement made to the Japanese Privy Council between 10 a.m. and 11 a.m. on 8th December 1941 (Tokyo time) that an agreement for the passage of the troops was being negotiated, (2) a Japanese broadcast announcement that they had commenced friendly advancement into Thailand on the afternoon of the 8th December (Tokyo time) (Washington time, 7th December), and that Thailand had facilitated the passage by concluding an agreement at 12.30 p.m., and (3) a conflicting statement, also introduced by the prosecution, that Japanese troops landed at Singora and Patani in Thailand at 3.05 in the morning of 8th December (Tokyo time). On 21st December 1941 Thailand concluded a treaty of alliance with Japan. No witness on behalf of Thailand has complained of Japan's actions as being acts of aggression. In these circumstances we are left without reasonable certainty that the Japanese advance into Thailand was contrary to the wishes of the Government of Thailand and the charges that the defendants initiated and waged a war of aggression against the Kingdom of Thailand remain unproved.

Count 31 charges that a war of aggression was waged against the British Commonwealth of Nations. The Imperial Rescript which was issued about 12 noon on 8th December 1941 (Tokyo time) states "We hereby declare war on the United States of America and the British Empire." There is a great deal of lack of precision in the use of terms throughout the many plans which were formulated for an attack on British possessions. Thus such terms as "Britain", "Great Britain", and "England" are used without discrimination and apparently used as meaning the same thing. In this case there is no doubt as to the entity which is designated by "the British Empire". The correct title of that entity is "The British Commonwealth of Nations". That by the use of the term "the British Empire" they intended the entity which is more correctly called "the British Commonwealth of Nations" is clear when we consider the terms of the Combined Fleet Operations Order No. I already referred to. That order provides that a state of war will exist after 0000 hours X-Day, which was 8th December 1941 (Tokyo time), and that the Japanese forces would then commence operations. It is provided that in the very first phase of the operations the "South Seas Force" will be ready for the enemy fleet in the Australia area. Later it was provided that "The following are areas expected to be occupied or destroyed as quickly as operational conditions permit, a, Eastern New Guinea, New Britain. These were governed by the Commonwealth of Australia under mandate from the League of Nations. The areas to be destroyed or occupied are also stated to include "Strategic points in the Australia area". Moreover, "important points in the Australian coast" were to be mined. Now the Commonwealth of Australia is not accurately described as being part of "Great Britain", which is the term used in the Combined Fleet Secret Operations Order No. I, nor is it accurately described as being part of "the British Empire", which is the term used in the Imperial Rescript. It is properly designated as part of "the British Commonwealth of Nations". It is plain therefore that the entity against which hostilities were to be directed and against which the declaration of war was directed was "the British Commonwealth of Nations", and Count 31 is well-founded when it charges that a war of aggression was waged against the British Commonwealth of Nations.

It is charged in Count 30 of the Indictment that a war of aggression was waged against the Commonwealth of the Philippines. The Philippines during the period of the war were not a completely sovereign state. So far as international relations were concerned they were part of the United States of America. It is beyond doubt that a war of aggression was waged against the people of the Philippines.

For the sake of technical accuracy we shall consider the aggression against the people of the Philippines as being a part of the war of aggression waged against the United States of America.

PART C
CHAPTER IX
FINDINGS ON COUNTS OF THE INDICTMENT

In Count I of the Indictment it is charged that all the defendants together with other persons participated in the formulation or execution of a common plan or conspiracy. The object of that common plan is alleged to have been that Japan should secure the military, naval, political and economic domination of East Asia and of the Pacific and Indian Oceans, and of all countries and islands therein or bordering thereon, and for that purpose should, alone or in combination with other countries having similar objects, wage a war or wars of aggression against any country or countries which might oppose that purpose.

There are undoubtedly declarations by some of those who are alleged to have participated in the conspiracy which coincide with the above grandiose statement, but in our opinion it has not been proved that these were ever more than declarations of the aspirations of individuals. Thus, for example, we do not think the conspirators ever seriously resolved to attempt to secure the domination of North and South America. So far as the wishes of the conspirators crystallised into a concrete common plan we are of opinion that the territory they had resolved that Japan should dominate was confined to East Asia, the Western and South Western Pacific Ocean and the Indian Ocean, and certain of the islands in these oceans. We shall accordingly treat Count I as if the charge had been limited to the above object.

We shall consider in the first place whether a conspiracy with the above object has been proved to have existed.

Already prior to 1928 Okawa, one of the original defendants, who has been discharged from this trial on account of his present mental state, was publicly advocating that Japan should extend her territory on the Continent of Asia by the threat or, if necessary, by use of military force. He also advocated that Japan should seek to dominate Eastern Siberia and the South Sea Islands. He predicted that the course he advocated must result in a war between the East and the West, in which Japan would be the champion of the East. He was encouraged and aided in his advocacy of this plan by the Japanese General Staff. The object of this plan as stated was substantially the object of the conspiracy, as we have defined it. In our review of the facts we have noticed many subsequent declarations of the conspirators as to the object of the conspiracy. These do not vary in any material respect from this early declaration by Okawa.

554

Already when Tanaka was premier, from 1927 to 1929, a party of military men, with Okawa and other civilian supporters, was advocating this policy of Okawa's that Japan should expand by the use of force. The conspiracy was now in being. It remained in being until Japan's defeat in 1945. The immediate question when Tanaka was premier was whether Japan should attempt to expand her influence on the continent - beginning with Manchuria - by peaceful penetration, as Tanaka and the members of his Cabinet wished, or whether that expansion should be accomplished by the use of force if necessary, as the conspirators advocated. It was essential that the conspirators should have the support and control of the nation. This was the beginning of the long struggle between the conspirators, who advocated the attainment of their object by force, and those politicians and latterly those bureaucrats, who advocated Japan's expansion by peaceful measures or at least by a more discreet choice of the occasions on which force should be employed. This struggle culminated in the conspirators obtaining control of the organs of government of Japan and preparing and regimenting the nation's mind and material resources for wars of aggression designed to achieve the object of the conspiracy. In overcoming the opposition the conspirators employed methods which were entirely unconstitutional and at times wholly ruthless. Propaganda and persuasion won many to their side, but military action abroad without Cabinet sanction or in defiance of Cabinet veto, assassination of opposing leaders, plots to overthrow by force of arms Cabinets which refused to co-operate with them, and even a military revolt which seized the capital and attempted to overthrow the government were part of the tactics whereby the conspirators came ultimately to dominate the Japanese polity.

As and when they felt strong enough to overcome opposition at home and latterly when they had finally overcome all such opposition the conspirators carried out in succession the attacks necessary to effect their ultimate object, that Japan should dominate the Far East. In 1931 they launched a war of aggression against China and conquered Manchuria and Jehol. By 1934 they had commenced to infiltrate into North China, garrisoning the land and setting up puppet governments designed to serve their purposes. From 1937 onwards they continued their aggressive war against China on a vast scale, overrunning and occupying much of the country, setting up puppet governments on the above model, and exploiting China's economy and natural resources to feed the Japanese military and civilian needs.

In the meantime they had long been planning and preparing a

war of aggression which they proposed to launch against the
U.S.S.R. The intention was to seize that country's Eastern territories when a favourable opportunity occurred. They had also long
recognized that their exploitation of East Asia and their designs on
the islands in the Western and South Western Pacific would bring
them into conflict with the United States of America, Britain, France
and the Netherlands who would defend their threatened interests and
territories. They planned and prepared for war against these countries also.

The conspirators brought about Japan's alliance with Germany
and Italy, whose policies were as aggressive as their own, and
whose support they desired both in the diplomatic and military fields,
for their aggressive actions in China had drawn on Japan the condemnation of the League of Nations and left her friendless in the
councils of the world.

Their proposed attack on the U.S.S.R. was postponed from
time to time for various reasons, among which were (1) Japan's
preoccupation with the war in China, which was absorbing unexpec-
tedly large military resources, and (2) Germany's pact of nonaggression with the U.S.S.R. in 1939, which for the time freed the
U.S.S.R. from threat of attack on her Western frontier, and might
have allowed her to devote the bulk of her strength to the defence
of her Eastern territories if Japan had attacked her.

Then in the year 1940 came Germany's great military successes
on the continent of Europe. For the time being Great Britain, France
and the Netherlands were powerless to afford adequate protection
to their interests and territories in the Far East. The military
preparations of the United States were in the initial stages. It
seemed to the conspirators that no such favourable opportunity could
readily recur of realising that part of their objective which sought
Japan's domination of South-West Asia and the islands in the Western and South Western Pacific and Indian Oceans. After prolonged
negotiations with the United States of America, in which they refused to disgorge any substantial part of the fruits they had seized
as the result of their war of aggression against China, on 7th December 1941 the conspirators launched a war of aggression against
the United States and the British Commonwealth. They had already
issued orders declaring that a state of war existed between Japan
and the Netherlands as from 00.00 hours on 7th December 1941.
They had previously secured a jumping-off place for their attacks
on the Philippines, Malaya and the Netherlands East Indies by forcing their troops into French Indo-China under threat of military
action if this facility was refused to them. Recognising the exist-

ence of a state of war and faced by the imminent threat of invasion of her Far Eastern territories, which the conspirators had long planned and were now about to execute, the Netherlands in self-defence declared war on Japan.

These far-reaching plans for waging wars of aggression, and the prolonged and intricate preparation for and waging of these wars of aggression were not the work of one man. They were the work of many leaders acting in pursuance of a common plan for the achievement of a common object. That common object, that they should secure Japan's domination by preparing and waging wars of aggression, was a criminal object. Indeed no more grave crimes can be conceived of than a conspiracy to wage a war of aggression or the waging of a war of aggression, for the conspiracy threatens the security of the peoples of the world, and the waging disrupts it. The probable result of such a conspiracy, and the inevitable result of its execution is that death and suffering will be inflicted on countless human beings.

The Tribunal does not find it necessary to consider whether there was a conspiracy to wage wars in violation of the treaties, agreements and assurances specified in the particulars annexed to Count I. The conspiracy to wage wars of aggression was already criminal in the highest degree.

The Tribunal finds that the existence of the criminal conspiracy to wage wars of aggression as alleged in Count I, with the limitation as to object already mentioned, has been proved.

The question whether the defendants or any of them participated in that conspiracy will be considered when we deal with the individual cases.

The conspiracy existed for and its execution occupied a period of many years. Not all of the conspirators were parties to it at the beginning, and some of those who were parties to it had ceased to be active in its execution before the end. All of those who at any time were parties to the criminal conspiracy or who at any time with guilty knowledge played a part in its execution are guilty of the charge contained in Count I.

In view of our finding on Count I it is unnecessary to deal with Counts 2 and 3, which charge the formulation or execution of conspiracies with objects more limited than that which we have found proved under Count I, or with Count 4, which charges the same conspiracy as Count I but with more specification.

Count 5 charges a conspiracy wider in extent and with even more grandiose objects than that charged in Count I. We are of opinion that although some of the conspirators clearly desired the achievement of these grandiose objects nevertheless there is not sufficient evidence to justify a finding that the conspiracy charged in Count 5 has been proved.

For the reasons given in an earlier part of this judgment we consider it unnecessary to make any pronouncement on Counts 6 to 26 and 37 to 53. There remain therefore only Counts 27 to 36 and 54 and 55, in respect of which we now give our findings.

Counts 27 to 36 charge the crime of waging wars of aggression and wars in violation of international law, treaties, agreements and assurances against the countries named in those counts.

In the statement of facts just concluded we have found that wars of aggression were waged against all those countries with the exception of the Commonwealth of the Philippines (Count 30) and the Kingdom of Thailand (Count 34). With reference to the Philippines, as we have heretofore stated, that Commonwealth during the period of the war was not a completely sovereign State and so far as international relations were concerned it was a part of the United States of America. We further stated that it is beyond doubt that a war of aggression was waged in the Philippines, but for the sake of technical accuracy we consider the aggressive war in the Philippines as being a part of the war of aggression waged against the United States of America.

Count 28 charges the waging of a war of aggression against the Republic of China over a lesser period of time than that charged in Count 27. Since we hold that the fuller charge contained in Count 27 has been proved we shall make no pronouncement on Count 28.

Wars of aggression having been proved, it is unnecessary to consider whether they were also wars otherwise in violation of international law or in violation of treaties, agreements and assurances. The Tribunal finds therefore that it has been proved that wars of aggression were waged as alleged in Counts 27, 29, 31, 32, 33, 35 and 36.

Count 54 charges ordering, authorising and permitting the commission of Conventional War Crimes. Count 55 charges failure to take adequate steps to secure the observance and prevent breaches of conventions and laws of war in respect of prisoners of war and civilian internees. We find that there have been cases in which crimes under both these Counts have been proved.

Consequent upon the foregoing findings, we propose to consider the charges against individual defendants in respect only of the following Counts: Numbers 1, 27, 29, 31, 32, 33, 35, 36, 54 and 55.